# Orthodoxy and Orthopraxis

# Orthodoxy and Orthopraxis
*Essays in Tribute to Paul Livermore*

EDITED BY
Douglas R. Cullum
AND
J. Richard Middleton

☙PICKWICK Publications · Eugene, Oregon

ORTHODOXY AND ORTHOPRAXIS
Essays in Tribute to Paul Livermore

Copyright © 2020 Wipf and Stock Publishers. All rights reserved. Except for brief quotations in critical publications or reviews, no part of this book may be reproduced in any manner without prior written permission from the publisher. Write: Permissions, Wipf and Stock Publishers, 199 W. 8th Ave., Suite 3, Eugene, OR 97401.

Pickwick Publications
An Imprint of Wipf and Stock Publishers
199 W. 8th Ave., Suite 3
Eugene, OR 97401

www.wipfandstock.com

PAPERBACK ISBN: 978-1-5326-7256-9
HARDCOVER ISBN: 978-1-5326-7257-6
EBOOK ISBN: 978-1-5326-7258-3

## *Cataloguing-in-Publication data:*

Names: Cullum, Douglas R., editor. | Middleton, J. Richard, editor.

Title: Orthodoxy and orthopraxis : essays in tribute to Paul Livermore / Edited by Douglas R. Cullum and J. Richard Middleton.

Description: Eugene, OR: Pickwick Publications, 2020. | Includes bibliographical references.

Identifiers: ISBN 978-1-5326-7256-9 (paperback). | ISBN 978-1-5326-7257-6 (hardcover). | ISBN 978-1-5326-7258-3 (ebook).

Subjects: LCSH: Livermore, Paul. | Bible. O.T.—Criticism, interpretation, etc. | Bible. N.T.—Criticism, interpretation, etc.

Classification: BS1192.5 O78 2020 (print). | BS1192.5 (ebook).

Scripture quotations marked NRSV are from New Revised Standard Version Bible, copyright © 1989 National Council of the Churches of Christ in the United States of America. Used by permission. All rights reserved worldwide.

Scripture quotations marked NRSVCE are from New Revised Standard Version Bible: Catholic Edition, copyright © 1989, 1993 National Council of the Churches of Christ in the United States of America. Used by permission. All rights reserved worldwide.

Scripture quotations marked NIV are taken from the Holy Bible, New International Version®, NIV®. Copyright © 1973, 1978, 1984, 2011 by Biblica, Inc.™ Used by permission of Zondervan. All rights reserved worldwide. www.zondervan.com The "NIV" and "New International Version" are trademarks registered in the United States Patent and Trademark Office by Biblica, Inc.™

Scripture quotations marked NKJV are taken from the New King James Version®. Copyright © 1982 by Thomas Nelson. Used by permission. All rights reserved.

Scripture quotations marked MSG are taken from *THE MESSAGE*, copyright © 1993, 2002, 2018 by Eugene H. Peterson. Used by permission of NavPress. All rights reserved. Represented by Tyndale House Publishers, Inc.

Scripture quotations marked NLT are taken from the Holy Bible, New Living Translation, copyright ©1996, 2004, 2015 by Tyndale House Foundation. Used by permission of Tyndale House Publishers, Inc., Carol Stream, Illinois 60188. All rights reserved.

Scripture quotations marked ESV are from the ESV® Bible (The Holy Bible, English Standard Version®), copyright © 2001 by Crossway, a publishing ministry of Good News Publishers. Used by permission. All rights reserved.

Scripture quotations marked KJV are from The Authorized (King James) Version. Rights in the Authorized Version in the United Kingdom are vested in the Crown. Reproduced by permission of the Crown's patentee, Cambridge University Press.

Scripture quotations marked NASB are taken from the New American Standard Bible® (NASB), Copyright © 1960, 1962, 1963, 1968, 1971, 1972, 1973, 1975, 1977, 1995 by The Lockman Foundation. Used by permission. www.Lockman.org

Scripture quotations marked RSV are from Revised Standard Version of the Bible, copyright © 1946, 1952, and 1971 National Council of the Churches of Christ in the United States of America. Used by permission. All rights reserved worldwide.

Scripture quoted by permission. Quotations designated NET are from the NET Bible® copyright ©1996–2016 by Biblical Studies Press, L.L.C. http://netbible.com/. All rights reserved.

Scripture texts marked NAB in this work are taken from the New American Bible, revised edition © 2010, 1991, 1986, 1970 Confraternity of Christian Doctrine, Washington, D.C. and are used by permission of the copyright owner. All Rights Reserved.

Scripture quotations marked NEB taken from the New English Bible, copyright © Cambridge University Press and Oxford University Press 1961, 1970. All rights reserved.

Scripture marked CEB taken from the Common English Bible®, CEB® Copyright © 2010, 2011 by Common English Bible.™ Used by permission. All rights reserved worldwide. The "CEB" and "Common English Bible" trademarks are registered in the United States Patent and Trademark Office by Common English Bible.

Scripture quotations marked NJB are taken from The New Jerusalem Bible, published and copyright 1985 by Darton, Longman & Todd Ltd and Les Editions du Cerf, and used by permission of the publishers.

Scripture quotations marked NETS are taken from A New English Translation of the Septuagint, ©2007 by the International Organization for Septuagint and Cognate Studies, Inc. Used by permission of Oxford University Press. All rights reserved.

Manufactured in the U.S.A.  04/01/20

*For Alice Livermore, whose life with Paul has made all the difference in making him the person we know and love.*

# Contents

*List of Contributors* | xi

*Introduction* | xiii

## Part 1: Grappling with Scripture in Ancient and Contemporary Contexts

1. More Than a Faithful Treaty Partner: Why Covenant Is Not Enough for God | 3
   —Joseph Coleson

2. *Akedah* as Apologia: The Function of Genesis 22 for Second Temple Jews | 11
   —Karen Strand Winslow

3. The Irony of Reading the Book of Joshua as Christian Scripture | 27
   —Frank Anthony Spina

4. The Blessing of Abraham and the *Missio Dei*: Reframing the Purpose of Israel's Election in Genesis 12:1–3 | 44
   —J. Richard Middleton

5. Trauma not Triumph: Reading the Hebrew Bible as Disaster and Resistance Literature | 65
   —Louis Stulman

6. False Worship as a Gateway to Social Injustice in Jeremiah 7:1–8:3 | 84
   —T. L. Birge

7   Daniel as an "Historical" Sign of the Eschatological Ancient of Days and Most High God? Reading *Bel et Draco* in Eschatological Contexts—Apocalyptic, Prophetic, and Sapiential | 101

—Eugene E. Lemcio

8   The Wild and the Cultivated Olive: Embarrassing or Brilliant? | 109

—Margaret G. Flowers

9   "Because of Transgressions" (Galatians 3:19): Reassessing Jerome | 120

—Timothy Dwyer

10  Interpreting the Epistle to the Hebrews as a Pastoral Letter | 132

—Wayne McCown

11  A Survey of Attempts to Tackle an "Unsolved Problem": The Literary Structure of Hebrews in Contemporary Scholarly Discussion | 146

—James P. Sweeney

## Part 2: Insights from the History of the Church

12  "Study to Show Thyself Approved": B. T. Roberts's Reading Record, 1852–1855 | 169

—Douglas R. Cullum

13  Body Matters: Re-Examining Ascetic Practice in John Climacus's *The Ladder* | 185

—Rebecca S. Letterman

14  At Home among the Stars: An Athanasian Perspective on Natural Theology | 196

—Linda S. Schwab

15  See How They Love One Another: A Short History of Medieval and Reformation Poor Relief and Its Significance for the Church Today | 209

—Elizabeth L. Gerhardt

16  Spiritual Direction in the Early Eastern Orthodox Church and in Twentieth Century Classical Pentecostalism | 226

—John R. Miller

17  John Wesley's Appropriation of *Theosis*: An Exercise in
    Contextual Theology | 236
    —David Belles

18  Aging in the Light: The Patristic Writers' Views on Aging though, with,
    and in Christ | 251
    —Suzanne Pearson

19  The Recapitulation of the Tree of the Knowledge of Good and Evil | 262
    —Mark W. McMonagle

20  A Most Unbearable Commandment: Adolf Schlatter and Jewish Piety | 273
    —James E. McNutt

## Part 3: Exploration and Reflections—Theological and Otherwise

21  Biblical Interpretation: Why Are There So Many Interpretive Disagreements
    among Christians with the Same High View of Scripture? | 291
    —David Basinger

22  The Renewing of the Mind: Cognitive and Developmental Implications
    of Romans 12:2 | 304
    —Jeffery H. Altman

23  Beauty Will Save the World: Literary Imagination and Ministry | 322
    —Thomas R. Worth

24  Strong *Nabû*: The Form and Meaning of an Ancient Mesopotamian Prayer | 330
    —Joel H. Hunt

25  Is Pastoral Visitation a Thing of the Past? | 358
    —Donald N. Bastian

# Contributors

**Jeffrey H. Altman**, Professor of Psychology, Emeritus, Roberts Wesleyan College, Rochester, NY.

**David Basinger**, Professor of Philosophy and Chief Academic Officer, Roberts Wesleyan College, Rochester, NY.

**Donald N. Bastian**, Bishop Emeritus of the Free Methodist Church, USA and Canada.

**David Belles**, Academic Dean, International Fellowship of Christian Assemblies Bible College, Richmond Heights, OH.

**T. L. Birge**, Assistant Professor of Biblical Studies, Azusa Pacific University, Azusa, CA.

**Joseph Coleson**, Professor of Old Testament, Emeritus, Nazarene Theological Seminary, Kansas City, MO.

**Douglas R. Cullum**, Professor of Historical and Pastoral Theology, Vice President and Dean, Northeastern Seminary at Roberts Wesleyan College, Rochester, NY.

**Timothy Dwyer**, Professor of Bible and Ministry, Chair of the Ministry Department, Warner University, Lake Wales, FL.

**Margaret G. Flowers**, Professor Emerita of Biology, Wells College, Aurora, NY. Ordained elder in the Free Methodist Church of North America.

**Elizabeth L. Gerhardt**, Professor of Theology and Social Ethics, Northeastern Seminary at Roberts Wesleyan College, Rochester, NY.

**Joel H. Hunt**, author, Athens, GA.

**Eugene E. Lemcio**, Professor Emeritus of New Testament, School of Theology, Seattle Pacific University, Seattle, WA.

CONTRIBUTORS

**Rebecca S. Letterman**, Professor of Spiritual Formation, Northeastern Seminary at Roberts Wesleyan College, Rochester, NY.

**Wayne McCown**, Provost Emeritus of Roberts Wesleyan College and Founding Dean Emeritus of Northeastern Seminary at Roberts Wesleyan College, Rochester, NY.

**Mark W. McMonagle**, Vicar, St Brendan Orthodox Mission, Honeoye Falls, NY.

**James E. McNutt**, Professor of History and Chair of the Department of History, Thomas More University, Crestview Hills, KY.

**J. Richard Middleton**, Professor of Biblical Worldview and Exegesis, Northeastern Seminary at Roberts Wesleyan College, Rochester, NY.

**John R. Miller**, Professor and Program Chair, Elim Bible Institute and College, Lima, NY.

**Suzanne Pearson**, Spiritual Director, Rochester, NY.

**Linda S. Schwab**, Professor Emerita of Chemistry, Wells College, Aurora, NY. Ordained elder and Endorsed Chaplain in the Free Methodist Church of North America.

**Frank Anthony Spina**, Professor Emeritus of Old Testament, Seattle Pacific Seminary and School of Theology, Seattle Pacific University, Seattle, WA.

**Louis Stulman**, Professor of Religious Studies, University of Findlay, Findlay, OH.

**James P. Sweeney**, J. Russell Bucher Professor of New Testament, Director of the Master of Divinity Program, Winebrenner Theological Seminary, Findlay, OH.

**Karen Strand Winslow**, Professor of Biblical Studies, Chair of Biblical and Theological Studies, Director of Master of Arts in Theological Studies, Azusa Pacific Seminary at Azusa Pacific University, Azusa, CA.

**Thomas R. Worth**, Pastor, Community Covenant Church, Manlius, NY.

# Introduction

## The Career and Contribution of Paul Livermore

――――――― Douglas R. Cullum and J. Richard Middleton

This volume celebrates the life and ministry of Professor Paul W. Livermore. Its pages are written by friends, colleagues, and former students in recognition of Professor Livermore's many contributions to the church and academy. The chapters to follow represent the broad trajectory of influence that Professor Livermore has had on our lives and in the honing of our own varied practices of scholarship on behalf of the church. They testify to Livermore's commitment both to an ecumenical orthodoxy and to an orthpraxis that embodies faithfulness to Christ.

Professor Livermore's long tenure at Roberts Wesleyan College and Northeastern Seminary was unflinchingly tied to twin commitments that characterized the whole of his vocation: He was and is a pastoral theologian, a scholar on behalf of the church. In the church, he consistently served as a *resident theologian*. In the academy, he faithfully serves as a *churchly scholar*. These two pillars of Livermore's identity and calling encapsulate the unique, enduring, and extraordinary contribution he made throughout his career.

Livermore's career, of course, would not have been possible without Alice—a name that every one of Paul's students over the years has heard many times. Paul and Alice first saw each other in Mound Valley, Kansas, when Paul's father, the Rev. Dr. Harry Livermore, took the family with him on one of his visits as a Free Methodist conference superintendent to the church where Alice's family worshiped. Paul and Alice were three years old. A decade later, Alice's family moved to McPherson, Kansas, and Central College, where Paul and Alice met again. They were married seven years later at the tender age of twenty.

In 1966, Paul received his bachelor's degree from Greenville College (a Free Methodist College in Greenville, Illinois) with a double major in two double fields of study: History and Political Science; and Religion and Philosophy—a true liberal arts education! While at Greenville, Paul and Alice pastored Zion Free Methodist Church in

Durley, Illinois (1964–66). Also, in 1966, their oldest child Geoff was born, and Paul was ordained deacon in the Kansas Conference of the Free Methodist Church.

From 1966 to 1969, Paul and Alice were in Wilmore, Kentucky, where Paul pursued his MDiv degree at Asbury Seminary. Their pastoral ministry continued as Paul and Alice pastored the New Columbus Methodist Church in New Columbus, Kentucky, during seminary days (1967–69). After seminary, the Livermores moved to the Central Illinois Conference where they pastored at Aldersgate Free Methodist Church, in McComb, Illinois (1969–72). Their daughter Alicia was born there. And Paul was ordained as an elder in the Central Illinios Conference in 1970.

From 1972–1976, Paul and Alice were at Princeton where Paul would earn both the ThM and PhD degrees. During these years, their pastoral engagement continued as they served a two-point United Methodist circuit in Broadway and Montana, New Jersey (1972–75).

Paul's doctoral program at Princeton involved the study of Second Temple Judaism and the dialogue between early Christianity and Judaism. While working on his PhD, Paul served as a graduate assistant to Bruce Metzger, well known for his text-critical work on the New Testament.

In 1976, Paul was invited to join the faculty of Roberts Wesleyan College, where he served initially for five years, as well as serving 1980 to 1981 as interim pastor at Buchanan Park Free Methodist Church, Hamilton, Ontario, Canada. In 1981, Paul and Alice responded to the call to serve the Ransomville Free Methodist Church, where they served for four years until returning to Roberts Wesleyan College in 1985. Paul returned to the faculty as the George L. Skinner Professor of Religion.

Professor Livermore's career at Roberts Wesleyan College was stellar. It included his nearly decade-long tenure as chair of the Division of Religion and Humanities (1990–99) and consistent involvement in the articulation of the mission and vision of the College for the late-twentieth century. At the same time, Paul's commitment to serve as a scholar on behalf of the church continued unabated. Over the years, his academic endeavors were applied to the needs of the church through service on the Genesee Conference Commission on Ministry (1978–1989), the Board of Ministerial Education and Guidance (1978–1998), the Study Commission on Doctrine of the Free Methodist Church USA (1979–2015), delegate to the General Conference (1985, 1989, and 1999), and council member at the Seventh World Methodist Conference in Rio de Janeiro, Brazil (1996). In addition, Dr. Livermore served as interim pastor, pulpit supply, and member of the adult curriculum committee for the denomination.

Professor Livermore's role in the founding of Northeastern Seminary at Roberts Wesleyan College cannot be understated. It was his vision and passion for theological education that launched the generative conversations that resulted in the birth of a new institution. Livermore's seminal insight was then matched with founding Dean Dr. Wayne McCown's administrative skill and the support leadership of and President Dr. William Crothers and Provost Dr. John Martin. It was an incomparable combination. Apart from Dr. Livermore's vision and prophetic imagination it is unlikely that Northeastern Seminary would exist today.

Professor Livermore's scholarly contributions in the classroom and in writing have made their mark. Although he started out teaching primarily biblical studies, his expertise has expanded to include patristic Christianity and the theology of John Wesley. In his capacity as a member of the Study Commission on Doctrine of the Free Methodist Church., he authored *Foundations of a Living Faith: The Catechism of the Free Methodist Church* and the first of a two-volume systematic theology, *The God of Our Salvation* (1995). He has also authored journal articles and book chapters on the New Testament, early Judaism, patristic Christianity, and John Wesley.

Livermore continues to work on a fresh, systematic re-formation of the Christian message for the twenty-first century. The need for his work amid the rapidly changing context of evangelicalism in North America cannot be overstated. His deep grasp of both Scripture and the development of Christian theology gives his work a depth of perspective that is often lacking in our day. His work provides a breathtaking, balanced response to the often shrill and un-nuanced pronouncements of those theologies that lie at either end of the theological spectrum.

While Livermore's work is deeply rooted in both Scripture and the historical church, the reader immediately recognizes that she or he will not be expected to "check one's brains at the door," ignoring the insights of the best of scientific study in order to track with Livermore's treatment of a vibrant Christian faith. Professor Livermore's ongoing research seeks to take seriously the insights and implications of science—whether evolutionary biology or neuroplasticity—for theology and the Christian life. His work is precisely the sort of theology that many young evangelicals are yearning for, but too often find unavailable in today's polarized church and commercialized culture.

## The Essays in This Volume

The essays in this volume testify to the various areas of scholarship with which Paul Livermore has been engaged throughout his career.

Part 1 contains eleven chapters on Scripture and its interpretation, beginning with six specifically on the Old Testament. Whereas Joseph Coleson digs beneath "covenant" to find its basis in God's love and faithfulness, Karen Winslow offers a veritable history of early Jewish interpretation of the binding of Isaac (Genesis 22), and Frank Spina dares to read Joshua positively as Christian Scripture. J. Richard Middleton explores a missional, yet non-supersessionist, interpretation of the call of Abraham, Louis Stulman reads the Hebrew Bible as literature of trauma and resistance, and T. L. Birge suggests that Jeremiah helps us understand how false worship leads to injustice in human relations.

INTRODUCTION

The next chapter addresses the Apocrypha, followed by four chapters on the New Testament. Eugene Lemcio proposes an eschatological reading of the addition to Daniel found in *Bel et Draco* (Bel and the Dragon), while Margaret Flowers defends Paul's use of the botanical metaphor of the olive tree in Romans 11 against its detractors in the commentary tradition, and Timothy Dwyer explores Jerome's understanding of a crucial Pauline phrase in Galatians 3. Finally, Wayne McCown and James Sweeney discuss aspects of the interpretation of the letter to the Hebrew—its function as a pastoral letter (McCown) and its complex literary structure (Sweeney).

Part 2 contains eleven chapters that mine the history of the church for theological and ethical insights. Douglas Cullum examines the extensive reading program of B. T. Roberts, the founder of the Free Methodist Church, after whom Roberts Wesleyan College is named, while Rebecca Letterman explores the role of the body in the ascetic practices of the early medieval text, *The Ladder of Ascent*, and Linda Schwab turns to Athanasius, the fourth-century bishop of Alexandria, for his profound understanding of the place of humanity in a complex cosmos held together by the divine *Logos*. Elizabeth Gerhardt examines the significance of Medieval and Reformation poor relief for the church today, while John Miller draws parallels between spiritual direction in early Eastern Orthodoxy and twentieth-century Pentecostalism, and David Belles proposes John Wesley's appeal to *theosis* in the Eastern Fathers as a model of contextualization. Next, Suzanne Pearson draws on the Church Fathers for insights about aging in the light of Christ, while Mark McMonagle explores the meaning of the tree of the knowledge of good and evil among the Eastern Fathers, and James McNutt critiques the myth of Jewish legalism perpetuated by the influential biblical scholar Adolf Schlatter.

Part 3 contains six chapters that range beyond biblical interpretation (Part 1) and church history (Part 2). Philosopher David Basinger analyzes the phenomenon of significant disagreement in biblical interpretation among Christians, Jeffery Altman applies insights from cognitive and developmental psychology to the transformation of the person enjoined in Romans 12:2, and pastor-poet Thomas Worth explores the place of literary imagination in pastoral ministry. Joel Hunt turns his expertise in ancient Near Eastern languages and literature to the interpretation of an ancient Mesopotamian prayer, and Donald Bastian reflects on the continuing role of pastoral visitation in the church today.

These essays, from a wide variety of disciplines and perspectives, testify to the wide and diverse impact of Paul Livermore on his colleagues, friends, and students. They are offered with deep appreciation and admiration for his outstanding life and ministry.

# Part 1: **Grappling with Scripture in Ancient and Contemporary Contexts**

# 1

# More Than a Faithful Treaty Partner: Why Covenant Is Not Enough for God

— Joseph Coleson

It is a privilege and a joy to contribute to this volume for my dear friend and colleague, Paul Livermore. Paul's life, work, and friendship have influenced the ideas presented. I think of this as a brief programmatic essay, a prolegomenon, anticipating fuller treatment as time and providence may allow. Several recent already-influential works in various aspects of Old Testament/Biblical Theology, blending overview with more detailed exegetical work, have encouraged me to utilize a similar approach. Whether successful here, or not, the reader will discern. In any event, I offer it with thanks to the God of new beginnings, and in the hope that this modest beginning may add in some measure to the honor accorded Professor Livermore in these pages.

## The Popularity of Covenant as the Central Theme of the Bible

Historically, much popular Protestant expression of the Christian faith has been enamored of covenant as *the* central theme of the Hebrew/Christian Scripture. Applying too broadly a select set of biblical passages, many preachers and popular writers have been content to see biblical salvation history as a series of covenants. The series usually includes the Adamic, Noahic, Abrahamic, Mosaic, and Davidic covenants of the Hebrew Bible/Old Testament. God's new covenant in Christ either sets aside or incorporates some or all of them, depending on the particular covenant theology employed. As popular expositors interpret persons, places, circumstances, and events in and by their relationships to one or more of these covenants, they often appear to see the hermeneutical task as finished.

Biblical scholars have not embraced these covenant theologies so uniformly, but enough have done so that many popular expositors have seen them as legitimated by the academy. The premier and best-known proponent in Hebrew Bible scholarship is Walter Eichrodt, one of the two most important Old Testament theologians of the mid-twentieth century; his influence still runs deep. In his two-volume *Old Testament*

*Theology*, Eichrodt answered the question, "Does the Old Testament have a center (*Mitte*)?" with a resounding, "Yes, and the *Mitte* is covenant." Pressing the point, Eichrodt likened this "First Covenant" to a "headless torso" unless taken together with the "New Covenant," because the New Covenant reveals Christ.

## Covenant: Necessary, but Insufficient

As the reader has fathomed, I intend to suggest a case for a different understanding. First, though, allow me a charitably-intended "concession": Covenant is important. Because God has forged covenantal relationships, we need to acknowledge and understand them. Nevertheless, covenant is not the be-all and end-all of the biblical witness.

At its purest and simplest, a "covenant" is a contract: nothing less, and hardly, if ever, anything more. Because covenant *does* figure prominently in the scriptural narrative, and because God is the Divine Initiator of all the really important covenants, we tend to invest the term "covenant" itself with the aura of the faithful lovingkindness (*ḥesed vě'ĕmet*), the righteousness, the justice, the grace, and the mercy that are rightfully associated with the person and character of God. Yet, the fact remains that by simple definition—in faithfulness to reasonable semantic methodologies and findings—a "covenant" is simply a contract. Over the last two centuries, the wealth of discoveries from the social/economic/political world of the ancient Near East (biblical Israel's world) has revealed that covenant was an important and familiar instrument for the establishment and maintenance of relationships on all levels of society. It made eminent sense for God to use covenant in reassuring early Israel of God's long-term faithful intentions toward them and their progeny. Yet, it is equally important to note that God did not use covenant to *introduce* Godself and God's redemptive design for eternal relationship with Israel and ultimately—in Christ who came by way of Israel—with all creation.

Let me use an everyday example to illustrate what a covenant is and is not. Buyers often approach the purchase of a pre-owned motor vehicle skeptical of the salesperson's good faith—not only initially, but throughout the transaction. On the other side, the "associate" (previously, the "used car salesman") may view the prospective buyer as naïve, an easy mark, someone to take advantage of. Purchaser and seller may approach the transaction with mutual disdain.

Of course this is as much caricature as accurate characterization, but it does happen. Yet even with all the baggage a vehicle-purchase contract can be made to carry, in an overwhelming majority of cases both seller and buyer faithfully fulfill their respective obligations. A contract (covenant) is a contract (covenant). How the parties feel, think, speak, or act while fulfilling its stipulations, is of no consequence—so long as they *do* fulfill its stipulations.

A foundational principle of the scholarly enterprise is to avoid weighting a term with a semantic load it cannot carry. Careful precision in definition and usage is necessary even—we should say, rather, *especially*—with terms, phrases, and concepts that we "know." A comparable example may help. One evening early in my undergraduate years, I attended a Bible study focused on Jesus's exchange with Peter, in John 21:15–19. The primary insight of the session was that Greek *agape* is a "special" kind of God-given love, higher and more spiritual than *philia* love, and certainly to be prized over the basest love of all, *eros*.

Since that time, I have heard and seen (as has the reader, no doubt) many expositions of that lexical "fact," both in speech and in print. I also was blessed to learn better before I began to preach, teach, or write that idea myself. Plenty of New Testament passages require a different understanding of *agape*; one example—to my mind the most dramatic of all—suffices to rule out this one completely. In 2 Tim 4:10, Paul reported to his protégé, "Demas has forsaken me, having loved [*agapesas*] this present world."[1] For good measure, John, the beloved elder, instructed the faithful, "Do not love (*agapate*) the world, nor the things of the world" (1 John 2:15). Whatever it is, "*agape* love" is *not* a special love sent from heaven, that only Christians can possess, experience, and manifest. (What *agape* is, is to be "all in" on desiring and acting for the total wellbeing/flourishing/*shalom* of the beloved—including, but also extending far beyond, "mere" attitude or emotion. *Agape* is centered in intention, will, and action.)

Semantically, so it is with covenant: A covenant is a contract, period. Certainly, we may believe the best of any contract initiated and signed off on by God. However, that inviolability does not reside in the basic concept of covenant (contract) itself—no matter how fervently both parties may desire their mutual and lasting fidelity. Nor does it lie in the idea that God somehow transformed the ordinary covenant/contract of the ancient world into something different, greater, or special, by the mere fact of its becoming part of the divine transaction with creation, and thus a part of the biblical record—any more than *agape* somehow is a uniquely "spiritual" love. The quality of specialness (holiness) in the biblical covenants is not inherent in covenant, but in Yahweh, the quintessential covenant Partner. Plenty of contracts are nullified by the transgression of one or another (sometimes, all) of their signatories. The concept of covenant is necessary to a proper understanding of God's dealings, especially those with *'ādām*, the human species, but covenant is far from sufficient for a full understanding. Covenant alone cannot meet even human relational aspirations—to say nothing of God, who did not give up on us when we turned our backs on God. Covenant is necessary, but it falls far short of being sufficient.

Moreover, covenant is insufficient because covenant is secondary in God's dealings with God's good creation, including *'ādām*. Covenant never has been the starting point of God's interaction with any individual, nor with any group of persons. If not covenant, then what?

---

1. All translations are the author's.

## Ḥesed: Kin(d)ness Displayed as Attitude-in-Action

If, as Gen 1:26–27 avers, God formed 'ādām in God's own image, we do well to consider what that image is. I take the Hebrew Bible to affirm ḥesed as the defining expression of God's character, and of God's attitude and actions in relationship with, and on behalf of, God's creation. What, then, is ḥesed?

Because Glueck's definition of ḥesed as "covenant loyalty" seems to dominate popular understanding—students quite frequently cite it in my classes, for example—a brief excursus is necessary. Among other considerations, this definition overlooks an important association. The phrase ḥesed wě'ĕmet occurs only a few times in Scripture, but I understand it to be the primary Hebrew summation of God's character; the second noun, 'ĕmet, denotes "loyalty/faithfulness." If ḥesed meant "covenant loyalty," the entire phrase ḥesed wě'ĕmet would mean "covenant loyalty and loyalty." Taking the phrase as a hendiadys, as most do, we would translate it, "loyal covenant loyalty." What kind of sense does that make as the most important Hebrew description/definition of God's character?

Approximately one-quarter of the uses of ḥesed occur in narrative contexts of human interaction. Specifically and originally, ḥesed is the normative attitude, and its resulting actions, of lovingkindness expected and usually exhibited between family members within a healthy complex of family dynamics. Lovingkindness—love expressed as kindness—seems a felicitous rendering when we recall that English "kindness" itself designates the attitude-resulting-in-action expected and normally exhibited, in the first instance, toward one's own kin/kind. When nurtured in healthy families, humans learn ḥesed from the womb. As the sphere of our relationships widens, so does our arena for expressing the ḥesed we have learned and practiced in the generous intimacy of family.

Sometimes the term occurs, sometimes it does not, but the attitudes and actions of ḥesed between husband and wife are enjoined throughout the collections we call the Torah, the Prophets, and the Writings. In and for Israel's cultural context, the Torah's instruction on marital matters generally is forward-looking. In the mostly narrative material of the Prophets, pride of place in demonstrating ḥesed may go to Ruth; she consistently acted in ḥesed toward her successive husbands Mahlon and Boaz, as well as toward her mother-in-law Naomi. In the Writings the exemplary wife of Proverbs 31, and both the lovers of the Song of Songs, immediately catch our attention as living out an ethos of ḥesed unstintingly.

We expect fathers and mothers to show/do/act in ḥesed toward their children; both Torah and Wisdom provide considerable instruction toward that end. Several mothers—e.g., Jocheved; Hannah; here also, the unnamed woman of Proverbs 31—are presented as exemplars of ḥesed. Disappointingly, the narratively prominent fathers tend rather to demonstrate what ḥesed is not, with respect to their children; Jacob and David come readily to mind.

Early in life, the twin brothers Jacob and Esau certainly did not relate to each other in *ḥesed*, but the scene of their reconciliation (Genesis 33) demonstrates *ḥesed* to a degree matched by few other passages, whether narrative or didactic. The brothers-in-law David and Jonathan displayed an extravagant *ḥesed* toward each other, even at the risk of both their lives.

## The *Ḥesed* of *Shaddai*

Most of the remaining three-fourths of its occurrences posit *ḥesed* as belonging to and/ or coming from God. God chose the *ḥesed* of the family circle to introduce Godself to us. We most adequately understand God's redemption intentions when we see them as the divine expression of the *ḥesed* we first experience in the intimate atmosphere of a healthy family. We could illustrate this extensively, citing any number of family relationships, but one will suffice. For every human, it is our earliest relationship; for most of us, it dominates the first years of our childhood—vital, intimate, virtually all-consuming. If we can demonstrate that God is the God of *ḥesed* in this relationship, we almost could say we need no further evidence. We are speaking of God under the title, *Shaddai*—the birthing, nursing, tactile, comforting Mother, the earliest and most intimate of all the manifestations of *ḥesed*.

First, and just to set it aside so as to get on to the reality. The usual English translation of *Shaddai* as "Almighty" simply no longer is tenable (if ever it was). The vast body of Akkadian documents was not yet known when "Almighty" began to emerge as the "default" English rendering. Still, it has become common to justify it by resorting to Akkadian *shadû*, "mountain"; i.e., *Shaddai* is the God of the mountains, either by virtue of having God's divine residence within/upon the (mighty) mountain(s) or, even better, of being their Creator. However, the chances that *Shaddai* derives from *shadû* are less than miniscule. Moreover, even if it did, *shadû* itself almost certainly is from an Akkadian form meaning "breast," bringing us back to where we are bound, anyway. Akkadian *shadû*, "mountain," is a metaphorical extension of the Semitic root, *šad*, "breast," in the same way the Grand Tetons range of the American Rockies is a metaphorical naming by early French explorers. (This analogy has been cited so often, I am embarrassed to use it; still, it is apt.)

To my mind, the most basic "negative" reason Hebrew *Shaddai* does not derive from Akkadian *shadû* is that Hebrew has several forms, from at least three different roots, to indicate mountains, hills, heights, etc. None is either derived from or related to Akkadian *shadû*. Hebrew uses no cognate of, nor loan-word from, Akkadian *shadû* to designate mountains or heights.

Positively, and more importantly, Hebrew *does* have a root *šad*, meaning "breast." Four further assertions are possible: 1. No etymological, philological, grammatical, syntactical, or other linguistic argument can be adduced to prevent *Shaddai* from being derived from this root. 2. As is well-known, *Shaddai* occurs but forty-eight times in the Hebrew canonical corpus—the distribution of these occurrences makes eminent sense when considered within the semantic horizon of a derivation from *šad*, "breast." 3. The distribution of these occurrences is entirely meaningless if taken as originating within the semantic horizon of a derivation from Akkadian *shadû*, "mountain." 4. Several explicit punning uses of *Shaddai* paired with another similar-sounding root *šod*, "destruction," make excellent sense if *Shaddai* derives from *šad*, "breast," no sense at all if *Shaddai* means "Almighty." We proceed to the most salient of the details.

First, the basic meaning of *Shaddai* is "The Breasted One." Obviously, as a title for God, it conveys a feminine image. God is the Mother, the all-nourishing Provider. Throughout most of human history, and often yet today, the newborn infant is entirely dependent upon its nursing mother for every need—for its smallest increment of nourishment, for warmth, for the security of the mother's total, all-encompassing embrace, for the reassurance of touch and its importance to our early emotional, psychological, and even mental growth, for *every* need. Just so, human dependence upon God is all-encompassing and all-inclusive. Ultimately, we are nothing, we have nothing, except as it comes from God, to the same (or greater) degrees both of totality and of intimacy as we see in the nursing mother's care of her newborn infant. As surely and completely as God is the Divine Father, God also is the Divine Mother.

The first occurrence of the title *Shaddai* is in Gen 17:1, as God came to Abraham and entered into the most extensive conversation with him recorded in the narrative of his life. The other occurrences in Genesis are: 28:3; 35:11; 43:14; 48:3; 49:25. It is not too much to call the last reference paradigmatic. The climax of Jacob's blessing upon Joseph is the "blessings of the breasts and the womb." The descendents of fruitful Joseph would have the all-encompassing nurture, the formational security and confidence, begun at and symbolized by a mother's breast.

Alongside this intrinsic "literal" meaning, we note also that the storyline of the Patriarchal Narratives is a saga of wandering, the classic narrative of a quest, but one in which these questers do not, cannot, come to the satisfying successful conclusion of the quest. Where else would the figuring of God as the all-caring, all-providing Mother be more appropriate? Wandering in the sure hope of the Promise, but in the equally sure knowledge that this hope would not be realized in their lifetimes, who more than Israel's Patriarchs and Matriarchs needed to lean upon the breast of the Divine Mother?

The largest cluster of occurrences of *Shaddai*, nineteen in all, is in the book of Job. Has anyone in all history and all literature ever needed to call upon God in God's character as sustaining and comforting Mother than did Job?

Isa 13:6 and Joel 1:15, both speaking of the "Day of Yahweh," say, "It will come as destruction (*šod*) from *Shaddai*." If this meant, "as destruction from the Almighty," the words themselves (as distinguished from the concept these prophets intended them to convey) would have no particular power, carry no particular pathos. But if this predicted destruction—and *shod* connotes a very large, thorough, complete destruction, indeed—if such devastation comes at the hand (or even only with the permission) of *Shaddai*, the nursing Mother, who can stand? Who can endure it? This is precisely the point of this pun of deep pathos in both these prophets.

In Ruth 1:20–21, upon her return to Bethlehem after at least a ten-year absence, Naomi lamented her bitter lot in similar terms. In a short speech, she used first the title *Shaddai*, then the name Yahweh, then reversed the order chiastically—*Shaddai*:Yahweh::Yahweh:*Shaddai*). Naomi charged *Shaddai*, the nursing Mother, with dealing "*very* bitterly" with her (v. 20), and with "testifying against" her. How could *Shaddai* do such a thing? In these depth-of-her-soul complaints, as well as in the intentional puns of Isaiah and Joel, if *Shaddai* meant "Almighty," these three are saying almost nothing. But if, as truly is the case, *Shaddai* means "The Breasted One," "God-the-nursing-Mother," they are speaking to the limit of human language to convey, not a neutral and sterile pietude, but feeling, anguish, pathos, loss, what-possibly-can-we-do-now? If God-the-nursing-Mother is against us, all *is* lost.

That we discover God's nature, character, and image so profoundly in God's title *Shaddai* is one of the great graces of all these passages. Do we wish to understand *ḥesed*? When we look to God as *Shaddai*, we find the deepest, most tender expressions of *ḥesed*.

## Conclusion

All scholars of the ancient Near East know that the language of covenant relationships in the treaties of the Second and the First millennia BCE is cast in family terms. The suzerain was "father"; the vassal king was "son." Parity treaties were concluded between "brothers." The evidence is abundant that these treaties rested on shifting sand. No vassal "son" died in battle alongside his suzerain "father" if he could avoid it. Many times at the death of a suzerain, their "father," vassal "sons" rebelled against the late suzerain's real son, whom they should have acknowledged as their new "father" had their allegiance been genuine. In virtually every ancient Near Eastern political/military context, the "family" language was a pretext, its rituals a charade. Suzerains maintained "covenant loyalty" at the point of the sword; when the sword-point dipped (or even appeared that it might), many vassals' "loyalty" evaporated. Even dressing a covenant (contract) fraudulently in the clothing of family language almost never was enough to preserve it.

(As an aside, the political notion of a human king as "father" is at best a cobbled-together, makeshift stopgap. At its worst—as Caesar, Kaiser, Tsar, der Feuhrer, Il Duce, Supreme Leader, Big Brother, and many more—it becomes a perversion on the largest scale.)

God used the language of "covenant" because that political apparatus was coin of the realm through most of the history of the ancient Near East. Rescuing Israel from Pharaoh's hegemony, and offering them status as God's own people made "covenant" a term Israel could understand in their new political circumstances. But political covenant was neither the beginning nor the end of God's ḥesed toward Israel. Covenant—conditioned as it is on historical, cultural, social, political circumstances—was and is but a small feature of ḥesed's far grander scope.

God's ḥesed involves nothing less than an invitation into God's eternal family. We are not vassals, and covenant is not enough for God. We are not even only "kingdom citizens." We are family, God's adopted daughters and sons, younger brothers and sisters of our elder Brother who entered into death to rescue us from death. God invites us into the eternal perfection and joys of *God's* family ḥesed—lovingkindness, i.e., family love and kindness in thought, attitude, and intention, in word and in deed.

# 2

## *Akedah* as Apologia: The Function of Genesis 22 for Second Temple Jews

— Karen Strand Winslow

### Translation of Genesis 22[1]

1 After these things God tested Abraham. "Abraham," he called. "Here I am, he replied." 2 He said, "Take *your son*, the one with whom you are one, Isaac, whom you love, and go to the land of Moriah, and offer him there as a burnt-offering on one of the mountains that I shall show you." 3 So Abraham rose early in the morning, saddled his donkey, and took two of his young men with him, and *his son* Isaac; he cut the wood for the burnt-offering, and set out and went to the place in the distance that God had shown him. 4 On the third day Abraham looked up and saw the place far away. 5 Then Abraham said to his young men, "Stay here with the donkey; the young man and I will go over there; we will worship, and then we will come back to you." 6 Abraham took the wood of the burnt-offering and laid it on *his son* Isaac, and he himself carried the fire and the knife. *So the two of them walked on as one.* 7 Isaac said to *his father* Abraham, "*My father!*" And he said, "Here I am, *my son.*" He said, "The fire and the wood are here, but where is the lamb for a burnt-offering?" 8 Abraham said, "God himself will see to the lamb for a burnt-offering, *my son.*" *So the two of them walked on as one.* 9 When they came to the place that God had told him, Abraham built an alar there and laid out the wood, bound *his son* Isaac, and laid him on the altar, on top of the wood. 10 Then Abraham reached out his hand and took the knife to kill *his son.* 11 But the angel of the Lord called to him from heaven, and said, "Abraham, Abraham!" And he said, "Here I am." 12 He said, "Do not lay your hand on the youth or do anything to him; for now I know that you fear God, since you have not withheld *your son, the one with whom you are one,* from me." 13 And Abraham looked up and saw a ram, caught in a thicket by its horns. Abraham went and took the ram and offered it up as a burnt-offering instead of *his son.* 14 So Abraham called that place "The Lord will see"; as it is said to this day, "On the mount of the Lord it shall be

---

1. All translations of the Old Testament are the author's. Italics represent repeated relational terms (father-son) and those that show the oneness of Abraham and Isaac.

seen."15 The angel of the Lord called to Abraham a second time from heaven, 16 and said, "By myself I have sworn, says the Lord: Because you have done this, and have not withheld your son, *the one with whom you are one*, 17 I will indeed bless you, and I will make your offspring as numerous as the stars of heaven and as the sand that is on the seashore. And your offspring shall possess the gate of their enemies, 18 and by your offspring shall all the nations of the earth gain blessing for themselves, because you have obeyed my voice." 19 So Abraham returned to his young men, and they arose and went together to Beersheba; and Abraham lived at Beersheba.

## Introduction

What is the meaning of Genesis 22, "The Binding (*Akedah*) of Isaac" for the Jews of Persian Yehud? Why would Jewish scribes in the Second Temple period have preserved or composed this cryptic account of a traumatic trial of Abraham that has raised many challenges for later recipients of Scripture? Did not the shapers and preservers of the sacred texts—whether they were recorders of oral tradition, redactors of written sources, creative artists, or some combination of the above—hesitate before including this passage in the Torah?[2] Are contemporary moral sensitivities so removed from those of Second Temple scribes that the latter could include—without qualms—this tradition about God initiating a cruel ordeal for his elected servant so that God could see the extent of Abraham's loyalty? Many honest readers have been revolted by this story and some of them admit it.

Immanuel Kant wrote:

> In some cases one can be sure that it is *not* God whose voice a man may believe he hears, namely when what this voice says is opposed to the moral law. However majestic and supernatural an apparition may seem to be, one must then regard it as a delusion. Take as an example the sacrifice which Abraham was to make on allegedly Divine command by slaughtering and burning his only son. Abraham ought to have replied to the pretendedly divine voice: "That I must not kill my good son is quite certain, but that you who appear to me as God are indeed God, of this I can never become certain, even if your voice came down to me from the visible Heaven."[3]

---

2. Although there are a number of theories about the processes of oral and written sources that comprise the Pentateuch, and linguistic analysis is helpful, we have little certainty about which Torah traditions were transmitted from earlier eras and which were composed by Second Temple scribes. Whatever its origin, the *Akedah* as we know it was produced by Jewish scribes for Persian period—and later—Jews. It is not referred to elsewhere in the Hebrew Bible, but it appears in extra-canonical literature beginning in the second century BCE According to Documentary critics, Genesis 22 is composed of pre-exilic E (Elohist) and J (Yahwist) sources, and redacted by the Elohist.

3. Kant, *The Quarrel between the Faculties*, 334–35.

Certainly, Kant would have altered this plot or left it out of the Bible entirely. This is impossible, however, once a text had attained the status of Scripture. However, during the Jewish Scriptures' formative period, when a fixed canon of Jewish "Scripture" did not yet exist, this tradition was not excised from the collective memory of Jews, but rather preserved—or even produced—and became the text as we now read it. The fact that the story of Genesis 22 is in the Bible indicates that it was affirmed repeatedly in the scripturalization process as an important component of Jewish tradition.[4] How then did this text function for the framers of the Jewish Scriptures? What was this "wrenching little tale" attempting to demonstrate in Second Temple times?

We cannot point to inner-biblical exegesis to answer this question, because "The Binding of Isaac" is not cited, questioned, altered, expanded, explained, or even alluded to by other biblical authors. Extra-canonical texts, however, such as *Jubilees*, 4 Maccabees, the works of Philo and Josephus, the New Testament (first century CE), and Midrashim and Targumim (from the rabbinic period), do treat the *Akedah*.[5] By adding numerous characters, contacts, conversations, and incidents, the imaginative expansions of the interpreters attempt to resolve some of the same moral and theological issues that perplex us. In so doing, they transform the story in light of their developing theological understandings, thus defend—develop an apology for—their brand of Judaism for their Graeco-Roman contexts.

For example, Philo and Josephus are first century apologists for Judaism who provide a defense of the attributes of Judaism in their renditions of Genesis 22.[6] Philo demonstrates that Abraham, the founder of Judaism, is more pure and performs more difficult feats than the gods of the myths or the citizens of the nations who sacrifice their children for their country out of custom or fear. They do so, not only as soldiers but as actual victims of ritual sacrifice "in order to deliver it from war or drought." Others give their children for glory at the time and renown in the future. However, according to Philo, "Abraham was not mastered by custom or love of honor or fear; but rather through obedience and acting as the priest himself and not from a position

---

4. The Torah, of which Genesis 22 is a part, was probably compiled and relatively fixed around the middle of the fifth century, although it may have been subject to revision and editing for some time after that. We may observe the transformations of this tradition in the later literature of the Jews and Christians, but we have no way of knowing if there were traditions behind the one we read in Genesis 22, or how it reached its final form. One of the criteria for determining which of several versions is earliest is brevity. This is based on an assumption that later receivers of texts are prone to embellish and explain enigmas. This criterion alone sets Genesis 22 earlier than all of the other (extra-biblical) versions of this story.

5. 4 Maccabees is in the canon of Eastern and Roman Catholicism and was written in the first century between 18 and 55; perhaps during the reign of Caligula around 40 CE. It is about Antiochus IV Epiphanes giving Jews the choice to eat pork and other forbidden meat or die in 167 BCE. Some sections of the *Targumim* post-date the fall of the Second Temple. *Jubilees*, a rewritten Torah, was composed in the second century BCE and is among the earliest extant interpretations of this story. Some of the New Testament epistles were written before the fall of the Temple in 70 CE, and most of the rest of the NT was written by 100 CE.

6. Philo, *Abraham*, 32–36 (167–207) (trans. Yonge); Josephus, *Ant.* 1:8 (1–4, 218–39).

removed." Thus, Philo continues, everyone who is not "envious and a lover of evil must be overwhelmed with admiration for his excessive piety." Any small action of "the Sage" was "enough to show the greatness and loftiness of his soul" (*Abr.* 35). Josephus's father and son's actions are suited to Roman filial custom; Isaac responds to Abraham's explanation of his need to die by rushing to the altar (*Ant.* 1:7.4 [234]).[7]

After outlining some the dilemmas this brief tale creates and showing how other early recipients of Scripture discovered meanings in the story that were crucial to their own circumstances, we will turn to those early Jews of the Second Temple period who enfolded Abraham's "last trial" into the rest of his story. I will imagine the answers they might give to questions that arise from our honest distress over this tale, answers that suggest apologetic motives of the scribes of early Judaism as they framed Scripture in the Persian period. We will see that the single exchange between Isaac and Abraham provides a link between this story and other Torah portraits of God as See-er and Provider and points to a defense of the God of the Jews and his first servant and friend, Abraham. In addition, it advances a defense of the God of the Jews and of Abraham, their founding father.

## Dilemma I: God's Cruelty, Doubt, and Jealousy

The problems with this text begin with God. God, the Holy One Blessed be He, who is revered above all else for His goodness, love, mercy, and knowledge, appears anything but compassionate in this strange tale. Instead, we might suspect Him of ignorance, mistrust, and jealousy. When Abraham was finally reaping the fruits of waiting and believing, believing and waiting, for he now had the son of Sarah as promised, God initiated the movement of the story by telling Abraham to offer up his beloved son as an ʽ *olâ*—a whole burnt offering. This same God who had made Sarah a mother when she was not only barren but *old* and barren, ordered Abraham to make a *holocaust* of the bringer of laughter, the would-be father of a great nation.[8] Giving a child to an aged, infertile couple is what we might expect from God: "For to God nothing is too incredible!" (Gen 18:14).[9] Asking this father to slaughter this son, however, seems very unlike the God we know from the rest of the Bible, a God who is known for creating and preserving life and honors those who do the same.[10]

---

7. Josephus, *Ant.* 1:7.4 (234).

8. *Holocaust* is the Greek term for ʽ *olâ*, whole burnt offering.

9. This announcement made to Sarah about the birth of Isaac by the angel is nearly identical to the one made to Mary about the birth of Jesus in Luke 2:37.

10. Among the many examples, see Genesis 1–5 and the Joseph story of Genesis 37–50, which includes the story of Tamar in Genesis 38. See also Exodus 1 about the midwives who were honored for disobeying Pharaoh and saving babies. There are a few exceptions, however: God destroyed most of creation in a flood (Genesis 6–9) and attempted to slay Moses in Exod 4:24–26, after sending him back to Egypt to deliver all of God's people there.

Another difficulty, which at first seems like a resolution to the previous problem, is that the entire episode is construed as a test. "After these things God *tested* Abraham" is the introduction to the story (Gen 22:1). While we might be relieved that God never intended to see Isaac's blood, we are surprised that God could not know Abraham's heart without trying him in this cruel way. We are horrified to consider that God would put his faithful follower through such an ordeal so that He would see and learn the extent of Abraham's devotion to Him.

God did not know Abraham's heart when he arose early in the morning, saddled his donkey, cut the wood, or gathered the three young men. God did not stop him as the little company walked along the way or when two separated from two (Gen 22:5). Not even when God saw Abraham build the altar or bind Isaac and lay him on it did God know Abraham's heart. Not until Isaac was as good as dead to Abraham—he had stretched out his son to grasp the knife to slay his son—did the angel of the LORD tell him to proceed no further: "for *now I know* that you fear God in that you have not withheld your son, your beloved, from me." God did not, until that last moment of seeing, *know* Abraham. Apparently God feared that Abraham loved Isaac more than he feared God, and God was determined to ascertain the truth; so that God could see whether Abraham truly feared God or not (Gen 22:12). In Genesis 22, God initiated a test to discover Abraham's devotion. This un-omniscient God asked the impossible of his covenant partner—he tried him in order to search and know him.[11] This is a problem for those who believe God knows all things, including the future, or—if not the future—at least the present character of individuals, which, in this chapter, God did not know except by seeing what Abraham did. The God of the *Akedah* is a God who sees what humans do at the moment they do it and thus knows them, but *not* a God who knows what they would do without a trial.

Subsequent to the test, the angel of the LORD promised Abraham wonderful rewards for passing the test: blessings, descendants numbered like the stars and sand, possessing enemy gates, and that in him all nations (*gôyim*) shall bless themselves (Gen 22:16–18). This is less consolation, however, when we remember that most of these promises had been promised earlier to Abraham in previous vignettes (Gen 12:1–6 [self-blessing nations], 15:1–21 [descendants like the stars, this land], and 17:1–27 [many descendants]). The descendants, land (implied in possessing enemy gates), and the universal blessings promised again in 22:18 had been presented to Abraham earlier at God's initiative without paradoxical and outrageous demands. God previously intended to do all this, and Abraham was *already* reckoned righteous because he believed the LORD (Gen 15:6). Why should Abraham have to do something so terrible in order to confirm a bequest already promised? Did God become uncertain and jealous as Abraham received this son and delighted in him?

---

11. The paradox of a knowing God who may also try and search a human is framed in Ps 139:13–24: "You know me well . . . in thy book were written every one of the days that were formed for me when they were not yet . . . Search me O God and know my heart, try me and know my thoughts."

Certainly, from the Genesis storyline, we note growing expectations for Abraham each time the covenant was renewed. Conditions are implied in Genesis 12 in that Abraham must go to receive the promises. In Genesis 15, he must be a person of integrity who raises his household well. Here Abraham believed God and this was merited to him as righteousness. In Genesis 17, the promises are set in terms of the covenant that Abraham and his son by Sarah and all their descendants must keep: circumcision. Circumcision is a sacrifice and represents further, more costly sacrifice.[12] Nonetheless, it is a great leap in scale when God demands that Abraham sacrifice to him the embodied fruit of his loins, the son of promise, Isaac. Furthermore, at the conclusion of Genesis 22, we are under the impression that offering his son was required in order to receive these promises, that the previous versions of the promise would have been revoked had he not passed *this* test—it was his "last trial." To do justice to the text, we must accept that God initiated this ordeal because God did not know of Abraham's "fear" until he grabbed the knife, which proved it to Him. Only when God saw this did God re-confirm the promises.

As later Second Temple literature and even later Midrashim indicate, God's doubt and mistrust that led to this severe ordeal were challenges for early interpreters. In order to absolve God of responsibility for initiating the trauma, the authors of *Jubilees* and the rabbinic Midrashim extend the cast of the drama to include other characters who challenged God about Abraham just as *hasatan* did about Job. In their rewritten Bibles, the incident becomes the result of boasts, quarrels, and/or challenges of Prince Mastema (*haśśāṭān*), angels, the nations of the world, Ishmael and Eliezer, or Isaac himself.[13] God was compelled to prove Abraham and Isaac's total devotion (of which God was already thoroughly aware) to these additional figures. For example, the story concludes in *Jubilees* 18:9–13 this way:

> And I stood before him, and before the prince Mastema, and the Lord said, "Bid him not to lay his hand on the lad, nor to do anything to him, for I have shown that he fears [10] the Lord." And I called to him from heaven, and said unto him: "Abraham, Abraham;" and he [11] was terrified and said: "Behold, (here) am I." And I said unto him: "Lay not thy hand upon the lad, neither do thou anything to him; for now I have shown that thou fearest the Lord,

---

12. Several phenomena were involved in both circumcision and blood sacrifice that served to link the two rituals: cutting flesh, shedding blood, the maleness of the victims and the priests, and the fact that the commandment to perform both comes from the deity to mark the victim as belonging to the deity. Whereas sacrifice (devotion to deity) was associated with the firstborn (Exod 4:21–23, Exod 13:15, Exod 34:19, Gen 22:13), circumcision became necessary for all males (Gen 17:4–7, 9–10, 14; Lev 12:3). In Isaiah 56, even Gentiles who are circumcised may join the community. Circumcision took over from sacrifice the indexing of male descent lines when many—then all—Jews lived without a temple. See Hoffman, *Covenant of Blood*, 32–50.

13. *Jub.* 17:15—18:12, *b. Sanh.* 89b, *Gen. Rab.* 55–6, *Tanh. Bub. Vay.* 42, *Ber. Rab.* to Gen 22:1; *Tanh. Vay.* 18 and *Sefer ha-Yashar* 22–23. In a modern midrash by Jakov Lind, Abraham blames Sarah for his action. "It is not him I wanted to kill. It's your doubt, your laughter, I wanted to destroy." See Lind, "The Near Murder," 147–148.

and hast [12] not withheld thy son, thy first-born son, from me." And the prince Mastema was put to shame; and Abraham lifted up his eyes and looked, and, behold a ram caught . . . by his horns, and Abraham [13] went and took the ram and offered it for a burnt-offering in the stead of his son.

In *Jubilees*, Mastema challenged God concerning Abraham and was shamed when Abraham demonstrated fear of the LORD to him.

The first line in the biblical account, "after these things" is the means by which the Midrashim introduce these new players and scenes, contributing various events and circumstances that are not in the biblical text. By answering the question: what things?, they clear God of blame for setting up the test and appearing unknowing and mistrustful. According to these accounts, God is interested in demonstrating, not for Himself, but to *others*, the faithfulness of Abraham. I am suggesting here that the biblical account has much the same motive. Within the world of the story, God is trying Abraham to prove Abraham's devotion to God, but to hearers and readers, the story demonstrates Abraham's devotion to God at the cost of his beloved son, who is more to him than his own life. Certainly, Abraham's commitment to God and God's consequent obligation to him and his progeny is dramatically affirmed. Before we further examine the *Akedah's* apologetic purpose, we will observe another of its puzzles: the problem of Abraham's obedience.

## Dilemma II: Abraham Obeyed God

For interpreters who stand back from the story, God is not the only questionable figure in the *Akedah*; Abraham is as well. Although *God* was pleased with Abraham's mute obedience, early midrashic interpreters found his silence so incredible (albeit sometimes commendable), they were compelled to put a multitude of words into Abraham's heart and mouth. In the various accounts, he dialogues with himself, with God, Sarah, Satan/Mastema, and/or his young men as he processes the command and carries it out. Abraham's conversation with Isaac is prolonged. All of these dialogues stress his obedience, which is highly regarded.[14]

On the other hand, when we step out of a stance that unthinkingly accepts any biblical pronouncement as good, we are amazed that Abraham would and could obey such an immoral demand. If we are honest, we would call out with Kant early in the drama: "Abraham, Abraham, what on earth are you doing? You cannot kill your son no matter who orders you to do it! Why would God want a dead Isaac anyway—He promised that your seed would be engendered through him—Isaac cannot be a father if he's dead!" Or: "Stop! This cannot be God; it is your worst nightmare and you must resist it. No good God is bloodthirsty!" And, "what about his mother? She carried him;

---

14. See especially *Gen. Rab.* 55–6 (also *Sefer ha-Yashar* 22).

do you have any right to take him from her forever? God must know your devotion by now! Besides, the penalty for shedding human blood is death!" (Gen 9:6).

Most preaching and commentary on the subject, however, avoid such reactions and instead commend Abraham for his obedience to this horrid request. They follow in the path of the Midrashim who put resisting responses into the mouth of *haśśāṭān* in his attempts to thwart Abraham's obedience.[15] Nonetheless, in our most honest moments, we find it difficult to shake our views on the value of human life and strength of parental love in order to glorify a man for his willingness to slay his son. How can we join God in praising Abraham when we put people in prison (or worse) for pre-meditated killing? Abraham retains a puzzling, reprehensible profile for those who believe it cannot be good to obey God if this means killing your child to offer him to God.

## Dilemma III: Isaac's Question and Abraham's Answer

Isaac is the least culpable of all the actors. In the spare biblical text, the concern is not with Isaac's willingness to die, but Abraham's willingness to obey the order to sacrifice his beloved son. From the first, we know Isaac was the object of the sacrifice, not the sacrificer. Isaac was a trusting child, at one with his father as they walked the way together (Gen 22:6 and 8; *yaḥdāw*, "as one"). Isaac was the heart of his father torn slowly from his bosom with each step of the journey, each gathered stone for the altar, each wrap of the rope around beloved limbs. Nevertheless, he cannot be understood as totally passive. He was, after all, a youth, not a toddler or lamb.[16] He chose to walk toward Moriah at one with his father, and, recognizing at last his fate, allowed himself to be bound and laid upon the altar. Thus, we wonder to Isaac, "We can understand why you would go; but why did you not run or plead for your life when you realized what was happening?" However, this is precisely what walking *as one* with his father means. While Abraham was demonstrating to God that he feared God, a mostly silent Isaac was demonstrating his oneness with his father.

Like Abraham, Isaac said very little in the biblical story and we are given no insight to his thoughts. These silences are filled by the *daršān*; the sages are captivated with Isaac's role and they give us a loquacious, enthusiastic character. In their re-tellings, Isaac becomes an active co-offerer of his life. This transformation of the tradition has repercussions in Judaism and Christianity, which we will discuss after examining the single line in the passage in which Isaac breaks his silence by asking his father the piercingly pertinent question: "Where is the lamb for the ʿolâ?"[17]

---

15. See *Jub.* 17:15—18:12 and *Sefer ha-Yashar* 22:47—23:39.

16. No age is given in the biblical text, of course, but soon after Abraham acquires a wife for him (Genesis 24). Some strands of rabbinic tradition set his age at 37, others at 25.

17. Isaac's question shows that the customary victim of an ʿolâ was a lamb or kid. No one in the story considered the idea that Abraham might be intending to sacrifice his child—except God. Receivers of the text are expected to find this an unusual, shocking ordeal.

Abraham responded: "God *will see* for himself—'*ĕlohîm yir' eh*—the lamb for the burnt offering, my son." This answer may be considered evasive or explicit; either "God will see to that, my son," or "God will see (and find out), my son," or "God will see that the lamb for the burnt offering *is* my son." The response may show Abraham's hope that God would provide a lamb—in the place of Isaac. However, it seems to me that the *peshat*, the plain meaning, is that "my son" is direct address to Isaac, not an appositive to the lamb. "My son," as direct address is consistent with the rest of the passage that repeats the relational terms in order to highlight the closeness, the at-oneness of son and father. In any case, the important term is: '*ĕlohîm yir' eh*—"God will see." Most translations use: "God will provide" for God's seeing, for God's growing awareness is connected with God's response, which includes divine action, and often provision, His "seeing to it." God as See-er and See-er-to (responder) is a tie that binds this tale to its place in the Genesis and the rest of the Torah. God's seeing and response has pervaded the narratives of Genesis and continues into Exodus and beyond. We will look at a few examples.

## The God Who Sees

In the beginning, God saw—*yar'*—that his work was good, "*wayyar' ĕlohîm ki-tôb*" (Gen 1:10). He saw—*yar'*—the great wickedness of man and the corruption of the earth in Noah's time (Gen 6:5, 11, 12) and acted. In Genesis 18, the LORD came down *to see* about Sodom and Gomorrah and acted. In the Abraham cycle, when Hagar ran from Sarah's abuse and the angel of the LORD found her by a spring, he promised that the LORD would greatly multiply her descendants. Hagar called the name of the LORD: The God of seeing, "' *l rŏ' î*" (Gen 16:13). God provided sustenance for Ishmael and Hagar when Abraham cast them out (Genesis 21). When the sons of Israel had been enslaved by the Egyptians, God saw the people of Israel and knew their condition and developed a plan of action (Exod 2:24–25). God saw that Moses turned to see the burning bush and called to him: "Moses, Moses." Like Abraham before him, he replied, "Here am I." God said, "I have seen the affliction of my people who are in Egypt" (Exod 3:4), which led to a series of moves for God and Moses.

In these and other Torah texts, God sees what people do and only then responds. This seeing God is not the omniscient God of the philosophers and medieval theologians, but a God who sees and hears within the world of the story and human history. Second Temple "theologians" were not presenting a god who knows the future, but a god who becomes aware, who investigates. This God is not cavorting with other gods, hunting and fighting, distracted, or engaged elsewhere. Neither is Israel's God senseless, immutable, beyond feeling, change, or passion, but a God who sees the suffering that was initiated by demanding this ordeal, just as the same See-er will know the suffering of Abraham's descendants under Pharaoh.

PART 1: GRAPPLING WITH SCRIPTURE IN ANCIENT AND CONTEMPORARY CONTEXTS

## The Place Moriah: "The Lord Will See"

This is further emphasized by the name Abraham called the place: "*YHWH yir' eh*, the Lord will see, as it is said today: 'On the mount of the Lord it shall be seen'" (Gen 22:14). Abraham's name for his place of testing ("*YHWH* Will See") is similar to Moriah, the land to which God ordered Abraham to take his beloved son at the outset of the trial: "that which is seen" (Gen 22:2). According to 2 Chr 3:1–2, Moriah is the site of Solomon's Temple.[18] Chronicles are the Second Temple annals that rewrite the story of Israel, depending heavily on 1–2 Samuel, 1–2 Kings, and genealogies of the Torah. In Chronicles, the scribes connected the mountain of Isaac's binding, Moriah, to the place of prayer and sacrifice for later Jews.[19] There they will pray and God will hear from heaven; He will see and provide. In Solomon's dedication of the (first) Temple at Jerusalem in 2 Chr 6:12–42 (based on 1 Kgs 8:22–53), he prays that when God's servants (and strangers, etc.) pray toward this place; that God will hear in heaven his dwelling place; and when he hears he will forgive.[20] Whether the term Moriah of Gen 22:2 was retrojected by Second Temple scribes into an older tradition of the *Akedah* or was part of a transmitted tradition does not matter for our interest in the meaning of the tale for Second Temple Judaism. Before we turn back to that era, we will look at the Jewish interpretive texts that draw out the implication of Abraham's naming of the place "*YHWH yir'eh*."

The *Mishnah*, Midrashim, and Targumim depict Abraham imploring God to remember his silent obedience on Moriah for the sake of Isaac's future children. Abraham's prayer after the ram had been slain in place of Isaac in the *Fragmentary Targum* says: "Now I pray for mercy before You, O Lord God, that when the children of Isaac come to a time of distress You may remember on their behalf the Binding of Isaac their father, and *loose and forgive* them their sins and deliver them form all distress."[21] *Mishnah Ta'anit* records the prayer of public fast days: "May He that answered Abraham our father on Mount Moriah answer you and hearken to the voice of your crying this day."[22] *Genesis Rabbah* elaborates on Genesis 22 this way:

> The moment You said to me, "Take now your son, your favored one," I could have retorted, yesterday You said to me, "For it is through Isaac that offspring shall be continued for you," and now you say to me, "Take now." But, heaven

---

18. "Moriah" of 2 Chr 3:1 is not connected there to Abraham's test, but to the threshing floor where the Lord appeared to David.

19. A full discussion of Moriah as cult site is in "The Aqedah as Etiology" by Jon Levenson in his book, *The Death and Resurrection of the Beloved Son*, 111–24. See pp. 115–16 about retrojecting "Moriah" into Genesis 22.

20. 1 Kgs 8:30, 32, 34, 36, 39, 43, 45, 49. Although no direct archaeological evidence for Solomon's Temple exists, the existence of a Jewish community in Persian Yehud in the fifth and following centuries is certain.

21. Speigel, *The Last Trial*, 206. My emphasis.

22. M. Ta'an. 2:4.

forbid I did not act that way, on the contrary, I suppressed my feelings of pity in order to do Thy will. So may it be Thy will, O Lord our God, whenever Isaac's children get into distress, to recall that *Akedah* on their behalf, and do Thou be filled with compassion for them.[23]

The plea for mercy, compassion, and forgiveness as expressed in the *Fragmentary Targum*, the Mishnah, and *Genesis Rabbah* ultimately transcends any attachment to a particular place. According to *Leviticus Rabbah* 2:11, the institution of the two daily lamb sacrifices while the temple stood was a reenactment of Isaac's binding. After the fall of the Second Temple, when anyone reads Lev 1:11 about the ram's slaughter on the north side of the altar, God remembers the binding of Isaac. These Midrashim underscore the theme that every sacrifice of the lips offered ever after must be a reminder of Abraham's gift of his beloved son. God saw Abraham's sacrifice; God will see and heed the prayers of Isaac's seed.

Later Jewish interpreters view the Moriah event as Isaac's self-sacrifice as much as it was Abraham's son-sacrifice. The tradition of the Second Temple becomes transformed for the templeless times. Prayers of the people—anywhere, anytime—implore a seeing God to remember the sacrifice of Abraham, which became the sacrifice of Isaac. Isaac's willingness to lay down his life must be remembered and applied to their descendants. Before we return to the function of the *Akedah* for early Jews, we will look at a few more examples of the transformation of this tradition for later Jews and Christians subsequent to the fall of the Second Temple and further dispersion of the Jews.

## Isaac's Self-Sacrifice in Later Jewish and Christian Texts

Isaac is represented as a co-offerer with Abraham of his life to God in 4 Maccabees, most of the Midrashim, and in Josephus and other Hellenistic rewrites of the story. Isaac was not a passive victim, but eager to lay down his own life.[24] As these interpretations invent Abraham's thoughts and conversations, so they put words into Isaac's mouth. In this way, he is understood as complicitous in the testing of Abraham; Isaac is tested too. 4 Maccabees is among the earliest references to Isaac as offerer of his own life and is an obvious example of scribes addressing current crises and movements to serve apologetic purposes for the context of its production.

---

23. *Gen. Rab.* 56:10; see *J. Ta'an.* 2:4, 16a (about the ashes of Isaac) and *Lev. Rab.* 29:9 in Speigel, *The Last Trial*, 90–91. See also the *Zikhronot* prayer of *Rosh HaShanah* ("*Musaf* of the New Year Service"), which Vermes and others find associated with the same festival in the first century CE. There is definite evidence that the commemoration of the *Akedah* was an established tradition in the third century. See Vermes, "Redemption and Genesis 22," 197–227, esp. 206–9.

24. In *Ant.* 1 (233), Isaac "rushed to the altar and his doom. And the deed would have been accomplished had not God stood in the way, for He called upon Abraham by name, forbidding him to slay the lad . . . Now that He know the ardour and depth of his piety, He took pleasure in what He had given him and would never fail to regard with the tenderest care both him and his race."

In 4 Maccabees, Isaac becomes the prototype of the Jewish martyr and may be compared and contrasted to Christian representations of Jesus's self- sacrifice.[25] According to these first century CE texts, both Isaac and Jesus were offered up by their fathers, but they also give themselves up to death. In 4 Maccabees, Isaac has given himself as an ' olâ, not a near-sacrifice, but a whole burnt offering. Compare passages in 4 Maccabees to verses from the New Testament: The seven sons and their mother who were martyrs "became ransom for the sin of our nation. Through the blood of these righteous ones and through the propitiation of their death the divine providence rescued Israel" (4 Macc 17:21–22). And: "Remember whence you came and at the hand of what father Isaac *gave himself* to endure immolation for piety's sake" (4 Macc 13:10; see also 16:18–20). And: "[Your father] read to you of Abel, done to death by Cain, of Isaac offered as a holocaust" (4 Macc 18:11–12).

The New Testament illustrates these themes as well.[26] "God . . . did not withhold his own Son, but gave him up for us all" (Rom 8:32). And: "For God so loved the world that he gave his only Son, that whoever believes in him should not perish but have eternal life" (John 3:16). And: "I am the good shepherd. The good shepherd lays down his life for the sheep . . . and I lay down my life for the sheep . . . For this reason the Father loves me, because I lay down my life, that I may take it again. No one takes it from me, but I lay it down of my own accord" (John 10:11, 15b, 17–18a). And: "No one has greater love than this, to lay down one's life for one's friends. You are my friends" (John 15:13–14a).

Like 4 Maccabees, the New Testament carries the concept of propitiation, the death of a martyr who purifies and redeems many others. The theme of the letter to the Hebrews, repeated many times throughout the first ten chapters, is illustrative of the benefits of self-sacrifice: For example, to paraphrase Hebrews 9: Christ offered himself once for all to bear the sins of many to put away sin by the sacrifice of himself (Heb 9:12–14, 24–28). Compare: "In Christ we have redemption through his blood, the forgiveness of our trespasses" (Eph 1:7). And: "one man's act of righteousness leads to justification and life for all . . . by the one man's obedience many will be made righteous" (Rom 5:18b, 19b).

These New Testament verses allude to life after death wrought by expiatory atonement. The family of martyrs in 4 Maccabees also stands with God, Abraham, Isaac, and Jacob in eternity. Fourth Maccabees and the New Testament thus call the Deuteronomistic criteria of success into question. Although they suffer and die in this life, they are blessed in the next for what they have done for others. Death is not the end and rewards remain imminent, even though they come only in the age to come: "On account of their endurance they now stand beside the divine throne and live the life of the age of blessing" (4 Macc 17:18).

---

25. John's Gospel is usually dated around 90 CE and Romans is dated to 56–57 CE. Ephesians is probably earlier.

26. All New Testament quotes are from the NRSV.

This literature develops received traditions to represent perspectives that emerged in Palestine and its surroundings about martyrdom, the immortality of the soul, and the resurrection of bodies in the two centuries that surround the turn of the era. Like the victims of Antiochus Epiphanies IV, Isaac of 4 Maccabees willingly gave himself as a martyr. His offering was applied to all Israel; God remembers Isaac's self-sacrifice and redeems his descendants just as the present-day Jews are rescued because of these martyrs' courage. The martyrs live with God after death because a life after death becomes more necessary, more foundational for the hope for recompense.[27]

Furthermore, the experience of Jesus's resurrection informs the views of first century Christian writers concerning traditions about the ancestors and origins. For example, according to the book of Hebrews, whose author recognized resurrection from the dead, Abraham believed that God would raise Isaac back to life as God had raised Jesus back to life (Heb 11:17–19). Those who transformed this tradition followed Second Temple scribes in using the *Akedah* to make claims about the founders of Israelite religion and Judaism that were relevant to their times. Let us return to these scribes and emerging Judaism in Persian Yehud.

## *Akedah* as Apologia

Second Temple period scribes were establishing an identity and parameters for their community by composing a history and a constitution. They knew their history included child sacrifice; the people had practiced it (Jer 19:5–6). Certainly their prophets had denounced it, saying God never commanded, never decreed it; it never even entered God's mind (Jer 7:31; Mic 6:6–9; Isa 57:5). Their law traditions included the demand by God for the firstborn from the womb, animal and human. Exod 22:28–29 says that the firstborn sons shall be given to God just as the first born of oxen and sheep shall be given. Exod 34:19–20 calls for the redemption of the firstborn sons (probably with a sheep), but the pericope of Exodus 22 makes no such substitution provision.

Ezekiel, the exilic prophet, claimed that God gave Israel "statutes that were not good and ordinances by which they could not live" as a punishment for breaking previous life-giving commandments, to render them desolate.[28] Knowing that prophets often use sarcasm, hyperbole, and shocking reenactments of their message, I cite this taxing passage to further demonstrate that: 1) the concept and practice of sacrificing children was known to the Second Temple Jews associated with the formation of the Bible, and 2) they considered child sacrifice strictly prohibited. This literary collection of the Jews represents a Mediterranean culture that did not avoid entanglement

---

27. See Levenson, *Death and Resurrection*, 173–99; and Milgrom, *The Binding of Isaac*, 82–89.

28. "Moreover I gave them statutes that were not good and ordinances by which they could not live. I defiled them through their very gifts, in their offering up all their firstborn, in order that I might horrify them, so that they might know that I am the Lord" (Ezek 20:25–26).

with this universal structure. The ancient mythic expectation that the gods require the pouring out of human life to effect military or agricultural success or as evidence of their followers' devotion and/or expiation for sin is both reflected in and countered by the Jewish Scriptures.[29]

Most biblical texts imply or declare that God did not require Jews to sacrifice their children after the manner of Moab, Phoenicia, Carthage, and other Mediterranean cultures.[30] Genesis 22 is an exception. There God ordered "the first Jew" to do just that, although the narrator informs the reader that God was only testing Abraham. Nonetheless, the *Akedah* demonstrates that the founding father of all Jews was willing and able to offer up his son to his God.[31] Abraham, the progenitor of the Jews, is put to the test in this story because the founding figure must demonstrate that he is capable of the most extreme self-sacrifice. The original servant of Israel's God, Abraham, must—for his part—give up his much beloved son to God.

Thus, the early scribes of Judaism can have it both ways. As the apology goes, Abraham, the father of all Jews, sacrificed his dearest possession—his beloved son—to God; but from God's end it was only a test. Abraham has a thoroughly devoted heart, but the LORD, unlike other gods, does not desire Isaac's blood or ashes. The man selected to be the father of the Jews was no less devoted to his god than the pious of surrounding cultures. Such a performance was a sign of honor and the test an opportunity to prove one's devotion.

The biblical rendition of the tradition serves to justify Abraham's merit as much as Philo's and Josephus's explanations of the story. It is a defense of Abraham's absolute worthiness to be known as a God-fearer and the first Jew. Genesis 22 says that if God had asked (and God did), Abraham would have slain his own son, his own heart, for God's sake—(and he did). Abraham proved he could have pierced and incinerated his son, save God intervened, after seeing that Abraham passed the test, and—only then—"seeing to" or providing the ram in the place of Isaac and in the place of the lamb that Isaac expected.

My students, seeing the difference between the lamb of Isaac's question (Gen 22:7) and the ram provided in v. 13, have wondered over the disparity. Indeed, the offered ram is of profound significance. Isaac, the lamb, was *not* sacrificed that day on Mount Moriah, but Abraham, the ram, was. Abraham was laying himself upon the altar as he bound his own beloved son. Isaac, the lamb, was saved, but Abraham, the ram, was not. In subsequent chapters in Genesis, Isaac marries, has children, digs

---

29. Levenson's *Death and Resurrection* is a full treatment of child sacrifice in Israel and its surrounding cultures.

30. See, for example, 2 Kgs 3:26–27 in which the king of Moab offers the crown prince on the city wall, which dispersed Israel.

31. Levenson presents the evidence from Carthage in North Africa. Twenty thousand urns filled with bones of young children and lambs were deposited between 400–200 BCE. Child sacrifice increased as the civilization of Carthage "advanced" (20–24). This was the period of formation, preservation, and sanctifying of the Jewish Scriptures.

wells, and receives the covenant, but in *this* story Abraham returns to his young men alone. This is another way the story indicates Abraham completely gave his beloved son to God. With that gesture, he gave up himself; he is an utterly lonely, depleted figure, spent and bereft. On one level, the story ends well—God has seen to a sacrifice in place of his son, Isaac. On another, darker, level the ram symbolizes an ' *olâ*, a whole offering of Abraham himself, given fully over to God.

## Conclusion

The explicit statements of Genesis 22 create perplexities for later readers: "God tested Abraham"; "Offer up your son as a burnt offering to me"; "Now I know . . ." But for the scribes who incorporated this story into the Torah, its contributions to Jewish self-understanding and Judaism far outweighed any theological anxieties that it provoked for later hearers and readers. The framers of the Torah took their seeing God to a new height through the climb of Abraham and Isaac to Moriah. There God—who had seen Hagar and Ishmael, the sons of Sodom, and the corruption of Noah's world, who would see the suffering of the Hebrew slaves—saw this unprecedented act of obedience. The God who saw the *Akedah* will see the sacrifices and prayers ever after offered on or toward this mountain, even when this mountain is controlled by other nations. Abraham's obedience gave him the right to be the father of Israel, the patriarch of Jews and of other Abrahamic peoples. *Genesis Rabbah* argues that God did not select the Jews to be His people on a whim; neither did they deserve their election. Nonetheless, Abraham's choice in his final trial, his work of righteousness, earned the Jews' election as the people of God.[32]

As we have seen, Jewish texts, including Josephus, explicitly expanded the sacrifice made by Abraham to enfold Isaac as a willing sacrifice, which has a basis in the biblical text, although it is a silent complicity. The "Binding of Isaac" became a sacrifice made by Isaac.[33] Drawn this way, Isaac is the prototype of the servant of the LORD who lays down his life for others (Isaiah 53), whose self-offering is remembered on every *Rosh Hashanah*, a tradition beginning before the first century.[34]

This view of Isaac has repercussions in Christian theology. Because oral traditions of interpretation may far precede (as well as parallel) their written versions, we can only affirm that Judaism and Christianity of the first century obtained corresponding notions. The result of Isaac's and Jesus's sacrifice in both traditions is deliverance from distress, answers to prayer, and ultimately redemption from sin. The Christian story ensnares God himself into the ancient mythic demand that the first born son be sacrificed to the gods. For Christians, God, like Abraham, sacrificed his son, and Jesus, like Isaac, sacrificed himself. Jesus, as God's beloved son, was the one with whom God

32. *Gen. Rab.* 55:1.
33. In *Sefer ha-Yashar* 23:61, a far later document from 1553, it became Isaac's idea to be bound.
34. Vermes, "Redemption and Genesis 22," 217.

was one. And God, like Abraham, was not immune from the deep structural mythic demand to give up a son to a sacrificial death. To do so, God handed over God's own beloved son to the world and risked losing him. The Christian texts supplement Judaism's apologetic claim that their original patriarch passed the ultimate test, by affirming that God himself submitted to such an ordeal. The New Testament reshaped this Scripture to make meaningful circumstances and defend interpretations that occurred in the first century CE. The theology expressed in the literature of Judaism and Christianity claims that those who benefit from such sacrifice owe everything to those who gave everything. The worthiness of the central characters—the founding figures—is, by extension, the worthiness of those who follow in their footsteps to Moriah, to Calvary, and beyond.

## Bibliography

*Babylonian Talmud.* Edited by Isidore Epstein. 34 vols. London: Soncino, 1935–48.

Charles, R. H., trans. *Jubilees.* In *The Apocrypha and Pseudepigrapha of the Old Testament.* Oxford: Clarendon, 1913. http://wesley.nnu.edu/sermons-essays-books/noncanonical-literature/noncanonical-literature-ot-pseudepigrapha/the-book-of-jubilees/.

Hoffman, Lawrence. *Circumcision and Gender in Rabbinic Judaism.* Chicago: University of Chicago Press, 1996.

*Josephus.* Translated by H. St. J. Thackeray et al. 10 vols. Loeb Classical Library. Cambridge: Harvard University Press, 1926–1965.

Kant, Immanuel. *The Quarrel between the Faculties.* 1798. *Kant.* Translated by Gabriele Rabel. Oxford: Clarendon, 1963.

Levenson, Jon D. *The Death and Resurrection of the Beloved Son: The Transformation of Child Sacrifice in Judaism and Christianity.* New Haven: Yale University Press, 1993.

Lind, Jakov. "The Near Murder." In *Gates to the New City—A Treasury of Modern Jewish Tales*, edited by Howard Schwartz. Northvale, NJ: Aronson, 1991.

*Midrash Rabbah: Genesis.* Translated by H. Freedman and Maurice Simon, vols. 1–2. London: Soncino, 1939.

Milgrom, Jo. *The Binding of Isaac: The Akedah, a Primary Symbol in Jewish Thought and Art.* Berkeley: Bibal, 1988.

*Pesiqta Rabbati: Discourses for Feasts, Fasts, and Special Sabbaths.* Edited by W. G. Braude. 2 vols. New Haven: Yale University Press, 1968.

Philo. *The Works of Philo.* Edited and translated by C. D. Yonge. Peabody, MA: Hendrickson, 1995, 1997.

*Sefer ha-Yashar.* Berlin: Hartz, 1553, 1923.

Speigel, Shalom. *The Last Trial.* New York: Behrman, 1979.

Vermes, Geza. "Redemption and Genesis 22." In *Scripture and Tradition in Judaism: Haggadic Studies.* Leiden: Brill, 1961.

# 3

# The Irony of Reading the Book of Joshua as Christian Scripture

— Frank Anthony Spina

I am deeply honored to contribute to a Festschrift celebrating Paul Livermore's career as a university and seminary professor, biblical scholar, theologian, and pastor. Our friendship (with Alice as well) goes back over fifty years to our undergraduate days at Greenville College. We also spent two years together at Asbury Theological Seminary. To me, Paul has been a model of a scholar whose academic work first and foremost is offered in service to the church, the body of Christ. Hoping to emulate Paul's orientation to the church, I offer this modest essay.

## Introduction

The Christian church views few biblical books as more theologically inconvenient than Joshua. Notwithstanding the Church's neglect of if not disdain for the Old Testament generally, the book of Joshua is often seen as especially egregious. After all, it seemingly depicts Israel as engaged in a holy war whose goal was nothing short of genocide. This horrific depravity is moreover sanctioned by YHWH, Israel's God. If this is a fair reading, then Joshua could not be more problematic. How could genocide or anything comparable to it be compatible with Christian faith? *Inconvenient* is not a sufficiently strong word. Joshua's vile content mocks the very notion of a loving and gracious God. Consequently, surely the Church must reject Joshua as a *revelatory text*.[1]

Granted, some passages might be salvaged on an individual basis. Rahab (Joshua 2) is a compelling example of an outsider responding positively to Israel's God. As well, Joshua's stunning victory over Jericho perhaps teaches us—at least metaphorically—to rely on God when facing overwhelming odds. Equally exemplary is Joshua's impressive obedience throughout the book, accented finally by his famous declaration, "as

---

1. I am using the phrase *revelatory text* in the sense suggested by Schneiders in *The Revelatory Text: Interpreting the New Testament as Sacred Scripture*. Though she concentrates on the New Testament, in my view her arguments apply equally well to the whole of Christian Scripture.

for me and my house, we will serve the Lord" (Josh 24:15).[2] But we can find similar teaching elsewhere in Scripture without having to deal with Joshua's abhorrent content. The unpalatable truth is that there is no way to soften biblical material in which God commands Israel to annihilate the entire population of Canaan down to the last man, woman, child, and beast.

As might be expected, content this appalling engenders hermeneutical moves designed for damage control. As long as Joshua remains a formal part of Christian Scripture, it has somehow to be rendered innocuous. To that end, some have appealed to the concept of *progressive revelation*, an outlook maintaining that God accommodated divine self-disclosure to a people developmentally unable to comprehend initially the deity's true, presumably pacifistic, nature. On this view, God incrementally reveals through time until eventually in the revelatory process God's actual nature becomes known. This stance suggests that the God of the Old Testament is bellicose and judgmental while the God of the New Testament is peace–loving and gracious. Those who espouse this position overlook the consistent testimony of the writers of the New Testament that Jesus was the incarnation of the God of Abraham, Isaac, and Jacob, that is, the very deity who also acts in Joshua.

Still others see Joshua as evidence of God's judgment on an utterly immoral population. Certainly, this is in keeping with other texts in which God uses one nation or people to inflict punishment on another. Even Israel is punished by God's use of other peoples. The exile at the hand of the Assyrians and later the Babylonians is perhaps the prime example of Israel being the object of divine wrath rather than its instrument. While allowing for the important motif of punishment to explain Joshua, problems remain. Why should God's wrath be extended even to Canaanite animals, not to mention innocent children? Equally, why is the vocabulary so specialized in Joshua? The text uses the language of putting the inhabitants of the land "to the Ban" (*ḥerem*), terminology that is virtually never used to describe warfare or military violence generally. Is this the language of *Holy War* or ethnic cleansing?

Given these seemingly insurmountable difficulties, others state unequivocally that this awful book simply has no revelatory content. Joshua may remain in the canon, but ought not be considered part of the *canon within the Canon*. In effect, Joshua is retained for traditional reasons but finally of no practical use for the Church. Accordingly, Joshua reflects nothing more than ancient Israel's militaristic projections. This ostensibly lets God off the hook, but fails to explain how other parts of Scripture were immune to human projection. However, regardless of the tack taken, efforts such as these end up in the same place: Joshua cannot function as Christian Scripture. In a sense, it does not matter whether any of these approaches succeed

---

2. Douglas S. Earl has pointed to classical efforts on the part of Christian interpreters to use the text of Joshua theologically or for homiletical purposes. For example, the crossing of the Jordan has been seen symbolically in the rite of baptism, the falling of Jericho's walls reflects the destruction of *worldly* values, and Rahab's being rescued as a prefiguring of Christian salvation. See *Reading Joshua as Christian Scripture*.

since all of them effectively undermine the text's pertinence to the community that recognizes its canonical status.

## Redeeming Joshua as Christian Scripture

In what follows I argue that Joshua not only *is* Christian Scripture, but that it—as well as the Old Testament in general—is a *per se* witness to what God has done in and through Israel not only for their benefit but for the benefit of the created order.[3] As a corollary, I reject the idea of progressive revelation, the necessary implication of which is that the Old Testament is not only theologically inferior to the New, but has to be corrected by the latter as well. I take with utmost seriousness the claim made both implicitly and explicitly by the writers of the New Testament that what God did in Christ was "according to the Scriptures," that is, the Jewish Scriptures of the Synagogue, which eventually became the Christian Old Testament (1 Cor 15:3).[4] In addition, the New Testament writers depict Jesus as having this same view of the Synagogue's Scriptures (e.g., Luke 4:16–21; 24:13–27).

At the outset I concede that if, in fact, Joshua is a straightforward historical narrative in which Israel annihilates the Canaanites, the book is beyond theological redemption. If Joshua indeed reflects genocide, holy war, jihad or the like, then I side with those who conclude that such deplorable material cannot function as Scripture, not only for Christianity, but for Judaism as well.

I also contend that if Joshua is to function as Christian Scripture its interpretation must be based on the text itself. Regardless of the validity of external arguments, they are not finally determinative for explicating Joshua *as Scripture*. For example, the historical reconstructions that have been proposed to explain Israel's emergence in Canaan in the thirteenth century BCE—whether a full frontal assault, a peaceful infiltration over time, or part of a social revolt—are not constitutive of the meaning of the biblical text.[5] The *text* of Joshua is authoritative Scripture, not the historical reconstructions that allegedly lie behind the text. Likewise, even if Joshua were originally composed as state propaganda to induce political compliance among the general populace in the time of Josiah that also says nothing about the material's final canonical status or its theological import.[6] Indeed, though it is probably the case that at the time Joshua underwent its final editing none of the so-called *seven nations* even existed in a recognizable socio-political form—their having been transformed into stereotypical Israelite enemies for literary and theological purposes—the negative

---

3. For understanding the Old Testament as a *per se* theological witness, see Seitz, *Word without End*.

4. Seitz, *Word Without End*, 51–60.

5. Though dated, Norman K. Gottwald's rehearsal of these various reconstructions remains helpful. *The Tribes of Yahweh*, 191–219.

6. Rowlette, "Inclusion, Exclusion and Marginality," 15–23.

sentiments of Joshua would remain. These and other potential arguments do not solve the dilemma of Joshua being part of Scripture. Thus, Joshua's role as Scripture can only be resolved on the basis of the present text.

## Joshua's Content

Until quite recently, biblical scholars have been primarily interested in the book of Joshua in terms of its portrayal of Israel's *conquest* of either Canaan or Palestine.[7] This is hardly surprising since Joshua narrates Israel's acquiring the land that God had promised to give them since the time of the ancestors. But at another level, approaching Joshua in terms of *conquest* is somewhat problematic in that it gives the impression that this biblical book simply recounts a military takeover of the land. In truth, viewing the content of Joshua in this manner is largely simplistic, not to mention paying insufficient attention to the complexities and nuances of the received canonical text.

The literary structure of Joshua, including its allocation of textual space, militates against seeing this material as merely descriptive of conventional military activity. Joshua 1 notes that Israel is about to inherit the land that YHWH long ago promised (1:6; Gen 12:7). But the extent of this land—which encompasses territory much more extensive than *historical Israel* ever possessed (Josh 1:4)—suggests that at a literary and theological level the promised land is something of an idealization.[8] This supposition is reinforced by the fact that the text simultaneously emphasizes that God gave the entirety of the land as promised (21:43–45) *and* that considerable land remained to be possessed (13:1–7; 23:4–5; see also Judg 1:19, 21, 27–28, 29, 30, 31–32, 33, 34–36). In fact, the inhabitants who remain in the land after the so-called conquest pose a perpetual temptation for the Israelites, who are warned not to intermarry with these people and thereby follow their gods (23:7, 12–13).[9]

The allocation of textual space in Joshua is also revealing. Following Joshua 1, the conquest proper—if we may for the sake of convenience call it that—is narrated in Joshua 2–12. Yet, even though the conquest involves Israel's defeating thirty-one cities and their kings (12:31), the text concentrates on only two cities: Jericho (chaps. 2–6) and Ai (chaps. 7–8). Another extended narrative (Joshua 9) relates how the Gibeonites via an elaborate ruse got themselves exempted from Israel's target list. Consequently, most of the conquest is relegated to Joshua 10–12, and a major portion of this section is a summation (12:7–31). Add to this the fact that chapters 2, 7–8, and

---

7. See, for example, the several titles with this designation in the bibliography provided by Childs, *Introduction to the Old Testament as Scripture*, 239–41.

8. As one might expect, Solomon is said to have been king over this extensive territory (1 Kgs 4:20; 5:1 [Kgs: 4:20–21]).

9. According to 1 Kings, the descendants of the peoples whom Israel had not conquered were used as forced laborers during the time of Solomon (9:20–21).

9 raise important theological issues completely unrelated to conventional warfare. At the very least, the manner in which Joshua tells the story requires that we account for its structure and allocation of textual space.

The subject matter found in chapters 3–5 also makes it difficult to regard Joshua as fundamentally a war chronicle. Two chapters (3–4) describe an elaborate procession in which the people follow the Ark of the Lord being carried by Levitical priests through the Jordan River, the waters of which the Lord dries up in a manner reminiscent of God's drying up the waters of the *Yam Suf*/Sea of Reeds.[10] The next chapter makes clear that the Amorite and Canaanite kings are dispirited not by the prospect of facing Israel's formidable army but by hearing of YHWH's actions in drying up the river (5:1). At this point three events unfold that make virtually no sense if we are to understand this material as a straightforward war report.

First, at YHWH's behest Joshua arranged to have all the males born in the last forty years during Israel's wilderness trek undergo circumcision (Josh 5:2–7). Even though time was allowed for healing (5:8), performing this rite on the proverbial eve of a great military campaign stretches credulity to the limits.[11] Second, Israel took the time to observe Passover, on the appointed day and at the proper time (5:10; see Exod 12:18). Again, such behavior in a war context is, to say the least, strange. Third, when Joshua was "in Jericho" (*bîrîḥô*; RSV: "by Jericho"; JPS: "near Jericho") he encountered a man (*'îš*) with a drawn sword (Josh 5:13). Apparently, sensing that the man was more than a man, Joshua asked, "Are you for us or for our adversaries?" The man's answer is perplexing, "No! But as the commander of YHWH's army I have now come" (5:14a).[12] At the very point where a military leader was seeking divine confirmation for the genocide he was presumably poised to carry out, this odd reply is startling. However we are to interpret this enigmatic response, it appears unwarranted to conclude that the story we are reading is an unambiguous example of God's demanding an absolutely blessed Israel to destroy an absolutely damned enemy. Appropriately, Joshua does not press the matter. He merely falls to the ground, worships, and asks for further instruction, which he receives: "Take off your shoes, for the place where you are standing is holy" (5:14b–15).

The question may therefore be posed: "What is Joshua about if it is not about *the Conquest*?" This is where irony has a role to play. When I use the word *irony* in the context of this chapter I mean the word in its most obvious, common sense. That is, I am not using the term in a literary or dramatic sense in which a character says something that a reader or audience understands while the character who is speaking

---

10. In spite of the conventional translation *Red Sea*, the body of the water over which Israel miraculously crossed in the escape from Egypt is consistently referred to as the *Sea of Reeds*.

11. The folly of undergoing circumcision prior to engaging in battle is well illustrated in Gen 34:18–29.

12. All translations of the Old Testament in this essay will be the author's, unless otherwise indicated.

is oblivious. Irony is simply the use of language in which meaning refers to something more or less opposite to what that language or topic normally means. In light of this definition, in what sense is it ironic to read Joshua as Christian Scripture?

## Joshua as the Worst Example of God's Judgment

One source of irony regarding Joshua is to ask why this book is singled out as the most horrific expression of divine judgment in the Old Testament. Is it because its content is unique? Or, is it primarily because it has been considered an ancient version of genocide, holy war, jihad, and the like—most of which assault modern sensibilities? To be sure, the destruction recounted in the book of Joshua is portrayed as an act of the Lord's judgment on the Canaanite population. That is clear in Lev 18:24–29; 20:22–26 and Deut 7:1–26. In these programmatic passages the Canaanites, or more specifically the *seven nations* (Hittites, Girgashites, Amorites, Canaanites, Perizzites, Hivites, Jebusites), are depicted as engaging in abominable religious practices and thus are subject to divine condemnation.[13] That divine judgment is operative in Joshua cannot be gainsaid. But does that justify either seeing the book as a singular instance of God's judgment or as deserving of special condemnation?

Actually, the ultimate story of judgment in the Old Testament is the flood story (Gen 6–8). Because the emphasis typically in a Sunday School approach to this episode has featured Noah and the Ark—which is a divine act of grace—the judgmental aspect has been somewhat sanitized. But this awful episode of worldwide destruction is not for the squeamish. The Lord states unequivocally the divine intention to blot out humanity, the animal kingdom, including creeping things and birds (Gen 6:7). Just in case there is any doubt, God informed Noah that the target of this terrible judgment was *all flesh* (6:12–13). This particular punishment will not be limited to a mere *seven nations*, as in Joshua, but to every living being on the planet, excepting, of course, those on the ark. Joshua is not even a close second in describing devastation on this scale. Why, then, does Joshua receive such disproportionate opprobrium?

The closest parallel to the destruction depicted in Joshua is what God did to Egypt as described in Exodus. As is well known, God wreaked havoc on Egypt because it had enslaved Israel (Exod 1:11). But this was no simple matter of Egyptian sin and their

---

13. Only three references name all seven groups: Deut 7:1; Josh 3:10; 24:11. The order of the lists, however, is not consistent. In Josh 3:10 the order is: Canaanites, Hittites, Hivites, Perizzites, Girgashites, Amorites, and Jebusites. The order in 24:11 is: Amorites, Perizzites, Canaanites, Hittites, Girgashites, Hivites, and Jebusites. There is no discernible reason for preferring one ordering over another. Besides these three references there are combinations of somewhat smaller lists of the inhabitants, from at least six groups to no more than three (Gen 15:18–21; Exod 3:8, 17; 13:5; 23:23, 28; 33:2; 24:11; Deut 20:17; Num 13:28–29; Josh 9:1; 11:3; 12:8; Judg 3:5; Neh 9:8). Ezra 9:1 mentions these same residents of Canaan (excepting Hivites and Gigashites) along with Ammonites, Moabites, and Egyptians. But this listing is representative of peoples with whom Israelites who had avoided exile intermarried. Finally, 2 Chr 8:7 includes five of the seven nations (excepting Canaanites and Girgashites) who were subjected to forced labor by Solomon.

consequent punishment. For one thing, though Pharaoh stubbornly refused to release the Israelite slaves (8:15, 32; 9:34), an action already known to the Lord (3:19), the Lord inexplicably seemed to make matters worse by hardening the king's heart (4:21), something that the Lord did more than once (Exod 9:12; 10:20, 27; 11:10; 14:4, 8, 17). This action on God's part was part of a motif emphasized throughout Exodus, namely, that in the contest between the Lord's sovereignty and Egyptian sovereignty, the Lord comes out on top. Indeed, God is sufficiently powerful to *make sport* (*hitʻ allaltî*) of this great nation (10:2). The Lord's power vis-à-vis Egyptian power, as expressed by its military and its gods, is the primary issue dealt with in this incident. The issue of free will is more or less tabled at this point. In fact, the Lord's power extended not only to *hardening* hearts, but *softening* them as well. The Lord did the latter in making ordinary Egyptians amenable to Israelite requests for money, jewelry, and clothing on the eve of their escape (3:21–22; 11:2–3; 12:35–36). Unfortunately for Egypt, this softening had the goal of impoverishing the whole land. At the end of the day, the Egyptian king's stubbornness, coupled with the Lord's hardening of hearts, led to the plagues that ruined Egypt (7:14—12:32). Egypt also suffered the humiliation of being induced by the Lord to hand over their wealth to the escaping slaves, not to mention the loss of their military forces (12:35–36; chap. 14). Though a great power by any standards, Egypt had no chance against Israel's deity.

The comparison between what God did in Egypt and what God did when enabling Israel to occupy the Promised Land is made explicit in Deut 7:17–19. The book of Joshua even explains the Lord's response to the inhabitants residing in the Promised Land in terms reminiscent of Exodus, namely, the hardening of hearts (Josh 11:20).[14] Though the two events are presented in tandem in the final canonical text, arguably the portrayal of God's fierce assault on Egypt is even greater than what happened to the Canaanites, at least at an emotional or psychological level. The suffering caused by the plagues in the Exodus episode, affecting not only people but animals, not to mention the anguish of every family (even animal families!), losing a first-born child to divine wrath would have caused unspeakable anguish (Exod 11:4–6). Would not death have been preferable to pain on this scale? At the very least, it is ironic that we respond to the book of Joshua as though it were the supreme example of divine anger, even though it is not even close to the horrors of the flood story, or for that matter any worse than what Egypt experienced. Again, why single out the book of Joshua as especially reprehensible?

## Joshua, Militarism, and Genocide

As we said at the beginning of the essay, Joshua's theological inconvenience is related not only to Israel's alleged extreme bellicose posture but because they supposedly used

---

14. Stone, "Ethical and Apologetic Tendencies," 25–36.

military force not for defense or other justifiable reasons, but to commit genocide. Notwithstanding, I suggested that the allocation of textual space to the battles, as well as Joshua's literary structure, perhaps point in another interpretive direction. Why does the text spend so much time on Jericho (chaps. 2–7)? Why would a chronicle of conventional warfare feature so many non-military matters (chaps. 3–5)? What sense does it make to describe unconventional or even absurd military tactics such as marching around a city, blowing trumpets, and shouting (chap. 6)? And, finally, is the charge of genocide accurate when the text makes it clear not only that the resident population will have to be dealt with gradually over years but, in fact, their existence represents a perpetual temptation to Israel when it takes over the Land of Promise (Deut 7:22; Josh 13:2–6; 23:4–5, 12–13; 1 Kgs 9:21)? In addition, why are these essentially *historical* questions put forward as a way of understanding Joshua *as Scripture*?

Then again, why is the vocabulary used in Joshua so specialized? Why does the text seem to avoid, systematically, ordinary military jargon? If the book of Joshua presents Israel as the epitome of bellicosity and the architect of genocide, what accounts for the strange terminology that is employed? In fact, why is the language that is so prominent in Joshua virtually never used to depict conventional military activity elsewhere in Old Testament narratives?

This specialized language is related to a Hebrew word in nominal and verbal constructions for which it is all but impossible to find an English equivalent. When Israel takes over the land that the Lord has promised, the operative term comes from a Hebrew root *ḥrm*, whether it is used as a noun or as a verb.[15] When used nominally, the term is translated as *devoted things* (RSV; NRSV; NIV), something that is *proscribed* (JPS), or the *Ban*. In its verbal form, the word is typically translated as *annihilation* or being *doomed*. More specifically, in the capture of the Promised Land, neither people nor goods are to be retained as spoils, as they would be in conventional warfare (e.g., Deut 13:12–18). Conversely, even when populations are killed off in territory that is not part of the land of Canaan (i.e., the Land of Promise), the taking of booty *is* permitted (Deut 2:34–35).

In short, using *ḥrm* nominally or verbally virtually never refers to conventional military activity. More than that, the term never seems to describe an actual practice of Israel *in the present*. It is either about the past, in which it depicts strategic foundational events, or the future, in which it speaks to eschatological or apocalyptic periods (Isa 34:2, 5; 43:28; Jer 25:9; 50:21, 26; 51:3; Mic 4:13; Zech 14:11; Dan 11:44).[16] This

---

15. This particular Semitic root is not used in extra-biblical texts to refer to regular practices of warfare or conquest. See Earl, *Delusion*, 57. One exception to this is when the Assyrian official during the siege of Jerusalem bragged about his kings having destroyed the nations who had resisted Assyrian aggression (2 Kgs 19:11). Still, this terminology is never used in a regular war context related to Israel.

16. Sometimes the Lord's wrath is directed against the nations pitted against Israel and sometimes against Israel itself. In both cases, the accent is on divine action in circumstances of profound judgment. These contexts are not about conventional warfare as such.

usage underscores the symbolic use of ḥrm.[17] Interestingly, the concept is not used for military activity even in Samuel, Kings, or Chronicles, where stories of so-called conventional Israelite military excursions are commonplace.[18] The exceptions to this are Judg 1:17; 21:11; and 1 Samuel 15. Judges 1:17 is a continuation of the Joshua motif of eliminating the population to prepare the land for Israel's entrance. In Judg 21:11 a particular purging of disloyal Israelites is in view. And 1 Samuel 15 is, again, on a par with the Joshua material. Arguably, most interesting is the fact that ḥrm is never used in imprecatory psalms. In these psalms, in which calumnies are uttered against a variety of enemies this word—so very prominent in Joshua—is conspicuously absent.[19] The book of Joshua has the lion's share of citations of this critical specialized term and univocally presents the subject matter (Josh 2:10; 6:17, 18, 21; 7:1, 11, 12, 15; 8:26; 10:1, 28, 35, 37, 39, 40; 11:11, 12, 20, 21; 22:20).

There are several items to consider that are related to the ḥrm root as it is employed in Joshua. One involves the Lord's activity, as opposed to Israelite efforts. A second one has to do with eliminating all sinful activities from the Land of Promise. A third issue, which is closely related to the second, is the elimination of the Canaanites or, more precisely, the *seven nations*, all of which have contributed to the sinful pollution of the land that God had promised as Israel's inheritance. Finally, the primary goal of Israel's takeover of the Promised Land was not genocide but *rest*.

For all the negative talk about Israel's military prowess and the uses to which it was put, the text accents exactly the opposite. The Lord is powerful; Israel is weak. Of course, Israel did not lift a hand in the escape from Egypt—that was all the Lord's doing. Even the great Moses was reluctant at first (Exod 3:1–4:17). Throughout the Exodus narrative, far from glorying in the Lord's power, Israel consistently either did not believe that God was capable of rescuing them or actually preferred the status quo (Exod 5:20–21; 6:12; 13:17; 14:10–12, 25, 30–31; 15:3).[20] The juxtaposition of the Lord's strength with Israel's weakness is also stressed in Deuteronomy. The Lord is providing the land for Israel; the Lord will enable them to be victorious; the Lord will control this process from front to back (Deut 7:17–24). Israel dare not think that their election is due to any merit or ability that they possess (7:7; 9:4–6)—their election was a function of the inscrutable will of God. God, and God alone, likewise supplied the power needed

17. Earl, *Delusion*, 60.

18. I use the term "so-called" because of my conviction that these materials are equally theological, symbolic, metaphoric, or figural, and thus are to be read *as Scripture*, as opposed to straightforward historical annals. There is indeed a historical component to Scripture, but this is a rather more complex manner than merely accepting biblical narratives as historical or non-historical in the ordinary sense either of describing what happened or simply being fictional. See the treatments of historical readings of canonical or theological texts by Van Leeuwen, "Quest for the Historical Leviathan," 145–57; Green, "Rethinking 'History' for Theological Interpretation," 159–73.

19. Earl, *Reading Joshua*, 106.

20. Ironically, in spite of this emphasis on Israel's relative weakness, God has them change their route assuming their extreme fear in the face of warfare, yet they still leave Egypt *equipped for battle* (Exod 13:18)!

to accomplish the divine plan. The Lord will see to it that Israel gets great cities, which they did not build themselves, houses full of good things, no thanks to their efforts, cisterns, which they had not hewn out, and vineyards and olive trees, which they had not planted (6:10–11). Every military and domestic benefit had to be attributed to the Lord. Not surprisingly, this motif is also present in Joshua (23:9–10; 24:12–13). Again, any criticism of Israel's militarism needs to be addressed to the Lord.

Items number two and three may be treated in tandem. These have to do with the Canaanite population—the *seven nations*—and the abominable religious practices that they regularly perform. In this contest the text presents the Canaanites as so unholy as to be beyond redemption, whereas Israel is consummately holy because of the Lord's election. As we shall see, neither the stereotypical portrayal of reprobate Canaanites nor the idealistic depiction of Israel as a *kingdom of priests and a holy nation* (Exod 19:6) is the complete truth. But in this part of Israel's story it is, more or less, the whole truth. In the baldest of terms, the Canaanites and their abhorrent rites and rituals, and the beliefs these collectively express, are to be exterminated so as to cleanse the whole land of religious filth. This is why when Israel enters the land it is commanded to break down Canaanite altars, dash their pillars into pieces, cut down their Asherim, and burn their graven images with fire (Deut 7:5). Under no circumstances is Israel to make covenants with this population, not to mention the unthinkable outrage of intermarriage, because such a posture would inevitably and inexorably lead to religious compromise (7:2–4, 23–26; 20:16–18). Deuteronomy announces the wickedness of the Canaanite population (9:5) and the divine judgment that is thereby to be carried out, while Joshua implements this judgment by presenting Israel as God's instrument.

The last item to be treated in this section is the notion of *rest* (the Hebrew root *nwḥ*). Three times in Deuteronomy, in slightly different contexts, the Lord's bringing Israel into the land has *rest* as the goal for Israel in the land (3:20; 12:10; 25:19). A similar emphasis is found in Joshua (1:13, 15; 21:44; 22:4; 23:1). The term is also used in a slightly different manner in a number of sacerdotal, liturgical, or religious actions that are related to the overall aims of Israel's taking over the land of promise (3:13; 4:3, 8; 6:23). Elsewhere in the Old Testament, *rest* occurs in strategic places involving God's plans for Israel (e.g., Isa 14:3, 7; 28:11–12; 32:18; 64:14; Ps 95:11; Dan 12:13). Of course, the writer of the epistle to the Hebrews makes much of the idea of *rest* (*katapauō*; *katapausis*) for the ultimate work of Jesus the Christ (Heb 3:11, 18; 4:1, 3, 4, 5, 8, 10, 11). In brief, Israel's reception of the land that God had promised to them had nothing to do with hegemonic claims or outright land confiscation. It had instead to do with a land in which Israel could *rest* (not *relax!*) in alignment with God's overall purposes related to the community's divine election.

All these ideas are highly metaphorical, even *mythical*. *Myth* in this sense has nothing to do with being fictional, unhistorical, and certainly not untrue.[21] Rather,

---

21. Earl, *Reading Joshua*, 17, 33.

mythological language is required when the subject matter accents God's actions. Technical terminology in this instance will not do the job. I am using *myth* at this point as equivalent to the early Christian Fathers' appealing to the *spiritual sense* of Scripture.[22] Apart from such an approach to the Bible, the text is able to refer only to the past, whereas Scripture is oriented to the present and future of the community who recognizes it canonically. By all means, Scripture is emphatically rooted in actual people and events, but a theological reading demands reading metaphorically, symbolically, figurally, parabolically, and mythically. Such an approach allowed the writers of the New Testament to read their Scripture *Christologically*.

Accordingly, we recognize another irony in accepting the book of Joshua as Christian Scripture. Joshua emphasizes not Israel's powerful army or its glorious military accomplishments, but the Lord's sovereignty. In the battles themselves, Israel is depicted for the most part either engaging in liturgical activities—the people following the Ark of the Covenant being carried by Levitical priests (Josh 3:1–13), miraculously crossing over the Jordan River on dry ground (3:14–17), setting up monuments to be used in the future to teach younger generations (4:1–10), God's exalting Joshua as Moses had been exalted (4:11–14), Joshua's presiding over the miraculous crossing just as Moses once did (4:15–24), circumcising those who had not been circumcised during the wilderness journey (5:2–9), celebrating Passover and the cessation of manna (5:10–12), Joshua's learning from the *man* who was the commander of *YHWH's army* that the question as to what side God was on was not an appropriate question (5:13)—or defeating Jericho in a singularly absurd manner in terms of conventional military tactics (6:1–27). Add to this the stress on God's judgment on the Canaanites, the specialized vocabulary of ḥrm, the cleansing of the land of abominable religious practices, and the motif of *rest*. All these matters militate against interpreting the book of Joshua as narrative promoting holy war, genocide, ethnic cleansing or, for that matter, usual military activity. Ironically, the text is replete with clues not to view Israel in conventional military terms. Instead, it recognizes and celebrates divine power.

## The Ultimate Irony

In my judgment, the most ironical feature of reading the book of Joshua as Christian Scripture is that its content in entirely compatible with classic Christian thought. Joshua deals with the serious question of *belonging*. Is identity with Israel a closed book? Might someone not part of the original elected group become one with Israel? Is Israel's election for their benefit only, or might others benefit as well? What are the requirements for being included with Israel? What circumstances might lead to exclusion? Of course, I submit that these questions are consonant with questions the New Testament poses. But why should that be surprising? The Old Testament

---

22. Earl, *Reading Joshua*, 37.

was after all, before it was an *Old Testament,* the only Scripture recognized by Jesus or by every writer of the New Testament, who all claimed in one way or another that what God did in and through Jesus the Christ was *according to the Scripture* (1 Cor 15:4). That in and of itself should make us regard the two testament Christian canon as primarily conjunctive rather than disjunctive. Otherwise, I repeat, how could New Testament writers read Scripture (i.e., the Jewish Scriptures, later called the Old Testament by the church) *Christologically*?

The issue of identity in Israel in sharply put by the antipodal relationship between Joshua 2 and Joshua 7. In Joshua 2 we encounter Rahab, who is a quintessential Canaanite. Indeed, she is a prostitute. Her profession is reinforced by her salaciously provocative name as well as the several sexual innuendoes found in the story.[23] Though Rahab's *house* apparently lured the spies to book lodging there, she did not make use of her wiles to insure her and her family's safety when Jericho fell. Instead, she expressed faith in Israel's God with a confession that made it seem like she had read Deuteronomy cover to cover. In fact, her statement of faith was a model of Israelite orthodoxy. Had Joshua believed as Rahab had, he would not have seen any need to send spies who, it should be noted, gathered no strategic intelligence whatsoever when they spent the night at her *house*.[24] In effect, this episode is a conversion story. She and her family became part of Israel *to this day* (Josh 6:25), even though the explicit command of Deuteronomy 20 had to be violated to make this happen (20:16–18). Famously, Rahab eventually ended up in Jesus's genealogy (Matt 1:5).

Achan is the mirror image of Rahab. She is the quintessential Canaanite; conversely, he is the quintessential Israelite. This is indicated by his impressive pedigree, which is traced back four generations to none other than Judah, from whom David (and Jesus) derived (Josh 7:1). Unlike Rahab, who confidently believed in Israel's God, what this deity had done and what this deity would do, Achan violated faith by treating the *devoted things* as ordinary booty good for the taking (7:1, 13–21). When Israel discovered the culprit and confirmed that he was by all means guilty, he and his family suffered the ultimate penalty of death (7:22–24). Just as Rahab and her family remained with Israel *to this day*, Achan's and his family's destruction was memorialized with an infamous place name that exists *to this day* (7:25).

These two antipodal episodes are stunning in what they teach. Unlike the prejudice typically registered against the book of Joshua as a narrative in which one *pure* ethnic group commits genocide against the *other* ethnic groups, the pericopes featuring Rahab and Achan respectively dramatically illustrate exactly the opposite situation. A quintessential Canaanite, with a most unsavory occupation, confesses faith in Israel's God so that she and her family may now identify with God's elect people, Israel. A quintessential Israelite, whose genealogy provides him with elite status, commits a transgression against the Israelite God in such a manner that the deity threatens Israel with being

---

23. Spina, *Faith of the Outsider*, 54–56.
24. Spina, *Faith of the Outsider*, 58–61.

under the *Ban* themselves unless the guilty party is punished (Josh 7:12). Even though Israel's election by the Lord is, in one way, irrevocable—at the least a remnant of Israel will always be preserved even when the most serious forms of judgment are administered—this does not prevent terrible punishments being executed against Israelites. At the same time, even outsiders, even Canaanite prostitutes, can, with proper faith, become part of elect Israel—grafted in to the tree, as it were (Rom 11:17).[25]

Joshua 2 and 7 are not the only narratives in this book that show how porous the boundaries to Israelite identity are. The story of the Gibeonite ruse demonstrates how an entire group, indeed a whole people, may also become part of Israel (Joshua 9). The story starts by noting that various kings who ruled throughout the Land of Promise had arrayed as one to combat Israel (9:1). That was the typical Canaanite response, to which Rahab's had been the anti-type. The Gibeonites took a completely different tack, hoping above hope to penetrate Israel's boundary and fuse with them.

Just as Rahab conducted herself as though she was intimately acquainted with Deuteronomy, the Gibeonites somehow knew about the rules for engagement found in Deuteronomy 20. This explains their efforts to convince Israel that they are outsiders—"from a far country" (Josh 9:6)—not indigenous residents of Canaan. To this end, they displayed worn-out sacks on their donkeys, well used wineskins, patched sandals, ratty clothing, and food that was dry or moldy (9:4–5). When questioned about their origins by the Israelites, the Gibeonites not only stated their desire to make a covenant with the Israelites, but also declared what they believed about the Israelite deity. Their confession was not as elaborate or fulsome as Rahab's had been, but it was adequate (9:9–10). In the end, the trick worked. Israel accepted that the Gibeonites were not part of Canaan's native population—and therefore subject to the *Ban* (Deut 20:15–18)—and made a covenant with them, with Joshua's compliance (Josh 9:15).

Almost immediately, the Gibeonites were found out as having been deceptive (Josh 9:16–17). This led to Israelite disgruntlement, but nothing else (9:18). Israelite leaders kept the agreement they had made, notwithstanding the Gibeonites' false pretenses (9:19). Thus, Israel granted, however reluctantly, permission to be part of Israel, once again, *to this day* (9:27). But Israel's allowance came with a twist, a twist that is an irony within a larger irony. The leaders insisted that the Gibeonites had to undergo some discipline for their prevarications. According to the leaders, the Gibeonites were to be hewers of wood and drawers of water for the whole community (9:21). How this happened is elaborated by discussion of Joshua's role in assigning this apparently menial job to the Gibeonites. Joshua, obviously angry, pronounced a curse on the Gibeonites and sentenced them to lives as slaves, hewers of wood and drawers of water (9:22–23). This concords with what the leaders had earlier said.

---

25. I have argued in *Faith of the Outsider* that this motif is central to the idea of election in the Old Testament and not a peripheral issue that may be dismissed as involving *exceptions*. See Earl, *Reading Joshua*, 41.

But the ironical twist comes in the form of two particular terms, used by the leaders and Joshua respectively. The leaders had told the Gibeonites that their services as hewers of wood and drawers of water was to be for *all the congregation* (Josh 9:21). The term *'ēdāh* is very commonly used to describe Israel not only collectively, but especially as God's congregation. It is a synonym of *qāhāl*, which also refers to Israel as a *people*. Interestingly, the Greek Old Testament (the Septuagint) often translates these words with *ekklēsia*, or *church*. Joshua is even more explicit. He relegates the Gibeonite service to *the house of my God*, then a little later specifies that their activity is geared for the *congregation* and the *Lord's altar* (9:23, 27). Neither the Israelite leaders nor Joshua thought this was anything but a punishment, perhaps not as severe as they would have liked, but a punishment nonetheless. Keep in mind that no one consulted the Lord before entering into this agreement (9:14).

But was this a punishment? What was so terrible about serving the congregation, or at the Lord's altar or, more pointedly, at the *house of my God*? This is temple service, indicated by the statement that this activity was to occur at the place where the Lord would choose (Josh 9:27). The phrase has normally been considered the manner in which Deuteronomy speaks of the temple site (e.g., Deut 12:5, 11, 14, 18, 21, 26; 14:23, 24, 25; 15:20; 16:2, 6, 7, 11, 15, 16; 17:8, 10, 15; 18:6; 26:2; 31:11).

Perhaps more poignantly, when Joshua referred to the location of this labor he uses an odd designation, namely, the *house of my God* (*lĕbēt 'ĕlōhay*; Josh 9:23). There is only other place where this phrase is found in the Old Testament: Ps 84:10 (84:11 MT). In that verse we read, "For a day in your courts is better than a thousand I might choose (elsewhere), / (better) tending to the threshhold in *the house of my God* than residing in the tents of wickedness."[26]

From a strictly Israelite perspective, what Joshua and the leaders envisioned as punishment ironically gave the Gibeonites an opportunity to participate in a most sacred milieux. Joshua and the leaders did not countenance this, but the narrator of Joshua surely did.[27]

Ironically, in a narrative that ostensibly pits the Israelites against outsiders who are not only beyond redemption but assigned for complete extermination, we encounter stories that celebrate the inclusion of a Canaanite prostitute and a whole people, the Gibeonites, who lied through the teeth to be included with God's elect. These stories accent the radical graciousness of Israel's God. It should not be ignored that the inclusion of these outsiders actually trumped strict adherence to the Torah, which, over and over, Israel was commanded to obey. The salvation of Rahab and the Gibeonites,

---

26. The Masoretic editors of the Hebrew text even marked the two verses in Josh 9:23 and Ps 84:11 (Eng 84:10) as designed to be read in the light of each other.

27. Joshua usually spoke in a voice that aligned with the narrator, but not always. He may have been, for example, remiss in sending the spies in the first place and in this setting failed to see the possibilities for including the Gibeonites in the Israelite family. Spina, "Moses and Joshua," in *Go Figure!*, 65–92.

however, took precedence.[28] One might make a case for ethnic chauvinism in Ezra and Nehemiah, but not the book of Joshua, notwithstanding the withering criticism directed at it especially in relatively modern times.[29] In a most delightfully ironic way, the despicable Canaanites, represented by Rahab and the Gibeonites, manage to get themselves included in God's elect people, Israel, in a story where God's grace trumps even obedience to the Torah. If this does not qualify reading the book of Joshua as Christian Scripture, nothing does.[30]

## Conclusion

I have spoken of the irony involved in reading the book of Joshua *as Christian Scripture*. It is ironical in the first instance in that what we Christians refer to as the *Old Testament* was thought of only as *Scripture* to Jesus of Nazareth and all his earliest followers. Jesus himself and every writer of the New Testament materials held these Scriptures as authoritative and decisive. Indeed, in historical terms none of these writers even considered the necessity of adding to the Jewish Scriptures. There was intense debate about how to read them, but no dispute whatsoever about their authority. Including the New Testament documents was a function of a subsequent church decision. Why is it necessary to make a case for reading Jesus's Bible precisely *as Scripture*?[31]

A second irony has to do with the constant criticism of Joshua as being beyond the pale of what a Christian can accept. Yet, we do not flinch at other stories featuring judgment on a much broader scale, such as the Flood narrative in Genesis. Does that imply that our problems with Joshua have much more to do with modern sensibilities than its specific content? At least, I should think we would be willing to assess our extremely negative attitudes in that light.

It is also deeply ironical, thirdly, that the text does not present Israel in terms of its military prowess or its chauvinistic attitudes. The commands are from God, the battles are waged by God, and the land is given by God. Why, then, should not our truck be with *God*? Moreover, we have generally ignored the multiple features in the text that are patently absurd if the intention is to chronicle conventional warfare. In our haste to

---

28. Salvation biblically (and theologically) means so much more than going to heaven when you die! Charry, *By the Renewing of Your Minds*, 121; Middleton, *A New Heaven and a New Earth*; Wright, *Surprised by Hope*.

29. Blenkinsopp, *Judaism: The First Phase*.

30. In an essay in which Ellen Davis observes that according to Deuteronomy "the only good Canaanite is a dead Canaanite," she nevertheless points out the positive and faithful actions on the part of Canaanites in Joshua. See "Critical Traditioning," 733–51.

31. It has been customary to argue that Jesus refuted Scripture in the antitheses of the Sermon on the Mount (Matt 5:21–48). But in my judgment Jesus in this context is contesting popular interpretations found in Second Temple Judaism. In no place in the New Testament is Scripture ever introduced with the words, "You have heard that it was said," or a variation of this formula (5:21, 27, 31, 33, 38, 43).

dismiss Israel as the epitome of ancient barbarism we have paid correspondingly little or no attention to the actual details of the text.

The final irony in reading Joshua as Christian Scripture is that this book is so radical in its presentation of God's grace for the very Canaanites who have been targeted for extermination. Rahab is saved; Achan is damned, if not eternally than at least provisionally. Including only a single Canaanite and her family might be passed off as exceptional. But the inclusion of the Gibeonites belies that interpretation. The book of Joshua deals with the enormously important topic of what it means to be Israel.[32] As it turns out, Israel's boundaries are ultimately porous. This is not due to socio-political matters, but to the astounding grace that was operative already at God's initial call of Abraham and Sarah (Gen 12:1–3). The book of Joshua *is* Christian Scripture, and should be read as such. It is ironical that we Christians have to reminded of that.

## Bibliography

Blenkinsopp, Joseph. *Judaism: The First Phase: The Place of Ezra and Nehemiah in the Origins of Judaism*. Grand Rapids, MI; Cambridge, UK: Eerdmans, 2009.

Charry, E. *By the Renewing of Your Minds*: The Pastoral Function of Christian Doctrine. Oxford: Oxford University Press, 1997.

Childs, Brevard S. *Introduction to the Old Testament as Scripture*. Philadelphia: Fortress, 1979.

Davis, Ellen. "Critical Traditioning: Seeking an Inner Biblical Hermeneutic." *Anglican Theological Review* 82 (2000) 733–51.

Earl, Douglas S. *The Joshua Delusion? Rethinking Genocide in the Bible*. Eugene, OR: Cascade, 2010.

———. *Reading Joshua as Christian Scripture*. Journal of Theological Interpretation Supplement 2. Winona Lake, IN: Eisenbrauns, 2010.

Gottwald, Norman K. *The Tribes of Yahweh: A Sociology of the Religion of Liberated Israel, 1250–1050 BCE*. Maryknoll, NY: Orbis, 1979.

Middleton, J. Richard. *A New Heaven and a New Earth: Reclaiming Biblical Eschatology*. Grand Rapids: Baker Academic, 2014.

Rowlette, L. L. "Inclusion, Exclusion and Marginality in the Book of Joshua." *Journal for the Study of the Old Testament* 55 (1992) 15–23.

———. *Joshua and the Rhetoric of Violence: A New Historicist Analysis*. JSOT Supplement 226. Sheffield: Sheffield Academic Press, 1996.

Schneiders, Sandra M. *The Revelatory Text: Interpreting the New Testament as Sacred Scripture*. 2nd ed. Collegeville, MN: Liturgical, 1999.

Seitz, Christopher R. *Word without End: The Old Testament as Abiding Theological Witness*. Grand Rapids: Eerdmans, 1998.

Spina, Frank Anthony. *The Faith of the Outsider: Exclusion and Inclusion in the Biblical Story*. Grand Rapids: Eerdmans, 2005.

---

32. Other places in Joshua accent this theme. For example, Joshua 22 recounts a dispute between the Israelites on the western side of the Jordan River and the Israelites on the eastern side. The threat is of not only a civil war but of schism. The issue of belonging to Israel involves not only outsiders but insiders as well. I am treating Joshua 22 and other similar texts in a book length study, with the provisional title: *Multiplying Divisions: The Fractious Nature of Elect Israel*.

———. "Moses and Joshua: Servants of the Lord as Purveyors of the Word." In *Go Figure!: Figuration in Biblical Interpretation*, edited by Stanley D. Walters, 65–92. Princeton Theological Monograph Series. Eugene, OR: Pickwick Publications (Wipf and Stock), 2008.

Stone, Lawson G. "Ethical and Apologetic Tendencies in the Redaction of the Book of Joshua." *Catholic Biblical Quarterly* 53 (1991) 25–36.

Wright, N. T. *Surprised by Hope: Rethinking Heaven, the Resurrection, and the Mission of the Church*. New York: HarperOne, 2008.

# 4

# The Blessing of Abraham and the *Missio Dei*: Reframing the Purpose of Israel's Election in Genesis 12:1–3

### J. Richard Middleton

For many years I have understood the call of Abraham (Gen 12:1–3) as fundamentally missional or instrumental, in the sense that the ultimate purpose for which God calls this ancestor of Israel is to mediate the blessings of salvation to the nations.[1] Not only have I taught the book of Genesis with this orientation, but this understanding of Gen 12:1–3 has played an integral role in my framing of the canonical narrative of Scripture in my published writings, from *Truth Is Stranger than It Used to Be: Biblical Faith in a Postmodern Age* (1995) through *A New Heaven and a New Earth: Reclaiming Biblical Eschatology* (2014); it can be found also in a variety of essays written in the intervening years. There is, however, an important qualification to the way I articulated Abraham's role in the *missio Dei* in *A New Heaven and a New Earth*, which calls for clarification.

When Brian Walsh and I wrote *Truth Is Stranger Than It Used to Be*, we were attempting to contextualize the biblical message as a critique of western understandings of the centrality of the human subject, including the oppositional stance of the modernist subject vis-à-vis nature and the growing tribalism of postmodern culture, which pits one idealized group over against demonized others. This contemporary context (to which the church has become acculturated) attuned our ears to the way that Scripture often relativised the subject, challenging notions of exclusive privilege and oppositional identity. Instead, we highlighted the way the Bible reframed privilege as one moment in a larger framework of ethical responsibility toward others. We saw this as central to the prophetic critique of Israel in the Old Testament, which itself reflected the way that Israel's election or chosenness was framed in a variety of biblical texts. In this light, our missional reading of Gen 12:1–3 was meant to call into

---

1. Technically, his name is Abram, until Gen 17:5 when it is changed to Abraham. For convenience, I will use the name Abraham throughout this essay.

question any self-serving notion of Christian identity, challenging the church instead to its ethical vocation in the world.

## Challenges to My Missional Reading of the Call of Abraham

However, my missional/vocational interpretation of Gen 12:1–3, and thus my instrumental understanding of Israel's election, was itself called into question—no less than three times.

The first time was after I presented a paper on an ethical reading of the canonical narrative of Scripture at the annual meeting of the Canadian Theological Society (CTS). The year was 1995 and the paper was a draft of material I was working on for *Truth Is Stranger than It Used to Be*.[2] After the conference I received a long, passionate, respectful letter from Canadian theologian Gregory Baum, who had attended my presentation. Baum interacted with my paper and called me to repent of my Christian supersessionism towards my Jewish brothers and sisters. I was humbled and challenged by this letter, since I had no inkling of such a point of view in the paper. Baum and I wrote back and forth a few times; it was a cordial exchange as I tried to understand his challenge and take it to heart.[3]

Later that year *Truth Is Stranger than It Used to Be* was published (with my CTS paper integrated into the analysis).[4] A year after that (1996) I began teaching at Colgate Rochester Divinity School. In my very first year at Colgate, my colleague in Old Testament, Werner Lemke, took me to lunch and had a long discussion with me about the book, in which he challenged me in a manner similar to Baum. It turned out that both Baum (a Catholic theologian) and Lemke (a Protestant Old Testament scholar) had been engaging in regular dialogue with Jews on matters of Jewish-Christian relations. They were thus intensely attuned to the often-superior attitudes of Christians toward "Judaism," which many Christians viewed an outdated religion that has been superceded by faith in Christ. A significant part of this attitude was rooted in an instrumentalist understanding of Israel's election. Now that Israel had produced the Messiah and the church was founded, Judaism had fulfilled its function and was now irrelevant.

---

2. The paper, entitled "Whose Story? Which Tradition? The Counter-Ideological Character of the Biblical Metanarrative," was originally written for a conference on ethics and narrative in the thought of Alasdair MacIntyre, at Brock University, in St. Catharines, ON, February 1993. I presented it two years later at the Canadian Theological Society annual meeting at Université du Québec à Montréal, in Montréal, QC, June 1995.

3. I later discovered that Gregory Baum and I had similar backgrounds, in that we were both immigrants to Canada (him from Germany, me from Jamaica), and that we both had a Jewish mother and a gentile father.

4. Middleton and Walsh, *Truth Is Stranger than It Used to Be*. The title of the CTS paper ("Whose Story? Which Tradition?") makes a brief appearance on p. 73.

Of course, the issue of the legitimate differences between Christianity and Judaism is a complex matter, as is an accurate account of the famous "parting of the ways" of these sister religions in the first centuries of the Christian era. The checkered history of Christian persecution of Jews and the silence of many German Christians during the Holocaust only complicates matters further.

The third event that challenged my missional interpretation of Gen 12:1–3 took place via an email exchange with Old Testament scholar Walter Moberly in 2007. That year I had planned to present a paper at the Society of Biblical Literature (SBL) on the call of Abraham, in which I wanted to give a nuanced account of my missional reading (taking into account the challenges of Baum and Lemke). I never did give the paper, since I found myself bogged down in the analysis, unable to complete the argument in the required 25 minutes of paper presentation. Instead, I gave a paper on a different subject.

Moberly, however, who did not attend the SBL that year, read the announcement of my paper and sent me an email requesting a copy; he was working on a book on the theology of Genesis, with a chapter on Gen 12:1–3, and was interested in what I had to say.[5] Since I never completed the paper, Moberly asked if I would be interested in reading his draft chapter and giving my feedback.

I read the chapter and returned my feedback the following day. I was quite taken with Moberly's analysis of the issues. I described his chapter as: "Absolutely brilliant—and gripping." I concluded by telling him that he had *almost* persuaded me of his point of view; and that he had certainly "nudged and prodded me in ways that are extremely helpful."[6] It turned out that *this* was the analysis of the call of Abraham that I had been searching for in my own (incomplete) paper. Moberly's chapter, with his forceful, yet gracious, challenge to Christian interpreters of Genesis 12, forced me to reconsider the basis for my missional/vocational interpretation of the text.

The result was that when I was composing my chapter on the plot of the biblical story for *A New Heaven and a New Earth*, I wrote a lengthy excursus on the call of Abraham that attempted to take into account Moberly's analysis of the issues, while still maintaining (in the end) a missional reading of Abraham's call.[7] Once I had completed the excursus, however, I judged that it was too much of a sidetrack from the flow of the chapter and so I ended up simply summarizing the fruits of my analysis in two brief sections—one about the call of Abraham,[8] the other about the place of the exodus from

---

5. Published as ch. 8: "Genesis 12:1–3: A Key to Interpreting the Old Testament?" in Moberly, *Theology of the Book of Genesis*. The book contained another chapter devoted to Gen 12:1–3, which addressed questions of Zionism and the land promise given to Abraham/Israel.

6. Email from J. Richard Middleton to R. W. L. Moberly, November 29, 2007.

7. Ch. 3 ("The Plot of the Biblical Story") in *A New Heaven and a New Earth* was based on the plot summary I had given in an earlier essay (2006), entitled "A New Heaven and a New Earth" (esp. 81–82 on the call of Abraham).

8. Middleton, *A New Heaven and a New Earth*, 61–62. Here I affirmed that God's blessing was intended first for the flourishing of Abraham and his family and secondarily that Abraham's flourishing

Egypt in the larger biblical story.[9] Although I did not abandon a missional reading of the role of Abraham/Israel in the story of salvation, I did affirm God's purposes for the flourishing of Abraham/Israel—on the way to this larger purpose.

Ever since writing this excursus, I intended to work it up into a published essay on the subject, but never got around to the task. I was, however, recently encouraged to do this by New Testament scholar Andy Johnson, who drew on my unpublished analysis for his chapter on the call of Abraham in *Holiness and the Missio Dei* (2016).[10] I was further motivated to work on this material by my participation in an ecumenical Jewish Institute in New York City called Hadar, through which my respect has been greatly enlarged for Jews seeking to respond in faithfulness to God's covenant.[11] But the decisive impetus to rework the excursus for publication comes from my participation in this *Festschrift* dedicated to my colleague, Paul Livermore. I am delighted to offer the current essay in tribute to Paul, who has always been interested in how the New Testament and the early Christian tradition (articulated by the Church Fathers) are related to the Jewish context in which they were birthed.

## The Problem of Interpreting Abraham's Call in Genesis 12:1–3

Let us begin by noting the explicit claims of Gen 12:1–3. Although I will later provide my own translation of the text, here I quote the NRSV; I have italicized two clauses (at the end of verses 2 and 3) that will require special investigation.[12]

> ¹ Now the LORD said to Abram, "Go from your country and your kindred and your father's house to the land that I will show you. ² I will make of you a great nation, and I will bless you, and make your name great, *so that you will be a blessing*. ³ I will bless those who bless you, and the one who curses you I will curse; *and in you all the families of the earth shall be blessed*." (Gen 12:1–3)

At the beginning of Genesis 12 God instructs Abraham to leave behind his safe and secure land, along with his extended family of origin, in order to journey to an as-yet-unspecified place. To assure Abraham that this will be a worthwhile endeavor,

---

was in the service of God's purposes for the nations.

9. Middleton, *A New Heaven and a New Earth*, 63. Here I noted that the exodus was first for the sake of the flourishing of Israel as God's elect, but that it was also for the sake of Israel's vocation in the wider world.

10. Johnson, *Holiness and the Missio Dei*, ch. 2.

11. My connection to Hadar (formerly Mechon Hadar) came through one of its founding Rabbis, Shai Held. Having had email correspondence and an initial phone call with Rabbi Held (in 2015), and then reading many of his writings. I have twice participated in the week-long Executive Seminar sponsored by Hadar (in 2016 and 2017). At my request, Walter Moberly, along with other Christian Old Testament scholars, joined me in writing endorsements for Held's recently published two-volume commentary on the Pentateuch, entitled *The Heart of Torah*. I then organized a panel of Jewish and Christian scholars to discuss *The Heart of Torah* at the Society of Biblical Literature in November 2019.

12. All translations of the Bible in this essay will be the NRSV, unless noted otherwise.

God promises (not only in Genesis 12, but also on other occasions) to bless Abraham in a variety of ways.

The word *bless* occurs in some form no less than five times in Gen 12:1–3. God promises to *bless* Abraham (12:2) and to *bless* those who *bless* Abraham (12:3). In the NRSV (along with many other English versions), God also promises that Abraham will be a *blessing* (12:2) and that the entire human family will be *blessed* in Abraham (12:3). Although these last two occurrences of *bless* are the ones that will require further investigation, it is nevertheless clear that God wants to shower Abraham with blessing.

These blessings start with a promise of a *new land* (initially only hinted at in Gen 12:1), a promise that is repeated with more specifics in Gen 12:7; 13:14–17; 15:7, 18–19; 17:8; 22:17; 26:3–4; 28:4, 13; and 35:12. God also promises Abraham that he will have *many descendants* (Gen 12:2), a promise repeated in Gen 13:16; 15:5; 17:4–6; 22:17; 26:4, 24; 28:3, 14; and 35:11. Despite the initial childlessness of Abraham and Sarah, which we are informed of at the outset of the story (11:30), God promises that Abraham's descendants will become as multitudinous as the dust of the earth (13:16; 28:14), the sand on the seashore (22:17), and the stars of the heavens (15:5; 26:4). More specifically, God promises that from Abraham, Isaac, and Jacob will come a great nation (12:2), indeed, many nations (17:4–6), even a company of nations (28:3; 35:11), including kings (17:6; 35:11).

In short, God promises to establish Abraham's family as a flourishing people in their own land—as a microcosm of God's intent for humanity. This can be seen by the analogy between God's initial blessing on humanity, who are to multiply and fill the earth (Gen 1:28), and the various depictions of God's blessing on Abraham's descendents, which involves their multiplying and filling the earth (Gen 47:27; 48:4, 16; Exod 1:7); some of the very wording from Genesis 1 is used.

Beyond promising Abraham a people and a land, God promises to magnify Abraham's "name" or reputation (12:2), and pledges to protect him by affirming that those who bless Abraham will themselves be blessed, but that anyone who treats Abraham disdainfully will be cursed (12:3). God is thus committed to the extraordinary flourishing of Abraham and his family, in the context of a world of threat.

But this raises an important hermeneutical question: Is the flourishing of Abraham's family the sole (or even primary) focus of Gen 12:1–3? Or is Abraham's family *also* to have a redemptive function in the larger biblical story?

## The Meaning of the Blessing in Genesis 12:3b

An answer to that question might be inferred from the promise given at the end of our text: "and in you all the families of the earth shall be blessed" (Gen 12:3b). This promise, given here to Abraham for the first time, is repeated in Gen 18:17–18 (in a divine soliloquy) and then restated to Abraham in 22:17–18. The promise is then given to Isaac in Gen 26:4–5 and to Jacob in Gen 28:14. This repeated statement of blessing vis-à-vis the nations seems to suggest that the ultimate purpose of the call of Abraham (and his descendants) is to be a mediator or channel of blessing to the entire human race (as if this new family will function as God's priests in the world).

However, a missional interpretation of the call of Abraham is not as obvious as I have typically assumed. In response to Walter Moberly's incisive challenge for Christian interpreters to do justice to what the text actually says, instead of imposing a Christian reading from the outside, I intend to take a hard look at whether a missional reading of the call of Abraham is in fact supported by Gen 12:1–3.[13] Here the discussion will, by necessity, become somewhat technical, as I examine issues pertaining to the translation of these verses.

Although Gen 12:3b is translated in many Bibles as "and in you all the families of the earth shall be blessed," matters are not that simple. As is well known by biblical scholars, Gen 12:3b may legitimately be translated "and by you all the families of the earth shall *bless themselves*" or possibly "*bless each other*."

The issue is that the Hebrew verb for "bless" (*bārak*) occurs in Gen 12:3 in the Niphal stem.[14] The Niphal may generally be rendered either by the *passive* ("be blessed") or by the *reflexive* ("bless themselves") or the *reciprocal* ("bless one another"), depending on the verb in question.[15] Whereas the passive involves the subject of the verb receiving, rather than, performing the action, the reflexive involves the subject of the verb acting on himself/herself (the reciprocal is a variant of this, where the plural subject of the verb, the nations, act on each other).

A *passive* translation of "bless" in Gen 12:3 ("be blessed") would be compatible with viewing Israel as an instrument or channel of blessing to the nations (in the sense that blessing will somehow reach the nations through Abraham or Israel's being blessed by God). However, a *reflexive* or *reciprocal* translation ("bless themselves" or "bless one another") suggests something quite different.

The most likely reflexive or reciprocal understanding would be that the nations will pronounce (verbal) blessings on themselves or on each other, by citing Abraham or Israel as a paradigm or model of blessing ("May we/you be as blessed as Abraham/Israel!"). If this is the meaning, the point isn't that the nations themselves will *receive* blessing through Abraham/Israel, but that they will *recognize* that Abraham/Israel has been blessed (Abraham and his descendents would be, for them, a prime exemplar of blessing); and it means, further, that they desire such blessing for themselves.

---

13. Moberly cites a variety of Christian interpreters who take the text as basically missional, including Gerhard von Rad, Claus Westermann, Brevard Childs, Richard Bauckham, and Christopher J. H. Wright. See Moberly, *Theology of the Book of Genesis*, 142–48.

14. The stems or *binyanim* of verbs in Semitic languages have no structural equivalent in English grammar, though they do have translation equivalents.

15. With some verbs it is translated as the simple active (equivalent to the Qal stem).

PART 1: GRAPPLING WITH SCRIPTURE IN ANCIENT AND CONTEMPORARY CONTEXTS

"Be Blessed" / "Bless Themselves" Passages in Genesis (NRSV)[16]

| YHWH to Abraham (12:1–3) | Niphal | ¹Now the LORD said to Abram, "Go from your country and your kindred and your father's house to the land that I will show you. ²I will make of you a great nation, and I will bless you, and make your name great, so that you will be a blessing. ³I will bless those who bless you, and the one who curses you I will curse; *and in you all the families of the earth shall be blessed*." |
|---|---|---|
| YHWH to Abraham (18:17–18) | Niphal | ¹⁷The LORD said, "Shall I hide from Abraham what I am about to do, ¹⁸seeing that Abraham shall become a great and mighty nation, *and all the nations of the earth shall be blessed in him*? |
| YHWH to Abraham (22:17–18) | Hittpael | ¹⁷I will indeed bless you, and I will make your offspring as numerous as the stars of heaven and as the sand that is on the seashore. And your offspring shall possess the gate of their enemies, ¹⁸*and by your offspring shall all the nations of the earth gain blessing for themselves*, because you have obeyed my voice." |
| YHWH to Isaac (26:4–5) | Hithpael | ⁴I will make your offspring as numerous as the stars of heaven, and will give to your offspring all these lands; *and all the nations of the earth shall gain blessing for themselves through your offspring*, ⁵because Abraham obeyed my voice and kept my charge, my commandments, my statutes, and my laws." |
| YHWH to Jacob (28:14) | Niphal | ¹⁴And your offspring shall be like the dust of the earth, and you shall spread abroad to the west and to the east and to the north and to the south; *and all the families of the earth shall be blessed in you and in your offspring*. |

Of the five occurrences in Genesis of this promise of blessing vis-à-vis the nations, three are in the Niphal stem (12:3; 18:18; 28:14), while the remaining two are in the Hithpael stem (22:18; 26:4). There is widespread agreement that the Hithpael of the verb for "bless" (as found in 22:18; 26:4) is reflexive or reciprocal.[17] The question is what to do about the Niphal.

## Is There a Difference in Meaning between the Niphal and Hithpael of Bless?

We thus have a choice before us. Either we view the variation of the Niphal and Hithpael in the five Genesis texts as insignificant grammatically; they both mean basically the same thing, which would likely be reflexive or reciprocal. Or we view the variation

16. Chart adapted from Bandstra, *Reading the Old Testament*, ch. 2.

17. There are six occurrences of "bless" in the Hithpael stem in the Hebrew Bible (Gen 22:18 and 26:4; Deut 29:19; Ps 72:17; Isa 65:16; and Jer 4:2). A reflexive or reciprocal meaning makes best sense of all of these.

as significant and translate the Hithpael as reflexive or reciprocal (in two cases) and the Niphal as passive (in three cases).

Some modern translations, such as the RSV and the NJPS translate all five occurrences as reflexive ("shall bless themselves"), while the NET Bible translates all five as reciprocal ("will pronounce blessings on one another using your name" [or "his name" or "the name of your descendents"]).

Many translations, however (such as the NIV, NASB, NLT, and Robert Alter[18]), continue to use the passive for all occurrences ("be blessed"). The TNIV and the most recent edition of the NIV (2011) also include a footnote in each case with the alternative rendering, "will use your name [or "his name" or "the name of your offspring"] in blessings."

The reflexive sense of "bless," however, might not require the specific idea of pronouncing verbal blessings. It could simply mean that the nations will "gain blessing for themselves," although it is left open how exactly this is to be accomplished. This is the NRSV's rendering in the case of Gen 22:18 and 26:4 (the two occurrences of the Hithpael).

The NAB is similar to the NRSV, in that it renders all five verses as "shall find blessing," though it omits "for themselves." The NAB thus opts for the middle voice (somewhere between the passive and the reflexive). A similar middle translation ("find blessing") is proposed by Gordon Wenham in his Genesis commentary.[19] While also opting for the middle voice, Everett Fox translates the Niphal and Hithpael somewhat differently; he renders the Niphal as "will find blessing" and the Hithpael as "shall enjoy blessing."[20]

Translations such as "gain," "find," or "enjoy" blessing suggest a meaning that goes beyond merely verbal blessing and could be compatible with viewing Abraham/Israel as a mediator of blessing. However, it would grant the nations a more active role in the process than the passive "be blessed," perhaps by having them take the initiative in seeking this blessing.

The NRSV is the rare example of a modern translation that distinguishes between the meanings of the Niphal (as passive) and the Hithpael (as reflexive). Although it is possible to find scholarly arguments in favor of different meanings for the Niphal and Hithpael stems of "bless,"[21] this is not typical. Against such a distinction is the fact that the three cases of "bless" in the Niphal stem (Gen 12:3; 18:18; 28:14) constitute the only such occurrences in the entire Bible. Hebrew typically has a different way of

---

18. Alter, *Genesis*.

19. Wenham, *Genesis 1–15*, 277. Wenham acknowledges that a reflexive or reciprocal translation is justified since the text probably means that the nations will use Abraham's name to pronounce blessings, but still claims that it implies a middle sense, because through this they will themselves be blessed (278).

20. Fox, *Five Books of Moses*.

21. See the argument in Grüneberg, *Abraham, Blessing and the Nations*.

expressing the passive of "bless."[22] This strongly suggests that the traditional passive rendering ("be blessed") found in many modern translations is suspect.

While I tend to think that a reflexive or reciprocal meaning in all five cases has the most plausibility as a translation option, the continuing disagreement among biblical scholars makes this a very difficult issue to resolve on linguistic grounds alone.[23] This requires us to look to the idiomatic meaning of being a blessing.

## The Meaning of the Blessing in Genesis 12:2b

Along with the contested meaning of Gen 12:3b is the related issue of the meaning of the last line of Gen 12:2, "so that you will be a blessing."[24] The English idiom of "being a blessing" suggests the idea of being a *source* of blessing to others (which would fit well with the passive interpretation of Gen 12:3b).

However, that is not the idea of the Hebrew idiom, which means to be a *model or exemplar* of blessing, someone that others may cite as a positive example or paradigm, whom they might desire to emulate (this fits well with the reflexive or reciprocal interpretation of Gen 12:3b). A good example of this meaning is found later in Genesis when Jacob says concerning Joseph's two sons: "By you Israel will invoke blessings, saying, 'God make you like Ephraim and like Manasseh'" (Gen 48:20).[25]

This idiomatic sense of "being a blessing" is confirmed when we look at cases of *being a curse* (the opposite of blessing) in the Bible. These are clearly references to being cited by others as an example of curse, a byword, a negative example to be avoided. Thus, God says that after he has judged king Zedekiah and the inhabitants of Judah by the Babylonian exile, "I will make them a horror, an evil thing, to all the kingdoms of the earth—a disgrace, a byword, a taunt, and a curse in all the places where I shall drive them" (Jer 24:9). This sense of being a curse is further elaborated in Jeremiah's letter to the exiles, concerning the fate of two false prophets, Ahab and Zedekiah (not to be confused with the Judahite king of the same name), who are claiming an early

---

22. Since the active sense of "bless" in Hebrew is communicated by the Piel stem (often thought of as having an intensive meaning), the passive of "bless" usually uses the Pual (the passive of the Piel) or the Qal passive participle (in statements such as "blessed be x").

23. Although Moberly also admits that the translation question is "probably insoluble on philological grounds," he thinks there that the Niphal and Hithpael most likely have the same meaning. Not only is there nothing in the context of the five versions of the repeated promise to suggest a difference in meaning, but there are other cases of verbs in Genesis where the variation between the Niphal and Hithpael does not change the meaning (such as the two forms of the verb for "hide" in Gen 3:8 and 3:10). Moberly, *Theology of the Book of Genesis*, 151.

24. While the verb is technically an imperative or command ("be a blessing!"), Hebrew syntax allows this line to be translated as a result or purpose statement ("so that you will be a blessing"). I will return to this point.

25. Rashi, the famous eleventh-century Rabbinic commentator, cites Gen 48:20 to illustrate the meaning of Gen 12:3b. The TNIV and NIV 2011 also cite this verse in the footnotes that give the alternative rendering of 12:3b, "will use his name in blessings."

end to the exile: "And on account of them this curse shall be used by all the exiles from Judah in Babylon: 'YHWH make you like Zedekiah and Ahab, whom the king of Babylon roasted in the fire'" (Jer 29:22). To be a curse in these cases is clearly to be cited verbally as a negative example.

This understanding of being a curse makes sense of God's promise in Zech 8:13 concerning the reversal of Israel's fortunes: "Just as you have been a cursing among the nations, O house of Judah and house of Israel, so I will save you and you shall be a blessing." In the context of the oracle of Zech 8:1–17, this prophecy means that Israel will fully experience God's salvation (deliverance from exile with consequent restoration to wholeness), thus becoming an exemplar of blessing that the nations will look up to.

Given the complexity of the issues concerning the meaning of "blessing" in Gen 12:2b and 12:3b, we should perhaps be cautious in taking the call of Abraham as unproblematically specifying a vocation to the nations. Especially because of the idiomatic sense of being a blessing in Hebrew, we may be justified in taking the overall thrust of Gen 12:1–3 as assurance to Abraham of God's faithfulness in bringing about the fulfillment of the promises of 12:2a and 12:3a. This assurance would be needed, given the evident difficulty and uncertainty involved in Abraham leaving his country, kindred, and father's house and traveling to an unspecified land (Gen 12:1). The point seems to be that God's promises of blessing in 12:2 (that Abraham will become a great nation with a famous reputation) and of protection in 12:3 (blessing those who bless Abraham and cursing anyone who disdains him) will be so effective that in the end all nations will recognize Abraham's descendants as "a model of desirable existence" (a prime instantiation of blessing).[26] God's promises in Gen 12:1–3 would be given in the first place *for the benefit of Abraham*, not the nations.[27]

## Evidence for the Priestly Vocation of Israel among the Nations

While this interpretation makes eminent sense of the text from the perspective of the one receiving the promises, the question remains whether the benefit or blessing of the nations themselves could also be in view in Genesis 12 (even if only distantly, on the horizon).

Within the book of Genesis itself we find the king of Gerar explicitly recognizing that YHWH has richly blessed Isaac (Gen 26:28–29; also 26:12–14). Other biblical texts, like Isa 61:9, claim that the nations will come to recognize the true source of Israel's blessing: "Their descendants shall be known among the nations, / and their offspring among the peoples; / all who see them shall acknowledge / that they are a people whom the LORD has blessed."

---

26. Moberly, *Theology of the Book of Genesis*, 154.
27. Moberly, *Theology of the Book of Genesis*, 149–50.

Moberly, however, makes the important point that just because the nations may come to recognize that Israel's blessing is due to YHWH (Israel's God), there is no assumption that the nations will accept Israel's frame of reference and seek blessing by appeal to YHWH. Rather, given that the nations have allegiance to other deities, they might well say: "May Chemosh make you like Abraham."[28] The consequence of this is there is no guarantee that invoking blessing by citing Abraham/Israel will result in the nations actually receiving blessing.[29] This is a powerful argument, and it is correct as far as it goes.

However, when we go beyond Gen 12:1–3 and the Abraham story, we find a variety of prophetic texts that envision a day when the nations will actively seek YHWH and join Israel in allegiance to the one true God (for example, Isa 2:2–4, 19:18–25, 60:3; Jer 3:17; Mic 4:1–4; Zech 2:11, 8:20–23). Zechariah 8:20–23 is an instructive example, since it follows the Zech 8:13 passage about Israel becoming a blessing instead of a curse.

According to Zech 8:23, "In those days ten men from nations of every language shall take hold of a Jew, grasping his garment and saying, 'Let us go with you, for we have heard that God is with you'" (Zech 8:23). Given the placement of this oracle, we are warranted in thinking that it is precisely Israel's being an example of blessing that will attract the nations to YHWH. Therefore, whether or not the blessing of the nations is an explicit concern in Gen 12:1–3, such a concern becomes part of the larger vision of Scripture beyond Genesis 12 (and that is even before we get to the New Testament).

Do we then have to acknowledge Moberly's point that Genesis 12 itself does not envision the actual blessing of the nations? Or is there some way that Genesis 12 itself leads to the expectation that the nations may move beyond recognizing that YHWH has blessed Israel, and even beyond wanting this blessing for themselves, to actively seeking Israel's God as the source of this blessing—with the result that they themselves are blessed?

The fact that the reflexive of "bless" in Gen 12:3b could be translated to mean that the nations will gain/attain blessing for themselves (rather than verbally bless one another using Abraham as an example) opens the door to a positive answer. This is, however, only a translation possibility (it may not be the best rendering),

## The Narrative Placement of the Call of Abraham

Instead, we would do better to attend to the narrative placement of Gen 12:1–3 immediately after the Primeval History (which culminates in the dead-end of Babel). Due to this placement, Terence Fretheim calls Gen 12:1–3 a "fulcrum text"

---

28. Moberly, *Theology of the Book of Genesis*, 151–54. The quote about Chemosh is from 154.
29. Moberly, *Theology of the Book of Genesis*, 155.

that links the family of Abraham with God's purposes for humanity and creation.[30] This suggests that the larger purpose of Abraham and his descendents is, narratively speaking, to aid in reconciling humanity to God and thus restoring humanity to its original purpose, by helping to remove or overcome the impediment of sin and violence, which has become endemic.[31]

If it is objected that Fretheim is a Christian interpreter (so this sort of reading is to be expected), we should remember the famous Jewish midrash on the creation of humanity in Gen 2:7 that links Adam and Abraham in terms of plot. According to *Genesis Rabbah* 14:6, God thought: "I will create Adam first, so that if he sins, Abraham may come and set things right."[32]

Beyond *Genesis Rabbah*, the Jewish biblical scholar and theologian Martin Buber also links the election of Israel to creation, via the Bible's presentation of one comprehensive macro-narrative. According to Buber:

> We are to trace the meaning of [Israel's] origin back to the meaning of the origin of the world, and back to the intention of the Creator for His creation. To be sure, the Bible does not present us with theological statements about this intention and this meaning; it presents us with a story only, but this story *is* theology; biblical theology is narrated theology. The Bible cannot be comprehended if it is not comprehended in this way.[33]

In other words, while it might be theoretically possible to read Gen 12:1–3 as an independent literary unit focusing simply on the blessing of Abraham, to the exclusion of the nations, the placement of the Abraham story after the dispersion of Babel significantly reframes the meaning of Abraham's call in terms of God's purposes for the larger human family.

Abraham's own family comes from Ur (Gen 11:31), an important city in southern Mesopotamia, which is clearly intended to connect Abraham to the Primeval History, since Babel/Babylon is located in the same region (compare Gen 11:1 with 10:10). The fact that Gen 11:31 states that Abraham's family (led by his father, Terah) had already made the trip from Ur (in southern Mesopotamia) to Haran (in Aram/Syria) might even suggest they were part of the dispersion of Babel. It is only when Terah dies in Haran (11:32), and the journey seems to have come to a standstill, that God speaks to Abraham in Gen 12:1 about moving on.

---

30. Fretheim, *God and World in the Old Testament*, 92.

31. Although how this is to be done is not explicitly stated in Gen 12:1–3, God later reveals that Abraham is to "charge his children and his household after him to keep the way of the Lord by doing righteousness and justice" (Gen 18:19), which would enable God's promises to Abraham to be fulfilled. I will come back to this.

32. *Genesis Rabbah* 14:6. Translation taken from Freedman, *Midrash Rabbah*, 114. This quote is meant to answer the question of why God didn't just start with Abraham, given his preeminent stature in Judaism (indeed, the text says he was worthy of being created before Adam).

33. Buber, "Abraham the Seer," 25–26 (his emphasis).

This narrative placement of the call of Abraham in the context of universal history from creation to Babel is clearly meant to indicate that Abraham's God is no petty national or regional deity, but the creator of the heavens and the earth.[34] Before he was Abraham's God, YHWH was already the God of all humanity with a concern for the blessing or flourishing of all people.

The narrative question therefore becomes: Is the creator God intending to ignore the needs of the human race and to focus now only on this one family? Or does God's calling of Abraham/Israel (with intent to bless) address in some way his creational purposes for human flourishing, which have been stymied by sin?[35]

Or we could ask the question from the point of view of Israel's responsibility. Just as it would be unethical for humans to use their distinctive privilege and power as God's image to abuse (or ignore the needs of) their earthly environment, rather than caring for and positively developing the earth, so wouldn't it be illegitimate for Israel to hoard their privilege as God's elect people, rather than aiding the rest of humanity in attaining God's purposes for human life?

A positive answer to this question seems indicated; it suggests that Israel's vocation vis-à-vis the nations is analogous to the human calling as *imago Dei* vis-à-vis the earth. In fact, it makes sense to view election as a particular concentration of the human calling, a subplot in the service of the larger narrative. Whereas the human calling to image God was originally focused on faithful cultural development of our earthly environment (a calling which has not ceased), in a post-fall world the power of *imago Dei* is meant to be directed *also* towards redemptive living, to address the problem of human evil and brokenness, at personal, social, even international levels.[36]

## The Global Purpose of Israel's Salvation

That God's purposes for Israel are in the service of his concern for all humanity is evident when we turn to the book of Exodus.[37] There we find that Israel's deliverance from Egyptian bondage is framed with a global or universal purpose. The universal scope of the exodus is alluded to in numerous statements during the narrative of the plagues and the Sea crossing to the effect that not just Israel (Exod 6:7; 7:17; 10:2), but

---

34. Note also Gen 14, where the king of Salem calls God Most High (*'ēl 'elyôn*) "the creator of heaven and earth" (14:19), something then affirmed by Abraham, who identifies *'ēl 'elyôn* with YHWH (14:22).

35. Moberly himself admits the tension between what is explicit in Gen 12 and what is required by the larger narrative of Scripture: "The relationship between exegetical precision and canonical frame of reference is finely balanced here." *Theology of the Book of Genesis*, 148.

36. For an analysis of the parallel between the human vocation and Israel's purpose, see Middleton, *A New Heaven and a New Earth*, 62.

37. The next two paragraphs are adapted from Middleton, *A New Heaven and a New Earth*, 91–92.

also Pharaoh and all Egypt (Exod 7:5; 8:10, 22; 9:14, 29; 10:7; 14:14, 18), would come to know who YHWH is through these miraculous events.

This broad scope of the exodus is especially emphasized in connection with the seventh plague, when YHWH affirms that his name will be proclaimed in all the earth (Exod 9:14). Indeed, at this point universal statements accumulate: Pharaoh will come to know that there is no one like YHWH in all the earth (9:16) and that the earth belongs to YHWH (9:29). That is, the exodus is not just for Israel's sake (though it surely is for that), but also for the sake of the wider world.[38]

After the exodus, when Israel arrives at Mt. Sinai, a universal claim precedes God's affirmation of Israel's calling. Although "the whole earth is mine" (19:5), says YHWH, Israel is to be "a priestly kingdom and a holy nation" (19:6). While this could be taken to mean that Israel alone (from all the nations) is granted the privilege of ministering to God (like priests in his temple), the global scope of the exodus suggests that a better interpretation is that Israel has the vocation of mediating divine blessing and presence in a world that belongs to God.[39]

The universal purpose of Israel's election becomes most explicit during the Babylonian exile in the so-called servant songs of Isaiah, where God, who identifies himself as creator of the cosmos and all humanity (Isa 42:5), articulates the calling of Israel (God's servant) to be "a covenant to the people, a light to the nations" (Isa 42:6; also 49:6), which will include their release from blindness and bondage (Isa 42:7). To speak of Israel as God's "covenant" to the peoples of the world is surely unusual, suggesting that the covenant God makes with the nations *is* Israel; the very existence of the elect constitutes God's covenantal pledge or oath to the nations that he hasn't given up on them or left them in the dark. The final servant song (Isa 52:13—53:12) even suggests the need for Israel's vicarious and efficacious suffering as God's servant on behalf of the world, something that the New Testament understands as fulfilled in Christ, the ultimate servant of the Lord (Acts 8:32–34).[40]

## The Witness of the Septuagint and the New Testament

But the case for understanding Abraham and his descendents in Genesis 12 as a source of blessing for the nations becomes even stronger when we turn to the Septuagint (LXX),

---

38. The best elucidation of this theme is found in the works of Terence Fretheim. See Fretheim, *Exodus*; "Plagues as Ecological Signs"; "Reclamation of Creation"; "Because the Whole Earth Is Mine"; and his *magnum opus*, combining the insights from many of his earlier studies, *God and World in the Old Testament*, esp. ch. 4: "Creation and the Foundation Narratives of Israel."

39. In his essay "The Election of Israel: A Biblical Inquiry" (*On the Bible*, 80–92), Buber understands Exodus 19:5–6 as connecting Israel's vocation as God's elect to the failed royal vocation of humanity. Whereas humanity was originally called to "serve as [God's] delegated governors on earth" (86), Israel is God's "unmediated dominion" (kingdom of priests), whose obedience is intended "to begin the preparation of humanity for [the reestablishment of God's] kingdom" (89).

40. For a brilliant study of the status and vocation of the servant of YHWH in Isaiah, see Janzen, "Ecce Homo."

which translates the Hebrew of "bless" in Gen 12:3b by what is clearly a passive verb in Greek. Indeed, the Septuagint translates all the repeated occurrences of this promise (in Gen 18:18, 22:18, 26:4 and 28:14), whether in the Niphal or the Hithpael, by the same passive Greek verb, meaning to "be blessed." Whatever the original sense of the Hebrew in these passages, it is clear that some post-biblical Second Temple Jewish interpretation (represented by the LXX of Genesis) had come to understand the importance of the gentiles in God's plan and read Israel's election as instrumental to that purpose, mediating God's blessings to all the nations or families of the earth.[41]

This instrumental or mediational understanding of the call of Abraham (which is not a Christian innovation) then finds its way into the New Testament. Both Gal 3:8–9 and Acts 3:25–26 explicitly quote the promise from Gen 12:3b combined with its restatement in 22:18 (the Greek combines elements of the LXX of both texts). The Galatians passage takes this to mean that the gentiles who believe will receive the same blessing Abraham did (he also believed God, according to Gen 15:6), while the Acts text understands Jesus as *the* descendent (or seed) of Abraham *par excellence* through whom blessing comes, first to Israel and then to the gentiles. Both texts, furthermore, interpret the blessing that comes through Abraham as equivalent to salvation.

## The Vocation of Abraham according to Genesis 12

For a variety of reasons, then, we are warranted in viewing Abraham and his descendents as entrusted with the task of participating with God in the *missio Dei* to address (and overcome) the obstacle of sin among the nations, thus restoring the human race to its original purpose. That this is a *task* or *calling* given to Abraham, and not simply a promise of what God will unilaterally do, is suggested by the fact that the verb for "be" a blessing at the end of Gen 12:2 is technically in the form of an imperative or command (thus, "be a blessing!"). Although according to the rules of Hebrew syntax, the full sentence structure of verse 2 allows this line to be translated as a result or purpose statement ("so that you will be a blessing"), it might be important to feel the full force of this "unprecedented imperative," as Martin Buber puts it.[42]

Let us fully grant that the Hebrew idiom of *being a blessing* means to live as an example of blessing and not to be a source or channel of blessing to others. Nevertheless, if we let this imperative stand (as Buber thinks we should), this means that Israel's living as an example is not simply a promise that God will bring about, but a calling or vocation that Israel must live up to.[43] Thus, in the midst of amazing promises of

---

41. Even Moberly admits this; *Theology of the Book of Genesis*, 157.

42. Buber, "Election of Israel," 87. Another Jewish scholar who agrees with Buber on translating Gen 12:2b as an imperative ("be a blessing!") is Fox, *Five Books of Moses*, 55, while Shai Held suggests "You must be a blessing" as a possible translation (Held, *Heart of Torah*, 2:304, n. 29). Christian scholars who render Gen 12:2b as an imperative include Wright, *Mission of God*, 213, 216; Alexander, *From Paradise to the Promised Land*, 152, 175; and Goldingay, *Old Testament Theology*, 213.

43. Buber, "Election of Israel," 87.

blessing, protection, and flourishing for Abraham and his descendants, Buber nevertheless thinks that God expects "Abraham will bid the people he begets to adhere to the way of the God who strides before them by its practice of righteousness and its proof of worth."[44] And this moral example will decisively benefit the nations. As Buber puts it: "This is what becoming a blessing for the other peoples means: setting a living example of a true people, a community."[45]

Thus, instead of taking the end of Gen 12:2 as a purpose statement, concluding the prior promises in that verse, it is possible to see "Be a blessing!" as a parallel imperative to "Go!" (at the start of 12:1), which thus begins a new thought (after all, verse numbering is a later phenomenon in the biblical text, and does not always represent the best division of ideas). God's initial words to Abraham would then be structured by two imperatives, followed by a series of promises. The following is my proposed translation of Gen 12:1–3.

> [1] YHWH said to Abram:

> "GO from your country, and from your kindred, and from your father's house, to the land that I will show you. [2] And I will make of you a great nation, and I will bless you, and I will make your name great.

> BE a blessing! [3] And I will bless those who bless you, (but the one who disdains you I will curse[46]); and by you all the families of the earth shall bless one another."

Although I have left the promises (in 12:2 and 12:3) joined with what precedes them by the non-committal word "and," these promises could be plausibly construed as consequences or even purpose statements—what God will do if Abraham obeys these two commands.[47] The basis for this interpretation is the paratactic character of Hebrew prose. Parataxis is the phenomenon of laying down a string of clauses joined only by the multiple-duty conjunction *vav* (typically, "and") attached to the beginning of the next word. The translation value of *vav* in any particular case must be interpreted by the context. It may have a conjunctive force ("and"); it may be contrastive

---

44. Buber, "Election of Israel," 87. Here Buber cites Gen 18:19, where God reflects on the need for Abraham to teach his children and household "the way of YHWH," which includes "righteousness and justice," as a condition for God fulfilling his promises to Abraham.

45. Buber, "Election of Israel," 87. See also 86.

46. Many translations correctly distinguish between the plural of "those" who bless Abraham from the singular of "the one" who disdains him. I have also kept the distinction between the verb for "disdain" (or treat lightly) and the verb for "curse" (which is stronger).

47. *Purpose* may be communicated by the fact that many of these verbs are in the cohortative, which communicates God's intent or desire to accomplish what is stated (as opposed to just a statement of fact that it will happen). Two verbs that are not in the cohortative are God's statement about cursing (which is why I rendered it as a parenthetical statement) and the final line about the families of the earth blessing themselves (this is technically excluded from being a cohortative since it is not a first person verb about what God will do); the end of verse 3 thus describes the ultimate *consequence* of Abraham's obedience.

("but," "yet"); it may represent temporal sequence ("then," "now"); it is often simply omitted in translation. But *vav* attached to an imperfect or cohortative verb may also signify consequence or purpose ("that," "so that").[48]

This interpretation of Gen 12:1–3 (organized around two imperatives) would place significant responsibility on Abraham, not only to leave Haran and travel to Canaan (something he does in Gen 12:4), but also to live as a model of blessing. Blessing, for either Abraham or others, would not be an automatic outcome.

This is consistent with other texts in Genesis where Abraham has a positive role to play in living according to righteousness ("walk before me and be blameless"; Gen 17:1) and in teaching his family God's ordinances for right living (Gen 18:19). At least three times in Genesis the fulfillment of God's promises (including the nations blessing each other by Abraham and his offspring) is made dependent on Abraham's obedience to God (Gen 18:18–19; 22:18; 26:4–5). And Exod 19 explains that it is only through obedience to God and faithfulness to his covenant that Israel will fulfill their elect role as "a priestly kingdom and a holy nation" (Exod 19:5–6).[49]

## Does Abraham's Family Fulfill Their Calling?

The narrative question then arises as to whether Abraham (and Israel) will live in such a way as to mediate the blessing of God to the rest of humanity, thus enabling the nations to overcome the impediment of sin, which has prevented their fulfillment of the original human vocation. In the narrative of Genesis this question comes down to the issue of the righteousness of Abraham and his offspring.

While it is traditional to view Abraham as a paradigm of righteousness, the text portrays him as a more ambivalent figure. Having received specific directives from God, to *go* (Gen 12:1) and *be a blessing* (12:2), we find that Abraham does in fact go (12:4–9), thus obeying the first directive. In the very next narrative episode (12:10–20), however, he becomes a paradigm not of blessing but of *curse* (a negative example), when he deceives the king of Egypt out of fear, by pretending that Sarah is his sister, not his wife (she is technically both). This allows the king's courtiers to take Sarah for the royal harem, which results in diseases coming on Pharaoh and his household (thus Abraham prevents, rather than mediates, blessing to the nations).

48. Alexander translates God's promises as purpose statements, dependent on the two commands, "go" and "be a blessing" (Alexander, *From Paradise to the Promised Land*, 152, 175). Wenham views these promises as the purpose or consequence of Abraham's obedience to the command to "go" (Wenham, *Genesis 1–15*, 275).

49. I realize that my reading of Gen 12:2b as an imperative ("be a blessing!") goes against the grain of the majority of Genesis commentaries. It is, therefore, worth noting that my interpretation of Abraham's vocation to the nations does not depend on this reading. Nor does it depend on the New Testament. It is, rather, grounded in the narrative placement of Gen 12:1–3, the universal scope of the exodus articulated in the plague narrative and at Sinai, the prophetic vision of the nations turning to YHWH via the witness of Israel, and the LXX translation of Gen 12:3b. To which we can add the Genesis references to the necessity of Abraham's obedience, referenced in the preceding paragraph.

Paradoxically, Abraham (who doesn't seem to learn from this experience) goes through the same charade again with Abimelech the king of Gerar (20:1–18), which results in barrenness on the king's household and a death threat from God, who offers the king mercy in a dream, but is nevertheless constrained by his promise to curse anyone who treats Abraham lightly (12:2). In both cases Abraham's actions (which are motivated by lack of trust in God's promises) have disastrous consequences for the royal families in question, consequences prevented or ameliorated only by the return of Sarah untouched by the king. In the second episode (with Abimelech), Abraham intercedes for the healing of those he affected adversely (20:17–18), thus functioning, in the end, as a mediator of blessing to counter the curse his own actions generated.

Similar ethical ambivalence dogs Abraham's descendents. Jacob deviously gets his older brother Esau (who is certainly not a faultless character) to give up his birthright for a pot of stew (25:29–34) and deceives his aging father Isaac into giving him the blessing reserved for the firstborn (27:1–40). Thus the sibling rivalry that began in the womb (25:21–26), abetted by parental favoritism (25:27–28), flowers into the desire of one brother to kill the other (27:41–45). Yet the deceiver can also positively impact others, as when the increase of Laban's flocks is attributed to blessing brought by Jacob (Gen 30:27–30).

In many ways Joseph is a more complex example. He endures the animosity of his brothers, which leads to his enslavement in Egypt (37:18–36), then a wrongful accusation of attempted rape, resulting in prison (39:6–20). We shouldn't forget, however, that it was Joseph's own adolescent boasting to his older brothers about his dreams of privilege (influenced perhaps by the favoritism shown him by his father) that led to (or fueled) their animosity in the first place (37:2–11). Yet Joseph undergoes significant character transformation over the course of the narrative, which ends with his emotionally fraught reconciliation with his brothers (Gen 42–45)—the very ones who sold him into slavery.[50]

Even during his slavery Joseph brings blessing and prosperity to Potiphar's household (39:2–6); and after he is released from prison his rise to the position of Pharaoh's second-in-command allows him to preserve the life of the Egyptians (indeed, "all the earth") during a time of extreme famine (41:53–57). Blessing certainly comes to others through Joseph.

Yet Joseph seems to have instituted debt slavery in Egypt as a way for those impoverished by famine to receive food. After they had depleted their silver (47:13–15), then their livestock (47:16–17) to pay for the grain he stored, the text says that Joseph took their land and their "bodies" as payment (47:18–22), and instituted a one-fifth taxation rate for the yield they received from this grain (47:23–26). I

---

50. For an astute study of Joseph's character transformation, see Sykora, "The Mission that Transforms." For a profound reading of how the narratives of Genesis subvert sibling rivalry (including a study of Joseph's transformation), see Sacks, *Not in God's Name*, Pt. 2: "Siblings" (chaps. 6–9).

believe we are justified in wondering whether this is the very institution of slavery that the Israelites were later subjected to.[51]

And one could go on to read the entire history of Israel in terms of whether or not (and to what degree) Abraham's descendants live up to their calling to live as an exemplar of blessing. Indeed, the pervasive prophetic critique of Israel's failure to keep YHWH's covenant may be viewed in this light.

Jeremiah 4 even specifies that if God's people repent and turn to him in faithfulness, the result will be that Gen 12:3b will finally be fulfilled, in that the nations will bless themselves by Israel—or possibly even by YHWH himself (depending on the referent of "by him" in v. 2). YHWH declares through the prophet:

> If you return to me,
> if you remove your abominations from my presence,
>    and do not waver,
> and if you swear, "As YHWH lives!"
>    in truth, in justice, and in uprightness,
> then nations shall bless themselves by him,
>    and by him they shall boast" (Jer 4:1b–2; NRSV adapted).

## A Jewish Understanding of Israel's Vocation to the Nations?

It is fascinating that having argued against a missional reading of Genesis 12 as a Christian distortion, Moberly concedes (at the end of his chapter on the blessing of Abraham) that there are prominent Jewish scholars who affirm the universal purpose of Israel's election, even in Genesis 12. He cites the commentaries of Nahum Sarna, Umberto Cassuto, and Jacob Benno.[52] Although Sarna and Cassuto think that Gen 12:3b should probably be translated as passive, and Jacob takes its meaning as reflexive, all three affirm that Abraham's election is ultimately for the benefit of the entire world.[53] According to Jacob, the blessing that Abraham is to mediate to the nations "is an expression of a great-hearted religious universalism, not surpassed by any of the prophets. It is stated at the beginning of Israel's history."[54]

To these three Jewish voices I would add Martin Buber, whose writings on the election of Israel first helped me see the role of Abraham in the wider biblical story.[55] Particularly striking is Buber's elucidation of the line YHWH speaks (via Moses) to

51. For a nuanced analysis of this point, see Held, *The Heart of Torah*, 1:104–108.

52. Moberly, *The Theology of the Book of Genesis*, 159–161.

53. Sarna, *Genesis*, 89; Cassuto, *Commentary on the Book of Genesis*, Pt. 2, 315; Jacob, *Genesis*, 85–87.

54. Jacob, *Genesis*, 87. Moberly's version of this quote diverges somewhat from my own, since he gives his own translation of the 1934 German edition, whereas my quote is taken from the published English translation.

55. It is paradoxical that my missional reading of the Israel's election was initially prompted by reading Buber in the early nineties.

Israel at Sinai: "I bore you on eagles' wings and brought you to myself" (Exod 19:4). Noting that the entire book of Deuteronomy could be viewed as a midrash on Exod 19:1–5 (which he designates "the eagle passage"),[56] Buber highlights the Song of Moses (Deuteronomy 32) for its elaboration of the eagle imagery:

> As an eagle stirs up its nest,
>   and hovers over its young;
> as it spreads its wings, takes them up,
>   and bears them aloft on its pinions,
> the LORD alone guided him;
>   no foreign god was with him. (Deut 32:11–12)

The text vividly imagines God as an eagle teaching its young to fly. Although the "God-eagle," Buber explains, has many offspring (the nations), he nevertheless "spreads his wings and sets one of the young upon his pinion, carries it away, and, by throwing it into the air and catching it, teaches it to fly freely."[57] Teaching the young to fly is an allusion to obedience, even to *imitatio Dei*, learning God's righteousness.

But then Buber asks: "Why the one?" In other words, why the election of Israel from among the nations?

I will let Buber have the last word: "Why else but that it may fly ahead, leading the way for the others!"[58]

## Bibliography

Alexander, T. Desmond. *From Paradise to the Promised Land: An Introduction to the Pentateuch*. 3rd ed. Grand Rapids: Baker Academic, 2012.

Alter, Robert. *Genesis: Translation and Commentary*. New York: Norton, 1996.

Bandstra, Barry L. *Reading the Old Testament: An Introduction to the Hebrew Bible*. 4th ed. Belmont, CA: Wadsworth Cengage, 2009.

Buber, Martin. "Abraham the Seer (Genesis 12–25)." In *On the Bible: Eighteen Studies*, edited by Nahum N. Glatzer, 22–43. New York: Schocken, 1968.

———. "The Election of Israel: A Biblical Inquiry (Exodus 3 and 19; Deuteronomy)." In *On the Bible: Eighteen Studies*, edited by Nahum N. Glatzer, 80–92. New York: Schocken, 1968.

Cassuto, Umberto. *A Commentary on the Book of Genesis*, Pt. 2: *From Noah to Abraham*. Translated by Israel Abrahams. Chicago: Varda, 2012.

Fox, Everett. *The Five Books of Moses*. The Schocken Bible. New York: Schocken, 1995.

Freedman, H. *Midrash Rabbah: Genesis*, vol. 1. London: Soncino, 1939.

Fretheim, Terence E. "Because the Whole Earth Is Mine: Narrative and Theme in Exodus." *Interpretation* 50 (1996) 229–39.

———. *Exodus*. Interpretation. Louisville: Westminster John Knox, 1991.

---

56. Buber, "Election of Israel," 89.
57. Buber, "Election of Israel," 90.
58. Buber, "Election of Israel," 90.

———. *God and World in the Old Testament: A Relational Theology of Creation*. Nashville: Abingdon, 2005.

———. "The Plagues as Ecological Signs of Historical Disaster." *Journal of Biblical Literature* 110 (1991) 385–96.

———. "The Reclamation of Creation: Redemption and Law in Exodus." *Interpretation* 45 (1991) 354–65.

Goldingay, John. *Old Testament Theology: Israel's Gospel*. Downers Grove, IL: InterVarsity, 2003.

Grüneberg, Keith N. *Abraham, Blessing and the Nations: A Philological and Exegetical Study of Genesis 12:3 in Its Narrative Context*. Beihefte zur Zeitschrift für die alttestamentliche Wissenschaft 332. Berlin: de Gruyter, 2003.

Held, Shai. *The Heart of Torah: Essays on the Weekly Torah Portion*. 2 vols. Philadelphia: Jewish Publication Society, 2017.

Jacob, Benno. *Genesis: The First Book of the Bible*. Translated by Ernest I. Jacob and Walter Jacob. New York: Ktav, 2007.

Janzen, J. Gerald. "*Ecce Homo*: The Servant of YHWH as *Imago Dei* in Second Isaiah." *Canadian Theological Review* 2/2 (2013) 1–14.

Johnson, Andy. *Holiness and the Missio Dei*. Eugene, OR: Cascade, 2016.

Middleton, J. Richard. "A New Heaven and a New Earth: The Case for a Holistic Reading of the Biblical Story of Redemption." *Journal for Christian Theological Research* 11 (2006) 73–97.

———. *A New Heaven and a New Earth: Reclaiming Biblical Eschatology*. Grand Rapids: Baker Academic, 2014.

Middleton, J. Richard, and Brian J. Walsh, *Truth Is Stranger than It Used to Be: Biblical Faith in a Postmodern Age*. Downers Grove, IL: IVP Academic, 1995.

Moberly, R. W. L. *The Theology of the Book of Genesis*. Old Testament Theology. Cambridge: Cambridge University Press, 2009.

Sacks, Jonathan. *Not in God's Name: Confronting Religious Violence*. New York: Schocken, 2015.

Sarna, Nahum M. *Genesis: The Traditional Hebrew Text with New JPS Translation*. JPS Torah Commentary. Philadelphia: Jewish Publication Society, 1989.

Sykora, Josef. "The Mission that Transforms: A Development of Joseph's Character in Genesis 37–50." *Canadian Theological Review* 4/2 (2015) 1–18.

Wenham, Gordon J. *Genesis 1–15*. Word Biblical Commentary 1. Waco, TX: Word, 1987.

Wright, Christopher J. H. *The Mission of God: Unlocking the Bible's Grand Narrative*. Downers Grove, IL: IVP Academic, 2006.

# 5

## Trauma not Triumph: Reading the Hebrew Bible as Disaster and Resilience Literature[1]

— Louis Stulman

"The ordinary response to atrocities is to banish them from consciousness."

—Judith Herman, *Trauma and Recovery*

The Hebrew Bible largely is literature of loss.[2] Sometimes this loss is palpable (synchronic presence) as in Abel's gratuitous death, Sarai's infertility, Hagar's banishment, and the threat of massacre in Egypt. It is evident in the defeat of Israel's and Judah's kings, the suffering of God's servant Israel in Isaiah, the imagined collapse of the order of creation in Jeremiah, the deportation of the prophet-priest Ezekiel, and diaspora stories in Daniel and Esther. At other times, however, pain bubbles beneath the text (i.e., diachronic presence) as in the priestly account of creation, the divine promise of land in Genesis, the concern for ritual purity in Leviticus, well-defined insider-outsider boundaries in Deuteronomy,[3] and the blanket denunciations of the

---

1. Author's note: Paul Livermore was my first college instructor in Hebrew. A fellow student Jay McDougal and I met with Professor Livermore at 7:30 A.M. Tuesdays through Fridays for nearly two years during which we translated every Hebrew to English/English to Hebrew exercise in Weingreen's *Grammar* and then worked through Deuteronomy. In one of those early-morning tutorials, Jay and I discovered Professor Livermore asleep at his desk, due not to boredom but to another late night devoted to his Princeton dissertation. Years later when I returned to Roberts to give a lecture, Paul introduced me as "the only student"—at which point I thought he was going to say something flattering but instead conceded—"in whose class I ever fell asleep as teacher!" I take some pride in that, although since then, I'm sure, a good number of students have fallen asleep in my own classes.

I am indebted to Paul Livermore for his wondrous theological insight, for his abiding commitment to the church and the academy, and for a sustaining friendship over forty years old.

2. See the ground-breaking works of Smith-Christopher's *A Biblical Theology of Exile* and Carr's *Holy Resilience*. See Boase and Frechette, *Bible through the Lens of Trauma*, as well as O'Connor's *Jeremiah: Pain and Promise* and her recent commentary *Genesis 1–25A*. See also Brett, *Political Trauma and Healing*; Kelle et al., *Interpreting Exile*; and Becker et al., *Trauma and Traumatization*; and Garber, Jr., "Trauma Theory and Biblical Studies"; Kim and Stulman's *You are My People*; Stulman, "Art and Atrocity, and the Book of Jeremiah," in *Jeremiah Invented*.

3. Stulman, "Encroachment in Deuteronomy."

people Israel by the prophets. Although loss may not be readily apparent, the trauma of land confiscation, physical displacement, and confinement, as well as the existential need to make sense of the nonsense of war, also inform these texts.

Whether the pain is on or below the surface of the text, much of the Bible is the literary legacy of the disempowered, the complex and conflicted witness of communities across time and space that have suffered the wreckage of violence, most often in the form of war. Rarely does the literature of the historical losers survive. Rarely do we read the stories of the defeated and testimonies of their gods. The geo-political winners too often frame the narrative and monopolize memory. The losers, as W. G. Sebald observed, demonstrate an uncanny ability to "forget what they do not want to know . . . and carry on as if nothing happened."[4]

The Hebrew Bible is a notable exception. It summons surviving communities to remember the hardship and humiliation of captivity in Egypt (Deut 15:15; 24:18; see also 5:15). It evokes the memory of "the long way the LORD your God led you in the wilderness these forty years" (Deut 8:2a). The psalmists summon God to remember Israel's hardships (Pss 74:2, 18; 89:50). More often than not, the Bible refuses to deny deep ruptures in life. It embraces disorienting moments as part of its national narrative (e.g., Deut 26:4–10).[5] It speaks on behalf of the dispossessed, the disappeared, the displaced and bears witness to their pain. It even envisions God entering the fray and casting God's lot with the weak and easily discarded.

> Father of orphans and defender of widows is God in his holy habitation.
> God settles the lonely in their homes;
> he sets prisoners free with happiness,
> but the rebellious dwell in a parched land. (Ps 68:5–6)[6]

This literary artifact of loss also endures as a rich meaning-making map. In this capacity, it strives to sustain those suffering a cascade of direct and indirect (second and third generational) traumas including military invasion, occupation, the loss of homeland and family, shaming, displacement, and resettlement. Although these forms of traumatic violence often numb the senses and reduce the world to silence, the *voice* returns in the Hebrew Scriptures in the dialect of lament, rage, resistance, and resilience. Liberation theologians and post-colonial, feminist, and LGBTQ readers have long deciphered this voice, as have myriad women, men, and children living on the margins.

The Bible's varied expressions of pain, especially when read by minority and indigenous peoples, unite ancient text and contemporary readers in ways unlike most

---

4. Sebald, *On the Natural History of Destruction*, 41.

5. Deut 26:5, "My father was a Syrian refugee," throws into sharp relief current anti-immigrant ideologies and policies of exclusion. This biblical text apparently embraces the community's identity as an immigrant people. It is not scandalized by the painful memories of exile and loss. It even dares to recognize itself in the face of outlier Syria/Aram.

6. CEB. All other Bible translations are the author's.

other idioms. This language captures something elemental about life.[7] It sheds light on human vulnerability and brokenness. It provides words when there are none and pathos when we grow callous. It reveals God's face in the stranger, the estranged, and the wounded (see, e.g., Gen 18:1–15), but also exposes base human inclinations to dominate, exclude, and victimize others.

Many on the margins—the powerless, the defeated, the so-called losers—have long found solace in the Bible's deep ruptures and cries for justice. African slaves looked to its stories of suffering and liberation for hope and consolation even though their oppressors used the Bible to justify their economic enterprise. Many blacks during apartheid South Africa read the Old Testament as a text of resistance even though the Dutch Reformed Church used the same text to legitimatize its racist ideology. Today in the U.S., despite its misappropriation by white nationalists and others, this same text resonates with the marginalized and sometimes becomes their solitary voice of hope.

This essay attempts to read the Hebrew Bible through the lens of trauma. It seeks to shed light on biblical Israel's history of damage while exposing First World reading strategies rooted in power. Undoubtedly, this overview fails to do justice to the Hebrew Bible's rich cacophony of voices. It says nothing, for example, of priestly concerns for purity, the importance of ancient law codes, or the David and Zion traditions. It does not explore the Israelite religion as a religion of blessings, fertility, and good life. Nor does it deal with victory literature in the Bible (see, e.g., the stories of Joshua's military campaigns or the celebration of King Cyrus in the final words of 2 Chronicles), nor even diatribes against outsiders (see, e.g., Jeremiah 50–51; Ezra 9–10). *It merely suggests that the Old Testament occupies a place of trauma, mystery, and grief. Specifically, it interprets the Hebrew Scriptures as disaster and survival literature—literature that explores artful refractions of Israel's history of marginality and resilience especially during the years ca. 586–330 BCE.* In those turbulent years, survivors struggled with the loss of homeland, the destruction of the central shrine, and the normalization of diaspora. By every account, these national disasters leave an indelible mark on much of Bible.[8]

---

7. Placher, *Narratives of a Vulnerable God*, xi. Placher follows the lead of Moltmann and others who argue that language of divine vulnerability, the power of love, not divine impassibility, captures something core and primal about the Christian tradition, something capable of inspiring believers to acts of kindness.

8. Most interpreters have long argued that the Torah was shaped during the Babylonian exile and early Persian period. The (exilic or, more likely, *post-exilic*) priestly community of the Torah was more or less responsible for the formation of the tradition. Its macro-narrative begins with the creation of the world, tells the story of Israel's earliest challenges, and culminates in Deuteronomic regulations given to a landless people. The penultimate scenes of the Former Prophets, also assembled during this time of exigency, depict Babylonian armies invading Jerusalem, ravaging the city, burning the temple, and deporting Judeans. Its final vignette describes Babylon's King Evil-merodach releasing Judah's exiled King Jehoiachin from prison, although the Judean ruler remains under Babylonian control (2 Kgs 25:27–30). War, exile, and theodicy are never far from the purview of this writing/reading community nor the Latter Prophets, which address survivors of Babylonian and Persian hegemony. And many books of the Writings are diaspora and survival texts emerging from the contingencies of the Achaemenid Persian era.

Corinna Guerrero poignantly observes, "The metanarrative of salvation is laced with loss."[9] The biblical story of God's revelation in Israel pulsates with collective and intimate pain no less than Marc Chagall's lithograph of *Sorrow* or Picasso's *Guernica*. Certainly there are moments of joy, even ecstasy, as when Miriam dances before God (Exod 15:20–21) or when Hannah erupts in praise (1 Sam 2:1–10), but rarely are expressions of rapture divorced from deep ruptures.

Even biblical recitals of faith are rooted in pain. Life-threatening experiences of war and exile, confinement and diaspora are integral parts of ancient Israel's theological testimony and national narrative. Rather than scandalizing the community, as noted above, these moments of liminality and accompanying stories of rescue bear witness to the character and piety of God's people. "Remember this day, the day you left Egypt, the house of slavery, because Yhwh liberated you with a mighty hand; you shall eat no leavened bread" (Exod 13:3). "When your children ask you, 'What is the meaning of the laws, the regulations, and the rules that Yhwh our God has commanded you?' tell them, 'We were Pharaoh's slaves in Egypt, but Yhwh brought us out of Egypt with a mighty hand'" (Deut 6:20–21). "You saw the affliction of our ancestors in Egypt and heard their cry at the Sea of Reeds . . . But look, we are slaves today, slaves in the land you gave our ancestors" (Neh 9:9, 36). "When Israel was a child, I loved him, and out of Egypt I called my son" (Hosea 11:1).

Israel's story of trauma not only creates its identity; it also gives rise to its ethical compass.[10] It calls for solidarity with victimized people based on the memory and experience of disempowerment. Richard Kearney contends that "[t]he entire Bible . . . is a story of struggles between different ways of responding to the alien."[11] "Do not mistreat or oppress the stranger, for you were strangers in Egypt" (Exod 22:21). "Do not oppress a stranger, for you know what it is like, having yourselves been strangers in the land of Egypt" (Exod 23:9). "Treat the stranger residing among you as a citizen. Love them as yourself, for you were strangers in Egypt. I am the Yhwh your God" (Lev 19:34). "You must look after the stranger, for you were strangers in the land of Egypt" (Deut 10:19). "Remember that you were a slave in Egypt and Yhwh your God rescued you. That is why I give you this command today" (Deut 15:15). "You shall not deprive the rights of the stranger or the orphan of their rights; you shall not take a widow's garment in pledge. Remember that you were a slave in Egypt and Yhwh your God redeemed you there; therefore, I command you to follow this instruction" (Deut 24:17–18).

---

9. Guerrero, "Costly Scripture," 19.

10. Pivotal works on trauma theory include: Van der Kolk, *The Body Keeps the Score*; Van der Kolk et al., "History of Trauma in Psychiatry," in *Traumatic Stress*; Erikson, *A New Species of Trouble*; Alexander, *Trauma: A Social Theory*; Herman, *Trauma and Recovery*; Caruth, *Unclaimed Experience* and *Explorations of Memory*; Scarry, *The Body in Pain*.

11. Kearney, *Anatheism*, 20.

We can discern signs of loss and survival, trauma and resilience, in the three major parts of the Hebrew Bible: the *Torah*, the *Nevi'im*, and the *Ketuvim*.

## Refractions of Trauma and Resilience in the Torah

There are few utopian visions in the *Torah*. Although the Bible opens with a world virtually unscathed by scarcity (Gen 1:1—2:4a),[12] almost immediately we find our primal selves estranged from this idyllic setting and banished east of Eden (Genesis 3). The residual world of the text, the world we know all too well, is broken, at times beyond repair. Its fissures emerge in the brisk, spiccato-like movement from estrangement, shame, and alienation (Genesis 3) to rage, violence, and idolatry, namely the unrestrained pursuit of power and renown, perhaps even the passion to win at any cost, in the so-called story of the Tower of Babel (Genesis 4–11). The opening act of the biblical drama, therefore, takes us on an existential journey from Eden to Babel (Babylon), that is, from a well-ordered and symmetrical world culminating in the Sabbath to the chaos of exile. Ironically, this life-threatening world of diaspora provides the context for the birth of the people Israel: God calls Abram and Sarai *from the nations*, specifically from Ur of the Chaldeans (Gen 11:31). And it is no literary accident that the Judean people face their greatest challenges in Babylon.

In their journey out of Babylon, Abram and Sarai encounter a God who promises to create or recreate the people Israel (Gen 11:10—12:9).

> Yhwh said to Abram,
> Leave your country, your kin, and your father's family,
> and go to the land I will show you.
> I will make you a great people,
>   I will bless you;
> I will make you famous,
>   and you will be a blessing.
> I will bless those who bless you,
>   and curse those who harm you.
> And all the families on earth
>   will be blessed through you. (Gen 12:1–3)

From the very start, however, barrenness, violence, rival nations, internal rivalries, and food shortages put the future of God's people at risk. The ancestral narratives bristle with anxiety. Will the promised child be born (Gen 11:26—20:18)? Will the child survive (Gen 21:1—22:24)? Will God come to the aid of the small vulnerable family (Gen 25:19—50:26)? Will cooperation/collusion with the empire lead to its

---

12. I say "virtually" because the priestly account of creation alludes to the primordial conflict between chaos and order and it employs royal language in its depiction of God and the *imago Dei*. Nonetheless, Gen 1:1—2:4a is perhaps as close as the Hebrew Bible gets to a utopian world replete with symmetry, coherence, and beauty.

demise (Gen 39:1—50:26; Exod 1:8–22)? Will the Israelite people, now facing Pharaoh's malevolent actions, endure the empire's brutality (in the book of Exodus) and the perils of landlessness (in Leviticus through Deuteronomy)? These disaster stories not only speak of a distant past, as we often assume; they also give voice to the pressing concerns of exilic and post-exilic communities facing the exigencies of war and the hardships of a pariah people.

At the same time, these disaster stories function as survival texts. They testify to God's fidelity in the most trying of times. They bear witness to One for whom nothing is too wonderful (Gen 18:14).[13] They tell of God inverting hierarchical arrangements (e.g., first-born, gender, and hegemonic).[14] These diasporic narratives claim, in the words of Bob Dylan, "for the loser now / will be later to win" (from "The Times They Are A-Changin'") or, in more familiar terms, that God humbles the proud and lifts up the needy. War-ravaged Judeans whose country has been devastated and whose future is in grave danger hear Abraham affirm, "Yhwh will provide" (Gen 22:14) and hear an audacious Sarah uttering her child's name (Isaac/Laughter), and they testify that God sustains struggling people and sees to their survival. Text and reader converge in the nadir of loss and vulnerability, survival and hope.

The book of Exodus drives home this point with force. It gives voice to God's response to and immersion in Israel's first national disaster: Egyptian slavery. The story of the Israelite people begins with the dreadful treatment of the Hebrew people (Exod 1:8–14). In order to destroy the Israelites, the king of Egypt exaggerates the threat of the minority people; he labels them "dangerous foreigners"; he seeks to slaughter Hebrew baby boys; and eventually commoditizes their value. Like barrenness and food scarcity in Genesis, these powerful forces threaten the future of God's people. Despite the empire's systematic attempts to destroy outlier Israel, the narrative asserts that the God of Abraham, Isaac, and Jacob, Yhwh, sees the distress of suffering people and acts on their behalf. God "knows about their pain," and "comes down to rescue them" (Exod 3:7–8). In this way, text and reader again converge in the nadir of loss and vulnerability, survival and hope.

The books of Leviticus, Numbers, and Deuteronomy continue the litany of grave threats to outlier Israel. Leviticus accentuates the dangers of living in close proximity to this holy God. Defilement or pollution rules, or put positively, purity rites, create order and defined boundaries for a community under assault from within and outside the borders (likely in the exilic and post-exilic eras). Numbers outlines the hazards of the wilderness or landlessness. Deuteronomy expresses concern with Israel's existence over against foreign nations.[15] As von Rad observed, Israel "is constantly

---

13. See also, Jer 32:27, a passage that explicates what is "too wondrous" or implausible: "Houses, fields, and vineyards will again be bought in this land."

14. See Zakovitch, "Through the Looking Glass."

15. Von Rad, *Studies in Deuteronomy*, 59.

brought into relationship with the existence of other people" in Deuteronomy.[16] More often than not, the text perceives this contact as dangerous. And so all of these formative writings depict Israel at risk. All depict the line between life and death as porous. All represent the people Israel as outliers. Again, text and reader converge in the nadir of loss and vulnerability.

## Refractions of Trauma and Resilience in the Prophets

Interpreters have often read Joshua, Judges, Samuel, and Kings, so-called the Former Prophets or the Deuteronomistic History, as a history of salvation (*Heilsgeschichte*). Some interpret this literature as an invitation to return (*šûb*) to God during and after the Babylonian exile (see, e.g., 1 Kgs 8:35, 48; 2 Kgs 17:13). Others focus on land, the centrality of David, the monarchy, and the temple. However, tribal and national losses complicate the salvific landscape. Israel fails to seize the whole land (Judges), creating so-called enemies within the borders. Philistine warlords (1 Samuel 4–7) along with Syrian, Assyrian, and Babylonian rulers wage war against Israel/Judah (see 2 Kings 16–17, 18–19, 20–21). More pressing, Israel/Judah must contend with its own failures and those of its reckless leaders. In due course the monarchy splinters (1 Kings 11–12) in part due to royal exploitation and idolatry (1 Kgs 5:13–18). Eventually the entire monarchic experiment collapses under the weight of Babylonian hegemony as troops attack Jerusalem and destroy the holy temple (2 Kings 25).[17] Together these crippling forces create a theological topography riddled with failure. The text still asserts that God is at work sustaining the people Israel in fulfillment of the divine promises. But by the end of the corpus little remains of Israel's pre-exilic structures. By the time we reach the final chapters of 2 Kings, there is no land, no monarchy, and no temple as the axis mundi. To heighten the level of anxiety, the corpus makes a sweeping claim that Israel, not God, is responsible for its national disasters. In other words, it places Israel/Judah's losses within coherent (Deuteronomic) contexts of meaning.

The Latter Prophets are no less literature of loss and resilience, trauma and hope.[18] The books of Isaiah, Jeremiah, Ezekiel, and the Twelve are complex theological responses to the collapse of Israel's social and symbolic worlds, due in large part to military loss, forced relocation, and captivity. Covering the span of at least three centuries, from the eighth century BCE to at least the fifth century BCE, the focal points of these writings are the fall of Samaria in the eighth century BCE (by the Assyrian military machine) and the collapse of Jerusalem in the sixth century (by the neo-Babylonian armies).[19] Michael H. Floyd maintains that "[t]he prophetic books

---

16. Von Rad, *Studies in Deuteronomy*, 58.

17. King Evil-merodach's kind treatment of deposed Jehoiachin (2 Kgs 25:27–30), the book's very last vignette, hints at the prospect of restoration, although this hopeful overture is modest at best.

18. See Kim and Stulman, *You are My People*.

19. Gowan, *Theology of Prophetic Books*, 9-16.

are concerned with developments that led to exile under the Babylonians and/or developments that followed from the reversal of exile under the Persians. Each book mines Israel's prophetic tradition to interpret theologically some aspect(s) of exile and restoration."[20] Building on these and other studies, Paul Kim and I have suggested this corpus is "the disaster literature of those who survived the onslaught of the three great world powers—Assyria, Babylon, and Persia—and their imperialistic designs."[21] If there is a *Mitte* or center of this literary tradition, it might well be the trauma of war and a concerted attempt to survive it.[22]

The Book of the Twelve is replete with language of divine and human violence. To the surprise (and disappointment) of many readers, violence is present at almost every juncture. Hosea opens the Book of the Twelve with an ominous allusion to the violence of Jehu's house (Hos 1:4–5). Joel's metaphorical world is consumed by invading armies, imagined as "cutting locust," "swarming locust," "hopping locust," and "destroying locust" (Joel 1:4). Abuses in warfare inform the initial oracles against the nations in Amos; and the threat of military invasion is present throughout the book (e.g., Amos 5:1–2). Obadiah is an expression of rage against Edom for "the slaughter and violence done to your brother Jacob" (Obadiah 10). In contrast to Nahum, Jonah elicits a more amenable response to the empire that annihilated his country. Micah imagines Yhwh coming from his dwelling to punish Israel and Judah. "The mountains melt beneath him and the valleys split apart, like wax before fire, like water running down a slope" (1:4). Habakkuk laments the violence done to God's people and the apparent idleness of God. Zephaniah announces sweeping destruction on earth—"I will sweep everything away from the earth, declares Yhwh" (1:2)—although the devastation centers on Judah and its capital city Jerusalem. Less enamored of violence, Haggai encourages a flagging community to rebuild the temple but at the same time speaks of God shaking heaven and earth, sea and land, as well as all the nations (2:6–7a). Zechariah begins with a plea for repentance and concludes with nations waging war against Jerusalem (14:1–2), as a prelude to Yhwh's war against the rebellious nations (14:3–21). Malachi closes the Twelve with a cryptic allusion to the "awesome, fearful day of Yhwh" (3:24).

This language of war is no less apparent in the scrolls of Isaiah, Jeremiah, and Ezekiel. Although Isaiah's lyrical expressions of hope are well known, violence also scars its landscape, violence that is inextricably tied to human arrogance and abuse of power. Isaiah of Jerusalem urges listeners/readers not to trust in the military machinery of super-powers. "Woe to those who go down to Egypt for aid, and who rely on horses, who depend on chariots. . . but do not depend on the Holy One of Israel or seek God" (Isa 31:1). The prophet insists that relying upon "horses and chariots" (the ancient equivalent of drones and AK-47s) carries a great cost (29:1–10). Even

---

20. Floyd, "The Production of Prophetic Books," in *Prophets, Prophecy, and Prophetic Texts*, 277.
21. Kim and Stulman, *You are My People*, 6.
22. Kim and Stulman, *You are My People*, 6.

more dreadful, Isaiah envisions the loss of order and beauty in the world, even the end of culture (Isaiah 24).

> The earth is breaking, breaking; the earth is crumbling, crumbling. The earth is reeling, reeling; the earth is swaying like a drunkard; it is rocking back and forth like a hut. Weighted down and about to fall, and rise no more. (Isa 24:19–20)

The wreckage of war likely informs this haunting image of a return to primeval chaos (also Jer 4:23–28).

Forced migration and homecoming from exile are center stage in the second half of Isaiah (Isaiah 40–66). In chapters 40–55, the prophet assures discouraged refugees that Babylon's downfall and their return to Jerusalem are imminent (e.g., 40:27–31; 47:1–5). In the remaining chapters of the book, the text addresses Judean repatriates negotiating the challenges and disappointments of their new life as a small province in the Persian Empire. Throughout the book, we find God fully engaged in the struggles and pain of God's people.[23]

To read Jeremiah is to enter the world of trauma frontally: we encounter wounded communities, a devastated earth, a tormented prophet, and a suffering God. Their voices are sometimes indistinguishable as if clear and unambiguous categories break down when worlds collapse.

My suffering, my suffering! Pain unbearable; my heart in turmoil; throbbing nonstop" (Jer 4:19). "No healing, only grief; my heart is broken" (8:6). "If only my head were a spring of water, my eyes a fountain of tears, I would weep day and night for the wounds of my people" (Jer 9:1). These ancient laments, these cries of anguish, remind us that war leaves nothing unscathed.

War completely envelops the exilic book of Ezekiel. It frames the text; it defines the text; it engulfs the text in suffering and leaves an indelible mark on virtually every word and image. Signs of trauma surface in the prophetic persona and in Ezekiel's God despite the book's stable and well-defined torah-regulated categories. One can detect these deep fractures in the text's landscape of death and in Ezekiel's traumatized body and prophetic utterance. The net result is a text, prophet, God, and implied readership no less impervious to suffering than Ezekiel's contemporary Jeremiah and Jeremiah's God.[24]

In sum, the violence of war and the idiom of trauma informs memory, social construction, and *even theological imagination*.[25] They throw virtually everything

---

23. Kim, *Reading Isaiah*.

24. See the insightful treatment of the book of Ezekiel in Sharp, *Prophetic Literature*.

25. Scholars who employ trauma analysis in biblical studies often do so as a window into biblical Israel's social and political worlds. For example, trauma and disaster analysis clarifies the communal and individual effects of forced migration and prolonged captivity, harrowing experiences in ancient and modern times. Rarely, however, have scholars engaged trauma studies in the service of theology, that is, to ponder the "elusive presence" (Samuel Terrien) from the perspective of the wounded. To

into question, including and especially divine fidelity. They shatter beliefs about self and community; they rob the wounded of language; they undermine hope and destroy faith. The prophetic literature inhabits this trauma-laden space. It is the legacy of the defeated whose countries have been reduced to "inconsequential places" in vast empires.

## Refractions of Trauma and Resilience in the Writings

The *Ketuvim* is by far the most wide-ranging collection of religious expressions in the Bible. It includes narrative, love poetry, wisdom material, apocalyptic literature, liturgy, history, and philosophy. Dated, for the most part, to the Persian and Hellenistic periods, this residual corpus explores topics as varied as prayer and theodicy, exile and assimilation, diaspora and domination, community identity and insider/outsider boundaries, most of which represent real threats to community life.

Much of this literature responds to deep anxieties over individual and collective survival. More than sixty of the one-hundred-and-fifty psalms, as is well known, are laments in which petitioners cry out to God during times of overwhelming distress. Vulnerable to internal and external forces beyond their control (often in the form of "enemies"), they plead for the restoration of justice and equilibrium. Job and Qoheleth call into question longstanding understandings of God. The former examines the ethical workings of the universe, divine reliability, and innocent suffering. The latter reflects on divine inscrutability and human limitations. Both maintain that God's ways are beyond human control. Daniel and Esther are diaspora stories that address the challenges of minority communities, including resistance to repressive policies and subversion of the empire's absolute claims (often in the form of government edicts). Deploying the funeral dirge as its principal genre, the book of Lamentations mourns the destruction of Jerusalem. Ezra and Nehemiah show deep signs of stress as conflicting parties grapple with temple restoration, political loyalty, purity, and intermarriage. Chronicles reimagines the Judahite identity during the late Persian Period. This last book in the Jewish canon develops an alternative narrative and worldview for a displaced community.

The *Ketuvim*, accordingly, expresses loss and no less than the Torah and the Prophets. This polyphonic corpus struggles with life and death issues: internal

---

move in this direction is dangerous because *theology is at stake*. It is one thing to employ trauma and disaster studies to elucidate the social and psychological dimensions of suffering communities; it is another to shed light on the attendant language for God. But suffering is difficult to parse. It is too raw and unmanageable to control and compartmentalize. Even if it were not, language of divine vulnerability, an immersion of God in human suffering "captures something core and primal about the Christian tradition [and I would suggest the Jewish and Muslim traditions as well], something capable of moving us deeply and inspiring us to action" (Placher, *Narratives of a Vulnerable God*). This "domestication of transcendence" (Placher's term) situates the sacred as the province of the wounded, the weak, the disempowered, the survivors.

rivalries, diaspora, the breakdown of long-established structures, and disturbing questions about individual and community survival. It fosters counter-worldviews, acts of defiance, and survival strategies for disempowered Jews. Although scribal elites frame various parts of the Writings, this literature still speaks on behalf of the displaced people. In the first place, the pen of the scribe plays a key role in the future of the people.[26] That is to say, as buoyant testimony, the act of writing affirms that the community's dire circumstances are not the end of the line. Scribal efforts to maintain the status quo in the service of the surviving ruling elite,[27] moreover, do not mute the pain and dislocation that erupt in the text.

Existential threats of war and prolonged confinement as well as the assault upon the people's sense of integrity, security, and meaning all play a determinative role in the Hebrew Scriptures. This is not to say that exilic and post-exilic communities invented the traditions, only that these emergencies play a seminal role in the text's formation and metanarrative. Consequently, the Tanak functioned, and still functions, as disaster and survival literature for communities on the margins, dislocated and defeated. Haunted by violence of war and its aftermath, indeed the existential threat of annihilation, this wounded/trauma-laden literary tradition gives expression to a torrent of national disasters, including military assault, foreign occupation, and forced relocation. Its varied expressions of liminality and loss give testimony, preserve memory, and address deep disjunctions in life. This literature of trauma, not triumph, refuses to banish the memory of war. Its multiplicity of voices—poetry and prose, male and female, individual and communal—moves beyond cognitive numbness and emotional shock to an attempt to make sense of war and hegemony.

## Textual Art and Trauma

It is noteworthy that this speech presents the community's ordeals in the form of poetry and artistic prose (*Kunstprosa*) or "textual art."[28] Not art for art's sake, but art for the sake of survival, art that throbs with pain and speaks of worlds on the brink of destruction; art that dares to confront human brutality, insisting that raw human power is not ultimate power; art that trades in words not weapons.

For communities ravaged by violence, as ancient Israel was for much of its history, art has long served as a way to survive the unimaginable. Whether that artistic expression takes the form of poems by Garcia Lorca, simple arts and crafts by Japanese Americans held in internment camps in the United States from 1942 to 1946, haunting

---

26. I am indebted to Professors Mark Brummitt and Julie Claassens for this observation.

27. As evident, for example, in their proclivity to uphold moral symmetry and cosmic coherence (see, e.g., Job 42:7–17, Psalms 1 and 150, and in the concluding words of Ecc, 12:13–14; as well as in the doctrine of retribution, i.e., linking rewards and punishments with obedience and disobedience, e.g., Chronicles and Proverbs).

28. Diamond and Stulman, *Jeremiah (Dis)Placed*, 28.

drawings in the camps, or musical "inflection for darkness,"[29] art and atrocity converge to create a matrix for healing. In the speech of the wounded, or what Oscar Romero called "the violence of love," victims discover a source of resilience. Art is capable of capturing this unspeakable pain and creating glimpses of hope.

In other words, the Bible does far more than *report*. It articulates horrors of violence and strategies for survival in artistic expression. Whether written in poetry or prose, this textual art shifts the worst of circumstances to a bearable distance. It removes the trauma of violence from "naked reality,"[30] which is often too much to bear, to the symbolic world of language. We see this symbolic shift in Jeremiah the Deuteronomic preacher, for example, who invites Judean casualties of war to revisit the unthinkable: the destruction of the temple and its liturgical world (7:1—8:3), the end of the covenant (11:1–17), an assault on the election tradition (18:1–12), the reconfiguration of the Davidic dynasty (21:1–10), and the normalization of life in diaspora (25:1–14). This reenactment of Judah's most devastating moments, the end of its once sure and certain cultural and sacred world, allows victims of war to "return" to the pain-filled scenes of violence: to name the disaster, to rage and mourn, to recognize God's presence in it, and to survive the dismantling of their worlds of meaning.

The attempt to confront radical suffering (i.e., to construct theodicy), as we have seen in the book of Jeremiah, is one of the most distinguishing features of the Hebrew Bible.[31] This meaning-making-grief-driven work assumes various forms. Sometimes prophets, priests, and sages attempt to make sense of tragedy by drawing direct correlations between conduct and condition, a nexus between behavior and recompense (Ps 1; Jer 17:5–8). The Torah imagines this kind of morally exacting universe in its formulations of the Sinai and Deuteronomic covenants. When the Former and Latter Prophets pronounce Judah's sacred world under divine siege, when they accuse Israel of wholesale wrongdoing, they are placing the wreckage of war within a context of meaning and are not merely engaging in social commentary. The sage does likewise when connecting morality and circumstance based on observation, tradition, and experience.

Although this kind of retributive or punitive speech often blames the victim rather than perpetrators of violence, it engages in the meaning-making-grief-laden struggle of making sense of radical suffering for survivors. It grapples with the effects of individual and collective trauma and seeks to discern God's presence and purposes in experiences that defy moral logic.[32] As Gregory Orr notes personally, it is often less

---

29. Leonard Cohen's term.

30. Zimmermann, "Introduction," in *Reimagining the Sacred*, 2.

31. See Sweeney, *Hebrew Bible After the Shoah*. My understanding of the term "radical suffering" derives from Farley, *The Wounding and Healing of Desire*.

32. Those ravaged by violence sometimes struggle their entire lives to make sense of their trauma. Trauma theorists and therapists argue that viable explanations are crucial to individual and community survival. Survivor Victor Frankl put it directly, "To live is to suffer, to survive is to find meaning in this suffering." See *Man's Search for Meaning*, 11. These trauma and resilience impulses are visible

painful to live in a coherent moral universe that one can negotiate, *even with guilt*, than in a morally arbitrary world spiraling out of control. Daniel Smith-Christopher observes that self-incrimination, or self-blame, is a common survival strategy of traumatized people, employed to make sense of senseless acts of violence. The attempt to create symbolic and social order in the face of inexplicable suffering is one of the most enduring characteristics of the Hebrew Bible. It affirms a sense of meaning in the world. It restores dignity and autonomy to victims of debilitating trauma. This ordering of chaos empowers victims of disaster to take back their lives and carve out a future in the face of unwieldy loss.

Still, not all meaning making insists on moral coherence. Walter Brueggemann has made a strong case for the central place of disputation in the Hebrew Scriptures.[33] The book of Job tells the story of a paragon of virtue suffering for no fault of his own. The laments in the Psalter rarely attribute distress to moral lapse. The prophet Amos objects to God's scathing indictments against God's people: "O Lord, forgive, I beg you! How can Jacob stand? He is so small!" (Amos 7:5). The prophet Jeremiah imagines taking God to court for injustice in the world (Jer 12:1–3). On occasion this same prophet is more certain of his own innocence than God's (see Jeremiah's so-called Confessions). Habakkuk interrogates God about evil and violence in the world. Overall, theological constructions of coherence and incoherence, theodicy and anti-theodicy, attempt to help victims of traumatic violence, often victims of war and its aftermath, come to terms with incomprehensible loss.

Still the Tanak does more. It moves beyond speech, art, and even meaning making to liturgy or performance. We know little about the social realities behind scroll recitation in the life of ancient Judahite communities,[34] but it is difficult (for me) to imagine the act of reading sacred texts apart from public worship. Through ridicule and affirmation, scorn and celebration, worshipping congregations would reenact texts in which God subverts and disassembles pretentious world powers as a way to carry out justice and salvation. Prophetic oracles against the nations (see, e.g., Isaiah 13–23, Jeremiah 46–51; Ezekiel 25–32; Joel 3) are a case in point. Perhaps the most violent utterances in the Bible, these utterances likely represent the liturgy of war victims incapable of confronting their oppressors apart from their deployment of liturgical expression. As Stephan Wyss puts it, "'the mighty speech' of the powerless, which laughs at massive claims to power, serves as the coping strategy of the defeated and

---

in the text's framing traditions: the Exodus and the Exile, the pivotal points of the metanarrative of Scripture. Although the historical fingerprints of the exodus and the exile are not as impressive as the text purports, both play a massive role theologically in the Old Testament. Both anchor the metanarrative of Israel in loss and liberation, disaster and survival. Both drive home the centrality of the lament. Both affirm that God hears the cries of the wounded and acts on their behalf. Both place the most serious threats to the people Israel within contexts of meaning.

33. Brueggemann, *Theology of the Old Testament* is one of many of Brueggemann's books that accentuates the importance of disputation/counter-testimony in the Bible.

34. Stulman, *Jeremiah*, 349–87.

subordinated who are able to fight injustice only by words and to leave the revenge to God."[35] In liturgical theater, the so-called historical losers engage in the subversive enterprise of envisioning God at work in the moral ambiguities of history; affirming God's involvement in communities saddled with pain; anticipating God dismantling oppressive power arrangements for the sake of the oppressed. Refugees wield the only weapons they have to survive, words and worship.

## Conclusion

When Daniel Smith-Christopher asked at the 2010 SBL Meeting in Atlanta whether the entire scope of 20th century biblical scholarship should be reconsidered in light of what we now know about trauma, many thought he was trading in hyperbole. But there is at least anecdotal evidence to demonstrate that trauma changes everything. Ask anyone who has suffered from sexual violence, lived through war, or endured the assault of a life-threatening disease. Trauma ravages and debilitates; it numbs the senses and renders ordinary language useless. It shatters dreams and constructions of self and community. It violates bodies and splinters families. It destroys trust in God and belief in any semblance of moral coherence in the world. David Carr is surely correct that "The Jewish and Christian scriptures arose out of and speak to catastrophic human trauma."[36] The Bible also maps out avenues of resilience and hope under the most intractable of conditions.

In this essay, I have called attention to the presence of tangible pain at many junctures of the Hebrew Bible. I have argued for the convergence of text and reader in the nadir of loss and vulnerability, survival and hope. Although this is clearly a literary exercise, it also reflects a history of damage bubbling beneath the text. When considering the destruction of the Second Temple of Jerusalem in 70 CE, Eli Weisel muses, "All people usually celebrate victories. The Jewish people also remember [and mourn] defeat."[37] I realized this point when I first read John Bright's and Martin Noth's reconstructions of ancient Israel. I was struck by their construal of Israel's humble origins. Both rejected the historicity of a mass exodus and invasion of Canaan. Bright made a plausible case for early Israel as a disparate people on the periphery of the Near East, namely, as semi-nomadic clans comprised of refugees and run-away slaves who eventually united in covenant (Apiru/Habiru)—a motley group ("mixed multitude") of outliers, without legal rights and vulnerable to the exploits of dominant world power structures.

Recent biblical scholarship has only confirmed this liminal social location. Douglas Knight and Amy-Jill Levine note that ancient Israel was "invaded and occupied

---

35. Quoted in Fischer, "On Writing a Feminist-Postcolonial Commentary," in *Prophecy and Power*, 249–50.
36. Carr, *Holy Resilience*, 5.
37. *The Jewish People: A Story of Survival*.

repeatedly, each time becoming *small provinces* in vast empires."[38] The Israel behind the text, they note, was "a tiny country buffeted by geopolitical forces it could scarcely repel."[39] In addition, biblical scholars have come to pay increasing attention to exile and diaspora, especially the Persian period (ca. 550–330 BCE), as the formative social location of the literary corpus. It is quite likely that the Hebrew Bible took shape in post-war settings in which Yehudite communities were negotiating their identities under foreign rule. Consequently, any plausible *historical reconstruction* must take into consideration the enormous toll exacted on this "little country" by empires on the Tigris and the Euphrates. Moreover, any moving *theological construction* must take seriously a protracted history of war, exile, and captivity. History and theology converge in language of loss and vulnerability.

I have not always appreciated this fact. When my children were young, their public school teachers introduced them to the great empires on the Tigris and Euphrates, in Asia Minor, and on the Nile: Sumer, Egypt, Babylon, Anatolia, Assyria, neo-Babylonia, Persia, Media, Greece, and Rome. I recall my frustration that their textbooks mentioned ancient Israel only in a footnote, referencing its considerable impact on the Western canon. It took some time for me to grasp the significance of this lacuna: Israel never belonged in the company of the powerful. It inhabited the space of the displaced and disempowered who were battered and bruised by the imperialistic exploits of the ancient super powers.[40] Biblical Israel's legacy is the testimony of those on the margins, not at the center, the so-called historical losers, or more accurately, survivors.

To ignore this history of damage and its literary iterations is to risk misconstruing the Jewish and Christian Scriptures. Some interpreters, for example, still read the Bible as the story of the winners. They are wedded to biblical images of power and privilege: multitudes leaving Egypt as a massive military machine, conquering "wicked Canaanites" and occupying their land by divine decree, appointing kings who erect renowned temples and palaces and leave an indelible mark on the world. Granted, reading the Bible as triumph literature is to some extent inspired by the text itself, but *reading one's sacred text—any sacred text—as an expression of power from a position of power is a deadly combination.* It all too often incites hatred, begets bigotry, and fosters intolerance in the name of God. It elevates power and privilege over generosity and hospitality. It implicates God in political alignments that have little concern for the stranger, the lonely, the homeless. It co-opts and misappropriates the biblical mandate for justice, kindness, and humility. As observes Jean Vanier, the founder of L'Arche,

---

38. Knight and Levine, *The Meaning of the Bible*, 27.

39. Knight and Levine, *The Meaning of the Bible*, 143.

40. Almost two decades before Bright and Noth's historical reconstructions, Artur Weiser made the rather innocuous observation, "The history and civilization of Palestine are largely determined by the fact that. . . its inhabitants were drawn into the political and cultural struggles of the powers on the Euphrates, in Asia Minor and on the Nile." Weiser, *Formation and Development*, 11. Ancient Israel, whose God is still worshipped by millions, whose God I invoke in my prayers, was *utterly vulnerable* to the great empires of the Near East.

a network of communities for persons with disabilities, the "religion of winning . . . leaves behind those who are weaker."[41] Winning more than implies that there are losers, and the losers are often the most vulnerable among us.

The impact of this religion of winning reaches far and wide. It rips apart the social fabric of communities at home and abroad. It has legitimized various forms of *Realpolitik*, such as the doctrines of American exceptionalism and unilateralism, ideologies at work, for example, in the 2003 preemptive invasion of Iraq, a war that resulted in the death of tens of thousands of Iraqis and over four thousand U.S. soldiers. It fosters domestic policies that disparage programs of social uplift in the name of religion.

One can also recognize its influence in the "Make America Great Again" banner, which many interpret as nostalgia for a time when white heterosexual men held sway over minorities, women, and immigrants. Donald Trump's campaign slogan is a perfect fit for one who by his own admission likes only winners. Peter Wehner, who has served in three Republican administrations, has called this fascination with raw power a "Nietzschean morality" (a celebration of the *Übermensch*), an approach to life that is incompatible with an ethic that honors human dignity and embraces the poor and weak.[42]

In stark contrast to Trump, Henri Nouwen imagines "no countries to be conquered, no ideologies to be imposed, no people to be dominated. There are only children, women, and men to be loved . . . Love is not made manifest in power but in powerlessness."[43] Leonard Cohen gave voice to this sentiment in his famous song "Hallelujah": "Love is not a victory march. / It's a cold and it's a broken Hallelujah."

When winning, or the perception of winning, carries more weight than the welfare of people, when access to central institutions of power takes precedence over the most vulnerable, something has gone terrible awry.[44] "For what profits one to gain the whole world but lose their own soul?" (Matt 16:26; Mark 8:36)

Reading the Bible as a story of the winners, I have argued, ignores a multiplicity of biblical voices that imagines it otherwise. Instead of depicting Israel as triumphant, many Tanak texts, perhaps most, envision Israel on the margins: dislocated and out of sorts, colonized yet defiant, vulnerable yet resilient, at risk and wounded by war, yet survivors against all odds. Its varied utterances of loss leave an indelible mark on much of the corpus and often testify that God is who is at home on the periphery with the wounded.[45]

---

41. Salai, S.J., "God Chooses the Despised," 1.

42. Wehner, "The Theology of Donald Trump."

43. Nouwen, *Peacework*, 94.

44. See the incisive piece by Molly Worthen, "A Match Made in Heaven." See also the incisive work of Jacques Ellul, *Violence*, 27–79, esp. 27–30.

45. When the powerful hijack these narratives, liturgies, and poetry, they often exploit them to do violence to the weak and vulnerable. There is a long and sad history to support this claim. We witness this misappropriation in our contemporary world, when white nationalists employ the civil rights

## Bibliography

Alexander, Jeffrey. *Trauma: A Social Theory*. Cambridge: Polity, 2012.

Becker, Eve-Marie, et al., eds. *Trauma and Traumatization in Individual and Collective Dimensions: Insights from Biblical Studies and Beyond*. Studia Aarhusiana Neotestamentica 2. Göttingen: Vandenhoeck & Ruprecht, 2014.

Boase, Elizabeth, and Christopher G. Frechette, eds. *Bible through the Lens of Trauma*. Atlanta: SBL Press, 2016.

Brett, Mark G. *Political Trauma and Healing: Biblical Ethics for a Postcolonial World*. Grand Rapids: Eerdmans, 2016.

Brueggemann, Walter. *Theology of the Old Testament: Testimony, Dispute, Advocacy*. Minneapolis: Fortress Press, 2012.

Carr, David. *Holy Resilience: The Bible's Traumatic Origins*. New Haven: Yale University Press, 2014.

Caruth, Cathy. *Unclaimed Experience: Trauma, Narrative and History*. Baltimore: Johns Hopkins Press, 1996.

———, ed. *Explorations of Memory*. Baltimore: Johns Hopkins Press, 1995.

Diamond, A. R. Pete, and Louis Stulman, eds. *Jeremiah "(Dis)Placed": New Directions in Writing/Reading Jeremiah*. Library of Hebrew Bible/Old Testament Studies 529. London: T & T Clark, 2011.

Ellul, Jacques. *Violence: Reflections from a Christian Perspective*. New York: Seabury Press, 1969.

Erikson, Kai. *A New Species of Trouble: Explorations in Disaster, Trauma, Community*. New York: Norton, 1994.

Farley, Wendy. *The Wounding and Healing of Desire: Weaving Heaven and Earth*. Louisville: Westminster John Knox, 2005.

Fischer, Irmtraud. "On Writing a Feminist-Postcolonial Commentary: A Critical Evaluation." In *Prophecy and Power: Jeremiah in Feminist and Postcolonial Perspective*, edited by Christl M. Maier and Carolyn J. Sharp, 234–51. Library of Hebrew Bible/Old Testament Studies 577. London: T. & T. Clark, 2013.

Floyd, Michael H. "The Production of Prophetic Books." In *Prophets, Prophecy and Prophetic Texts in Second Temple Judaism*, edited by M. H. Floyd and R. D. Haak, 276–97. Library of Hebrew Bible/Old Testament Studies 427. London: T. & T. Clark, 2006.

Frankl, Victor. *Man's Search for Meaning*. New York: Washington Square, 1985.

Garber, David G., Jr. "Trauma Theory and Biblical Studies." *Currents in Biblical Research* 14 (2015) 24–44.

Gowan, Donald E. *Theology of the Prophetic Books: The Death and Resurrection of Israel*. Louisville: Westminster John Knox, 1998.

Guerrero, Corinna. "Costly Scripture: Encountering Trauma in the Bible." *America: The Jesuit Review* 213 (2015) 19–22.

Herman, Judith Lewis. *Trauma and Recovery: The Aftermath of Violence from Domestic Abuse to Political Terror*. New York: Basic Books, 1999.

*The Jewish People: A Story of Survival*. Produced by PBS Home Video, 2009.

Kearney, Richard. *Anatheism: Returning to God after God*. New York: Columbia University Press, 2011.

---

language of the 60s, when the church reads its sacred text to justify an agenda of bigotry, and when the Bible is deployed as a canonical warrant for dominance, acquisition, and moral hegemony.

Kelle, Brad E., et al., eds. *Interpreting Exile: Displacement and Deportation in Biblical and Modern Contexts*. Ancient Israel and Its Literature 10. Atlanta: Society of Biblical Literature, 2011.

Kim, Hyun Chul Paul, and Louis Stulman. *You Are My People: An Introduction to Prophetic Literature*. Nashville: Abingdon, 2010.

Kim, Hyun Chul Paul. *Reading Isaiah. A Literary and Theological Commentary*. Macon, GA: Smyth & Helwys, 2016.

Knight, Douglas A., and Amy-Jill Levine. *The Meaning of the Bible: What the Jewish Scriptures and Christian Old Testament Can Teach Us*. New York: HarperOne, 2011.

Nouwen, Henri. *Peacework: Prayer, Resistance, Community*. Maryknoll, NY: Orbis, 2008.

O'Connor, Kathleen M. *Genesis 1-25A*. Smyth & Helwys Bible Commentary 1A. Macon, GA: Smyth & Helwys, 2018.

———. *Jeremiah: Pain and Promise*. Minneapolis: Fortress, 2011.

Placher, William. *Narratives of a Vulnerable God: Christ, Theology, and Scripture*. Louisville: Westminster John Knox, 1996.

Rad, Gerhard von. *Studies in Deuteronomy*. Translated by D. Stalker. Studies in Biblical Theology 1/9.Chicago: Regnery, 1953.

Salai, Sean, SJ. "God Chooses the Despised: An Interview with 2015 Templeton Prize Laureate Jean Vanier." *America: The Jesuit Review* (August 2015) 1–5. https://www.americamagazine.org/content/all-things/god-chooses-despised-interview-2015-templeton-prize-laureate-jean-vanier.

Scarry, Elaine. *The Body in Pain*. Oxford: Oxford University Press, 1985.

Sebald, W. G. *On the Natural History of Destruction: With Essays on Alfred Andersch, Jean Améry and Peter Weis*. New York: Random House, 2003.

Sharp, Carolyn J. *Prophetic Literature*. Nashville: Abingdon, 2019.

Smith-Christopher, Daniel L. *A Biblical Theology of Exile*. Overtures to Biblical Theology. Minneapolis: Fortress, 2002.

Stulman, Louis. "Art and Atrocity, and the Book of Jeremiah." In *Jeremiah Invented: Constructions and Deconstructions of Jeremiah*, edited by Else K. Holt and Carolyn J. Sharp, 92–103. Library of Hebrew Bible/Old Testament Studies 595. London: T. & T. Clark, 2015.

———. "Encroachment in Deuteronomy: An Analysis of the Social World of the D Code." *Journal of Biblical Literature* 109 (1990) 613–32.

———. *Jeremiah*. Abingdon Old Testament Commentaries. Nashville: Abingdon, 2005.

Sweeney, Marvin A. *Reading the Hebrew Bible after the Shoah: Engaging Holocaust Theology*. Minneapolis: Fortress, 2008.

Van der Kolk, Bessel A. *The Body Keeps the Score: Brain, Mind, and Body in the Healing of Trauma*. New York: Viking, 2014.

Van der Kolk, Bessel A. et al. "History of Trauma in Psychiatry." In *Traumatic Stress: The Effects of Overwhelming Experience on Mind, Body, and Society*. New York: Guilford, 2007.

Wehner, Peter. "The Theology of Donald Trump." *The New York Times* (July 2016). https://www.nytimes.com/2016/07/05/opinion/campaign-stops/the-theology-of-donald-trump.html.

Weiser, Artur. *The Old Testament: Its Formation and Development*. New York: Association Press, 1963.

Worthen, Molly. "A Match Made in Heaven. Why Conservative Evangelicals Have Lined up behind Trump." *The Atlantic* (May 2017). https://www.theatlantic.com/magazine/archive/2017/05/a-match-made-in-heaven/521409/.

Zakovitch, Yair. "Through the Looking Glass: Reflections/Inversions of Genesis Stories in the Bible." *Biblical Interpretation* 1 (1993) 139–52.

Zimmermann, Jens. "Introduction." In *Reimagining the Sacred*, edited by Richard Kearney and Jens Zimmermann, 1–5. New York: Columbia University Press, 2016.

# 6

## False Worship as a Gateway to Social Injustice in Jeremiah 7:1–8:3

——————————————————————————————— T. L. Birge

Prophetic literature offers many warnings to the people of God, but there two primary rebukes: false worship and social injustice.[1] It is no surprise that these indictments are central to prophetic critique as they are essential to the very core of Torah Law itself. For example, in Exodus 20 the first three of the Ten Commandments involve fidelity of worship, while the remaining seven regulate human relationships and social actions. Proper worship and healthy social interactions *should* characterize the covenant people. The nature of belief does, in fact, matter to the prophets. Therefore, regardless of the time, place, and circumstances of the prophetic oracle, the consequences described by the prophets revolve around the various ways in which the people violate these fundamental aspects of Israelite law.

While the punishment Israel receives as a result of their covenant violations seem straightforward, many cannot help but question the morality of a God who would wound, maim, and humiliate an entire nation just because they worshiped the wrong god (or worshiped Yhwh incorrectly). For example, in prophetic literature Judah's idolatry is often likened to an adulterous wife and God the cuckolded husband. According to the text, "her" behavior warrants destruction, humiliation, and death, often delivered by God himself.[2] Feminists critics, like Carleen Mandolfo, question the ethical implications of this metaphor, stating that God's insecurity and anger as a cuckolded husband reflects cruelty, rather than love—punishing a woman who *just happens* to

---

1. This paper uses the term "false worship" to describe any violation of the first two commandments from Exod 20:1–17. These commandments require absolute loyalty to YHWH (v. 2), as well as a prohibition from creating idols (either to worship YHWH or another deity). Both commandments deal with the correct forms of worship, violations of which may be termed idolatry or false worship. I prefer to use "false worship" because this text is not always clear whether the people are worshipping other deities or worshipping YHWH in a manner inconsistent to his commands and this term better fits the ambiguity. Either way, this worship is condemned.

2. Most notably are the passages in Ezekiel 16, 23 and most of Hosea.

love someone else.³ Western law believes that murdering a cheating spouse is wrong; which is the ethical standard? Mandolfo presses modern readers to reflect on their assumptions on the character of God; is it not possible that a God of love and grace could overlook a case of infidelity and false worship? Therefore, it seems apt for both modern and ancient readers to wonder, *what's the big deal* with false worship?

Furthermore, if false worship is enough to condemn God's people, Israel should have received destruction long before Babylon. According to the book of Kings, Israel had been guilty of false worship long before the Babylonian exile, yet God's wrath was reserved for this time and place; but what was he waiting for?

This paper seeks to understand a theological thread present in Jeremiah's oracles, which shows the power of worship. False worship is never benign; instead, it reshapes our behavior and ethics until we become like the gods we serve.⁴ More specifically, this paper will discuss the nature of false worship and its effects on the people of God as seen in Jer 7:1—8:3. Using rhetorical analysis and narrative characterization to understand the impact of the passage on the reader, I will demonstrate that this passage presumes a deep connection between worship and action. As Jeremiah struggles with the weight of his message, God lays bare what is really happening in Jerusalem. God has chosen to hold his judgment until, *the iniquity of the Israelites had been complete*,⁵ and the infidelity of worship is fully manifest in the lives of the people. Essentially, Jeremiah's rhetoric demonstrates that false worship, when fully adopted, leads to social injustice and abuse.

## Establishing the Literary Unit

It is imperative to first establish the pericope boundaries, as the book of Jeremiah has long proven to be a structurally complicated text. Jer 7:1—8:3 is not one narrative account, but a series of short stories, oracles, and prayers that explore the fidelity of worship in Israel and ultimately the reason for exile. Scholarship is divided on the structural integrity of the book of Jeremiah, and these vignettes are sometimes seen as a random collection of material rather than a literary unit. In his commentary on Jeremiah, John Bright argues that Jer 7:1—8:3 represents a series of prose sayings that are loosely combined, yet their structure remains irrelevant for interpretation.⁶ Bright is not alone in this assumption, but joins other scholars, like Robert Carroll, who argue that the final form of the book of Jeremiah is a hopeless hodgepodge of topics, events, and poorly connected sources.⁷ If Bright and Carroll are correct, the final redactor of

---

3. Mandulfo, *Daughter Zion Talks Back to the Prophets*. See also Dempsey, *The Prophets*. Weems, *Battered Love*. Yee, *Poor Banished Children of Eve*.
4. This theological concept is introduced in Yhwh's indictment of the people in Jer 2:5b.
5. This is a re-articulation of the famous indictment of the Canaanites in Gen 15:16.
6. Bright, *Jeremiah: Introduction, Translation, and Notes*.
7. Carroll, *Jeremiah*.

Jeremiah (whether in the Greek or Hebrew tradition) paid little attention to the literary and rhetorical shaping of these accounts and the text offers little more than loosely connected bits of theological nuance and emphasis.[8]

More recently, scholars like Louis Stulman and Terence Fretheim have argued convincingly that the final form of Jeremiah shows intentional shaping and development.[9] Rather than a loose collection of stories, Stulman aptly demonstrates that the prose sections are not random at all, but the overall structure of Jeremiah's text is rhetorically driven, with the prophetic speeches systematically deconstructing false belief in Israel and, later, offering hope of restoration.[10] Therefore, Jer 7:1—8:3 is an intentional grouping of small stories around the theme of worship, acting as an interpretive guide for the oracles that follow.[11]

Jeremiah 7:1—8:3 seems to be a cohesive rhetorical unit for a variety of reasons. First, the change in literary genre suggests a cohesive unit: from poetry in chapters 2–6, to prose in 7:1—8:3, and back to poetry again in 8:4—9:11. Likewise, each of these shifts in genre (chapters 2–6; 7:1—8:3; 8:4—9:11) seem to focus on a different topic and timeframe; while Jer 2–6 depicts the coming destruction of Jerusalem and Judah in cryptic language, Jer 7:1—8:3 demonstrates a concrete example of what kind of destruction is coming and its specific cause.[12] The poetic session which follows then shifts its focus to the existential questioning over Israel's deep-seated transgression and its woeful implications.

This pericope includes five scenes in which the infidelity of Israel is unpacked with an increasingly direct connection to their ramifications, exile and death (7:1–15; 7:16–20; 7:20–26; 7:27–29; 7:30—8:3). These speeches build upon and interact with one another. The initial scene in 7:1–15 offers a stinging rebuke for the covenant transgressions of God's people as well as a clear connection to the consequences of their failure. From there, God responds to Jeremiah's seeming resistance to this rebuke by unpacking the idolatry of Judah and its implication on their social

---

8. This paper will not address the larger structural issues with the book of Jeremiah as a whole for the purpose of time. The major structural issues happen long after this passage, and are only tangentially relevant to this passage. Furthermore, though LXX and MT do disagree on certain details (at various points, the MT embellishes the texts with adverbs, adjectives, demonstratives, appositional modifiers, etc), but the differences are minor. They do not affect the structure and, at most, further emphasize points shared between the two. This paper will use the MT unless otherwise noted.

9. In his commentary on the book of Jeremiah, Louis Stulman has aptly demonstrated that the book of Jeremiah is not a miscellaneous collection of oracles and stories, but has a distinct literary framework. Stulman argues that the prose sermons are placed strategically throughout the book and are used to introduce important motifs for the following poetic material. The narrative in 7:1–15, then, is the literary link to understanding the larger section (Jer 7–10). This literary unit dismantles the temple culture and its misleading belief that Yhwh is bound to the building regardless of Israel's actions. Stulman, *Jeremiah*, 86.

10. Stulman, *Jeremiah*, 15–16. Stulman uses the MT, but argues that the LXX is also shaped for the needs of its audience.

11. Stulman, *Jeremiah*, 16.

12. Stulman, *Jeremiah*, 86.

system, culminating in the practice of sacrificially killing their children. The unifying theme that connects each account is an exploration of false worship in Israel and the people who participate.

Furthermore, there are several indications within the text itself that these accounts should be placed together. Quite a few key words are repeated and are elaborated upon throughout the text: the use of "place" (*maqôm*) as an operative word,[13] "poured out" (in vv. 18 and 20, two different Hebrew words, but resonating similarity), and "your ancestors" (' *ăbôtêkem* in vv. 7, 14, 22), as well as the deviant acts of the people described as generational (in vv. 30, 31). In their own rhetorical analysis of this passage, Isbell and Jackson argue that 7:2 and 8:2 form an inclusio due to a contrasting repetition to the verb for "worship" (*lĕhištaḥăwôt* in 7:2; *hištaḥăwû* in 8:2). According to Isbell and Jackson, the movement from worshiping "Yhwh of hosts" in 7:2 (the title occurs in 7:3) is deconstructed and abandoned by 8:2, as the people have broken their covenant with God and now worship the "hosts" (sun, moon, and stars) instead.[14] The oral resonance between 7:2 and 8:2 acts as bookends for this passage, connecting the material throughout as it moves from false worship to outright idolatry.

## Exploring the Literary and Rhetorical Connection Between Worship and Action in Jeremiah 7:1—8:3

A literary-rhetorical analysis seems best suited for this study because prophetic literature is persuasive by nature. It assumes that the biblical text is trying to persuade *someone* (God, Jeremiah, the people, or the reader) of *something* (to look, repent, act, etc.). The text is not a flat, textbook-like rendering of what happened to Israel and why, but it is structured to make the reader/hearer feel something and respond. For example, prophets (like Jeremiah) described the painful realiy of exile before it happened, not because they were trying to prove they knew the future, but because they were trying *to persuade* the people to repent and *to avoid* its painful reality.

This particular passage utilizes short stories intended to persuade Jeremiah (and the reader) of the depth of Israel's negative transformation through narrative characterization. Early in the passage, Jeremiah is conflicted in delivering an oracle of such extreme judgment to his people. God's response to Jeremiah's complaint is rhetorically driven, persuading him to see what the people have truly become. The people didn't simply misunderstood Yhwh's demand for loyalty, instead the speech leads Jeremiah to see their idolatry for what it is—they have become as worthless and corrupt as their

---

13. The use of the word *maqôm* as an interpretive thread throughout these scenes is widely attested. Mark Leuchter's treatment of this term is helpful in understanding its use in this text as well as throughout the book of Jeremiah. Leuchter, "The Temple Sermon and the Term *Mqm* in the Jeremianic Corpus," 93–109.

14. Isabell and Jackson, "Rhetorical Criticism and Jeremiah 7:1—8:3," 23.

faulty belief system. Idolatry, when fully manifest, can be seen in the people's social abuse and injustice that becomes conflated with worship.[15]

## The First Vignette: Jeremiah, Jerusalem, and God (Jeremiah 7:1–15)

The narrative begins with the longest episode in 7:1–15, by introducing the reader to the characters of Jeremiah, the people of Judah, and God. They are depicted in the most sacred of places: the Jerusalem temple. The temple was the hub of both religious and social life in Jerusalem, and crowds of worshipers would pass through these gates on their way to various temple activities.[16] Those who hear Jeremiah's oracle have not yet completely abandoned Yhwh for another (which is why they are in the temple grounds to begin with), so why was God so upset?

In this section, little is said about Jeremiah's character. His speech (an often used tool in Hebrew characterization) is predicated by the phrase, "thus says Yhwh," and is therefore intended to be the words of God, not the prophet.[17] He is simply portrayed as an obedient messenger, delivering an unpopular (perhaps even treasonous) message in a highly-populated location.

The characterization of Judah, however, is more fully developed. The people who hear Jeremiah's speech are those present at the temple, who thus undoubtedly perceive themselves to be worshipers of Yhwh—*at least* they have shown up. The temple was a physical representation of Yhwh's presence among his people and (on some readings) his unconditional promise to the Davidic king. The people's assurance of Yhwh's commitment to defend the city is expressed by their overused refrain, "This is the temple of Yhwh, the temple of Yhwh, the temple of Yhwh." For the observers, the temple did not symbolize the presence of Yhwh; it was his presence, and any denial of this "simple fact" was akin to blasphemy or treason (just ask Jeremiah).[18] However, these same people entered the temple gates with the intention of worshiping Yhwh, only to hear that their faith claim, "this is the temple of Yhwh," was based on a deceptive half-truth. The significance of this phrase is amplified by the conventions of Hebrew narrative, which points to the significance of speech in shaping character.[19] The only words put

---

15. I acknowledge that this is specified only in the MT, yet the scope of this paper is limited to an analysis of only one tradition. Although I believe both the MT and OG present valid text traditions, this paper will focus on the MT unless otherwise noted.

16. Craigie et al., *Jeremiah 1–25*, 120.

17. While an argument can be made that prophets are not simply dictating the message of God, but relaying the message in their own words, these words reveal obedience to God's call above all else. Jeremiah's reservations, seen in v. 16, demonstrate his reluctance to deliver the message. If the dialogue reveals anything about Jeremiah's character it is that he is rhetorically gifted and willing to use this talent to deliver God's message in a powerful way, regardless of how he might feel about it.

18. Brueggemann, *A Commentary on Jeremiah*, 77.

19. For a full treatment of the use of dialogue and action in shaping characters, see Alter, *The Art of Biblical Narrative*, 63–84.

in the mouth of the people are words of self-deception. Yes, God's presence dwells with his people, but what makes them his people?

The passage may begin by describing the people as "trusting in deceptive words" (vv. 4, 8), but it moves on to characterize the people as much more deliberate covenant-breakers. In 7:5–6, God calls Judah to "amend your ways and your doings." What are their "ways and doings"? The prophet provides a list: they do not promote justice, they oppress those marginalized in society, shed innocent blood (either a reference to murder or human sacrifice), and go after other gods. These elements represent the antithesis of the Sinai Law and the failed distinction of Yhwh's covenant partners, both in their loyalty to Yhwh and their social responsibility to each other. Those who are worshiping at this temple have forsaken the most basic elements of their covenant commitments and have become morally-ambivalent, polytheistic patrons.

Significantly, false worship is the only indictment tied to a consequence in the passage; God asks if they will choose to go after other gods "to your own hurt" in 7:6, amplifying its intensity. Jeremiah's rebuke is clear, false worship is always tied to consequences and though it may seem harmless (perhaps they feel they are hedging their bets in the pantheon), the consequences are clearly seen in their broken social relationships. Rather than leading them to a genuine faith in God, their blind trust in the temple has led them to break the law of the God they assumed would protect them.

Yet, at this point, the passage holds out hope that the people are not beyond repair with the use of conditional language: to paraphrase verses 5–7: *"if"* you change your ways (protasis), *"then"* I (God) will remain with you (apodosis). One question remains: does the conditional language suggest that the fate of Jerusalem has not been sealed, or is this a rhetorical tool of the oracle? Or is it possible that both are true? The consequence is the same either way. If they meet destruction, they are the only ones to blame.

That note of hope for redemption quickly dies away. Once again, Yhwh describes the people as "trusting in deceptive words" then pronounces a list of indictments that echo the Sinai covenant. The people are breaking six of the ten commandments. Initially, the prophet simply lists their abhorrent social injustices (they steal, murder, commit adultery, swear falsely), but he reverses the order of these famous prohibitions, discussing false worship last. This shift in the anticipated order of a well-known list of commandments highlights the importance of these final indictments (worshipping other gods). Furthermore, these final violations are not merely checked off on a list, but the prophet elaborates on the deviant acts of worship themselves. They did not simply make idols and bow down to them (as the Ten Commandments prohibits), but they make offerings to Baal, a specific god. Rather than just worshipping other gods, they are *chasing after* other gods; and the oracle sdds emphatically that these are gods "you have not known." Their sinful actions are condemned and idolatry is emphasized as the central issue in their indictment.

Loyalty to Yhwh is essential to biblical faith, but why? Perhaps the prohibition of idolatry begins the Ten Commandments because all other commands flow from it. The people are called to imitate the God that they worship, to "be holy, for I am holy" in Lev 11:45. Inversely, Psalm 135 states that those who worship idols become worthless, like the gods that they serve. A similar sentiment is found in Jer 2:5, which states that the people "went after worthless things [*hahebel*], and became worthless themselves [wa*yyehbalû*]." It makes sense that if the gods of the ancient Near East do not follow an ethical standard consistent with biblical faith, neither will their followers.

The characterization of Judah continues and, after the list of their trespasses, the people are chastised for their flawed faith that the temple will shelter them from all harm, even that which is self-inflicted. The people sin; they then have the audacity to come to the temple to receive protection from their own wrongdoings. The passage likens their actions to that of hardened criminals who, rather than seeking the temple to restore them to God, have used it as a safe-house to escape retribution. However, it is precisely because of their actions that the temple no longer houses the presence of Yhwh, but instead shelters thieves, liars, and murderers.

The rhetoric reaches its fever pitch in verses 12–15 where Judah (in particular, Jerusalem) is compared to Shiloh, the previous holy place where the Ark of the Covenant and the presence of God had dwelt when Eli was High Priest. The sons of Eli were wicked and the elders of Israel assumed they could manipulate God to do their bidding, using the Ark as a lucky rabbit's foot in battle, but they were sorely mistaken.[20] There is no story that recounts the details of the destruction of Shiloh, only the ominous hint of an ending: a soldier, torn and dirty, running from the battle with the Philistines to the city, with the report of the great slaughter (1 Sam 4:12–17)—and Shiloh never again reenters the biblical narrative as an important city of God.

The comparison between Judah and Shiloh would have shocked and enraged the temple crowds, and perhaps even offended Jeremiah himself. Their faith centered on their trust that God's presence would never leave "the place I gave you."[21] It is *this* assumption, that the place guarantees presence, which brings them to the point of no return. Their actions are no longer described as passively "trusting in deceptive words" (vv. 4 and 8), but as actively disrespecting and misrepresenting the holy place to their own demise, just like Shiloh. Like members of the mafia who would never miss communion, but who lie, cheat, steal, and murder—their faith is called out for what it is, a meaningless facade.

Narrative critics often point out the use of contrast between words and actions in Hebrew characterization, and this passage offers a clear example of this technique. The actions of Judah (they lie, steal, murder) contrast with their faith claim ("this is the temple of Yhwh") and cause the reader to do a double take. How can faith in Yhwh allow

---

20. To read this story, see 1 Samuel 4–6.

21. Note the use of "place" [*maqôm*], repeated throughout the passage to refer to both the temple when God is the subject, and the land when the people are the subject.

for such injustice and evil to exist in Judah? The characterization of Judah, then, elicits a mixture of sympathy and antipathy. They are both deceived by cliché wisdom and hardened in their rejection of the covenant stipulations. They may believe themselves to be worshiping Yhwh, but their actions reveal that they do not know him.

The oracle also begins to shape the characterization of Yhwh through his interactions with Judah. God's patience with his people is clearly on display as the oracle begins, with God imploring the people to change their actions in order to maintain their relationship. His use of conditional language suggests that he is awaiting their response, perhaps even hoping for a positive outcome. He gives the people the benefit of the doubt, that they are trusting in a deceptive half-truth (rather than out-right rejection of Yhwh) and calls on them to amend their ways. Even his punishment (no longer dwelling in this place, vv. 3, 7) shows great restraint, describing the consequence of their sin as a removal of his presence (or a veiled reference to their eviction from the land) rather than a scene of death and decay.

However, God's patience is wearing thin after the people of God, generation upon generation, have rejected his covenant and profaned his holy place. Their self-deception has changed the way they see God as well as each other; rather than a nation defined by its protection of the poor, widowed, outsiders, and orphans, they have allowed and perpetuated systems of abuse to become normative in Israel.

God's rhetoric shifts in 7:8, from imploring to disgust. Although there is no indication that time has passed, God's tone shifts as if Judah's defiance has continued and they have rejected God's second chance. The conditional language used in 7:5–7 is replaced with a statement in the simple present in 7:8, "here you are, trusting in deceptive words to no avail." God is outraged that the people continue to bury their head in the sand and ignore his voice in order to perpetuate this false adage. He describes their actions and lingers on their idolatry. God seems baffled that they would go on chasing other gods "that you have not known" (7:9). For God, idolatry is a personal rejection, not simply a violated stipulation of the law. The text continues, describing God's alarm that "this house, *which is called* by my name" (perhaps echoing the clichéd adage, *this is the temple of Yhwh*, with a truer refrain, *the house is Yhwh's in name only*), has become their hiding place from the repercussions of their sin (7:10). God reminds the people that though he desires to protect them, their actions will not go unnoticed because "I too am watching" (7:11).

Finally, God's mood reaches its breaking point as the conditions of repentance are removed and God pronounces the destruction of Judah. The people trust in the temple like they would a superstitious talisman, but their so-called faith has enabled them to commit "all kinds of abominations" (v. 10) without fear of guilt or reprisal. God has warned them, speaking persistently (v. 13), without an answer or response. The people have chosen God's protection without choosing God and God is done.

## The Second Vignette: God Shows Jeremiah What is Happening in Judah (Jeremiah 7:16–20)

The rhetorical scene then shifts to a seemingly private moment between God and Jeremiah. God's focus moves from proclamation at the temple ("thus says Yhwh") in verse 2, to words addressed directly to his prophet in verse 16 ("as for you"). Although Jeremiah does not speak to God here, his perspective is clearly seen in God's response to his unasked question. Through this implicit dialogue, the characterizations of both God and Jeremiah are further nuanced. Jeremiah has an intense desire to intercede for the people, which is evident in God's repeated reminder (three times) *not* to pray for them. It is also clear that Jeremiah sympathizes with the people, wondering if their actions truly warrant the destruction God intends to bring. The previous section describes them as trusting in deception rather than truth, but could their behavior be misguided and unintentional? Can good people simply misunderstand the requirements of God? Jeremiah seems to wrestle with the question of divine justice, asking God the same question modern interpreters struggle with: "what's the big deal" with false worship?

God's characterization seems resolute, yet he cares that Jeremiah would understand his decision. God instructs Jeremiah not to intercede. First, God explains that the intercession will not work, stating "I will not hear you" (7:16). Then, God suggests that Jeremiah's intercession will come from a place of misunderstanding ("do you not see?"; 7:17). His judgment is not based on petty frustrations or a sense of patriarchal right to retribution (as suggested by Mandolfo), but rather is a legitimate response to those who have taken advantage of his favor and used to bring harm. He asks Jeremiah, "do you not see what they are doing in the streets?" (7:17). This question, not of their beliefs but of their actions, becomes a pivot point in the discourse as God draws back the curtain to allow Jeremiah (and the reader) to see what he has seen and thus to recognize that Judah is not the people he expects them to be. God cares what Jeremiah thinks; God's judgment is imminent, but it matters to God that Jeremiah understands why it is unavoidable. It is through God's narration of the events in Judah that Jeremiah (and the reader) see the full effects of false worship on the people of God.

The narrative in 7:18–19 turns to the streets of Judah. Tension builds as God begins his persuasive argument to convince Jeremiah that the justice of God requires action. The text first examines the family unit (the most basic element to society) as they enjoy a festive occasion together, but instead of worshiping Yhwh, they are celebrating the Queen of Heaven. Each family member is involved in this shared idolatry. The children gather wood, the fathers kindle the fire, and the women make cakes for the goddess (7:18). What is striking about the passage is not the extreme measures the family has taken to worship the Queen of Heaven, but how utterly mundane this deviant religious practice has become. Idol worship is not relegated to distant high places with foreign priests, but has incorporated itself fully into the everyday lives of regular people. Judah claimed to be the people of Yhwh, yet at the most elemental levels of society idolatry flourished.

Furthermore, their actions seem aimed to provoke God to anger, suggesting that the people were aware of their own covenant violations. Perhaps they believed that in extending their worship to include several gods, they would better protect their interests (in the event Yhwh would not or could not do so). Yhwh points out the ridiculousness of such a practice, rather than protecting self, or even successfully creating problems for Yhwh, they "bring trouble upon themselves and to their own shame" (v. 19). God's rebuke reiterates that the coming destruction is both avoidable and self-inflicted. The consequences of such false worship are all encompassing, affecting all of the created order: human beings, animals, trees, and crops (7:20).

## The Third Vignette: God Speaks to Judah in Jeremiah 7:21–26

Once again the scene shifts in 7:21–26, evident by the shift from God speaking to Jeremiah in 7:16 (regarding "this people") to a direct oracle to the people in 7:21 ("thus says Yhwh"). Here, God humbles an arrogant crowd of pseudo, temple-worshipers, telling them that their cultic practice is meaningless. Through God's indictment the religious practices of the people become clear. The people are characterized by a fundamental misreading of the Torah. Rather than understanding the call to obedience and holy living, they have focused solely on burnt offerings and sacrifices as a means of holiness. Unfortunately, thes practices miss the point. The Torah was about walking in the way of Yhwh, not simply placating him with gifts. God warns them that this fundamental misunderstanding has made the sacrifices worthless, go ahead, says Yhwh, "add your burnt offerings to your sacrifices, and eat the flesh" (7:21), because the gifts are meaningless without obedience.

The people are then compared to ter foolish ancestors, specifically the exodus generation, who were notoriously "stiff-necked" and disobedient. Both generations were called to "obey my voice" as a precondition of "be[ing] my people" (v. 23) but both generations have failed. However, this generation was not simply like the exodus generation; their disobedience and stubbornness far exceeds the infamous ancestors. They have arrogantly assumed they were right in the eyes of God, they have ignored God, and they have not taken any of their many chances to repent. The text says that God warned them through prophets "persistently" and "day after day" (v. 25). But Judah, like children with their fingers stuck in their ear, only ignored the voice of God. They did not listen and therefore God deems them "worse" than their ancestors.

God is simply exasperated. He has persistently sent prophets, messengers, and whispered in their ear, but they have ignored his call for hundreds of years. God does not want their false postures of worship; he wants covenant partners.

### The Fourth Vignette: The Futility of Jeremiah's Task is Revealed (Jeremiah 7:27-29)

God's argument moves from the people's normalizing of idolatry (vv. 18-20) to the irony that their current Yhwh worship cannot save them (vv. 21-26). Here, God speaks again to Jeremiah with a series of rhetorical statements: speak to them, but they will not listen; call to them, but they will not answer. God's persuasive argument that began in vv. 16-17, ("do you not see what they are doing?") is now becoming clear. Jeremiah's attempt to speak and call to Judah will be as futile as God's own attempt to reach out to his people for generations. At the climax of his argument, God sums up the problem: when idolatry is normalized, and faith misses the point, "truth has perished" (v. 28). The combination of these elements makes the death of Judah inevitable and in v. 29 the funeral dirge begins before the death blow has been felt. "Cut off your hair and throw it away; / raise a lamentation on the bare heights, / for the Lord has rejected and forsaken / the generation has provoked his wrath" (7:29).

### The Fifth Vignette: Horror at Topheth and Impending Destruction (Jeremiah 7:30—8:3)

So what does this faulty religious framework produce? Horror at Topheth. Finally, God deals his crushing rhetorical blow to the persona of Judah. The abominations of the people are not relegated to the streets of Jerusalem, or the high places abroad, but invade the high places of Jerusalem, and the house "called by my name" (v. 30). The line between the worship of other gods and Yhwh becomes blurred and these "abominations" insult God and "defile" worship. The revelation that worshipers were entering the temple to worship other gods casts the bystanders in the temple gate in a new light. Where before they seemed like worshipers of Yhwh who were struggling in obedience, now they brought their evil inside the temple walls. Though they may call this building "the temple of Yhwh," it is no longer safe to assume it is Yhwh they came to worship.

Circling back to the imagery of the Judean family from 7:16-17, the scene has fundamentally changed. No longer are the children collecting twigs, men stoking fires, and women humming as they shape their breads. Now the family worships at the valley of Topheth, literally "fire pit" in Aramaic.[22] It is here that the implications of Judah's false worship reach their climax as the children of Judah come to die at the hands of their "pious" parents. Is it even possible to feel sympathy for such evil? God's own horror is clear in his exasperated refrain, "which I did not command, nor did it come into my mind" (v. 31). False worship is united with brokenness and abuse as the children of Judah are sacrificially murdered.

---

22. Fretheim, *Jeremiah*, 141. Fretheim points out, further, that the it is pronounced with the same vowels (both accented on the first syllable) as the Hebrew word "shame," thus carrying an implicit judgment.

Both horror and ambiguity dominate the text. Who exactly do the people intend to worship with such a heinous act? Perhaps they are worshipping Baal, who was known to require child sacrifice and has already been referenced in 7:9. There are indications in the book of Kings that child sacrifice had previously been introduced to Judah by kings Ahaz and Manasseh, but the practice was outlawed (along with Baal worship) by King Josiah. Could it have made its way back into Israelite worship? Or perhaps their horrendous acts have been committed in the name of Yhwh, a perversion of the command to consecrate their first born child to God, a deluded attempt to fulfill God's command to give the firstborn to Yhwh from Exod 22:29.

Did the people of Judah murder their children in the name of Yhwh? The text is shrouded in purposeful ambiguity. False worship, whether worshiping other gods, worshipping Yhwh incorrectly, or trying to combine the worship practices together, will lead to darkness and death. God's rhetorical strategy is finally achieved. This final glimpse into Judah's religious life pushes Jeremiah and the reader to reject Judah and beg for God to stop the madness. False worship may have been initially presented as simply baking "cakes to the queen of heaven," but now it is seen in its fullest form as making the unthinkable a reality in God's Promised Land and holy temple.

In 7:32—8:3, God concludes his plea with Jeremiah and the reader. Judah's true nature has been exposed in their idolatry, religious perversion, and moral crimes. They are no longer sympathetic characters, but despised and rejected for their own cruelty. They are not victims, but violent offenders. In this context, God announces the depth of his judgment on Jerusalem. The deaths at Topheth will no longer be those of their sacrificed children, but the corpses of Judah piled up from battle; their instruments of destruction will be used against them. The sound of joy and celebration will end, and even fundamental life events, like weddings, will no longer be celebrated. God's judgment extends beyond the living to those who are nothing but bones. Even they will be disgraced, with bodies strewn on the ground like dung. God's voice echoes with poetic justice in 8:2, these bones "shall be spread before the sun and the moon and all the host of heaven, which they have loved and served, which they have followed." Therefore their bodies will be desecrated in worship of the very gods they chose (above Yhwh) to protect them. Their rejection of God culminates in violence, but begins and ends in idolatry.

## Character Summaries

The characterization of the three primary actors (God, Jeremiah, and the people of Judah) are essential in understanding the connection between false worship and social injustice. Hebrew narrative uses characterization to help drive the plot, develop complexity, and impact the reader. Characters are not merely a sum of the literary parts that shape them, but multi-dimensional and even unpredictable.[23] The power of the narrative is found in the way it mirrors life as the inscrutability of character resonates with the reader as they wrestle to understand self.[24] Hebrew narrative, in particular, utilizes the interplay between the speech and actions of the characters to shape perception. It is through these characters that the mimetic force of the narrative takes hold of the reader as they are able to reflect upon the complexity of the moral and ethical dilemmas faced by the people of God.

## God

God's character develops through his speech to two different audiences: the people of Judah and Jeremiah. The prophesies directed to the people offer assessment of wrongs, an urge to repent, and warnings of possible action he may take if the people do not heed his warning. Repeatedly, three major elements of God's character are demonstrated in this account: he is merciful, responsive, and just. First, Yhwh is portrayed as a generous and merciful God. His speech is directed to a people who are described as liars, cheaters, and murderers, yet God still delivers a conditional call for repentance (7:1–5). There is still hope for a restored relationship before destruction. Furthermore, these prophesies are not his final word, but they represent *another* attempt by God to get the people to listen. God's response offers a measured reply to the people and their situation. The character of God may be unchanging, but God's response to his human creation is adapted to their actions and circumstances. The people of Judah are not being punished for the sins of their ancestors, but for their own repeated and habitual Torah failings. Yet God still engages them, working through his prophet to persuade them to change, and he is willing to respond to them *if* they do change their ways. Finally, the justice of God demands that he not allow for the weakest to be victimized any longer. Mercy for the perpetrator of violence against the weakest among them (children in 7:30—8:3) would be devoid of justice. God will act.

## Jeremiah

Jeremiah's character is particularly impactful because the narrative is told from the first person perspective of the prophet himself. First person narrative is rare in Hebrew narrative and it allows the reader to further identify with the thoughts and actions of the prophet. Readers are not simply relating to another external person; rather they are cast in the role of the faithful prophet himself. His thoughts are their thoughts, his actions are their actions. The text anticipates that the reader, like Jeremiah, would be

---

23. Alter, *The Pleasures of Reading*, 49.

24. The concept of the mimetic force of literature traces back to Auerbach, *Mimesis*; this idea was more specifically applied to biblical literature in the work of Robert Alter. Alter, *The Pleasures of Reading*, 64.

aghast at the call to destroy Jerusalem. Perhaps the first person narrative serves to urge the reader to ask the pressing ethical questions that began this paper: Can't a God of mercy forgive his own people?

There is no personal speech or direct actions that shape Jeremiah's character, yet his disposition is demonstrated indirectly through God's speech to him. Jeremiah's discomfort with his prophecy (7:16–17) mirrors the internal struggle of the reader as they come to terms with the destruction of Jerusalem at the hand of Babylon. *Was the faulty worship system really bad enough to warrant total destruction by the hand of Babylon?* While the people have clearly broken the covenant law, they are still God's people and it is Jeremiah's prophetic responsibility to intercede for them to avoid destruction. Like Jeremiah, we desire to turn the people away from their destructive path, but God denies this possibility (7:21–29). Rather than simply demand Jeremiah's (and our) loyalty to his plan, Yhwh shows him what he has seen: false worship and social injustice have fully corrupted the people, "do you not see?" (7:17).

The People

The final characterization of the people unfolds in three stages, as God shows Jeremiah (and the reader) what they could not see. After the opening oracle of destruction (7:1–15) comes Yhwh's response to Jeremiah, which demonstrates corruption of family and temple (7:16–29), and then the corruption of family and temple, which lead to death at Topheth (7:30—8:3).

The characterization begins with a list of Torah failures due to self-deception in Jeremiah 7:1–15. The oracle begins by shaping a self-deceptive persona as the people repeat the refrain "this is the temple of Yhwh" (7:1–3). Speech is often one of the most powerful tools of Hebrew characterization; therefore, when the only spoken words of the people are those of self-deception, the actions that follow seem shaped by that statement. The many acts of covenant violations that follow may be a result of that self-deception. With this notion of self-deceptive faith, Jeremiah's desire to intercede for the people (and avoid the fate of Shiloh, 7:12–15) seems natural.

The second section (7:16–29) shifts focus as God responds to the implicit hesitation of Jeremiah, offering him a glimpse into the reality the people's broken faith claims. In 7:18–20, Yhwh shows Jeremiah the extent of the idolatry, which has been fully integrated into the lives of the family. It is especially important to notice the participation of the parents and children in their illicit worship practices. In 7:21–26, the people once again receive an oracle of rejection, pointing out through their actions (rather than speech) that they have fundamentally misunderstood their covenant obligations. Rather than living like the people of God, they have focused their rituals on sacrifices and offerings as if Yhwh were any other pagan God to be placated. They, once again, have misunderstood what God has asked them to do and their faulty worship has negatively affected the holiest of places, the Temple, rendering it void. It is in this context that Yhwh once again turns his attention to Jeremiah (therefore the reader) that their current faith and worship cannot save them.

The final scene (7:30—8:3) demonstrates the result of the misleading faith characterized above. The idolatry that has been integrated into family and temple becomes corrupt and violent. The people are no longer characterized by self-deception (as in the previous two sections), rather they are rejecting *Yhwh* as their God. In the previous scene, God's speech revealed the idolatry in the family and the corruption of them temple. In this last scene these two idolatrous practices combine to produce violence and death. The children reappear in the final vignette, but it is only to be murdered in the name of god; but which god?

The "worship" at Topheth causes the reader to reconsider the earlier characterization of Judah in 7:1–15. Are the people entering the gates of the temple simply misunderstanding God's call to his people or are they at the Temple in order to worship another god altogether? The narrator seems to leave this detail purposefully vague. Perhaps they are rejecting Yhwh for Baal; maybe they have attempted to worship both deities; or maybe they have simply forgotten who the God of Israel really is. Whether self-deceptive faith or idolatry, the result is the death of the most vulnerable among us.

Much like Alice in Wonderland, the developing characterization of Judah in Jeremiah 7:1—8:3 proves that seemingly simple concessions to idolatry send the people of God tumbling down the rabbit hole into a strange world of wide-spread and institutionalized injustice. In God's persuasive response to Jeremiah, he reshapes his sense of sympathy for the people into disdain, leading him to fully understand the implications of false worship: death and violence.

## Theological Implications of Jeremiah 7:1—8:3

This passage demonstrates the power of belief and worship to shape action. We act in ways consistent with our belief, therefore when we forget who God really is and we become corrupt and perverse like our belief system. False worship (or idolatry) is both a rejection of God to worship another and the false beliefs that distort our picture of who God really is. This literary unit serves as a caution to people of faith in both the ancient and modern worlds; worshipping God requires that we know him first, rather than fake piety and assume we are the favored people.

Much like Judah before the exile, modern Christianity often struggles with idolatry, but perhaps not in the most obvious way believe. We speak of idolatry as manifested vice: the love of money, pride, or entertainment, etc. But those issues seem more consistent with the social and ethical issues that *result* from idolatry, rather than with idolatry itself. False worship in Judah is sometimes the rejection of God for the worship of Baal, but more often it is takes root in half-truths and self-deceptive proclamations of God. Today we fill in the gap of knowledge with culturally glorified renderings of what we believe God *should* be, while ignoring God's own self-revelation in Scripture. For Judah, it may have started as an "open-mindedness" to Canaanite culture and piety, but it quickly spiraled out of control, devaluing the commandments of God and eroding their sense of loyalty to Yhwh until the only thing that was required of them were outward acts of piety (burnt offerings).

Like Judah, our failure to understand God is reflected in our fractured social structures. The painful truth is that racism, sexism, violence, and all forms of xenophobia dominate American culture, and are painfully evident in the American evangelical movement. According to Jeremiah's oracle, these social injustices are rooted in our own distortions of the God of Scripture and what he asks of us. Like the people of Judah, we join the refrain, "American evangelicalism is the temple of Yhwh," to our own demise. Perhaps the first step in healing our social wounds may be to remember that we do not simply serve god, but a specific God—Yhwh, and he has revealed himself for a reason.

This oracle serves as a warning to a modern culture that consistently emphasizes faith, while failing to take the time to see who or what their faith is in. If Psalm 135 is correct, and we become like what we serve, what do our injustices perpetuated against each other say about the god we actually serve? If we are not careful, we may become like the Judahites before Babylon who exchanged genuine faith for superficial trappings of piety. Thus we would end up deceiving ourselves and forsaking the God we claim to serve.

## Bibliography

Allen, Leslie C. *Jeremiah: A Commentary*. Old Testament Library. Louisville: Westminster John Knox, 2008.

Alter, Robert. *The Art of Biblical Narrative*. New York: Basic Books, 1981.

———. *The Pleasures of Reading in an Ideological Age*. New York: Norton, 1996.

Auerbach, Erich. *Mimesis: The Representation of Reality in Western Literature*. Translated by Willard Trask. Princeton: Princeton University Press, 2003.

Bright, John. *Jeremiah: Introduction, Translation, and Notes*. Anchor Bible 21. Garden City, NY: Doubleday, 1965.

Brueggemann, Walter. *A Commentary on Jeremiah: Exile and Homecoming*. Grand Rapids: Eerdmans, 1998.

Carroll, Robert P. *Jeremiah*. Old Testament Guides. Sheffield: Sheffield Phoenix, 2006.

Craigie, Peter C., et al. *Jeremiah 1–25*. Word Biblical Commentary 26. Dallas: Word Books, 1991.

Dempsey, Carol J. *The Prophets: A Liberation-Critical Reading*. A Liberation-Critical Reading of the Old Testament. Minneapolis: Fortress, 2000.

Fretheim, Terence E. *Jeremiah*. Smyth & Helwys Bible Commentary. Macon, GA: Smyth & Helwys, 2002.

Gitay, Yehoshua. "Rhetorical Criticism." In *To Each Its Own Meaning: An Introduction to Biblical Criticisms and Their Application*, edited by Stephen R. Haynes and Steven L. McKenzie, 135–149. Louisville: Westminster John Knox, 1993.

Isbell, Charles, and Michael Jackson. "Rhetorical Criticism and Jeremiah 7:1—8:3." *Vetus Testamenum* 30 (1980) 20–26.

Leuchter, Mark. "The Temple Sermon and the Term *Mqm* in the Jeremianic Corpus." *Journal for the Study of the Old Testament* 30 (2005) 93–109.

Mandolfo, Carleen R. *Daughter Zion Talks Back to the Prophets: A Dialogic Theology of the Book of Lamentations*. Semeia Studies 58. Atlanta: Society of Biblical Literature, 2007.

Meynet, Roland. *Rhetorical Analysis: An Introduction to Biblical Rhetoric*. Rev. ed. Journal for the Study of the Old Testament Supplement Series 256. Sheffield: Sheffield Academic, 1998.

Stulman, Louis. *Jeremiah*. Abingdon Old Testament Commentaries. Nashville: Abingdon, 2005.

Weems, Renita J. *Battered Love: Marriage, Sex, and Violence in the Hebrew Prophets*. Overtures to Biblical Theology. Minneapolis: Fortress, 1995.

Yee, Gale A. *Poor Banished Children of Eve: Women as Evil in the Hebrew Bible*. Minneapolis: Fortress, 2003.

# 7

## Daniel as an "Historical" Sign of the Eschatological Ancient of Days and Most High God? Reading *Bel et Draco* in Eschatological Contexts— Apocalyptic, Prophetic, and Sapiential

Excursus: Daniel as Judge in Susanna—a Similar Role?[1]

———————————————— Eugene E. Lemcio

THE SORT OF SIGNALING or signing that I propose is not entirely without precedent. Hosea's/Hosee's marital relations with Gomer functioned as an explicit analogy of God's on-going covenantal relation with Israel (chapters 1–3, esp. 3:1).[2] However, the prophet's enacted parable is addressed to the Israel of his day, whereas the scope of Daniel's activities in these narratives is international and "futuristic."

Within the body of Daniel itself (but without the future reference), the lines become somewhat blurred. In chapter 2, there is the astonishing account of Nebuchadnezzar's/ Nabouchodonosor's falling on his face and worshiping [סְגִד, προσεκύνησεν] the Seer because of his interpreting the dream about four kingdoms and their demise—both historical and eschatological (2:46). However, neither the MT nor Θ goes as far as the OG translator in recounting a kind of devotion ordinarily reserved for the divine. The king, it continues, ἐπέταξε θυσίας καὶ σπονδὰς ποιῆσαι αὐτῷ ["ordered

---

1. A version of this article was read to the Graduate Seminar of the Institute for Septuagintal Studies at Trinity Western University on February 27, 2013. I am indebted for helpful responses by both students and colleagues, in particular to the Director of the Institute, Professor Rob Hiebert. By "historical" in this context, I mean an account of a person purported to have existed and a narrative of events purported to have occurred at a particular place and time. However, on the basis of genre and other considerations, parts or all of the narrative might come to be regarded as legendary. Names of biblical books and persons are spelled according to Pietersma and Wright, *A New English Translation of the Septuagint* [NETS].

2. For the Massoretic Text (MT), I have used Elliger and Rudolf, *Biblia Hebraica Stuttgartensia* [HB]. I have used two critical texts of the LXX, which I am regarding as a critical reconstruction of the Old Greek (OG): Rahlfs, *Septuaginta* and Ziegler and Munnich, *Susanna. Daniel. Bel et Draco*. Unless otherwise indicated, all translations of the OG and Theodotian [Θ] are from the NETS.

that sacrifices and libations be made to him"].³ Θ has καὶ μαναα καὶ εὐωδίας εἶπεν σπεῖσαι αὐτῷ ["and manaa [מנחה] ('grain offering') and fragrances be poured out to him"]. Surprisingly, nothing is said about Daniel's shrinking back in horror at the prospect of such reverential treatment.⁴ So far as I am aware, this is about as far as the Jewish Scriptures in Greek go in blurring the lines between obeisance rendered to God's human agent and that offered to God.⁵ Perhaps only the stunning assignment given to Moses at Exod 7:1 provides something of a comparison with OG Dan 2:46, though it lacks the element of worship:

ראה נתתיך אלהים לפרעה ואהרן אחיך יהיה נביאך. Ἰδοὺ δέδωκά σε θεὸν Φαραω. καὶ Ααρων ὁ ἀδελφός σου ἔσται σου προφήτης. "See, I have given you [as/to be a] god to Pharao, and Aaron your brother will be your prophet."⁶

In the following, I have attempted to answer the questions, "What is the effect upon interpretation when the 'historical' accounts of Bel et Draco are read in their Danielic and Septuagintal eschatological contexts? How does the role of the Seer emerge in their light"?⁷ So far as I have been able to determine, no one has posed these queries before. Consequently, my answers are also unique—and therefore subject to the limitations that such "firsts" entail. For heuristic purposes alone, I have reordered the sequence thus: Draco et Bel.⁸ Three ways of approaching the future organize the

---

3. Translation mine.

4. See 2 Suppl 35:3, where Iosias commands the Leuites to serve [λειτουργήσατε] both God and the people. This term and προσκυνεῖν are used interchangeably at Dan 3:10 and 18 in connection with τῇ εἰκόνι and τῷ εἰδώλῳ. At v. 95 [in Greek translations only], τῷ θεῷ is the object of both verbs—as it is in 6:27 (but not in Θ).

5. The availability of OG Daniel throughout "Hellenistic Judaism" of the "Second Temple" period should not be confined to the Jewish Diaspora. Only rarely does either expression embrace Greek-speaking Judaism on *Palestinian* soil. This remains largely the case despite the lip-service paid to the indisputable fact that the region had been Hellenized (with varying degrees of effort and success) for three centuries, both in Galilee and Judea (including Jerusalem) by the time of the Common Era. A mountain of evidence in support of this view has been marshaled by Martin Hengel, chiefly through his magisterial work, *Judaism and Hellenism*. Lesser-known is the author's smaller survey of the 300-year gap between this and the Bar Kochba revolt, *The "Hellenization" of Judaea in the First Century After Christ*. Before Hengel, Jan Sevenster had come to similar conclusions: *Do You Know Greek?*. For the most recent amassing of the data, see Cotton *et al.*, *Corpus Inscriptionum Palestinaeae et Judaeae*, pp. 1–704. Furthermore, the Theodotus synagogue inscription (1st c. CE) from the Ophel ("a high place to climb to"), the area between the City of David and the Temple Mount, provides dramatic evidence of reading and teaching the Law in Greek for pilgrims in the heart of the Old City itself. A photograph and edited text may be found in Frey, *Corpus Inscriptionum Judaicarum*, #1404, 332–35. The inscription is discussed in Meyers and Chancery, *Alexander to Constantine*, 208–9.

6. Translation mine.

7. While one should not presume to speculate about the joiner's *intent* in appending Bel et Draco to the main body, I can suggest what the resultant *effect* on subsequent readers might be.

8. Because they are so highly speculative, I have avoided engaging in discussions about possible Semitic and Greek *Vorlagen*. Although such conversations are entirely legitimate as historical exercises, they sometimes interfere with encountering the text *qua* text in its various contexts. Doing the latter is somewhat more straightforward when working with the Greek text of Daniel—which

argument: eschatology from the perspectives of apocalyptic, prophecy, and wisdom.[9] In the Excursus, I tentatively suggest that Daniel in Susanna (given the contexts of both Daniel 7 and Bel et Draco) is functioning as an "historical" sign of the eschatological Assize to be conducted by the Ancient of Days.

## Eschatological Contexts for the "Historical" Daniel in Bel et Draco

### Draco

*Apocalyptic Eschatology*

In the apocalyptic vision of 7:9–11, the Ancient of Days first deposes and then destroys four θηρία that arise from the sea and oppose the Most High and God's holy people (vv. 8c [OG]–11, 21, 25, 27). Although none is described as having "draconian" or serpentine features, their association with the sea reminds one of the dragon-snake that will be destroyed "in the sea" (see the discussion of Esa 27:1, below.)

One of the attendants in the vision interprets the unnatural beasts as representing four kingdoms that are to arise from/upon the earth (vv. 16–17). Scholars have regularly associated these with the four empires envisioned in Nabouchodonosor's dream of the statue composed of four different substances (chapter 2), the first representing the king himself. Although Θ of Bel et Draco sets the stage during the subsequent Persian era (v. 2), the deed in both versions occurs in Babylon. Viewed within the larger context, the Seer's destroying the Dragon of this imperial city, the alleged "living" god, whom king and people worshiped (vv. 23–24, 27), suggests that, in the action of Daniel in the heart of the Empire, one looks through a lens by which to glimpse its divinely-ordained future demise. When Daniel causes the Dragon to explode, he is accomplishing proleptically, in an "historical" narrative, that which the apocalyptic vision of chapter 7 (reinforced by chapter 2) imagines the Ancient of Days/Most High God doing in the future.

*Prophetic Eschatology*[10]

Only two instances in prophetic literature look forward to the eschatological slaying of a dragon figure. The first contains an historical referent (the Pharaoh), the

---

has itself come down to us in two versions: the OG/LXX and Θ. The differences between the latter, regularly identified in critical discussions, do not affect my thesis.

9. It is important to recall that, while all apocalyptic is necessarily eschatological, not all eschatology is of the apocalyptic variety. Furthermore, the fulfillment of eschatological expectation can be near as well as remote, so far as timing is concerned. Its scope can vary, too: from the particular (local and ethnic) to the universal (global, international, and even cosmic).

10. The OG alone opens with the statement that what follows is ἐκ προφητείας Αμβακουμ. The NRSV and NEB follow Θ (with support from C. Vaticanus). NETS translates both in parallel columns.

fulfillment of its prediction being more proximal and the scope more local: the land of Egypt and its people (Iez 29:1–2): "Son of man, set your face against Pharao, king of Egypt, and prophesy against him and against all Egypt, and say, This is what the Lord says: Behold, I am against Pharao, the great dragon who is ensconced in the midst of his streams and the one who says, 'The streams are mine, and I made them.'" The pronouncement of judgment that follows in the wake of such hubris further employs reptilian and aquatic imagery to make the point (vv. 4–7).[11]

In the second passage (Esa 27:1), God is described as finally destroying the dragon-snake in what appears to be the more distant future: "On that day, God will bring his holy and great and strong dagger against the dragon, a fleeing snake—against the dragon, a crooked snake—and he will kill [ἀναλεῖ] the dragon": ἐπὶ τὸν δράκοντα ὄφιν [לויתן נחש] φεύγοντα, ἐπὶ τὸν δράκοντα ὄφιν σκολιόν. (C. Sinaiticus, following the HB, adds "in the sea" [τὸν ἐν τῇ θαλάσσῃ].) Clearly, the scope is broader than the Iezekiel passage in that neither particular place nor people is mentioned. Politics seems to have been entirely left behind in this case. Nor does the conflict appear to be limited to the earth. The language of myth (regarding foundational issues) has taken over completely, thereby including the cosmos.

In this context, Daniel promises to slay [ἀνελῶ] the dragon of Babylon—revered [σεβέσθαι] and worshiped [προσκυνεῖν] by its subjects—without benefit of any instrument: neither iron nor club (vv. 26–27). Ingesting a combustible cake does the deed, accomplishing in "history" a fore"taste" of that which God will do at the end of days. That the translator of OG used the same verb [ἀναιροῦν] as in Esaias may indicate a deliberate allusion.[12] Was the translator of Θ also being similarly allusive by employing μαχαίρας (καὶ ῥάβδου) as the chosen eschatological instrument (the same word in Esa 27:1) rather than σιδήρου (καὶ ῥάβδου)?[13]

---

See Moore, *Daniel, Esther, and Jeremiah: The Additions*, 139. While not all prophecy is of the predictive variety, one cannot help wondering if the OG (which, accompanied by Θ, closes with Hambakoum's rescuing Daniel) hints that what occurs in between has eschatological implications.

11. Dragon imagery is applied to Nabouchodonosor for attacking Sion (LXX Ier 28:34. NB the reference to Babylon's sea and fountain in v. 36) and, by inference, to the Roman general Pompey for conquering Jerusalem (Pss Sal 2:25). However, from the authors' viewpoint, each of these events had occurred in the past.

12. Θ has ἀποκτείνειν, as does OG at v. 28 in reported speech.

13. For a treatment of how reptilian imagery was adopted and adapted in antiquity, see Daniel Ogden's *Dragons, Serpents, and Slayers*. Pages 189–90 provide a brief treatment of Bel et Draco, which does not include the point being made here. The closest statement about a future slaying to be found in wisdom or poetic literature appears in Iob 3:8 (cited by Ogden, p. 188): "May the one that will subdue the great sea monster... [he transliterates κῆτος, the Hebrew לויתן] curse it (author: '[sc. the day of my birth].'"

# Bel

## Apocalyptic Eschatology

Up to this point, the scope of idol destruction in non-eschatological and non-apocalyptic biblical texts is more local and ethnic. Late in the history of Iouda, the ardent reformer-kings Hezekias and Iosias had removed and pulverized images of foreign idols on *home* territory—including the Ierousalem Temple (4 Reigns 18:4, 23:4–6; 2 Suppl 34:4). Ultimately, God will destroy all idols in *Israel and that city*—the vocabulary ranging from συντρίβειν ['to break in pieces'] (Iez 6:6); ἐξολεθρεύειν ["to destroy utterly"] (Zech 13:2); τιθέναι εἰς ἀφανισμόν ["to set for destruction"] (Mic 1:7). So far as a broader scope is concerned, Samson is the only one on record to demolish a pagan idol (Dagon) in the god's own temple, in the enemy's own city of Gaza—himself perishing in the process along with thousands of worshipers (Judges A and B 16:21, 23–31). Impressive as this was, it was limited to one of the Philistine cities strung along the Mediterranean's eastern coast.

So far as the context in Daniel itself is concerned, the ruler from the north will overturn [καταστρέψει] the idols of his rivals (11:8). Furthermore, because the relationship between image and idol is clear in Daniel 3 (Nebuchadnezzar's/Nabouchodonor's image is to be worshipped: vv. 5–18), one can infer an implicit link between them in chapter 2. The king envisions the destruction "at the end of days" [באחרית יומיא/ἐπ' ἐσχάτων τῶν ἡμερῶν] (vv. 28–29) of an image [צלם/εἰκών] made of four substances by a stone uncut by human hands (vv. 34–35). The prophet reveals [גלה/ἀποκαλύπτειν] its meaning thus: the kingdom of God will destroy four human empires, itself taking their place but becoming global in scope and eternal in duration (v. 44). Given this near eschatological context (in an apocalyptic mode), it is not unlikely that chapter 2 would have provided the foil for which Daniel's encounter with Bel could have been seen as an "historical" sign or anticipation.

Thus, Daniel brought to ruin [κατέστρεψε] the idol of the god Bel in the heart of the vast Empire (vv. 1–22)[14]—in the "belly of the beast," both metaphorically and literally.[15] The act recorded in this "Addition" can be construed as fitting retaliation against that earlier, quintessential Gentile ruler, Nabouchodonosor, who had transferred some of the temple vessels into his idol temple [τῷ εἰδωλίῳ] (1:1–3). More significantly, no other human had ever been credited with destroying both an idol and a dragon, much less the idol and the dragon in their temple and in Babylon itself. Each belongs to that class of gods (Marduk) and monsters (Tiamat)[16] who were

---

14. The OG makes Daniel companion to the king of Babylon (v. 2). Θ identifies him as Cyrus the Persian (vv. 1–2).

15. In the OG, the king destroyed Bel. Θ reports that Daniel destroyed Bel and the idol's temple as well (v. 22). Moore, *Additions*, 138.

16. Moore, *Additions*, 122–25, 143 and Collins, *Commentary on Daniel*, 412 discuss these in relation to the original myth.

primeval in origin and subsequently of great consequence: together, they had laid the foundations for both the created and political orders. Therefore, I infer that here, too, Daniel signifies in the present age, that which God in his awesome might will accomplish in the age to come.

*Sapiential Eschatology*

It is not clear that the first Greek translators/editors themselves had known the Wisdom of Salomon—in which case my using it as a larger context regarding Bel is contestable. Nevertheless, at some point during the course of its *Wirkungsgeschichte*, the text eventually found a home in the Greek Scriptures. In keeping with what we observed in Daniel 2, but with special reference to the actual destruction of idols (rather than of those in the metaphorical dream image), we have what appears to be the only time that God is said to bring about their universal demolition in the end-time. The Sage looks forward to the era when "there will be a visitation upon the idols of the nations": ἐν εἰδώλοις ἐθνῶν ἐπισκοπὴ ἔσται (v. 11). "Visitation" is so much more in Scripture than dropping by for tea. It means a momentous encounter with God—bringing either rescue or retribution. In this case, "a speedy end was planned for them": σύντομον αὐτῶν τὸ τέλος ἐπενοήθη (v. 14). However, unlike the instances cited above, there does not seem to be an intimate connection between idol worship and politics. Rather, according to this author, the former has been from the outset the foundation of moral degradation (vv. 12–13).

## Conclusions

When this "Addition" to Daniel is read in the contexts of the entire book and that of related texts within the LXX as a whole, then it emerges as something more than an awkward appendage to the body. Using the dynamic interplay of "history" and eschatology, the editor (and translator?) painted a richer and fuller portrait of his subject.[17]

## EXCURSUS: Daniel as Judge in Susanna—a Similar Role?

I pose (but with greater tentativeness) the same questions as before, this time with regard to the account of Susanna: "What is the significance of prefixing this 'historical' account to the main narrative, concerned as the latter is with eschatological and

---

17. The portrait is richer still when one takes into account that the translator of Greek Daniel went further, as I also argued in a paper to the Institute for Septuagintal Studies at Trinity Western University (see note 1, above) and in "Daniel and the Three," 43–61 that the Prophet appears as an "historical" sign of the eschatological Son of Man. Together, these studies show that, in Hellenistic Judaism (encompassing both Judea and Galilee), the Seer was meant to function as an "historical" sign of both the eschatological Son of Man *and* Ancient of Days/Most High God a century or so before the Christian era.

apocalyptic themes? Do the phenomena described in the suffixed Bel et Draco also play a role in its interpretation? Is there at least a possible relationship between the terms for *judging*, which occur thirteen times each in OG and Θ (along with punishment by fire in the former), and identical terminology—within Dan 7:10–11, 22, 26?[18] (See Table 7.1, below.) Could it be that Daniel as a judge in Israel's past 'history' signals the future Assize that the Ancient of Days/Most High God (envisioned with apocalyptic symbols) will conduct among the nations and in the universe?[19]

Table 7.1 Terms for Judgment/Judging

|  | Susanna[20] | Daniel 7 |
|---|---|---|
| ἀνακρίνειν | 48, 51(Θ), 52 (OG) | |
| κατακρίνειν | 41 (Θ), 48, 53 | |
| κρίμα | 9 | |
| κρίνειν | 6 (Θ), 53 | |
| κρίσις | 6, 53 | |
| κριτήριον | 49 (Θ) | 10 |
| κρίτις | 5 (Θ: 2x), 29 (OG), 34 (OG), 41 | 22, 26 |
| πῦρ | 62 (OG) | 9–11 (3x) |

If this suggestion holds as well, then one could supplement the conclusion above with an analogous one. When this "Addition" to Daniel is read in the contexts of both Daniel 7 and Bel et Draco, then it too emerges as something more than a "mere" attachment to the entire work. Here, also, by means of the dynamic interplay between "history" and eschatology, the translator-editor provided an even richer and fuller rendering of his Subject.

## Bibliography

Collins, John J. *Daniel: Commentary on the Book of Daniel.* Hermeneia. Minneapolis: Fortress, 1993.

Cotton, Hannah M., et al., eds. "Inscriptions from the Hellenistic period up to the destruction of the Second Temple." *Corpus Inscriptionum Palestinaeae et Judaeae*, vol. 1, part 1: *Jerusalem*. New York: de Gruyter, 2010.

18. Between vv. 6 and 62 of Susanna, a juridical term occurs on an average of every fourth verse. Between vv. 10 and 26 of Daniel 7, a form of that term occurs on an average of every three verses.

19. Although only once is the forensic vocabulary directly applied to Daniel (OG v. 52, Θ v. 51), he *functions* as judge (vv. 44–64), using the spectrum of terms to indict the two wicked judges.

20. Verses followed by parentheses are found only there. Otherwise, both OG and Θ contain the expressions.

Elliger, K., and W. Rudolph, eds. *Biblia Hebraica Stuttgartensia*. 3rd rev. ed. Stuttgart: Deutsche Bibelgesellschaft, 1997.

Frey, Jean-Baptiste. *Corpus Inscriptionum Judaicarum: Receuil Des Inscriptions Juives Qui Vont Du IIIe Siècle Avant Jésus-Christ Au VIIe Siècle de Notre Ère*, vol. 2, Asie-Afrique. Rome: Pontifico Instituto di Archeologica Cristiana, 1952.

Hengel, Martin. *Judaism and Hellenism: Studies of the Encounter in Palestine in the Early Hellenistic Period*. Translated by John Bowden. Philadelphia: Fortress, 1975.

———. *The "Hellenization" of Judaea in the First Century after Christ*. Translated by John Bowden. 1989. Reprint, Eugene, OR: Wipf & Stock, 2003.

Lemcio, Eugene E. "Daniel and the Three (Principally in the Old Greek): 'Historical' Signs of the Apocalyptic Son of Man and Saints of the Most High?—a Paradigm for Christology and Discipleship." In *A Man of Many Parts: Essays in Honor of John Westerdale Bowker*, edited by Eugene E. Lemcio, 43–61. Eugene, OR: Pickwick Publications, 2015.

Meyers, Eric M., and Mark A. Chancery. *Alexander to Constantine: Archaeology of the Land of the Bible*. Vol. 3. New Haven: Yale University Press, 2012.

Moore, Carey A. *Daniel, Esther, and Jeremiah: The Additions*. Anchor Bible 44. Garden City, NY: Doubleday, 1977.

Ogden, Daniel. *Dragons, Serpents, and Slayers in the Classical and Early Christian Worlds: A Sourcebook*. Oxford: Oxford University Press, 2013.

Pietersma, Albert, and Benjamin G. Wright, eds. *A New English Translation of the Septuagint*. Oxford: Oxford University Press, 2007.

Rahlfs, Alfred, ed. *Septuaginta*. 7th ed. Stuttgart: Württembergische Bibelanstalt, 1962.

Sevenster, J. N. *Do You Know Greek? How Much Greek Could the First Jewish Christian Have Known?* Novum Testamentum Supplements 19. Leiden: Brill, 1968.

Ziegler, J., and O. Munnich, eds. *Susanna. Daniel. Bel et Draco*. 2nd ed. Septuaginta: Vetus Testamentum graecum 16/II. Göttingen: Vandenhoeck & Ruprecht, 1999.

# 8

## The Wild and the Cultivated Olive: Embarrassing or Brilliant?

MARGARET G. FLOWERS

> and if the root is holy, so are the branches. But if some of the branches were broken off, and you a wild olive shoot, were grafted in their place to share the richness of the olive tree, do not boast over the branches . . . it is not you that supports the root, but the root that supports you . . . For if God did not spare the natural branches, neither will he spare you . . . And even the others, if they do not persist in their unbelief will be grafted in again, for God has the power to graft them in again. For if you have been cut from what is by nature a wild olive tree, and grafted, contrary to nature, into a cultivated olive tree, how much more will these natural branches be grafted back into their own tree. (Rom 11:16b–18, 21, 23–24)[1]

IN SETTING AFTER SETTING, Paul chose the words of his arguments with care. In Antioch of Pisidia, his "word of exhortation" in the synagogue brought "almost the whole city to hear the word of God on the following Sabbath" (Acts 13:16–44); in Athens, he turned the culture of idol worship to an advantage in preaching the gospel on the Areopagus (Acts 17:22–34); and the well-timed affirmation of his belief in the resurrection of the dead sent the Sanhedrin into confusion (Acts 23:6). Indeed, his way with words was a critical element in his desire to "become all things to all men, that [he] might by all means save some" (1 Cor 9:22b). What is the likelihood, then, that Paul would stumble at a critical time in his ministry, when he was in need of the assistance of the entire Roman church—both Jewish and Gentile—to support him in prayer as he prepared to take the collection to the dangerous setting of Jerusalem and to seek the material aid of the Romans in his anticipated missionary expedition to Spain?

In an apparent disregard for this evidence, interpreters of Paul's letter to the Romans frequently pass by the metaphor of the wild and cultivated olives either

---

1. Translations of the Bible are RSV.

without comment, or with an embarrassed note on the "confused and confusing figure of the olive tree,"[2] or with the disclaimer that Paul described a procedure that was "contrary to what is practiced,"[3] that he "had the limitations of a town-bred man . . . [who] had not the curiosity to inquire what went on in the olive-yards which fringed every road he walked,"[4] or that "as almost always in Paul, imagery is shaped by the intended subject matter, so that statements are made which it is best not to check out from the standpoint of agriculture."[5] Despite such an admonition, I propose to examine that very point.

## Selection of the Olive

Of all of the plants cited in the Hebrew Scripture as illustrative of the chosen people of God, why did Paul select the olive, rather than, say, the grapevine? In the Gospel of John, Jesus uses the grapevine in what appears to be a similar fashion:

> I am the true vine, and my Father is the vinedresser. Every branch of mine that bears no fruit, he takes away, and every branch that does bear fruit he prunes that it may bear more fruit. . . If a man does not abide in me, he is cast forth as a branch and withers; and the branches are gathered, thrown into the fire and burned. . . These things I have spoken to you, that my joy may be in you and that your joy may be full. (John 15:1–2, 6, 11)

While both grape and olive were cultivated, which included pruning for increased fruitfulness (Lev 25:3; Rom 11:18–19), and both are also found growing wild in the region (Hos 9:10; Rom 11:17), there are several critical differences between Jesus's selection of the grape and Paul's choice of the olive. Jesus's reference to himself as the *true* vine is indicative of the manner in which the grape is sometimes used to refer to the people of Israel. The vineyard that is Israel has degenerated despite all God's attention to it (Isa 5:2–4); indeed, even the wood is useless except for anything other than a fuel (Ezek 15:2–7). It was not even used for an altar fire in the temple.[6]

In contrast, the olive, as a symbol of a faithful Israel, is described as "green . . . fair with goodly fruit" (Jer 11:16); the Israel that has returned to faith will have "beauty like the olive" (Hos 14:6). While the *branches* of a disobedient Israel will be consumed with fire, the trunk will remain (Jer 11:16). And unlike the wood of the grape, that of the olive was highly prized, being specified for construction of the cherubim, doors and posts of the temple (1 Kgs 6:23, 30–31), and for the booths at the Feast of Tabernacles (Neh 8:15).

2. Donfried, *The Romans Debate*, 322.
3. Wesley, *Notes on St. Paul's Epistle to the Romans*, 11.7.
4. Dodd, *The Epistle of Paul to the Romans*, 180.
5. Käsemann, *Commentary on Romans*, 308.
6. M. *Tamid* 2:3.

## Horticultural Practices

From the perspective of modern science, what do we know about olives and olive culture? A point of special interest for the student of economic botany is the origin of crops cultivated and domesticated by ancient civilizations: the olive, cultivated in the eastern Mediterranean for several millennia BC and known to the Romans by 600 BC, is such a tree.[7] Written records are lacking, but such information may be surmised with great accuracy by examination of the chromosome number and morphology of the domesticated plant as compared with possible progenitors. On the basis of such studies, it has been determined that the wild olive (*Olea europaea* var. *oleaster*) that is found in the eastern Mediterranean represents a cultivated olive (*Olea europaea* var. *sativa*) that has escaped from cultivation to the wild rather than one of the two or three distinct species ancestral to the cultivated olive.[8] Indeed, recent studies of archaeological sites have shown that it is impossible to distinguish between wild and cultivated olives on morphological grounds.[9] However, through quantitative inorganic elemental analysis, this distinction is possible; cultivated trees would have been fertilized, and, therefore, contain higher quantities of these elements.[10] This close relationship between the cultivated and wild olives was, in fact, recognized by Irenaeus:

> For as the good olive, if neglected for a certain time, if left to grow wild and to run to wood, does itself become a wild olive; or again, if the wild olive be carefully tended and grafted, it naturally reverts to its former fruit-bearing condition.[11]

Thus, not only would grafting be possible and relatively easy, but also the fruit produced by a "wild" tree engrafted onto the "cultivated" would be identical (or nearly so) to that of the cultivated. Differences at the level of the variety ("var.") usually involve subtle differences in vegetative, rather than flower or fruit characteristics. One such difference between the types of olive may be the water content of the wood. The oleaster, but not the olive was used for the construction of altar fires;[12] furthermore, "what is made from olive-tree branches is not susceptible [to uncleanliness] unless the wood has been heated to drive out moisture."[13]

From Columella, a first century contemporary of Paul, we have a description of pruning of olive trees:

---

7. Fabbri et al., *Olive Propagation Manual*, 4.
8. Simmonds, "Olive," 219.
9. Liphschitz et al., "The Beginning of Olive," 441.
10. Terral, "Wild and Cultivated Olive," 396.
11. Irenaeus, *Against Heresies*, 5.10.1 (ANF 1.536).
12. *M. Tamid* 2:3.
13. *M. Kelim* 12:8.

> The olive-grove must be pruned at intervals of several years; for it is well to remember the old proverb "He who ploughs the olive-grove asks it for fruit; he who manures it begs for fruit; he who lops it, forces it to yield fruit." However, it will suffice to have pruned it every eighth year, so that the fruit-bearing branches may not be from time to time cut off.[14]

There is also a description of grafting of a wild olive onto a cultivated trunk:

> It happens also frequently that, though the trees are thriving well, they fail to bear fruit. It is a good plan to bore them with a Gallic auger and to put tightly into the hole a green slip taken from a wild olive-tree; the result is that the tree, being as it were impregnated with fruitful offspring, becomes more productive. But it must also be assisted by being dug round and by unsalted lees of oil mixed with pigs' urine or stale human urine, a fixed quantity of each being observed . . . Olive trees also refuse to bear fruit because of the badness of the soil . . . [This is remedied by application of lime] . . . If there is no result from this remedy, we shall have to have recourse to the assistance of grafting.[15]

This is followed by detailed descriptions of three standard methods of grafting generally applicable to all tree species.[16] They are known today as cleft, side and bud grafts.[17]

Olive groves are maintained by a combination of practices. Trees are extremely long-lived, and ancient trunks are often used as support of young grafted shoots.[18] In addition, cuttings are taken from old trees; these are allowed to become rooted and to grow in a nursery.[19] This practice was also known in the first century:

> Take from the most fruitful trees tall and flourishing branches, such as the hand can grasp when it takes hold of them—that is to say the thickness of a handle—and cut off from these the freshest slips in such a way as not to injure the bark or any other part except where the saw has made its cut . . . The slips should then be cut to the length of a foot and a half with a saw . . . and sunk into the ground.[20]

---

14. Columella, *Res Rustica*, 5.9.15.
15. Columella, *Res Rustica* 5.9.16–17.
16. Columella, *Res Rustica* 5.11.1–11.
17. Janick, *Horticultural Science*, 368–3671; Columella, *De Arboribus*, xxvi–xxvii.
18. Kinman, *Olive Growing*, 19.
19. Hood, *Farm Horticulture*, 93; Kinman, *Olive Growing*, 17.
20. Columella, *Res Rustica* 5.7.2–4.

Figure 1. One-year-old scions grafted to a 30-year-old trunk, photographed May 1920. This is an example of cleft grafting, practiced in the ancient world (Kinman, *Olive Growing*, 19).

In this way, it was be possible, and even common, to produce a number of young trees identical in their makeup and qualities to the parental "old" tree: what we would today refer to as "cloning."

PART 1: GRAPPLING WITH SCRIPTURE IN ANCIENT AND CONTEMPORARY CONTEXTS

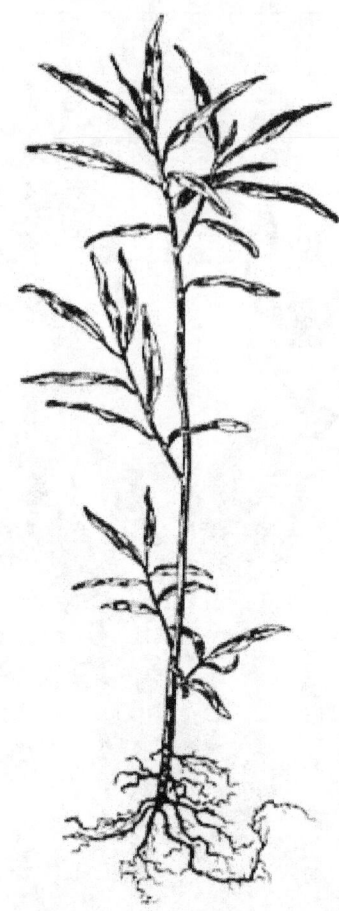

Figure 2. A softwood cutting, the "flourishing branch," taken from an old tree and rooted to produce another plant that is genetically identical to hte parent (Bergen and Caldwell, *Introduction to Botany*, 90).

## The Church of First-Century Rome

At the time of Paul's composition of his letter to the Romans, the Christian church was somewhat fragmented, both ethnically and physically. The edict of banishment issued by Claudius in AD 49 resulted in a several-year absence of both Jews and Jewish-Christians from Rome; during those years the Christian community in Rome would have been derived entirely from the gentiles, many—if not all—of whom would have had no recollection of the overlay of the practice of the Jewish law on Christian doctrine. The return of the Jewish-Christians, beginning in AD 54, likely brought back to Rome what we have come to call a Judaizing influence, which Paul frequently condemned.[21]

---

21. Note that my use of the term "Christian" is somewhat anachronistic, since followers of Jesus were not commonly known as Christians at this time (this is a later designation).

In addition to the divisions based on the controversy concerning keeping the cultic and national laws of Israel as a prerequisite for Christian belief, the community was also physically divided. Based on contemporary inscriptions, several synagogues are known to have existed in Rome, including two that were likely to have included Jewish-Christians. Of these, the Synagogue of the Olive Tree has been proposed as the headquarters of the Jewish-Christians in Rome.[22] The name of this synagogue might have been a reflection of the messianic passage of Zechariah:

> Then I said to him [the angel], "What are these two olive trees on the right and the left side of the lamp stand?" And a second time I said to him, "What are these two branches of the olive trees, which are beside the two golden pipes from which the oil is poured out?" He said to me, "Do you not know what these are?" I said, "No, my lord." Then he said, "These are the two anointed who stand by the Lord of the whole earth." (Zech 4:11–14)

## The Allegory of the Olive Tree: Romans 11:16–24

and if the root is holy, so are the branches.

As a prelude to the metaphor of the grafted olive, Paul first establishes a background picture of the holiness of the olive tree from one extremity to the other. The olive tree has been interpreted as the true Israel,[23] with the root representative of Abraham,[24] the patriarchs,[25] or the remnant of the present believing community of Israel (the Jewish-Christians).[26] The longevity of the olive correlates well with history of the God's chosen people; further, just as in nature the health of the visible portion of the tree is dependent on the health of the unseen root, the holiness of the branches of the tree of Israel depends ultimately on the stock from which it arises. To view the holiness of the branches as an absolute requires this be interpreted in a national, rather than individual sense,[27] or as an "eschatological possibility;"[28] to consider the branches as individuals[29] or as "all of them who believed"[30] would contradict Paul's next statement.

---

22. Barnes, *Christianity at Rome*, 87.
23. Bruce, *Apostle of the Heart Set Free*, 334.
24. [Pseudo-]Constantius, "The Holy Letter of St Paul to the Romans," 293.
25. Dodd, *Epistle of Paul to the Romans*, 179; Chrysostom, "Homily 19," *Homilies* (NPNF 1.11.490); Donfried, *The Romans Debate*, 321.
26. Johnson, *Reading Romans*, 169.
27. Calvin, *The Epistles of Paul*, 249.
28. Barth, *The Epistle to the Romans*, 407.
29. Bruce, *Apostle of the Heart Set Free*, 334.
30. Chrysostom, "Homily 19," *Homilies* (NPNF 1.11.480).

> But if some of the branches were broken off, and you a wild olive shoot, were grafted in their place to share the richness of the olive tree.

Was the reference to a branch broken off a warning to the Jewish members of the Synagogue of the Olive Tree? The branches broken from the tree, similar to the process of pruning, have generally been understood to represent individual Jews removed from the tree because of their unbelief. The "disease" of these branches, requiring their removal, occurs independently of the health of the root. Unlike the branches of the vine (John 15), they are not cast into the fire; the implication here is that they continue to live.[31] While this passage was likely directed to the gentile-Christians as Paul's primary audience, it is probable that he also had the Jewish-Christians in view as well. His description of the pruning of "some" of the branches (rather than "most") may be regarded as a gentle treatment of the Jews, whom he has no wish to alienate.[32]

The grafting of the wild olive shoot has presented one of the greatest difficulties for an interpretation of this passage, even when the authors of commentaries were aware of the practice reported by Columella. While one early writer used the metaphor of different types of grafts commonly practiced to illustrate different methods of Christian instruction,[33] in the opinion of another, this is an "ambitious horticultural analogy, which is not terribly successful at the level of science."[34] I would disagree.

Whether or not the grafting of a wild scion onto a cultivated stock was common practice, it was a procedure known during the first century; the detailed accuracy of reports of other horticultural practices strongly suggest the validity of this description as well. The closeness of the relationship between the cultivated and wild olives, although unknown in modern scientific detail, would have been understood in principle by first century arborists from the ability of these plants to be grafted one onto another. Indeed, based on a reading of the *Mishnah*, these may well have been considered to be the same tree: "One kind of tree may not be grafted onto another kind."[35] The fruits of these trees would be very similar, if not identical (just as there are not separate "fruits of the Spirit" for Jewish and gentile Christians); because the wild tree was commonly unfruitful, as it began to bear fruit, it would have appeared to have been "changed into the good olive-tree."[36] This close relationship would also suggest that while Hodge's understanding of the "Jewish church [as an] olive tree, one of the most durable, productive and valuable of the productions of the earth" is certainly accurate, his description of the wild olive—the gentiles—as "one of the most worthless of trees to express the degradation of their state, considered as estranged from God"[37] may be a bit harsh. Indeed, it is the very

---

31. Donfried, *The Romans Debate*, 322.
32. Chrysostom, "Homily 19," *Homilies* (NPNF 1.11.490); Calvin, *The Epistles of Paul*, 249–50.
33. Clement of Alexandria, *Stromata*, 6.15 (ANF 2.507–508).
34. Johnson, *Reading Romans*, 169.
35. M. Kilaim 7–8.
36. Irenaeus, *Against Heresies*, 5.10.1 (ANF 1.536).
37. Hodge, *Commentary on the Epistle to the Romans*, 579.

nearness of relationship that allows the wild shoot (the gentiles) to be able to partake of the benefits of the cultivated root grounded in Israel.

> Do not boast over the branches . . . it is not you that supports the root, but the root that supports you.

Had Paul addressed the gentiles in scientific terms, he might have pointed out that the grafted scion receives not only its physical support, but also its water and nutrients from the rootstock (via the xylem). Since only "some" of the cultivated branches were removed, those remaining, as well as the wild grafted branches, will contribute to maintain the life and function of the rootstock by the transport of sugars (via the phloem). Indeed, it was this life-giving function of the wild scion that was responsible for the rejuvenated stock to which it was grafted; by analogy, was it this rejuvenation created by the gentiles that would provoke the jealousy of the Jews (Rom 11:11)? And was this another way to caution the "strong" gentile Christians against despising the "weak" Jewish Christians (Rom 14:3–4; 15:1) of the Synagogue of the Olive Tree?

A constant in Paul's botanical metaphor is the place of the patriarchal root; whether supporting the "cultivated" Jews or the "wild" gentiles, it continues to impart its life-giving continuity with the holiness of God. In short, there is no church of gentile Christians apart from the root of Israel.[38] There is certainly no scriptural basis for gentiles who "are so utterly stupid in their zeal that . . . in their inarticulate and inept literary products they unblushingly call the Jew accursed."[39]

> For if God did not spare the natural branches, neither will he spare you.

A grafted branch that does not bear fruit (i.e., is guilty of unbelief) is just as subject to pruning as a natural branch! Irenaeus noted that the grafted wild branch, in becoming fruitful, did not lose its other "wild" characteristics; if not truly grafted in, it would be useless for anything other than burning.[40]

> And even the others, if they do not persist in their unbelief will be grafted in again, for God has the power to graft them in again. For if you have been cut from what is by nature a wild olive tree, and grafted, contrary to nature, into a cultivated olive tree, how much more will these natural branches be grafted back into their own tree.

If the earlier reference to grafting proved difficult for interpretation, the idea of regrafting the natural branches has been more so. According to Bruce, the "analogy with horticultural practice has been strained to the limit, but the link snaps completely when Paul says that God can graft the original branches which were lopped off back

---

38. Käsemann, *Commentary on Romans*, 309.
39. Luther, *Lectures on Romans*, 314.
40. Irenaeus, *Against Heresies,* 5.10.2 (ANF 1.536).

onto their parent tree, to derive life from it anew."[41] The improbability of this event in nature presumes that the pruned natural branches are either burned or left on the ground to wither and dry. Paul, however, does not specify either of these fates; this leaves open the possibility that the pruned natural branches could have been rooted to produce new young cultivated olive trees. Natural branches taken from this source could, indeed, be grafted back into a tree that was their own in every sense.

Grafting, by definition, is a process that is "contrary to nature." No one, for example, would mistake a tree grafted with five varieties of apple as "natural"; it would be an obvious deviation from the natural condition. A single variety so grafted, however, might escape notice. In a similar way, the regrafted natural branch of the Jews might fail to draw comment, whereas, the grafting of the "wild" gentile onto the stock of the Jewish patriarchs is to create something remarkable.

## Conclusion

Based not only on the symbolic value of the olive tree as representative of Israel, but also on the characteristics of the wild and cultivated varieties of this tree, the common horticultural practices of the first century, and the state of the Christian church in Rome, Paul's use of the botanical metaphor is characteristic of his careful use of words and images. Indeed, it is difficult to conceive of a substitute that would so precisely speak to the issues facing the Jewish- and gentile-Christians in Rome. Paul's words to the church of Corinth might well be addressed to the critics of his imagery:

> For we write you nothing but what you can read and understand; I hope you will understand fully as you have understood in part, that you can be proud of us as we can be of you on the day of the Lord Jesus. (2 Cor 1:13–14)

## Bibliography

*The Ante-Nicene Fathers*. Edited by Alexander Roberts and James Donaldson. 1885–1887. 10 vols. Peabody, MA: Hendrickson, 1994.
Barnes, Arthur S. *Christianity at Rome in the Apostolic Age*. Westport, CT: Greenwood, 1971.
Barth, Karl. *The Epistle to the Romans*. 6th ed. Translated by Edwyn C. Hoskyns. New York: Oxford, 1933.
Bergen, Joseph Y., and Otis W. Caldwell. *Introduction to Botany*. Boston: Ginn, 1914.
Bruce, F. F. *Apostle of the Heart Set Free*. Grand Rapids: Eerdmans, 1977.
Calvin, John. *Calvin's Commentaries. The Epistles of Paul the Apostle to the Romans and to the Thessalonians*. Translated by Ross Mackenzie. Grand Rapids: Eerdmans, 1960.
Columella, Lucius Junius Moderatus. *De Arboribus*. Translated by E. S. Forster and Edward H. Heffner. Loeb Classical Library. Cambridge: Harvard University Press, 1955.
———. *Res Rustica*. Translated by E. S. Forster and Edward H. Heffner. Loeb Classical Library. Cambridge: Harvard University Press, 1954.

---

41. Bruce, *Apostle of the Heart Set Free*, 334.

Dodd, C. H. *The Epistle of Paul to the Romans*. London: Hodder & Stoughton, 1932.

Donfried, Karl P., ed. *The Romans Debate*. Rev. ed. Peabody, MA: Hendrickson, 1991.

Fabbri, Andres, et al. *Olive Propagation Manual*. Collingwood, Victoria: CSIRO, 2004.

Hodge, Charles. *Commentary on the Epistle to the Romans*. Philadelphia: Martin, 1873. https://archive.org/stream/commentaryon1873hodg#page/578/mode/2up/.

Hood, George W. *Farm Horticulture: Prepared Especially for Those Interested in Either Home or Commercial Horticulture*. Philadelphia: Lea & Febiger, 1921.

Janick, Jules. *Horticultural Science*. San Francisco: Freeman, 1979.

Johnson, Luke Timothy. *Reading Romans: A Literary and Theological Commentary*. New York: Crossroad, 1997.

Käsemann, Ernst. *Commentary on Romans*. Translated and edited by Geoffrey Bromiley. Grand Rapids: Eerdmans, 1980.

Kinman, C. F. *Olive Growing in the Southwestern United States*. United States Department of Agriculture Farmers' Bulletin 1249. Washington, DC: United States Government Printing Office, 1922.

Liphschitz, Nili, et al. "The Beginning of Olive (*Olea europaea*) Cultivation in the Old World: A Reassessment." *Journal of Archaeological Science* 18 (1991) 441–63.

Luther, Martin. *Luther: Lectures on Romans*. Translated and edited by William Pauck. Library of Christian Classics 15. Philadelphia: Westminster, 1961.

*The Mishnah*. Translated by Herbert Danby. Oxford: Oxford University Press, 1933.

*The Nicene and Post-Nicene Fathers*, Series 1. Edited by Philip Schaff. 1886–1889. 14 vols. Peabody, MA: Hendrickson, 1994.

[Pseudo-]Constantius. "The Holy Letter of St. Paul to the Romans." In *Romans*, edited by Gerald Bray. Ancient Christian Commentary on Scripture 6. Downers Grove, IL: InterVarsity Press, 1998.

Simmonds, N. W. "Olive." In *Evolution of Crop Plants*, edited by N. W. Simmonds. Essex, UK: Longman Scientific & Technical, 1976.

Terral, Jean-Frédéric. "Wild and Cultivated Olive (*Olea europaea* L.): A New Approach to and Old Problem Using Inorganic Analysis of Modern Wood and Archaeological Charcoal." *Review of Paleobotany and Palynology* 91 (1996) 383–97.

Wesley, John. *Notes on St. Paul's Epistle to the Romans*. Notes on the Whole Bible: The New Testament. http://wesley.nnu.edu/john-wesley/john-wesleys-notes-on-the-bible/notes-on-st-pauls-epistle-to-the-romans/#c5577/.

## List of Figures

Figure 1. One-year-old scions grafted to a 30-year-old trunk, photographed May 1920. This is an example of cleft grafting, practiced in the ancient world (Kinman, *Olive Growing*, 19).

Figure 2. A softwood cutting, the "flourishing branch," taken from an old tree and rooted to produce another plant that is genetically identical to the parent (Bergen and Caldwell, *Introduction to Botany*, 90).

# 9

## "Because of Transgressions" (Galatians 3:19): Reassessing Jerome

— TIMOTHY DWYER

"WHAT THE LAW WAS meant to do, what it does and cannot do: the debate on Paul's view of these matters is endless." So says Stephen Westerholm in a comprehensive 2004 book on Paul.[1] Likewise, James Sanders commented in 1987 that "Paul's attitude toward the law has been one of the most puzzling and seeming insoluble in biblical study."[2] Similarly, H. J. Schoeps wrote in 1961 that the law is the "most intricate doctrinal issue in Paul's theology."[3] Whether it is the exegesis of individual verses, or synthetic approaches to the broader question of Paul and the law, a veritable flood of texts has worked at the subject with little or no consensus.[4]

This essay proposes to examine one of the more enigmatic statements of Paul on the Torah, Gal 3:19, where the question is asked, "Why therefore the law?"[5] (*ti oun ho nomos*) The answer is given in four parts or definitions: 1. The law was added because of transgressions. 2. Until the promised seed might come. 3. It was commanded through the angels. 4. By the hands of a mediator.[6] The first part of the definition, "It was added on account of transgressions" (*ton parabaseon charin prosetethe*), is notoriously obscure, but also has great significance for Paul's view of the law, so much so that Daniel Wallace has labeled it a *crux interpretum*.[7] How is *charin* ("on account of") used here? Whose transgressions are in view? This essay proposes to reassess the ancient view of Jerome, namely, that it is not general human transgressions which caused the law to be given, but the specific sins of Israel following the exodus. It seems

---

1. Westerholm, *Perspectives Old and New*, 261.
2. Sanders, "Paul and the Law," 115.
3. Schoeps, *Paul the Apostle to the Gentiles*, 168.
4. For example, Dunn, *Paul and the Mosaic Law*; Sanders, *Paul, the Law and the Jewish People*; Räisänen, *Paul and the Law*; Das, *Paul, the Law and the Covenant*; Schreiner, *The Law*; Thielman, *Paul and the Law*; Hubner, *The Law*; Kuula, *The Law, the Covenant and God's Plan*; Hong, *The Law*.
5. All translations of the Bible are the author's, unless otherwise indicated.
6. Betz, *Paul's Letter*, 163.
7. Wallace, "Galatians 3:19–20," 225–45.

appropriate, then, to proceed in three steps. Our first will be to examine how more recent commentators have viewed the verse and the use of *charin*; then we will proceed to some grammatical considerations; and finally, we will discuss and evaluate Jerome's view and compare it to some Jewish exegetical traditions.

## Recent Views

### To Make Transgressions Known

A first way that Gal 3:19 has been interpreted relates to the use of *charin*, and understands the preposition to be used in a cognitive sense: the law or Torah was given to make transgressions known. Jeffry A.D. Weima, noting that there is a deprecation of the law in Galatians 3, believes that the temporal clause makes best sense with a cognitive view, namely, the law was added to make humanity "more fully aware of its sinfulness, thereby heightening the significance of the coming of the promised seed, Jesus."[8] Weima's view also adduces the evidence of the subsequent imagery of the law as a supervisory custodian or pedagogue (3:24–25 and 4:2), and believes the law has a cognitive function in Rom 3:20 and 7:7 as well. Likewise, Burton emphasizes a cognitive view, focusing on his understanding of *parabaseon* as the violation of an explicit law, so the recognition of sinful deeds is in view as sin is converted into transgression.[9] Weima and Burton follow the older view of Calvin, in his 1548 commentary on Galatians, where he stated that like Rom 3:20 and 5:13, by the law comes the knowledge of sin. With their transgressions made obvious, people will or can acknowledge their guilt. In more recent years, Philip Esler followed this train of thought (though Esler recently is more explicit that he sees the restraining view of the law in view in 3:19).[10] The law was established to provide a collection of norms in relation to which human behavior would have an altered character, in particular that the breach of the norms would bring punishment. Virtually any legislation wants to label certain conduct reprehensible and discourage such conduct, says Esler.[11]

### To Provoke or Stimulate Transgressions

A second way that Gal 3:19 and especially *charin* has been understood is that the law has been given to *cause* transgressions rather than to define or make them known. After a rather lengthy discussion of Hellenistic and Jewish parallels, Betz, for example, presents the idea that Paul takes a decidedly non-Jewish position in Gal 3:19. In contradistinction to the idea that the Torah was a "fence of protection" around Israel (*Let. Arist.* 139;

---

8. Weima, "The Function," 227.
9. Burton, *Galatians*, 188.
10. Esler, "Paul's Contestation," 31.
11. Esler, *Galatians*, 195–6.

142; 3 Macc 3:1–7), Betz believes that Paul here thinks that the Torah was given "for the purpose of transgressions," with a wholly negative connotation.[12] Paul's view is that the purpose of the Torah was to produce transgressions, not prevent them. Betz rejects the ideas of Schlier, Oepke, Lightfoot, Zahn, Mussner, and others that the law was supposed to prevent transgressions. With the possibility that the notion that the law was given "in addition" may be pre-Pauline, Betz thinks that the gift of the law produced transgressions, since without the law there were no transgressions (citing Rom 4:15), and the law intensified them until the intervention of God's grace became necessary. Rather than preventing transgressions, the law produced them, according to Betz.[13]

A similar view is held by Louis Martyn. Martyn notes that *charin* (evaluated as the accusative of *charis* and used here as a preposition) could be followed by a cause or a goal. Understanding "transgressions" as the breaking of a recognized command, Paul is thinking of the law as antedating the transgressions, and "very probably producing them."[14] If the gospel is now eliciting faith (3:22 and 3:25), the law, as a parallel, entered the picture in order to elicit transgressions (as in Rom 5:20). For Martyn, "This is a view of the law for which there is no proper parallel in Jewish tradition; where the law is thought to increase resistance to transgressions."[15]

Betz and Martyn follow the fuller argument of Räisänen in the idea that the law was given in order to produce transgressions. Räisänen admits that the context in Gal 3:19 does not provide enough information to understand the use of *charin* with *ton parabaseon*, but the talk of the law being added parallels the idea of Rom 5:20, as Räisänen sees it. So, the law was added to bring about or increase transgressions. This contradicts the following image of the law as a pedagogue, which points to the law as preventing transgressions, but Paul's thought on the law here is "artificial and conflicting" because he deduced the statements from his Christological insights.[16]

Another interpreter who follows the train of thought that the law was given in order to produce transgressions is Thomas Schreiner. He notes the negative evaluation of the law in Galatians 2–4, and says that in light of that, it is unlikely that Paul speaks here positively of the law as restricting transgressions (in 3:19). Thus, the context of Galatians and the parallel in Rom 5:20 indicate that Paul is saying here that the law was given to cause sin.[17] In the context, salvation cannot come from the law since all are under the power of sin, and Gal 3:10 indicates (for Schreiner) that the law cannot be kept and brings a curse. Since the law confines all under the power of sin in 3:21–22, it is unlikely that the law restrains sin in 3:19. Also, nowhere else in Galatians is it said that the law prevents people from sinning (and that would be an odd argument to make

---

12. Betz, *Galatians*, 165.
13. Betz, *Galatians*, 165.
14. Martyn, *Galatians*, 354.
15. Martyn, *Galatians*, 354.
16. Räisänen, *Paul and the Law*, 144–5, 153.
17. Schreiner, *The Law*, 74–5.

when Paul is trying to argue against the use of the law by the Galatians).[18] In relation to the contention by some that Romans should not be used to interpret Galatians (to which Schreiner is sympathetic), Schreiner responds that the letters of Paul should not be hermetically sealed off from each other. Thus, Rom 5:20 and Gal 3:19 communicate the same message, namely, that the law provoked more sinning.[19]

I will leave aside counter arguments for the moment (as interesting as they are; Longenecker wonders why God would want an increase of sin building up to the coming of Christ,[20] and Esler wonders if the command not to kill was really given so that men might commit homicide[21]), and note a third approach to understanding *ton parabaseon charin prosetethe*. This approach takes a decidedly more positive tone than the idea that the purpose of the law was to produce or even define transgressions.

## To Provide a Temporary Remedy in the Sacrificial System

In over a decade's worth of work on Galatians, James Dunn has covered most every topic in the book. In his commentary on Galatians and his work on the theology of Galatians, he discusses 3:19.[22] Dunn notes the view of those like Betz who take the verse in a negative sense. He notes that the main reason is the parallels between Gal 3:19 and Rom 4:15 and 5:20, but says that Galatians should be read in light of Romans because Romans may be a revision in Paul's thought.[23] Dunn does not think Paul's view of the law is as negative as often portrayed in Galatians (his well-known view on "works of law" is that it is those identity markers of the law such as circumcision, Sabbath-keeping, and the food laws); and 5:14 shows a highly positive view of the law for Christians also. Thus, Dunn thinks that 3:19 presents a positive view of the law prior to the coming of Christ. The law was given to provide a remedy for transgressions, that is, the sacrificial system provided a means for transgressions to be dealt with and atonement made before the coming of Christ.[24] One of the alternate views, namely that the law provoked transgressions for nearly a millennium without a remedy, presents a "remarkably heartless view of God who so failed to provide." The law, then, was instead an interim measure to deal with the problem of transgression until it could be definitively dealt with in the cross of Christ.[25]

A related positive twist on Gal 3:19, though not identical with the view of Dunn, is the interpretation of E. P. Sanders in *Paul, the Law, and the Jewish People*. For

18. Schreiner, *The Law*, 76.
19. Schreiner, *The Law*, 77.
20. Longenecker, *Galatians*, 138.
21. Esler, *Galatians*, 196.
22. Dunn, *The Theology of Paul's Letter to the Galatians*; *The Epistle to the Galatians*.
23. Dunn, *Epistle*, 189.
24. Dunn, *Epistle*, 190.
25. Dunn, *Epistle*, 190.

Sanders, the question of Gal 3:19 is triggered by the statement of 3:18, namely that the promise or inheritance does not come by law. So, Sanders notes the progression in the answer: 1. It was given because of transgressions and temporarily. 2. It consigned all things to sin (3:22). 3. It kept us in restraint (3:23). 4. It was our custodian (3:24). 5. It can be compared to a guardian of a minor.[26]

While the law was part of God's providence, it did not provide for salvation because it was connected to sin in a negative place in God's plan of salvation. Sanders finds it hard to determine whether 3:19; 3:22; 3:23; and 3:24 are synonymous, but says that it is not fully necessary to determine whether the verses are. So, the simplest reading for Sanders is that the law deals with transgressions until the coming of Christ.[27] However, not too much weight should be put on the statement because it is not one that Paul very carefully worked out. Rather, he worked from solution to plight: salvation was from Christ, so it was not from the law, whose place was a temporary remedy or solution.

To Restrain Transgressions

A fourth option which has been presented is to see Gal 3:19, "The law was added because of transgressions" in another fairly positive way, that is, the law was given to restrain or prevent transgressions. This has been tied by some to the pedagogue language in the following paragraph, or the guardianship language in the first eight verses of Galatians 4. This view has a long heritage, and goes back as far as Thomas Aquinas.

Aquinas commented on the letters of Paul between 1259 and 1265 and again between 1272 and 1273. In his thoughts on Galatians, he presents four reasons for the "old law" being given. His first reason includes the idea that the "old law" was given to suppress wickedness, since by forbidding and punishing sin, the law would restrain people from sin. In other words, those ill-disposed to God need to be kept from sin and are so kept by the manner that sin has penalties attached to it.[28] In addition, then, to other uses of the "old law," such as disclosing human weakness and taming human concupiscence, Aquinas emphasizes the idea that the law was given as a restraint to sin in his comments on Gal 3:19.

This has found modern supporters also. For example, in his work on the pedagogue in Gal 3:19–25, David Lull exegetes *ton parabaseon charin prosetethe* as indicating the law in its pedagogical function served to restrain or control transgressions.[29] The preposition *charin* is understood by Lull in a causal sense as introducing the prior condition that caused God to "add" the law. So, the law was added because of

---

26. Sanders, *The Law*, 65.
27. Sanders, *The Law*, 66.
28. Aquinas, *Commentary*, 95–96.
29. Lull, "The Law," 482.

transgressions, or to deal with transgressions that had occurred.[30] Doubting the clarity of Rom 4:14–15, 5:13 and 20, Lull hesitates to make use of them in interpreting Gal 3:19. The pedagogue was certainly not charged with luring his charges into transgression! Rather, the pedagogue curbed youthful desires for a designated and limited period of time. So, the law was given for a designated and limited period of time to restrain prior transgressions until the promised seed should come.

Richard Hays is attracted to the view of the law as given to restrain transgressions given the following pedagogue metaphor,[31] but given the brevity of Paul's statement, finds it difficult to decide exactly what is meant in Gal 3:19, and opts for a solution that involves both restraining and identifying human sin as explicit, revealed transgressions of a revealed divine will.[32] Likewise, as stated earlier, Esler follows the view of the law as restraining transgressions.[33]

With four major interpretive options before us for Gal 3:19a, namely that the law was given 1. *to make transgressions known*; or 2. *to provoke and stimulate transgression*; or 3. *to provide a remedy in the sacrificial system until the seed should come*; or 4. *to restrain transgressions*, let us consider briefly some exegetical and textual details, and then assess Jerome's view, which is rarely referred to in modern scholarship.

## Textual and Exegetical Matters

There are three minor variants in the textual tradition that we should briefly note. D* has *paradoseon* ("traditions") instead of *parabaseon*, a two-letter difference that Wallace identifies as a scribal blunder. Also, *ton praxeon* ("of deeds") is found instead of *ton parabaseon* in P 46, F, G, and some other minor texts. "Why then the law of deeds" was added by some "Western" scribes, Wallace thinks.[34] Likewise, D, F, and G (later and western) have *etethe* (some with *praxeon*), but this reading is also less likely because of the geographical and chronological limits.

There are three main grammatical/lexical issues. One question is the use of *charin*, the accusative of *charis* used as a preposition, elsewhere. In the Pauline corpus, it is found in Ephesians 3:1 and 14 with the identical expression *toutou charin*, probably best translated as "for this reason." 1 Timothy 5:14 is probably causal: *didonai to antikeimeno loudorias charin*; Titus 1:5 is identical to Eph 3:1 and 14; and Titus 1:11 probably presents a goal or telic sense: "for the purpose of gain" (*kerdous charin*). Luke 7:47 is probably less relevant, and Jude 16 probably also presents the preposition in a telic sense: *ofeleias charin*, "for the purpose of profit." 1 John 3:12 is the only place in the New Testament where *charin* actually precedes the word it governs (which is the more

---

30. Lull, "The Law," 483.
31. Hays, "Galatians," 267.
32. Hays, "Galatians," 267.
33. Esler, "Abraham," 31.
34. Wallace, "Crux," 233.

normal pattern in the Greek versions of the Hebrew Scripture). There, *kai charin tinos esfaxen auton* ("And for this cause killed him") probably indicates the reason.

The accompanying interrogative *ti* is probably to be taken adverbially here ("why then the law?"), indicating an inquiry about the purpose of the law, rather than a pronominal sense which would inquire of the nature of the law.[35] Then, *parabasis* is used in the Pauline corpus in Rom 2:23, indicating a transgression of the law, and in Rom 4:15, which also links the two: *ou de ouk estin nomos oude parabasis* ("Where there is no law, there is no transgression"). However, Rom 5:14 speaks of the *parabaseos Adam*, so apparently a transgression could also be of a verbal command. Likewise, 1 Tim 2:14 speaks of the transgression of Eve. Outside of the Pauline corpus, the noun is found in Heb 2:2 and 9:15. What the lexical study is unable to tell us, however, is *whose* transgressions are in view in Gal 3:19. Modern interpreters seem to assume either general human transgressions or general transgressions of Israel. Jerome raises the possibility for us that the transgressions for which the law was added were more specific.

## Jerome

Robert Payne has pictured Jerome as "tender and violent, gentle and rude, viciously proud and childishly humble, a man of deep hates and morbid passions whose brain was nevertheless permanently clear. He was a tissue of contradictions and he seems to have been perfectly aware of it himself."[36] A bit of a flavor of the man can be seen in his attack on the priest Onasus. Jerome makes fun of his name, misshapen nose, and speech impediment, and comments with cruelty, "Oh, cover your nose and shut your mouth; that is the best thing for you."[37] Jerome was that interesting and hard to live with combination of being both brilliant and a stinker. He lived from 347 to 419/20 AD, was born in Dalmatia, or possibly in a corner of Italy, and after a series of travels, settled for the last thirty-four years of his life in Bethlehem.[38] He was a man of three languages, the rare church father who knew Hebrew as well as Greek and Latin.

Lightfoot said of Jerome's commentary on Galatians, that it is "the most valuable of all the patristic commentaries on the Epistle to the Galatians: for the faults are more than redeemed by extensive learning, acute criticism and lively and vigorous exposition." Grutzmacher said, "In spite of all imperfections and in spite of the dependence upon Greek exegetes, Jerome's commentary on the Epistle to the Galatians is worthy of respect, and is considerably superior to his later exegetical products."[39] It is one of his commentaries on Paul's short letters (Philemon; Galatians; Ephesians; Titus) and is sometimes dated between 389 and 392, near the beginning of his time

---

35. Wallace, "*Crux,*" 231.
36. Payne, *The Fathers,* cited in Hall, *Reading Scripture,* 109.
37. Hall, *Reading Scripture,* 109.
38. Von Campenhausen, *The Fathers,* 130, 158.
39. Grutzmacher and Lightfoot are quoted by Schatkin, "The Influence of Origin," 52.

at Bethlehem, or slightly earlier.[40] Jerome shows dependence on a mostly lost work of Origen on Galatians, refers to a variety of Greek versions of the Scripture, but also shows some fruit of his studies in Hebrew with a Jewish convert (he had also studied later with a Jew named Baraninas in Bethlehem).[41] Much of the work of the commentaries on Galatians and Ephesians are compilations of other exegetes, says J. N. D. Kelley.[42] Jerome's biblical work is an example of the riches able to be mined for exegesis in patristic sources.

Of interest to us presently is Jerome's interpretation of Paul's comment in Gal 3:19a that the law was added "because of transgressions." Jerome's comment is "*Post offensam enim eremo populi, post adoratum vitulum et murmur in Dominum, lex transgressiones prohibitura successit* ("it was after the offense of the people in the wilderness, after the adoration of the calf and the murmurings against God, that the law came to forbid transgressions"). A quotation from 1 Tim 1:9 follows, and Jerome indicates that the law was not given for the righteous man, but for the lawless and disobedient, godless and sinful, unholy and profane.[43] For Jerome, it was the specific transgressions of Israel in the golden calf incident, and the murmurings in the wilderness that caused the law to be added.

At first glance, a question arises. Did Jerome forget the order of the book of Exodus? Since the book of the covenant (given in Exod 20–23) actually precedes the golden calf incident in chapters 32–34. So, how could the law have been given on account of the golden calf and murmurings which follow? Three options seem possible. First, it is possible that Jerome is following the dictum that "There is no earlier or later in the Torah," so that the canonical sequence is not to be determinative. Another option is that Jerome is referring to subsequent laws, such as those of the tabernacle construction in chapters 35–40 (though the instructions were in chapters 25–31), and Leviticus and Deuteronomy, which indeed follow the golden calf and the murmurings. Another option is simply that Jerome was confused or wrong in his assumed sequence.

What are we to make of this interpretation, namely that the law was not given to reveal, provoke, deal with, or restrain transgressions, but because of specific transgressions of Israel in the wilderness? It is interesting to note that there are some Jewish exegetical traditions, unrelated to Jerome, which also indicate that the law was added in a sort of *ad hoc* way because of specific transgressions of Israel in the wilderness. One tradition depends on Jer 7:22, "For when I freed your ancestors from the land of Egypt, I did not speak with them or command them concerning burnt offerings and sacrifices." On this, Rabbi Isaac Abravanel, a fifteenth-century Spanish philosopher

40. Schatkin, "The Influence of Origin," 53.
41. Kelly, *Jerome*, 134.
42. Kelly, *Jerome*, 145.
43. Jerome's commentary on Galatians is found in Milne, *Patrologia Latina* 26, 331–468; on 3:19, it is 26, 391C [440].

and biblical commentator, in his commentary on Jer 7:21–22 says that the command to build the tabernacle was a response to Israel's worshipping of the golden calf.[44] This idea goes back to Rabbi Ishmael (early second century; a counterpart of Rabbi Akiva), who understood that the command to build the tabernacle was actually given after, and as a response to, the making of the golden calf in Exodus 32–34.[45] One tradition has the gold of the tabernacle atoning for the gold of the calf.[46] Another tradition linked with Rabbi Ishmael notes that in Lev 17:7 it speaks of Israel not offering any longer sacrifices to goat-demons, and the conclusion is drawn that the first command is against idolatry because of Israel's proclivity to idolatry in the wilderness.[47] Another tradition has the sacrificial system as a whole instituted to combat idolatry. A lamb was chosen for the Passover to combat idolatry because lambs were worshipped as gods in Egypt[48] and another midrash answers the question as to why the command to purchase the paschal lamb preceded the slaughtering by four days, and the answer is given that the reason is the people were steeped in idolatry.[49]

No genetic relations can be drawn between Jerome and the varieties of Jewish tradition which relate the laws as an *ad hoc* response to various sins of Israel in the wilderness, especially that of the golden calf. However, it is interesting that both Jerome and some strains of Jewish exegetical tradition relates the laws to specific, not general, transgressions of Israel, and do not reflect an idea that the law was given to produce or define transgressions. What are we to make of this possibility for Gal 3:19a?

## Evaluation

One of the few modern commentators to notice Jerome's views on 3:19 is Richard Hays. Hays notes that Jerome's view is possible because in 3:19–20 Paul is thinking about the Exodus narrative of the giving of the law, but if Paul intends to allude to the golden calf incident, "He has given no clues to that effect."[50] But, has Paul given broader clues as to the Exodus story and wilderness apostasy in Galatians?

Recently, several writers have thought so. Todd A. Wilson and Sylvia C. Keesmaat have independently written on Exodus and wilderness traditions in Galatians.[51] In particular, I will pay attention to some suggestions by Wilson and relate them to Jerome's thesis. Wilson sees Exodus/redemption motifs in Gal 1:3–4, "rescued from this

---

44. Noted in Heschel, *Heavenly Torah*, 82.

45. *YS Pekudei* 414, *Tanhuma Terumah* 8; *TB Pekudei* 2, *Midrash on Ps* 3:6, referred to in Heschel, *Heavenly Torah*, 77.

46. *Sifre Devarim* 1, *PT Shekalim* 45 D, noted in Heschel, *Heavenly Torah*, 79.

47. *BT Horayot* 8 a–b, noted in Heschel, *Heavenly Torah*, 74.

48. *Exodus Rabbah* 16:3, in Heschel, *Heavenly Torah*, 84.

49. *MI Pisha* 5, cited in Heschel, *Heavenly Torah*, 84.

50. Hays, *Galatians*, 266.

51. Wilson, "Wilderness Apostasy," 550–71; Keesmaat, *Paul and His Story*.

present evil age"; 4:3, 7, "God redeemed and adopted us"; and 4:21—5:1a, "Christ has set us free"; along with 5:13a, "called to freedom." He sees wilderness apostasy motifs in 1:6–7, "so quickly turning away"; 4:8–9, "turn back again to become slaves"; 5:1b, "Do not submit again to a yoke of slavery"; and 5:13b–26, "not an occasion for the flesh."[52] For our purposes, it is telling that Wilson links "so quickly turned" (*tacheos*) to "They have quickly turned aside" (Greek *tachu*) in Exod 32:8. After experiencing an Exodus-like redemption, the Galatians are now contemplating a return to an Egyptian-like bondage through a golden-calf like apostasy.[53] So, is Hays wrong that Paul has given clues to Exodus motifs and the golden-calf incident after all?

Aside from the questions of how one identifies motifs, and whether interpreters have been overly clever in spotting allusions and echoes (about which a minor growth industry has arisen), with others countering that audience competence, not to mention literacy, is vastly overrated by many New Testament scholars, there seems to be a problem in sequence. The movement from *exodus* to *threatened apostasy* sounds different than *promise* to *law/temporary tutor/pedagogue* to *fulfillment of promised seed being given*. In other words, the sequence both extends back farther and farther into the future. Even if we go further back, it is unclear how the movement from *Abrahamic promise and covenant* to *temporary tutor* to *fullness of time and arrival of the promised seed* in Galatians 3 overlaps an *exodus story* to *wilderness apostasy story* stretching from Galatians 1–5. The best we may be able to do is say that specifying the rapid turning away of the Galatians could be alluding to the quick turning away of the Israelites in Exod 32:8 at the golden calf incident. To assert much more than that may be over-exegesis of the text.

However, there is another intriguing possibility that should be mentioned. In the Greek versions, it is interesting to note how the calf incident is described. In Exod 32:8, *parebesan tachu*; in the retelling of Deut 9:12, God tells Moses that *parebesan tachu*; then, in Deut 9:16, Moses says he saw that *kai parebete apo tes hodou*. It is very striking that all three cases use forms of the verb *parabaino*, related to Paul's word in Gal 3:19a, *parabasis*! While too much weight should not be placed on a single word, the narrative sequence, related word in Gal 3:19a, and Jewish and Christian exegetical tradition must give us pause here. The most famous "turning aside" or "transgression," after all, was the golden calf incident. Though this doesn't explain the plural in Gal 3:19, it is not out of the question that the murmurings mentioned by Jerome and part of the Exodus narrative are included, since both murmurings and the golden calf incident are together spoken of by Paul in 1 Corinthians 10.

---

52. Wilson, "Wilderness Apostasy," 532–3.
53. Wilson, "Wilderness Apostasy," 570.

## Conclusion

So, is Jerome right in his understanding of this maddening terse expression in Gal 3:19a? My hunch is that Paul is walking a tightrope between two things: wanting to downgrade the law for his rhetorical and pastoral purposes, and wanting to preserve the law in 4:21, 5:13–15, and 6:2, not to mention his parenesis elsewhere. Following a reference to Abraham, and given the splitting off of the covenant and promised seed from the law, it is not impossible that Paul is referring to specific transgressions between the promise of the seed and the "fullness of time." Those specific transgressions could indeed be those of Israel, and I think it less likely that general transgressions are in view. However, it is not possible to be certain nor is it provable. So, exegetes and historians will continue having work to do, and church fathers and mothers will continually surprise us by their fascinating insights into the biblical text. It is such insights that Paul Livermore discovered in his studies in both the New Testament and Patristics. This essay honors his commitment to both, and his long ministry at Roberts Wesleyan College and Northeastern Seminary.

## Bibliography

Aquinas, Thomas. *Commentary on St. Paul's Epistle to the Galatians.* Albany, NY: Magi, 1966.
Betz, Hans Dieter. *Galatians: A Commentary on Paul's Letter to the Churches of Galatia.* Hermeneia. Philadelphia: Fortress, 1979.
Burton, Ernest de Witte. *The Epistle to the Galatians.* International Critical Commentary. Edinburgh: T. & T. Clark, 1921.
Campenhausen, Hans von. *The Fathers of the Latin Church.* Translated by Manfred Hoffman. Peabody, MA: Hendrickson, 1998.
Das, A. Andrew. *Paul, the Law, and the Covenant.* Peabody, MA: Hendrickson, 2001.
Dunn, James D. G. *The Epistle to the Galatians.* Black's New Testament Commentaries. Peabody, MA: Hendrickson, 1995.
———, ed. *Paul and the Mosaic Law.* Wissenschaftliche Untersuchungen zum Neuen Testament 89. Tübingen: Mohr/Siebeck, 2001.
———. *The Theology of Paul's Letter to the Galatians.* New Testament Theology. Cambridge: Cambridge University Press, 1993.
Esler, Philip F. *Galatians.* New Testament Readings. London: Routledge, 1998.
———. "Paul's Contestation of Israel's (Ethnic) Memory of Abraham in Galatians 3." *Biblical Theology Bulletin* 36 (2006) 23–34.
Hall, Christopher A. *Reading Scripture with the Church Fathers.* Downers Grove, IL: InterVarsity Press, 1998.
Hays, Richard B. "The Letter to the Galatians." In *The New Interpreter's Bible,* edited by Leander E. Keck, et al., 11:181–348. Nashville: Abingdon, 2000.
Heschel, Abraham. *Heavenly Torah: As Refracted through the Generations.* New York: Continuum, 2006.
Hong, In-Gyu. *The Law in Galatians.* Journal for the Study of the New Testament Supplement Series 81. Sheffield: Sheffield Academic, 1993.

Hübner, Hans. *The Law in Paul's Thought*. Translated by James C. G. Grieg. Edited by John Riches. Studies of the New Testament and Its World. Edinburgh: T. & T. Clark, 1984.

Keesmaat, Sylvia. *Paul and His Story: (Re)Interpreting the Exodus Tradition*. Journal for the Study of the New Testament Supplement Series 181. Sheffield: Sheffield Academic, 1999.

Kelly, J. N. D. *Jerome*. 1975. Reprint, Peabody, MA: Hendrickson, 1998.

Kuula, Kari. *The Law, the Covenant, and God's Plan*. Vol. 1, *Paul's Polemical Treatment of the Law in Galatians*. Proceedings of the Finnish Exegetical Society 72. Göttingen: Vandenhock & Ruprecht, 1999.

Longenecker, Richard. *Galatians*. Word Biblical Commentary. Waco: Word Books, 1990.

Lull, David. "'The Law Was Our Pedagogue': A Study in Galatians 3:19–25." *Journal of Biblical Literature* 105 (1986) 481–98.

Martyn, J. Louis. *Galatians: A New Translation with Introduction and Commentary*. Anchor Bible 33A. New York: Doubleday, 1998.

Migne, J. P. ed. *Patrologia Latina*. 217 vols. Paris: Imprimeria Catholoque, 1844–1857.

Räisänen, Heikki. *Paul and the Law*. Philadelphia: Fortress, 1983.

Sanders, E. P. *Paul, the Law, and the Jewish People*. Philadelphia: Fortress, 1983.

Sanders, James. "Paul and the Law." In *From Sacred Story to Sacred Text: Canon as Paradigm*, 115–23. Philadelphia: Fortress Press, 1987.

Schatkin, Margaret A. "The Influence of Origin upon St. Jerome's Commentary to the Galatians." *Vigiliae Christianae* 24 (1970) 49–58.

Schoeps, H. J. *Paul the Apostle to the Gentiles in Light of Jewish Religion and History*. London: Lutterworth, 1961.

Schreiner, Thomas. *The Law and Its Fulfillment: A Pauline Theology of Law*. Grand Rapids: Baker, 1993.

Thielman, Frank. *Paul and the Law: A Contextual Approach*. Downers Grove, IL: InterVarsity Press, 1994.

Wallace, Daniel. "Galatians 3:19–20: A *Crux Interpretum* for Paul's View of the Law." *Westminster Theological Journal* 52 (1990) 225–45.

Weima, Jeffrey A.D. "The Function of the Law in Relation to Sin: An Evaluation of the View of H. Räisänen." *Novum Testamentum* 32 (1990) 219–35.

Westerholm, Stephen. *Perspectives Old and New on Paul: The "Lutheran" Paul and His Critics*. Grand Rapids: Eerdmans, 2004.

Wilson, Todd A. "Wilderness Apostasy and Paul's Portrayal of the Crisis in Galatians." *New Testament Studies* 50 (2004) 550–71.

# 10

## Interpreting the Epistle to the Hebrews as a Pastoral Letter

WAYNE McCOWN

THE PURPOSE OF THIS essay is to set forth, in succinct form, six theses respecting the epistle to the Hebrews. Presented in ascending order, each thesis builds on those preceding it: the first are foundational to those which follow; the argument culminates in the final theses, which are more expansively developed.

### 1. The Exhortatory Purpose of the Letter

Heb 13:22 reads, "I urge you to bear with my word of exhortation, for I have written you only a short letter." In our view, this statement constitutes the author's definition of purpose.[1] On the one hand, it identifies Hebrews as an epistle, not an essay. (This inference is based on the writer's use of the verb *episteila*, generically translated "I have written.") Further, it describes this *letter* as a message of *exhortation*.

What is (or, was) a "word of exhortation"?[2] The Greek term underlying "exhortation" is *paraclesis*; the same root is used to describe the Holy Spirit, as *Paraclete*. The literal meaning, as most readers know, is to call (or be called) alongside, with a view to rendering help or assistance. In actual usage, the idea has a wide range of applications: from (stern) admonishment to comfort (in bereavement); exhortation, counsel, and encouragement represent the continuum between these boundaries. In brief, the basic

---

1. In support of this assertion, see Spicq, *L'Épître aux Hébreux*, 437; Lane, *Hebrews*, c; Cockerill, *Hebrews*, 313.

2. Exactly the same phrase is used in Acts 13:15 to describe Paul's synagogue address at Antioch of Pisidia. Some commentators infer that Hebrews belongs to the same "genre." Spicq states: "The Epistle to the Hebrews represents the classical type of the missionary preaching of the early church" (see *L'Épître aux Hébreux*, I, 18–20). Bruce (*The Epistle to the Hebrews*, xlviii) suggests that the phrase "word of exhortation" represents "a form of sermon or homily." Lane (*Hebrews*, lxx) elaborates on this idea: "'Word of exhortation' appears to be an idiomatic, fixed expression for a sermon in Jewish-Hellenistic and early Christian circles." An extended discussion follows (lxx–lxxv), which includes summary of an excellent work by Thyen, *Der Stil des jüdisch-hellenistichen Homilie*. Lane concludes: "Hebrews is a sermon prepared to be read aloud to a group of auditors."

notion is to come alongside another and render what help is most needed, be that a stern warning, spiritual encouragement, or personal comforting.[3]

A fairly wide range of meaning is found in Hebrews: notably, stern admonishment; but so too, exhortatory instruction; and also, pastoral encouragement. Thus, Heb 13:22 may be translated as a "message of encouragement," or paraphrased as a "letter of instruction and exhortation."

## 2. The Author's Concern for the Readers

Taking seriously the author's stated purpose in Heb 13:22 elevates significantly the importance of identifying the readers' needs. Here the focus is on discerning from his exhortations the author's expressed concerns for his readers. Although our historical knowledge of the readers is quite limited, the author knew them well: According to Heb 13:19, he had been with them and hopes to be "restored" to them soon. In each of two statements (5:12–13 and 10:35–36), the author expressly cites aspecific "need": their failure to thrive (i.e., to grow spiritually) and a lackadaisical attitude as regards their faith. Further, the author reflects his concern for certain persons within the audience, through the repeated use of "so that none" clauses: in 2:1; 3:12, 13; 4:1, 11.[4]

The author's clearest expression of intent for these readers (in positive as well as negative terms) is found in 6:11–12 (author's translation): "*We desire each one of you to show the same earnestness in realizing the full bearing of hope, until the end—so that you may not be (or, lest you become) sluggish, but imitators of those who through faith and patience inherit the promises.*" The author takes a serious view of the spiritual condition of his friends and readers. Despite their good beginnings, they now stand in danger of drifting away from the way of salvation, to their ruin and utter loss. They have grown disheartened and discouraged in the persistence of persecution, the length of the way, and their familiarity with the Word.[5] A tendency now exists (especially on the part of some) to slackness, doubt, even apostasy from the "confession" of faith (see 4:14).[6]

---

3. Lane (*Hebrews*, c) adds: "Intrinsic to all the meanings of *paraclesis* is the notion of earnest appeal."

4. Many translations render the two Greek phrases used in these texts as "lest," which represents more strongly the author's sense of "fear" for his audience (see particularly 4:1; KJV, NKJV, NAS, RSV).

5. Grässer ("Der Herbräerbrief 1938–1963," 198) summarily states: "Tiredness and a weakening of faith have befallen the community." Erdman (*The Epistle to the Hebrews*, 14–15) extends the application: "No matter where these Christians lived, their counterpart can be found in every land and every age . . . there is indifference, languor, weariness, practical unbelief. Whoever the original readers may have been, this epistle is addressed in a true sense to the Church of the present day."

6. Whereas NIV and NJB render *homologia* as "the faith we profess," NKJ, NAS, RSV, and NRS translate it as "confession." I prefer the latter, and interpret it—in the context of the epistle to the Hebrews—as referring to the affirmation "Jesus is the Son of God," one of the earliest confessions of faith (see thesis 5 below).

Some comment that the addressees manifest attributes characteristic of second generation Christians (see 2:3).[7] Clearly, in this particular situation, a condition of mental stagnation has set in, or possibly worse yet, of spiritual deterioration. The community does not exhibit the level of spiritual growth and maturity that might be expected (5:12–14). And, for want of solid food and strengthening exercise, their arms have become "feeble" and their knees "weak" (12:12–13). Moreover, they have become "lazy" (5:11).

This lack of spiritual vitality, with its resultant concomitants, has brought the addressees to the brink of disaster. They stand in acute danger of actually spurning the grace of God (6:4–6), of deliberately sinning after receiving the knowledge of the truth (10:26), of totally selling out like Esau "who for a single meal sold his inheritance rights" (12:16).[8] Already, "some" are habitually neglecting the assembling of the Christian community (10:25).

## 3. The Delimitation of Seven Exhortatory Sections

A careful delimitation of the exhortatory sections is important to a proper interpretation of this epistle as a "word of exhortation."[9]

Most commentators regard 10:19 to the end of the epistle as exhortatory.[10] This includes chapter 11, although it contains neither direct imperative ("do this") nor cohortative appeal ("let us"). On the other hand, the exhortatory intent of the chapter is clear, particularly in view of its present framework, 10:35–39 and 12:1–4.[11] Structurally and substantively, however, chapter 11 is sufficiently distinctive to set it off as a separate section within this larger block of exhortatory material.[12] The same is true of chapter 13, which opens with a series of brief exhortatory reminders (quite unlike the preceding discourse from Scripture, 12:18–29).[13] Thus, four "exhortatory" sections (i.e., units of exhortatory material) may be delimited at the end of Hebrews: 10:19–39; chapter 11; chapter 12; and chapter 13.

Additionally, commentators universally acknowledge the presence of exhortation earlier in Hebrews, interspersed with the author's exposition of theology. The first such section is almost universally delimited as 2:1–4. The next is recognized as occurring

---

7. Note Kuss, "Der Verfasser des Hebräerbriefes als Seeslsorger," in *Auslegung und Verkundigung*, 332.

8. See McCown, "Unforgivable Sin," 9–23.

9. See McCown, *Nature and Function of the Hortatory Sections*.

10. E.g., Purdy, "The Epistle to the Hebrews," 709.

11. See Calvin, *Hebrews and I and II Peter*, 157; Spicq, *L'Épître aux Hébreux*, I, 334 and II, 382; Kuss, *Der Brief an die Hebräer*, 200; Lane, *Hebrews*, ci and 316.

12. See Michel, *Der Brief an die Hebräer*, 228.

13. See esp. Filson, *"Yesterday": A Study of Hebrews in the Light of Chapter 13*.

within chapters 3–4, although variously divided and delimited. Similarly, chapters 5–6 are recognized as containing exhortation, but again variously delimited and labeled.

As regards chapters 3–4, three observations are germane. First, these two chapters belong together; they are a literary unit (not two, as many outlines demand). Excluding the first and final paragraphs, this material (3:7–4:13) consists of a continuous exposition on Ps 95:7–11.[14] Second, the first and final paragraphs are transitional, and serve to "fit" the exposition of Psalm 95 (God's Promise of Rest) into its present context. Third, the first imperative occurs in 3:1 and the last (a cohortative) in 4:16. So (however the intervening material is interpreted!), it is beyond dispute that 3:1–4:16 are exhortatory. Thus, we consider it proper to delimit the second hortatory section as chapters 3–4.

As regards chapters 5–6, almost all commentators agree that 5:11 marks the beginning of this exhortatory section. The ending is harder to establish: Should 6:13–20 be included? Many think so, for three reasons. First, the repetition of the phrase "in the order of Melchisedek" at 6:20 clearly returns the reader to the thesis set forth in 5:10 and brackets the intervening section. Second, this intervening material constitutes the author's address to the readers' needs. This includes exhortation in the form of direct address in 5:11–6:12, as well as the illustration from Scripture which follows in 6:13–20. Third, 6:13–20 is closely connected to the author's statement of concern and desire in 6:11–12: The exhortatory intent expressed there is clearly continued in presenting Abraham as a model of faith and patience for the readers to imitate.[15] (Note: The inclusion of 6:13–20 among the exhortatory materials of the epistle is based on considerations very similar to those argued for chapter 11.) For these reasons, most commentators agree that the proper delimitation of this exhortatory section is 5:11–6:20.

To summarize, the exhortatory letter called Hebrews contains seven exhortatory sections:

1. 2:1–4;
2. chapters 3–4;
3. 5:11–6:20;
4. 10:19–39;
5. chapter 11;
6. chapter 12;
7. chapter 13.

---

14. See esp. Clemen, "The Oldest Christian Sermon (Hebrews III and IV)," 392–400.
15. Note Moffatt, *Epistle to the Hebrews*, 85.

## 4. The Literary Outline Viewed Inductively

Hebrews has often been outlined deductively from the vantage point of some expository theme, such as the Superiority of Christ.[16] Viewed inductively (i.e., exegetically), these outlines usually prove half-satisfying.

Christ's Superiority over Angels, while fitting for chapter 1, is not an appropriate title for chapter 2. Students not prejudiced by this theme label 2:5–18 (more accurately) Jesus's Incarnation, or Jesus's Identification with Us. As regards angels, it is Jesus's (temporary) inferiority that is asserted in chapter 2, not his superiority.[17]

Extended into chapters 3–4, the theme approach becomes even more problematic. First, it usually requires a division in the exposition on Rest (which continues uninterrupted across the two chapters). Second, while Christ's Superiority over Moses is argued in 3:1–6, to utilize this as the title for the whole of chapter 3 again is to extend it too far. Moreover, in doing so, especially when chapter 4 is then titled Christ's Superiority over Joshua, the point of the exposition on Psalm 95 is completely lost. Third, it is doubtful that anyone reading chapter 4 on its own terms would ever come up with the required title, as representing the author's main idea or point. Admittedly, these titles contain a measure of truth, but viewed inductively, they do not fit well.

It should be remembered that Hebrews is a pastoral *letter*, not a theological essay. It should also be recalled that the author describes his letter as a message of *exhortation*. At the least, this description should alert us to give proper respect to the exhortatory sections.

Utilizing the seven exhortatory sections previously delimited as integral units in the author's letter, the following structural outline unfolds: chapter 1 (exposition); 2:1–4 (exhortation); 2:5–18 (exposition); chapters 3–4 (exhortation); 5:1–10 (exposition); 5:11–6:20 (exhortation); 7:1–10:18 (exposition); 10:19–39 (exhortation); chapter 11 (exhortation); chapter 12 (exhortation); chapter 13 (exhortation).

## 5. The Use of a Previously-Prepared Theological Treatise

Admittedly, there is a strong sense of theme development and continuation of argument in the expository sections of Hebrews. So much so, that a few commentators refer to some of the exhortatory sections as follows: 2:1–4 as a "digression" (in the argument of chapters 1–2)[18]; 5:11–6:20 as an "interlude" (in the treatment of Jesus's priesthood, to address the spiritual immaturity of the readers).[19]

---

16. See, e.g., Guthrie, *New Testament Introduction*, 54–59.
17. See Héring, *L'Épître aux Hébreux*, 30.
18. E.g., Robinson, *The Epistle to the Hebrews*; Moffatt, *Epistle to the Hebrews*, 12.
19. E.g., Moffatt, *Epistle to the Hebrews*, 85. Note the counter argument of Spicq (*L'Épître aux Hébreux*, I, 8): "It is necessary to guard against considering these [exhortatory passages] as digressions, accidental considerations... In reality it is these [passages] which 'constitute the veritable *raison d'être* of our epistle'" (quoting A. Lemonnyer, *Épîtres de Saint Paul*, 207).

It is our thesis that the expository sections, taken together, reflect a previously-prepared theological treatise. It would take too much space to reproduce it here in its entirety. It should suffice to show the key points of continuity (by bridging over the exhortatory sections): from 1:13–14 to 2:5; from 2:17–18 to 5:1–2; from 5:8–10 to 7:1–3.

> 1:13–14 "To which of the angels did God ever say, 'Sit at my right hand until I make your enemies a footstool for your feet'? Are not all angels ministering spirits sent to serve those who will inherit salvation?"

> 2:5 "[For][20] it is not to angels that he has subjected the world to come, about which we are speaking."

> 2:17–18 "For this reason he had to be made like his brothers in every way, in order that he might become a merciful and faithful high priest in service to God, and that he might make atonement for the sins of the people. Because he himself suffered when he was tempted, he is able to help those who are being tempted."

> 5:1–2 "Every high priest is selected from among men and is appointed to represent them in matters related to God, to offer gifts and sacrifices for sins. He is able to deal gently with those who are ignorant and are going astray, since he himself is subject to weakness."

> 5:8–10 "Although he was [Son],[21] he learned obedience from what he suffered and, once made perfect, he became the source of eternal salvation for all who obey him and was designated by God to be high priest in the order of Melchizedek."

> 7:1–3 "This Melchizedek was king of Salem and priest of God Most High. He met Abraham returning from the defeat of the kings and blessed him, (and) Abraham gave him a tenth of everything. First, his name means 'king of righteousness'; then also, 'king of Salem' means 'king of peace.' Without father or mother, without genealogy, without beginning of days or end of life, like the Son of God he remains a priest forever."

---

20. NIV ignores the explanatory Greek *gar*. It is included and translated "For" in several other translations: KJV, NAS, RSV.

21. NIV stands alone in rendering *huios* "a son"; KJV, NKJV, NAS, NJB, RSV and NRSV all translate it "a Son." Both translations are problematic. For one thing, the Greek language has no indefinite article. More significantly, to declare "although he was a son, he learned obedience" contradicts 12:5–8; and to describe Jesus as "a Son" is theologically nonsensical. The author has established, particularly in ch. 1, that Jesus is God's Son. The point of argument here in 5:8 is well stated in the following two paraphrases: NLT, "even though Jesus was God's Son, he learned obedience from the things he suffered"; NJB, "he learnt obedience, Son though he was, through his sufferings." See Bornkamm, "Sohnschaft und Leiden," in *Judentum-Urchristentum-Kirche*, 198; see Grässer, "Der Herbräerbrief 1938–1963," 221.

The continuity of argument, from one expository section to the next, reflects that sense of theme development so many commentators have tried to express in outlining Hebrews.

The key to understanding the thesis of this theological treatise is found in Hebrews 5:5–6.[22]

> "The One who said to his Anointed One, 'You are my Son . . .' Similarly in another place says,
>
> 'You are a high priest . . .'"

As every student of Hebrews knows, the author moves from an affirmation of Jesus's exalted status as God's Son (in chapter 1) to a description of his eternal ministry as our high priest (in chapters 7–10). The former doctrine was commonplace in the New Testament church: the declaration "Jesus is the Son of God" (rooted in Ps 2:7) constituted one of its earliest confessions of faith (see 1 John 4:15). The latter doctrine—that concerning Jesus's priesthood—is unique to Hebrews.

Heb 5:5–6, having applied the declaration in Ps 2:7 to Jesus, similarly applies the declaration in Psalm 110:4 to him. (The parallelism between the two divine declarations forms part of the argument.) Both psalms were well-known—and interpreted christologically—in the early church.[23] Linking divine affirmations concerning the Christ from these familiar psalms, the author sets forth his unique christological thesis: God's Son is our priest.

Such is the theological treatise embedded within the Epistle to the Hebrews. Since it comes from the same hand as the rest of Hebrews, we presume it was previously prepared by the author. Other materials in the epistle also appear to have similar origins: most notably 3:7–4:13, God's Promise of Rest; and chapter 11, The Exemplars of Faith. On the occasion of writing this exhortatory letter, the author selected these materials, which he had developed in the course of his ministry, as especially pertinent to the situation at hand.[24] Artfully, he wove them into his epistle, adding transitions and exhortations which fit them into the letter and apply them to the readers' situation.

## 6. The Role of Theology in the Service of Exhortation

The author describes his letter as a "word of exhortation." Thus, a proper understanding of the theology of Hebrews requires recognition of its alignment with and relation

---

22. This paragraph is dependent on insights derived from Bornkamm, "Das Bekenntnis im Hebräerbrief," in *Studien zu Antike und Urchristentum*, 188–203.

23. Hebrews relies heavily on these two OT psalms: Ps 2:7 in 1:5; 5:5 (scripturally grounding the numerous additional references to Jesus as Son); Ps 110:1 in 1:13 (see also 1:3; 8:1; 10:12; 12:2) and Ps 110:4 in 5:5, 6, 10; 7:7, 17, 21.

24. Gyllenberg ("Die Komposition des Hebräerbriefes," 137–147) argues a similar hypothesis to our own, but postulates that the theological treatise was inserted after the writing of the letter.

to the exhortatory purpose of the letter.[25] In Hebrews, theology stands in the service of exhortation—and in this role, it makes a significant contribution.[26]

The author is addressing a congregation that has grown lackadaisical spiritually. He warns them sternly about the dangers of this condition. But he also deploys other means at his disposal. One of them—an important one—is the quickening of their theological imagination. He sets before them Christ and his saving work, in a new way. He paints for them a grand vision of what God is doing in the world, then speaks directly to them about their participation in it.[27] The objective of this final thesis is to view the theology of Hebrews from this perspective.

## Eschatology

The eschatological element in Christian faith is emphasized in this epistle with a practical purpose in view. Three aspects are portrayed: past fulfillment in the person of Jesus Christ; present participation in the new aeon and community by faith; and, future expectation of judgment and/or salvation.

The turning-point, at the center of God's speaking and acting in history, has happened in the person and work of the Son-priest: "He has appeared once and for all at the climax of history to abolish sin by the sacrifice of himself" (9:26 NEB; see prologue, 1:1–4). A new aeon has been inaugurated, the eon of God's new covenant with his people. Jesus has secured an eternal redemption, which requires no repeated sacrifice for sins (9:11–12; 10:14, 18).

Nothing can surpass the greatness of this accomplishment, which constitutes the basis of Christian faith. The author's emphasis on the superiority of this salvation, which Christ not only wrought but promises to believers, surely should strengthen this disheartened congregation.

On the other hand, the finality, the decisive once-for-all character of Jesus's death for sin evokes a serious rejoinder against allowing any relapse back into sin. The Cross is planted in past history and will not be repeated; God has no other means of grace in store than those revealed in his Son. For apostates (those who deny Jesus), the future holds only the prospect of divine judgment. Thus, each member of the pining community is reminded of the theological ultimacy of the Christ-event.

Also appropriate in addressing the reader's situation, the author accentuates the present or "realized" aspects of eschatology. In Jesus Christ, "a better hope is

---

25. See Michel, *Der Brief an die Hebräer*, 29–35; Nauck, "Zum Aufbau des Hebräerbriefes," in *Judentum-Urchristentum-Kirche*, 2013–203; Lane, *Hebrews*, c: "An appreciation of the vital interrelationship between exposition and exhortation is crucial to an adequate understanding of the function of either component of the discourse."

26. See Kuss, *Hebräer*, 16.

27. See Spicq, *L'Épître aux Hébreux*, I, 1–2.

introduced, through which we draw near to God" (7:19)[28]; by his blood, the way into the very presence of God has been opened to us (10:19–22). "Crowned with glory and honor because he suffered death" (2:9), Jesus has become "the source of eternal salvation for all who obey him" (5:9). As recipients of "such a great salvation" ("which was first announced by the Lord," 2:3), those who hear the message with believing hearts (see 4:2) can be described as "those who have once been enlightened, who have tasted the heavenly gift, who have shared in the Holy Spirit, who have tasted the goodness of the word of God and the powers of the coming age" (6:4–5). What more inspiring affirmation could be set before this disheartened congregation?

And what incentive could be more effective? The blessings of God's eschatological salvation have been only "tasted," the better hope only "introduced," the way to God only "opened." Their realization is proleptic, an anticipation of larger fulfillment. Moreover (this point is brought to the fore several times), "We have come to share in Christ *if* we hold firmly till the end the confidence we had at first" (3:14).[29]

In the meanwhile, for those "who share in the heavenly calling" (3:1) but are tempted, Jesus is able to help. As our great high priest, he has entered into the heavenly sanctuary and now intercedes for those who draw near to God through him (7:25). He is not unable to sympathize with our weaknesses, for he too has been tempted as we are, yet without sinning (4:15; see 2:17–18). "Let us then," the author exhorts, "approach the throne of grace with confidence, so that we may receive mercy and find grace to help us in our time of need" (4:16). Obviously, theology here stands in the service of exhortation, giving it substance and significance.

Eschatological expectation for the future is emphasized especially, but not exclusively, in the exhortatory sections. Jesus Christ, having offered for all time a unique sacrifice for sins, "sat down at the right hand of God," thereafter to await the consummation of the divine eternal kingdom, "until his enemy should be made a stool for his feet" (1:13; 10:12–13). And as he has appeared at the climax of history "once-for-all . . . to "bear sin," he will appear "a second time . . . to bring salvation to those who are waiting for him" (9:26–28). Thus shall he bring many sons "to glory" (2:10), consummating the deliverance of his brethren from death and the destruction of the devil's power (2:10, 14–16).

The congregation of Christ can look forward to "being greatly rewarded" for its confidence (10:35; see 11:26). The destination to which faith's gaze is directed is described as a heavenly fatherland (11:16), a city prepared by God (11:16; see 13:14), an unshakable kingdom (12:28), the abode (resting-place) of God himself into which his people also shall enter (4:9–10). But only through the pursuit of peace and holiness can anyone see the Lord (12:14).[30]

---

28. See Robinson, "Eschatology of the Epistle to the Hebrews," 37–51.

29. The conditional *if* is also found in 3:6, 7, 14; 4:7. See Calvin, *Hebrews and I and II Peter*, 49: "believers enter [God's rest], but on condition that they continuously run and press on."

30. See McCown, "Holiness in Hebrews," 58–78.

There is also the prospect of judgment: "man is destined to die once, and after that to face judgment" (9:27). Aside from this one instance, this motif occurs only in conjunction with exhortatory appeal: 2:2–3; 3:7–4:13 passim; 6:7–8; 10:37–38; 12:4. It serves to intensify the (emotional) force as well as to support the validity of the warning against apostasy. In 13:4 and 13:17, it informs the "grounds"[31] for moral and obedient conduct among the brotherhood. And at 10:25, the author admonishes the congregation to increasing exhortation (*paraclesis*) among themselves in anticipation of God's judgment: "let us encourage one another—and all the more as you see the Day approaching."

By using this theological theme, Hebrews endeavors to stimulate the imagination of these readers, in order to incite them to faithful and persevering progress forward "unto the saving of soul"; it strives to preclude the (imminent?) possibility of shrinking back "unto perdition" (10:39 KJV). The readers have need of endurance, "so that when you have done the will of God, you will receive what he has promised" (10:36). The pertinence of theology to the exhortatory purpose of the epistle is obvious here. Both come to focus on one issue, the nature and meaning of the Christian life (see below): "For in just a very little while, 'He who is coming will come and will not delay. But my righteous one will live by faith. And if he shrinks back, I will not be pleased with him'" (10:37–38, quoting Habakkuk 2:3–4).

## Christology

The eschatological emphases in Hebrews are closely intertwined with its christological convictions. The depiction of the work of Christ on earth and in heaven, although complex, is not presented as speculation in the abstract. Christology, too, serves the pastoral purpose of this letter.

The confessional designation of Jesus as "Son" relates not only to his exalted position in the heavens at the right hand of God, higher than the angels. It also, according to Hebrews, characterizes his participation in humanity, for a little while made lower than the angels, so that in bringing "many sons" to glory he might make the pioneer (forerunner) of their salvation perfect through suffering and death: "Although he was Son, he learned obedience through what he suffered; and being made perfect he became the source of eternal salvation to all who obey him" (5:8, author's translation).

Such affirmations supply a theological basis for and give a depth of meaning to the exhortations in Hebrews for those who feel disheartened at hardships and hostilities (see 12:1–4). Jesus has left an Example[32] to be followed; he has opened up a pathway through suffering, and given new meaning to obedience.

The priestly interpretation distinctive of Hebrews makes the paradox of Jesus's offering more meaningful: "He suffered although he was the Son, but because he was

31. German: *Begründung*.
32. German: *Vorbild*.

to become high priest."[33] The Christological presentation, therefore, accords well and fittingly promotes the exhortatory intention of the epistle. Encouragement for this weakened suffering community flows from its Christology.

Central to Jesus's priestly accomplishment is the purification from sins wrought by his self-offering. This fact is set forth thematically in the prologue and exposited extensively in this epistle. The referent, clearly, is the earthly death of Jesus; the topic, its eternal significance.

Through the blood of this personal sacrifice, we have a superior and unique atonement. By his singular death, Christ Jesus has validated God's new covenant, in which there is provision for an effectual forgiveness of sins, cleansing of the conscience, and complete sanctification for all who believe.[34]

"By the blood of Jesus," too, we have the privileged assurance of access before the heavenly throne of grace, into the very presence of God (4:6). And for those who thus draw nigh to God through him he makes intercession as our exalted and eternal high priest. And he is able to save (7:25). Here again, exhortation presents the logical consequences of theology: "Therefore, brothers, since we have confidence to enter the Most Holy Place by the blood of Jesus, by a new and living way opened for us through the curtain, that is, his body, and since we have a great priest over the house of God, let us draw near to God with a sincere heart in full assurance of faith, having our hearts sprinkled to cleanse us from a guilty conscience and having our bodies washed with pure water" (10:19–22). Exhortation is obviously informed, quite amply, by theology, here summarily.[35]

The Christology of Hebrews serves the exhortatory purpose. Ernst Kasemann has exemplified the intention, at the conclusion of his study, as follows: "An objective confirmation of hope is needed and offered: first, the example of Christ as our Pioneer evokes the necessity of following in his steps; second, the glimpse of him as our heavenly High priest points to the certainty of the goal."[36]

## Christian life

In the "exhortatory" sections, the theology of the "expository" treatise is not only extended and applied, but a theology of Christian life is presented as well.

Faith is central to this theology.[37] Faith means, in the first instance, affirmative response to the divine Word of promise, but then also tenacious perseverance on the way entered (see chapter 11). The contrast to faith and faithfulness is apostasy. Sin deceitfully entangles its victim (see 12:1) and hardens his heart (see 3:13–14), and thus achieves

---

33. Bornkamm, "Das Bekenntnis im Hebräerbrief," in *Studien zu Antike und Urchristentum*, 201.
34. See McCown, "So Great a Salvation," in *An Inquiry Into Soteriology*, 169–194.
35. See Schierse, *Verheissung und Heilsvollendung*, 201.
36. Käsemann, *Das wandernde Gottesvolk*, 156.
37. See Grässer, *Der Glaube im Hebräerbrief*.

its goal—apostasy from the living God. And for such an apostate—the exhorter would sound a stern warning—there exists no possibility for a second repentance.

Thus, the Christian, on her way under the Word, finds herself confronted with a decisive decision: Will she diligently pursue faith or fall prey to sin? That is to say, will he continue in his pilgrimage with God's people, obeying God's Word and pursuing its promise, or will he disobey, give up on the promise, and fall away from God and his people?

Moreover, it must be noted that the health of the entire community stands at stake wherever there be "feeble arms" and "weak knees" (12:12). The peace and holiness of the church are threatened if anyone "misses the grace of God," or if a "bitter root" springs up and causes trouble or if (God forbid!) someone sells out to the world (12:15–17). The members, therefore, must exercise responsibility one for the other and take oversight for those in danger of collapsing and/or relapsing. Through the stimulus of mutual exhortation, the congregation should be goaded onward, its faith kept lively. The hardened heart, unless roused, will grow torpid, susceptible to the evil deceit of sin, which thrives where faith has become dormant.

## Conclusion

It was his pastoral concern for the readers that prompted the author to write Hebrews.[38] His purpose in sending them this exhortatory letter was practical,[39] to quicken their faith. That was a critical need in the congregation, especially among some of the members.

The purpose of this letter is expressly exhortatory. Its exhortations are not merely parentheses nor digressions in the theological argument. Rather, it is in these sections that the concerns of this pastor and the needs of his audience are most explicitly revealed and addressed. Thus, the exhortatory sections provide us with the keys to a proper interpretation of the theological expositions in this pastor's "word of exhortation."[40]

Hebrews is a pastoral letter. That is not to denigrate the role of theology. Rather, theology makes a significant contribution to the letter's exhortation, giving it substance and significance. On the other hand, it is necessary to give the primacy to exhortation if Hebrews is to be properly interpreted on its own terms.

---

38. Lane (*Hebrews*, 567) characterizes the motivating factor as "sustained pastoral concern."

39. The ultimate purpose of this letter is labeled "practical" by Windisch, *Der Herbräerbrief,* 131; Spicq, *L'Épître aux Hébreux,* I, 4.

40. Michel (*Der Brief an die Hebräer,* 5) concludes: "The chief weight lies on exhortation (paranesis), not on a theological framework; here is where the theological ideas reach their end." Schierse (*Verheissung und Heilsvollendung,* 11) asserts: "Perhaps the long-sought 'key' to the Epistle to the Hebrews can be found in the exhortatory texts which it contains."

## Bibliography

Bornkamm, Günther. "Das Bekenntnis im Hebräerbrief." In *Studien zu Antike und Urchristentum*, Gesammelte Aufsatze 2. Munich: Kaiser, 1959.

———. "Sohnschaft und Leiden." In *Judentum-Urchristentum-Kirche*. Berlin: Töpelmann, 1960.

Bruce, F. F. *The Epistle to the Hebrews*. New International Commentary on the New Testament. Rev. ed. Grand Rapids: Eerdmans, 1990.

Calvin, John. *Hebrews and I and II Peter*. Translated by W. B. Johnston. Calvin's New Testament Commentaries. Grand Rapids: Eerdmans, 1970.

Clemen, Carl. "The Oldest Christian Sermon (Hebrews III and IV)." *The Expositor* 5 (1896) 392–400.

Cockerill, Gareth L. *Hebrews*. Indianapolis: Wesleyan Publishing House, 1999.

Erdman, Charles R. *The Epistle to the Hebrews*. Erdman Commentary on the New Testament. Rev. ed. Grand Rapids: Baker, 1983.

Filson, Floyd V. *"Yesterday": A Study of Hebrews in the Light of Chapter 13*. Studies in Biblical Theology 2/4. Naperville, IL: Allenson, 1967.

Grässer, Erich. *Der Glaube im Hebräerbrief*. Marburg: Elwert, 1965.

———. "Der Herbräerbrief 1938–1963." *Theologische Rundschau* 30 (1964) 138–236.

Guthrie, Donald. *New Testament Introduction: Hebrews to Revelation*. Chicago: InterVarsity Press, 1962.

Gyllenberg, Rafael. "Die Komposition des Hebräerbriefes." *Svensk Exegetisk Årsbok* 22/23 (1957/58) 137–47.

Héring, Jean. *L'Épître aux Hébreux*. Commentaire du Nouveau Testament 12. Neuchatel: Delachaux & Niestlé, 1954.

Käsemann, Ernst. *The Wandering People of God: An Investigation of the Letter to the Hebrews*. Translated by Roy A. Harrisville.. Minneapolis: Augsburg, 1984.

———. *Das wandernde Gottesvolk: Eine Untersuchung zum Hebräerbrief*. Forschungen zur Religion und Literatur des Alten und Neuen Testaments 55. Göttingen: Vandehoeck & Ruprecht, 1957.

Kuss, Otto. *Der Brief an die Hebräer*. Regensburger Neues Testament 8. Regensburg: Puset, 1953.

———. "Der Verfasser des Hebräerbriefes als Seeslsorger." In *Auslegung und Verkundigung*. Regensburg: Puset, 1963.

Lane, William L. *Hebrews*. Word Biblical Commentary 47. Dallas: Word Books, 1991.

McCown, Wayne. "Holiness in Hebrews." *Wesleyan Theological Journal* 16/2 (1981) 58–78.

———. *The Nature and Function of the Hortatory Sections in the Epistle to the Hebrews*. Ann Arbor, MI: University Microfilms, 1970.

———. "So Great a Salvation: The Soteriology of the Epistle to the Hebrews." In *An Inquiry into Soteriology*, edited by John E. Hartley and R. Larry Shelton, 169–194. Anderson, IN: Warner, 1981.

———. "Unforgivable Sin." *Kardia: A Journal of Wesleyan Thought* (1985) 9–23.

Michel, Otto. *Der Brief an die Hebräer*. Kritisch-exegetischer Kommentar über das Neue Testament 13. Göttingen: Vandenhoeck & Ruprecht, 1955.

Moffatt, James. *Epistle to the Hebrews*. International Critical Commentary. Edinburgh: T. & T. Clark, 1963.

Nauck, Wolfgang. "Zum Aufbau des Hebräerbriefes." In *Judentum–Urchristentum–Kirche: Festschrift für Joachim Jeremias*, edited by Walter Eltester, 2013–203. Beihefte zur Zeitschrift für die neutestamentliche Wissenschaft und die Kunde der älteren Kirche 26. Berlin: Töpelmann 1960.

Purdy, Alexander C. "The Epistle to the Hebrews." In *The Interpreter's Bible*, edited by George Arthur Buttrick, vol. 11. New York: Abingdon-Cokesbury, 1955.

Robinson, Theodore B. *The Epistle to the Hebrews*. Moffatt New Testament Commentary. London: Hodder & Stoughton, 1933.

Robinson, W. "Eschatology of the Epistle to the Hebrews. A Study in the Christian Doctrine of Hope." *Encounter* 22 (1961) 37–51.

Schierse, Franz Joseph. *Verheissung und Heilsvollendung: Zur theologische Grundfrage des Hebräerbriefes*. Müchener theologische Studien, I: Historishe Abteilung 9. Munich: Zink, 1955.

Spicq, C. *L'Épître aux Hébreux*. Vol. 2. Sources bibliques. Paris: Lecoffre, 1952.

Windisch, Hans. *Der Herbräerbrief*. Handbuch zum Neuen Testament 14. Tübingen: Mohr/Siebeck, 1931.

# 11

## A Survey of Attempts to Tackle an "Unsolved Problem": The Literary Structure of Hebrews in Contemporary Scholarly Discussion[1]

— James P. Sweeney[2]

The document known traditionally as "The Epistle of Paul to the Hebrews"[3] is both intriguing and challenging. Many of the traditional questions of historical introduction resist certain answers.[4] Hebrews lacks the distinctive introductory elements common to ancient letters.[5] Unlike the Pauline and Catholic letters of the New Testament, moreover, there is no explicit designation of authorship. It is thus formally an anonymous document.[6] Additionally, there is no internal textual reference to the recipients.[7] Literary issues like structure, genre, and purpose also pose their own

---

1. I acknowledge Logos Bible Software (http://www.logos.com) with appreciation for granting me permission to incorporate into this essay some previously published material from my article, "Hebrews, Letter to the, Critical Issues," in *Lexham Bible Dictionary*.

2. I count it a privilege to contribute the following essay in honor of Professor Paul Livermore. I had the privilege of studying with Paul in 1987–1988. His broad interests in the Hebrew Bible, Second Temple Judaism, New Testament, Patristic Studies, Christian History, and Christian Doctrine were an impetus to me as an undergraduate to cast the proverbial net widely. In an age of increasing specialization, Paul is a reminder of the importance of breadth of learning. In the present essay I'll examine a subject that has received a good deal of attention since the late 1980s when I first studied with Paul: namely, the problem of the literary structure of Hebrews.

3. This is the traditional title affixed in various editions of the Authorized (or King James) Version.

4. I survey historical matters like authorship, provenance, date, recipients, and destination at some length in the aforementioned article, "Hebrews, Letter to the."

5. Ancient Greco-Roman letters had a conventional three-part structure: an opening, body, and closing. See esp. White, "Epistolary Literature," 1731; and "Greek Letters," 97. On more general matters related to letter writing, see also Richards, *Letter Writing*.

6. The author's reference to Timothy (Heb 13:23), however, does suggest someone in, or at least familiar with, the Pauline circle.

7. The earliest (extra-textual) testimony to the recipients' identity is found in the title heading of the Chester Beatty Papyrus II collection (P46): namely, "To the Hebrews" (πρὸς Ἑβραίους). The Beatty collection is the oldest Greek manuscript tradition preserving the letters of Paul and is dated to the late second century AD. In this collection Hebrews is placed after Romans.

difficulties for interpreters. The primary focus of the present essay will be the first of these: namely, the literary structure of Hebrews.

Interpreters of the early twentieth century commonly acknowledged difficulties in identifying the divisions in the literary structure of Hebrews. Brooke Foss Westcott (1825–1901), in the posthumously published third edition of his commentary (1903) noted that the general progress of Hebrews was "clear." He nonetheless conceded that "in a writing so many sided, with subjects unnaturally foreshadowed and recalled, differences of opinion must arise as to the exact divisions of the argument."[8] William Wrede (1859–1906), likewise, in a work published the year of his death, characterized Hebrews as a "literary riddle."[9] James Moffatt (1870–1944), in his 1924 commentary in the ICC series, maintained it was "artificial" even to divide up a writing of the kind of Hebrews. Consequently, he "deliberately abstained from introducing any formal divisions and subdivisions in the commentary."[10]

Late twentieth century scholars similarly acknowledge the similar difficulties regarding the literary structure of Hebrews. In 1986 David Alan Black published an essay entitled (in part), "The Problem of the Literary Structure of Hebrews."[11] The following year, David E. Aune characterized the literary structure of Hebrews as "an unsolved problem."[12] As a consequence, a variety of methodological approaches has been applied to Hebrews. The present essay will survey representatively a broad selection of these approaches as interpreters attempt to press forward toward greater clarity. Attention will at points be given to the interconnected question of *genre* (type of literature) only insofar as it bears on the matter of the literary structure of Hebrews.

## A Broad Survey of the Application of Differing Types of Analysis to the Literary Structure of Hebrews

The ensuing survey will examine representative types of literary analysis that contemporary scholars have applied to the literary structure of Hebrews. For convenience, the types of analysis will be grouped under the following seven headings: thematic, structural, text linguistic, rhetorical, socio-rhetorical, discourse, and chiastic.

### The Application of Thematic Analysis to the Literary Structure of Hebrews

A thematic approach is perhaps the most common type of literary analysis applied to Hebrews. F. F. Bruce (1910–1990) applied this form analysis to Hebrews in the first and second editions of his widely-used commentary on Hebrews in the New International

---

8. Westcott, *Epistle to the Hebrews*, xlviii.
9. Wrede, *Das literarische Rätsel*.
10. Moffatt, *Epistle to the Hebrews*, xxiii–xxiv.
11. Black, "Literary Structure of Hebrews," 163–77.
12. Aune, *Literary Environment*, 213.

Commentary of the New Testament.[13] Bruce organized the content of Hebrews under eight thematic headings: The Finality of Christianity (1:1–2:18); The True Home of the People of God (3:1–4:14); The High Priesthood of Christ (4:15–6:20); The Order of Melchizedek (7:1–28); Covenant, Sanctuary, and Sacrifice (8:1–10:18); Call to Worship, Faith, and Perseverance (10:19–12:29); Concluding Exhortation (13:1–22); and Postscript (13:23–25).[14] Bruce's understanding of the literary structure of Hebrews clearly influenced Paul Ellingworth's commentary in the New International Greek Testament Commentary series.[15]

In a detailed two-volume contribution to the Word Biblical commentary series, William L. Lane (1931–1999) stressed the oral, sermonic character of Hebrews.[16] He organized its content thematically in five major sections. He further indicated the prominent role of the author's warnings throughout the argument: 1. The Revelation of God through His Son (1:1–2:18 [*The First Warning*: The Peril of Ignoring the Word Delivered by the Son (2:1–4)]); 2. The High Priestly Character of the Son (3:1–5:10 [*The Second Warning*: The Peril of Refusing to Believe God's Word (3:7–19)]); 3. The High Priestly Office of the Son (5:11–10:39 [*The Third Warning*: The Peril of Spiritual Immaturity (5:11–6:12) and *The Fourth Warning*: The Peril of Disloyalty to Christ (10:19–39)]); 4. Loyalty to God through Persevering Faith (11:1–12:13); and 5. Orientation for Life as Christians in a Hostile World (12:14–13:25 [*The Final Warning*: The Peril of Refusing God's Gracious Word (12:14–29)]).[17]

The noted Roman Catholic scholar Raymond Brown (1928–1998) likewise preferred a form of thematic analysis to more formal approaches like that of Vanhoye (see below).[18] Brown identified "superiority" as the principal motif of Hebrews 1:4–10:18. It was clearly reflected in his seven-part outline: 1. Introduction (1:1–3); 2. Superiority of Jesus as God's Son (1:4–4:13); 3. Superiority of Jesus's priesthood (4:14–7:28); 4. Superiority of Jesus's sacrifice and his ministry in the heavenly tabernacle inaugurating a new covenant (8:1–10:18); 5. Faith and endurance: availing oneself of Jesus's priestly work (10:19–12:29); 6. Injunctions about practice (13:1–19); and 7. Conclusion: blessing and greetings (13:20–25).[19]

---

13. F. F. Bruce's NICNT commentary was originally published in 1964 and reissued in a second edition (1990). The second edition has been replaced by Gareth Lee Cockerill's contribution. See below.

14. Bruce, *Hebrews* (1990), viii–x; see xix–xxii. Other than differences of typeset and the removal of the superfluous Ch./Chs. designations of the 1964 edition, the second (1990) edition retains the same outline as the first edition.

15. Paul Ellingworth, *Epistle to the Hebrews*. Ellingworth cites the entirety of Bruce's outline from the first edition (50–53). Ellingworth's own six-part outline exhibits many similarities: see, e.g., vi, 89, 107, 193, 297, 558, 661.

16. Lane, *Hebrews 1–8*, lxix–lxxv. He was admittedly indebted to the work of H. Thyen, *Der Stil*.

17. Lane, *Hebrews 1–8*, viii–ix *et passim*.

18. Brown, *Introduction*, 691.

19. Brown, *Introduction*, 684.

Gareth Lee Cockerill provides a more recent thematic analysis.[20] He favors a division of Heb 1–12 into three parts, owing to the parallel character of 4:14–16 and 10:19–25. He further notes that Christ's high priesthood, the author's main theme, dominates the central portion. Cockerill's outline attempts to emphasize the author's imagery and the concrete way he has arranged his material to motivate his hearers.[21] Cockerill organizes his outline around a narrative storyline in which the Son's high priesthood is central (see figure 1 below).

Table 11.1: Cockerill's Thematic Outline of Hebrews

---

I. A Very Short History of the Disobedient People of God (1:1–4:13):

  A. Sinai Revisited: God Has Spoken in the Eternal, Incarnate, Now Exalted Son (1:1–2:18)

  B. Tested at Kadesh-Barnea: Avoid the Congregation of the Disobedient (3:1–4:13)

II. The Son's High Priesthood—Resource and Urgency of Perseverance (4:14–10:18):

  A. The Life of Faith and the High Priesthood of the Son (4:14–5:10)

  B. Don't Be Unresponsive But Grasp What Christ Has Provided (5:11–6:20)

  C. Our High Priest's Legitimacy and Eternity (7:1–28)

  D. Our High Priest's All-Sufficient Sacrifice: A Symphony of Three Movements (8:1–10:18)

III. A History of the Faithful People of God from Creation to Consummation (10:19–12:29):

  A. The Life of Persevering Faith and the High Priesthood of the Son (10:19–39)

  B. The Past History of the People of God until the Coming of Jesus (11:1–12:3)

  C. The Present History of the People of God until the Consummation (12:4–29)

IV. Instructions for the Life of Gratitude and Godly Fear (13:1–25)[22]

---

The advantage of thematic approaches to the literary structure of Hebrews is that they often provide a good indication of what a given commentator takes to be the central themes of the book. The potential disadvantage, however, is that this form of literary analysis is commonly driven by identified themes rather than grammatical and structural markers that the author employed.

---

20. Cockerill, *Epistle to the Hebrews*. As noted above, it replaces Bruce's second (1990) edition in the NICNT series, in keeping with Gordon D. Fee's goal, as series editor at that time, of keeping the series up-to-date.

  21. Cockerill, *Epistle to the Hebrews*, 61–62.

  22. Cockerill, *Epistle to the Hebrews*, 78–81.

### The Application of Structural Analysis to the Literary Structure of Hebrews

The most prominent scholar who applied structural analysis to Hebrews is the noted Jesuit scholar Albert Vanhoye (b. 1923). He authored a wide number of works on the literary structure of Hebrews.[23] He identified six structuralizing techniques that the author employed:

1. Announcement of the subjects to be discussed.
2. Inclusions which indicate the boundaries of the developments.
3. Variation of literary genre (exposition or paraenesis).
4. Words which characterize a development.
5. Transition by immediate repetition of an expression or of a work (i.e., a "hook word").
6. Symmetric arrangements.[24]

Vanhoye organized the central content of Hebrews as a tightly arranged chiasm (literary inversion) exhibiting five key points (see figure 2 below).

Table 11.2: Vanhoye's Chiastic Structure of Hebrews[25]

| |
|---|
| 1:1–4 Exordium |
| 1:5–2:18 First Part (The Name of Christ) |
| 3:1–5:10 Second Part (Christ, the High Priest Merciful and Worthy of Faith) |
| 5:11–10:39 Third Part (The Unequaled Value of the Priesthood and of the Sacrifice of Christ) |
| 11:1–12:13 Fourth Part (Faith and Endurance) |
| 12:14–13:19 Fifth Part (Straight Paths!) |
| 13:20–21 Peroration (Conclusion) |
| 13:22–25 Word in Parting |

Reactions to Vanhoye's work have been mixed. Many German and American scholars have viewed his work with varying levels of reservation. This has been prompted by what has been viewed as its complexity and the artificial nature of the elaborate chiasm for which he argued.[26] David Alan Black, by contrast, was favorably

---

23. Vanhoye's many analyses included: "De structura litteraria," 73–80; "Discussion sur la structure," 349–80; *La structure littéraire*; *Structure and Message*; and "Hebräerbrief," 498–99. The following references will refer to his fullest (1989) work, *Structure and Message*; see also "Hebräerbrief" (1993).

24. Vanhoye, *Structure*, 19–20.

25. Vanhoye, *Structure*, 18–36, 80–109.

26. Kümmel, for example, considered Vanhoye's chiastic structure "contrived" (*Introduction*, 390); see also Brown, *Introduction*, 691; and Cockerill, *Hebrews*, 60.

disposed toward it. He observed that "the detailed literary and stylistic investigation attempted by Vanhoye has resulted in the amassing of a phalanx of objective literary facts which simply cannot be ignored."[27]

A major alternative to Vanhoye's structural approach is a tripartite approach to the literary structure of Hebrews. There is some contemporary debate as to who should be credited with introducing this approach. Cynthia Long Westfall credits Otto Michel's commentary with first suggesting a tripartite structure.[28] Udo Schnelle, by contrast, maintains Wolfgang Nauck was the originator.[29] Albert Vanhoye identified the still earlier example of Otto Kuss.[30]

Hans-Friedrich Weiß is a more recent example of a tripartite approach to the literary structure of Hebrews: 1:1–4:13: God's Final Word in his Son (*Gottes endgültige Rede in seinem Sohn*); 4:14–10:18: The Christological Foundation of the Earnest Appeal of Faith (*Der christologische Grund der Glaubensparaklese*); and 10:19–13:25: The Earnest Appeal of Faith (*Die Glaubensparaklese*).[31] Udo Schnelle also offers three-part analysis: 1:1–4:13; 4:14–10:31; and 10:32–13:25.[32]

## The Application of Text-Linguistic Analysis to the Literary Structure of Hebrews

George H. Guthrie analyzes Hebrews according to textual linguistics.[33] Textual linguistics is a branch of linguistics which seeks to approach texts as communication systems. Its original aim was to uncover and describe text grammars. The application of text linguistics has evolved from this approach in that texts are viewed in much broader terms that go beyond a mere extension of traditional grammar towards an entire text. Guthrie seeks to understand Hebrews as an interplaying of units of text in a discourse. He seeks further to be sensitive to the literary and

27. Black, "Literary Structure of Hebrews," 163–77; here 176.

28. Michel, *Der Brief*, 29–35, as noted in Cynthia Long Westfall, *Discourse Analysis*, 12 and n. 56.

29. Nauck, "Zum Aufbau," 199–206, as noted by Udo Schnelle, *History and Theology*, 371 n. 21.

30. Kuss, "Der Brief," as noted by Albert Vanhoye, "Hebräerbrief," 494–505 (here 498), where Vanhoye credits Kuss, Michel, Nauck (in that order). Vanhoye references both editions of Kuss's commentary ("Hebräerbrief," 503). Werner Georg Kümmel (*Introduction*, 390 n. 1) had earlier credited Kuss, Michel, and Nauck, but provided no bibliographic details on Kuss.

31. Weiß, *Der Brief*, 8–9. For a similar recent assessment of Hebrews' structure, see Allen, *Hebrews*, 87–94. Allen follows the same divisions, but additionally marks out a prologue (1:1–4) and conclusion/final greetings (13:22–25).

32. Schnelle, *History and Theology*, 370. Schnelle simply entitles these sections Part One, Two, and Three. He does not provide titles for the parts. Note that his delineations of the parameters of sections two and three differ slightly from those of Weiß.

33. George H. Guthrie has contributed widely to the study of Hebrews. This doctoral dissertation was devoted to the subject of "The Structure of Hebrews" (Ph.D. diss., 1991), the substance of which was published as *Structure of Hebrews*. He has additionally written a popular-level commentary on Hebrews (*Hebrews* [NIV Application Commentary]) and a number of related articles on Hebrews: "Old Testament in Hebrews," 841–50; "The Case for Apollos as Author of Hebrews," 41–56; "New Testament Exegesis of Hebrews," 591–605; and "Hebrews," in *Commentary on the New Testament Use*, 919–95.

oratorical conventions of the first century.[34] As is common, Guthrie identifies 1:1–4 as an introduction. He argues that the literary structure of Hebrews consists of a combination of expository units and hortatory units. The expository units develop step-by-step, both spatially and logically.[35] The hortatory units do not develop in the same way, but reiterate certain key topics.[36] The author seeks to challenge the recipients through them.[37] Guthrie identifies two major expository portions in Hebrews 1:5–10:25. Both are related to the Son's position: 1. The Position of the Son in Relation to Angels (1:5–2:18) and 2. The Position of the Son, Our High Priest, in Relation to the Earthly Sacrificial System (4:14–10:25). Guthrie sees key turning points (overlaps between exposition and exhortation) at 4:14–16 and 10:19–25.[38] He views 4:14–16 as the opening to section II; 10:19–25 closes it. Hebrews 10:32–39 and 11:1–40 offer positive examples. Hebrews 12 provides exhortations (12:1–2, 3–17, 18–24) and a warning (12:25–29). Hebrews 13 concludes with exhortations (13:1–19), a benediction (13:20–21), and a closing (13:22–25).[39]

The Australian New Testament scholar Peter O'Brien maintains that Guthrie has made a substantial contribution to the understanding the structure of Hebrews.[40] O'Brien's own commentary outline (largely thematic) is clearly and admittedly indebted to Guthrie.[41] Cockerill similarly considers Guthrie's work "insightful," but with more qualification.[42]

### The Application of Socio-Rhetorical Analysis to the Literary Structure of Hebrews

Socio-Rhetorical analysis draws on a form of interpretation which Vernon K. Robbins developed.[43] It attempts to draw upon a broad spectrum of methodologies in the study of texts. The methodologies employed involve literary forms of analysis (literary, narrative, intertextual, and rhetorical) and the application of the social sciences.

David A. deSilva applies a form of this kind of analysis to Hebrews in a socio-rhetorical commentary. deSilva suggests that the author of Hebrews has two primary foci. First is the author's rhetorical strategy in seeking to persuade the recipients to

---

34. Guthrie, *Structure*, xviii.
35. Guthrie, *Structure*, 126.
36. Guthrie, *Structure*, 127.
37. Guthrie, *Structure*, 139.
38. Guthrie, *Structure*, 117; see also his *Hebrews*, 39–40.
39. Guthrie, *Structure*, 131–4; see *Hebrews*, 39–40.
40. O'Brien, *The Letter to the Hebrews*, 30–34.
41. O'Brien, *The Letter to the Hebrews*, viii–x; see 34. O'Brien's structural outline has nine points.
42. Cockerill, *Hebrews*, 61 (see below).
43. Vernon K. Robbins is a prominent interpretive theorist. His works include *Tapestry*; *Texture of Texts*; *Jesus the Teacher*; and *Sea Voyages*. His influence is further seen in several works: Jack N. Lightstone, *Mishnah and the Social Formation*; and Kayle B. De Waal, *A Socio-Rhetorical Interpretation*. See too David B. Gowler et al., eds., *Fabrics of Discourse*.

remain committed to the Christian faith. The second are the social effects of the recipients' acceptance of the author's message.[44] deSilva first profiles the recipients and the author.[45] He then traces the rhetorical goal and socio-rhetorical strategy of Hebrews.[46] deSilva maintains that the author of Hebrews employs elements of both epideictic and deliberative oratory.[47] The author confronts his recipients with two opposing courses of action: remain committed or turn away. The author's argument is calculated to heighten the advantages and positive consequences of commitment. The author likewise exposed the disastrous consequences of turning away.[48] In terms of structure, deSilva outlines Hebrews in ten segments: 1. Responding to God's Word and Work in the Son (1:1–2:18); 2. The Inexpediency of Distrust (3:1–4:13); 3. Jesus, Our Guarantor of God's Favor (4:14–5:10); 4. Honoring God Necessitates Perseverance (5:11–6:20); 5. Jesus, the Better-Qualified Mediator of God's Favor (7:1–8:13); 6. The Decisive Removal of Sin's Defilement (9:1–10:18); 7. Draw Near to God and to Each Other (10:19–39); 8. Faith's Orientation in the World (11:1–12:3); 9. In Training for the Kingdom (12:4–29); and 10. Living in Gratitude to God (13:1–25).[49]

## The Application of Rhetorical Analysis to the Literary Structure of Hebrews

A growing number of commentators have applied rhetorical criticism to Hebrews. Rhetorical analysis seeks to apply the New Testament writings the rules of ancient Graeco-Roman rhetoric that governed speeches.[50] Harold W. Attridge identifies Hebrews as a form of epideictic rhetoric.[51] Epideictic rhetoric was one of three principal species of rhetoric attested in the rhetorical handbooks. A speaker employed it to persuade the audience to hold or reaffirm some viewpoint in the *present*.[52] Attridge maintains Hebrews begins with an Exordium [i.e., Introduction] (1:1–4) followed by an argument of five parts: 1. Christ exalted and humiliated, a suitable High Priest (1:5–2:18). 2. Christ faithful and merciful (3:1–5:10). 3. The difficult discourse

---

44. deSilva, *Perseverance in Gratitude*, xiv; see his earlier *Despising Shame*.

45. deSilva, *Perseverance in Gratitude*, 1–39.

46. deSilva, *Perseverance in Gratitude*, 39–80.

47. deSilva, *Perseverance in Gratitude*, 48. Epideictic was a species of (oral) rhetoric used to persuade an audience to hold or reaffirm some viewpoint in the *present*. Deliberative rhetoric was a species of (oral) rhetoric used to persuade an audience to take some action in the *future*. See below.

48. deSilva, *Perseverance in Gratitude*, 56.

49. deSilva, *Perseverance in Gratitude*, 83–483.

50. Kennedy, *Rhetorical Criticism*; Classen, *Rhetorical Criticism*, chs. 1–3; Watson, *Rhetoric of the New Testament*; Black and Watson, eds., *Words Well Spoken*; and Witherington, *New Testament Rhetoric*. Classen notes that Melanchthon (AD 1497–1560) and others applied a type of this analysis to the New Testament texts (*Criticism*, chs. 1 and 5).

51. Attridge, *Epistle to the Hebrews*, 14.

52. See Kennedy, *Rhetorical Criticism*, 19.

(5:11–10:25). 4. Exhortation to faithful endurance (10:26–12:13). 5. Concluding exhortations (12:14–13:21).[53]

Craig S. Koester maintains that characterizing Hebrews as either deliberative or epideictic rhetoric is not helpful.[54] Rather, it functions as both simultaneously, depending on where the recipients are in relation to the message. For those who remain committed, Hebrews is epideictic. For those who are drifting away, it is deliberative.[55] Koester organizes Hebrews in a fully rhetorical outline: 1. Exordium (1:1–2:4). 2. Proposition (2:5–9). 3. Arguments (2:10–12:27) in three series (2:10–6:20; 7:1–10:39; 11:1–12:27); 4. Peroration [i.e., Closing] (12:28–13:21); and 5. Epistolary Postscript (13:22–25).[56]

Ben Witherington III, like Attridge, views Hebrews as a form of epideictic rhetoric.[57] As is common with this kind of analysis, Witherington views 1:1–4 as an exordium (introduction). He next identifies two rounds of exposition and exhortation (1:5–2:4 and 3:1–19), a reflection on rest (4:1–14), a further round of exposition and exhortation (4:14–5:10), an exhortation against apostasy (5:11–6:12), a *transitus* (literary transition) (6:1–20), and a central exposition in two parts (7:1–8:6 and 8:7–10:18). Following this is an exhortation to adhere (10:19–39). 11:1–12:17 calls for faithfulness. Witherington maintains 12:18–29 is a peroration (concluding portion) describing theophanies behind and before the recipients. He suggests that Hebrews closes with final exhortations and an epistolary closing (ch. 13).[58]

James W. Thompson applies another form of rhetorical analysis to Hebrews. Thompson notes the author's indebtedness both to the Jewish homiletical tradition and Greek rhetoric. He detects several Greek rhetorical devices. *Synkrisis* (comparison) is predominant. Other devices include his mode of argumentation, abundant use of terminology from logical proof, and in arguments based on what is necessary (7:12; 9:16, 23),[59] impossible (6:18; 10:4),[60] and appropriate (2:10).[61] Thompson combines a common tripartite division along with Aristotelian rhetorical analysis (see figure 3 below).

---

53. Attridge, *Epistle to the Hebrews*, 19.

54. Speakers employed deliberative rhetoric to persuade the audience to take some action in the *future* (see Kennedy, *Rhetorical Criticism*, 19).

55. Koester, *Hebrews*, 82.

56. Koester, *Hebrews*, 84–85.

57. Witherington, *Letters and Homilies*, 127.

58. Witherington, *Letters and Homilies*, 97–351.

59. In these passages the noun ἀνάγκη ("necessary"—Heb 7:12) is employed. In Heb 9:16, 23 ἐστίν is understood: "[it is] necessary."

60. Both passages begin with the same language: Ἀδύνατον γὰρ ("for it is impossible . . ."); see too 6:18 and 11:6.

61. ἔπρεπεν γὰρ αὐτῷ ("for it was fitting for him"); see too 7:26.

Table 11.3: Thompson's Structural Outline of Hebrews

---

Hearing God's word and faithful endurance (1:1–4:13): *Exordium* [Opening]: Encountering God's ultimate word (1:1–4); and *Narratio* [The facts to be argued]: Hearing God's word with faithful endurance (1:5–4:13)

*Probatio* [The major argument or proof section]: Discovering certainty and confidence and the word for the mature (4:14–10:31): Drawing near and holding firmly: following the path of Jesus from suffering to triumph (4:14–5:10); Preparing to hear the word that is hard to explain (5:11–6:20); Grasping the anchor in the word for the mature: the sacrificial work of Christ as the assurance of God's promises (7:1–28); and drawing near and holding firmly in an unwavering faith (8:1–10:31)

*Peroratio* [Concluding portion]: On not refusing the one who is speaking (10:32–13:25): Enduring in hope: the faithfulness of Jesus and the faithfulness of the ancestors (10:32–12:13); Listening to the one who is speaking from heaven (12:14–29); and Bearing with the word of exhortation (12:30–13:25)

---

## The Application of Discourse Analysis to the Literary Structure of Hebrews

Cynthia Long Westfall applies discourse analysis to the text of Hebrews.[62] It is a form of systemic functional linguistics developed for the study of Hellenistic Greek. She also draws on additional linguistic studies. As many prior to her, Westfall maintains that the literary structure of Hebrews is tripartite: 1. 1:1–4:16. 2. 4:11–10:25 (two parts: 4:11–7:28 and 8:1–10:25). 3. 10:19–13:25.[63] She further views 4:11–16 and 10:19–25 as transitional units. They stand respectively between the second and third sections. Each unit has three hortatory subjunctives (the "Let us . . ." structures). These two triads of hortatory subjunctives "are both the destination and point of departure of the surrounding units—they tend to belong to both units."[64] The resultant structure emerging from Westfall's study can be represented, for convenience, in figure 4.

---

62. Westfall, *Discourse Analysis*.

63. Westfall, *Discourse Analysis*, chs. 4–6; see similarly Weiß, *Der Brief*, 8–9, and the earlier discussion.

64. Westfall, *Discourse Analysis*, 297.

Table 11.4: Westfall's Tripartite Analysis of Hebrews with
Interlocking Literary Transitions

---

I. Jesus—the Apostle of Our Confession (1:1–4:16)

< Literary transition between sections I and II: 4:11–16 >

II.A. Jesus the High Priest of Our Confession, Part 1: A Priest according to the Order of Melchizedek (4:11–7:28)

II.B. Jesus the High Priest of Our Confession, Part 2: A Priest who Equips Us to Draw Near to God (8:1–10:25)

< Literary transition between sections II and III: 10:19–25 >

III. Partners in a Heavenly Calling—The Priesthood of the Believers (10:19–13:25)

---

David L. Allen's 2010 commentary on Hebrews in the New American Commentary series reflects Westfall's influence. Between a prologue (1:1–4) and conclusion/final greetings (13:22–25), he identifies three sections: I. The Superiority of the Son (1:5–4:13); II. Obligations of Jesus's Priestly Office and Saving Work (4:14–10:18); and III. Exhortation to Draw Near, Hold Fast, and Love One Another (10:19–13:21).[65]

One of the potential weaknesses of her analysis is her interpretation of Psalm 95 in Heb 3:7–4:1. She maintains that Jesus is the speaker. Cotterill questions whether this is sustainable at the exegetical level.[66]

## The Application of Chiastic Analysis to the Literary Structure of Hebrews

In a 2010 publication, John Paul Heil treats Hebrews as an elaborate chiasm.[67] He determines the chiasms throughout Hebrews by applying a list of nine criteria which Craig Blomberg delineated in a 1989 article on 2 Corinthians 1–7.[68] Blomberg's nine criteria are as follows: 1. There must be a problem in perceiving the literary structure of the text in question, which more conventional outlines fail to resolve. 2. There must be clear examples of parallelism between the two "halves" of the hypothesized chiasmus, to which commentators call attention even when they propose quite different outlines for the text overall. 3. Verbal (or grammatical) parallelism as well as conceptual (or structural) parallelism should characterize most if not all of the corresponding pairs of subdivisions. 4. The verbal parallelism should involve central or dominant imagery or terminology, not peripheral or trivial language. 5. Both verbal and conceptual parallelism should involve words and ideas not regularly found elsewhere within the

---

65. Allen, *Hebrews*, 87–94.

66. See Cotterill, *Hebrews*, 60–61.

67. Heil, *Hebrews*. As noted above, Vanhoye also identified the structure of Hebrews as chiastic, but not with the elaborateness exhibited by Heil.

68. Blomberg, "Structure of 2 Corinthians 1–7," 4–20, esp. 4–8. Heil summarizes these criteria in *Hebrews*, 2.

proposed chiasmus. 6. Multiple sets of correspondences between passages opposite each other in the chiasmus as well as multiple members of the chiasmus itself are desirable. 7. The outline should divide the text at natural breaks which would be agreed upon even by those proposing very different structures to account for the whole. 8. The center of the chiasmus, which forms its climax, should be a passage worthy of that position in light of its theological or ethical significance. 9. Ruptures in the outline should be avoided if at all possible.[69]

Heil divides Hebrews into three macrochiastic levels. Heil identifies the entirety of Hebrews as having a basic three-part A-B-A' structure at the first macrochiastic level (see figure 5 below).[70] In addition, he identifies second and third macrochiastic levels which are much more involved. He maintains that the second macrochiastic level divides the three main sections of the first level into an elaborate eleven-part unit (A-B-C-D-E-F-E'-D'-C'-B'-A').[71] The third macrochiastic level divides the first five as well as the final five units of each of these main sections into a total of six patterns of A-B-C-B'-A'.[72]

Table 11.5: Heil's Outline of the First Macro-chiastic Level of the Structure of Hebrews[73]

| |
| --- |
| A) Heb 1:1–5:10: Be Faithful in Heart to Grace from the Son and High Priest |
| B) Heb 5:11–9:28: We Await the High Priest Who Offered Himself to Intercede |
| A') Heb 10:1–13:25: By Faith with Grace in Heart Let Us Do the Will of the Living God |

## Some Brief Reflections on the Contemporary Application of Differing Types of Analysis to the Literary Structure of Hebrews

Contemporary scholarship is by no means agreed on either the results of the varying forms of literary analysis applied to Hebrews or even the best way forward among the approaches. In the late 1980s David Alan Black saw Vanhoye's structural analysis as the way forward.[74] Vanhoye's structural proposal certainly influenced Attridge's Hermeneia commentary.[75] Raymond Brown, however, expressed concern that

---

69. Blomberg, "Structure of 2 Corinthians 1–7," 5–7. Blomberg also expands further on each of these basic points. I've cited only his initial statements.

70. Heil, *Hebrews*, 4–5.

71. Heil, *Hebrews*, 4, 13–14.

72. Heil, *Hebrews*, 4, 14–15.

73. Heil, *Hebrews*, 5.

74. Black, "Literary Structure of Hebrews," 176: "the point of departure for the discussion of [the structural criticism of Hebrews] today—at least in my opinion—must be the thesis of Albert Vanhoye."

75. Attridge, *Epistle to the Hebrews*, 19.

"too formal an approach may be in danger of divorcing Heb[rews] from the clear apologetic goal that it seeks to achieve by stressing the superiority of Christ."[76] Peter O'Brien maintains recently that George Guthrie offers the best way forward.[77] Others favor Westfall's analysis.[78] In assessing the influential works of Vanhoye, Westfall, and Guthrie, however, commentator Gareth Lee Cockerill is more circumspect:

> Although each of these analyses has its values, none of them appear to be fully satisfactory. Vanhoye's insistence on using literary features alone seems artificial. His attempt to force Hebrews into a chiastic mold breaks down in the central section of the book. Westfall's insistence that Jesus is the speaker of Psalm 95 in Heb 3:7–4:1, while essential to her structural analysis, finds no support in the text. Guthrie's insightful work would have been more helpful had he analyzed the expository and hortatory sections as a unity.[79]

Despite the varying conclusions relative to the differing approaches to the literary structure of Hebrews, however, there are some important observations to take away from the contemporary scholarly discussion. One is the wide acknowledgment of the interweaving of exposition and exhortation in Hebrews, with exposition providing the basis for the exhortation that follows.[80] Another is the rich combination of sermonic style and rhetorical features. A wide number of contemporary scholars have stressed the oral character of Hebrews. In contrast to an epistle, Albert Vanhoye suggested Hebrews would be better called "'Preaching on the Priesthood of Christ,' or 'The Priestly Sermon.'"[81] Owing to the parallel language in Acts 13:15 (with 13:16–41), William L. Lane maintained that the author's "word of exhortation" (Heb 13:22) was an "idiomatic expression for a sermon in Hellenistic-Jewish and early Christian circles."[82] With H. Thyen, Lane described Hebrews as "a paraenetic homily in the Hellenistic-Jewish synagogue tradition."[83] Luke Timothy Johnson similarly stresses the oral nature of Hebrews. He notes that it "most resembles a homily."[84] Johnson points to four stylistic features that indicate the oral character of Hebrews. First is the author's use of the first person throughout. Second are the various references to

---

76. Brown, *Introduction*, 691.

77. O'Brien suggests that Guthrie offers "the most satisfying approach" literary structure of Hebrews (*Hebrews*, 34). In his 1991 commentary, William L. Lane was favorably disposed toward Guthrie's analysis and devoted an addendum to Guthrie's text linguistic approach (*Hebrews 1–8*, xc–xcviii).

78. As noted above, David L. Allen's 2010 commentary on Hebrews clearly reflects Westfall's influence (*Hebrews*, 87–94). Andreas Köstenberger, L. Scott Kellum, and Charles L. Quarles are likewise sympathetic to Westfall (*The Cradle*, 680–83).

79. Cockerill, *Hebrews*, 60–61.

80. Guthrie, *Structure*, 139–46.

81. Vanhoye, *Structure*, 5.

82. Lane, *Hebrews 1–8*, lxix–lxxv, and "Hebrews," 449–51. The citation is from "Hebrews," 450.

83. Lane, "Hebrews," 450; see Thyen, *Stil*.

84. Johnson, *Writings*, 458.

speaking (2:5; 6:9; 8:1; 11:32) and hearing (5:11). Third is the masterful alternation between exposition and exhortation. Fourth is the way in which the author introduces and later develops prominent themes.[85]

The works of Vanhoye, Lane, and Johnson are surely on the right track in highlighting the oral character of Hebrews. Lane was further correct in observing a connection with the ancient Jewish homily tradition.[86] More recently, James W. Thompson also acknowledges the author's indebtedness to the Jewish homiletic tradition along with the author's rhetorical background. The homily tradition accounts for the author's rich use of scriptural traditions and pointed admonitions.

Given the oral character of Hebrews, moreover, insights from rhetorical analysis prove quite helpful if kept in perspective. While there are ongoing questions about the applicability of rhetorical analysis in application to the Pauline letters beyond that of matters of style,[87] the implied oral character of Hebrews renders rhetorical analysis quite useful. However, the differences among the rhetorical analyses of the content of Hebrews raise the question of to what degree Hebrews was intended as a thoroughly rhetorical piece. Commentators are not in agreement on the identity of the species of rhetorical invention that the author employed. Was it one or even a combination of species? In the light of this, it may be more accurate to suggest that the author of Hebrews employs rhetorical features at various points throughout the work without intending Hebrews as a formally rhetorical document. As Thompson shrewdly observes, "The author's artistry is evident in the fact that he skillfully avoids displaying the scaffolding of this work as one topic blends into another."[88]

At the structural level, moreover, a tripartite structure continues to prove the most adaptable template for analyzing the content of Hebrews. The principal debate has to do with where to draw the points of delineation between sections two and three. It is here that Westfall offers the helpful suggestion that 4:11–16 and 10:19–25 serve as literary transitions between sections I and II and sections II and III respectively.[89]

The application of differing methods of approach to the literary structure of Hebrews demonstrates how complex and challenging it proves to be for contemporary scholars. No two approaches and no two analyses agree completely in all the details.

---

85. Johnson, *Hebrews*, 10.

86. With Lane (see above), it should be observed that the author of Hebrew's "word of exhortation" (ὁ λόγος τῆς παρακλήσεως; 13:22) certainly has much in common with the epitomized (Pauline) synagogue sermon of Acts 13:16–41, introduced under the same rubric ("a word of exhortation": λόγος παρακλήσεως—Acts 13:15).

87. Scholars like Walton ("Aristotle," 229–50), Weima ("Aristotle," 458–68), and Green (*Thessalonians*, 69–74) question the suitability of applying the rules governing speech to the Pauline letters.

88. Thompson, *Hebrews*, 13.

89. She notes that each unit has three hortatory subjunctives ("Let us . . .") and each triad functions as "both the destination and point of departure of the surrounding units—they tend to belong to both units" (Westfall, *Discourse Analysis*, 297). Guthrie too rightly sees key turning points (overlaps between exposition and exhortation) at 4:14–16 (somewhat narrower than Westfall's 4:11–16) and 10:19–25 (*Structure*, 117).

Yet many of the analyses have provided helpful insights into various aspects of the literary features and argument of Hebrews.

## Challenging Interpretive Matters in Approaching the Literary Structure of Hebrews

Having surveyed the wide variety of methodological approaches to the literary structure of Hebrews, in what follows I will outline very briefly three important areas that have direct relevance for understanding the literary structure of Hebrews.

### The Author's Wide Use of the Scriptures

A commonly recognized feature of Hebrews is the author's wide use of the Scriptures. The precise number of identified Scriptural references varies considerably from interpreter to interpreter. More than thirty direct citations, however, are commonly identified.[90] Richard N. Longenecker well characterizes the challenge that the author's use of Scripture poses to the interpreter of Hebrews:

> Nowhere in the New Testament is the listing of biblical quotations more difficult than in Hebrews. Not only are we faced with the usual problem of distinguishing between direct quotations, on the one hand, and what may be called allusions, employment of biblical phraseology, or reference to Old Testament history, on the other hand, but we are also confronted in Hebrews with certain passages that are formally quoted again and again in the same discussion (e.g., Pss 95:7–11; 110:1–4) and other passages that are so elusively introduced as to frustrate any confident enumeration (e.g., Isa 8:17–18; Jer 31:33–34; Deut 32:35–36).[91]

Some of the author's citations are rather lengthy (1:10–12; 3:7–11; 8:8–12; 10:5–7). Some are quite brief (e.g., 1:5a; 4:4b). Some are repeated (e.g., 3:7, 13, 15 and 4:7 [Ps 95:7–11]; and 8:8–12 and 10:16–17 [Jer 31:31–34]). It is also possible that some of the shorter verbal links were not intended as conscious citations (e.g., 10:37a reflecting Isa 26:20 LXX). They nonetheless attest that the author was deeply steeped in the language of the Scriptures. Contemporary scholars correctly acknowledge that "a proper understanding of the uses of the Old Testament in Hebrews is of fundamental importance for understanding the structure of the book."[92]

---

90. Some representative estimates include the following: Spicq suggested 36 quotations (*L'Épitre aux Hébreux*, 1.133); Lane suggested 31 citations (*Hebrews 1-8*, cxvi); Longenecker proposed 38 citations (*Biblical Exegesis*, 147–48); Guthrie counted roughly 37 ("Hebrews," in *Commentary*, 919).

91. Longenecker, *Biblical Exegesis*, 146.

92. Guthrie, *Structure*, 7 n. 11.

## The Literary Role of the Author's Employment of Hortatory Injunctions

The author of Hebrews likewise employs a wide range of exhortations throughout the argument cast in the form of the hortatory subjunctive (see figure 6 below).

Table 11.6: Hortatory Subjunctives in Hebrews

| Theme | Exhortation |
| --- | --- |
| Entering God's "rest" | 4:1, "... let us fear [φοβηθῶμεν]..." |
| Entering God's "rest" | 4:11, "Let us therefore strive [Σπουδάσωμεν] to enter that rest..." |
| Holding fast to (the believing community's) confession | 4:14, "... let us hold fast [κρατῶμεν] our confession." |
| Drawing near to God with confidence | 4:16, "Let us then with confidence draw near [προσερχώμεθα] to the throne of grace..." |
| Leaving elementary matters and pressing on to maturity in Christ | 6:1, "Therefore leaving the elementary teaching about the Christ, let us press on [φερώμεθα] to maturity..." |
| Drawing near to God in worship | 10:22, "let us draw near [προσερχώμεθα] with a true heart in full assurance of faith..." |
| Holding fast to (the believing community's) confession of hope | 10:23, "Let us hold fast [κατέχωμεν] the confession of our hope without wavering..." |
| Considering one another to spur on to love and good deeds | 10:24, "And let us consider [κατανοῶμεν] one another in order to stir up love and good works" |
| Running the race (of faith) with endurance | 12:1, "Therefore,... let us run [τρέχωμεν] with endurance the race that is set before us" |
| Being thankful and offering acceptable worship to God | 12:28, "Therefore let us be grateful [ἔχωμεν χάριν]... and ... let us offer [λατρεύωμεν] to God acceptable worship..." |
| Going to Christ outside the camp bearing the approach he did | 13:13, "Therefore let us go out [ἐξερχώμεθα] to him outside the camp and bear [lit. bearing] the reproach he endured." |
| Offering a sacrifice of praise | 13:15, "Through him then let us continually offer up [ἀναφέρωμεν] a sacrifice of praise to God..." |

Westfall observes that the greatest concentration of the hortatory statements is found in 4:11–16 and 10:19–25. She further maintains, as noted earlier, that these statements function as transitional statements between 1:1–4:16 and 4:11–10:25, and between 4:11–10:25 and 10:19–13:25 respectively.[93]

---

93. See Westfall, *Discourse Analysis*, 297.

## The Literary Function of the Warning Passages of Hebrews

Hebrews contains a series of admonitions commonly described as "warning passages." Here the interpreter faces two challenges. The first is to identify the passages themselves. The second is to determine their literary function in the author's argument and their theological import. George Guthrie identifies five warning passages: 2:1–4; 4:12–13; 6:4–8; 10:26–31; and 12:25–29.[94] Howard Marshall, following Lane, identifies six such passages: 2:1–4; 3:1–4:14; 5:11–6:12; 10:19–39; 12:1–13; and 12:14–13:25.[95] C. Adrian Thomas identifies approximately twice as many: between eleven and thirteen.[96] An identification and assessment of these warnings commonly involves Christian readers in controversial theological questions about Christian "assurance."[97] Portions of Hebrews 6:4–8 and 10:26–31 in particular have proved particularly challenging for Christian readers. A volume edited by Herbert W. Bateman IV provides a helpful overview of different theological approaches taken to the warning passages.[98] This is a reminder that even structural matters related to a document like Hebrews involve contemporary Christian readers in theological implications. In terms of the role of these warnings in the author's structure, however, there is broad agreement among contemporary interpreters, as noted earlier, that the expositional portions serve as the basis for the exhortations and not vice versa.[99]

## Concluding Comments

Hebrews proves highly resilient in resisting contemporary interpreters' valiant efforts to capture its complexity in a mutually-agreed-upon surface-structure outline, however detailed. Harold W. Attridge proposes that "Some of the difficulty in analyzing the structure of Hebrews is due not to the lack of structural indices, but to their overabundance."[100] This should not imply, however, that contemporary interpreters should discontinue their pursuit. There is still room in contemporary study to address more fully the author's wide employment of and interpretive approach to the Scriptures, the literary role of the hortatory injunctions, and the literary function of the

---

94. Guthrie, *Structure*, 128–33.

95. Marshall, *Theology*, 606, following Lane, *Hebrews 1–8*, cii–ciii.

96. Thomas, *Case for Mixed-Audience*, 5 n. 10: 2:1–4; 3:1–6; 3:7–19; 4:1–13; (probably 4:14–16); 5:11–6:20; (probably 10:19–25); 10:32–39; 11:1–12:4; 12:5–17; 12:18–24; 12:25–29; and 13:1–19.

97. See Carson, "Assurance."

98. Bateman, ed., *Four Views*. The following views are represented: Classical Arminian (Grant R. Osborne), Classical [Swiss] Reformed (Buist M. Fanning), Wesleyan Arminian (Gareth Lee Cockerill), and Moderate [Swiss] Reformed (Randall C. Gleason). See Cortez's review. Thomas's *Case for Mixed-Audience* contends that the key to making sense of the warning passages is its intended mixed audience (see Steyn's review).

99. Guthrie rightly observes that the two genres work well together in the author's execution of the overall semantic program behind the macro-discourse (Guthrie, *Structure*, 139).

100. Attridge, *Epistle to the Hebrews*, 16.

warning passages, to name but a few issues. Such matters are beyond the scope of this or any essay. What the present essay does hope to communicate, however, is that there is no substitute for constant engagement with the author's challenging text presented to the original recipients as the ultimate word of revelation which "God ... has spoken to us by a Son" (Heb 1:1–2a, NRSV).[101]

## Bibliography

Allen, David L. *Hebrews*. New American Commentary. Nashville: Broadman & Holman, 2010.

Attridge, Harold W. *The Epistle to the Hebrews: A Commentary on the Epistle to the Hebrews*. Hermeneia. Philadelphia: Fortress, 1989.

Aune, David E. *The New Testament in Its Literary Environment*. Library of Early Christianity 8. Philadelphia: Westminster, 1987.

Bateman, Herbert W., IV, ed. *Four Views on the Warning Passages in Hebrews*. Grand Rapids: Kregel, 2007.

Black, C. Clifton, and Duane F. Watson, ed. *Words Well Spoken: George Kennedy's Rhetoric of the New Testament*. Studies in Rhetoric and Religion. Waco: Baylor University Press, 2008.

Black, D. A. "The Problem of the Literary Structure of Hebrews: An Evaluation and a Proposal." *Grace Theological Journal* 7 (1986) 163–77.

Blomberg, Craig. "The Structure of 2 Corinthians 1–7." *Criswell Theological Review* 4 (1989) 4–20.

Brown, Raymond E. *An Introduction to the New Testament*. Anchor Bible Reference Library. New York: Doubleday, 1997.

Bruce, F. F. *The Epistle to the Hebrews*. New International Commentary on the New Testament. Grand Rapids: Eerdmans, 1964.

———. *The Epistle to the Hebrews*. Rev. ed. New International Commentary on the New Testament. Grand Rapids: Eerdmans, 1990. (Unless otherwise noted, references to Bruce's commentary above are to this edition.)

Carson, D. A. "Reflections on Assurance." In *Still Sovereign: Contemporary Perspectives on Election, Foreknowledge, and Grace*, edited by Thomas R. Schreiner and Bruce A. Ware, 247–76. Grand Rapids: Baker, 2000.

Classen, C. J. *Rhetorical Criticism of the New Testament*. Wissenschaftliche Untersuchungen zum Neuen Testament 128. Tübingen: Mohr/Siebeck, 2000. Reprint, Leiden: Brill Academic, 2002.

Cockerill, Gareth Lee. *The Epistle to the Hebrews*. New International Commentary on the New Testament. Grand Rapids: Eerdmans, 2012.

Cortez, Felix H. Review of *Four Views on the Warning Passages in Hebrews*, edited by Herbert W. Bateman IV. Review of Biblical Literature. http://www.bookreviews.org.

---

101. This brief treatment, of course, is by no means intended as the last word in an ongoing issue of debate. It is simply an attempt to provide a representative (and hence necessarily incomplete) sketch of the contours of contemporary scholarly discussion.

deSilva, David A. *Despising Shame: Honor Discourse and Community Maintenance in the Epistle to the Hebrews.* Society of Biblical Literature Dissertation Series 152. Atlanta: Scholars, 1995.

———. *Perseverance in Gratitude: A Socio-Rhetorical Commentary on the Epistle "to the Hebrews."* Grand Rapids: Eerdmans, 2000.

De Waal, Kayle B. *A Socio-Rhetorical Interpretation of the Seven Trumpets of Revelation: The Apocalyptic Challenge to Earthly Empire.* Foreword by Vernon K. Robbins. Lewiston, NY: Mellen, 2012.

Ellingworth, Paul. *The Epistle to the Hebrews.* New International Commentary on the New Testament. Grand Rapids: Eerdmans, 1993.

Gowler, David B., et al., eds. *Fabrics of Discourse: Essays in Honor of Vernon K. Robbins.* Valley Forge: Trinity, 2003.

Green, Gene L. The *Letters to the Thessalonians.* Pillar New Testament Commentary. Grand Rapids: Eerdmans, 2002.

Guthrie, George H. "The Case for Apollos as Author of Hebrews." *Faith and Mission* 18 (2001) 41–56.

———. "Hebrews." In *Commentary on the New Testament Use of the Old Testament*, edited by Gregory K. Beale and Donald A. Carson, 919–95. Grand Rapids: Baker Academic, 2007.

———. *Hebrews.* NIV Application Commentary. Grand Rapids: Zondervan, 1998.

———. "New Testament Exegesis of Hebrews and the Catholic Epistles." In *Handbook to the Exegesis of the New Testament*, edited by Thomas E. Renz and Stanley E. Porter, 591–605. Leiden: Brill Academic, 2002.

———. "Old Testament in Hebrews." In *Dictionary of the Later New Testament and Its Developments : A Compendium of Contemporary Biblical Scholarship*, edited by Ralph P. Martin and Peter H. Davids, 841–50. Downers Grove, IL: Intervarsity Press, 2010.

———. *The Structure of Hebrews: A Text-Linguistic Analysis.* Novum Testamentum Supplements 73. Leiden: Brill, 1994.

———. "The Structure of Hebrews: A Text-linguistic Analysis." Ph.D. diss., Southwestern Baptist Theological Seminary, 1991.

Heil, John Paul. *Hebrews: Chiastic Structures and Audience Response.* Catholic Biblical Quarterly-Monograph Series 46. Washington, DC: Catholic Biblical Association of America, 2010.

Johnson, Luke Timothy. *Hebrews: A Commentary.* New Testament Library. Louisville: Westminster John Knox, 2006.

———. *The Writings of the New Testament: An Interpretation.* 2nd ed. Minneapolis: Fortress, 1999.

Kennedy, George A. *New Testament Interpretation through Rhetorical Criticism.* Chapel Hill: University of North Carolina Press, 1984.

Koester, Craig R. *Hebrews.* Anchor Yale Bible Commentaries 36. New York: Doubleday, 2001.

Köstenberger, Andreas, et al. *The Cradle, the Cross, and the Crown: An Introduction to the New Testament.* Nashville: Broadman & Holman, 2009.

Kümmel, Werner Georg. *Introduction to the New Testament.* Rev. ed. Translated by Howard Clark Kee. Nashville: Abingdon, 1975.

Kuss, Otto. "Der Brief an die Hebräer." In *Der Brief an die Hebräer und die Katholischen Briefe*, edited by Otto Kuss and Johann Michl. Regensburger Neues Testament 8. Regensburg: Friedrich Pustet, 1953. 2.Aufl., 1966.

Lane, William L. *Hebrews*. 2 vols. Word Bible Commentary 47A, 47B. Dallas: Word, 1991.

———. "Hebrews." *Dictionary of the Later New Testament and Its Developments*, 443–58.

Lightstone, Jack N. *Mishnah and the Social Formation of the Early Rabbinic Guild: A Socio-Rhetorical Approach*. Studies in Christianity and Judaism. Appendix by Vernon K. Robbins. Waterloo, ON: Wilfrid Laurier University Press, 2002.

Longenecker, Richard N. *Biblical Exegesis in the Apostolic Period*. 2nd ed. Grand Rapids: Eerdmans, 1999.

Marshall, I. Howard. *New Testament Theology: Many Witnesses, One Gospel*. Downers Grove, IL: InterVarsity Press, 2004.

Michel, Otto. *Der Brief an die Hebräer*. Kritisch-exegetischer Kommentar über das Neue Testament 13. 7.Aufl. Göttingen: Vandenhoeck & Ruprecht, 1975.

Mitchell, Alan C. *Hebrews*. Sacra Pagina. Collegeville, MN: Liturgical Press, 2007.

Moffatt, James. *A Critical and Exegetical Commentary on the Epistle to the Hebrews*. International Critical Commentary. Edinburgh: T. & T. Clark, 1924.

Nauck, Wolfgang. "Zum Aufbau des Hebraerbriefes." In *Judentum–Urchristentum–Kirche: Festschrift für Joachim Jeremias*, edited by Walter Eltester, 199–206. Beihefte zur Zeitschrift für die neutestamentliche Wissenschaft und die Kunde der älteren Kirche 26. Berlin: de Gruyter, 1960.

O'Brien, Peter T. *The Letter to the Hebrews*. Pillar New Testament Commentary. Grand Rapids: Eerdmans, 2010.

Richards, E. Randolph. *Paul and First-Century Letter Writing: Secretaries, Composition and Collection*. Downers Grove, IL: InterVarsity Press, 2004.

Robbins, Vernon K. *Exploring the Texture of Texts: A Guide to Socio-Rhetorical Interpretation*. Valley Forge, PA: Trinity, 1996.

———. *Jesus the Teacher: A Socio-Rhetorical Interpretation of Mark* (with a New Introduction). Minneapolis: Fortress, 2009.

———. *Sea Voyages and Beyond: Emerging Strategies in Socio-Rhetorical Interpretation*. Emory Studies in Early Christianity 14. Blandford Forum, UK: Deo, 2010.

———. *The Tapestry of Early Christian Discourse: Rhetoric, Society and Ideology*. London: Routledge, 1996.

Schnelle, Udo. *The History and Theology of the New Testament Writings*. Translated by M. Eugene Boring. Minneapolis: Fortress, 1998.

Spicq, Ceslas. *L'Épître aux Hébreux*. 2 vols. Sources biblique. Paris: Gabalda, 1952–1953.

Steyn, Gert J. Review of *A Case For Mixed-Audience with Reference to the Warning Passages in the Book of Hebrews*, by C. Adrian Thomas. Review of Biblical Literature. http://www.bookreviews.org.

Sweeney, James P. "Hebrews, Letter to the, Critical Issues." In *Lexham Bible Dictionary*, edited by Lazarus Wentz et al. Bellingham, WA: Lexham. http://www.lexhampress.com. Logos Bible Software. http://www.logos.com.

Thomas, C. Adrian. *A Case for Mixed-Audience with Reference to the Warning Passages in the Book of Hebrews*. New York: Lang, 2008.

Thompson, James W. *Hebrews*. Paideia Commentaries on the New Testament. Grand Rapids: Baker, 2008.

Thyen, H. *Der Stil der jüdisch-hellenistischen Homilie*. Forschungen zur Religion und Literatur des Alten und Neuen Testaments 47. Göttingen: Vandenhoeck & Ruprecht, 1955.

Vanhoye, A. "De structura litteraria Epistulae ad Hebraeos." *Verbum domini* 40 (1962) 73–80.

———. "Discussion sur la structure de l'Épître aux Hébreux." *Biblica* 55 (1974) 349–80.

———. "Hebräerbrief." In *Theologische Realenzyklopädie*, edited by Gerhard Krause and Gerhard Müller, I/14:494–505. Berlin: de Gruyter, 1993.

———. *La structure littéraire de l'Épître aux Hébreux*. 2nd ed. Studia neotestamentica 1. Paris/Bruges: de Brouwer, 1976.

———. *Structure and Message of the Epistle to the Hebrews*. Subsidia Biblica 12. Rome: Pontificio Instituto Biblico, 1989.

Walton, Steve. "What Has Aristotle to Do with Paul: Rhetorical Criticism and 1 Thessalonians." *TynBul* 46 (1995) 229–50.

Watson, Duane F. *The Rhetoric of the New Testament: A Bibliographic Survey*. Tools for Biblical Study. Blandford Forum, UK: Deo, 2004.

Weiß, Hans-Friedrich. *Der Brief an die Hebräer*. Kritisch-exegetischer Kommentar über das Neue Testament 13. 15.Aufl. Göttingen: Vandenhoeck & Ruprecht, 1991.

Weima, Jeffrey A.D. "What Does Aristotle Have to Do with Paul? An Evaluation of Rhetorical Criticism." *Calvin Theological Journal* 32 (1997) 458–68.

Westcott, B. F. *The Epistle to the Hebrews*. 3rd ed. London: Macmillan, 1903.

Westfall, Cynthia Long. *A Discourse Analysis of the Letter to the Hebrews: The Relationship between Form and Meaning*. Library of New Testament Studies 297. London: T. & T. Clark, 2005.

White, John L. "Ancient Greek Letters." *Greco-Roman Literature and the New Testament*, edited by David E. Aune, ch. 5. Society of Biblical Literature Sources for Biblical Study 21. Atlanta: Scholars, 1988.

———. "New Testament Epistolary Literature in the Framework of Ancient Epistolography." In vol. 2 of *Aufstieg und Niedergang der römischen Welt: Geschichte und Kultur Roms im Spiegel der neueren Forschung*, 1730–56. Berlin: Walter de Gruyter, 1984.

Witherington, Ben, III. *Letters and Homilies for Jewish Christians: A Socio-Rhetorical Commentary on Hebrews, James and Jude*. Downers Grove, IL: InterVarsity Press, 2007.

———. *New Testament Rhetoric: An Introductory Guide to the Art of Persuasion in and of the New Testament*. Eugene, OR: Cascade, 2009.

Wrede, William. *Das literarische Rätsel des Hebräerbriefs: Mit einem Anhang über den literarischen Charakter des Barnabasbriefes*. Forschungen zur Religion und Literatur des Alten und Neuen Testaments 8. Göttingen: Vandenhoeck & Ruprecht, 1906.

Part 2: **Insights from the History of the Church**

# 12

## "Study to Show Thyself Approved": B. T. Roberts's Reading Record, 1852–1855

DOUGLAS R. CULLUM

ALL WHO KNOW DR. Paul Livermore know that he is a consummate reader. He is truly a renaissance person whose interests range broadly across a plethora of subjects and disciplines. In honor of the intellectual life so richly modeled by professor Livermore, this chapter seeks to offer a glimpse into the intellectual life of the principal founder of the early Free Methodist Church, the tradition in which Dr. Livermore was born and through which he lived out his calling.

In the early years of his ministry, B. T. Roberts included a record of his reading in his personal diary. His later diaries tend to focus primarily on the location, people, and circumstances of his preaching and superintending itinerancy, a fact due probably to the increased travel required in his role as leader of the new denomination. Thus the bibliographic notations of the early diaries provide a rather unique window through which to view Roberts's intellectual development in the formative years of his ministry.

The years 1852 through 1855 were foundational in many ways for B. T. Roberts. Having become a full clergy member of the Genesee Conference of the Methodist Episcopal Church in 1850, Roberts was in the process of finalizing his preparations for elder's orders, which he received in 1852. And, most significantly, it was also during these years that the ferment in the Genesee Conference that eventually burst forth in the organization of the Free Methodist Church was beginning to grow in earnest, and during which Roberts began to use the press to speak out publicly on issues of concern in the church.

Though Roberts did not make note of everything he read in these years, he did provide enough information to give a clear sense of his literary interests and patterns of intellectual engagement during these formative years. A summary analysis of his reading in this period indicates that Roberts spent his time working in five broadly-conceived areas of academic endeavor in relation to his pastoral ministry. This analysis not only offers insight into the actual content of Roberts's study in this period, it also provides a glimpse into his struggle to maintain a vibrant intellectual life amid the rigors of nineteenth-century pastoral ministry.

## The Methodist Episcopal Course of Study

It is readily apparent from Roberts's reading notations is that he spent a significant portion of his study time in spring and summer of 1852 completing the course of study for ministers in the Methodist Episcopal Church. Five of the ten non-periodical items that Roberts recorded having read that year were a part of the required reading for the ministerial course of study.[1] The major focus of his work on the course of study for this period was in the area of Christian history.

He began in early April to work his way through the Mosheim's *Ecclesiastical History* and Ruter's *A Concise History of the Christian Church*—over 1200 pages total, depending on which editions he actually used.[2] On the days that he could carve out for this task, Roberts was able to work through forty to fifty pages of these texts in his morning study time. Yet, it is clear that his efforts were neither as often nor as productive as he expected of himself. By mid-June, Roberts was regularly bemoaning his lack of progress. "I do not seem to accomplish much," he wrote. "I begin to fear that I never shall." Again, the following day, Roberts confessed, "My progress in Church History is not very rapid." He was troubled that he found his "mind easily diverted" from his studies, with the net result that by the end of the week he often felt that he had only "completed incomplete preparations for the Sabbath."[3] Nonetheless, Roberts was able to plow through his church history studies with sufficient success to complete the course of study and be ordained as an elder in September 1852.

During this same period, Roberts completed requirements for the course of study in the areas of biblical and theological studies by working his way through James Townley's *Illustrations of Biblical Literature* and John Wesley's *Plain Account of Christian Perfection*.[4] Later in the year Roberts also read—or re-read—Joseph Butler's *Analogy of Religion*. Though Butler was required reading in the course of study, it is unlikely that Roberts's use of Butler was related to his completion of the course of study because he read it in December—after his ordination as elder in September.

Roberts's completion of the ministerial course of study for the Methodist Episcopal Church is another indicator of his thorough immersion in the Methodist ethos and culture of his day. Through both his university training and his church-authorized

---

1. For an analysis of the development of the ministerial courses of study in the Methodist Episcopal Church and its successors, see Patterson, "The Ministerial Mind of American Methodism." For insight into the early development of the course of study, see Rowe, "New Light on Early Methodist Theological Education," 58–62.

2. For Roberts's record of reading Mosheim, see Roberts, "Diary," 8, 13, 15, 19, 27 April 1852; 12 May 1852; and 8 June 1852. For Ruter, see 8 April 1852.

3. Roberts, "Diary," 8–19 June 1852.

4. Roberts, "Diary," 6 April 1852 and 2 February 1852.

preparation for ministry, Roberts participated fully in the educational expectations of the church.[5]

## Methodistica and Denominational Interest

Roberts's churchly commitment was also nurtured through his regular reading of Methodist literature, including theology, history, and church periodicals. His regular engagement in these materials is indicative of an interest in both the primary sources of the Methodist tradition and its contemporary expressions.

As might be expected for a Methodist minister, Roberts made regular use of the *Works of John Wesley*.[6] In early 1852, Roberts seems to have been enamored enough with Wesley to have attempted to put into practice the Wesleyan discipline of rising early for study and prayer, but—at least on one occasion—without much success. On Saturday, February 28, 1852, Roberts recorded his faltering effort: "Rose at four. Read in Wesley's *Plain Account of C[hristian] P[erfection]* and prayed by 7. Slept over it." His summary comment for that day revealed his sense of failure. "I am very dull most of the time," Roberts confessed. "Accomplished in my study poor preparation for the Sabbath."[7] Two years later, in an afternoon service at Brockport, Roberts recorded having fulfilled the requirement of the Methodist Episcopal Book of Discipline that Wesley's sermon on evil speaking be read annually in the hearing of every congregation.[8]

Roberts was an avid reader of the *Methodist Quarterly Review*.[9] When this welcome journal reached his parsonage, he does not seem to have read it directly through in the order of its table of contents. Rather, Roberts gravitated to those articles that most captured his attention. Such was the case in January 1852. The first article he recorded having read was editor John McClintock's discourse on glories of "the old Methodist school of preaching."[10] Roberts was impressed, noting that he "read in the *Quarterly* a good article by the editor on Methodist preaching that will make McClintock bishop."[11] Though Roberts's hunch about McClintock becoming a bishop did not materialize, Roberts clearly enjoyed the intellectual stimulation that the *Quarterly* brought to his

---

5. For a full bibliography of the texts that Roberts is likely to have used in the 1848 course of study's four-year curriculum, see Appendix 1, in Cullum, "Gospel Simplicity," 373–382.

6. See, for example, Roberts, "Diary," 2 April 1852 and 28 April 1854, where Roberts simply recorded that he had read Wesley, without indicating the actual document.

7. Roberts, "Diary," 28 February 1852.

8. Roberts, "Diary," 19 March 1854.

9. For a brief sketch of the history of the *Methodist Quarterly Review*, see Lippy, ed., *Religious Periodicals of the United States*, 353–57.

10. McClintock, "Methodist Preaching," 81. For an overview of McClintock's life, and his role in the Methodist Episcopal Church, see Ryan, "John M'Clintock (1814–1870)," in *Something More Than Human*, 141–57.

11. Roberts, "Diary," 16 January 1852.

study every three months. McClintock's treatise on Methodist preaching continued with additional installments in each of the April and July issues of the journal. Given his positive response to the first article, it is fairly certain that Roberts devoured them as well. In the same issue as McClintock's first article, Roberts recorded also having read the articles on Dante Alighieri and William Penn only a few days later.[12]

Roberts's use of the *Methodist Quarterly Review* indicates that it served well in accomplishing one of its intended purposes: that of providing intellectual stimulation and educational direction for those in the Methodist itinerancy. Roberts regularly looked to the *Quarterly* to point him toward worthwhile materials for his personal study. For example, the January 1854 issue included a review article on three recent works related to the life of the late Stephen Olin: *The Life and Letters of Stephen Olin*, *The Works of Stephen Olin*, and his *Travels in Egypt, Arabia, Petraea, and the Holy Land*.[13] By April, Roberts had gotten his own copy of Olin's *Life and Letters* and recorded having read it in the following months.[14] In the same issue, Dr. Charles Collints's article on Austen Layard's second exploring expedition to the ruins of Nineveh and Babylon appeared.[15] In March, Roberts recounted that he had "bought Layard's Second Expedition to Nineveh for $2.00," and that he had begun reading it the following day. He continued to work on Layard as he had opportunity, finally completing it in June of that year.[16]

Again, after the *Quarterly* had reviewed Albert Bledsoe's *Theodicy* in the April 1854 issue, Roberts spent a good part of his study time in the months of June and July reading the actual text.[17] Bledsoe's book was a substantial volume of 365 pages that offered a tightly-woven argument on the perennial question of how the twin truths of God's absolute perfection and the existence of evil can be satisfyingly harmonized.[18] Bledsoe's personal pilgrimage from an indefinite Arminianism to a committed Calvinism, and then back toward the Arminian side, made his text especially fertile in its presentation of these ideas.

Perhaps most interesting for Roberts was Bledsoe's strong rebuttal against Jonathan Edwards's position on divine necessity in relation to human sin. This arduous question was seen finally to boil down to only two alternatives. "[One] must either conclude that [sin] exists by God's permission while he might have prevented it, or else against his will, because he could not hinder it."[19] Unlike Edwards, Bledsoe was

---

12. Roberts, "Diary," 19 January 1852. For the articles on Dante and Penn that Roberts read, see Hyde, "Dante," 49–66; and Moore, "William Penn," 119–35.
13. McClintock, "Stephen Olin," 9–33.
14. Roberts, "Diary," 28–29 April and 6 June 1854.
15. Collins, "Layard's Second Exploration," 113–31.
16. Roberts, "Diary," 8–9, 13 March, 12 April, and 7 June 1854.
17. Curry, "A Theodicy," 263–87; and Roberts, "Diary," 3, 9, 14 June and 12, 17 July 1854.
18. Bledsoe, *A Theodicy*, 9; and Curry, "A Theodicy," 265.
19. Curry, "A Theodicy," 272.

compelled to choose the latter option, arguing that the human free will, if it is truly free, must be "a self-actuating cause."[20] Daniel Curry, the author of the review of Bledsoe's book for the *Quarterly*, balked at Bledsoe's conclusion, preferring rather to leave the ultimate answer in the mystery of the divine. Roberts, on the other hand, simply noted that he had "finished reading *Theodicy*" and that he had "derived benefit from its perusal."[21] It is clear that he was honestly wrestling with the knotty problems of theological inquiry.

In addition to *The Methodist Quarterly Review*, Roberts was also a regular reader of other denominationally sponsored periodicals. In early May 1852, just before he began his journey to Boston for General Conference, Roberts "received the first n[umber] of the *Daily Zion's Herald*, dated May 3rd."[22] This paper was a special edition of the *Christian Advocate* issued every day except Sunday during the quadrennial sessions of General Conference. His reading of the news surrounding General Conference must have incited his motivation to attend, because two days later, after having read again in the *Zion's Herald*, Roberts spoke to ministerial colleague, Rev. Walter Gordon, about his decision to make the trip to Boston.[23]

Another Methodist serial that Roberts found time to read was the *National Magazine*. This monthly publication, edited by Abel Stevens, was launched in July 1852 and included an eclectic mix of "literature, art, and religion."[24] Though he did not indicate which articles he read, he did record on November 30, 1852 that he "read some in the *National Magazine*.[25] And, while it cannot be determined with certainty whether he was reading the November or the December issue, Roberts was certain to have found many pieces that captured his attention. For example, the lead article in November 1852 was an essay on the life and work of the poet-politician, William Cullen Bryant, whose literary, editorial, and abolitionist efforts Roberts would undoubtedly have found stimulating. The November publication also included a piece on Washington Irving, and, again, though there is no way to know with certainty if there was a direct connection, it is perhaps more than coincidence that Roberts read Irving's *Life of Mahomet* and *Mahomet and his Successors* early the following year.[26]

If Roberts had been reading the December issue, similar connections to his life and interests are readily apparent. Among the articles that Roberts would likely have gravitated toward were an editorial on "The Christianity Required by the Times," and

20. The phrase, "self-actuating cause," is that of Thomas A. Langford in an essay that is very helpful for locating the significance Bledsoe's thought in the larger context of nineteenth-century theology; see Langford, *Practical Divinity*, 102. For Bledsoe's extended discussion, see Bledsoe, *A Theodicy*, 98–126.

21. Roberts, "Diary," 17 July 1854.

22. Roberts, "Diary," 5 May 1852.

23. Roberts, "Diary," 7, 10 May 1852.

24. *The National Magazine: Devoted to Literature, Art, and Religion* 1–13 (1852–58) (New York).

25. Roberts, "Diary," 30 November 1852.

26. "William Cullen Bryant," 385–89; "Washington Irving," 444; and Roberts, "Diary," 30 March and 4 April 1853.

biographical sketches of the lives of Charles Elliott and Daniel Webster.[27] The first of these articles discussed themes that resonated with Roberts throughout his whole ministry: the need for a recovery of the "primitive ideal" of early Christianity and the necessity of "an abatement of the sectarianism of the Church."[28] In addition, the article on the life of Charles Elliott would certainly have drawn Roberts's attention because the ministerial course of study for 1848 made Elliott's *Delineation of Roman Catholicism* required reading for those pursuing ordination: this volume undoubtedly played a significant role in early Free Methodism's participation the anti-Catholic nativism that impacted nearly all of American Protestantism in the mid-nineteenth century.[29] In July 1853 Roberts found himself immersed in Elliott again as he began reading "in Elliott on Slavery."[30] As for the Daniel Webster article, Roberts would have come to this piece with the fresh memories and impressions of his recent trip to Boston, where he had availed himself of the opportunity to hear Daniel Webster in person.

Roberts's regular reading of Methodist periodical literature reveals a strong sense of intellectual and emotional connection with the denomination. He was quick to acquire and read new books on Methodist topics. In November 1852 Roberts gave a close reading to Isaac Taylor's recently published *Wesley and Methodism*. His initial assessment of this latest book on Methodist history was hardly enthusiastic. "[Taylor] gives W[esley] a high character for sanctity, learning, and logical ability," wrote Roberts, "but thinks him destitute of the higher faculty, the abstract quality."[31] Less than a week later when Roberts finished reading the book, his three-point evaluation was more precise, but no more flattering: "[Taylor] leans too strongly to Calvinism. He does not do full justice to Wesley. He looks for the advent of a new Methodism."[32]

More enjoyable for Roberts was his reading of James B. Finley's *Autobiography*, detailing Methodism's pioneer life in the West. Roberts read Finley's account of his exploits in the westward expansion of Methodism "with a good deal of interest."[33] So great, in fact, was Roberts's interest that he was quickly drawn to Finley's next book, *Sketches of Western Methodism*, which he also read within the first year of its publication.[34] Finley's vivid accounts were undoubtedly a factor in Roberts's attraction

---

27. "The Christianity Required by the Times," 501–5; "Charles Elliott, D.D.," 560–62; and "Daniel Webster," 559.

28. "The Christianity Required by the Times," 501.

29. For a general overview of anti-Catholicism in nineteenth-century American life, see Roy, *Rhetorical Campaigns*; Bennett, *The Party of Fear*; Franchot, *Roads to Rome*; Schwartz, *The Persistent Prejudice*; Davis, *The Fear of Conspiracy*; and Cross, *The Burned-Over District*, 231–33.

30. Elliott's text was *The Sinfulness of Slavery* (1850/51). For a review of Elliott's *Delineation of Roman Catholicism*, and a further indicator of nineteenth-century Methodism's interest in Elliott's work, see Eddy, "The Claims of Romanism," 533–52.

31. Roberts, "Diary," 23 November 1852.

32. Roberts, "Diary," 29 November 1852.

33. Roberts, "Diary," 28 March 1854.

34. Roberts, "Diary," 25 May 1855.

to a primitive, revivalistic form of Methodism. Certainly, Roberts could not have imagined as he was reading Finley's second book that in five years he and J. W. Redfield would be involved in yet another westward expansion of the Methodist movement.[35] But when the time came that Roberts was actually involved in the organizing stages of the western branch of Free Methodism, Finley's work was still fresh in his memory. The April 1860 issue of the *Earnest Christian* included Roberts's own reflections on Finley's *Autobiography*. "We have seldom been more entertained with any work than with the autobiography of this pioneer of the west," wrote Roberts. "He contributed as much perhaps as any other man to the establishment and spread of Methodism at [*sic*] the west."[36]

## Biblical and Theological Studies

Yet, Roberts's appetite for intellectual development was much broader than things Methodist. His study habits in the early years of his ministry reveal a disciplined pattern of reading and study in a variety of areas, but always around a center of biblical and theological studies. Roberts was regularly engaged in the exegetical study of the biblical text, studying biblical history, and reading on theological topics.

Often up by 5:00 a.m., B. T. Roberts's daily morning discipline included the reading of the scriptures in their original languages. His statement of 21 April 1852— "Read as usual in my Hebrew and Greek Test[aments]"—may stand as a summary of numerous diary entries.[37] He regularly recorded having spent time working with scripture in the original languages. The focus of Roberts's study in the biblical languages in the early years was the mastering of Hebrew. Having studied both Greek and Latin at Wesleyan University, Roberts seems to have taken it upon himself to learn the language of the Old Testament.[38] Even though it was tough going, Roberts was relatively pleased with his progress. In early 1852 he recorded that he was making "slow progress in Hebrew"; but it was progress nonetheless, because on another morning later in the same week Roberts noted that he had "read Hebrew with good

---

35. For discussion of the Western movement and the various other independent "Free" churches that formed prior to the official formation of the Free Methodist Church, see Roberts, *Why Another Sect*, 263–78; Roberts, "A Sketch of the Life of Rev. J. W. Redfield, M.D.," 323–24; Terrill, *The Life of Rev. John Wesley Redfield, M.D.*, 419–39; Hogue, *History* [Vol. 1], 265–87, 323–24; Zahniser, *Earnest Christian*, 145–47, 162–76; and Marston, *From Age to Age*, 207–52.

36. Roberts, "Rev. James B. Finley," 113. See also the evidence of acquaintance with Finley's work in Cooley, "Order and Confusion," 81–83.

37. Roberts, "Diary," 21 April 1852.

38. Hebrew was not offered at Wesleyan University when Roberts was there as a student, though it had been in earlier years. Nathan Bangs had added Hebrew, biblical literature, and ecclesiastical history to the curriculum when he came as president. But, due to budgetary constraints and a desire to focus on the classical liberal arts curriculum, Olin omitted these departments in 1843—just two years before Roberts arrived. See Price, *Wesleyan's First Century*, 66–67, 77.

success."[39] By the end of the year, Roberts's diligence was beginning to pay off. He felt that he was "making some proficiency in Hebrew" through his discipline of having "read carefully a chapter in the Hebrew Bible" in the course of a week's time.[40] Yet, he was sober about his accomplishment; later the same month he underscored his need for disciplined study when he confessed that he found "it necessary to read some every day to get along well."[41]

His discipline seems to have served him well because the following spring Roberts expressed his satisfaction in being able to use the primary languages of scripture. "I find more delight than ever in studying the Bible in the original," he recorded and then was immediately prompted to include a prayer for his own responsiveness: "O, may I find grace to obey it!"[42] The following year, Roberts had progressed to the point that he was reading nearly a chapter a day. On 22 March 1854 he noted that he had "finished the 31st chap[ter] of Deut[eronomy] in Hebrew." On another day he "read half a chap[ter] in Hebrew."[43] Reading the Old Testament in Hebrew had finally become just another part of Roberts's regular daily routine, along with working in the garden, making pastoral visits, and leading a class meeting: "Planted some early potatoes in my garden. Reviewed a chap[ter] in Hebrew. Read a chap[ter] of Blair's *Rhetoric*. Called at Bro. Hitchcock's and Sis. Church's. Took tea at Bro. Perry's. At class meeting this eve. 26 present. An excellent meeting."[44]

Roberts often read his Hebrew Bible along with the Septuagint, Josephus's *History of the Jews,* and, sometimes, Townley's *Illustrations of Biblical Literature.* In Roberts's use of these resources one can see a penchant for textual studies and the critical analysis of historical materials. Early in January 1852, Roberts read passages from the Old Testament in both Hebrew and Greek, "compared their chronology with Josephus," and then noted his conclusion that "Josephus and the Septuagint agree in the main."[45] He also ventured a tentative judgment regarding the presuppositions of Josephus's history. "He seemed anxious to conciliate the Greek philosophers," Roberts observed.[46]

A final glimpse into Roberts's engagement in biblical studies is offered by his reading of the works of Nathaniel Lardner (1684–1768). Lardner was an English Dissenter whose most famous work was *The Credibility of the Gospel History* (1727–57), in which he sought to reconcile "the discrepancies in the biblical narratives."[47] While

---

39. Roberts, "Diary," 21, 23 January 1852.
40. Roberts, "Diary," 9, 13 November 1852.
41. Roberts, "Diary," 30 November 1852.
42. Roberts, "Diary," 17 March 1853.
43. Roberts, "Diary," 22 March and 4 May 1854.
44. Roberts, "Diary," 16 May 1854.
45. Roberts, "Diary," 3 January 1852.
46. Roberts, "Diary," 21 January 1852; for Roberts's reading of Josephus, see also Roberts, "Diary," 1–2, 23 January and 2 April 1852.
47. "Lardner, Nathaniel," in *The Oxford Dictionary of the Christian Church*, 800.

Roberts did not indicate whether he was reading this or another of Lardner's works, he was absorbed enough to have spent "most of the day in Lardner" on one rainy and snowy day in May 1855.[48]

The broad-ranging nature of Roberts's theological interests has already been suggested in the foregoing discussion of his use of the *Methodist Quarterly Review* as a guide for his own study. It remains to sample Roberts's exposure to a handful of other theological texts in order to offer a clearer understanding of the scope of his interests. First, Roberts appears to have found a congenial theological conversation partner in the writings of Jonathan Edwards. While one could wish that Roberts had made more precise notes regarding the actual texts that he read, in 1855 Roberts did offer that he was reading "in Edwards's *Works*."[49] The impact that Edwards made on Roberts almost certainly centered around Edwards's affirmation and clear articulation of an experiential religious faith. In 1860, when Roberts began the publication of the *Earnest Christian*, he often included short quotations attributed to "Pres. Edwards" as filler text. These were succinct and penetrating statements, usually only a sentence or two in length, that Roberts clearly appreciated for their ability to drive home a point with great economy of words.

For example, in January 1860 the first issue of the *Earnest Christian* included three quotations credited to Edwards, two of which have been verified as actual Edwards texts. The first was presented as a motivational one-liner: "Slothfulness in the service of God is as damning as open rebellion," excerpted from Edwards's *Treatise Concerning Religious Affections*. Edwards's original sentence continued, "for the slothful servant is a wicked servant, and shall be cast into outer darkness among God's enemies, Matthew 25:26, 30."[50] In the same issue, Roberts also excerpted the following long Edwardsian sentence and gave it the caption, "Work of the Spirit":

> To rejoice that the work of God is carried on calmly, without much ado, is in effect to rejoice that it is carried on with less power, or that these is not so much of the influence of God's Spirit; or though the degree of the influence of the Spirit of God on particular persons, is by no means to be judged of by the degree of external appearances, because of the different constitutions, tempers, and circumstances of men; yet, if there be a very powerful influence of the Spirit of God on a mixed multitude, it will cause some way or other a great visible commotion.[51]

---

48. Roberts, "Diary," 8 May 1855.

49. Roberts, "Diary," 12 January 1855.

50. Edwards, "[Slothfulness]," 10; for the full text of Edwards's statement, see *A Treatise Concerning Religious Affections* (III.12.3), 315.

51. Edwards, "Work of the Spirit," 20; and *Thoughts on the Revival of Religion in New England* (III.4), 394.

Though Roberts would have had some fundamental theological differences with Edwards,[52] he was strongly drawn to Edwards's insistence that authentic Christianity must involve both the head and the heart.

In April 1853, Roberts recorded that he had "commenced reading 'The Eclipse of Faith.'"[53] In this case, it is difficult to know whether Roberts had gotten his own copy of Henry Rogers's anonymously-published *The Eclipse of Faith; or, a Visit to a Religious Skeptic,* or whether he was reading the review article that was published the same month in the *Methodist Quarterly Review*.[54] Either way, it is indicative of Roberts's interest in the current theological debates of his day. Using conversations between fictitious characters, Rogers's text offered a creative refutation of nineteenth-century religious skepticism. It was given a glowing review in the *Quarterly*. "The author has done for the disciples of [David] Strauss, [Francis] Newman, [Theodore] Parker, and the rationalists and spiritualists of the present age," wrote Floy, "what Butler did, and Paley, and Watson, for the skeptics of former times: he has swept away their subtle cavils, unveiled their sophistries, and shown the pillar of revelation unharmed by their malignity."[55] While Roberts's own evaluation of Rogers's book remains unknown, that he read either the book itself, the review, or both, is evidence of his exposure to and interest in the theological currents of his day.

The presupposition and goal of all such study for Roberts and those of similar religious piety was the belief that it would lead to authentic and ever-deepening religious experience. Their motivation for studying theology and reading the scriptures in their original languages was to gain authoritative guidance for the life of faith. A hint of this commitment was inscribed in the flyleaf of Roberts's diary for 1854. In addition to his name and his town (Brockport), there were only three words written on the page: "Σεαυτὸν ἁγιὸν τήρει."[56] Here Roberts had used his skills in biblical languages to appropriate for himself the command of 1 Tim 5:22: "Keep thyself pure" (KJV).

## World and National Interest

In addition to his churchly and theological interests, Roberts's reading record reveals a person very much engaged in the national and international issues of his day. In the early 1850s, the exploits of Hungarian freedom fighter, Louis Kossuth, had captured the democratic imaginations of the American people. B. T. Roberts was no exception.

---

52. See, for example, Edwards's discussions of the divine decrees, the efficacy of grace, and the perseverance of the saints in which he takes on what he understood as the Arminian position, in Edwards, *The Works of Jonathan Edwards*, 525–65, 596–603. On these issues, Roberts stood firmly in the Arminian camp, as mediated through Wesley and the American Methodist tradition.

53. Roberts, "Diary," 16 April 1853.

54. Dr. Floy, "The Eclipse of Faith," 169–91.

55. Dr. Floy, "The Eclipse of Faith," 169.

56. Dr. Floy, "The Eclipse of Faith," flyleaf, 1854.

Kossuth was the insurgent leader of the 1849 revolution in which the Magyar Slovaks won independence from Austria in a battle that was often compared in the popular mind to the American revolution of 1776.[57] Because Hungarian freedom was initially short-lived due to the strength of the combined Austrian and Russian armies, Kossuth fled the country and eventually made his way to the United States. In December 1851, Kossuth was received to a hero's welcome in many cities of the American northeast, and "Kossuth fever" began to spread through the country.[58]

The general public interest in Kossuth and his role in Hungary's fight for independence was apparent in the *Methodist Quarterly Review*. The April 1852 issue included an article reviewing one of the latest volumes on the Hungarian revolution, this one by Benjamin F. Tefft of Genesee Wesleyan Seminary. Tefft wanted his readers to know that his was "not a hastily-prepared production" published prematurely in the hope that it could capitalize on "the current of Kossuth's personal popularity." Rather, Tefft is said to have begun his research in 1842, and had his manuscript to the press before "it was known that the world-renowned Magyar would visit this country."[59] Roberts, along with other Methodists and Americans in general, was rapt with interest in the Kossuth story. On 29 March 1852 Roberts "commenced reading P. C. Headley's *Life of Kossuth*" in the same year as its publication, noting that he found it "very turgid yet interesting owing to its subject."[60] In less than four days Roberts had finished the book, now perhaps more impressed with Kossuth than he was at the start. "[Kossuth] is the wonder of the age—devout, patriotic, eloquent, and brave," glowed Roberts. "May he be successful in giving liberty to the enslaved millions of Hungary and Europe."[61]

Closer to home, Roberts was passionately interested in another problem of human oppression: the blight of American slavery. His reading of Elliott's text on *The Sinfulness of Slavery* in 1853 has already been noted above. Another book he read on the subject of slavery in this period was L. Maria Child's recently published, *Isaac T. Hopper: A True Life*. In the first few weeks of January 1855, Roberts devoured this narrative of Hopper's life and antislavery activities.[62] Isaac Tatem Hopper—"Friend Hopper," as he was affectionately known—was a Quaker activist who began assisting fugitive slaves in his teenage years. From those early beginnings, the rest of his life was given to the task of working against the institution of slavery. Child's book is filled with anecdotes of Hopper's aid to fugitive slaves, drawn largely from his own accounts that

---

57. May, "Seward and Kossuth," 268.

58. May, "Seward and Kossuth," 267–71.

59. Perry, "Hungary and Kossuth," 262, a review article of Benjamin Franklin Tefft, *Hungary and Kossuth*.

60. For the Headley volume, see appendix 1, bibliography II. For Roberts's comments, see Roberts, "Diary," 29 March 1852.

61. Roberts, "Diary," 2 April 1852.

62. See Roberts, "Diary," 1, 4, 12, 19 January 1855.

were serialized in newspapers under the title of "Tales of Oppression."[63] In addition to his antislavery activities, Hopper was an advocate against capital punishment and the unequal treatment of women.[64] Roberts found the story of Hopper's life fascinating, and particularly laudable for his commitment to social activism. On January 19, 1855, when Roberts had "finished reading the life of Isaac T. Hopper," he recorded two succinct sentences of sincere admiration: "His was a life abounding in good works. He was a friend of the oppressed."[65] This admiration, while not at all surprising for the issues involved, reveals in Roberts both a capacity and a willingness to make finely nuanced theological judgments. That is, Roberts was quite willing to embrace Hopper as a model for social justice advocacy, while at the same time rejecting some of his theological positions, particularly his Hicksite Quakerism. Child's book makes it abundantly clear—so clear that Roberts could not have missed it—that Hopper was a part of the theologically progressive branch of the Friends movement. In fact, Hopper was a younger contemporary and friend of Elias Hicks, whose views precipitated the split among American Quakers in 1827. Hicks and most of his followers embraced those very views of inward light and its ultimate primacy in relation to the Christian Scriptures that Roberts specifically rejected.[66]

A final glimpse of Roberts's interest in world and national issues may be seen in his leisure reading of Charles Wilkes' *Exploring Expedition*, an account of the famous United States oceanic exploring voyages of 1838–1842. A new edition of the five-volume narrative was published in 1851, perhaps the edition that Roberts had access to in July 1855.[67] Though he recorded no specific response to his reading, the simple fact that the text was among the self-selected materials on Roberts's reading list is again indicative of a far-reaching intellectual curiosity.

## Language and Rhetoric

A final area of Roberts's intellectual engagement as indicated by his reading habits of 1852–1855 was in the field of language and rhetoric, broadly conceived. It is in this arena that the influence of Roberts's education at Wesleyan University is especially apparent. One of the marks of a liberally educated person in the nineteenth century was a grasp of the structure and use of language, including both one's native tongue and other languages. The mastery of foreign languages, in particular, was thought to be one of the most productive means of disciplining the faculties of the mind for critical thinking.

63. Child, *Isaac T. Hopper*, v–vi.
64. Child, *Isaac T. Hopper*, 383–84.
65. Roberts, "Diary," 19 January 1855.
66. For the views of Elias Hicks, and Hopper's relation to Hicks, see Child, *Isaac T. Hopper*, 274–86, 381, 394–96. On Roberts's rejection of the priority of inward light, see Roberts, "Diary," 20 April 1853.
67. Roberts, "Diary," 16, 18 July 1855.

Having been trained under the tutelage of this educational philosophy, Roberts fully embraced the value of the study of foreign languages. In addition to his disciplined attention to the biblical languages of Hebrew and Greek, Roberts sought to keep up with his Latin and German. On 22 March 1853 Roberts recorded having "read some" in the Latin text of Caesar's *Commentary*. "He was a man of remarkable industry," reflected Roberts. "The battles he fought would alone have occupied the lives of most men."[68] Nearly six years later, when Roberts was in the midst of his own difficult struggle with his relationship with the Methodist Episcopal Church, he again found encouragement in drawing upon his knowledge of classical materials. On January 23, 1859, Roberts inscribed only one sentence and an author's name on his diary page for that day: "*Quod si ea mihi maxime impenderet, tamen hoc animo semper fui ut invidiam virtute partam gloriam, non invidiam putarem.* Cicero." The original context of this quotation from Cicero's *Orations* was the author's speech against Lucius Catilina in which he argued that he had no reason to fear unpopularity for his position. This then was followed by the sentence that the now unpopular Roberts gravitated toward: "And if it did threaten me to ever so great a degree, yet I have always been of the disposition to think unpopularity earned by virtue and glory, not unpopularity."[69]

In March 1854 Roberts set himself to the task of brushing up on his reading knowledge of German. He had evidently learned or begun to learn the language at some point in the past but had allowed it to fall into disuse. Though it is unknown what triggered his renewed motivation, he recorded on March 9, 1854 that he had "recommenced the German." The following days often included the simple notation that he had "studied German."[70] That he did not have as much facility in German as he did in the other languages is implied by his use of the term "studied" rather than "read," as was normally the case when he spoke about his use of Hebrew, Greek, or Latin texts.

Roberts was also interested in the areas of the English language and the arts of communication. Early in 1852 he had opportunity to review William Kenyon's freshly published *Elements of English Grammar*. Roberts's diary note was simple but conclusive: "I examined Kenyon's *Grammar*. Dislike it."[71] Two years later, Roberts's engagement with a different kind of text was almost certainly more positive. In May 1854 Roberts spent time reading Hugh Blair's nearly classic *Lectures on Rhetoric*.[72] Originally published in 1783, Blair's text gained a short-lived new popularity among Methodists in the mid-nineteenth century. Though it was not a part of the ministerial course of study when Roberts was pursuing ordination, it became a required text

---

68. Roberts, "Diary," 22 March 1853.

69. For Roberts's text, see Roberts, "Diary," 23 January 1859. For Cicero's text, see Cicero, *Orationes*, Catil. 1, speech 1. The translation is that of C. D. Yonge, see Cicero, *Orations*, Catil. 1, speech 1.

70. Roberts, "Diary," 9–10, 13 March 1854.

71. Roberts, "Diary," 2 January 1852.

72. Roberts, "Diary," 4, 16 May 1854. For bibliographical information on Blair, see appendix 1, bibliography IV.

in 1860 and remained so for the next quadrennium. Among Methodist Protestants, however, Blair's text was placed on the list of recommended texts in 1858 and remained there for a full twenty years.[73]

This sketch of the reading patterns of B. T. Roberts has revealed a broad set of intellectual and social interests. He was a lover of ideas who immersed himself deeply in the resources of his religious tradition and broadly in contemporary developments in theology, pastoral ministry, and society. Roberts read many of these materials within one or two years of their publication dates, revealing his intentionality to keep current with the literature in his areas of interest. Moreover, Roberts functioned in such a way that there was not a disjunction between scholarly endeavors and pastoral ministry; in fact, intellectual engagement for Roberts seems always to have been at the service of his churchly calling, but never in conflict with it. Indeed, B. T. Roberts sought to living out his calling as a *churchly theologian,* or *scholarly pastor.* As a result of the leadership role that he would hold in the Free Methodist Church in the first generation of its existence, Roberts's intellectual and churchly formation became formative also for the young denomination. There is no doubt that Dr. Paul W. Livermore stands firmly and faithfully in this stream of scholars on behalf of Christ's church.

## Bibliography

Bennett, David H. *The Party of Fear: The American Far Right from Nativism to the Militia Movement.* 2nd ed. New York: Vintage, 1995.

Bledsoe, Albert Taylor. *A Theodicy; or, Vindication of the Divine Glory as Manifested in the Constitution and Government of the Moral World.* New York: Carlton & Phelps, 1854.

"Charles Elliott, D.D." *The National Magazine* 1 (1852) 560–62.

Child, L[ydia] Maria Francis. *Isaac T. Hopper: A True Life.* Boston: J. P. Jewett, 1853.

"The Christianity Required by the Times." *The National Magazine* 1 (1852) 501–5.

Cicero, M. Tullius. *Orationes: Pro Sex, Roscio, de Imperio Cn. Pompei, Pro Cluentio, in Catilinam, Pro Murena, Pro Caelio.* Edited by Albert Clark. Perseus Project, Tufts University. http://www.perseus.tufts.edu.

———. *Orations: Three on the Agrarian Law, the Four Against Catiline, the Orations for Rabirius, Murena, Sylla, Archias, Flaccus, Scaurus, Etc.* Edited by C. D. Yonge. Perseus Project, Tufts University. http://www.perseus.tufts.edu.

Collins, Charles. "Layard's Second Exploration." *Methodist Quarterly Review* 36 (1854) 113–31.

Cooley, William C. "Order and Confusion." *Earnest Christian* 1 (1860) 81–83.

Cross, Whitney R. *The Burned-Over District: The Social and Intellectual History of Enthusiastic Religion in Western New York.* Ithaca, NY: Cornell University Press, 1950.

Cullum, Douglas R. "Gospel Simplicity: Rhythms of Faith and Life Among Free Methodists in Victorian America." PhD diss., Drew University, 2002.

Curry, Daniel. "A Theodicy." *Methodist Quarterly Review* 36 (1854) 263–87.

"Daniel Webster." *The National Magazine* 1 (1852) 559.

---

73. Patterson, "The Ministerial Mind of American Methodism," 285, 366–67.

Davis, David Brion. *The Fear of Conspiracy: Images of un-American Subversion from the Revolution to the Present*. Ithaca, NY: Cornell University Press, 1971.
Eddy, T. M. "The Claims of Romanism." *Methodist Quarterly Review* 36 (1854) 533–52.
Edwards, Jonathan. "[Slothfulness]." *Earnest Christian* 1 (1860) 10.
———. "Work of the Spirit." *Earnest Christian* 1 (1860) 20.
———. *The Works of Jonathan Edwards*, vol. 1. With a memoir by Sereno E. Dwight and revised and corrected by Edward Hickman. 1834. Carlisle, PA: Banner of Truth Trust, 1974.
Elliott, Charles. *Sinfulness of American Slavery*. 2 vols. Cincinnati: Swormstedt & Power, 1851.
Floy, Dr. "The Eclipse of Faith." *Methodist Quarterly Review* 35 (1853) 169–91.
Franchot, Jenny. *Roads to Rome: The Antebellum Protestant Encounter with Catholicism*. Berkeley: University of California Press, 1994.
Hogue, Wilson T. *History of the Free Methodist Church*. 2 vols. Chicago: Free Methodist Publishing, 1915.
Hyde, A. B. "Dante." *Methodist Quarterly Review* 34 (1852) 49–66.
Langford, Thomas A. *Practical Divinity: Theology in the Wesleyan Tradition*. Nashville: Abingdon, 1983.
"Lardner, Nathaniel." In *The Oxford Dictionary of the Christian Church*, edited by F. L. Cross and E. A. Livingstone, 800. 2nd ed. 1974. Oxford: Oxford University Press, 1983.
Lippy, Charles H., ed. *Religious Periodicals of the United States: Academic and Scholarly Journals*. New York: Greenwood, 1986.
Marston, Leslie R. *From Age to Age a Living Witness: A Historical Interpretation of Free Methodism's First Century*. Winona Lake, IN: Light & Life, 1960.
May, Arthur J. "Seward and Kossuth." *New York History* 34 (1953) 267–83.
McClintock, John. "Methodist Preaching." *Methodist Quarterly Review* 34 (1852) 66–81.
———. "Stephen Olin." *Methodist Quarterly Review* 36 (1854) 9–33.
Moore, T. V. "William Penn." *Methodist Quarterly Review* 34 (1852) 119–35.
*The National Magazine: Devoted to Literature, Art, and Religion* 1–13 (1852–58). New York.
Patterson, Louis Dale. "The Ministerial Mind of American Methodism: The Courses of Study for the Ministry of the Methodist Episcopal Church, the Methodist Episcopal Church, South and the Methodist Protestant Church: 1880–1920." PhD diss., Drew University, 1984.
Perry, James H. "Hungary and Kossuth." *Methodist Quarterly Review* 34 (1852) 262–80.
Price, Carl F. *Wesleyan's First Century: With an Account of the Centennial Celebration*. Middletown, CT: Wesleyan University, 1932.
Roberts, Benjamin Titus. "The Diary of Benjamin T. Roberts." Collected papers of Benjamin T. Roberts Family (covering the years 1832–1924). Library of Congress.
———. "Rev. James B. Finley." *Earnest Christian* 1 (1860) 113–17.
———. "A Sketch of the Life of Rev. J. W. Redfield, M.D." In *History of the Origin of the Free Methodist Church*, by Elias Bowen. Rochester, NY: Roberts, 1871.
———. *Why Another Sect: Containing a Review of Articles by Bishop Simpson and Others on the Free Methodist Church*. Rochester, NY: Earnest Christian Publishing House, 1879.
Rowe, Kenneth E. "New Light on Early Methodist Theological Education." *Methodist History* 10 (1971) 58–62.
Roy, Judy M. *Rhetorical Campaigns of the 19th Century Anti-Catholics and Catholics in America*. Lewiston, NY: Mellen, 2000.

Ryan, Michael D. "John M'Clintock (1814–1870)." In *Something More Than Human: Biographies of Leaders in American Methodist Higher Education*, edited by Charles E. Cole. Nashville: United Methodist Board of Higher Education and Ministry, 1986.

Schwartz, Michael. *The Persistent Prejudice: Anti-Catholicism in America*. Huntington, IN: Our Sunday Visitor, 1984.

Tefft, Benjamin Franklin. *Hungary and Kossuth: Or, an American Exposition of the Late Hungarian Revolution*. Philadelphia: Ball, 1852.

Terrill, Joseph Goodwin. *The Life of Rev. John Wesley Redfield, M.D.* Chicago: By the author, 1890.

"Washington Irving." *The National Magazine* 1 (1852) 444.

"William Cullen Bryant." *The National Magazine* 1 (1852) 385–89.

Zahniser, Clarence Howard. *Earnest Christian: Life and Works of Benjamin Titus Roberts*. Published by the author, 1957.

# 13

# Body Matters: Re-Examining Ascetic Practice in John Climacus's *The Ladder*

———————————— Rebecca S. Letterman

## Why Reexamine Christian Ascetic Practices?

In formative Christian spirituality, our human bodies matter.[1] Human bodies matter to Christians because they matter to God. Not only did God create, delight in, and promise to resurrect human bodies, but God became a human in the incarnation of God the Son, Jesus Christ. Through the life, death, resurrection, and ascension of Jesus Christ, God has exhibited his investment in and love of humanity for eternity. Despite God's affirmation of the bodies of humanity, historically Christians have struggled to articulate and understand the relations of our mortal physicality experienced alongside dimensions of human living that seem to extend beyond physicality. Throughout Scripture, the terminology of "spirit" has many different meanings, but it has traditionally been understood as expressing something distinguishable from human physicality alone, distinguishable from "flesh," and distinguishable from "body."[2] At times, such distinction has been assumed to mean separateness, such that body and spirit in much of the literature of Christian spirituality have been viewed as unequal parts of what it means to be Christian human persons, with the spirit taking clear precedence.

One highly critiqued aspect of historic Christian understandings of the relationship of body and spirit, especially from the Protestant perspective, has been Christian ascetic movements of the early and medieval eras, which arguably involved both an unhealthy exaltation of ascetic practices and a tendency to view such practices as in some ways requiring God to respond to human initiatives and a kind of "works righteousness." Of course, one may counter that such criticisms come from a rather

---

1. I will be utilizing the Formative Spirituality Theory of Adrian van Kaam, as articulated in his six volume *Formative Spirituality Series* and four volume *Formative Theology Series*.

2. Scripture is at times ambivalent in the use of terms that are translated into English as "flesh," although most contemporary theological exegetes are careful to distinguish between "flesh" in the literal sense of body and "flesh" in the sense of that which resists God.

shallow understanding of such practices and their sociohistorical underpinnings. Still, judgmentalism towards those who did not practice asceticism, terrible degradation of human sexuality along with concomitant misogynistic views of women, and failures to delight in the creation of God as evidenced by the human body all flourished amid the milieu of Christian ascetic traditions for over a millennium. Thus, the Protestant correctives as well as reforms that have occurred within the Roman Catholic and Orthodox branches of the church in regard to some of these unhealthy trajectories have been warranted.

Despite some correctives in regards to understandings of the gifts of our bodies, arguably there are still often rather dismissive and ambiguous views of the human body among many Christians. Residual matter-spirit dualism still exists in theologies and liturgies that exalt spirit over body, that imply femaleness as less than maleness, and that emphasize only the dignity of Jesus Christ as Son of God and minimize the vulnerability of Jesus Christ as Son of Man. The church is in need of a more robust theology of the body, informed by a better understanding of the ways in which the dimensions of what classically have been understood as body and spirit exist in relation with one another, and the ways in which they constantly form and interform with one another.[3] Though perhaps it might seem unlikely, arguably there is wisdom to be gleaned in this regard from the Christian ascetic tradition, based on at least two premises.

First, classic Christian ascetic practices that desert monks and nuns recommended as means of taming vices and nurturing virtues came from years of experience across diverse communities. Recommended spiritual practices were not the suggestions of armchair Christians. They were instead based on the experiences of women and men across time and geographies who practiced and reflected on the results of the ways that physical, embodied practices affected their attentiveness to and love for God, themselves, and others.

Second, contemporary explorations of neuroscience are demonstrating that what have often been conceived of as so-called spiritual aspects of Christian living, such as experiences of reflection, transcendence, and compassion, are in point of fact physical experiences with correlative observable effects in the brain.[4] Neuroscience is also discovering that while there are certain locations for specific types of neural-processing (e.g., Broca's or Weirneke's areas for language, the pre-frontal cortex for complex

---

3. van Kaam, *Traditional Formation*, 82. To "form" is here understood as to influence or give shape to something. To "interform" is a van Kaamian term that describes the dynamics by which all aspects of living carry the capacity to influence each other. Hence, to "interform" refers to the action of various dynamics influencing one another in always on-going dynamism.

4. For examples of contemporary understandings of neuroscience in regard to aspects of humanity that have been traditionally considered as spiritual, see: Hall, "Repairing Bad Memories"; Sacks, "Seeing God in the Third Millennium"; Simon-Thomas et al., "An fMRI study of caring vs self-focus during induced compassion and pride"; and Immordino-Yang et al., "Neural Correlates of Admiration and Compassion," 8021–26.

decision-making), it is at the same time the case that different physical areas of our brains simultaneously and diffusely are involved with many activities.[5]

I argue that Christian texts that recommend bodily ascetic practices can be read through the lens of description, rather than prescription, as ways in which physical experiences occur in relation to what have commonly been conceived of as spiritual experiences. From this perspective, such classic ascetic practices may provide experiential wisdom regarding the ways in which human body and spirit interform together. To this end, consider such a reading of the classic Christian text of John Climacus, *The Ladder of Divine Ascent*.

## John Climacus: *Ladder of Divine Ascent*

In his introduction to the text as presented by the Classics in Western Spirituality series, Bishop Kallistos Ware notes that *The Ladder of Divine Ascent* is not only read aloud in its entirety during every Lent in Orthodox monasteries, so that some monks will have listened to this text over fifty times in their lifetime, but that it is a perennial favorite among the laity throughout the orthodox world.[6]

*The Ladder* was written by a monk named John who lived in the desert of Sinai in either the late sixth or early seventh century. John most likely entered the monastery as a young man. After living over 40 years as a monastic, he became the abbot of the monastery at Moses's Mount, where a century earlier the Emperor Justinian had built a church.[7] It was while serving in the role of Abbot that John wrote *The Ladder*, at the request of a friend serving as a superior at a nearby monastery.[8] When John humbly submitted to his friend's request, he did so as a man for whom experiential encounter with God was of primary importance. Given John's sociohistorical situatedness, his asceticism drew both from his own experience and from the ascetic experiences of men and women across several centuries of Christian tradition before him.

While John wrote for a monastic audience, he was deeply convinced of God's love for all of humanity. He wrote that "God is the life of all free beings. He is the salvation of . . . monks or those living in the world, of the educated or the illiterate, of the healthy or the sick, of the young or the very old . . . 'For God is no respecter of persons' (Rom 2:11)."[9] John's understanding of "progress in the spiritual life" was not a matter of growing in "contemplation" or "knowledge of God," but of growing in love.[10]

---

5. Carr, *What the Internet is Doing*, 182–194. Advancement of our understanding of the diffuse areas of the brain involved in memory formation and recall has changed dramatically over the past decade. See Nobel Prize Winner Eric R. Kandel's *In Search of Memory* for a history of the development of "biology of mind" and an explanation of current understandings of the field.

6. Ware, "Introduction," in *The Ladder*, 1.

7. Ware, "Introduction," in *The Ladder*, 1–3.

8. Ware, "Introduction," in *The Ladder*, 5.

9. Climacus, *The Ladder*, 74.

10. Ware, "Introduction," in *The Ladder*, 12.

John's text does recommend a few specific practices, including fasting and vigil. He did not lay out detailed directions for ascetic practices, for John was not primarily concerned with specific to-do lists of techniques, but instead John wanted to commend a way of life for his readers to assist them in discerning a way of walking in intimacy with Jesus. For John, this was not only a way of imitation of the Master, but a way of sharing the life experiences of Jesus through one's own life experiences, and through that shared experience to know union with the Trinity through Jesus Christ. John would have conceived of such union as being "spiritual."

To structure his text, John used the image of a ladder with thirty rungs. The number thirty represented for John the thirty years of the life of Jesus Christ before his baptism, with each rung corresponding to one of thirty main chapters in the text.[11] John titled his chapters with the virtues and vices that he explored, such as "On Renunciation of Life" and "Patience," and "Malice" and "Gluttony." Each chapter begins with a definition of the topic to be explored, followed by John's observations and recommendations for Christian response in relation to each topic.

### John's Understanding of the Body: Enemy, Helper, or Both/And?

Given the overall need to bring greater wholeness to the church's understanding of the body, it is of crucial importance to begin by identifying John's perspective on the body in *The Ladder*. Among the thousands of lines of the text, there are approximately a dozen lines in which John clearly treated the body as an enemy, found in about a half-dozen or so of the thirty chapters. For example, in the chapter "On Mourning," which focused on contrition, confession, and repentance, John observed that people who are gifted with godly mourning "regard their lives as detestable, painful and wearying, as a cause of tears and suffering, and they turn away from their body as from an enemy."[12] In his chapter "On Malice," which focused on harboring unforgiveness and anger, he wrote, "Treat your body always as an enemy, for the flesh is an ungrateful and treacherous friend. The more you look after it, the more it hurts you."[13] In his chapter entitled "On Chastity," which addressed what it is like to live life driven by unbridled passions, he wrote, "So as long as you live, never trust that clay of which you are made and never depend on it until the time you stand before Christ himself."[14] In his chapter entitled "On Discernment," he proclaimed, "A monster is this gross and savage body."[15] Clearly for John, the body is "other than" that part of him that is expressing the *imago Dei*.

---

11. Ware, "Introduction," in *The Ladder*, 11.
12. Climacus, *The Ladder*, 139.
13. Climacus, *The Ladder*, 153.
14. Climacus, *The Ladder*, 173.
15. Climacus, *The Ladder*, 232.

In one final particularly poignant example, in his chapter "On Meekness, Simplicity, Guilelessness, and Wickedness," John referenced the original, pre-Fall, childlike simplicity of Adam as that which "saw neither the nakedness of his soul nor the indecency of his flesh."[16] This is a particularly significant disparaging of the body, as it named the body as indecent before sin entered the world. There is no disputing that John expressed a disdain for the body—a view that is unbiblical and reflects the philosophical and cultural dualism of John's time, and which is representative of many (though not all) Christian ascetics.

If that were all there was to say, we might rightly proclaim "can anything good come from John's Christian ascetic tradition?" However, alongside John's dualism exists at the same time real insight into the human complexities of expressing the life of God in our bodies.

Alongside disdain for the body, John also expressed awe at the complexity of the human condition in relation to the ways in which the body (while assumed by him to be an "enemy") in actuality participated in healthy formation of what he conceived of as spirit. For example, in his chapter "On Gluttony," John wrote: "It is truly astounding how the incorporeal mind can be defiled and darkened by the body. Equally astonishing is the fact that the immaterial spirit can be purified and refined by clay."[17] While John's dualism is clear here, so is his acknowledgement that body and spirit interform with each other, and that for the Christian the body can be instrumental in the ongoing purification of "spirit."

Another example of John's ambiguous view of the body may be seen from John's chapter "On Chastity": "I was told once about an astonishing level of chastity attained by someone. 'There was a man who, having looked on a body of great beauty, at once gave praise to its Creator, and after one look was stirred to love God and to weep copiously, so that it was marvelous how something that could have brought low one person managed to be the cause of a heavenly crown for another . . . The same guideline ought to direct us when we sing songs and hymns, for the lovers of God are moved to holy joy, divine love, and tears by songs both worldly and spiritual, just as lovers of pleasure are moved to the opposite."[18] While John's asceticism would by default tend to make him suspicious of looking at a beautiful human body, or singing worldly songs, in point of fact John recognized that for those whose lives were free from inordinate passions, beauty and even worldly songs could lead them to love and praise to God.

Another example where John's observations of the ways in which human body and spirit form one another for ill or for good is found in his chapter "On Discernment," where he cautioned: "One man's medicine can be another man's poison, and something can be a medicine to the same man at one time and a poison at another. So I have seen an incompetent physician [of the soul], who by inflicting dishonor on

16. Climacus, *The Ladder*, 216.
17. Climacus, *The Ladder*, 169.
18. Climacus, *The Ladder*, 179.

a sick but contrite man produced despair in him."[19] Notice that John's understanding that cures for the soul must be carefully discerned so as not to do harm are based on his observations, on what he has "seen." From this same chapter "On Discernment" comes a short quip, a literary device for which John is well loved: "There are many roads to holiness—and to hell. A path wrong for one will suit another, yet what each is doing is pleasing to God."[20] This same theme of persons having various paths to wholeness is echoed in John's chapter "On Prayer," when he acknowledged: "We are not all the same, either in body or soul. Some profit from singing the psalms quickly, others from doing so slowly, the [first] one fighting distraction, the other[s] coping with ignorance."[21]

Such advice to those who are responsible to serve as guides to others in discerning the best ways to grow in love is hardly a shallow application of some activity assumed to produce a virtue or to lessen an inordinate passion. In his chapter "On Vainglory," John emphasized the foolishness of assuming one could earn things from God through human effort: "There are men who wear out their bodies to no purpose in the pursuit of total dispassion, heavenly treasures, miracle working, and prophetic ability . . . The man who seeks a quid pro quo from God builds on uncertainty, whereas the man who considers himself a debtor will receive sudden and unexpected riches."[22]

As do many in the Christian ascetic tradition upon careful reading, John acknowledged the complexity of the human condition that necessitates loving, prayerful discernment in any guidance provided to persons regarding receptivity to spiritual gifts from God. While John clearly was influenced by Greek dualism and Stoicism, at the same time John's experience and observations of the ascetic experiences of others led him to recognize a "mingling of spirit and clay."[23] For John, the relationship between what he viewed as two separate parts of humanity was a complex one in which one did not acquire, simply by physical exertions through ascetic practices, guaranteed spiritual fruit. There is more subtlety to John's thought than oversimplification too often ascribes to him and his ascetic ilk. That is, while ascetic Christians like John Climacus held a philosophic dualism between what they viewed as two different and clearly unequal parts of humanity (body and spirit), at the same time by their experiments with and observations of ascetic practices, they recognized that physical practices could be formative of their life in God and their relationships with one another. This contrasts with contemporary Protestant perspectives that dismiss entirely the formation potential of the body in Christian living, including those who would assume, for example, that physical position is irrelevant to prayer, or that what

---

19. Climacus, *The Ladder*, 233–4.
20. Climacus, *The Ladder*, 243.
21. Climacus, *The Ladder*, 281.
22. Climacus, *The Ladder*, 204.
23. Climacus, *The Ladder*, 248. John is here referring to a quotation of Gregory of Nazianzus.

and the amount that we have or have not eaten (e.g., caffeine) might affect our ability to attend to others with compassion.

While many Christian ascetics viewed the body philosophically as an enemy, in their actual practices they experientially acknowledged an implicit unity of body and spirit. For example, common to many of the ancient Christian ascetics is the linking of inordinate eating and sins of fornication and other sins of inordinate desire. John reflected this tradition, too, and wrote in his chapter "On Gluttony": "The man who looks after his belly and at the same time hopes to control the spirit of fornication is like someone trying to put out a fire with oil."[24] He went on to note that "most food that inflates the stomach also encourages desire."[25] He recommended fasting not only as a practice that helped to lessen lust and bad thoughts, but also as a means by which to nurture a host of attitudes and dispositions that he considered spiritually formative. He wrote, in his chapter "On Gluttony": "Fasting ends lust, roots out bad thoughts, frees one from evil dreams. Fasting makes for purity in prayer, an enlightened soul, a watchful mind, a deliverance from blindness. Fasting is the door of compunction, humble sighing, joyful contrition, an end to chatter, an occasion for silence, a custodian of obedience, a lightening of sleep, health of the body, an agent of dispassion, a remission of sins, the gate, indeed, the delight of Paradise."[26] For our sisters and brothers of past eras, there was a widely held assumption, based on observation and experience, that fasting helped in dealing with temptations of a host of inordinate desires, along with related sins, such as fornication.

In his chapter "On Placidity and Meekness," John noted that fasting in some people might actually increase their passions. For example, he wrote, "You will note that many irritable persons practice vigils, fasting, and stillness, For the devils are trying to suggest to them, under cover of penance and mourning, what is quite likely to increase their passion."[27] So while John upheld the idea of fasting as a practice that could assist one in not only resisting but lessening passionate temptations, he was not a simpleton. He was simply recommending the tried and true physical practice of fasting, in carefully discerned situations, that he and others for centuries before him had observed as being helpful in living a free and loving, "spiritual," life.

In his chapter "On Chastity," John advocated in regard to resisting sexual passions a mixture of physical practices alongside the practice of nurturing dispositions of wise moderation and humility: "The man who struggles against this enemy [of sexual passions] by sweat and bodily hardships is like someone who has tied his adversary with a reed. If he fights him with temperance, sleeplessness, and keeping watch, it is as if he had put fetters on him. If he fights [sexual passions] with humility, calmness and thirst,

---

24. Climacus, *The Ladder*, 169.
25. Climacus, *The Ladder*, 167.
26. Climacus, *The Ladder*, 169.
27. Climacus, *The Ladder*, 149.

it is as though he had killed the enemy and buried him in sand."[28] Clearly to John, bodily hardships and sweat provide but a flimsy response to sexual temptation, while when certain physical practices are joined with dispositions of moderation, attentiveness, humility, and equanimity, more efficacious results might be expected.

## Neuroscience and John's Ascetic Tradition

John's recommendation of combining a physical embodied experience within a broader context of human intention and humility echoes what current medicine is discovering about the nature of addressing addictions (what John would call the working out of disordered passions). Contemporary medicine has come to the understanding that addictions result from a complex set of factors, and that in fact human behaviors and experiences themselves may be triggers in addiction, not only drugs and other chemicals. Current neuroscience research in fact links to the same region of the brain all human experiences of addiction, whether inordinate sexual desires, inordinate desires for food, or inordinate desires for alcohol and other drugs.[29]

For example, Donald Hilton and Clark Watts in their 2011 article "Pornography Addiction: A Neuroscience Perspective," argue that current research is demonstrating that "process addictions" (such as a gambling addiction) and "natural addictions" (addictions resulting from excesses of normal biological processes like eating or sexual attraction) have parallel effects in the brain with drug addiction. Researchers are discovering that all addictive behaviors change brain chemistry and brain structures in ways that then impair the ability of subjects to resist repeating the addictive-compulsive behaviors in question.[30]

Harvard researcher Dr. Howard Shaffer wrote back in 2001: "I had great difficulty with my own colleagues when I suggested that a lot of addiction is the result of experience . . . repetitive, high-emotion, high-frequency experience. But it's become clear that neuroadaptation—that is, changes in neural circuitry that help perpetuate the [addictive] behavior—occurs even in the absence of drug-taking."[31] That is, human activities, not just the ingestion of chemicals or drugs, potentially have the power to foster addictive behavior.[32] Our physical activities can indeed influence what has classically been conceived of as the spiritual dynamic of "inordinate desires."

---

28. Climacus, *The Ladder*, 172.
29. Hilton and Watts, "Pornography Addiction."
30. Hilton and Watts, "Pornography Addiction."
31. Holden, "Behavioral Addictions," 294.
32. Schaffer, "What is Addiction?"

## Revisiting Christian Asceticism

In light of such findings, rather than conceiving of ascetic advice from the Christian tradition as mere works righteousness, we might actually approach such ascetic texts with an eye toward finding observed and described experiential wisdom in the advice of our ancient sisters and brothers for physical practices that they witnessed as nurturing our bodies (including our "brains" and neural pathways) in their ongoing process of conversion, of "putting away your former way of life."[33] Such a change of perspective is likely to challenge some of our own contemporary body-spirit dualism.

For example, in another passage from "On Chastity," John collected together a number of different recommended practices in the intentional battle against specific temptations: "When temptation comes, our best weapons are sackcloth and ashes, all-night vigils, standing up, hunger, the merest touch of water when we are thirsty, time passed among the burial places of the dead, and most important of all, humility of heart; and if possible a spiritual director or a helpful brother, old in wisdom rather than years, should also support us. Indeed, it would come as a great surprise if anyone could, by his efforts alone, save his ship from the sea."[34] While most modern-day North American Christians would likely readily affirm the helpfulness of advice and friendship of a wise Christian, or the disposition of humility in responding to temptation, most of the same people would likely hesitate at the ideas that wearing certain textures of clothing, being in a certain physical environment like a cemetery, or purposefully minimizing our physical comfort, could play a role in helping us respond to temptation.

But our sisters and brothers of ancient faith recognized that not only do thoughts and dispositions find expression in behavior or actions, but in point of fact, physical behaviors and actions also form our thoughts. That is, they recognized the fact that physical activities can shape our thoughts, our so-called "inner life." We have already examined the fact that, in the case of classic texts like John Climacus's *The Ladder of Divine Ascent*, they do not expect across-the-board, simplistic one-to-one relationships of things like fasting in resisting temptation. But neither are they hesitant to acknowledge that there are formative relationships among all dimensions of embodied human living, including those classically understood as body and spirit.

By their observations of the interactions between physical practices and the effects those practices had on their growth in love, desires for God, and sometimes release from anger and pride and lust, our sisters and brothers of the Christian ascetic traditions were in point of practice attuned to the embodiedness of our life as Christians in ways that many contemporary Christians are not. While they often

---

33. Alongside the definitive work of Christ of "a circumcision not performed by human hands" (Col 2:11, NIV), there is a call to human action accompanying such conversion: "put away your former way of life, your old self, corrupt and deluded by its lusts" (Eph 4:22, NRSV).

34. Climacus, *The Ladder*, 179.

mistakenly disdained the body as being less than, or as an enemy of what they viewed as the separate and more important "spirit," the fact of the matter is that in many ways they understood these two dimensions of being human to be interformational in a more sophisticated way than many contemporary North American Christians do. They understood physical practices as shaping their prayerfulness, their attitudes, and their temptations, not just as expressing them. In his chapter "On Humility," John expressed this very idea in relation to the actions of Jesus Christ at the Last supper: "The Lord understood that the virtue of the soul is shaped by our outward behavior. He therefore took a towel and showed us how to walk the road of humility (see John 13:4). The soul indeed is molded by the doings of the body, conforming to and taking shape from what it does."[35]

## Conclusion

Our ancient sisters and brothers understood that spiritual formation happens all the time simultaneously in all the dimensions of what it means for us to be humans. Some of their connections seem at first blush to be rather bizarre to us: what could fasting have to do with tempting thoughts? In what possible ways could thirst or sleeplessness assist us in our ability to respond to temptations in Christ-like ways? But in a time when brain science is beginning to uncover that there is a basic quality of diffusion and interrelatedness of many brain functions, this makes such recommended practices of our ancient sisters and brothers of the ascetic tradition potentially less bizarre, and in fact, perhaps, very much worth studying more carefully from the perspective of a description of what kinds of bodily practices were effective for many people in shaping their spirits in freedom and love.

Such historical descriptions take on fresh significance when placed in dialogue with ongoing research in neuroscience that is uncovering the many ways that physical activities significantly shape our brains, our minds and hearts, our orientations and perspectives, and our behaviors. Because our bodies are the embedded context of what it means for us to be humans, created in the image of God, our ascetic Christian forbearers invite us to reconsider the role of our bodies in not only the expression of but the actual shaping of our redeemed humanity. This commends future research in the relationship between physical activities and their impact on the ways we experience and know God, ourselves, and one another. Such research would be, by necessity, inter-disciplinary, including but not limited to research in psychology, physiology, neuroscience, pastoral care, and a truly holistic formative spirituality.

---

35. Climacus, *The Ladder*, 227.

## Bibliography

Carr, Nicholas. *What the Internet is Doing to Our Brains*. New York: Norton, 2010.

Climacus, John. *John Climacus: The Ladder of Divine Ascent*. Translated by Colm Luibheid and Norman Russell. The Classics of Western Spirituality Series. Mahwah, NJ: Paulist, 1982.

Hall, Stephen S. "Repairing Bad Memories." *MIT Technology Review* (2013). http://www.technologyreview.com/featuredstory/515981/repairing-bad-memories/.

Hilton, D. L., and C. Watts. "Pornography Addiction: A Neuroscience Perspective." *Surgical Neurology International* 2 (2011). http://www.surgicalneurologyint.com/article.asp?issn=2152-7806;year=2011;volume=2;issue=1;spage=19;epage=19;aulast=Hilton.

Holden, C. "Behavioral addictions: Do they exist?" *Science* 294 (2001) 980–82.

Immordino-Yang, Mary Helen, et al. "Neural Correlates of Admiration and Compassion." *Proceedings of the National Academy of Sciences* 106 (2009) 8021–26.

Kandel, Eric R. *In Search of Memory: The Emergence of a New Science of Mind*. New York: Norton, 2006.

Sacks, Oliver. "Seeing God in the Third Millennium." *The Atlantic*. http://www.theatlantic.com/health/archive/2012/12/seeing-god-in-the-third-millennium/266134/.

Schaffer, H. J. "What Is Addiction? A Perspective." *Cambridge Health Division on Addiction*. http://www.divisiononaddictions.org/html/whatisaddiction.htm.

Simon-Thomas, Emiliana R., et al. "An fMRI Study of Caring vs Self-focus During Induced Compassion and Pride." *Social Cognitive and Affective Neuroscience* (advance access publication September 6, 2011). Stanford School of Medicine's The Center for Compassion and Altruism Research and Education. http://ccare.stanford.edu/article/an-fmri-study-of-caring-vs-self-focus-during-induced-compassion-and-pride/.

van Kaam, Adrian. *Formation of the Human Heart*. Formative Spirituality 3. New York: Crossroad, 1991.

———. *Fundamental Formation*. Formative Spirituality 1. New York: Crossroad, 1989.

———. *Human Formation*. Formative Spirituality 2. New York: Crossroad, 1989.

———. *Scientific Formation*. Formative Spirituality 4. New York: Crossroad, 1987.

———. *Traditional Formation*. Formative Spirituality 5. New York: Crossroad, 1992.

———. *Transcendence Therapy*. Formative Spirituality 7. New York: Crossroad, 1995.

———. *Transcendent Formation*. Formative Spirituality 6. New York: Crossroad, 1995.

van Kaam, Adrian, and Susan Muto. *Christian Articulation of the Mystery*. Formation Theology 2. Pittsburgh: Epiphany, 2005.

———. *Formation of the Human Heart*. Formation Theology 3. Pittsburgh: Epiphany, 2006.

———. *Foundations of Christian Formation*. Formation Theology 1. Pittsburgh: Epiphany, 2004.

———. *Living Our Christian Faith and Formation Traditions*. Formation Theology 4. Pittsburgh: Epiphany, 2007.

Ware, Kallistos. "Introduction." In *John Climacus: The Ladder of Divine Ascent*. Translated by Colm Luibheid and Norman Russell. Classics of Western Spirituality. Mahwah, NJ: Paulist, 1982.

# 14

## At Home among the Stars: An Athanasian Perspective on Natural Theology

LINDA S. SCHWAB

### This Fragile Earth

IN DECEMBER 1972 a member of the Apollo 17 crew snapped the picture of earth that soon became known as the "Blue Marble" photograph. This image became immediately famous, and almost as quickly changed the way we think about our planet. Suddenly, the place where everything human has happened looked small and vulnerable in a vast dark field. Some saw in this defining image a confirmation of scientific materialism: a magnificent example of the machinery of natural laws, but a machine without purpose.

At the same time, earth took on the qualities of a spaceship, with a complex internal life in delicate balance, perhaps alone in its journey: "this fragile earth, our island home,"[1] adrift in an endless sea, confirming the urgency of the environmental issues facing the 1970s. Since then, humankind has become increasingly able, and even apparently willing, to destroy the balance of nature. With this realization, many see such ecological homeostasis as conferring a kind of personhood on the earth, and, by extension, perhaps on the universe as well: though a personhood without personality.

Nor was such a personhood a completely new idea. Since the 1940s, discoveries leading to the neurotransmitter theory of affective disorders had made the kinds of human qualities and experiences formerly associated with the soul into mere epiphenomena of brain biochemistry. As both intentional and accidental human tests uncovered psychotropic effects, including visions and religious euphoria, in new medicines,[2] many felt justified in relegating faith itself to the status of an epiphenomenon. The ability to treat mental illnesses as chemical imbalances brought in its wake a view of the interior landscape as radically changed as the view of the exterior universe.

---

1. "Eucharistic Prayer C," in *The Book of Common Prayer*, 370.
2. Sneader, *Drug Discovery*, 109–110 and 186.

Contemporary Western culture shows a wide diversity of responses to these views of human place and person. For some, scientific materialism affords all necessary answers. Others, impressed by the complexity of ecological interdependences, find themselves drawn to pantheism or panentheism. Conferring agency on "the Universe"—whether its ability to reward or punish by a karma-like mechanism, or to act in unpredictable and perhaps random ways—is as common as an indefinite and personal polytheism drawn from neopaganism and interest in world aboriginal religions. Finally, although the contemporary view of the human person is so shaped by medical science, questions of healing, restoration, and value remain—and remain troubling.

## Unprecedented Challenges?

Given these developments, by the late twentieth century what had come to be familiar ground in Christian natural theology was often being ceded, if not abandoned outright, as writers and preachers became well aware of the God-of-the-gaps fallacy, the weaknesses of teleological analogies like the Watchmaker, and the neo-orthodox position that nothing about God can be known rationally. It seemed unlikely that works of the earliest Christian eras could offer any new and helpful insights. Many prominent concerns of the first four centuries today sound at best irrelevant and at worst tainted by prejudice and violence. The gods of Greece and Rome represent no threat; the philosophical schools have changed and changed again; and a defense of Christian faith against Jews is, even at its mildest, too much a family quarrel—not to mention being forever darkened by the smoke of the Holocaust.

But perhaps the greatest problem with such ancient sources, at least in the contemporary mind, is the idea that none of this even matters: that they are, all of them, irrelevant because they belong to the pre-scientific era. Here a careful distinction must be made between being pre-scientific and being anti-scientific. Ancient atomists did not use the modern scientific method to develop or confirm their model of the universe, either in whole or in part; they were philosophers, not experimentalists.

However, the Enlightenment did not make previous knowledge irrelevant or untrue. Modern physics, chemistry, and biology incorporate the observations that humans had made for millennia, for example (to name just a few areas) in mechanics, metallurgy, and agriculture. Furthermore, the human interest in creating mental models that provide a coherent explanation of diverse phenomena was not made obsolete by the development of experimental science in the Enlightenment. On the contrary, the experimental method brought coherence to increasingly diverse observations. As the chain of human reason extended farther and farther beyond the limitations of human senses and human history, working from hypotheses through theories to laws, it began to seem almost as if there were nothing that humans could not know. And yet, philosophical ideas like explanatory power and qualities like mathematical elegance had their roots long before the Enlightenment.

Indeed, for two and a half millennia or more before the present, the place of earth in the universe was also the subject of active and refined study. Philosophers explored the possibilities that the earth might be floating on water, poised in the air or coalesced from a vortex of particles spun together in a bright, airy membrane.[3] By the first century, these and other cosmologies were familiar to the educated Greek world, along with Plato's and Aristotle's critique of each. Such world views, in which matter was given at least equal place with the idea of God, comprised one of the major intellectual challenges to early Christianity. These challenges spurred intense efforts to vindicate the reasonableness of Christian belief, engaging opposing views on their own ground. Therefore, let us first consider these efforts in more detail.

## Examples of Engagement

The Christian thinkers of the second and third centuries known as the Apologists framed crucial arguments that outlined a distinctively Christian philosophy and formed the beginnings of theology, especially a theology of nature. Three key figures—Justin, Clement of Alexandria, and Origen—joined the ideas that Christians may use (pagan) philosophy in interpreting Scripture, and that Jesus the Word is central to creation as well as salvation. The counterbalancing voice of Tertullian raised critical questions that have come to the fore again in our own time.

The philosopher Justin Martyr (ca. AD 103–165) came to faith in Christ as a mature man, at least partly in response to the intellectual coherence of Christianity.[4] When prejudice against Christians ignited persecution, he turned his skills to a reasoned defense of the faith. "Christians serve God rationally," he declared in his *First Apology*.[5] Justin's pre-conversion studies furnished many examples of philosophers who said things remarkably in line with Christian thought, and he gladly appropriated philosophers' insights. As a result, his early work, *A Hortatory Address to the Greeks* was a *tour de force* of what was called "physical philosophy," by a specialist for specialists. His point-by-point treatment of influential works is still fascinating to anyone interested in the history of scientific ideas, and, knowingly or not, remains the pattern followed by many authors in the area of faith and science.

Also heavily reliant on Greek philosophy was Clement, bishop of Alexandria (ca. AD 150–215); indeed, his knowledge of philosophy was so wide and deep that some of the pre-Socratic philosophers are known today mainly or only by his citation.[6] Influential as the founder of the Alexandrian school of theologians, Clement found philosophy to be at once preparation for the gospel and training to understand

---

3. Kirk and Raven, *Presocratic Philosophers*. The philosophers referred to are, in order, Thales, 87–89; Anaximander, 134–135; and Leucippus, 409–411.
4. Justin Martyr, *Dialogue with Trypho*, 3–8.
5. Justin Martyr, *Apology*, 13.
6. Kirk and Raven, *The Presocratic Philosophers*.

it; Christ, being the perfection of both philosophy and the Law, may thus be called "*Logos* and *Nomos*."[7] Origen (ca. AD 185–254), arguably the most famous of the Alexandrian school, developed a Platonist *Logos*-Christology that gave effective expression to two influential themes: that "the admirable order of the world" is proof of its Creator and reason to worship Him,[8] and that humans, by communion with the divine through Jesus, "might rise to be divine" and be elevated "to friendship with God and communion with Him."[9]

These three writers had engaged the best knowledge of the time on how the world works, and drew these ideas, clothed in the pervasive Platonism of the era, into Christianity. Tertullian recognized a potentially fatal flaw in this engagement: there is no value-free vantage point from which to view the world. Heretics had invariably imposed a pagan philosophical system on Christian belief, he observed, and come up with a "mottled Christianity of Stoic, Platonic and dialectic composition."[10] With pit-bull tenacity and a fine forensic mind, Tertullian grappled with these influences in a way that remains provocative, concluding that Christians should take their stand in Scripture, "on Solomon's Porch," rather than in the fundamentally anti-Christian stoas of Athens.[11]

## For of His Becoming Incarnate, We Were the Object

The indispensable deacon at the Council of Nicea, the tireless foe of the Arian heretics, the oft-exiled Bishop of Alexandria, and the eloquent exponent of *homoousion* Christology, Athanasius (ca. AD 298–373) was from his early years a deep student of Scripture and a keen observer of the philosophies and beliefs of his time. Even as a young man, he evinced a "clear, forcible and persuasive" style of speaking and writing and the capacity for deep concentration; but "knowledge of human nature was his first and most important science."[12] As his admirer Gregory described him, Athanasius

> was brought up, from the first, in religious habits and practices, after a brief study of literature and philosophy, so that he might not be utterly unskilled in such subjects . . . From meditating on every book of the Old and New Testament, with a depth such as none else has applied even to one of them, he grew rich in contemplation, rich in splendor of life, combining them in wondrous sort by that golden bond which few can weave, using life as the guide of contemplation, contemplation as the seal of life.[13]

7. McGrath, *Historical Theology*, 89–90.
8. Origen, *Against Celsus*, 1.23.
9. Origen, *Against Celsus*, 3.28.
10. Tertullian, *Prescription Against Heretics*, 7.
11. Tertullian, *Prescription Against Heretics*, 7.
12. Gibbon, *Decline and Fall*, 3.350–52.
13. Gregory of Nazianzus, *On the Great Athanasius*, 6.

In his youthful treatises (written at about age 21) *Against the Heathen* and *On the Incarnation of the Word*—actually two parts of one work—Athanasius addressed the views of pantheists, panentheists and Epicureans, among others. How he understood these views, how he answered their adherents, and how he continued to form his response into a theology of Christ, nature and humanity, will prepare the way for exploring their contemporary relevance.

From the outset, Athanasius made clear the intent of his work: "the purpose of the book [is] a vindication of Christian doctrine, and especially of the cross."[14] Whereas the second-century Apologists tended to look at Christ within the framework of philosophy, associating John's *Logos* with the Platonic *Logos* and filling in the picture with all the cosmological associations that that entails, Athanasius looked at Christ first and foremost as Savior. Therefore, Athanasius's cosmology resulted from his soteriology.[15]

*Against the Heathen* opens with a brief view of the goodness of God's original creation, in which evil had no part; however, man became self-absorbed and sense-absorbed. In fact, evil consists in exactly this, Athanasius argued: choosing the lesser over the greater good.[16] Furthermore, he observed, this same focus on the material and sensual leads also to idolatry; not even the poets' finest portrayals of the Greco-Roman gods could withstand scrutiny without fundamental inconsistencies and deep moral problems becoming evident.[17]

So much for the crudities of popular paganism, which were relatively easy to dismiss; however, as Athanasius observed, some of those who repudiate that kind of idolatry believe that they are taking the high road in "worship of the universe and of the parts of the universe"[18]—in today's language, in pantheism or animism. In response, Athanasius pointed out that the parts of creation are mutually dependent and none is self-sufficient; in fact, many of these parts are opposites which would, taken separately, tend to destroy one another.[19]

Here, Athanasius assumed self-sufficiency as a requisite attribute of God. If God is in one part of nature, such as the sun or the moon, then God is not self-sufficient, because the sun requires the existence of the heavens and the moon requires the sun. Indeed, each part of nature requires some other part, so no one part can be God without making God dependent and not self-sufficient. But what if these sophisticated nature-worshippers "combine all [the parts of nature] together and . . . say that the whole is God"? This renders God "unlike Himself," being made of dissimilar parts. This part of the argument rests on assuming for God an essential unity, the oneness of Deut 6:4.

---

14. Athanasius, *Against the Heathen*, 1.
15. Robertson, "Prolegomena," xxiii.
16. Athanasius, *Against the Heathen*, 2–7.
17. Athanasius, *Against the Heathen*, 8–26.
18. Athanasius, *Against the Heathen*, 27:1.
19. Athanasius, *Against the Heathen*, 27:5–7.

Lacking such integrity, however, God could not be eternal; He would be "destined to be divided again, in accordance with the natural tendency of the parts to separation."[20] As a result, nature is not God, even taken collectively,[21] but God is recognized as the artist of nature, just as the "works of art by their symmetry and by the proportion of their parts betray Phidias [the sculptor] to those who see them."[22]

Athanasius's next argument will prove to be an extremely interesting one. He observed that the order of nature is, in fact, a harmony of opposing forces, which must be created, brought together, and what is more, sustained in this delicate tension, by the reason, Wisdom, or Word of God, as in Prov 8:27, John 1:1, and Col 1:15–18. Athanasius briefly presented three analogies to explain this: the Word works in the universe as the conductor leads a great chorus, or as the soul moves the body, or as the founding ruler of a kingdom directs the works of all its citizens as they engage in their occupations.[23] It is through this Word that human nature will be restored.

In *On the Incarnation of the Word*, Athanansius continued to develop the theme of creation and restoration, but also introduced another view that he intended to address. This is the Epicurean worldview, derived in part from the atomists Leucippus and Democritus; in it, the universe is understood as originating by the chance coalescence of atomic matter.

Again, Athanasius used what may be a novel argument to show a weakness of this philosophy. His description of the materialistic worldview identifies a key implication: "For if, as they say, everything has had its beginning of itself, and independently of purpose, it would follow that everything had come into mere being, so as to be alike and not distinct."[24] Perhaps drawing on his observation of the harmony of opposites in nature, he recognized that matter in random combinations is more likely to produce disorderly uniformity than complex differentiation, and that in fact the jump to complex differentiation is extremely unlikely to occur on its own; in the modern language of thermodynamics, it is not spontaneous.

Athanasius's critique of the Epicureans' beginning-less universe is essential to his argument: "so that it may be duly perceived that the renewal of creation has been the work of the self-same Word that made it at the beginning."[25] In creation, God set his image on humanity (Gen 1:26-27); as human self-absorption and rejection of God smeared and ruined this image, "He dealt so lovingly as to appear and be born even in a human body," just as the subject of a portrait would return so that the stained painting could be accurately restored.[26] Since it was humankind's self-

---

20. Athanasius, *Against the Heathen*, 28.
21. Athanasius, *Against the Heathen*, 29.
22. Athanasius, *Against the Heathen*, 35.
23. Athanasius, *Against the Heathen*, 36.
24. Athanasius, *On the Incarnation of the Word*, 2.
25. Athanasius, *On the Incarnation of the Word*, 1.
26. Athanasius, *On the Incarnation of the Word*, 4, 14.

centered absorption in the physical that caused the problem, God had to enter the physical and material, becoming incarnate; only this complete engagement with human senses and minds could redress the confusion and restore the human condition.[27] Having worked out this theme through the atonement and supported it with reference to Scripture, Athanasius returned to the objections of the era's intelligentsia. Given that most of them accepted a pervading Spirit or *Logos* (rationality) in the universe, what, he asked, is so difficult about accepting that the Spirit or *Logos* could be joined to one particular part of the universe, that is, to one particular person?[28] Anticipating the philosophers' objections, he explained that were the Word not in the whole of creation, it could not be in any one part.[29] Furthermore, since it was only humans who needed saving and restoring, it could only be through a human that this should happen.[30] So complete is this re-creation that humanity is reconciled with God, indeed lifted up to be rejoined to God; in summary,

> Let [one] marvel that by so ordinary a means things divine have been manifested to us, and that by death immortality has reached to all, and that by the Word becoming man, the universal Providence has been known and its Giver and Artificer, the very Word of God. For He was made man that we might be made God.[31]

In his following works, Athanasius continued to differentiate himself from his predecessors in his careful and perceptive avoidance of subordinationism on soteriological grounds. This would later become the cornerstone of his argument against the Arians. The nature of saving or redeeming—reconciling or restoring to God—is such that no fellow-creature can accomplish it fully for another; only God can do this. According to the Arians, Jesus was the first of the Father's creations, and therefore, less than fully God; hence he is incapable of saving and restoring. However, since Jesus Christ is Savior, he is also God. This argument also hinges on Christian worship of Jesus. Only God is to be worshipped; Christian worship of Jesus declares him Savior, Christ and God.[32] The key to this statement is Athanasius's appreciation of the tradition of worship and its formative quality. In this complex of interlinked arguments, he anticipated the quadrilateral of Scripture, tradition, reason, and experience.

Throughout these works, simply by his engagement with philosophies like Epicurean materialism, Athanasius showed himself open both to ways of addressing questions about the world and, occasionally, to specific ideas that continue to resonate

---

27. Athanasius, *On the Incarnation of the Word*, 15.
28. Athanasius, *On the Incarnation of the Word*, 41.
29. Athanasius, *On the Incarnation of the Word*, 42.
30. Athanasius, *On the Incarnation of the Word*, 43–45.
31. Athanasius, *On the Incarnation of the Word*, 54.
32. Athanasius, *Four Discourses Against the Arians*, Discourse 2 and 3; "On Worship," Discourse 2, 23–24.

in human thought. This extends to ideas that one might have thought to be not only modern but very recent, such as the possibility of multiple universes.[33] Though his era was pre-scientific, his approach was by no means anti-scientific, and we might profitably examine his works for insights of renewed significance.

## A Pastoral Apologetic

At the outset, it is important to observe the strongly pastoral character that marks both the expression and content of Athanasius's two-part work. His detailed address to the philosophies of the day is driven by the desire, as a physician of souls, to teach Christ as Savior and to bring to a disintegrating humanity a message of healing and restoration. Extending the direction of his thought to today's situation requires recognizing the pastoral component in its character.

Next, such a message of restoration must refer to the specific obstacles, misunderstandings or interests of real people: nothing replaces knowing the audience and addressing their specific issues in their own language. It is a practical expression of the pastoral approach to engage in dialogue fitted to the needs and understanding of one's conversation partner. As Gregory of Nazianzus observed, the qualities that resulted from Athanasius's immersion in Scripture showed through in his life,[34] giving him the ability, in everyday discourse, to identify the needs of individuals and respond to each, by turns inspiring, consoling, instructing, and protecting.[35] Rarely using classical rhetorical models or planning a highly systematic composition, Athanasius wrote with a conversational flow, often repeating important points or favorite examples.

Although much in these two works clearly belongs to a distant time and its equally distant cultural milieu, the books' recurring theme has recently increased in interest and importance: an exploration of the relationship among humankind, nature, and God. Two aspects of this exploration are especially relevant to today's concerns: the balance of nature and the meaning of embodied life.

## Harmony and Restoration

Among the Apologists, as among many since, the aspects of nature that most speak of God are nature's magnificence and the wisdom evinced in its details. For Athanasius, however, the essential quality of nature, the aspect that gives the clearest evidence of God, is nature's harmony: the creative tension of opposites. These opposing forces are brought together and sustained in dynamic balance by the Word of God. This idea is explored and reinforced in a second and more detailed exposition of the triple analogy of the harmony of nature: the universe as a chorus, and the Word as the conductor; the

---

33. Athanasius, *Against the Heathen*, 39.
34. Gregory of Nazianzus, *On the Great Athanasius*, 6.
35. Gregory of Nazianzus, *On the Great Athanasius*, 10.

universe as a body in action, and the Word as the soul; and the universe as a great city, and the Word as its ruler.[36] These analogies bear closer study.

In each, elements act individually under the direction of the Word as the common purpose uniting them. Furthermore, each describes a situation characterized by creative development rather than mechanistic reaction. In the first, the individuality of a chorus is in the singers—male and female, young and old—and the conductor elicits from each "sound according to his nature and power," but "a single harmony." "Harmony," in this example, is more than chordal: it is the music as a whole, including melody and rhythm as well. Furthermore, the Word is not the plan of the work, the mere score; rather, the Word is the conductor, who brings the plan to life with expression through dynamics and tempo.

The next deals with the harmony of the human body. To put Athanasius's simile in contemporary language, this harmony is the simultaneous modulation and integration of sensory inputs—sight, hearing, touch, smell, and taste—by one another to elicit a concerted sensorimotor response. Today we would speak of sensory and motor systems in terms of their physical substrates, that is, neural pathways. Each of these is indeed a system: that is, it comprises many neurons. The number of individual elements brought into common purpose is therefore much more in line with those in Athanasius's other analogies—a large chorus, a city—than he might have guessed. Furthermore, Athanasius presented the most complex possible case. It has become axiomatic in neuroscience that successive generations of neuroscientists have understood the nervous system in terms of the best technology of their time: nerve-to-nerve communication as working like a telegraph, neural systems as working like a telephone exchange, and neural integration as working like a computer. These models have assisted in mapping sensorimotor systems of two pathways, such as hand-eye coordination, but more extensive integration of sense and action, not to mention including the awareness of thought and feeling, is far more complex.[37]

Indeed, it would be more like the work of a great city, Athanasius's third example. Here, each individual has a particular role and condition, work and direction. All of this complex system is organized by the ruler's presence and management: the ruler's presence is throughout, though the ruler's management is indirect. The unity that results confers on each (as Athanasius earlier described it) "peace in the enjoyment of equal rights."[38] In his emphasis on God the Word's power to call into being and to sustain in balance a world or universe characterized by complex differentiation, Athanasius chose qualities that are closely linked to the question of healing and restoration,

---

36. Athanasius, *Against the Heathen*, 43.

37. Athanasius did not lack for a way to conceptualize complex integration; between the two choral analogies, he described the modulating role of the intelligent soul as being that of a "skilled musician," an "artist," playing upon the physical substrate of the senses as upon a lyre. Athanasius, *Against the Heathen*, 31.

38. Athanasius, *Against the Heathen*, 38.

since the action of the Word—conductor, soul, or ruler—by directing toward harmony directs away from disorder and decay.

The insights of experimental science over the last two hundred years have increasingly pressed the question of how complex systems can exist at all in a world in which (as Athanasius noted) "the natural tendency of the parts to separation"[39]—in other words, to undifferentiated disorder—is so strong. One way of answering the question comes from in the field of non-equilibrium thermodynamics. Explained very briefly, work in this area over the last half-century suggests that order develops in nature (for example, in snowflake patterns) along a many-branched path from a randomized state (like that which Athanasius calls "mere being"[40]) to a complex, ordered state. Precisely what causes the road taken at each branch is not only unknown but can be shown to be unknowable.[41] In other words, the cause is not subject to the God-of-the-gaps fallacy, but represents a specific physical type of unknowability. It should be reiterated that this experimental and mathematical answer is concerned only with the "how" of such apparently improbable order, and not the "why."

However, Athanasius's description of the Word's role in organizing mixed and disordered systems into complex, orderly ones represents more than an interesting set of comparisons with contemporary scientific thought. As noted above, one of the qualities of the early apologists was the tendency to approach Christ's saving action as developing from philosophical cosmology, whereas Athanasius chose the standpoint of Christ's salvation as that from which to develop a cosmology. In such an approach, sustenance and restoration play central roles. The former is especially seen in the balance of nature; the latter, in one part of the creation, that is, human life, which cannot be considered apart from the issue of having/being a body.

The pastoral dimension of Athanasius's work is especially evident in his discussion of the way in which the Incarnation saves, protects and restores everything human.[42] "Therefore the perfect Word of God puts around Him an imperfect body . . . that, paying the debt in our stead, He might, by Himself, perfect what was wanting in man."[43] Athanasius, in his later work Against the Arians, emphasized the relationship of this act to all of physical nature with his usual concreteness. He made it clear that when Jesus "transferred to himself all the affections of the body," these feelings included, in detail, all the physiological and psychological ills (such as hunger, thirst, weariness, "not knowing," pain, and fear of death) that needed to be corrected. By this, the human body can say:

---

39. Athanasius, *Against the Heathen*, 28.
40. Athanasius, *On the Incarnation of the Word*, 2.
41. Prigogine and Stengers, *Order Out of Chaos*, 131–76; 222–26; 291–313.
42. Athanasius, *On the Incarnation of the Word*, 10.
43. Athanasius, *Four Discourses Against the Arians*, Discourse 2; 21, 66.

"I am from earth, being by nature mortal, but afterwards I have become the Word's flesh, and He 'carried' my affections, though He is without them; and so I became free from them, being no more abandoned to their service because of the Lord who made me free from them"[44]

## At Home among the Stars

With the passage of time, the iconic image of earth as a "Blue Marble" may have come to represent more than the views it first prompted: of earthly life as a cosmic accident, and its planet as fragile, vulnerable and perhaps alone. It might someday be seen as emblematic of a time in which humankind acted as if it were possible to hold the natural world at arm's length. Certainly at no previous time in history has it been so easy to disregard the connection to nature as it is today for most people in the developed world, or to propose for nature's "problems" solutions that are increasingly technological and increasingly separate from daily life and experience.

This separation from the natural world extends to its most intimate expression, the human body. Ironically, as medical science has more and more erased the separation between mind and body, it has become more and more common for people to speak of "my body" as an entity separate from the self, a being capable of a sort of independent (perhaps even contrary) life and the rudimentary communication of its wants.

Without a knowledge of and a connection to nature, a theology of nature and of human bodily life, if possible at all, is bound to be stunted. Worse yet, so is Christian proclamation and care. One can hardly engage in dialogue a Deep Ecologist who may be an adherent of Gaia or science or "the Universe" without being on quite literally the same ground: the same patch of dirt. When the human body is seen as mere utilitarian clothing for the real self, those with less functional suits (which, sooner or later, is all of us) become of less value.

Athanasius's perspective, grounded in the saving work of Christ and weighting sustenance equal to creation, can address such divisions directly, because it is rooted in observation of the natural world and natural processes. Throughout *Against the Heathen*, Athanasius developed the idea that the most fundamental kind of order in nature is the productive tension of unlike properties—cold and hot, wet and dry—and that it is the dynamic balance and harmony in which these and their physical substrates are held that reveals the power of the Divine Word. Near the end of this first book, Athanasius showed this power at work in a sweeping scene in which

> the heaven revolves, the stars move, the sun shines, the moon goes her circuit, and the air receives the sun's light and the aether his heat, and the winds blow; the mountains are reared on high, the sea is rough with waves, and the living things in it grow, the earth abides fixed, and bears fruit, and man is formed

---

44. Athanasius, *Four Discourses Against the Arians*, Discourse 3; 33–34.

> and lives and dies again and all things whatever have their life and movement; . . . plants grow, and some are young, some ripening, others in their growth become old and decay, and while some things are vanishing others are being engendered and are coming to light.

And the Word holds not only this visible universe but also its "invisible powers"—including the mystery of life endowed with rational thought—at one.[45]

As this passage indicates, Athanasius saw no division between the natural world and human life, except insofar as life and thought are invisible; indeed, the comprehensive redemptive action of the Incarnation depends upon this unity. Such a vision is in accord with the contemporary recognition of the complexity of mind-body interactions. Therefore, Athanasius's picture can readily be re-expressed in today's language. For example, we are now used to thinking of human bodies at the level of systems and molecular processes. How important it is that Jesus "carried," redeemed, and restored all of these. The fact that Jesus had DNA makes him quite practically and specifically the Savior of the infant with a genetic metabolic disease and the middle-aged cancer patient; that he had a human brain and nervous system makes him the Savior of the young woman with bipolar disorder and the old man with Parkinson's. In that he carried the basic matter involved in all these cases, Christ carries the physical burden for each one, and for those who love them, that we might be "taken to him through his flesh, and henceforward inherit life everlasting."[46]

As Athanasius saw it, to try to count the ways in which the Savior worked and works in the world through the Incarnation is like trying to count the waves, as coming one upon another they crash on the shore.[47] Indeed, the Word's restorative sustenance is as much hope for earth's resilience as it is for individual lives. But this is restoration for a purpose: life guided by the Word. It can be known in no other way but by striving to express it in daily action, in one's way of life:[48] adding one's own voice to the Word's chorus, one's senses to the Word's hand, and one's own work to the unfolding Kingdom, in active praise to the God of our salvation.

---

45. Athanasius, *Against the Heathen*, 44.
46. Athanasius, *Four Discourses Against the Arians*, Discourse 3; 34.
47. Athanasius, *On the Incarnation of the Word*, 54.
48. Athanasius, *On the Incarnation of the Word*, 56–57.

PART 2: INSIGHTS FROM THE HISTORY OF THE CHURCH

## Bibliography

Athanasius. *Against the Heathen*. In vol. 4 of *The Nicene and Post Nicene Fathers*, Series 2. Edited by Philip Schaff and Henry Wace. 1886–1889. 14 vols. New York: Christian Literature Company, 1892.

———. *Four Discourses Against the Arians*. In vol. 4 of *The Nicene and Post Nicene Fathers*, Series 2. Edited by Philip Schaff and Henry Wace. 1886–1889. 14 vols. New York: Christian Literature Company, 1892.

———. *On the Incarnation of the Word*. In vol. 4 of *The Nicene and Post Nicene Fathers*, Series 2. Edited by Philip Schaff and Henry Wace. 1886–1889. 14 vols. New York: Christian Literature Company, 1892.

"Eucharistic Prayer C." In *The Book of Common Prayer*, 370. New York: Church Hymnal Corporation and the Seabury Press, 1977.

Gibbon, Edward. *The History of the Decline and Fall of the Roman Empire*, vol. 3. London: Murray, 1838.

Gregory of Nazianzus. *On the Great Athanasius*. In vol. 7 of *The Nicene and Post Nicene Fathers*, Series 2. Edited by Philip Schaff. 1886–1889. 14 vols. Reprint, Peabody, MA: Hendrickson, 1994.

Justin Martyr. *Apology 1*. In vol. 1 of *The Ante-Nicene Fathers*. Edited by Alexander Roberts and James Donaldson. 1885–1887. 10 vols. Reprint, Peabody, MA: Hendrickson, 1994.

———. *Dialogue with Trypho*. In vol. 1 of *The Ante-Nicene Fathers*. Edited by Alexander Roberts and James Donaldson. 1885–1887. 10 vols. Reprint, Peabody, MA: Hendrickson, 1994.

Kirk, G. S., and J. E. Raven. *The Presocratic Philosophers*. Cambridge: Cambridge University Press, 1969.

McGrath, Alister. *Historical Theology*. Oxford: Blackwell, 1998.

Origen. *Against Celsus*. In vol. 4 of *The Ante-Nicene Fathers*. Edited by Alexander Roberts and James Donaldson. 1885–1887. 10 vols. Reprint, Peabody, MA: Hendrickson, 1994.

Progogine, Ilya, and Isabelle Stengers. *Order Out of Chaos: Man's New Dialogue with Nature*. New York: Bantam, 1984.

Robertson, Archibald. "Prolegomena to St. Athanasius." In vol. 4 of *The Nicene and Post Nicene Fathers*, Series 2. Edited by Philip Schaff and Henry Wace. 1886–1889. 14 vols. New York: Christian Literature Company, 1892.

Sneader, Walter. *Drug Discovery: The Evolution of Modern Medicines*. Chichester: Wiley, 1985.

Tertullian. *Prescription Against Heretics*. In vol. 3 of *The Ante-Nicene Fathers*. Edited by Alexander Roberts and James Donaldson. 1885–1887. 10 vols. Reprint, Peabody, MA: Hendrickson, 1994.

# 15

## See How They Love One Another: A Short History of Medieval and Reformation Poor Relief and Its Significance for the Church Today

### Elizabeth L. Gerhardt

WHAT TO DO WITH the poor? The church has struggled throughout church history to create a theological and ethical response to poverty. This chapter is not an exhaustive study on poor relief during the Middle Ages and Reformation periods. Rather, it is a historical glimpse into the important transition from medieval to reformation theology, and the subsequent changes on the theory and practice of poor relief in the area of charity and social justice.

There are many possible avenues of study that could aid in understanding this important historical and theological transition, and its implication on policies regarding poor relief. However, for the purpose of identifying key social and theological influences on poor relief during these critical periods in church history, this chapter explores three representative influences: the medieval papacy, St. Francis and the Mendicants, and Luther's theology and its influence on community social change in Wittenberg. Both medieval and reformation theologies of charity and social justice can help inform the church in the twenty-first century on strategies to address poverty in both our local and global communities.

### The Intersection of West and East: Blessing the Poor

Prior to the rise of the market economy, the Western European church's primary function was liturgical. During the eighth to the eleventh centuries life was brief, and an agrarian society was vulnerable to the shift of political powers, the plight of weather, disease, and an insecure future. The poor populace relied on the security of liturgy and ritual. Within monasteries a daily rigorous schedule guided the services, meals, and work of the monks. Clergy offered Masses and blessings that offered not only comfort, but security from the fear of death.

The ritual of the "blessing" was a significant factor in providing the faithful with an appeasement to the wrath of God. Saintly people were viewed as those whose holiness could resist the temptation of the devil. However, most people needed the clergy to continue one of their main functions, the ritual of blessing. "They blessed people and things and places and occasions; they called upon various agents, divine, saintly, or ecclesiastical, to impart their respective blessings."[1] For the laity, these rituals created a system of great dependence on the clergy. The clergy and religious were the sole mediators between God and the lay people, and between the living and dead. The liturgy and rituals of blessing was the means to bestow their spiritual power to the repentant sinner. The religious blessing was indeed powerful. Prayers offered (or not offered) by the religious determined whether or not one was written into "the books of life." These books were real. Ledgers filled with names of the saved were kept near the altars in many monasteries and churches. As imagined, this system was open to political and ecclesiastical corruption.[2]

Due to the central role of worship and liturgy during the early medieval period, all church wealth was consecrated in luxurious sanctuaries with a vast use of gold, silver, and gems. Western monasticism from the seventh to the twelfth centuries was identified by the great riches the monasteries and church acquired.[3] During this same period the poverty of the masses was defined not only by a lack of wealth, but also by a lack of spiritual power. The relationship of the monks and religious who often claimed a voluntary poverty to the material poor masses was also based in ritual. Lester K. Little provides the following example of the close relationship between charity and ritual: that the death of a monastery donor would trigger the feeding of a set number of paupers who came to the door. The feeding of the poor was not determined by their needs, but rather by the liturgical needs of the religious and monastics.[4] Therefore, prior to the rise of the profit economy in the twelfth and thirteenth centuries, Christianity was centered on liturgy and ritual, with the religious as the sole intermediaries between God and the masses. Care for the poor was for the benefit of the institutional church, and deeply integrated into a spirituality that focused on acquiring divine blessing.

Like the West, the Byzantine church closely tied the work of charity to the achievement of holiness and blessedness. There is a rich history of poor relief in the Eastern Church and it is worthwhile to note a few exceptional examples of philanthropy. Both emperors and empresses were praised in official documents for their generosity to

1. Little, "Religion, Economy and St. Francis," 151.
2. Little, "Religion, Economy and St. Francis," 152.
3. Little, "Religion, Economy and St. Francis," 153. See also Chadwick, *The Early Church*, 267–8 for a description of development of liturgical riches in both the Eastern and Western Church.
4. Little, "Religion, Economy and St. Francis," 154. See also Chenu, *Nature, Man and Society*, for an extensive study on the interrelatedness of religion and societal development. He argues that religious rituals and spirituality had a direct impact on the familial and community relationships in Medieval Europe.

the less fortunate. They had little direct contact with the poor. Nevertheless, many viewed their state responsibility as one with their Christian mandate to provide charity through established institutions.

> In the fifth century Pucheria, the sister of Emperor Theodosios II and for a time his regent, is reported to have used her own funds to establish churches, shelters for beggars and the homeless, and monasteries. In the same century the exiled empress Athenais-Eudokia built in Jerusalem countless hospices for pilgrims, the poor, and the elderly. In the sixth century the empress Theodora, the wife of Justinian I, founded a specialized sort of institution, a reformatory for repentant prostitutes... One late ninth-century empress, Theophano, even achieved sanctity for her charitable activity and ascetic life-style.[5]

Financial gifts of land and money were considered acts of piety and frequently occurred when wealthy men and women entered monasteries and convents. Acts of charity were directly linked to the attainment of salvation of the donor.[6] The poor in medieval Byzantine were primarily ministered to by the deaconesses. These women visited the sick, distributed alms, worked in orphanages, poor houses, and hospitals.[7] In addition, there were large institutions supported by the wealthy and the church to serve the needs of the sick and indigent. Many were attached to monasteries, and there was one in Constantinople so large that it was called the "city for the poor." It included several buildings with hundreds serving the blind, lame, and destitute.[8] Like the West, the Byzantine monasteries and convents distributed food, clothing, and accepted donations on behalf of the families of the dead. These donations were regarded as a method of assuring the salvation of the deceased relative and of the nuns who supervised the distribution of food."[9]

Therefore, the chief motivation for charity was the search for salvation. Feeding and caring for the poor was considered to be identical to caring for Christ in a deeply spiritual and physical sense of Christian duty. In turn, to serve Christ concretely was to also hope for the reward of salvation. For the nuns, ministry to the needy also offered an opportunity to open the doors of the convents to serve the poor and mentally ill. They gained more individual freedom in contrast to those that lived the cloistered life. Lay women were also provided an occasion to leave the restrictions of their home life and interact with those outside their immediate households. The common thread holding together early medieval spirituality and care for the poor was this assumption

---

5. Talbot, "Byzantine Women, Saints, and Social Welfare," 107.
6. Talbot, "Byzantine Women, Saints, and Social Welfare," 109.
7. Malone, *Women and Christianity I*, 123. See Malone, pp. 123–28 for further information regarding the development of the deaconess movement from the third century to the eleventh. Malone argues that the deaconesses held great power in the early church, and became an increasing threat to the church hierarchy.
8. Talbot, "Byzantine Women, Saints, and Social Welfare," 115–16.
9. Talbot, "Byzantine Women, Saints, and Social Welfare," 119.

that the practice of charity assured sanctification and facilitated the quest for salvation. This common thread would strengthen and evolve into a strong rope that tied together theology, ecclesiology, and the assurance of salvation during later Middle Ages of the twelfth to the fifteenth centuries.

## Systematizing Poor Relief: The Significance of Papal Influence

Gregory the Great (590–604) and Innocent III (1198–1216) represent the beginning and the later papal authorities that determined ecclesial systematic care for the poor.

Accommodations were made for those held captive with ransoms for their safe return. Gregory I established an administrative process for feeding and caring for the poor (*miserabiles personae*) and sick. Gregory I also established hostels for pilgrims and poor strangers who were continually arriving in Rome.[10] Innocent III relied on these institutionalized responses to build a larger framework for addressing poor relief.

The eleventh and twelfth centuries witnessed the development of the church becoming more centralized due to a series of very powerful popes. The clergy assumed greater social and religious power, and the universities provided theological training limited to the clergy. There was also an increased emphasis on sin, and the demonic, with the addition of the sacrament of penance. This sacrament became very important in the lives of the people who were experiencing an increasing distance from a judgmental God who needed to be appeased. "People felt disenfranchised and orphaned and therefore less sure of their salvation. The increased sense of sin and of the demonic presence, which was one of the results of the development of the Sacrament of Penance, left people feeling far removed from a God who had become judgemental."[11] The clergy's increase in power as a result of their ability to now forgive sins and mediate between the common people and God led to spiritual and religious practices that helped ease the spiritual anxiety of the faithful. Charity and almsgiving, and later the indulgence trade, played an important role in appeasing an angry God while at the same time funding church projects and aiding the poor.

Innocent III represents the height of papal power, and his attempts to centralize power were realized in 1215 at the Fourth Lateran Council. His plan to centralize ecclesial power impacted his strategies for providing poor relief. Innocent III's concern for the poor and need for the church to provide hospitality and charity to the needy in a systematic way often caused friction with clergy who were not concerned about matters related to poverty. However, in his two treatises, *Book of Alms*, and *In Praise of Charity*, Innocent III outlines the effects of almsgiving by relying on Scriptural texts. The benefits from God include the blessing, perfection, protection, and liberation provided to the generous giver.[12]

---

10. Bolton, "Innocent III's Attitude to Social Welfare," 127.
11. Malone, *Women and Christianity*, 256.
12. Bolton, "Innocent III's Attitude to Social Welfare," 127.

The ultimate reward for charity was justification. "Almsgiving is a medicine of salvation that removes the stain of sin and helps to eradicate the desires of the flesh."[13] Interestingly, Gregory's emphasis on the good of charity was also integrated into a theology of the body. Prayer and fasting were considered essential to the well-being of both body and soul. However, fasting weakened the body and was completely a voluntary individual practice. Almsgiving was considered more essential to the Christian life because the practice focused on strengthening others' bodies and enabled the poor to gain health and physical restoration.[14] The exhortation for almsgiving extended to all Christians including the poor. Any small contribution added to the health of the other and provided spiritual security to the donor. For Innocent III almsgiving must go beyond the pietistic urge towards charity and be viewed as acts of justice. Alsmsgiving, therefore, needs practical organization. He provides four essential components to the practice:[15]

1. The cause: an urgent need, which must be met by an act of charity.
2. The outcome: should be a blessing for all concerned.
3. The means: alsmsgiving, which should be carried out joyfully. Here Innocent cites St. Paul (2 Cor 9:7), "God loves a cheerful giver."
4. The order: almsgiving should be performed regularly.

For Innocent III charity is a three-fold activity. Compassion must accompany almsgiving while encouragement must be spoken to the recipient and generosity must be shown through actions. In addition, almsgiving must not be determined by the worthiness of the poor person. Alms are given to both "the good and to the wicked, to the pious and impious, to friend and foe alike."[16] This understanding of not categorizing the poor into "the worthy poor" and the "unworthy poor" is carried throughout the later medieval period and highlighted in the work and teaching of St. Francis.

Innocent III initiated the construction of hospitals and used them as a means to collect alms and donations from kings, princes, and bishops. These hospitals, especially his hospital in Rome, *Santo Spirito*, cared for the sick and indigent and provided an avenue for the wealthy to give alms and do works of piety. These hospitals also provided a comprehensive church response for caring for the sick and poor. Much of the church's commitment to the poor rested with individual lay persons, priests, and voluntary organizations. However, there was a systemic effort by the church to alleviate poverty in the eleventh through thirteenth centuries. The leadership for providing a structural administrative framework was provided by both Pope Innocent III and the monastic communities. The development and extension of the medical and social

---

13. Bolton, "Innocent III's Attitude to Social Welfare," 123.
14. Bolton, "Innocent III's Attitude to Social Welfare," 127.
15. *Gesta Innocentii PP III* (PL), cols. 355–56.
16. Bolton, "Innocent III's Attitude to Social Welfare," 128.

systems under the direction of Innocent III is indeed remarkable. However impressive, the liturgical and theological supports for poor relief were also problematic. They created a church system that integrated care for the poor and sick with the remission of sins and salvation. This system sets the stage for the indulgence trade controversies that ultimately explode in the sixteenth century.

## The Impact of Historic, Economic and Social Developments on Medieval Charity

The last decade of the twelfth century and into the thirteenth century (1194–1207) witnessed a series of calamities. In addition to an epic famine and extreme weather conditions throughout what is today called Western Europe was the suffering caused by disease and the plague.[17] The subsequent devastation led to an increased number of the sick and destitute, with the indigent forced to move from town to town seeking provision. These crises set the stage for academic and spiritual debate in regards to the responsibility to aid the hungry and poor. In particular, at the University of Paris, scholars put forth a series of initiatives and urged both the governments and church to secure relief to the destitute.[18]

The academic debates and discussions also led to conscience raising and education. The laity was engaged in almsgiving, hospitality, and providing works of charity. As a result, lay confraternities became increasingly popular and were developed and established to organize voluntary efforts to ease the burden of the sick and poor.[19] The kings and princes were exhorted to provide both justice and charity to their subjects. There was a persistent and strong expectation on the royalty that they would ensure that their subjects would be provided adequate food and shelter. Church magistrates were also instructed to give generously as a result of their due belonging to the church, and therefore, they were to be good stewards of the riches.[20] There were direct benefits and immediate results for those who relied on the assistance of lay confraternities, royalty, church leaders, and the aristocracy. However, the numbers of poor did not decrease, and the social and religious structural supports for charity were not modified.

## The High Middle Ages: Transition to an Urban Economy

The eleventh to the fourteenth centuries marked the rise of the urban economy, and with it, changes in the forms of spirituality and ministry.[21] Prior to the twelfth

17. Bolton, "Pope Innocent III's Attitude to Social Welfare," 123–4.
18. Bolton, "Pope Innocent III's Attitude to Social Welfare," 124.
19. See Vauchez, "Confraternities and Guilds in the Late Middle Ages," 165–76, for a detailed analysis of the significance.
20. Bolton, "Innocent III's Attitude to Social Welfare," 124–25.
21. Marie-Dominique Chenu maintains that the profound economic and social changes during

century society was predominantly rural. With the rise of a profit economy and the increase in the social and economic distance between the destitute and the wealthy, a new spirituality and theology needed to emerge that addressed questions regarding the role of both the rich and poor in society and the church.[22] Late medieval theology pertaining to social problems was concerned with the problems that accompanied the growing market economy and the related problems of low wages and unemployment, the lack of education, medical care, and housing. As a result of the shift to a market economy, scholarly theological concerns regarding the ability of the medieval church to respond to the spiritual needs of the people were met by attempts to integrate theology, history, and social action.[23]

The growth of the preindustrial woolen cloth manufacturing and trade accompanied the rise of the urban economy during this time. The money supply increased and with it, a much greater circulation of both goods and currency. The handling of money became a work specialty done by the new banking class.[24] The market became more specialized and various trades became divided by skill level and competence. Rural life and poverty continued. However, there arose new social problems with the rise of the urban poor.

The wealth and luxury of the papacy, the grand churches, and aristocratic clergy offered a growing discomfort between the ubiquitous poverty of the urban areas and the flagrant showiness of the highly decorated altars and vestments, and the theatrical liturgical and feast day celebrations. Some of the old monastic orders retreated from urban life but did little to modify the religious and spiritual life to accommodate the great social changes taking place. There did exist, as noted above, increased scholarly questions and concerns related to the rise of the market economy and the role of poverty in the church and society. There was an increasing awareness that the church needed to better accommodate the social and economic changes in the wake of the new economic system. Accompanying this growing interest in a new spirituality and religious life that met the needs of an urban society was the development of new Mendicant Orders. Most noteworthy was the entrance of the Franciscans and the Dominicans onto the twelfth and thirteenth century scene.

---

the eleventh and twelfth centuries created a stressful spiritual and ministerial crisis. New religious reforms were needed and the development of the Mendicant Orders of the Franciscans and Dominicans helped to meet this need. See *Nature, Man, and Society in the Twelfth Century*. See also Little, "Religion, Economy and St. Francis," 148.

22. Little, "Religion, Economy and St. Francis," 148.

23. Little, "Religion, Economy and St. Francis," 149.

24. Little, "Religion, Economy and St. Francis," 155. See also Little, *Religious Poverty* for an in-depth discussion of the medieval shift from a "gift economy" to a "profit economy."

PART 2: INSIGHTS FROM THE HISTORY OF THE CHURCH

## The Virtue of Poverty: The Role of the Mendicants in the Late Middle Ages

The thirteenth century marked the rise of the Mendicant Orders, also known as the friars. One of the most well-known of these orders was the Franciscans. The Franciscan Order, officially known as the *Ordo Fratum Minorum* (Brothers Minor), was founded by Francis of Assisi (1181–1226). The Franciscans were not the first of the Mendicant Orders but their reputation and the popularity of their teaching and discipline provide a most relevant example of the medieval view of the role of poverty, religious life, and spirituality. Francis was born in the Italian hill town of Assisi in the upper valley of the Tiber. He was the son of a wealthy merchant, and by all accounts, had a reputation as being popular and charming. He had a reputation in town due to his participation in the youthful revelries of his time. As a result of illness and some disappointments he engaged in a religious pilgrimage.[25] He then devoted himself to the ministry of the poor, and, to the chagrin of his father, he publicly stripped himself naked as a symbol of renunciation of all worldly goods and as a sign of full devotion to Christ. In 1209, Francis accepted the call to be an itinerant preacher and desired to live his life in imitation to Christ.

In 1210 Francis and eleven of his companions went to Rome and received Papal permission to continue preaching, and subsequently, formally established his order. He preached on the love of God, forgiveness of sin, and the need to renounce worldly temptations of the body.[26] His call to poverty was in imitation of Christ, who entered the world in poverty. Francis also viewed voluntary poverty as an opportunity to engage in the life of grace in a way that made a social and religious difference in the lives of both the poor and the wealthy. The call to voluntary poverty was also an open invitation for women. Clare, a sixteen-year-old girl from Assisi joined Francis and established a second order of women, known as the Poor Clares. Later, a third lay order was established that linked those who lived a simple lifestyle with increased holiness due to their imitation of Christ.

The Rule of St. Francis (1223) describes the way of life that was to be observed by the Friars. The following excerpt reveals the underlying theology and spirituality that supported the Franciscans' understanding of the role of poverty and the Christian life.[27]

1. The brothers shall not acquire anything as their own, neither a house nor a place nor anything at all.

---

25. Latourette, *Christianity Through the Ages*, 111. See pp. 110–14 for a more detailed description of the development of the Franciscans and their relationship to the Dominican Order.

26. See Petry, "Medieval Eschatology and St. Francis," 54–69 for a more in-depth analysis of St. Francis' Christology, ethics, and eschatology.

27. "The Rule of St. Francis," Chapter VI, 1–6.

2. Instead, as pilgrims and strangers (see 1 Pet 2:11) in this world who serve the Lord in poverty and humility, let them go begging for alms with full trust.

3. Nor should they feel ashamed since the Lord made Himself poor for us in this world (see 2 Cor 8:9).

4. This is that summit of highest poverty which has established you, my most beloved brothers, as heirs and kings of the kingdom of heaven; it has made you poor in the things [of this world] but exalted you in virtue (see Jas 2:5).

5. Let this be your *portion*, which leads into *the land of the living* (Ps 141:6).

6. Dedicating yourselves totally to this, my most beloved brothers, do not wish to have anything else forever under heaven for the sake of our Lord Jesus Christ.

The Friars not only lived a simple lifestyle, but were models for others seeking to live out the *apostalica vita*. They drew large numbers of people who were attracted to living a simple lifestyle. They, along with other Mendicant orders, including the Dominicans, provided a late medieval framework for understanding the relationship between poverty and spirituality. It was understood to be virtuous to practice poverty in the imitation of Christ. "Let us pay attention, all [my] brothers, to what the Lord says: *Love your enemies* and *do good to those who hate you* (see Matt 5:44), For our Lord Jesus Christ, Whose footprints we must follow (see 1 Pet 2:21)..."[28]

This discipline drew the faithful to closeness to Christ and provided a way to heaven. Psychologically, it provided security in an insecure and perilous world. Communities of Mendicants also provided a social buffer from a dangerous world. The mendicant poverty movement was characterized by great communal solidarity.[29] However, this spirituality of poverty offered little in the way of relief to the masses of the involuntary poor. They benefitted by receiving alms and provisions, but there was no real effort to change the social and political structures that held the poor and suffering in their lower social class. Nevertheless, the idealization of poverty was compelling due to its theological connection to salvation. In a precarious world, voluntary poverty and almsgiving offered an opportunity for spiritual pilgrimage to heaven. The wealthy were comforted by the action of charity, which eased the moral discomfort of possessing wealth.[30]

The involuntary poor were also comforted by the idea that virtue was attached to the condition of economic poverty, and that there was hope of life in the hereafter. The Mendicants benefited by an assurance of salvation through a life of poverty and almsgiving. Ultimately, it was a system that was a means of social control. The Friars were the intermediaries between the wealthy and poor and provided distance for the wealthy away from the ugliness and reality of the ravages of poverty. "And this

---

28. "The Rule of St. Francis," Chapter XXII, 1–2.
29. Walter, "Pauperism and Illth," 247.
30. Bailey, "Religious Poverty," 459.

interaction, like all philanthropy, in turn both justified the rich in their wealth and helped maintain the poor in their poverty."[31]

## Martin Luther: Faith as the Foundation for Poor Relief

Before discussing the church response to poverty during the Reformation it is important to examine the radical *theological* shift that became the dawning of a new era in the sixteenth century. This shift fueled and rooted social ethics and poor relief in a newly defined theology of the cross. Martin Luther (1483–1546) created a paradigm that dramatically altered the view of poverty and poor relief. The early medieval understanding of "the justice of God" as one's struggle to achieve righteousness had led to years of struggle for Martin Luther. All his good works including fasting, prayers, and self-deprivations only led him to despair. It was while meditating on Romans 1:17 that "the justice of God" took on new meaning. Here Luther finally understood God's righteousness as passive righteousness, that is, as a gift, not a demand. There was nothing that one could do to merit salvation. God's gift of righteousness justified the sinner before God. The message of the cross is the paradoxical message of freedom as bondage to Christ. The new understanding of God's righteousness helped him to distinguish between law and gospel.[32] God's righteousness was not condemnation, but grace that justified and saved sinners.

This radical new understanding of righteousness as gift freed Luther from anxiety about salvation, and the accompanying effort of striving for salvation. This was to become central to Luther's development of every other aspect of his theology. For example, the role of works changes from being a requirement for salvation to an expression of the love of God. Love was no longer viewed as focused on our love toward God expressed through acts of merit, but rather as God's love toward us. In this new understanding Luther becomes aware of a radically different God than the One whom he had feared and hated.[33] God is now understood to be merciful, full of love and grace. This was a dramatic shift away from the theology of the medieval church and Innocent III's emphasis on charity being united with the "work" of salvation.

For Luther, this new perception of God changed everything. The incarnate Christ was now understood to be a loving Savior who sacrificed himself in order that sins are forgiven and new life is given to sinners. In realizing Christ's own righteousness captures human sin, Luther began to understand the nature of God. His entire paradigm of the relationship between faith and the good works of charity shattered. The medieval schema of works righteousness lost all power to persuade and was replaced by the life-giving release of God's freedom and Spirit. The predominant medieval view that valued poverty, and subsequently, poor relief through almsgiving and

---

31. Little, "Religion, Economy and St. Francis," 161.
32. Watson, *Let God Be God!*, 24.
33. Luther, *Luther's Works (LW)*, 34:336–337.

charity was on the precipice of a dramatic change with radical doctrinal focus on *sola fides*. Luther argued that viewing poor relief as a means of sanctification minimized the work that Christ had already been accomplished on the cross. He claimed that love and care for the neighbor is rooted in faith. God was to be no longer viewed, Luther argued, as a distant, cold, and judging Being needing to be placated with almsgiving, indulgences, and fasting. Condemnation had been lifted for believers. Christ was given "from a motive of pure love."[34] To refuse to trust in God's promise was to diminish Christ's work of salvation.

This theological perspective of the primacy of *sola crux* provided the foundation for Luther's teachings and activism in social welfare. Luther maintained that the church is the place through which God works to address evil in the world. "Luther had the boldness to address structural sources of injustice and to advocate legislative redress of them because his social ethics was rooted in the worship and proclamation of the community. The congregation is the local source in which God creates a new world."[35] Luther's concern for social welfare was a significant shift from medieval piety to social ethics.[36] For Luther, *Gottesdienst*, (translated literally as "worship") means "God's service." Worship is the root and context in which we are able to serve. Therefore, love for the neighbor is rooted in the creative love of God that we encounter in worship.

> Luther does not speak of social ethics per se, but that does not mean that in our sense of the phrase he did not develop it. What Luther does speak of is service to the neighbor, service that is inseparable from service to God—indeed, is service to God . . . It is because God serves us that we serve others. As Vilmos Vajta has emphasized in his thorough study of Luther's theology of worship, worship and service to others are inseparable. There is no doubt then that both worship and service are corporate and communal . . . The reform of worship included the renewal of social life . . . "Now there is no greater service of God [gottis dienst] than Christian love which helps and serves the needy" (LW 45:172; WA 12, 13, 26f). Worship creates the community and the community serves others. The work of the people does not stop at worship but rather begins there as the work of the people for the benefit of others—in what has been called "liturgy after the liturgy."[37]

Luther considered the daily work of the Christian as worship because it is rooted in obedience to God's will. Worship within the community is at the heart of all Christian

---

34. Watson, *Let God Be God!*, 20.

35. Lindberg, *Beyond Charity*, 163.

36. See Lindberg, *Beyond Charity*, 161–2 for a summary description of the widely held but erroneous theological viewpoint that Luther was a quietist and disinterested in worldly affairs.

37. Lindberg, *Beyond Charity*, 163–64. Lindberg refers to Luther's treatises "The Blessed Sacrament of the Holy and True Body of Christ and the Brotherhoods" (1519) and "To the Christian Nobility of the German Nation" (1520) to illustrate Luther's attack on the medieval institutions that promulgated rampant efforts at achievement piety.

work. For Luther, care for the poor emerges from the faith of the worshipping community. Only faith can guarantee ethical action." In medieval theology, self-denial was an important factor in achieving a piety that works with grace to attain the ultimate good. According to Luther, the emphasis on human effort needed to be shifted to God's work already achieved in Christ. There was a place for philosophy, and certainly reason, but the problem surfaced when philosophy entered the realm of theology. The focus on human effort undermined the centrality of justification by faith.[38] Luther argued that an ethic of the cross is based in God's revelation. The church's social ethics originate from grace received through Christ. The gospel issues the command to be for the other as God is *pro nobis*. Therefore, justification is the basis for all Christian ethics, social justice, and care for the poor.[39]

For Luther, the purpose of all service is to glorify God. Within Luther's understanding of a theology of the cross the medieval anthropocentric ethics dramatically shift. What Luther considers true Christianity is uncovered: Christ alone saves and transforms. In our worship we care for our neighbor as an act of love. The righteousness bestowed on the believer as a Godly gift enables a thirst for justice and love to be extended to the neighbor. Both exist together but it is faith that gives shape and power to the work of serving others. Luther's Christology is evident in his discussion on care for the poor. Christ saves and then empowers the church to serve in the

world. Luther's sacramental theology provides a framework for shaping the relationship between faith and love. The sacrament of communion shared together as a body reveals the basic principles of Christian life together. Faith is received and love activated by the Spirit. These two principles are inextricably linked together within the context of the worshipping body.

Luther's perspective on faith and works is one key to understanding the basis for his proposal for poor relief. The center of Christian life is the worship of God through the proclamation of the gospel and service to the neighbor. The source of all faith, and therefore works, is Christ. To believe and trust in the saving grace of God is also to receive the power authentically to address social problems.

## Reformation Initiatives for Poor Relief

Luther's theology of the cross and subsequent understanding of the role of faith and works had great practical implications for Reformation society.[40] There are a number of examples of specific efforts at poor relief during the Reformation as a result in

38. Forell, *The Proclamation of the Gospel in a Pluralistic World*, 128–9.

39. Forell, *Faith Active In Love*, 79–81. See 79–84 for a full discussion on Luther's opinion of Aristotle, scholasticism, and the influence of Greek philosophy on theology. See also George, *Theology of the Reformers*, for a more detailed analysis of Luther's theological development, 51–79.

40. Ozment, *Protestants: The Birth of a Revolution*. See Ozment's detailed argument that the theology of Luther and the other Reformers had a great influence on both the social and political arenas in sixteenth century Europe.

the shift of the underlying theology. Three of these are significant as representing the change in both theology and action in regards to caring for the poor: the outlawing of begging, the implementation of the common chest in churches, and the condemnation of usury. Since poverty is no longer viewed as a "good" worth pursuing, but rather, as a social problem, efforts are made to legally forbid begging in many area towns. Luther's strong conviction that one was to work if able-bodied coupled with the disintegration of theological supports for voluntary poverty led to legal orders outlawing the practice of begging. For those who were in true need the churches set up what was named "the common chest" for the collection and distribution of funds. An early example of this legislation is the *Order of the City of Wittenberg* (1522):

1. It is unanimously resolved that all income from the churches, all of the brotherhoods, and the guilds shall be collected together and brought into a common chest. Two from the city council, two from the community, and a secretary are to be delegated who shall receive and possess such income in order to provide for the poor people.

2. Moreover, henceforth the endowed income of priests, when it is freed through the death of a priest, will also be collected in the same common chest; and henceforth no one [no other priest] will be endowed by it.

3. Likewise, no beggars shall be tolerated in our city, rather one shall urge them to work or expel them from the city. But they who because of age or sickness or other misfortune have fallen into poverty shall be provided for from the common chest through the appropriate delegated manner.

4. Likewise, there shall be no *Terminey* [wandering mendicants] among us.

9. Likewise, loans shall be made from the common chest to poor artisans who without this are unable to support themselves daily by their trade, in order that they may be able to provide for themselves. When they are established, however, they can repay the loan without any interest, but if they are unable to repay the loan, it shall be pardoned for God's sake.

10. Likewise, the common chest shall provide for poor orphans, the children of poor people, and maidens who shall be given an appropriate dowry for marriage.[41]

The *Order of the City of Wittenberg* also condemned the sin of usury and allowed for borrowing from the common chest at a low interest rate: "In case our fellow citizens and residents are burdened by interest rates that are too high, for example, five to six percent, or do not have the means for a deposit, we will loan

---

41. Luther, "Order of the City of Wittenberg" (1522), in Lindberg, *Beyond Charity*, 200–201. See also Lietzmann, *Die Wittenberger und Leisniger Kastenordnung*; also in Sehling, *Die evangelischen Kirchenordnun*, 697–8.

them the main sum from the common chest, and they will repay the capital at four percent annually until it is repaid."[42]

The understanding that poverty is not merely an individual problem but a social one that has to be reduced by addressing the structural supports of poverty is most evident in Luther's and other civic leaders' condemnation of usury and a growing capitalism that preys on the vulnerabilities of the working poor. In a tract titled, "That Clergy Should Preach against Usury" (1540) Luther exhorts the clergy to preach against usury and asserts that unrestrained capitalism is a condemnation to the degree of *status confessionis*.[43]

> Because God wills it, we will let the princes do what they can or will. But it is not proper for us preachers to approve it [usury]. In this regard let us be bishops, i.e., be on guard and watch, for it concerns our salvation. First, we shall scold and condemn usury from the pulpit, and diligently and straight out repeat the text [see Neh 5 et al.], namely: Whoever loans something and gets more in return is a usurer and is condemned as a thief, robber, and murderer . . . This talk will perhaps seem to be somewhat harsh. Perhaps it will also be frightening to some. Above all it will appear frightening to the small usurers. I mean those who take only five or six percent. However, to the great devourers of the world, those who can never take a high enough percentage, one can never be sufficiently harsh, for they have given themselves over to mammon and the devil. They let us cry out and not once enquire about it. It is in particular of these I have spoken, they should be given over in life and death to the devil, and there should be no Christian fellowship with them.[44]

Imagine the Christian Church in America today condemning the practices of charging too much interest, the wealthy not paying their fair share of taxes, and the inadequate wage given to low income workers! The Reformers saw these prophetic shouts as integral to the well-being of the community, and therefore, to the life of the church. The dignity of each human being that the Medieval Church so richly highlighted is carried over into the life of the church of the Reformation. However, they also endeavored to ensure human dignity by extending individual mandates to care for the poor to the larger community and church institutions, both sacred and secular.

## Conclusion

There is a dramatic theological shift from the late medieval period to the sixteenth century Reformation, and subsequently, a change in how poverty was viewed and poor relief implemented. The primary contributions of medieval efforts toward

---

42. Luther, "Order of the City of Wittenberg" (1522), in Lindberg, *Beyond Charity*, 16.
43. Lindberg, *Beyond Charity*, 191.
44. Luther, "That Clergy Should Preach against Usury" (1540), in Lindberg, *Beyond Charity*.

charity were two-fold. First, there was the deeply held conviction that the Christian church plays a significant role in caring for the poor, and that all forms of works of charity, including almsgiving and care for the sick, must be holistic. There was no real dichotomy between meeting the physical needs of the body and the spiritual needs of the soul. The poor were approached in a holistic manner. Innocent III and St. Francis epitomize this understanding that Christians must care for the individual poor in imitation of Christ. Second, there was no negative view of the poor. There was no stigmatization of poverty on those that lacked material goods. They were not blamed for their physical and economic condition.

There was value created by the state of poverty to the extent that many, like St. Francis, chose voluntary poverty because they valued the simple life as the *vita apostolica*. However, the medieval approach to poverty also had negative consequences. Their approach was primarily moral, by way of patronizing the poor, or identifying with them through voluntary poverty. This did not allow for structural change, and therefore, realized no effective improvement in the status of the poor. The church's endorsement of poverty, by providing systematic spiritual support, created no social change in both urban and rural areas. This system was rooted in the medieval theological paradigm that integrated works of charity with salvation. The consciences of the wealthy were appeased through the pietistic offering of alms. This system grew, particularly under the rule of strong Popes such as Innocent III, and the Mendicant Orders.

This integration of faith and works led to the 1517 indulgence controversy, and under the leadership of Martin Luther, a break with the medieval understanding of charity, almsgiving, and indulgences as a means of salvation. This shift undercut the value of poverty. Faith in the righteousness of God removed the incentive to have a system that valued poverty as a good, and as a means toward gaining salvation. Luther rejected "the Church tradition (which) idealized poverty as the subject for good works by the rich and powerful, and as the condition which best allowed a person to lead an evangelic life."[45] Poverty was now viewed as a social problem to be addressed. The church supported efforts for structural change that would work to end the misery and dehumanization of the poor.

The medieval understanding of the worthiness of the poor and the requirement that Christians provide for both the spiritual and materialistic needs of the indigent offer the church today an approach that is both optimistic and holistic. The church today needs this reminder that the poor should not be divided into categories of the "worthy poor" and the "unworthy poor." We also need to integrate the works of charity into the life of our communities and understand the liturgical and Scriptural supports for serving all of those in need.

---

45. Lindberg, "No Beggars Among Christians," 317. See also Lindberg, "The Ministry and Vocation of the Baptized," 385–401 for an in-depth analysis of Luther's criticism of the medieval "idealization of poverty."

The Reformers, as represented in this chapter by Martin Luther, offer a radical understanding for the church in addressing poverty. They argued that Christians are free from the pietistic demands of works righteousness and free to serve the poor as a *response* to God's love. Poverty does not have value as a means toward salvation. Rather, poverty is a social problem that needs to be addressed both individually *and* systemically. Martin Luther reminds the church that the starting point for poor relief is in the worshipping community. He also reminds the church of its prophetic role in condemning practices such as usury that continue the structural supports for poverty. Reformation theology provides the framework for addressing the institution of poverty while medieval theology reminds us that all persons have inherent dignity given to them by our Creator, and subsequently, the poor should always be treated with respect and care. The Christian history of poor relief, in both the Medieval and Reformation periods, is a rich resource for the Christian church today.

## Bibliography

Bailey, Michael D. "Religious Poverty: Mendicancy, and Reform in the Late Middle Ages." *Church History* 72 (2003) 457–83.

Bethenser, Henry, ed. *Doctrine of the Christian Church*. New York: Oxford University Press, 1947.

Bolton, Brenda M. "Hearts Not Purses? Pope Innocent III's Attitude to Social Welfare." In *Through the Eye of a Needle: Judeo-Christian Roots of Social Welfare*, edited by Emily Albu Hanawalt and Carter Lindberg, 123–146. Kirksville, MO: Thomas Jefferson University Press, 1994.

Chadwick, Henry. *The Early Church: The Story of Emergent Christianity from the Apostolic Age to the Dividing of the Ways between the Greek East and the Latin West*. 2nd ed. New York: Penguin, 1993.

Chenu, Dominique-Marie. *Nature, Man and Society in the Twelfth Century: Essays on New Theological Perspectives in the Latin West*. Chicago: University of Chicago Press, 1968.

Forell, George W. *Faith Active In Love: An Investigation of the Principles Underlying Luther's Social Ethics*. New York: American Press, 1954.

———. *The Proclamation of the Gospel in a Pluralistic World: Essays on Christianity and Culture*. Philadelphia: Fortress, 1973.

George, Timothy. *Theology of the Reformers*. Nashville: Broadman, 1988.

*Gesta Innocentii PP III (PL)* cols. 355–366. Translated by Brenda M. Bolton. "Hearts Not Purses? Pope Innocent III's Attitude to Social Welfare." In *Through the Eye of a Needle: Judeo-Christian Roots of Social Welfare*, edited by Emily Albu Hanawalt and Carter Lindberg, 128. Kirksville, MO: Thomas Jefferson University Press, 1994.

Latourette, Scott. *Christianity through the Ages*. New York: Harper & Row, 1965.

Lietzmann, Hans, ed. *Die Wittenberger und Leisniger Kastenordnung*. Berlin: de Gruyter, 1935.

Lindberg, Carter. *Beyond Charity: Reformation Initiatives for the Poor*. Minneapolis: Fortress, 1993.

———. "The Ministry and Vocation of the Baptized." *Lutheran Quarterly* 6 (1992) 385–401.

———. "There Should Be No Beggars Among Christians." *Church History* 46 (1977) 313–334.

Little, Lester K. "Religion, Economy and St. Francis." In *Through the Eye of a Needle: Judeo-Christian Roots of Social Welfare*, edited by Emily Albu Hanawalt and Carter Lindberg, 123–146. Kirksville, MO: Thomas Jefferson University Press, 1994.

———. *Religious Poverty and the Profit Economy in Medieval Europe*. Ithaca, NY: Cornell University Press, 1978.

Luther, Martin. *Luther's Works (LW)*. Edited by Jaroslav Pelikan (vols. 1–30) and Helmut T. Lehmann (vols. 31–55). St. Louis: Concordia, 1968.

———. "Order of the City of Wittenberg" (1522). Translated by Carter Lindberg. In *Beyond Charity: Reformation Initiatives for the* Poor, 200–201. Minneapolis: Fortress, 1993.

———. "That Clergy Should Preach against Usury" (1540). Translated by Carter Lindberg. In *Beyond Charity: Reformation Initiatives for the* Poor, 191–2. Minneapolis: Fortress, 1993.

Malone, Mary. *Women and Christianity: The First Thousand Years*. Vol. 1. Maryknoll, NY: Orbis, 2001.

———. *Women and Christianity: The First Thousand Years*. Vol. 2. Maryknoll, NY: Orbis, 2002.

Ozment, Steven. *Protestants: The Birth of a Revolution*. New York: Image, 1991.

Petry, Ray C. "Medieval eschatology and St. Francis of Assisi." *Church History* 9 (1940) 54–69.

"The Rule of St. Francis." In *Francis and Clare: The Complete Works*. Translated by Regis J. Armstrong and Ignatius C. Brady. New York: Paulist, 1982.

Sehling, Emil, ed. *Die evangelischen Kirchenordnung des 16 Jahrhundert*. Vol. 1. Tübingen: Mohr/Siebeck, 1902.

Talbot, Alice-Mary. "Byzantine Women, Saints' Lives, and Social Welfare." In *Through the Eye of a Needle: Judeo-Christian Roots of Social Welfare*. Edited by Emily Albu Hanawalt and Carter Lindberg, 105–22. Kirksville, MO: Thomas Jefferson University Press, 1994.

Vauchez, André. "Confraternities and Guilds in the Late Middle Ages." In *Through the Eye of a Needle: Judeo-Christian Roots of Social Welfare*, edited by Emily Albu Hanawalt and Carter Lindberg, 165–176. Kirksville, MO: Thomas Jefferson University Press, 1994.

Walter, Eugene Victor. "Pauperism and Illth: An Archeology of Social Policy." *Sociological Analysis* 34 (1973) 239–54.

Watson, Philip S. *Let God Be God! An Interpretation of the Theology of Martin Luther*. London: Epworth, 1947.

# 16

## Spiritual Direction in the Early Eastern Orthodox Church and in Twentieth Century Classical Pentecostalism

— John R. Miller

This essay seeks to recognize a correlation or similarity between Eastern Orthodox and Pentecostal traditions, focused on the subject of spiritual direction. The discipline of spiritual direction recognizes both a formal discipline and an informal relationship between two people who seek intimacy with God and the ability to notice spiritual affect. It will notice the inferential language that describes the relationship between a spiritual mentor and a disciple, which antedates the formality of the discipline of spiritual direction as may be detected by the dawn of the second millennium, or as is noticed in, for example, the works of St. Ignatius. This research will examine, compare, and contrast the written record of the early Eastern Church, and it will specifically focus on the dynamic of spiritual direction in the various ministries of Elizabeth V. (nee Duncan) Baker and Susan A. Duncan, as exemplars of a classical Pentecostal tradition.

## Introduction

Spiritual direction is difficult to succinctly define. Irénée Hausherr defined spiritual direction as, "the relationship between *one* master, informed and experienced in the ways of the spirit, and *one* disciple who wishes to profit from such knowledge and experience."[1] Kallistos Ware posited that spiritual direction provides spiritual insight, spiritual discernment, burden bearing, and the ability to transform the inner spiritual environment of the disciple.[2] Unfortunately, the classical twentieth century Pentecostal Movement did not utilize this terminology to define its discipleship of new converts or of those who were entering into ministry. However, they did employ

---

1. Hausherr, *Spiritual Direction in the Early Christian East*, 1–2.
2. Ware, *The Spiritual Guide in Orthodox Christianity*.

the very same principles and thereby labeled them with various nomenclatures, such as disciple,[3] friend,[4] seeker,[5] or student.[6]

The following four questions guided this research project. First, if one proceeds on the premise that the discipline and expectation of spiritual direction developed over many centuries, then how might it have been understood before this formula was clearly defined? This premise notices the particular language that the early church writers employed when describing the relationship between mentor and protégé.[7] Second, how might the Eastern Orthodox understanding be significantly different from the Roman Catholic or Western concept and expectation for spiritual direction? This idea detects the Western bias towards the formal ecclesiastical requirement of spiritual direction, for the ordained, and the Eastern bias toward perpetual relationship between any two individuals.[8] Third, how did the early Eastern Church understand the discipline of Spiritual Direction? This concept explores the dynamic of one who seeks earnestly for the guidance of an elder.[9] Finally, how did the classical Pentecostal understand the concept of Spiritual Direction? This hypothesis searches for answers via the relational aspects, or mentoring paradigm, between the older church leadership and emerging leadership.[10]

During the early centuries the practice and expectation of spiritual direction is more loosely defined than it is presently in some western Christian churches.[11] Based

3. *Trust*, June 1908, 7.4, 16.
4. *Trust*, June 1908, 7.4, 19.
5. *Trust*, Oct. 1910, 9.8, 17.
6. *Trust*, June 1908, 7.4, 11.

7. "An old man had a disciple who for many years had obeyed him in everything." Heraclides, in Ward, *The Sayings of the Desert Fathers*, 72.

8. "If you are constantly upbraided by your director and thus acquire great faith in him and love for him, then you may be sure that the Holy Spirit has taken up residence invisibly in your soul and the power of the Most High has overshadowed you." Climacus, *Ladder of Divine Ascent*, Step 4 Obedience, 119.

9. "And even then, he would not dare accept this duty of office without the counsel and desire of his spiritual father. But let him humble himself, and let him do this because [his father] commands it, and with his prayers; and let him accept this charge only because of the salvation of his brothers. If he knows that his father partakes of the same Spirit and has been judged worthy to receive the same knowledge and wisdom so that he says nothing that is contrary to the will of God, but says what is pleasing to God and profitable to the soul, according to this same charism and degree. For want of this, he will be found to obey man and not God, and will be deprived of the glory and the charism that has been given to him. If he finds a good helper and spiritual advisor, his enterprise will be auspicious and more secure, and he himself will feel humble . . ." (Symeon, *Logos 88*, as quoted in Hausherr, *Spiritual Direction in the Early Christian East*, 128).

10. "We were led jot down in order one evening's service as it occurred during our meetings under divine leadership, no man on the platform or in the chair, and we pass it on, in brief, that you may understand something of our safety and liberty." *Trust*, Sept. 1908, 7.7, 12.

11. "How far is the Christian East sympathetic to a 'charismatic' understanding of the spiritual life? At first sight it might appear that there is but little affinity. Orthodoxy, it might be said, is liturgical and hierarchic, whereas Pentecostalism is grounded upon the free and spontaneous action of the Spirit;

PART 2: INSIGHTS FROM THE HISTORY OF THE CHURCH

on scriptural exegesis, spiritual intuitiveness, and experience with human nature, the discipline of spiritual direction is similar between the early Eastern Church and the classical Pentecostal tradition.[12] The present conception of discipleship or spiritual direction must inform the expectation that it carried in the early centuries of the church.

John Cassian has provided the contemporary reader with a wealth of information about the monastic lifestyle, and subsequently, about spiritual direction.[13] In many parallel passages, he alluded to the Desert Fathers and their particular relationships (not named as spiritual direction, but not unlike it either) with rigorous disciplines and submissive protégés.[14] One reads these accounts with wonderment at the willingness of the disciple to relinquish individual rights and personal judgment or discernment.[15] Yet, Cassian continues to instruct the spiritual directee as to the benefits of

---

Orthodoxy appeals to Holy Tradition, whereas Pentecostalism assigns primacy to personal experience." Ware, "Personal Experience of the Holy Spirit."

12. "We may claim to have found a large measure of convergence between our Patristic witnesses: (i) All agree that it is possible to possess the Holy Spirit within oneself, without being conscious of His presence. (ii) All agree that the 'second baptism'—the baptism of tears or 'baptism with the Holy Spirit'—is *an extension and fulfillment of the first baptism bestowed sacramentally with water.* 'Spirit baptism' is not to be seen as conferring an entirely new grace, different from that conferred through 'water baptism.' (iii) Some Eastern Christian authors, such as Mark the Monk, are reticent in describing the outward signs that may accompany conscious awareness of the Spirit. Others, such as Macarius and Symeon, enter into much fuller detail, referring in particular to the gift of tears, the vision of divine light and even on occasion to something that resembles the modem experience of speaking with tongues. But their allusions to this last are very infrequent. Of these three points, the second will surely prove of crucial importance in any future Orthodox-Pentecostal dialogue." Ware, "Personal Experience of the Holy Spirit," 9.

13. "He is brought to the midst of the council of the brothers, stripped of what is his in their midst, and clothed in the garb of the monastery at the hands of the abba . . . When, therefore, a person has been admitted . . . he is not permitted to join the community of the brothers immediately but is assigned to and elder . . . having been exposed to his first training . . . and is about to be admitted . . . he is given over to another elder . . . the chief concern and instruction of this man . . . to teach him to conquer his desires . . ." Cassian: *The Institutes* 4:5–9 (80–82).

14. "John submitted to his elder, and with such humility did he cling to his service that his obedience struck the old man himself with utter amazement." [Watering the dry stick story] Cassian: *The Institutes* 4:24 (90–91). A similar account is given of John the Dwarf §1, in Ward, *The Sayings of the Desert Fathers*, 85–86.

15. "In his reverence for the old man and in his sincere and simple dutifulness, which led him to believe with absolute confidence that the old man could give no order that was purposeless and unreasonable . . . I shall related a deed of Abba Patermutus . . . he ordered . . . throw him [the man's young son] into the river . . . given the fervor of his faith and obedience this would certainly have been brought to a bitter end were there not brothers purposefully stationed by the bank of the river, carefully watching . . . revealed to the elder that by this obedience he had performed the deed of the patriarch Abraham." Cassian: *The Institutes* 4:26–28 (92–93). A similar account is given of Abba Sisoes §10 in Ward, *The Sayings of the Desert Fathers*, 214. See [Narrative: Boys die carrying figs to the sick in the desert] "They had chosen to give up the ghost rather than the trust that had been placed in them, and to lose their temporal lives rather than to violate their elder's command." Cassian: *The Institutes* 5:40 (140–141). See "Some brothers came to find Abba Anthony to tell him about the visions they were having [donkey dying narrative] . . . the old man convinced them . . . that their visions came from demons." Anthony the Great §12, in Ward, *The Sayings of the Desert Fathers*, 3.

obedience and the pitfalls of disobedience.[16] He employed a variety of terms (abba, elder, old man, etc.) for the spiritual director, which reinforces the hypothesis that the formality of this discipline was still in nascent stages of development.[17] Cassian, who wrote for the instruction and establishment of new monastic houses, drawing from his extensive travels and encounters with the monasteries of Bethlehem and Egypt in the fourth and fifth centuries, continues to inform the contemporary reader. Additionally, as a Westerner, one ponders the influence of the cultural expectation and attitude of submission as an acceptable means of relationship between a superior and inferior, recognizing that out of this culture emerges the ready adoption of and rapid growth of the religion of Islam.

Irénée Hausherr focused extensively on the early Eastern approach to spiritual direction. He systematically delineated and compiled the attributes and expectations of the spiritual director and directee, and in this regard, he appeals consistently to the primary sources. Saint Symeon adjures the inward examination of the spiritual director, or of the one who advocated becoming a spiritual father, for he recognizes the impending weight of accountability.[18] Hausherr pointed to the necessity of one who would assume the office of spiritual father, and their recognition of its heavy responsibility, which will ultimately be reproduced in their protégé and in that an accountability to God.[19] Symeon proves to be a valuable primary source for Hausherr as he iterates these

---

16. "All of this [the spiritually dulling effect of avarice] makes a person no longer content to bear the yoke of the monastery or to be instructed by the teaching of any elder; he will not only deign to keep the rule of submission and obedience but will not so much as cock his ear when there is instruction in perfection." Cassian: *The Institutes* 12:27.2 (269).

17. He was "reproved by his abba because he had begun to depart from the humility that as a renunciant he had maintained for a very short time and was puffed up with diabolical pride, responded with the height of arrogance: 'Must I be constantly submissive because I have humbled myself for a while?' The elder was so stupefied at this unbridled and wicked response of his." Cassian: *The Institutes* 12:28 (271).

18. "Someone who examines himself diligently, and discovers that he is free of all desire for glory, without any trace of pleasure or of cupidity pertaining to the body, free of avarice and resentment, perfectly meek, unaware of anger; someone who is kindled by love and desire, event to tears, at the mere mention of the name of Christ, and who is, moreover, in mourning instead of his brothers and weighs the sins of others as his own, while he recons himself whole-heartedly as the greater sinner; and next, if he sees in himself the abundant grace of the Spirit shining instead of the sun, perfecting the inner heart; if he clearly perceives that the miracle of the Burning Bush is being repeated inside him, so that, united to the inaccessible divine fire, he burns without being consumed, because his soul is free of all passion; furthermore, if he humbles himself and judges himself by no means fit, but unworthy, knowing the weakness of human nature, but still trusting the grace from above, and the aptitude it confers; and if he undertakes this task eagerly because he is moved by grace, rejecting every human reasoning; next, if he risks his life for no other purpose than fulfilling God's commandment and loving his brothers; and if over and above what has been said, he has a mind that is free form all worldly thinking, and if he is wholly covered by the beautiful tunic of humility." (Symeon, *Logos 88*, as quoted in Hausherr, *Spiritual Direction in the Early Christian East*, 127–8).

19. "And even then, he would not dare accept this duty of office without the counsel and desire of his spiritual father. But let him humble himself, and let him do this because [his father] commands it, and with his prayers; and let him accept this charge only because of the salvation of his brothers. If

responsibilities of the spiritual parent, which in turn adjust the focal point off from the natural discernment and onto the genuine spiritual discernment that cannot be manufactured in the natural talents of the aspiring spiritual father.[20]

Kallistos Ware has proliferated the tenets of Eastern Orthodox doctrines in many contemporary venues; our current focus is no exception to his excellent ability of communication. In the forward to Hausherr's *Spiritual Direction*, Bishop Kallistos has posited five titles for the spiritual director: Doctor [ιατρος] Counselor [συμβουλος], Intercessor [πρεσβευτης], Mediator [μεσιτες], and Sponsor [αναδοχος].[21] These five descriptive titles are thereby reflected in various scripture contexts and emphasized by the Apostle Paul as attributes of a true leader.[22] Bishop Kallistos reiterated these concepts with his allusion to the Russian title of *starets* and of its manifold inference of charismatic attributes.[23] He pointed also to the inference of the *starets* in the context of Dostoevsky's *The Brothers Karamazov*, and to the role of the devoted disciple and the venerable spiritual director.[24]

Primary sources, such as the Bible and the Patristic authors have served to inform this research process and it is recognized that these weave intrinsically throughout the secondary sources. Masterfully, the allegorical and anagogical conceptualizations of director and directee emerge in the texts.[25] They expand on the theoretical and

---

he knows that his father partakes of the same Spirit and has been judged worthy to receive the same knowledge and wisdom so that he says nothing that is contrary to the will of God, but says what is pleasing to God and profitable to the soul, according to this same charism and degree. For want of this, he will be found to obey man and not God, and will be deprived of the glory and the charism that has been given to him. If he finds a good helper and spiritual advisor, his enterprise will be auspicious and more secure, and he himself will feel humble." (Symeon, *Logos 88*, as quoted in Hausherr, *Spiritual Direction in the Early Christian East*, 128).

20. "Virtues are preformed through assiduity and attention; they are acquired through our battles and toils, while the spiritual charismata are gifts accorded by Christ to those who struggle. For example, fasting and chastity are virtues, because they make pleasure wither and hold the fires of the body in check. They are the work of our free will and decision. But to practice these virtues without difficulty and to arrive at purity and perfect impassivity is the highest gift of God. On the contrary, to rule over irascibility and nascent anger is a great struggle, no moderate toil. But to arrive at the point where one experiences no commotion from them and one possess serenity of heart and perfect mildness is the work of God alone." (Symeon, *Logos 88*, as quoted in Hausherr, *Spiritual Direction in the Early Christian East*, 129–130).

21. Ware, foreword in Hausherr, *Spiritual Direction*.

22. The five scripture texts are: Col 4:14; Rom 11:34; Phil 1:9; Gal 3:20; and 2 Cor 11:1–10.

23. "The elder or *starets* is essentially a "charismatic" and prophetic figure, accredited for her or his task by the direct action of the Holy Spirit. Spiritual guides are ordained, not by human hands, but by the hand of God . . . The *starets* give advice, not only at confession, but on many other occasions. Moreover, while the confessor must always be a priest, the *starets* may be a simple monk . . . whether ordained or lay, frequently speaks with an insight and authority that only a very few confessor-priests possess." Ware, *The Spiritual Guide in Orthodox Christianity*.

24. "A *starets* is one who takes your soul, your will into his soul and into his will." Ware, *The Spiritual Guide in Orthodox Christianity*.

25. Abba Anthony said, "Nine monks fell away after many labors and were obsessed with spiritual pride, for they put their trust in their works and being deceived they did not give due heed to the

literal interpretations of familiar scripture texts.[26] The spiritual director and directee place themselves, with spiritual eyes that have been enlightened, in the middle of the mystical world of spiritual realities.[27] Moreover, the boundary line between the ordained clergy, the apostolic succession, and the spiritual lineage become blurred with Symeon's apt metaphor of the golden chain.[28] This golden chain exemplifies the mystical link between the spiritual parentage and ecclesiastical progression. Conversely, one is pressed to consider the Pentecostal and ecclesiastical attempt to formalize the concepts of spiritual direction in the venue of the Shepherding Movement, which ultimately nullified and repented of its own spiritual authority.[29]

The primary source for the twentieth century classical Pentecostal position will be limited in this essay to the articles and editorials published in the *Trust* magazine, by the Duncan sisters, Elizabeth V. (Duncan) Baker and Susan A. Duncan, who were located in Rochester, NY.[30] In these, one notices a plethora of interaction with the progenitors of the emerging Pentecostal Movement and the seekers of genuine spirituality. Invariably, the spiritual direction terminology of the emerging Pentecostal Movement lags behind the liturgical and established churches. Therefore, the reader must analyze the spiritual relationship and interactions between the spiritually mature and immature. This directs one to the process of research in order to discover the variety of roles and relationships that the spiritual director and directee engaged in. Special care is required to discern the network and cross-references made between the texts. Additionally, contemporary works were digested to discern the sociological dynamic that exists in both the Eastern Orthodox and Pentecostal traditions. Therefore, in this regard, each of the sources was scoured to discern the interrelation between the spiritually mature and the immature, which may or may not have been demonstrated to be a formal relationship in the venue of spiritual direction.

---

commandment that says, 'Ask your father and he will tell you.'" Ward, *The Sayings of the Desert Fathers*, 37 (9).

26. "From the moment you put yourselves completely in the hands of your spiritual father, you should know that you become a stranger to all that leads you outside, I mean to affairs and riches of men . . . (1:24) Unless your spiritual father allows it, do not give alms from the goods you have . . . abide by the decision of your spiritual father . . . (1:25) Never ask for water to drink even if thirst is burning you up. Wait until your spiritual father decides to offer you a drink." Symeon the New Theologian, *Theological and Practical Chapters*, 1:24–1:26 (39).

27. "A man who contradicts his [spiritual] father makes the devils rejoice, but when a man humbles himself even to death, he makes the angels stand amazed." Symeon the New Theologian, *Theological and Practical Chapters*, 1.62 (49).

28. "They [spiritual fathers] become just like a golden chain with each on of them a link, bound to all the preceding saints in faith, love, and good works." Symeon the New Theologian, *Theological and Practical Chapters*, 3.4 (73).

29. Moore, *The Shepherding Movement*.

30. I have collected 160 issues of the *Trust* publication (dating from 1908–1932) and have digitalized them for ease of data searching.

## PART 2: INSIGHTS FROM THE HISTORY OF THE CHURCH

| Attribute or Relationship | Eastern Orthodox | Duncan Sisters | Similarities | Contrasts |
|---|---|---|---|---|
| Elder/Disciple Relationship | ✓ | ✓ | Pentecostal reference to the James 5 motif. | Pentecostals seem to hedge this term with an independent choice. |
| Father/Mother Abba/Amma | ✓ | ✓ | Many inferential similarities | Pentecostals do not feel obliged to a perpetual relationship |
| Pastor Shepherd Leader | ✓ | ✓ | Many inferential similarities | Many inferential similarities |
| Presbyter Intercessor | ✓ | ✓ | Many inferential similarities | Many inferential similarities |
| Guide Director | ✓ | ✓ | Many inferential similarities | Many inferential similarities |
| Teacher Pedagogue | ✓ | ✓ | Many inferential similarities | Many inferential similarities |
| Counselor | ✓ | ✓ | Many inferential similarities | Many inferential similarities |
| Doctor | ✓ | | | Doctor is not used by the Pentecostal and is sometimes a pejorative term that stands in opposition to the miraculous |
| Mediator | ✓ | | | Pentecostals reserve this term for Christ |
| Sponsor God-parent | ✓ | | | Pentecostals disparage this term as too liturgical |

The above chart illustrates the similarities and contrasts between an Eastern Orthodox and a classical Pentecostal (the Duncan sisters) view of spiritual direction. While there is a communication gap over the definition of terminology, the inference of the role is abundantly evident.

The early Eastern perception of the discipline of spiritual direction rests on their interpretation of scriptural models. In reference to the sermon of Moses, they found a direct commandment to submit to ones spiritual director.[31] In reference to the injunction of Paul, they found an obligation for the spiritual director to maintain the relationship of spiritual dependence, even to the extent of securing the salvation of

---

31. [Abba Anthony] said, "Nine monks fell away after many labors and were obsessed with spiritual pride, for they put their trust in their works and being deceived they did not give due heed to the commandment that says, 'Ask your father and he will tell you.'" Ward, *The Sayings of the Desert Fathers*, 37 (9). "Ask your father and he will tell you, your elders, and they will explain to you." (Deut 32:7, NIV)

their protégé.[32] This overweening attitude of humility is evidenced by the initiatory rituals and patterns that preceded one being acceptable as a directee. Moreover, the perpetual submission to one's elder, *starets,* or spiritual director finds a correlation of interpretation in the apostolic injunction to care for, or to continually nurture, the churches that they had inaugurated.[33]

An early classical Pentecostal perception of the discipline of spiritual direction also rests on the interpretation of scriptural models. In Moses they perceived the great allegorical metanarrative of atonement, deliverance from bondage, baptism, and entrance into the fullness of the Spirit.[34] They longed for the early church experience to be revisited upon them, to return to the Upper Room paradigm, and to suffer the same as the first century church.[35] They saw themselves as the restoration of the archetypal church and in this also the prototype of ecclesiastical structure and discipleship of new believers. This they sought to establish in the venue and emphasis upon teaching sound doctrine and modeling signs, wonders, and miracles. The committed life-long relationship of director/directee, as per the Eastern model above, was lacking or it is inferred as informal.

If there is any benefit that can be gleaned from the investigation of the discipline of spiritual direction, it is in the wisdom that can be invested from the older generation into the lives of the younger generation. Further research topics might include the application of the discipline of spiritual direction into the Pentecostal church, the particular mystical expressions of spiritual direction, and the relational benefits of spiritual direction.

The primary recommendation recognized in this present research project would seek to incorporate this type of ministry into the Pentecostal and Charismatic traditions. First, the subject needs to be formally taught along with its function; benefits and pitfalls need to be explained. Second, there needs to be an education of both the director and directee so that any memory of the heartaches of the Shepherding Movement are neither associated with this practice, nor that they are recycled. Third, the attribute of humility must be fostered along with the spiritual disciplines and thereby resist the flamboyance and bombastic tendency of some associated with the Pentecostal movement. The longing for and renewed interest in the rich traditions of liturgy

32. "He is brought to the midst of the council of the brothers, stripped of what is his in their midst, and clothed in the garb of the monastery at the hands of the abba . . . When, therefore, a person has been admitted . . . he is not permitted to join the community of the brothers immediately but is assigned to and elder . . . having been exposed to his first training . . . and is about to be admitted. . . he is given over to another elder . . . the chief concern and instruction of this man . . . to teach him to conquer his desires." Cassian: *The Institutes* 4:5–9 (80–82).

33. 2 Cor 11:1–10 and 1 John 2:1.

34. *Trust,* Apr. 1911, 10.2, 6.

35. "Oh, for Spirit-touched eyes, and ears, and hearts, that will reveal the counterfeit experiences all about us, both in and outside the Pentecostal movement, and send us back to early church-power, even though it mean early church persecution and their badge of honor—'The offscouring of the earth.'" *Trust,* June 1908, 7.4, 11.

may well be accompanied by the renewed attraction of monasticism, or at very least the desire for inward reflection and spiritual formation.

## Bibliography

Behr, John. *Asceticism and Anthropology in Irenaeus and Clement*. Oxford: Oxford University Press. 2000.

Berthold, George C., ed. *Maximus the Confessor: Selected Writings*. Classics of Western Spirituality. New York: Paulist, 1985.

Burgess, Stanley M. *The Holy Spirit: Eastern Christian Traditions*. Peabody, MA: Hendrickson, 1988.

———. "Implications of Eastern Pneumatology for Western Pentecostal Doctrine and Practice." In *Experiences of the Spirit: Conference on Pentecostal and Charismatic Research in Europe at Untrecht University, 1989*, edited by Jan A.B. Jongeneel, 23–34. Studien zur interkultureen Geschichte des Christentums. Frankfurt: Lang, 1991.

Cassian, John. *John Cassian, the Institutes*. Edited by Boniface Ramsey. New York: Paulist, 2000.

Climacus, John. *John Climacus: The Ladder of Divine Ascent*. Translated by Colm Luibheid and Norman Russell. Classics of Western Spirituality. Mahwah, NJ: Paulist, 1982.

DeCatanzaro, C. J., ed. *Symeon The New Theologian: The Discourses*. New York: Paulist, 1980.

Goodier, Alban. S.J. *An Introduction to the Study of Ascetical and Mystical Theology*. New York: Benziger, 1938.

Greer, Rowan A., ed. *Origen: Selected Writings*. Classics of Western Spirituality. New York: Paulist, 1979.

Hall, Todd W. and Mark R. McMinn, eds. *Spiritual Formation, Counseling, and Psychotherapy*. New York: Nova Science, 2003.

Harton, F. P. *The Elements of the Spiritual Life: A Study in Ascetical Theology*. New York: MacMillian, 1957.

Hausherr, Irénée. *Spiritual Direction in the Early Christian East*. Kalamazoo, MI: Cistercian, 1990.

Lossky, Vladimir. *Orthodox Theology: An Introduction*. Crestwood, NY: St. Vladimir's Seminary Press, 1989.

Malherbe, Abraham J., and Everett Ferguson, eds. *Gregory of Nyssa: the Life of Moses*. Classics of Western Spirituality. New York: Paulist, 1979.

Maloney, George A. *Pseudo-Macarius: The Fifty Spiritual Homilies*. Classics of Western Spirituality. New York: Paulist, 1992.1

McVey, Kathleen E. *Ephrem the Syrian: Hymns*. Classics of Western Spirituality. New York: Paulist Press, 1990.

Meyendorf, George A. *Gregory Palamas: The Triads*. Classics of Western Spirituality. New York: Paulist, 1982.

Moore, S. David. *The Shepherding Movement: Controversy and Charismatic Ecclesiology*. Journal of Pentecostal Theology Supplement Series 27. London: T. & T. Clark, 2004.

Neufelder, Jerome M., and Mary C. Coelho. *Writings on Spiritual Direction by Great Christian Masters*. New York. Seabury. 1982

Rybarczyk, Edmund J. *Beyond Salvation: Eastern Orthodoxy and Classical Pentecostalism on Becoming Like Christ*. Carlisle, UK: Paternoster, 2004.

———. "Spiritualities Old and New: Similarities between Eastern Orthodoxy and Classical Pentecostalism." *Pneuma* 24 (2002) 7–25.

———. "What Are You, O Man? Theo-anthropological Similarities in Classical Pentecostalism and Eastern Orthodoxy." In *Ancient and Post-Modern Christianity*. Edited by Thomas C. Oden et al., 83–105. Downers Grove, IL: InterVarsity, 2002.

Symeon. *Symeon, the New Theologian: The Practical and Theological Chapters: and the Three Theological Discourses*. Kalamazoo, MI: Cistercian, 1982. Trust. Rochester, NY: Elim, 1908–1932.

Ward, Benedicta, trans. and ed. *The Sayings of the Desert Fathers: The Alphabetical Collection*. Kalamazoo, MI: Cistercian, 2004.

Ware, Kallistos Timothy. *The Orthodox Church*. New York: Penguin, 1993.

———. *The Orthodox Way*. Crestwood, NY: St. Vladimir's Seminary Press, 1995.

———. "Personal Experience of the Holy Spirit according to the Greek Fathers." Paper Presented at the Pentecostal-Charismatic Research Conference. Prague, 10–14 September 1997. http://philthompson.net/pages/library/wareonhs.html.

———. *The Spiritual Guide in Orthodox Christianity*. http://www.geocities.com/trvalentine/orthodox/spiritualguide.html?200617.

Wolff, Pierre. *The Spiritual Exercises of Saint Ignatius*. Liguori, MO: Triumph, 1997.

# 17

# John Wesley's Appropriation of *Theosis*: An Exercise in Contextual Theology

— DAVID BELLES

THEOLOGY IS OFTEN PERCEIVED as a stale and boring exercise that is merely a rehash of creeds or confessions written centuries ago, or bone-dry discussions on the nature of God, Christ, or the Trinity. Perhaps this attitude has developed from the belief that theology and theological formulations lack relevance. When presented in a manner that lacks creativity and imagination, theology fails to address contemporary problems and issues. To be relevant, theology must be applied to answer the question: So what? It must be put into a context that addresses the needs of the people of God, helping them live an authentic Christian life in the face of constant challenges. A contextual approach to theology takes the proven insights of the previous generations that helped define orthodoxy and applies those insights to the current generation. In the process it produces a new insight.

As the leader of a significant religious movement in the 17th century, John Wesley was faced with significant challenges to his methods and teachings. Churchmen in this century were concerned with whether the various doctrines and practices of the church were accurate representations of the faith and practice of first century Christians. Many churchmen scoured early Christian sources to discover what the early Church believed and practiced. They typically used what they found to defend those teachings and practices that they promoted as faithful to authentic Christianity. Wesley was no different. In the Wesley home, as well as at Oxford, John was encouraged to read the Church Fathers. The atmosphere in Britain guaranteed that an influential leader like Wesley had to be in dialogue with those sources in order to engage other clergy who were also in dialogue with them. We know that Wesley found many of those sources to be valuable. He recommended them to his Methodist ministers and included the works of some as abridgements in his Christian Library.[1]

Many scholars have examined the influence of ancient Eastern Patristic sources on Wesley's doctrine of sanctification, and have noted several affinities between it and

---

1. Maddox, "John Wesley and Eastern Orthodoxy," 30.

theosis. In this short article I will present the opinion that Wesley does manifest four key characteristics of theosis that are found in many of the early Eastern Church Fathers. These key characteristics are identified by Normal Russell in his book, *Fellow Workers with God: Orthodox Thinking on Theosis*. What this chapter will reveal is that Wesley's appropriation of theosis was contextual in nature. He gleaned from the insights of the Eastern Fathers and creatively applied those insights to address the concerns of his current context, and in doing so produced a new theological insight.

## Theosis

Norman Russell defines theosis as, "our restoration as persons to integrity and wholeness by participation in Christ through the Holy Spirit, in a process which is initiated in this world through our life of ecclesial communion and moral striving and finds ultimate fulfillment in our union with the Father—all within the broad context of the divine economy."[2] Russell's definition contains four important ideas that are integral to the concept of theosis. We engage in theosis by a process of participation. The process of participation brings about a transformation; as we are transformed we are restored to integrity and wholeness. The goal of theosis is union with the Father. From this definition it is evident that the Fathers used theosis as both a "theological theme and a spiritual teaching, both the goal of the divine economy and the process by which the economy is worked out in the believer."[3]

The term 'theosis' was created in the fourth century by Gregory of Nazianzus. In his Oration delivered shortly after the death of Emperor Julian the Apostate, he used the term as shorthand to describe the steps God took to restore humanity within the overall plan of salvation, or divine economy. First, God emptied himself and became a human being. Second, having become incarnate, he took up his assumed body into the divine life. Third, we appropriate his deified humanity at baptism. Fourth, we ascend to God through the contemplative life. Fifth, we reach the final fulfillment of our entire being in heaven.[4] Gregory's description contains elements found in many of the Eastern Father's description of theosis. The Son of God emptied himself and assumed a human body and nature that becomes representative for all humanity. Because the Son is divine, he possesses life in himself; as such, he communicated life (was life-giving) to the body that he assumed. We can participate in the Son's representative humanity and appropriate his divine life, overcoming death and corruption. The appropriation of the divine life (divinization) can progress in this life (in Gregory's case, through contemplation). Finally, the ultimate goal of divinization is union with the Father, which will accrue fully in the life to come.

2. Russell, *Fellow Workers with God*, 21.
3. Russell, *Fellow Workers with God*, 21.
4. Russell, *Fellow Workers with God*, 22.

While Gregory invented the term in the fourth century, the concept of theosis can be traced to the earlier second century Fathers: Clement of Alexandria, Hippolytus of Rome, and Irenaeus of Lyons. These early writers taught that through Jesus Christ human beings could achieve fellowship with God in a manner that "allowed them to be thought of as 'gods.'"[5] Irenaeus wrote that Christ "became what we are in order to make us what he is himself." In the fourth century Athanasius expressed the same idea in a different way when he said of Christ that "He became human that we might become divine."[6] This notion that Christ took upon himself our nature so that we might partake of his became known as the "exchange formula." In the fourth-century St. Ephrem the Syrian expressed this formula clearly and succinctly when he said that Christ "gave us divinity, we gave him humanity."[7]

Participation

We appropriate Christ's divinity by participating in his divine life. It was Origen who first distinguished two types of participation: natural and supernatural. Natural participation "belongs to the structure of our being," and is concerned with our being qua beings.[8] It refers to the fact that human beings are contingent and must rely on the existence of another for their existence. Metaphysically, humans must participate in the absolute because we have no existence in our own right.[9] Supernatural participation has to do with our activity as human beings.[10] It "belongs to our growth in the spiritual life."[11] In other words, it has to do with our moral progress and sanctification. According to Origen, because God is triune, he is personal; and because he is personal, he reaches out to his creation in order to reveals himself to us. If we freely respond in faith, his Spirit will transform us and make us partakers in the Son. Through the Holy Spirit we come to share in the divine attributes of the Son, and "arise to the right hand of the Father."[12] Without the Holy Spirit and the Son it is impossible to be a partaker in the Father.[13]

Later Church Fathers picked up Origen's notion of supernatural participation and developed it in different ways. For example, Gregory of Nyssa proposed the idea of a three-staged growth process based on Moses's ascent up Mount Sinai. In the third and final stage the soul begins to reflect the perfection of God as it participates in him

5. Russell, *Fellow Workers with God*, 23.
6. Russell, *Fellow Workers with God*, 23, 24.
7. Russell, *Fellow Workers with God*, 24.
8. Russell, *Doctrine of Deification*, 148; Russell, *Fellow Workers with God*, 129.
9. Russell, *Fellow Workers with God*, 127.
10. Russell, *Doctrine of Deification*, 148.
11. Russell, *Fellow Workers with God*, 129.
12. Russell, *Fellow Workers with God*, 127, 129.
13. Russell, *Doctrine of Deification*, 149.

and his image God is restored. The process is enabled by partaking of the Eucharist, which allows our mortal flesh to unite with immortality. Through the Eucharist we participate corporally with Christ's incorruption.[14]

Cyril of Alexander also emphasized this distinction between natural and supernatural participation. Like Origen, Cyril described natural participation as necessary because we are contingent and ontologically rely on God for our existence. When describing supernatural participation, Cyril's focus is on the deification of Christ's human flesh by the Word. Like Gregory, Cyril pointed out the need to partake of the Eucharist, which is a mirror of the incarnation. By partaking of Christ's deified flesh, we are transformed by the mystery and made to be more like God.[15] Cyril's use of participation was not focused only on our assimilation of Christ's divine attributes, but also upon our relationship with the Father; because we participate through the Spirit in the Son, like the Son we have a relationship with the Father.[16]

Transformation

Implicit in the idea of supernatural participation is the notion that human beings are not "self-contained."[17] In order to be truly human we must participate in the life of God and in doing so we will be transformed.

One of the favorite images used by the Eastern Fathers to illustrate our transformation was the transfiguration of Jesus. As they meditated on the meaning of the transfiguration event, they concluded that it signified more than just the transformation of Christ's physical body by the godhead. Those who observed the event were in some way transformed internally.[18] Those souls that experienced the transfiguration of Jesus were prepared by God to become his dwelling place.[19] In response to the revelation on Mount Tabor, the disciples followed Christ's example and emptied themselves by sharing in his Passion. They were able to follow Christ's example and lay down their lives because they saw the glory in Christ, a glory that they would one day share.[20] The revelation that the disciples experienced on Mount Tabor strengthened them so that they would have the courage to suffer and die for Christ's sake.

The transfiguration illustrates how God had emptied himself in an act of love so that human kind might participate in his glory. The transfiguration reveals God's act of love through the perceptible radiance that permeated Christ's physical body. In the transfiguration we do not encounter the very essence of God, but a physical

14. Russell, *Fellow Workers with God*, 130.
15. Russell, *Fellow Workers with God*, 131.
16. Russell, *Fellow Workers with God*, 132.
17. Russell, *Fellow Workers with God*, 113.
18. Russell, *Fellow Workers with God*, 102.
19. Russell, *Fellow Workers with God*, 107.
20. Russell, *Fellow Workers with God*, 110, 111.

manifestation of his creative energies in the form of a perceptible radiance. The proper human response to God's gift of love is to empty ourselves of those aspects of our humanity distorted by the fall.[21] Without willful co-operation, the process of transformation cannot take place.

Restoration

While the Eastern Fathers generally agreed that the goal of theosis was the restoration of what humanity lost in the Fall, they differed on what precisely was being restored. Clement of Alexandria, Basil the Great, and John of Damascus distinguished the image of God, which they said was not lost in the Fall, from the likeness of God, which was lost. They associated the image with the human rational capacity, while the likeness referred to the moral capacity.[22] Rather than distinguishing image from likeness, Athanasius distinguishes "the Image" from being in the image. Only the Son of God is "the Image" of the Father, while human beings were created to be "in the image" of the Son.[23] By participating in the Son's relation to the Father, human beings can become "images of the Image."[24] Gregory of Nyssa did not distinguish the image from the likeness; he placed the focus on the restoration of the moral goodness that was lost in the Fall.[25] Finally, Cyril of Alexandria described the need to restore the image of God, but he does not locate the image in humanities reasoning capacity. Instead, the locus for image of God is found in the will, which was distorted by the Fall.[26]

Union

The goal of theosis is union with God. However, as contingent beings we can never become essential like God. The gulf between created humanity and divinity can never be bridged. What we can become is *what God is*, except at the level of being.[27] This is how some of the eastern Fathers understood the notion of restoring "the likeness of God."[28] However, the Fathers differed on the degree to which you could attain likeness or union with God in this life.

21. Russell, *Fellow Workers with God*, 41.
22. Russell, *Fellow Workers with God*, 77.
23. Russell, *Fellow Workers with God*, 77.
24. Russell, *Fellow Workers with God*, 77.
25. Russell, *Fellow Workers with God*, 78.
26. Russell, *Fellow Workers with God*, 79.
27. Russell, *Fellow Workers with God*, 145.
28. Russell, *Fellow Workers with God*, 144.

## Summary

As we have described the concept of theosis, we have highlighted four key concepts found in Norman Russell's definition: participation, transformation, restoration, and union. In general, the Eastern Fathers understood God's grand plan of salvation as restoring the image or likeness of God that was lost in the Fall through a process of participation in the divine life of Christ, made available through the incarnation, until we come into perfect union with the Father. The acquisition of the life of God is not only necessary for mortal human beings to put on immortality, but also for our moral and spiritual development.

## Assurance

Wesley believed that having an assurance of faith was one of the blessings enjoyed by believers in the first centuries of the Church's existence. In a letter to Richard Tompson, he stated that although there is not much in terms of early Church doctrine on the subject, anyone who reads "Clemens Romanus, Ignatius, Polycarp, Origen, or any other of them" cannot doubt that they possessed an assurance of salvation.[29] Wesley considered the teaching of assurance to be "one grand part of the testimony which God has given . . . [to the Methodists] to bear to all mankind." It is a great evangelical truth that he and his fellow Methodists have recovered from being nearly forgotten.

Wesley's conviction that the assurance of faith was so prevalent in the early church makes his formulation of assurance an interesting test case to examine his contextual application of theosis. First, I will describe Wesley's doctrine of assurance. Then I will note how the four characteristics are found in that doctrine. Finally, I will conclude with a description of how Wesley's application of theosis to this issue is contextual in nature.

The Holy Spirit is integral in the formation of faith, the consciousness that the Father sent Jesus Christ to die "for me" because he "loved me." The presence of faith is a kind of supernatural "divine evidence" supplied by the Holy Spirit.[30] Its presence produces an assurance of salvation that is concurrent with justification and the new birth. However, is this consciousness the result of my own subjective religious or moral feelings, or does it come from somewhere outside of myself? This is an important question because Wesley defined faith in such a way that it requires one to have a subjective, personal conviction that Christ's salvific work is for *me*. If this form of faith is merely a product of my own subjective imagination, then there is no real faith and therefore no real salvation, certainly making Wesley and all his followers "men most miserable" (1 Cor 15:19).

---

29. Oden, *John Wesley's Scriptural Christianity*, 234.
30. Wesley, "Scripture Way of Salvation," II.2; John Wesley, "Justification by Faith," IV.2.

PART 2: INSIGHTS FROM THE HISTORY OF THE CHURCH

## Steering the Middle Course

Wesley described the believers' assurance as being due to the "Spirit itself" bearing witness "within our spirit that we are the children of God" (Rom 8:16). As he interpreted the meaning of this passage, he was careful to steer a middle course between two extremes: rationalistic skepticism and enthusiasm. The former consisted of an extreme doubt about whether it is ever possible to know God, and whether it is ever possible to be reconciled with him.[31] As such, it was skeptical of anyone who claimed to have a sense of assurance due to the influence of the Holy Spirit. Even the so-called "fruit of the Spirit" that characterized the outward changes in behavior subsequent to salvation were viewed as due to "naturalistic, psychological, sociological, or physical causes." Any Christian who claimed that they were talking to God, were in reality "talking to themselves."[32] Enthusiasts tended to confuse the voice of God's Spirit with their own "earthly hopes and despair, while at the same time their behaviors were closer to the 'works of the devil!'"[33]

In order to chart a middle course between the extremes of rational skepticism and enthusiasm, Wesley affirmed both the subjective internal witness of our own spirit, and the external witness of God's Spirit.[34]

## How does the Holy Spirit bear witness with our spirit?

When a person claims to be a Christian, there should be marks or indicators of transformation. According to Wesley, these include holy tempers (or attitudes) and actions, a successful desire to keep God's word and the commandments found in it, the presence of outward acts of righteousness, and a love for one's fellow brothers and sisters in Christ in word and deed. If all of these are present, then one is a child of God.[35] However, what makes the presence of these marks significant from the perspective of a personal assurance of salvation is not what they indicate to others, but that they indicate a change *to ourselves*.[36] Inwardly, a believer is conscious of these qualities or marks. The realization that "Yes, I am a child of God" comes about as the believer inwardly holds a mirror up to their life and reflected back they see the presence of the marks of salvation. According to Wesley, this realization is valid because these marks could never have been produced without the change that occurs at salvation and the

---

31. Oden, *John Wesley's Scriptural Christianity*, 229.
32. Oden, *John Wesley's Scriptural Christianity*, 230.
33. Oden, *John Wesley's Scriptural Christianity*, 229. Wesley, "Witness of the Spirit: Discourse I," Intro. 1.
34. Wesley, "Witness of the Spirit: Discourse I," Intro. 3.
35. Wesley, "Witness of the Spirit: Discourse I," I:2–4.
36. Wesley, "Witness of the Spirit: Discourse I," I:5.

enabling presence of the Holy Spirit. Assurance comes out of a consciousness of the *how* and the *why* a believer does the things that he does.

Wesley's less than optimistic view of human potential apart from God's help precluded him from concluding that these marks could be the result of human effort alone. The universal human condition due to the Fall is as it is described in the book of Genesis before the flood: Every imagination was evil, continually (Gen 6:5).[37] The Fall has made us prideful, self-worshipping idolaters dominated by the lust of the eye, the lust of the flesh, and the pride of life.[38] We have no love for God or our neighbor, no fear of God, and no knowledge of God.[39] Although it is possible through the use of natural reasoning to conclude that God does exist, we are completely estranged from him, having no relationship with him at all.[40] Fortunately, human beings are not left to themselves. We are capable of doing good because God, the author and worker of good, is with us.[41] The good that human beings do is due to the Holy Spirit striving with humanity against its evil desires.[42] It is the Spirit, operating freely "in us" that prevents humanity from descending into total chaos, and is the source of every good human work. The presence of those marks indicating a change in character toward being godly or Christ-like in nature are proof that a believer is being conformed into the image of Christ by the Holy Spirit.[43]

But how does the believer know that these changes are the work of the Holy Spirit as opposed to the natural causes proposed by the rationalist? According to Wesley, it is because they are accompanied by a joy that is the produce of having a good conscience toward God, which is produced when one has acted with simplicity and godly sincerity (2 Cor 1:12). The conscience is a "faculty or power, implanted by God in every soul . . . of perceiving what is right and wrong in his own heart and life, in his tempers, thoughts, rules or actions."[44] A conscience requires a rule or standard in order to judge. Using that rule, the conscience judges whether one's intentions and actions are in harmony with it and are therefore right or moral, or are out of harmony and are wrong or immoral. Everyone who is born into the world possesses a natural rule or moral sense that is written on their hearts by "the finger of God."[45] Christians, however, have a more fine-tuned moral sense that is informed by the word of God. This enhanced moral sense, informed by scripture, is present only because the gift of faith has activated the "spiritual senses" to comprehend scripture's truth.

37. Wesley, "Original Sin," I:1, 2.
38. Wesley, "Original Sin," II:7.
39. Wesley, "Original Sin," II:5, 6.
40. Wesley, "Original Sin," III:3.
41. Wesley, "Free Grace," 3.
42. Wesley, "Original Sin," I:4.
43. Wesley, "Witness of the Spirit: Discourse I," I:6.
44. Wesley, "Witness of Our Own Spirit," 5.
45. Wesley, "Witness of Our Own Spirit," 6.

Wesley described the gift of faith as a kind of light *for* the soul, and is a spiritual sight or perception *of* the soul. Those who have the gift of faith have the eyes of their understanding opened by the Holy Spirit so that their spiritual senses can become aware of God's presence. This corresponds to faith as perception by the soul. The Holy Spirit enables this aspect of faith so that the soul's spiritual sense mechanism can function. However, it is the Spirit who also enlightens the soul; thus, it is also the Spirit's function to provide for those with the gift of faith the light needed for the soul to operate with its now functioning spiritual senses.[46] The Holy Spirit provides both aspects of faith by enabling the spiritual eyes and enlightening those eyes to the truth: God has reconciled the world to himself by Jesus Christ; and that Christ "loved me" and died "for me."[47] The Spirit also supernaturally assists those who read God's word with earnest prayer. It is this supernatural assistance that makes scripture profitable in providing moral direction (2 Tim 3:16).[48]

For those whose spiritual senses are fully functional and enlightened whatever the word prescribes or directs is good, and whatever it forbids is evil.[49] Having a conscience informed by the word puts the Christian in a better position to avoid making errors in moral judgment. Additionally, they are in a better position to know specifically what God's righteous requirements consist of.

Beyond simply knowing that you have performed what God requires in his word, a good conscience also comes from knowing that one has acted in simplicity and godly sincerity. Wesley defined simplicity as a single-minded desire to serve God and him alone. One's intention is to glorify God and to do his will.[50] Godly sincerity refers to the fact that our actions align with our intentions; that we do in fact glorify God by doing his will.[51] It is not merely the doing of God's will that is the evidence of our transformation, but the doing coupled with intention.

By setting the criteria for having a good conscience well beyond mere adherence to the natural rule, including not only outward actions in conformance with the Word of God, but also the alignment of those actions with one's intentions, which must themselves be directed toward glorifying God, Wesley ensured that there is no possibility that a good conscience could come without the power of the Holy Spirit.[52] It is for this reason that a believer has joy, because the *only* way that one *could* have a good conscience is by the enabling power of the Spirit. Since the Spirit is at work to produce a good conscience, that believer must be a child of God.

---

46. Wesley, "Scripture Way of Salvation," II:1.
47. Wesley, "Scripture Way of Salvation," II:2.
48. Wesley, *Second Epistle to Timothy*.
49. Wesley, "Witness of Our Own Spirit," 6.
50. Wesley, "Witness of Our Own Spirit," 11.
51. Wesley, "Witness of Our Own Spirit," 12.
52. Wesley, "Witness of Our Own Spirit," 14, 15.

Wesley's answer to the rationalist was that the marks of salvation cannot be the result of natural ability because they are accompanied by the joy that comes from having a good conscience before God. If they were the work of natural ability, there would be no joy because according to the rationalist no one can know whether they are pleasing God, nor does a natural man care.

## The direct witness of the Spirit

The recognition that the marks of salvation are the work of the Spirit and therefore indicate that one is a child of God is what Wesley called the "indirect witness."[53] However, is there a witness that is "immediate" and "direct" that is not a result of reflection?[54] Wesley's answer was, "Yes, most assuredly." There is a witness that is prior to our spirit's witness; it is the direct witness of the Holy Spirit. It is the Holy Spirit who works prior to even our confession of faith, making the Holy Spirit's witness concurrent with justification and the new birth.[55] It is therefore not proof of a believer's confession, given that it is prior to that confession.[56]

The direct witness of the Holy Spirit is the cause of the indirect witness. Without the direct witness there can be no holiness of heart and life leading to the indirect witness.[57] There is a specific order of causal events that lead up to the indirect witness. Everything begins with the direct witness of the Holy Spirit to our spirit. This causes the love of God to be shed abroad in the believer's heart. The direct witness causes her to realize that the Father loved her enough to send his Son as a sacrifice for her sins, and that the Son loved her enough to give his life on her behalf.[58] The revelation of that love causes the believer to respond in love by living a holy life. As we have already pointed out, on her own she is incapable of manifesting the good works that are pleasing to God. It is the Holy Spirit who enables holy living. As the Holy Spirit works in the believer, enabling her to manifest good works, the Spirit "shines upon his own work."[59]

Finally, the holiness that is produced, as it is reflected upon, causes the indirect witness. The causal progression from the direct witness, to the realization of God's love, to manifestation of holiness as a response, to the indirect witness is what Wesley calls the testimony of the Holy Spirit "to and with our spirit."[60] If we grieve the Spirit by engaging in outward sin the Holy Spirit's testimony will be lost along with the inward

---

53. Wesley, "Witness of the Spirit: Discourse II," II:6.
54. Wesley, "Witness of the Spirit: Discourse II," II:4.
55. Wesley, "Witness of the Spirit: Discourse II," IV:4.
56. Wesley, "Witness of the Spirit: Discourse II," IV:4.
57. Wesley, "Witness of the Spirit: Discourse I," I:8.
58. Wesley, "Witness of the Spirit: Discourse I," I:9.
59. Wesley, "Witness of the Spirit: Discourse I," I:10.
60. Wesley, "Witness of the Spirit: Discourse II," II:1.

sense of assurance. As long as a believer repents when the Spirit reveals remaining sin, and continually relies on enabling grace to walk in love, hope, and faith, they will not sin. If a believer fails to avail themselves of God's grace in the face of temptation there is not an immediate abandonment by the Spirit, but there is a progressive loss of enabling grace.[61] When temptation is present, the Holy Spirit warns the believer of its presence and attempts to draw her away from its presence into prayer. If the believer does not heed the Spirit, but instead begins to give in to the temptation, the Spirit will be grieved. This will lead to a loss of faith and love, causing the Spirit to convict the believer more sharply. If the believer continues to follow the temptation, turning away from God, faith and love will vanish. At this point the enabling grace of God has departed and outward sin is possible.[62] As there is a loss of the enabling grace, faith, hope, and love as a Christian fails to flee from temptation, there is a loss of assurance as well. Assurance, as well as enabling grace, faith, hope, and love, requires the Spirit's presence to be maintained. As long as a believer works co-operatively with the Spirit, she will be maintained and grow.

The exact manner of how the direct witness of the Spirit works upon our spirit is a mystery.[63] The Spirit could witness to the human spirit in any number of ways; by an inward voice, or by bringing a scripture to mind. Primarily, the Spirit's direct witness is an inward "sense" or calm that comes because all one's sins are forgiven.[64] The immediate, visceral, and pre-reflective response to the direct witness is "Abba, Father"[65] and is due to the realization that reconciliation has taken place and God is now "my Father."

By proposing an objective external witness that is prior to any subjective witness on the believer's part Wesley avoided the charge of enthusiasm. His rejection of enthusiasm was due to his conviction that a personal subjective witness alone is insufficient. To illustrate, consider those who are under the Spirit's conviction, but they have yet to be justified. Those who are in this state realize that they need forgiveness and that only God can provide it. They have a personal witness to their own sin and their need for forgiveness, but without the direct witness of the Spirit they have no personal conviction that they *are* forgiven.[66] Those who are self-righteous have a personal witness to their own sincerity, but because they lack the direct witness of the Spirit they have no knowledge, and therefore no assurance that their sins are forgiven and that they are a child of God.[67] In both instances, the personal subjective witness is insufficient to bring about any assurance that one's sins are forgiven and that one is saved.

61. Wesley, "The Great Privilege," II:9.
62. Wesley, "The Great Privilege," III:9.
63. Wesley, "Witness of the Spirit: Discourse I," I:12.
64. Wesley, "Witness of the Spirit: Discourse II," II:4.
65. Wesley, "Witness of the Spirit: Discourse II," III:6.
66. Wesley, "Witness of the Spirit: Discourse II," III:7.
67. Wesley, "Witness of the Spirit: Discourse II," III:9.

Wesley's understanding of assurance maintained a balance between rationalistic skepticism and enthusiasm by affirming a personal, subjective, indirect witness that one is saved, which is grounded in an objective, direct witness of the Holy Spirit. To the question, is my consciousness that Christ died *for me* the result of my own subjective religious or moral feelings, or does it come from somewhere outside of myself, Wesley's answer was "Yes, both."

## Wesley's Contextual Use of Theosis

The purpose of the doctrine of assurance is to provide the believer with confidence in the hope of the future resurrection and new creation, culminating in our union with the Father. That day we will enjoy a life in the new creation that will be "a more beautiful paradise than Adam ever saw."[68] We will enjoy a "deep, an intimate, an uninterrupted union with God; a constant communion with the Father and his Son Jesus Christ, through the Spirit; a continual enjoyment of the three-in-one God, and all creation in Him!"[69] We have this hope because we know that we are children of God, and we know that we are his children because we believe that Christ loved each one of us and died for each one of us personally. The assurance of our faith in Christ's love is proven by the gift of the Spirit, given as a down payment of our future union. That same Spirit testifies to his own presence and activity by enabling each believer to manifest a holy life.

Like the Early Fathers who promoted the doctrine of theosis, Wesley did not hold to the notion that we had to wait until that future union before we could be conformed to the image of Jesus Christ. He taught that to a great extent we could be transformed into Christ's image in this life. As a believer reflects on their behavior, they are able to note this transformation in the presence of changes to his character manifested in outward acts of righteousness that conform to God's commandments. Further reflection reveals that these outward acts are motivated by a sincere desire to respond in love to God's love in Christ as it has been shed abroad in our hearts by the Spirit.

The alignment of our inward intention to respond in love and glorify God by doing his will elicits a sense of joy, since this could only happen if we are enabled by the Spirit. The transformation of our character is due to the presence of God's Spirit revealing to us God's love for us in Christ. We respond in love, enabled by the Spirit. This picture of how the indirect witness is produced is similar to how many of the Eastern Father's understood the transforming power of the transfiguration. Those who viewed the transfiguration witnessed a picture of God's self-emptying love so that one day they could participate in the glory revealed in the transfiguration. They responded by emptying themselves in love. The revelation of Christ's divinity in the transfiguration transformed both the intentions and behaviors of the disciples. In a

---

68. Wesley, "The New Creation," 16.
69. Wesley, "The New Creation," 18.

parallel way Wesley described the work of the Spirit to reveal God's love to our hearts, which in turn transforms our intentions and behaviors.

However, our transformation is not accomplished entirely in unilateral fashion. The moral transformation that Origin called supernatural participation required a free response of faith. Similarly, Wesley's description of the transformation to our character observed under the indirect witness and caused by the direct witness requires a willful response to the presence of the Holy Spirit. The moral transformation that Wesley referred to as "holy living" is a result of our loving response to the revelation of God's love in Christ by the Spirit. As long as the Spirit is not grieved to the point where he withdraws, we can willfully respond to his prompting and our assurance of salvation remains.

The one characteristic that was not mentioned specifically in my summary of Wesley's doctrine of assurance is restoration. Elsewhere, Wesley states that the goal of true religion is to "renew our hearts in the image of God."[70] Nevertheless I think that it is implicit in Wesley's doctrine. The Eastern Father's tended to locate the image or likeness of God in the human rational capacity, moral goodness, or will. Wesley described the work of the Spirit as a direct witness enabling our will to respond to God's love in Christ. As we respond in love, we begin to manifest holiness in outward acts or righteousness. These outward moral acts serve as the indirect witness to the transforming work of the Spirit upon our will. Wesley's description of the function of the direct and indirect witness is a description of the restoration of the image of Christ in the restoration of our will and our moral capacity.

As we can see, Wesley's balanced approach to the doctrine of assurance contains the four characteristics of theosis identified by Russell. God's proximate presence in the person of the Holy Spirit transforms us into the image of Christ through willful participation in his attributable attributes. This transformation creates an assurance of our eventual union with the Father. But how is Wesley's use of these characteristics contextual?

According to Russell, the Patristic Father's viewed theosis as both a "theological theme and a spiritual teaching, both the goal of the divine economy and the process by which the economy is worked out in the believer."[71] It supplies both the goal of God's salvific activities and the mechanism for our growth into the goal. It contains both the final as well as the efficient and instrumental causes of the economy of salvation. Wesley applied the characteristics of theosis to the narrower issue of how one knows that one is a child of God and therefore a partaker in God's economy. If, upon reflection, one observes in one's self the formation of traits that conform to God's teleological goal of re-forming in us his image, this constitutes evidence that we have a genuine faith. If we find that we are willfully co-operating with God in that transformation, and therefore fulfilling the role of instrumental cause in that

---

70. Wesley, "Original Sin," III:5.
71. Russell, *Fellow Workers with God*, 21.

process, this constitutes evidence that we have genuine faith. Assuming that our transformation into God's image and our willful participation in that transformation is not something that we could manufacture on our own without the immediate *presence* of God's Holy Spirit, this also constitutes real evidence that we have genuine faith and an assurance of one's future union with the Father. Theosis, in the form of transformation, restoration, and our willful participation are the evidences that give us an assurance of faith and a hope of union with the Father.

If contextual theology consists of taking biblical and theological insights and applying them to a current concern or issue, thereby producing a new theological insight, then Wesley's use of theosis is an exercise in contextual theology. Wesley applied the characteristics of theosis and from that application produced the doctrine of assurance. He addressed how it is we can be assured that we are a part of God's divine economy by examining whether there is evidence of progress toward the goal of that economy and whether we find that we are willfully participating in the mechanism that produces that progress. While Wesley would never have put it this way, in essence, he used the presence of theosis in the life of the believer as evidence for a valid assurance of faith.

What we have shown in this examination is that Wesley appropriated the theological insights of the Patristic Fathers regarding the goal and process of God's economy of salvation—Theosis—and applied it to his contemporary question of how one can have an assurance of faith. The result was a new insight, the Wesleyan doctrine of assurance. As we have defined it, Wesley's process in developing this doctrine was an exercise in contextual theology.

I began this paper by noting the importance of the "So what?" question to theological inquiry. This question opens the door to theological application and, in fact, makes a contextual theological discovery like Wesley's possible. Mentors and instructors who push students to ask the "So what?" question ensures that theology remains relevant and that new and creative theological discoveries take place. This volume is intended to honor a professor who made me ask the "So what?" question for every assignment. For that I have benefited and am grateful.

## Bibliography

Maddox, Randy L. "John Wesley and Eastern Orthodoxy: Influences, Convergences, and Differences." *Asbury Theological Journal* 45 (1990) 29–53.
Oden, T. C. *John Wesley's Scriptural Christianity: A Plain Exposition of His Teaching on Christian Doctrine*. Grand Rapids: Zondervan, 1994.
Russell, Norman. *The Doctrine of Deification in the Greek Patristic Tradition*. Oxford: Oxford University Press, 2004.
———. *Fellow Workers with God: Orthodox Thinking on Theosis*. Crestwood, NY: St Vladimir's Seminary Press 2009.
Wesley, John. "Free Grace."

PART 2: INSIGHTS FROM THE HISTORY OF THE CHURCH

———. "The Great Privilege of Those That Are Born of God."
———. "Justification by Faith."
———. "The New Creation."
———. *Notes on St. Paul's Second Epistle to Timothy.*
———. "Original Sin."
———. "The Scripture Way of Salvation."
———. "The Witness of Our Own Spirit."
———. "The Witness of the Spirit: Discourse I."
———. "The Witness of the Spirit: Discourse II."

# 18

## Aging in the Light: The Patristic Writers' Views on Aging though, with, and in Christ

*Suzanne Pearson*

When my 70-year-old father lay dying in a hospital bed after many long years of infirmity, he said to me, "Jesus never knew what it was like to grow old. He died when he was still young." While what my father said was true, I knew even though young, Jesus had suffered the insults to mind, body, and spirit my father was suffering. I knew my argument would be of little comfort to my father though, as he had been suffering for decades. So I said nothing and just sat with him. In the silence which followed, in my father's unspoken words, I heard the echo of the words of a dying Jesus, "My God, my God, why have you abandoned me?" (Matt 27:46).[1] Like Mary and Jesus's beloved disciple John, who stood at the foot of the cross of Jesus, I experienced a deep poverty of spirit that day and in the year to follow, as I watched my father die. I held his hand as he passed on peacefully, some months later, after having suffered silently in a world that did not understand the nature of his suffering. I continued to ponder his statement in my heart these subsequent decades in my life as I grew in faith without him.

### Idolatry of Death

Contemporary American popular culture portrays the ideal of aging as a restoration of youth at any price, even by measures as extreme as cosmetic surgical makeover. Senior years are seen as a time to retire from the demands of work to pursue play, and increasingly for some, when physical and mental health fail, as a time to actively pursue death through physician-assisted means. The moral confusion of our age has led to what Pope John Paul II warned is a "culture of death."[2] Late ethicist, William Stringfellow, identifies the living in defiance of death, as evidenced in our age

---

1. Unless otherwise noted, translations of the Bible will be taken from NRSVCE.
2. John Paul II, *Evangelium Vitae*, 12.

by everything from entertainment culture to euthansia, as the "idolatry of death."[3] Idolatry has been the primary problem in all cultures and in all times. In our culture and time Stringfellow suggests that if we are primarily concerned with defying death, then our primary reality must be death.[4] This cultural message is in direct opposition to the life-giving and life-affirming message of the gospel.

For the patristic writers, old age, like every other age, is a gift from God. For them it was not a given though, living in a time in history when many did not survive childhood. Even so, they did not see youth as something to hold on to at all costs, but something to surrender gracefully, if you were blessed with increasing years, to pursue a greater good. More valuable than a youthful appearance and lifestyle were growth in godly character, virtuous behavior, and spiritual maturity with the hope of gaining eternal life.

Unlike our culture, the patristic writers respected the physical appearance of the aging and found meaning in it. They considered clinging to the ways of youth a rebellion against the plan of God and living as the pagans do. Their words on the topic echoed those of Scripture, particularly, "Gray hair is a crown of glory; it is gained in a righteous life" (Prov 16:31). They viewed modern fashion and cosmetically altered appearance as fruitless vanity and reflective of the value system of the heathen. Patristic writers even advised against dying one's gray or white hair. Tertllian taught women about the futility of changing their God-given hair color, including their gray hair, and observed, "The more old age tries to conceal itelf, the more it will be detected."[5] Clement of Alexandria told men not to dye their hair for it was a mark of honor from God and their gray hair had a purpose. "God's mark of honor is to be shown in the light of day, to win the reverence of the young. For sometimes, when they have been behaving shamefully, the appearance of hoary hairs, arriving like an instructor, has changed them to sobriety, and paralyzed juvenile lust with the splendor of the sight."[6] Augustine suggested white hair reminds us of the abundance of the mercy of God and the restoration which comes from overcoming sin and gaining eternal life. "Ye see how the head groweth old, and whiteneth, as fast as old age approacheth. Though sometimes dost seek in the head of one who groweth old duly in his own course a black hair, yet though findest it not: thus when our life shall have been such, that the blackness of sins may be sought, and none found, that old age is youthful, is green, and ever will be green."[7] Clement of Alexandria called gray hair, "the admirable flower of venerable wisdom, conciliating confidence."[8]

---

3. Trulear, "Considering the Alternative," 4–5.
4. Trulear, "Considering the Alternative," 4–5.
5. Tertullian, "On the Apparel of Women," 41.
6. Clement of Alexandria, "Exhortation to the Heathen," 558.
7. Augustine, "On the Psalms, Psalm 92," 981.
8. Clement of Alexandria, "The Instructor," 535.

Athanasisus, who wrote on the life of St. Anthony, the founder of Christian monasticism, described the paradox of Anthony's appearance after a long, severely ascetic life. Included in his description was the fact Anthony retained his own teeth though, "They had become worn to the gums through the great age of the old man."[9] Anthony sought no physical comforts as he aged and eschewed the food, foot care, and comfortable clothes coveted by his aged counterparts. In spite of his asceticism, in comparison to his peers, "He appeared more cheerful and of greater strength."[10] Anthony's ascetism extended to his accomplishments in life which Athanasisus described as unrenowed save his piety toward God, which was what earned him fame, though he lived a hidden life. Athanasisus attributed the unlikely fame of Anthony to God, "For even if they work secretly, even if they wish to remain in obscurity, yet the Lord shows them as lamps to lighten all, that those who hear may thus know that the precepts of God are able to make men prosper and thus be zealous in the path of virtue."[11]

## Martyrdom

The patristic writers saw aging, suffering, and dying as a time to bear witness to Christ in a martyrdom, not of blood, but of the soul pouring out its faith for others and as a means to eternal life. Clement of Alexandria defined martyrdom as bearing witness to God by one's life or by words by the soul who sought in pureness of heart to know God and obey His commands. The essential element of martyrdom is an outpouring of faith. For some this included the shedding of blood but for all it is by faith that the soul is separated from the body before a person dies. He explained in the Gospels the reason the Lord praises the one who has left everything for Jesus and His Gospel is, "That person is blessed because he too is going to meet martyrdom simply by living in a way that is different from the crowd, because he is following the rule of the Gospel for the love of his Lord."[12] While all but one of the original disciples of Jesus died in a martyrdom of blood, as did many Christians in the first centuries of the Church, tradition has it that Jesus's beloved disciple, John, lived to an extreme old age. Entrusted with both the care of Jesus's mother, Mary, and evangelism of Christianity, John modeled the martyrdom of a long life lived through, with, and in Christ.

When witnessing to Christ included a martyrdom of blood, some of the most compelling testimonies of martyrs in the early Christian era were those of the elderly who approached their deaths with the ardor of youth. Not seeking exemption due to their advanced years, they suffered and died alongside their younger and more physically able sisters and brothers in Christ. Polycarp, a disciple of John the Evangelist and Bishop of Smyrna, refused to recant his Christian faith when offered

9. Athanasisus, "Life of St. Anthony," 631.
10. Athanasisus, "Life of St. Anthony," 631.
11. Athanasisus, "Life of St. Anthony," 631.
12. Clement of Alexandria, "Miscellaneous Studies," in *Hidden Fountain*, 39.

the opportunity to go free because of his advanced age. He declared, "Eighty and six years have I served Him, and He never did me any injury: how then can I blaspheme my King and Savior?"[13] Church historian, Eusibus, wrote of the brutal martyrdom of Pothinus, Bishop of Lyons. "He was more than ninety years of age, and very infirm, scarcely indeed able to breathe because of physical weakness; but he was strengthened by spiritual zeal through his earnest desire for martyrdom. Though his body was worn out by old age and disease, his life was preserved that Christ might triumph in it. When he was brought by the soldiers to the tribunal, accompanied by the civil magistrates and a multitude who shouted against him in every manner as if he were Christ himself, he bore noble witness."[14]

## Bearing the Image of Christ

Christian writers in the early church found meaning in aging and suffering and affirmed the dignity of the elderly and dying as bearing the image of Christ. Seim and Økland note, "It is clear that when the first Christians looked into the mirror, dimly, who they saw was not primarily themselves, but Christ, since their own selves in some sense had been replaced with Christ in baptism. They were being transformed into the same image from one degree of glory to another."[15] Augustine believed with the apostle Paul in the weakness of old age we assume the self-emptying of Christ on the cross that the strength of God may be revealed.[16] As Augustine meditated on the cross, he remembered the words of the Apostle Paul when he said on the cross, "Our old man hath been crucified together with Him" (Rom 6:6). Augustine said, "If there was there our old man, old age was there."[17] Through Christ's death and resurrection, the old sinful self and the physically dying self experience the reality of Ps 103:5, the renewal of our youth.[18]

Augustine saw Jesus in the Garden of Gethsemane in the old who anxiously await their deaths, begging the Father to let this cup pass (Matt 26:39). For our consolation, when Christ was actually about to be crucified,

> He had a desire for eternal life apart from the grievousness of death, to which grievous experience he was unwillingly carried, but from it [when all was over] he was willingly carried away; unwillingly he came to it, but willingly he conquered it, and left this feeling of infirmity behind that makes everyone unwilling to die,—a feeling so permanently natural, that even old age itself was unable to set the blessed Peter free from its influence, even as it was

13. Apostolic Fathers, "Martyrdom of Polycarp," 9.
14. Eusibus, "The Church History of Eusebius, Book 1," 293.
15. Seim and Økland, *Metamorphoses*, 5.
16. Augustine, "On the Psalms, Psalm 71," 694.
17. Augustine, "On the Psalms, Psalm 71," 694.
18. Augustine, "On the Psalms, Psalm 71," 694.

said unto him, "When thou shalt be old," thou shall be led "whither thou wouldest not."[19]

## Becoming Like Children

The patristic writers taught the process of sanctification through aging is becoming like children. Our childlikeness is perfected while our childishness is overcome. They again speak of the unhappy realities of the declines in the experience of aging as well as the hope of restoration of the vitality of youth. Old age is a time to take stock. First Cor 13:11 describes the call to grow up and put childish ways behind us. This theme is prominent in the writings of the patristic era.

Commodianus spoke of the right ordering of life, "Infancy is passed into maturity, old age does not enjoy trifles, the age of boyhood has departed; let the mind of youth in like manner depart. Your thoughts ought to belong to the character of men."[20] Clement of Alexandria exhorts the Greeks to become like children as well. "You have been boys, then lads, then youths, then men, but good you have never been. Have respect to your old age; become sober now you have reached the sunset of life; even at the end of life acknowledge God, so the end of your life may regain a beginning of salvation. Grow old to daemon-worship; return as young men to fear of God; God will enroll you as guileless children."[21]

Augustine found himself rebuked by his mentor Jerome when he sought to engage him in a war of wits in a show of his learning and found Jerome unwilling to engage. Jerome encouraged growth in the younger Augustine and explained, "To quote an instance from Scripture: Barzillai of Gilead, when he declined in favor of his youthful son the kindnesses of King David and all the charms of his court, taught us that old age ought neither to desire these things, nor to accept them when offered."[22] Augustine learned, "There is a kind of eloquence that is more becoming in youth, and a kind that is more becoming in old age."[23] For Augustine, to become like a child in one's old age was to possess the humility of a child without lacking the wisdom maturity brings while at the same time possessing the wisdom of old age without losing the humility of a child.[24]

The patristic writers saw the paradox of old age in the dying to the physically aging and sinful self as a restoration of a youthful and sanctified self being born into eternal life. Augustine spoke to this paradox of a life lived in Christ this way,

---

19. Augustine, "Gospel of St. John, Tractate 123," 897.
20. Commodianus, "The Instructions of Commodianus," 397.
21. Butterworth, "Clement of Alexandria," in *Metamorphoses* 230–33.
22. Augustine, "Letters, 72," 633.
23. Augustine, "On Christian Doctrine," 1207.
24. Augustine, "On the Psalms, Psalm 113," 1183.

> There are many complaints in old age; the cough, the rheum, the weakness of the eyes, fretfulness, and weariness. So then as when a man is old; he is full of complaints; so is the world old; and is full of troubles. Is it a little thing that God hath done for thee, in that in the world's old age, He hath sent Christ unto thee, that He may renew thee then, when all is failing? Choose not then to cleave to this aged world, and to be unwilling to grow young in Christ, who telleth thee, "The world is perishing, the world is waxing old, the world is failing; is distressed by the heavy breathing of old age. But do not fear, 'Thy youth shall be renewed as the eagle's.'"[25]

Clement of Alexandria spoke of the love of the Father for his aged people whom he affectionately calls children. In their helplessness, the Father cares for them as a mother does an infant. He defines the childhood of old age as, "a lifelong springtime, because the truth that is in us, and our habits saturated with the truth, cannot be touched by old age; but Wisdom is ever blooming, ever remains consistent and the same, and never changes."[26] Cyprian observed, "Life does not cease in old age, but it begins with old age."[27]

## Living with the End in Mind

The patristic writers were bluntly realistic about the suffering of aging while remaining hopefully optimistic that old age was part of a greater plan and purpose in Christ. Alexander said, "For what else is old age but the expectation of death?"[28] Augustine measured age by a different yardstick than the one used by the world, which sees after the age of 30, the bloom of youth has passed and humans begin, "to decline towards the defective and duller period of old age."[29] For Augustine, the measure of a human was not age or physical stature but rather "the measure of the age of the fullness of Christ."[30] For Chrysostom, age was irrelevant and today was what is important. He said, "Today, may be uttered at every time of life, even on the verge of old age, if you desire it: for repentance is judged not by quantity of time, but by disposition of the soul."[31] Whether young or old, he encouraged Christians to heed the counsel of the Scriptures and not harden their hearts should today they hear the voice of God (Ps 95:7–8).[32]

Living with the end in mind, living happily with God through eternity was the focal point the writers of the patristic era encouraged as one journeyed through this

---

25. Augustine, "Harmony of the Gospel, Sermon 31," 757–8.
26. Clement of Alexandria, "The Instructor," 411.
27. Cyprian, "Treatise 5," 939.
28. Alexander, "Epistle to Aeglon," 549.
29. Augustine, "City of God," 1044.
30. Augustine, "City of God," 1044.
31. Chrysostom, "Exhortation to Theodore," 158.
32. Chrysostom, "Exhortation to Theodore," 158.

life. As Psalm 103 tells us the life of mortals is like grass, Augustine noted no matter the length of life nor the suffering endured, the whole life of man is but a few days. "That labor being over, there is to come the Eternal Kingdom; there is to come happiness without end; there is to come equality with the Angels; there is to come Christ's inheritance, and Christ, our 'joint Heir,' is to come. How great is the labor, for which thou receivest so great a recompense?"[33] His words remind us of the promises of the new heaven and earth to come as described in Revelation 21.

In the writing of the patristic era, we find many of the same wisdom themes seen in the Book of Ecclesiastes. They speak of the futility of a life spent in self-indulgence, the wisdom and joy found in serving God, the seasonal nature of life, necessity of fidelity to duties of one's state in life, the value of friendship, proper attitudes for a godly person, nature of desire, sovereignty of God, and taking life a day at a time, to name a few. They speak of living this life well with the goal of eternal life in view as we progress through the natural seasons in life.

Defensor Grammaticus included in his collection of wisdom quotes one from Isidore who said, "Only in this life can you do good. What is awaiting you in the future life is not the opportunity of doing good but the reward of having done it."[34] Gregory of Nazianzus observed, "A true philosopher (i.e., Christian) welcomes the end of life as a time appointed for necessary liberation, and crosses over graciously to that life to come, where no one is immature or aged, but everyone shares the age of spiritual perfection."[35] He further stated, "If you are seeking long life, you ought to be seeking that life through which you come close to Christ, that is eternal life. That life is real life: this life is only mortal life."[36] Augustine taught true hope is found in the Word of Scripture. He urged the Christian, "To lift his hope off things which are mortal and transitory, and fix it on the word of the Lord; so that, cleaving to that which endures for ever, he may himself together with it endure forever."[37] Likewise, Chrysostom taught of heaven, "There is no old age there, nor any of the evils of old age, but all things relating to decay are utterly removed, and incorruptible glory reigns in every part. But greater than all these things is the perpetual enjoyment of intercourse with Christ in the company of angels, and archangels, and the higher powers."[38]

## Calling of Old Age

In our materialistic world, aging can be misinterpreted as God's version of planned obsolescence. To do so, is to hold both a false image of God and of humanity. Thomas

33. Augustine, "On the Psalms, Psalm 37, Second Part," 230.
34. Defensor Grammaticus, "Book of Sparkling Wisdom," in *Hidden Foundation*, 80.
35. Daly, "Gregory of Nazianzus," in *Metamorphoses*, 111–2.
36. Daly, "Gregory of Nazianzus," in *Metamorphoses*, 111–2.
37. Augustine, "Catechizing the Uninstructed," 582.
38. Chrysostom, "Exhortation to Theodore," 158.

Oden observes the meaning of suffering, which for the ancient Christians is a participation in the suffering of Christ, is a huge challenge to those holding a hedonistic value system.[39] The patristic writers believed suffering falls within the purview of the providential God who allows it for human growth and enables us to overcome it by grace. This reality is antithetical to a culture which sees itself entitled to health and wealth in this life, is attached to achievement and preaches a gospel of success. Basil the Great reminds us through the centuries as does Isaiah 55:8, our ways are not the ways of God. Basil said, "The 'way' does not belong to you nor is the present under your control. But as step succeeds step, enjoy each moment as it comes and then continue on your 'way.'"[40] He reminds us, though, "Pleasures do not last but pain is not permanent either."[41] May we heed Clement of Alexandria's exhortation to his heathen culture, "If you have respect for old age, be wise, now that you have reached life's sunset; and albeit at the close of life, acquire the knowledge of God, that the end of life may to you prove the beginning of salvation."[42] Lactantius reminds us, "We can take nothing with us, except a well and innocently spent life. That man will appear before God with abundant resources, that man will appear in opulence, to whom there shall belong self-restraint, mercy, patience, love, and faith. This is our inheritance, which can neither be taken away from any one, nor transferred to another."[43]

As I concluded this study, I was drawn to a story told by a contemporary Christian writer, Sister Mary Hester Valentine, in her book, *Aging in the Lord*. This story responded to both my father's perception of the lack of the suffering of old age in the life of Jesus and his feeling about the futility of his long years of suffering. Like the patristic writers, Sr. Mary wrote about a friend of hers who found meaning in the suffering of her advanced years. This elderly friend lived a solitary and serene life though nearly blind and deaf. She marveled in her friend,

> There is no disintegration of personality; her own comment on the situation revealed why she is so serene, so completely in control. She said to me before I left, "Now know what Paul meant when he said that we make up in our bodies what is lacking in the sufferings of Christ. Did it ever strike you that Jesus was a young man when he was crucified, and that horrible though that death was, he never experienced the gradual depletion of old age." She added quietly, "He lets me make up that deficiency in the redemptive plan. That's rather awesome, you know."[44]

---

39. Oden, "Bringing Forward Tradition," 13.
40. Basil the Great, "Commentary on Psalm 1," in *Hidden Fountain*, 39.
41. Basil the Great, "Commentary on Psalm 1," in *Hidden Fountain*, 39.
42. Clement of Alexandria, "Exhortation to the Heathen," 389.
43. Lactantius, "The Divine Institutes Book 7," 458.
44. Valentine, *Aging in the Lord*, 30–31.

Never treated for his life—long struggle with mental illness and alcoholism, my father died peacefully. Though he did not experience the permanent sobriety or healing he hoped for in this life, ten years before he died, he told me he believed God never stopped trying to help him no matter how much he failed. As I held his hand as he died from the catastrophic effects of his illnesses, he was at peace and continued to believe the Lord was still trying to help him. I understand the great gift of my father's faith to me now, a faith, ironically made more credible in his weakness. In my dreams these days, I see my father in his favorite blue sweater, looking like himself, but with a wellness I'd not known in him in his earthly life. Heaven is "swell" he tells me with a big smile on his face.[45]

My father's life-long suffering and death called him to faith and me as well. The faith of the patristic fathers calls us to faith too. Ancient faith lives anew most recently in the papacy of Pope Francis. In his recent encyclical letter on faith Pope Francis says, "Those who believe, see; they see with a light that illumines their entire journey, for it comes from the risen Christ, the morning star which never sets."[46] As we contemplate Christ's union with the Father, even as he suffered death on a cross, "Even death is illumined and can be experienced as the ultimate call to faith, the ultimate, 'Go forth from your land' (Gen 12:1), the ultimate 'Come!' spoken by the Father, to whom we abandon ourselves in the confidence that he will keep us steadfast even in our final passage."[47]

## Bibliography

Alexander. "Epistle to Aeglon, Bishop of Cynopolis, Against the Arians." In *Christian Library: Heritage Edition*, CD-ROM, version 4.0. Rio, WI: AGES Digital Library, 2005.

Apostolic Fathers. "The Martyrdom of St. Polycarp." http://www.ccel.org/ccel/richardson/fathers.vii.i.iii.html.

Athanasius. "Life of St. Anthony." In *Christian Library: Heritage Edition*, CD-ROM, version 4.0. Rio, WI: AGES Digital Library, 2005.

Augustine. "City of God." In *Christian Library: Heritage Edition*, CD-ROM, version 4.0. Rio, WI: AGES Digital Library, 2005.

———. "The Harmony of the Gospel, Selected Lessons of the Gospels, Sermon 31." In *Christian Library: Heritage Edition*, CD-ROM, version 4.0. Rio, WI: AGES Digital Library, 2005.

———. "Lectures on the Gospel of St. John, Tractate 123." In *Christian Library: Heritage Edition*, CD-ROM, version 4.0. Rio, WI: AGES Digital Library, 2005.

———. "Letters of St. Augustine, Second Division, Letter 72." In *Christian Library: Heritage Edition*, CD-ROM, version 4.0. Rio, WI: AGES Digital Library, 2005.

———. "On Catechizing the Uninstructed." In *Christian Library: Heritage Edition*, CD-ROM, version 4.0. Rio, WI: AGES Digital Library, 2005.

---

45. Pearson, "Advent Meditation 2013," 2.
46. Pope Francis, *Lumen Fidei*, 1.
47. Pope Francis, *Lumen Fidei*, 56.

———. "On Christian Doctrine." In *Christian Library: Heritage Edition*, CD-ROM, version 4.0. Rio, WI: AGES Digital Library, 2005.

———. "On the Psalms, Psalm 37, Second Part." In *Christian Library: Heritage Edition*, CD-ROM, version 4.0. Rio, WI: AGES Digital Library, 2005.

———. "On the Psalms, Psalm 71." In *Christian Library: Heritage Edition*, CD-ROM, version 4.0. Rio, WI: AGES Digital Library, 2005.

———. "On the Psalms, Psalm 92." In *Christian Library: Heritage Edition*, CD-ROM, version 4.0. Rio, WI: AGES Digital Library, 2005.

———. "On the Psalms, Psalm 113." In *Christian Library: Heritage Edition*, CD-ROM, version 4.0. Rio, WI: AGES Digital Library, 2005.

Basil the Great. "Commentary on Psalm 1, 4." In *Drinking from the Hidden Fountain: A Patristic Breviary, Ancient Wisdom for Today's World*, by Thomas Spidlik. Translated by Paul Drake. Kalamazoo, MI: Cistercian, 1994.

Butterworth, G. W., trans. "Clement of Alexandria: Exhortation to the Greeks." In *Metamorphoses: Resurrection, Body and Transformative Practices in Early Christianity*, 203–33. Berlin: Walter de Gruyter, 2009.

Chrysostom. "An Exhortation to Theodore After His Fall, Letter 1." In *Christian Library: Heritage Edition*, CD-ROM, version 4.0. Rio, WI: AGES Digital Library, 2005.

———. "Treatise Concerning the Christian Priesthood, Book 1." In *Christian Library: Heritage Edition*, CD-ROM, version 4.0. Rio, WI: AGES Digital Library, 2005.

Clement of Alexandria. "Exhortation to the Heathen." In *Christian Library: Heritage Edition*, CD-ROM, version 4.0. Rio, WI: AGES Digital Library, 2005.

———. "The Instructor [Paedagogus]." In *Christian Library: Heritage Edition*, CD-ROM, version 4.0. Rio, WI: AGES Digital Library, 2005.

———. "Miscellaneous Studies, 4, 4, 15." In *Drinking from the Hidden Fountain: A Patristic Breviary, Ancient Wisdom for Today's World*, by Thomas Spidlik. Translated by Paul Drake. Kalamazoo, MI: Cistercian, 1994.

Commodianus. "The Instructions of Commodianus In Favor of Christian Discipline Against the Gods of the Heathens." In *Christian Library: Heritage Edition*, CD-ROM, version 4.0. Rio, WI: AGES Digital Library, 2005.

Cyprian. "Treatise 5: An Address to Demetrianus." In *Christian Library: Heritage Edition*, CD-ROM, version 4.0. Rio, WI: AGES Digital Library, 2005.

Daly, B. E. "Gregory of Nazianzus." In *Metamorphoses: Resurrection, Body and Transformative Practices in Early Christianity*, 111–2. Berlin: de Gruyter, 2009.

Defensor Grammaticus. "Book of Sparkling Wisdom, 80." In *Drinking from the Hidden Fountain: A Patristic Breviary, Ancient Wisdom for Today's World*, by Thomas Spidlik. Translated by Paul Drake. Kalamazoo, MI: Cistercian, 1994.

Eusebius. "The Church History of Eusebius, Book 1." In *Christian Library: Heritage Edition*, CD-ROM, version 4.0. Rio, WI: AGES Digital Library, 2005.

Jackson-Jordan, Beth. "God's Call in Later Life: A Theological Reflection on Aging." *The Journal of the Association of Professional Chaplains* 17 (2001) 18–21.

John Paul II. *Evangelium Vitae, 12*. Libreria Editrice Vaticana, Rome, Italy: 1995. http://www.vatican.va/holy_father/john_paul_ii/encyclicals/documents/hf_jp-ii_enc_25031995_evangelium-vitae_en.html.

Lactantius. "The Divine Institutes, Book 7." In *Christian Library: Heritage Edition*, CD-ROM, version 4.0. Rio, WI: AGES Digital Library, 2005.

Oden, Thomas C. "Bringing Forward Tradition—An Interview with Thomas C. Oden." *Religion and Liberty* 21 (2011) 3, 12–13. http://www. acton. org/sites/v4. acton. org/files/pdf/RL_21_1_Web. pdf.

Pearson, Suzanne. "Advent Meditation 2013." Meditation presented at Morning Prayer at The Cathedral Community. Rochester, NY, December 20, 2013.

Pope Francis. *Lumen Fidei*. Libreria Editrice Vaticana, Rome, Italy: 2013. http://www.vatican.va/holy_father/francesco/encyclicals/documents/papa-francesco_20130629_enciclica-lumen-fidei_en.html.

Seim, Turid Karlsen, and Jorunn Økland. *Metamorphoses: Resurrection, Body and Transformative Practices in Early Christianity*. Berlin: de Gruyter, 2009.

Spidlik, Thomas. *Drinking from the Hidden Fountain: A Patristic Breviary, Ancient Wisdom for Today's World*. Translated by Paul Drake. Kalamazoo, MI: Cistercian, 1994.

Tertullian. "On the Apparel of Women." In *Christian Library: Heritage Edition*, CD-ROM, version 4.0. Rio, WI: AGES Digital Library, 2005.

Trulear, Harold Dean. "Considering the Alternative: Ageing and At-Risk Youth." *The Living Pulpit* (2001) 4–5.

Valentine, Mary Hester. *Aging in the Lord*. Mahwah, NJ: Paulist, 1994.

# 19

# The Recapitulation of the Tree of the Knowledge of Good and Evil

―――――――――――――――――――――― Mark W. McMonagle

There are many ways to interpret Scripture. Church history is chock full of examples. It is implied that the true interpretation saves souls and all other interpretations will have scant chance to achieve that. There is concomitant with this the assumption of mystery that the scriptures have hidden within them a message that is difficult to access. The revelation of that mystery is so compelling it has caused considerable mayhem in the world by those who did not find the message clearly enough. For those who have found it they have found a legacy of blessedness. This essay is an attempt to bring some clarity to the mystery by discussing two trees, typology, and the theology of recapitulation.

In Genesis 2 God tells the human he has made that "from the tree of the knowledge of good and evil you shall not eat, for in the day that you eat from it you will surely die" (Gen 2:17, NASB). However, in Genesis 3, "When the woman saw that the fruit of the tree was good for food and pleasing to the eye, and also desirable for gaining wisdom, she took some and ate it. She also gave some to her husband, who was with her and he ate it" (Gen 3:6, NIV).

By the standards of contemporary American culture what is happening in Genesis 3 is inoffensive and absurd. A snake approaches a woman who is convinced by it to take a piece of fruit that she now reckons has a fraudulent warning attached to it and eats a bite. After eating, she gives it to her husband who also eats. Perhaps on a higher, theological level one could even say this is a picture of communion: a man, a woman, and an animal dining together in a garden of utopian bliss and beauty. Certainly, mystery is tantalizing and what is forbidden is provocative. Forbidden fruit is eaten to access the out-of-reach mystery of God and, in knowing it, become like God.

Everything was created good and nothing was withheld from Adam and Eve except the fruit of this particular tree. The whole of earthly creation belonged to them, except for this tree. The prohibition against eating from the tree was a key mechanism in maintaining mankind's dominion over the world. The purpose of the prohibition was to be a negative good: a boundary that if not crossed, ensured blessing, dominion, and a bountiful life. To have dominion over the earthly creation meant he must have dominion over himself; the tree secured that for him as long as he did not eat from it. The proscription was a fast.

## Hunger

Scripture takes a surprising interest in hunger, appetite, and food. Alexander Schmemann explored this theme in his book, *For the Life of the World*, commenting at one point

> Man must eat in order to live; he must take the world into his body and transform it into himself, into flesh and blood. He is indeed that which he eats, and the whole world is presented as one all-embracing banquet table for man. And this image of the banquet remains, throughout the whole Bible, the central image of life. It is the image of life at its creation and also the image of life at its end and fulfillment: ". . . that you eat and drink at my table in my Kingdom."[1]

Yet in this very garden the fruit from the tree of the knowledge of good and evil is withheld in earnest. When Adam and Eve faced God over their transgression, the gravity of the command became clear. Now in peril of judgment, which came shortly thereafter, they tried to remedy their shame and guilt amidst other trees and with a covering of leaves. Nothing in the garden helped them; even seeking a cure among the trees was futile. They had done something that could not be undone: they broke their fast. St. Basil of Cappadocia considered the prohibition a spiritual discipline, a law that had a purpose beyond mere legal avoidance. There was a rationale for its imposition. "Fasting was ordained in Paradise," he wrote. "The first injunction was delivered to Adam, 'Of the Tree of the Knowledge of good and evil you shall not eat.' 'You shall not eat' is a law of fasting and abstinence."[2]

However, this was a peculiar fast unlike the ones that came later in history. The practice of abstinence to which Basil refers is certainly about restrained eating, but it infers something about man's hungers being more diverse than need for nutrients. In this, Basil assumes the presence of passions. The passions of men are hungers of a sort, the reaching out of oneself to consume something else, whether food, sex, material objects, adoration, purpose and meaning, or what have you. All of these things have something to do with hunger of some kind. Frankly speaking, these can be the lusts of the flesh, eyes, and the pride of life.[3] Hungers also propel us forward in life: in exploration, experimentation, in its joys and satisfactions, which are all quite normal. Fasting helps to restrain indulgence of these hungers but when restraint is removed there is

---

1. Schmemann, *For the Life of the World*, 11.
2. St Basil the Great, "On Fasting: Homily I," 6 para. 3.
3. 1 John 2:16.

only hunger and the will to satisfy. Everything then is vulnerable to brokenness, corruption, twisting, and whatever else the heart of man finds capable. The threat of death for eating from the tree had less to do with a cruel god than with the consequences of disorder and disobedience that come with indulgence.

John Calvin contends that eating from the tree because of hunger is a "puerile" theory held by the ancients. Why would hunger drive the two humans to eat from a forbidden tree when there were so many other fruits available to them? Consistent with Church dogma, their fault was unbelief.

> It is now asked, what was the sin of both of them? The opinion of some of the ancients, that they were allured by intemperance of appetite, is puerile. For when there was such an abundance of the choicest fruits what daintiness could there be about one particular kind?[4]

He preferred to see the whole affair forensically and dealt with it judicially. He was a lawyer, after all. Yet, more happened at this judgment than this and it relates to the nature of the tree and its effect on the humans. Of its nature, the tree gave knowledge of good and evil. With this knowledge Adam could judge and assert his dominion independent of God. Unfortunately, intimacy with the knowledge of evil had the consequence of influencing its bearer with deception, darkness, confusion, envy, greed, and manipulation. There was also the difficulty of determining the difference between good and evil, for evil can start to look reasonable and indistinguishable from good given the circumstances.

W. H. Auden wrote that "evil is unspectacular and always human, and shares our bed and eats at our own table."[5] Hannah Arendt concluded that evil is for the most part banal.[6] Evil does not necessarily presume physical violence, either. It also encompasses the thoughts and actions of erstwhile citizens, who, under their breath and brow, whisper thoughts of hatred, cheating, stealing, envying, and adultery; things that are unseen but destructive and distorting nonetheless. Given a second thought, evil is violence in all its aspects, seen and unseen, wounding the human soul and society at all levels. The antediluvian violence certainly had this element of the unseen, banal and subtle evils of the heart—things just as dire as physical violence is to the body. Suffice it to say that most evil passes by and through the individual with as much ease as any good. "The sad truth," wrote Arendt "is that most evil is done by people who never make up their minds to be good or evil."[7]

The tree of the knowledge of good and evil gave to mankind the ability to judge. In eating from the tree, Adam's and Eve's eyes were opened and they made their first judgment. How sterile that sounds. Their first "god-like" act was to condemn themselves.

---

4. Calvin, *Commentary on Genesis*, 3:6.4.
5. Auden, *Collected Poems*, n.p.
6. Arendt, *Eichmann in Jerusalem*, 231.
7. Arendt, "Thinking," in *The Life of the Mind*.

Shame is full exposure that causes all of the vulnerable parts of our soul to cringe in fear of harm. Despite their own efforts at healing and reparation (hiding and sewing fig leaves), fear-guilt betrayed them before God. If the prohibition was a tool for developing the man to be king over his dominion through restraint and self-control, then opening his eyes turned him into judge and convict at the same time. *Nolo contendere.*

It is not saying too much to see in all of this a foreshadowing of the Final Judgment. One can almost see Christ asking, "What have you done?" How we answer him in his unshielded, ultra-penetrating light will judge us; but the fact is that we will have already judged ourselves. It can be noted that God did not reject Adams self-judgment. He did not say to Adam, "Why are you blaming Eve?" Eve did, after all, give Adam the fruit to eat. Nor did Eve make any denials in her defense. She pointed to the serpent who answered not a word. They told the truth. Their own words were their judge. Only truth can stand in the presence of God and when that truth is the recounting of evil, it is addressed as such.

Death is a certainty for all of mankind; a condition shared with the rest of creation. Entropy and corruption: the lot of life. Sin is easier to do than doing well it seems, and often difficult to distinguish with its rationalizing and imaginative engine. Caught in an inescapable trap of temptations, self-deceptions, hungers and lusts, fears and longings, sorrows and fleeting envy and failure, the soul languishes in bondage. Yet passions are not the only concern here: his thinking-will became a complicated activity of unfettered thoughts commingled with passions informing and guiding his imagination, and it was always evil.[8] For them, unremitting indulgence of their passions led to the profaning of even the curse that was upon them.[9] The prospect for our contemporary world can fair no better, for we are them. We are the sons of Adam.

The beginning of sin in the world came from merely eating a piece of fruit, a frankly natural thing to do. Yet, the smallness and seemingly inconsequential nature of the deed was in truth a seed that grew into the undoing of mankind. What had been done could not be undone. A rich, modern comparison was the moment that Neil Armstrong set his foot on the surface of the moon. What appeared to be an improbable event for a man became a redefining moment for all. Because one man stepped onto the surface of the moon, all men through him have gone to the moon. It is simply impossible to undo now. Thus, one man ate from the tree and the boundary for all men was defeated. All have sinned, all suffer the same judgment, all live under the same curse and all die.

---

8. Gen 6:5
9. Rom 1:18–32

## Ambrose and Athanasius

Death defeats the glory of man. But another take on death can be seen in St Ambrose's homily, *On the belief in the Resurrection*,[10] written on the occasion of his brother Satyrus's death. Ambrose wrote that death came not so much as a penalty but as a remedy to the evils that would befall mankind from the moment the fruit was eaten; a reprieve from suffering. Death in this way becomes a kind of salvation from the bondage of sin. So, Ambrose was an optimist. This is not the usual understanding of death in any culture today and rarely seen even in the Church except in its earliest days. This is unfortunate because the belief that death is the result of the insinuation of the enemy, making them more victim than felon, posits salvation less in terms of wrath than liberation.[11]

Death is a grim fact, which is why resurrection is such a stunning proclamation to hear. The implication being that through death, death dies and the result confers eternal life. Certainly, then, Ambrose is correct that death brings a cessation to suffering and sin in the life of an individual. That is much like the medical proverb, death cures all ills. It is possible to see in his perspective that death as salvation is more than death as punishment or the judicial consequences of disobedience. Offering insight here he makes differentiation.

> Spiritual death, then is one thing, natural death another, a third death the death of punishment. But that which is natural is not also penal, for the Lord did not inflict death as a penalty, but as a remedy.[12]

> Death is given for a remedy, because it is the end of evils . . . You see that death is rather the goal of our penalties, by which an end is put to the course of this life.[13]

> So, then, death is not only not an evil, but is even a good thing.[14]

Athanasius is more severe in his consideration of death. He sees it as a result of our own making and as a logical end to our descent into natural law; a condition that is also inherently part of being human. Athanasius's development of thought in *De Incarnatione Verbi Dei* recognized that humanity is dust, divinely enlivened, and yet is quite serious about the dire and alarming state humanity is in under sin and death.

> But men, having turned from the contemplation of God to evil of their own devising, had come inevitably under the law of death. Instead of remaining in the state in which God had created them, they were in process of becoming corrupted entirely, and death had them completely under its dominion. For

---

10. Ambrose, *Belief in the Resurrection*, Book II.
11. Daniélou, *From Shadows to Reality*, 35.
12. Ambrose, *Belief in the Resurrection*, Book II, 37.
13. Ambrose, *Belief in the Resurrection*, Book II, 38.
14. Ambrose, *Belief in the Resurrection*, Book II, 39.

the transgression of the commandment was making them turn back again according to their nature; and as they had at the beginning come into being out of non-existence, so were they now on the way to returning, through corruption, to non-existence again.[15]

To demonstrate the need for the incarnation of God, Athanasius had to establish that humanity is part of the natural creation, and, while succeeding at that point, he acknowledged that in the beginning man had something no other creature had: "For, as I said before, though they were by nature subject to corruption, the grace of their union with the Word made them capable of escaping from the natural law."[16] That is, before they transgressed they would not have died because of their union with God through grace. The natural law is entropic, so all things have an end. While humans were in almost every respect animals, Athanasius understood that grace kept them from being touched by corruption.

> Then, turning from eternal things to things corruptible, by counsel of the devil, they had become the cause of their own corruption in death; for as I said before, though they were by nature subject to corruption, the grace of their union with the Word made them capable of escaping from the natural law, provided that they retained the beauty of innocence with which they were created.[17]

Without the grace of his first estate man became like the other animals subject to the inevitabilities of death, pain and disintegration. He did not know that once his passions were un-restrained he would succumb to all potential evil, existential and empirical. Athanasius proffered the question as to whether repentance on the part of Adam and Eve could have restored them to the garden and resoundingly denied its efficacy because corruption had been introduced and had to be healed in a way that repentance could not provide. As essential as repentance is for conversion, it can only cause a man to cease from sinning. He wrote:

> Nor does repentance recall men from what is according to their nature; all that it does is to make them cease from sinning. Had it been a case of a trespass only, and not of a subsequent corruption, repentance would have been well enough; but when once transgression had begun men came under the power of the corruption proper to their nature and were bereft of the grace which belonged to them as creatures in the Image of God.[18]

Because of his transgression and loss of grace, Adam (and we all) became subject to what he had previously been restrained and protected from, death and the dying process of corruption as was noted above. More is required: new flesh, a new life, and

---

15. Athanasius, *On the Incarnation*, ch. 1.
16. Athanasius, *On the Incarnation*, ch. 1.
17. Athanasius, *On the Incarnation*, ch. 1.
18. Athanasius, *On the Incarnation*, ch. 1.

a new beginning. A new, irreversible event was needed to reverse what could not be undone. This was, and is, Christ.

## Recapitulation

The work of Christ is a work of recapitulation, that is to say, salvation accomplished through the reinstatement of what was at the beginning, the reversal of the Fall and its components and the extension of the primeval state to the eternal state. Christ is placed as the head of humanity, the second Adam who restarts the human race by being what Adam was but could not do. Jesus, in this presentation of the gospel, reverses all the effects of the Curse and Transgression with his whole life, not singularly in his death on the Cross. This can also be viewed as the restoration or restitution of all things.

Robert Wilken's study of Cyril of Alexandria's theology of the Second Adam discussed Cyril's understanding of the gospel as recapitulation.

> Theologically, the Adam-Christ typology is rooted in Cyril's predilection to see redemption primarily in terms of creation-re-creation categories. In an early commentary on Genesis, the *Glaphyra*, Cyril writes: "Let us consider the state of things as they once were and perhaps we can say something of the restoration to a better state. For St. Paul said 'If anyone is in Christ he is a new creation,' and through the prophets God said, 'I will make all things new.' These passages mean that Christ's work is a recapitulation, (*anskephelaiosis*), that is to say a restitution (*anaphoitesis*) or a restoration (*epanorthosis*) of all things to their original state (*eis hoper en archi*)."[19]

Recapitulation is the re-creation of humanity which finds in the Advent of Christ the re-introduction of Adam who fulfills the will of God and thereby establishes the possibility of a humanity under a new head, Jesus instead of Adam. The importance of this should not be underestimated. Joseph P. Farrell says of recapitulation that "the doctrine of the Recapitulation in Christ bears implications not only for the exegesis and interpretation of Scripture and the understanding of the Incarnation, but implies also a general basis on which to interpret human history and the whole created order and their principles of activity."[20]

To see this more clearly one can look at types. Focusing on biblical usage, a type is a model or prefigurement in the historical past of a person living, or an event or circumstance that will happen in the future. The narrow application of this is reserved for the Old Testament foreshadowings of Christ in the New Testament. Types are bound by historical anchors and assume the historicity of the text to be an actual fact. Types function prophetically and fill the scaffolding of the economy of God's revelation. An allegory, in contrast, has a different function, as much as metaphors

---

19. Wilken, "Exegesis and the History of Theology," 142.
20. Farrell, *The Disputation with Pyrrhus*, iii–x.

and similes have differing functions. Jean Daniélou rejected the idea that allegory has any scriptural basis, claiming that it is a Philonian approach to interpreting scripture which gives a moralistic meaning, or perhaps even mystical connotation, to a verse of scripture.[21] In his opinion, allegory was not sufficiently Christological to warrant authoritative use.

The point of recapitulation theology is a Christology fully encompassing all referents in scripture, an interpretive norm that places Jesus as the fulfillment of that scripture, and in doing so establishes Christ as the new head of humanity by tracing the prefigurement of Adam and his potential and failure against the success of Christ. Jean Daniélou wrote in his oft-cited work, *From Shadows to Reality*:

> We may remember that in St Paul the parallelism between Adam and Christ bore a twofold aspect: Christ both accomplishes and restores what had been done by Adam. This is the exact meaning of recapitulation. We are concerned with a new beginning . . . which is a resumption of the first, while at the same time it both restores the broken harmony (here we have the idea of reparation for sin) and surpasses the original work (the aspect of accomplishment).[22]

The recapitulation is the reversal of the trespass of Adam and all its concomitant factors. St Gregory Nazianzen wrote in his second theological oration the importance of this reversal as the means of salvation.

> This is why . . . the tree is set over against tree, hands against hand, the one stretched out in self-indulgence, the others in generosity; the one unrestrained, the others fixed by nails, the one expelling Adam, the other reconciling the ends of the earth. This is the reason of the lifting up to atone for the fall, and of the gall for the tasting, and of the thorny crown for the dominion of evil, and of death for death, and of darkness for the sake of light, and of burial for the return to the ground, and of resurrection for the sake of resurrection. All these are a training from God for us, and a healing for our weakness, restoring the old Adam to the place whence he fell, and conducting us to the tree of life, from which the tree of knowledge estranged us, when partaken of unseasonably, and improperly.[23]

Jean Daniélou saw that St Cyril of Jerusalem viewed recapitulation similarly. Cyril wrote,

> Adam received the doom: "Cursed is the earth in thy work; thorns and thistles shall it bring for to thee." For this cause Jesus assumes the thorns, that he might cancel the doom, for this cause also was he buried in the earth, [that] the cursed earth might receive, instead of the curse, the blessing. At the time of

---

21. Daniélou, *From Shadows to Reality*, 24, 25.
22. Daniélou, *From Shadows to Reality*, 31.
23. Gregory Nazianzen, "Church Fathers: Letters, Division I," Letter 101.

> the sin, they clothed themselves with fig leaves: for this cause also Jesus made the fig-tree the last of his signs . . . And having touched on things connected with Paradise [,] I am indeed astonished at the truth of the types. In paradise was the fall, and in a Garden was our salvation. From the Tree came sin, and until the Tree sin lasted, in the evening they sought to hide themselves from the eyes of the Lord and in the evening the robber is brought by the Lord into paradise. The woman who was formed from the side, led the way to sin, but Jesus who came to bestow the grace of pardon on men and women alike, was pierced in the side for woman, that he might undo the sin.[24]

The life of Christ does more than set the stage for his sacrifice, so to speak. Rather, his life embraced all of human life, without which there is no complete salvation. Put another way, if there was some aspect of being human that was not in Christ, that aspect is not saved, it remains outside of redemption. An implication of this is that since there was no sin in Christ's life, sin is fully excised from the new creation. Gregory Nazianzen defended this and the fullness of Christ's humanity, and thus the totality of human salvation, where he writes: "For that which He has not assumed He has not healed; but that which is united to His Godhead is also saved."[25] He did not assume sin because the Godhead is sinless; in so doing those taking on his life are forgiven and begin their journey to *theosis*.

## Implications for the Trees

For the Christian, there must be an historical reality to the Fall for there to be a historically real *eschaton*. It is imperative that there have been a real tree in a garden around which a scandal of devastating proportions took place for the conclusion of the story (the gospels) to have its truest meaning. If the events of Eden were only metaphorical, then the gospel proclaims victory based on a metaphor, which means that the foundation for the gospels must be found elsewhere. Thus that real, dire, and grim reality of life, sin, death, and corruption experienced by humanity is left untouched. It offers a false hope. I will certainly still die. If, however, the cause of death was the result of an act by a very real man, then a very real, historical cure must counteract the cause. God's remedy is stridently comprehensive, touching on all aspects of the transgression. To conquer death, death must be a real phenomenon and any vestige of the curse of death must be expunged to elevate mankind to a new, spiritual state. In this way spirit is equated with life. Since death is a consequence of sin, sin must also be real. Similarly, since sin is forgiven and death vanquished, only life can remain. Sin, of course, must be vanquished and have no possibility of ever occurring again if there is to be a true defeat of sin. Something had to be done to reverse the tragedy and still keep the original intent of creation intact . . . or there is no victory and no salvation.

24. Daniélou, *From Shadows to Reality*, 42.
25. Gregory Nazianzen, *Oration 2*.

The tree of the knowledge of good and evil, its consequences, and recapitulation should be put together to make sense at this point. Above, it was explained that the Tree did two things; it set up a boundary of self-discipline for mankind to be trained under, and it bequeathed judgment to his mind (their eyes were opened). The former was a negative good; the good coming from abstinence. The latter was a negative consequence that needed to be repaired. The judgment of God was made and the curse, with its corruption, spread out across the vast panorama of history. It was during this time that *types* were established, covenants made, and prophecies proclaimed. God did not leave mankind without hope.

There is an antidote for the poison: another tree like the first. The recapitulation of the Tree of the Knowledge of good and evil is the Cross. Where the first tree was beautiful to behold and "offered" wisdom, the second was a horror[26] and foolishness.[27] The first fruit brought death, and the second brought life. The first exposed our shame and nakedness, but the second brought Christ who clothes us with himself. The first brought judgment; the second brought safety at the Judgment. The first tree was a scandal when it was trespassed; the second is a scandal when believed in. The first man was given dominion over the earth; the second is given dominion over all things. For the first tree, the command was "thou shalt not eat of it;" for the second, "you must eat."[28]

By the time Christ reached the Cross, that is, the recapitulated Tree of the Knowledge of Good and Evil, what awaited him was repugnant and humiliating, shameful and leafless, a human-fashioned, wooden trellis exuding the stench of death. It was a far cry from, a mere corrupt shadow of, the beauty of that first tree. Jesus's death transformed that foul tree into the sole means of salvation.[29] Only one tree was capable of sending a man into perdition, and only one could retrieve him from it. It turned out to be essentially the same one.

## Bibliography

Ambrose. "On Belief in the Resurrection." In *Church Fathers: On the Death of Satyrus, Book II (Ambrose)*. New Advent: Home. http://www.newadvent.org/fathers/34032.htm.

Arendt, Hannah. *Eichmann in Jerusalem: A Report on the Banality of Evil*. New York: Penguin, 2006.

———. *The Life of the Mind*. New York: Harcourt Brace Jovanovich, 1981.

Athanasius. *On the Incarnation*. Translated by Sister Penelope Lawson. http://www.spurgeon.org;~phil/histor/ath-inc.htm#ch_1.

Auden, W. H. *Collected Poems*. New York: Vintage, 1991.

Basil the Great. "On Fasting: Homily I." *Orthodox Tradition* 23 (2006) 6–16.

---

26. Isa 53:2–3
27. 1 Cor 1:18
28. John 6:53
29. 1 Pet 2:24b

Calvin, John. *Commentary on Genesis*. Grand Rapids: Baker, 1996. www.ccel.org/calvin/calcom01.ix.i.html.

Daniélou, Jean. *From Shadows to Reality: Studies in the Biblical Typology of the Fathers*. London: Burns & Oates, 1960.

Farrell, Joseph P. *The Disputation with Pyrrhus of Our Father among the Saints Maximus the Confessor*. South Canaan, PA: St. Tikhon's Seminary Press, 1990.

Nazianzen, Gregory. "Church Fathers: Letters, Division I (Gregory Nazianzen)." New Advent: Home. http://www.newadvent.org/fathers/3103a.htm.

———. "Church Fathers: Oration 2 (Gregory Nazianzen)." New Advent: Home. http://www.newadvent.org/fathers/310202.htm.

"Orthodox Apologetics: Christology and Recapitulation." *Orthodox Apologetics* (blog). February 16, 2012. http://orthodox-apologetics.blogspot.com/2012/02/christology-and-recapitulation.html.

Schmemann, Alexander. *For the Life of the World*. Crestwood, NY: St Vladimir's Seminary Press, 1998.

Wilken, Robert L. "Exegesis and the History of Theology: Reflections on the Adam-Christ Typology in Cyril of Alexandria." *Church History* 35 (1966) 139–56.

# 20

## A Most Unbearable Commandment: Adolf Schlatter and Jewish Piety

—— JAMES E. MCNUTT

[The Jews] expect nothing from faith, work must do it all. What that means, of course, is that they expect nothing from God and everything from themselves. They endeavor mightily after righteousness, but it hovers before them as their own achievement. They are blind to the revelation of divine righteousness. They do not want to receive it, but rather establish it as their own act.

—ADOLF SCHLATTER[1]

It can be set down as something destined to endure eternally that the usual Christian commentators will disparage Judaism and its supposed legalism, and Jewish Scholars will reply, usually fruitlessly . . . With those Christians who persist in deluding themselves about Jewish legalism, no academic communication is possible. The issue is not to bring these interpreters to love Judaism, but only to bring them to a responsible, elementary comprehension of it.

—SAMUEL SANDMEL[2]

SAMUEL SANDMEL'S BLUNT APPRAISAL of Christian perceptions of Jewish piety and his desire for a more conscientious understanding of Judaism expressed the frustration experienced by many Rabbinic specialists for much of the last century. The hermeneutical dominance of what could be termed the "legalism myth" so characterized Christian—especially Protestant—theology that Sandmel's pessimism concerning interreligious collaboration seemed justified. Fortunately, his hope for better Christian discernment in this matter was not lost on a number of twentieth-century biblical and Talmudic scholars.

1. *Erläuterungen, Römer*, 187.
2. Sandmel, quoted in Sanders, *Palestinian Judaism*, 35.

While experts in both Jewish and Christian circles point to the pioneering research of G. F. Moore in helping discredit the myth of Jewish legalism,[3] it would be E. P. Sanders's study on Palestinian Judaism that eventually prompted a decisive shift away from persistent Christian delusions regarding Jewish religious practice.[4] Sanders's careful reading of Rabbinic literature effectively laid to rest the misconception of Judaism's reliance on human-generated merit, pharisaical self-righteousness, spiritual pride, and fearful uncertainty of salvation. As with Moore, Sanders showed how the Rabbis gave preeminent place to concepts of "love, mercy, grace, repentance, and forgiveness"; while commitment to the Law, far from "earning" salvation, sought to honor God, who had graciously given the Law as guidance.[5] Framing Rabbinic thought in what he termed "covenantal nomism," Sanders credibly established that Judaism presupposed the immediacy of God's presence and grace within the commandments. Living under the yoke of the Law was not conceived as "earning" one's salvation, but seen as a faithful response to God's love.[6] Though Sanders's efforts have not escaped criticism,[7] he must be credited with helping refute the fallacious accusation that Jews thought they were saved by deeds or works.

An important aspect of Moore's and Sanders's works was their mapping out the theological origins of the modern legalism myth. Both found Ferdinand Weber's 1880, "The Theological System of the Ancient Palestinian Synagogue," to be the wellspring for the distorted view of Judaism as a legalistic religion completely antithetical to Christianity's reliance on trusting faith.[8] With prominent scholars such as Emil Schürer,[9] Wilhelm Bousset,[10] and a host of others[11] following suit, the Weberian model came to dominate Christian theology; ushering in what Solomon Schechter termed the "Night of Legalism."[12] Weber, Schürer, and Bousset, however, were not the only authoritative sources for the proliferation of this flawed perception of Jewish faith and practice. As a leading confessional voice within early 20th century, conservative German Protestantism, Adolf Schlatter contributed significantly to the stubborn tenacity

---

3. Moore, "Christian Writers," 197–254.

4. In addition to Sanders, *Palestinian Judaism*, see Sanders, *Paul, the Law*; Sanders, *Jesus and Judaism*. For the new perspective on Paul, together with an extensive bibliography, see, Das, *Paul*.

5. An excellent summary of Sanders's conclusions can be found in, Sanders, "Abstractions," here 360.

6. Sanders, *Palestinian Judaism*, 236–37.

7. Despite rejecting aspects of Sanders's work, Jacob Neusner emphasizes that, "Sanders takes up subjects with a virulent anti-Semitic tradition, and he has devoted his life to presenting Judaism in such a way as to help Christians overcome their ancient heritage of Jew-hatred and contempt for Judaism." Neusner, *Rabbinic Literature*, x, for critique, 106–24.

8. Weber, *System*. For background on Weber see, Zetterholm, *Approaches to Paul*, 63–7.

9. Schürer, *Geschichte*.

10. Bousset, *Religion*.

11. For a detailed discussion of the leading proponents see, Sanders, *Palestinian Judaism*, 33–59.

12. Schechter, *Aspects*, 117. For the permeation of "works righteousness" in 20th century Protestant theology see, Klein, *Anti-Judaism*, 39–66.

of the legalism myth. As professor of theology at the prestigious Tübingen University, this iconic figure's energetic personality exuded a dynamic influence in the hearts and minds of the multiple generations of clergy who travelled from all corners of the German nation to sit before his lectern.[13] Praised for his strong Biblicism and opposition to liberal theology, his work resonated with the common laity through venues of church conferences, Bible studies, published sermons, and devotionals. Commanding a reading audience far greater than his peers, his work was complicit in disseminating sharp and often disparaging assaults against what he saw as the spiritually bankrupt, legalistic, and self-serving piety of Judaism.

Paul Webster Livermore's doctoral work coincided with the discernable shift in perspectives toward Rabbinic religion, and his Pauline research compelled him to dig deeply into the Jewish understanding of the Law. Livermore's studied conclusions concerning Second Temple Judaism paralleled in large part Sanders's criticisms of Christian misrepresentations of Judaism, together with a sensitivity toward evaluating Rabbinic thought on its own terms.[14] Livermore echoed Sandmel by asserting that "the Jews have a right to speak for themselves, and we owe them a hearing. When they claim that Christians misrepresent what they understand it to mean 'to live under the yoke of the law,' they are largely correct."[15] More directly, Livermore argued that as a product of confessional myopia lacking historical and social contextualization: "Such caricatures of Judaism, however comforting to us because they may seem to buttress our conviction of having a superior faith, are inaccurate."[16] Livermore's patience could be tested when confronting simplistic and derogatory views of Judaism; as exhibited in his abrupt characterization of Old Testament scholar Walther Eichrodt's assessment of Judaism's teaching on sin and forgiveness.[17]

Eichrodt argued that post-exilic Judaism developed a piety stressing the individual trespass rather than a basic corruption of the will. Emphasis shifted to the doing of the Law, which was sufficient in itself to overcome guilt.[18] Although maintaining the idea of sin carrying personal guilt, Eichrodt posited Judaism's failure to sustain the radical seriousness in the concept of guilt which brought the entire life under judgment.[19] Through taking God's judgment seriously, the procurement of God's forgiveness and blessing became attached to the person's ability to obey the Law and thus attain God's favor. Fulfillment of the Law produced merit which balanced the debit of sinful acts,

13. Käsemann, *Questions*, 4.

14. Livermore, "Setting and Argument," 14–16.

15. Livermore, "The Precious Instrument," 18. This essay offers no pretense to expound on Livermore's theology as a whole, but rather deals with conclusions concerning Rabbinic piety reached early in his career.

16. Livermore, "The Precious Instrument," 31; for Evangelicals' lack of historical and social contextualization, 33.

17. Livermore was responding to Eichrodt, *Theology*, 420–23.

18. Eichrodt, *Theology*, 420.

19. Eichrodt, *Theology*, 421.

and conversion itself evolved into a good work which freed one from guilt; "thus juristic thinking triumphs over the religious condition of personal relationship."[20] For Eichrodt, this attempt to ease the burden of guilt ultimately failed, producing in its wake a devastating sense of uncertainty of one's standing before God.[21]

Livermore deemed Eichrodt's interpretation "offensive, smug, and inaccurate."[22] Strong words indeed, but words uttered to protect a hard won exegetical and theological position. Though formulated early in his career, Paul Livermore's cautionary voice against unjustified, triumphalist polemic toward the Jewish faith stands as a vital component of his legacy. It would appear, however, that this component merits serious attention today in that, as an Evangelical with unquestioned scholarly credentials, Livermore levels a direct challenge to the present endeavor by fellow Evangelicals to reestablish the theological prestige and authority of Adolf Schlatter.[23]

Schlatter's presentation of Jewish piety reveals a litany of conclusions nearly identical to those Livermore verbally skewered in Eichrodt. To be sure, Schlatter was a man of his time, with theological views common to his generation. Troublesome, though, is that despite volumes of Biblical and Rabbinic scholarship refuting the fallacy of Jewish works-righteousness, advocates appear intent on presenting him as a legitimate twenty-first century interpreter of Judaism. Potential readers may be well served by a brief overview of Schlatter's somewhat abrasive, confessional polemic that aimed less at Jewish compliance to the Law—which Schlatter did not see sinful in itself—than the illicit motives for obedience that stained the character of the Jews. As Livermore with Eichrodt, attentive readers may find in Schlatter a perspective that is "offensive, smug, and inaccurate."

Adolf Schlatter has been called "the most important figure in the Faculty of Protestant Theology at Tübingen" during the first third of the twentieth century.[24] Born August 16, 1852, in St. Gallen, Switzerland, Schlatter matured within a religiously conservative environment that shaped his entire life.[25] Following study of philosophy and theology at Basel and Tübingen, Schlatter's early academic career at Bern and Greifswald witnessed his emergence as a conservative defender of the faith. This reputation led to his appointment in 1893 to a newly created chair of Theology at Berlin for the sole purpose of balancing the influence of the famed liberal, Adolf von Harnack. Making his final career move to Tübingen in 1898, Schlatter's seemingly limitless

---

20. Eichrodt, *Theology*, 422.

21. Eichrodt, *Theology*, 422.

22. Livermore, "Precious Instrument," 36.

23. Examples of the movement: Dintaman, *Creative Grace*; Neuer, *A Biography*; Köstenberger, "Schlatter Reception Then"; Yarbrough, "Schlatter Reception Now"; Schlatter's translated works: *Romans: The Righteousness of God*; *The History of the Christ*; *The Theology of the Apostles*; *Do We Know Jesus?*

24. Stuhlmacher, "Schlatter's Interpretation," 434.

25. Schlatter, *Rückblick*, 13.

energy allowed him to continue emeritus lectures for eight years after his retirement in 1922. He died in 1938.[26]

Schlatter's profound influence cannot be overstated. Thousands of young scholars streamed to his lecture hall, with those testifying to his guidance in their lives, both personal and professional, forming a who's who list for 20th century theology: Paul Althaus, Ernst Käsemann, Otto Michel, Karl Heinrich Rengstorf, and Walter von Loewenich.[27] The renowned and controversial New Testament scholar, Gerhard Kittel claimed that for many—and most certainly himself—Schlatter was a "Father and Chariot of Israel." Kittel believed that few men in the Church or theology had decisively influenced so many people, both young and old, as had Schlatter.[28] Kittel's admiration was further evidenced by dedicating his massive *Theological Dictionary* to Schlatter, in hopes "that it expresses to this eighty year old scholar the thanks which the Church and theology and especially New Testament scholarship owe to his life's work."[29] In addition to his academic standing, Schlatter's dynamic personality and pastoral spirit bonded with the common layperson. Constantly speaking at Bible conferences and youth gatherings, his prodigious literary output and dynamic personality elevated him to one of the best-read conservative Protestants in Germany.[30]

Despite being overshadowed in most liberal academic circles by dialectical theology after World War I, Schlatter's popularity within conservative German Protestantism continued and remained steady even after his death. While his work resonated with only a few non-German speaking scholars during this period, the past quarter century has witnessed a "Schlatter renaissance" that has brought his work across the Atlantic. Dating roughly from the fiftieth anniversary of his death in 1988, and initiated by Tübingen New Testament scholar Peter Stuhlmacher, this renaissance culminated in a number of Schlatter's major works appearing in English translation.[31] American translator Robert Yarbrough has clearly stated the motivation behind the movement: "The fact is that like few scholars since the Enlightenment, Schlatter's work holds promise at multiple levels and in several areas for the wide range of concerns that converge when the questions of New Testament theology's methods, goals and practice arise."[32]

With due respect, if a goal of New Testament theology's method is to get things right in practice, then however well-intentioned the effort to introduce Schlatter to

---

26. For Schlatter's life see Neuer, *A Biography*; also, the much more detailed, Neuer, *Ein Leben*.

27. Harrisville and Sundberg, *Bible in Modern Culture*, 179.

28. Gerhard Kittel, "Gedenkrede," 19, 27.

29. See Kittel's preface in *Theological Dictionary*, ix.

30. Many of Schlatter's books went through multiple editions during his life time with new German reprints and editions continuing to this day. These stunning figures can be culled from the extensive bibliography in Neuer, *Ein Leben*, 832–841.

31. For the term "Schlatter Renaissance" see, Siegele-Wenschkewitz, "Schlatters Sicht," 108.

32. Yarbrough, "Schlatter Reception Now," 62.

American Evangelicalism, questions emerge concerning his disparagement of Judaism and the Jewish community. While unsurpassed in erudition of Second Temple Judaism within the field of German scholarship of his day,[33] Adolf Schlatter was equally unmatched in the intensity with which he presented Judaism as a dead religion of legalistic works-righteousness breeding spiritual pride and arrogance, yet ultimately mired in fear and uncertainty. While the problematic social and political ramifications of Schlatter's message during the Third Reich have been addressed elsewhere,[34] the following focuses on his confessional criticisms of what he saw as legalistic Jewish piety.

It is ironic that while Schlatter opposed the growing trend in contemporary German academia by respectfully acknowledging the people of Israel, the Old Testament, and unquestioned Jewishness of Jesus; his descriptions of Judaism expressed a consistent and aggressive negative religious polemic.[35] Marking his disparagement of Jewish piety was Schlatter's tendency to slip into ahistorical constructs by reading Jewish material with pietist Protestant eyes.[36] Foregoing any consideration of the contingencies of historical development, Schlatter plummeted into abstraction by positing a normative Judaism existing alongside a distinct Christianity in the earliest formation of the church.[37] Missed in this approach is the dynamic complexity and shifting sands of various decentralized messianic groups in various regions. As Luke Timothy Johnson has pointed out: "There was not period of stability during which self-definition could be consolidated . . . For at least the first fifty years of its existence, there was not one thing that could be called 'Christianity' as a standard by which to measure deviance." Judaism itself was not homogeneous, with a fully defined Pharisaic tradition, thus, Johnson continues, "No messianist in that period was in a position to adjudicate 'Judaism' as such."[38] Schlatter would have nothing to do with such complexity of concrete historicity and his theological work would be pockmarked with persistent anachronism.[39]

---

33. According to Joachim Jeremias, Schlatter should be considered "a leading authority in this field of religious history." Schlatter, *Synagoge und Kirche*, 5.

34. Siegele-Wenschkewitz, "Schlatters Sicht"; McNutt, "Schlatter and the Jews"; McNutt, "Vessels of Wrath"; McNutt, "Damning Truth"; Gerdmar, *Theological Anti-Semitism*, 253–326; Heschel, *Aryan Jesus*, 180–83.

35. Gerdmar, *Theological Anti-Semitism*, 253. For an excellent overview of the debates over Judaism and Jesus see, Heschel, *Abraham Geiger*.

36. Familiar with such confessional predispositions within his own community, Livermore's criticism of this flawed hermeneutic could be sharp and to the point: "most Evangelicals cannot think themselves behind the Aldersgate experience or the Westminster or Augsburg Confessions, let alone to Augustine, Nicea, or Paul. That is, what they call biblical is not really biblical but North American Evangelicalism read into the biblical text." "Precious Instrument," 33.

37. Schlatter clearly set this division in his claim that, "When Paul entered the community of Jesus, the controversy between Judaism and Christendom was already underway." Schlatter, *Theology of the Apostles*, 215.

38. Johnson, "Anti-Jewish Slander," 425, 426.

39. Examples of this type of ahistorical thinking are Schlatter's equating post-exilic Judaism's alleged degeneration of faith with "the old Catholic church," see, Schlatter, *Theologie des Judentums*, V.

Schlatter's foundational presuppositions which steered his interpretive approach to Judaism were systematically laid out in his 1885, *Faith in the New Testament*.[40] In Schlatter's mind, pre-exilic Jews lived in a divinely initiated relation to God who acted in their life and history. God bestowed his blessings upon his people and in their thankfulness for God's gifts faith was awakened.[41] Following the exile, however, Jewish religion shifted its attention away from God's gracious activity to God's given Law and posited human fulfillment of the commandment as the initiating premise for any relationship with God. Grounding true piety in the will and effort of the individual, the Synagogue inverted the divine-human relationship by bestowing a causal power upon the obedient act that prompted God's response.[42]

For Schlatter, with the human becoming the active agent and God becoming passive, Jewish piety marked the "death of faith,"[43] and their relationship to God became legal and distant. The pious Jew now stood before God as one contributing—not merely receiving.[44] Expanding this view in his *Christian Dogma*, Schlatter saw in the Jewish conferring of causal power to willful action the roots of a degrading merit system that prioritized human achievement and relegated God to a secondary factor.[45] Jewish "self-exaltation"[46] placed human will over and above God and made pious effort the arbiter of salvation. Such emphasis on the ability of one to fulfill the demands of the Law opened up in Schlatter's mind two divergent paths: Jewish egocentrism and pride in their legalistic achievements, or spiritual "despondency"[47] over potential failure which led to intense religious unrest, vacillation, and uncertainty.[48]

Schlatter's seeming inability to comprehend the impulse of Jewish submission to the Law as a faithful response to an antecedent act of grace shaped his entire theological and exegetical program. Devoid of any inclination that might find motivation in gratitude or humility, he saw Judaism's adherence to Torah as driven by "selfishness," or "selfish desires," giving "clear insight into the sinful character of Jewish piety."[49] Jesus broke with Judaism because he saw their religion as "mindless obedience to a

---

His merging Jewish and Catholic piety and the need for reformation was systematically laid out in, Schlatter, *Dogma*, 195–200.

40. Schlatter, *Glaube*.
41. Schlatter, *Glaube*, 9.
42. Schlatter, *Glaube*, 26.
43. Schlatter, "Absterben des Glaubens," in *Glaube*, 35.
44. Schlatter, "Absterben des Glaubens," in *Glaube*, 35.
45. Schlatter, *Dogma*, 198.
46. Schlatter, "Selbsterhöhung," in *Dogma*, 198.
47. Schlatter, "Verzagheit," in *Glaube*, 31.
48. "eine leidenschaftliche Unruhe und Schwankung . . . Durch dieses Verfahren wird alles ungewiss und die ganze religiöse Aktion, so eifrig sie betrieben wird, kommt um ihren Erfolg." Schlatter, in *Glaube*, 199.
49. "Klarer Einsicht in die sündliche Art der jüdischen Frömmigkeit . . ." *Glaube*, 473.

command . . . rooted in a sense of one's absolute power."[50] This spiritual failure produced a Jew that "was empty and weak inside, with an absent God with whom they had no connection," thus when confronted by these "sick theories . . . which formed the ground of Israel's life" Jesus "could not find God's work."[51] Such spiritually corrosive selfishness found its most powerful expression in the Pharisees who perverted the law and created a spiritual temperament separating the Jewish community from Christ and the church.[52] The crucifixion of Jesus at the hands of the Pharisees did not stem from Jesus's actions, but was a product of his enemies' religiosity.[53] Schlatter's Pauline interpretation followed suit with the apostle attributing guilt to the Jews for their belief that human effort attained righteousness.[54] A confidence that willful endeavor bore capacity to earn salvation, a confidence rooted in a selfish grasp for power, marked for Schlatter the fundamental sin of the Jew. Schlatter's Paul acknowledged that his former piety, shaped as it was by the Law, not only "did not hinder his battle against Christ, but was the very foundation of that struggle."[55] Within this context, Schlatter could begin speaking of the intrinsic character of the Jews, with some passages casting the "Jew" as a particular religious type, embodying actions specific to their unique nature rather than common to all humanity. Thus, Schlatter not only saw Paul placing guilt on the Jew "because of their already culpable Jewish piety," but understood the apostle as considering "the Jews rejection of Jesus to be the result of sin committed toward God by *the Jew as Jew*."[56]

Leaping the fence of academia, Schlatter's attack on Jewish legalism reached the average layperson through his popular pamphlets and published collections of devotional material. His readers learned that the Jews saw in the Bible only the obligations of the Law, the transgression of which brought guilt, while fulfillment engendered merit. Scripture's testimony to God's gracious work was relegated to secondary status and submerged under pious requirements.[57] God judged such Jewish piety as sin, since the Jew sought only his own greatness and desired to establish his own righteousness before God.[58] Judaism's decadence was rooted in the self–seeking person

---

50. Schlatter, "Bruch Jesu," 4.

51. Schlatter, "Bruch Jesu," 6.

52. Schlatter posited a thoroughly corporate understanding of the Jewish community acting with a unified will. Eschewing diversity, he funneled Jewish devotion entirely through the Pharisees who "represented what was at the time in Judaism not only natural activity and human selfishness [menschliche Eigensucht], but piety." Schlatter, *Glaube*, 473. See also, Schlatter, *Matthäus*, 668, where Schlatter speaks of the Pharisees' religious conduct always having a "self-seeking intention" [eigensüchtige Absicht].

53. Schlatter, *Glaube*, 472; *Dogma*, 198; *Matthäus*, 663.

54. Schlatter, *Glaube*, 336, 339.

55. Schlatter, *Bote*, 511.

56. Schlatter, *Apostles*, 215, emphases mine. For a list of spiritual characteristics Schlatter attributed to Jews that distinguished them from non-Jews, see McNutt, "Damning Truth," 297.

57. Schlatter, *Hülfe*, 102.

58. "die Frömmigkeit des Juden als sündlich," Schlatter, *Hülfe*, 138, see also 139.

slavishly pursuing their own well-being, and Schlatter saw this as the fruit of the Rabbinic takeover of the Jewish faith. In the centuries before Christ, Judaism fell into the hands of the Rabbis, and the study of the law became the Jewish science. The Law became the will of God revealed, and once the revelation of God was relegated to the past, the present remained vacant of divine grace. God demanded total obedience with no exceptions, thus the law no longer related to the human in their totality of thinking and willing, but rather with the preoccupation with thousands of details. The person is daily absorbed into following a law, and thus is not capable of being united with God in their whole heart and soul.[59] Pharisaical pursuit of perfection burdened their followers with a religion of arduous worship marked by never ending toil.[60] The Jew was ever and only concerned with himself and the thousand legal details that filled his day.[61] Jewish Law fashioned a religion that honored men alone,[62] created a human–centered righteousness, and produced a community based on compulsion, untruthfulness, and religious "exhibitionism."[63]

A close reading reveals that Schlatter's tethering Torah observance to self-seeking willfulness, together with his casting the Jew as a unique religious type, could take on darker shadings. He spoke of a "Jewish method" that strengthened the "selfish will," producing a culture that alienated men from nature, developed learning concerned only with the "I," and formed a religion involved only with human relationships. Schlatter left no doubt as to the spiritual ramifications of such a method: "Concerning this shift in Jewish history, Jesus said, 'it leads to hunger and swine.' . . . the empty soul-murdering poison of our culture confirms the judgment of Jesus."[64]

Similar polemical barbs found consistent expression in what would become his most famous and most expansive interpretive endeavor, "Commentary on the New Testament."[65] Through numerous editions both during and after his life, this multi-volume work has become a staple for pastors, church workers, and Bible readers even to this day. One finds throughout this commentary all the elements of Jewish spiritual failure; most notably the refusal to see humility or thankfulness as motivation for Jewish piety. The Jews' conviction that the Law was their salvation bred pride and self-seeking, making them great before God and elevated over all others.[66]

Presupposing the graceless character of the Law, Schlatter understood living under its yolk as thrusting the person back on themselves, on their own capabilities and

59. Schlatter, *Alte Testament*, 34–5.
60. Schlatter, *Gabe*, 13–14, 17.
61. Schlatter, *Alte Testament*, 35.
62. Schlatter, *Wir Christen*, 11.
63. "schauspielerei," Schlatter, *Wir Christen*, 21. Schlatter also could speak of false "pretense" [Shein], *Wir Christen*, 10; or "pious pretense" [frommen Schein], *Die Kirche*, 14.
64. Schlatter, *Ziel*, 353. Here Schlatter connects a Jewish type of religion to social decadence. For the ramifications of such a connection in 1920s and 1930s Germany see McNutt, "Vessels of Wrath."
65. Schlatter, *Erläuterungen zum Neuen Testament*.
66. Schlatter, *Erläuterungen, Galater*, 32–33.

powers. When Jews glorify God they are in fact glorifying their own person to whom God is now obligated. From this construction it is easy to see how Schlatter could separate Judaism from faith: "Jewish certainty says, 'I am righteous;' faith says, 'God is righteous.'"[67] It would be difficult to pinpoint a more precise summary of Schlatter's perspective on the nature and consequences of Jewish works-righteousness than that found in his *Erläuterungen* concerning Rom 9:30–10:2:

> Their worship of God has but one thought: Work! Work! Faith displeases them. To wait upon God, to listen for God, to seek help from God against sin and death . . . that all appears to them as an unbearable commandment. They expect nothing from faith, work must do it all; meaning they expect nothing from God and all from themselves . . . They are blind to the divine revelation of righteousness.[68]

Schlatter believed that the legalistic nature of Judaism, with its emphasis on human merit, could only lead to a restless heart and spiritual uncertainty. The clearest expression of this conviction was found in his study of Rabbi Jochanan Ben Zakkai.[69] As one of the most prominent first century Palestinian Rabbis, Schlatter saw in Jochanan the opportunity to place Pharisaical thinking over against the early Church.[70] Though initiating his study with respectful comments on Jochanan's commitment to a righteous life, tireless teaching, and life of prayer; Schlatter concluded by asserting the utter failure of the Rabbi's piety.

In describing Jochanan's death, Schlatter quoted from the Babylonian Talmud tractate *Berchot*, where the dying Rabbi speaking of his impending presence before the most holy King of kings confided to his disciples, "there are two ways before me, one to the Garden of Eden and the other to Gehinnon, and I do not know on which of them I am to be led . . . "[71] Pouncing on what he perceived as spiritual uncertainty, Schlatter extracted from this existential cry a devastating condemnation of Judaism *in toto*! Based on this deathbed utterance Schlatter indicted not only Jochanan but Judaism's entire system of merit-driven piety. He read from Jochanan's statement "Israel's entire worship was permeated by fear and remorse learned from the Law,"[72] thus confidence in works did not lead to certainty and "fear held victory over faith."[73] His ahistorical method of overlaying the narrative with Christian categories quickly became evident to Jewish scholars familiar with Talmudic literature.[74] Ludwig Blau justifiably complained

---

67. Schlatter, *Erläuterungen, Römer*, 50.

68. Schlatter, *Erläuterungen, Römer*, 187.

69. Schlatter, *Jochanan Ben Zakkai*. This work was an expansion on Zakkai found in Schlatter, *Glaube*, 32–5.

70. For Zakkai, see Neusner, *Yohanan Ben Zakkai*.

71. Schlatter, *Jochanan Ben Zakkai*, 72.

72. Schlatter, *Jochanan Ben Zakkai*, 75.

73. Schlatter, *Jochanan Ben Zakkai*, 73.

74. Jewish scholar Ludwig Blau reviewed Schlatter's book, finding translation errors and

that Schlatter injected too many preconceived Christian ideas into the narrative, thus producing a work more "homiletical" than historical.[75] Sanders's study of this same material based on a far broader grasp of Rabbinic literature reveals no basis for Schlatter's conclusion while noting Jacob Neusner's view that Jochanan's words reveal less uncertainty than humility before the judging God.[76]

Schlatter's work evaluated to this point has remained untranslated and inaccessible to English—only Evangelicals. Revealed is a man who embodied the spirit of an age carried along by the prevailing winds of Protestant theology's legalism myth. For scholars concerned with exegetical accuracy and historical credibility those days are gone. Yet, precisely because serious research has moved above and beyond the disparagement of Judaism so prevalent in Schlatter, his re-emergence is problematic. A cursory overview of Schlatter's translated works unearths the legalism myth expressed in a virulent polemical tone out of joint with contemporary biblical scholarship. Offered here are no isolated or random quotations, but rather illustrative crescendos of a larger unified theological composition. As such, one might ask: is not advancing Schlatter as an authority for 21st century Evangelicalism to risk advancing an image of Judaism that is, to harken back to Livermore, "offensive, smug, and inaccurate."

The most significant translation to appear was Schlatter's two-volume New Testament Theology, *The History of the Christ* and *The Theology of the Apostles*. Seen as "an ideal introduction to Schlatter's opus at large,"[77] these volumes depict Judaism as simply works-righteousness rooted in power-seeking selfishness. God rejected "the Jews' unrighteousness and callousness without reservation, considered the practical uselessness of Jewish piety to be guilt, shattered the prevailing religious arrogance, and attested to God's independence from all human actions."[78]

Far from finding motivation for adherence to the Torah in humble response to a gracious act from God, Schlatter focused on the Jews' "self-admiration that considered that one's own conduct to be superior."[79] Thus, "The rule of Law and the teaching regarding merit lent the desire for greatness considerable strength, so that the question of who would outdo the others by his religious achievements and be the greatest was continually discussed in Jewish circles."[80] Desire for righteousness was merely "Pharisaic pretense overshadowed by an entirely different desire, namely their selfish will that sought

---

"Christianizing reflections" (christianisirende Betrachtungen) injected into the Jewish sources. Blau, "christlicher Beleuchtung," 548. Jacob Neusner gave qualified praise to Schlatter but cautioned that that the work "should be read in the light of L. Blau's critical review." Neusner, *Yohanan*, XII.

75. Blau, "christlicher Beleuchtung," 558, 560.

76. Sanders, *Paul and Palestinian Judaism*, 225–30. Note Sanders's refutation of Schlatter's assertion that "Semitism has no precise parallel to *elpis*," 225–6.

77. Schlatter, *Christ*, 11.

78. Schlatter, *Christ*, 67.

79. Schlatter, *Christ*, 298.

80. Schlatter, *Christ*, 298.

their own greatness and glory."⁸¹ The Pharisees could not be freed from their "sensual desires," and they remained the "selfish ones"; while the "sensual tendency in their will that longed for affluence and well-being and the confidence that sought to establish God's kingdom through its own will power had the same root."⁸²

With an eye to the personal character of the Jewish leadership, Schlatter could claim that "they fought one another in hypocrisy . . . All was pretense and the desires for which they fought were exclusively selfish ones. They fought for money and women."⁸³ In his second volume, Schlatter proclaims "the Jew's piety turns into an inflated self-esteem, which leads to mercilessness toward others," while "external characteristics of piety replace the internal service of God."⁸⁴ With accusations that twist Jewish literature beyond recognition, the Jew's God is "supposed to overlook evil in his favorites and assign merit to their works."⁸⁵ Such religious chauvinism dominates because the Jew

> injects into his worship a selfish will that fights for man's right against God instead of longing for the revelation of God's righteousness. As his selfish will induces to break the love commandment of the Law and to do injustice to his neighbor, it also seduces him into glorifying himself on account of his piety and into attempting to subject God to himself.⁸⁶

When one turns to the most recent translation, Schlatter's final major work, *Do We Know Jesus?*,⁸⁷ works-righteousness is elevated to the dominant theme.⁸⁸ Schlatter persisted in uniting Jewish piety and selfishness: "The human arrogance and self-seeking will to power gave the rabbinate its existence and conferred upon it its stature."⁸⁹ Jesus stood in conflict with a people who in seeing nothing but God's law became both proud and despondent: "proud, when they hoped that the Law commended what they had done; despondent, when it convicted them of transgressions. *Yet always they dealt with nothing but works. God was distant.*"⁹⁰ Thus, for Schlatter:

> The outcome of this kind of worship [Pharisaic], however, was that their souls became restless, in continual uproar, for their piety lacked faith. It was their

---

81. Schlatter, *Christ*, 270.
82. Schlatter, *Christ*, 274.
83. Schlatter, *Christ*, 325. Schlatter reiterates "money and women" on p. 327.
84. Schlatter, *Apostles*, 217.
85. Schlatter, *Apostles*, 217.
86. Schlatter, *Apostles*, 217–218.
87. This is perhaps the most troublesome of Schlatter's works. Written in the shadow of the Third Reich's increased persecution of the Jewish community, Schlatter employs undeniable anti-Semitic stereotypes in shifting from theological polemic to social alienation. See McNutt, "Damning Truth," 296–300.
88. Schlatter, *Do We Know Jesus?* The clearest examples include—but are not limited to: 34–35, 45, 53, 111, 120, 135, 140, 156–57, 170, 172, 217, 222, 235, 244, 252, 220, 421.
89. Schlatter, *Do We Know Jesus?*, 317.
90. Schlatter, *Do We Know Jesus?*, 115. Emphasis mine.

work, which is why it did not bring them assurance. It remained uncertain whether they had attained their desired aim, the paradise of God. Added to this was fear, because there were numerous opportunities to sin, and although the spirit was willing, the flesh was weak. There was also bitter pain, for the state of the people was corrupt; and what was the use of a few turning to righteousness while the majority sinned and became objects of God's wrath? Hardly anyone steered clear of envy and misgivings. For each looked at the others and measured his achievements by theirs.[91]

In the end, Schlatter saw the pious Jew as unrepentant and lost since: "Judaism is pleased with its godless condition. It is afraid to encounter God more closely. It does not consider the rule of the sinful nature to be tyranny from which it wants to be released. It does not desire anything better than what it has."[92]

Concluding his review of Schlatter's study of Jochanan Ben Zakkai, Ludwig Blau stated that "In the interest of science it is wished that Professor Schlatter cast off his presuppositions and handle the rabbinic texts more carefully in his future work on Jewish history."[93] Unfortunately Blau's wish was not fulfilled. Schlatter continued to develop and propagate an abstract, ahistorical caricature of Jewish piety motivated by selfishness, egoism, and arrogance. At base, Schlatter simply refused to see the responsive character of Jewish devotion to the Law. His absolute conviction that sinful willfulness for self-glorification motivated Torah obedience flies in the face of the eminent Jewish Rabbi, Jacob Neusner's reminder that: "What we know about God and ourselves, Judaism maintains, we know because God's grace has permitted us to know—that alone."[94] As one of the twentieth century greatest Talmudic scholars, Neusner's assertion is rooted in a mastery of the literature far exceeding Schlatter. Louis Finkelstein was on target when he maintained that with Judaism's formation under various conditions over several centuries in differing places: "Inherent logical unity can be forced on Judaism only at the cost of distortion."[95] When Adolf Schlatter advances a single corporate view of Jewish piety and levels accusations of hypocritical religious arrogance, promotion of mercilessness to others, having a God who overlooks evil, and inevitable spiritual despondency; Rabbinic sources reveal his distortion.

On the level of practical piety, Schlatter's inability to think behind Augsburg, together with his confessional propensity to lay exclusive claim to the concepts of mercy and grace, sharpens the point of noted Jewish scholar, Solomon Schechter's questions:

> Is the Jew taught to confess his sins daily in the following words: "Forgive us, our Father, for we have sinned; pardon us, our King, for we have transgressed

---

91. Schlatter, *Do We Know Jesus?*, 143.
92. Schlatter, *Do We Know Jesus?*, 182.
93. Blau, "christlicher Beleuchtung," 561.
94. Neusner, *Judaism When Christianity Began*, 43.
95. Quoted in Neusner, *Judaism When Christianity Began*, xiii.

... blessed art thou our God, who art gracious and dost abundantly forgive": or is the formula borrowed from a non-Jewish liturgy? Has the Jew ever heard his mother at the bedside of a sick relative, directing prayers to God, and appealing to him as "the beloved name, the gracious helper, the merciful Father, and the dear God": or was it some Christian neighbor to whom he was listening?[96]

That the only truthful response to Schechter's query is "no" lends credence to Livermore's claim that Christians often do not understand Jewish piety and that we ought to turn a humble ear to what Judaism actually teaches. Such advice should guide any reading of Schlatter. Did some Jewish leaders who confronted Jesus possess a merit-driven, self-righteous, judgmental arrogance that masked inner insecurity and spiritual fear of their self-created God? Perhaps; possibly even in numbers matching the percentage of Christians today who burden themselves with self-justification. What can be said with a degree of certainty is that offering Schlatter as an authority on Judaism serves only to legitimize the exasperation expressed by Samuel Sandmel.

Despite fruitful research rendering his polemic obsolete, those rejuvenating Schlatter's legacy apparently have no intention of qualifying or even bringing attention to this matter. Are we to conclude that his advocates not only agree but seek to propagate the Tübingen icon's perspective? While Schlatter's past legacy of such inaccuracies was undoubtedly offensive to Jews, the apparent complacency of reaffirming such errors bears the marks of confessional smugness. In light of this problematic endeavor, respect and gratitude must be given to scholars such as Paul Livermore who utilize their academic skill and Christian integrity to confront the "offensive," rectify the "inaccurate," and perhaps humble the "smug."

## Bibliography

Blau, Ludwig. "Jochanan ben Zakkai in christlicher Beleuchtung." *Monatschrift für Geschichte und Wissenschaft des Judentums* 7 (1899) 548–61.

Bousset, Wilhelm. *Die Religion des Judentums im neutestamentlichen Zeitalter*. Berlin: Reuther & Reichard, 1903.

Das, Andrew A. *Paul, the Law, and the Covenant*. Peabody, MA: Hendrickson, 2001.

Dintaman, Stephen F. *Creative Grace: Faith and History in the Theology of Adolf Schlatter*. New York: Lang, 1993.

Eichrodt, Walter. *Theology of the Old Testament*, vol. 2. Translated by J. A. Baker. Old Testament Library. Philadelphia: Westminster, 1980.

Gerdmar, Anders. *Roots of Theological Anti-Semitism: German Biblical Interpretation and the Jews, from Herder and Semler to Kittel and Bultmann*. Studies in Jewish History and Culture 20. Leiden: Brill, 2010.

Harrisville, Roy A., and Walter Sundberg. *The Bible in Modern Culture: Baruch Spinoza to Brevard Childs*. 2nd ed. Grand Rapids: Eerdmans, 2002.

---

96. Schechter, *Aspects*, 22–23.

Heschel, Susannah. *Abraham Geiger and the Jewish Jesus*. Chicago: University of Chicago Press, 1998.

———. *The Aryan Jesus: Christian Theologians and the Bible in Nazi Germany*. Princeton: Princeton University Press, 2008.

Johnson, Luke T. "The New Testament's Anti-Jewish Slander and the Conventions of Ancient Polemic." *Journal of Biblical Literature* 108 (1989) 419–41.

Käsemann, Ernst. *New Testament Questions of Today*. Translated by W. J. Montague. Philadelphia: Fortress, 1979.

Kittel, Gerhard. "Gedenkrede bei der akademischen Feier." In *Ein Lehrer der Kirche: Worte des Gedenkens an D. Adolf Schlatter 1852–1938*. Stuttgart: Calwer Vereinsbuchhandlung, 1938.

———, ed. *Theological Dictionary of the New Testament*. Vol. 1. Translated by Geoffrey W. Bromiley. Grand Rapids: Eerdmans, 1964.

Klein, Charlotte. *Anti-Judaism in Christian Theology*. Translated by Edward Quinn. Philadelphia: Fortress, 1978.

Köstenberger, Andreas J. "Schlatter Reception Then: His *New Testament Theology*." *Southern Baptist Journal of Theology* 3 (1999) 40–51.

Livermore, Paul Webster. "The Precious Instrument: A Study of the Concept of Law in Judaism and Evangelicalism." *Wesleyan Theological Journal* 22 (1987) 17–37.

———. "The Setting and Argument of Romans 1:18–3:20: The Empirical Verification of the Power of Sin." PhD diss., Princeton University, 1978.

McNutt, James E. "Adolf Schlatter and the Jews." *German Studies Review* 26 (2003) 353–70.

———. "A Very Damning Truth: Walter Grundmann, Adolf Schlatter, and Susannah Heschel's *The Aryan Jesus*." *Harvard Theological Review* 105 (2012) 280–301.

———. "Vessels of Wrath, Prepared to Perish: Adolf Schlatter and the Spiritual Extermination of the Jews." *Theology Today* 63 (2006) 176–90.

Moore, George Foote. "Christian Writers on Judaism." *Harvard Theological Review* 14 (1921) 197–254.

Neuer, Werner. *Adolf Schlatter: A Biography of Germany's Premier Biblical Theologian*. Translated by Robert W. Yarbrough. Grand Rapids: Baker, 1995.

———. *Adolf Schlatter: Ein Leben für Theologie und Kirche*. Stuttgart: Calwer, 1996.

Neusner, Jacob. *A Life of Yohanan Ben Zakkai: Ca. 1–80 C.E.* Studia Post-Biblica 6. Leiden: Brill, 1970.

———. *Judaism When Christianity Began: A Survey of Belief and Practice*. Louisville: Westminster John Knox, 2002.

———. *Rabbinic Literature and the New Testament: What We Cannot Show, We Do Not Know*. Valley Forge, PA: Trinity, 1994.

Sanders, E. P. *Jesus and Judaism*. Philadelphia: Fortress. 1985.

———. "Judaism and the Grand 'Christian' Abstractions: Love Mercy and Grace." *Interpretation* 39 (1985) 357–72.

———. *Paul and Palestinian Judaism: A Comparison of Patterns of Religion*. Philadelphia: Fortress, 1977.

———. *Paul, the Law, and the Jewish People*. Philadelphia: Fortress, 1983.

Schechter, Solomon. *Aspects of Rabbinic Theology*. New York: Schocken, 1961.

Schlatter, Adolf. "Das Alte Testament und der Talmud." In *Das Alte Testament als Buch der Kirche*, 27–26. Bekennende Kirche 7. Munich: Kaiser, 1934.

———. "Der Bruch Jesu mit der Judenschaft: Joh. 5 u. 6." In *Aus Schrift und Geschichte*, 1–23. Basel: Reich, 1898.

———. *Das christliche Dogma*. Stuttgart: Calwer, 1911.

———. *Do We Know Jesus? Daily Insights for the Mind and Soul*. Translated by Andreas Köstenberger and Robert Yarbrough. Grand Rapids: Kregel, 2005.

———. *Erläuterungen zum Neuen Testament. Zweiter Band: Die Briefe des Paulus*. 4.Aufl. Stuttgart: Calwer Vereinsbuchhandlung, 1928.

———. *Der Evangelist Matthäus: Seine Sprache, sein Ziel, seine Selbstständigkeit*. 7th ed. Stuttgart: Calwer, 1982.

———. *Die Gabe des Christus: Ein Auslegung der Bergpredigt*. Essen: Freizeiten, 1928.

———. *Der Glaube im Neuen Testament*. 6th ed. Stuttgart: Calwer, 1982.

———. *The History of the Christ: The Foundation for New Testament Theology*. Translated by Andreas Köstenberger. Grand Rapids: Baker, 1997.

———. *Hülfe in Bibelnot: Neues und Altes zur Schriftfrage*. 2.Aufl. Essen: Freizeiten, 1928.

———. *Jochanan Ben Zakkai, der Zeitgenosse der Apostel*. Gütersloh: Bertelsmann, 1899.

———. *Die Kirche wie Jesus Sie Sah: Eine Auslegung seiner drei letzen Gleichnisse Matthäus 24, 45—25, 30*. Kassel: Neuwerk, 1936.

———. *Paulus, der Bote Jesu. Eine Deutung seiner Briefe an die Korinther*. 2.Aufl. Stuttgart: Calwer Verlag, 1956.

———. *Romans: The Righteousness of God*. Translated by Siegfried Schatzmann. Peabody, MA: Hendrickson, 1995.

———. *Rückblick auf meine Lebensarbeit*. 2.Aufl. Stuttgart: Calwer Verlag, 1977.

———. *Synagoge und Kirche bis zum Bar-Kochba-Aufstand. Vier Studien zur Geschichte des Rabbinats und der jüdischen Christenheit in den ersten zwei Jahrhunderten. Kleinere Schriften von Adolf Schlatter*. Stuttgart: Calwer Verlag, 1966.

———. *Die Theologie des Judentums nach dem Bericht des Josephus*. Gütersloh: Bertelsmann, 1932.

———. *The Theology of the Apostles: The Development of New Testament Theology*. Translated by Andreas Köstenberger. Grand Rapids: Baker, 1999.

———. *Wir Christen und die Juden*. Essen: Freizeiten-Verlag, 1930.

———. "Das Ziel der Geschichte." In *Gesunde Lehre: Reden und Aufsätz*. Essen: Freizeiten, 1929.

Schürer, Emil. *Geschichte des jüdischen Volkes im Zeitalter Jesu Christi*. Leipzig: Hinrichs, 1886.

Siegele-Wenschkewitz, Leonore. "Adolf Schlatters Sicht des Judentum." In *Christlicher Antijudaismus und Antisemitismus. Theologische und kirchliche Programme Deutscher Christen*. Edited by Leonore Siegele-Wenschkewitz, 95–110. Frankfurt: Haag & Herchen, 1994.

Stuhlmacher, Peter "Adolf Schlatter's Interpretation of Scripture." *New Testament Studies* 24 (1978) 433–46.

Weber, Ferdinand Weber. *System der Altsynagogalen Palästinenischen Theologie*. Leipzig, 1880.

Yarbrough, Robert W. "Schlatter Reception Now: His *New Testament Theology*." *Southern Baptist Journal of Theology* 3 (1999) 52–65.

Zetterholm, Magnus. *Approaches to Paul: A Student's Guide to Recent Scholarship*. Minneapolis: Fortress, 2009.

# Part 3: **Exploration and Reflections —Theological and Otherwise**

# 21

## Biblical Interpretation: Why Are There So Many Interpretive Disagreements among Christians with the Same High View of Scripture?

— David Basinger

No one denies that those who call themselves Christians often differ significantly in their understanding of what the Bible teaches. Nor is this surprising or even necessarily troubling, given that self-proclaimed Christians differ significantly on the extent to, and manner in, which they believe Scripture to be an authoritative divine communication and the role Scripture is to play in our lives.

But what of those Christians with a high view of Scripture—i.e., those who believe that the Bible contains God's authoritative teaching on all issues related to faith and life? Do significant interpretive disputes remain for those in this category? It is clearly the case that such disputes are somewhat minimized among those Christians who hold a high view of Scripture. For instance, those Christians in this category uniformly believe that there is one true God, that this God is personal and relational, that there is an afterlife, and that we are to love God and others. In fact, some have suggested that the majority of those interpretive disputes that remain are over minor, nonessential doctrinal issues. "Wherever the Bible has been the final authority, Christians have agreed on these important truths. Their disagreements with each other have been over issues which, while often important, are not crucial issues."[1] I disagree. It's been my personal and professional experience that those with a high view of Scripture continue to differ significantly on what most would agree to be some of the most important core (foundational) doctrines in Christian theology. I'll cite just three examples (to which I will return throughout this essay).

First, there is significant, widespread disagreement over the nature of God's power. Theological Determinists maintain that God *is all-controlling*. Humans are free and responsible for their actions, but all and only that which God has determined should happen does happen. Free Will Theists disagree. God *could be all-controlling*. But to the extent that God grants us meaningful freedom, God has voluntarily given

---

1. DeLashmutt, "How Can Anyone Be Certain?"

up control over what will occur. Moreover, even within this category, there are differing perspectives on the extent to which God retains control. Weak Free Will Theists hold that God frequently overrides our freedom to retain control; Strong Free Will Theists maintain that God seldom overrides our freedom, while Moderate Free Will Theists range somewhere in between.[2]

Second, there is a growing debate over the nature of God's knowledge. Historically, the majority of Christians who held a high view of Scripture affirmed one of two perspectives on this issue (whether they knew it or not). Some maintained (and many still do) that God possesses Simple Foreknowledge—that is, that God knows all that has occurred, is occurring, and will actually occur (for instance, in the life of a person).[3] Others maintained (and many still do) that God possesses Middle Knowledge. God knows not only all that has occurred, is occurring, and will actually occur, God also knows exactly what would have happened in every possible situation. A God with Middle Knowledge knows, for example, not only that a person will actually marry someone and all that will occur in their lives together, God knows what actually would have happened if this person had married someone else and thus can offer valuable comparative information beforehand.[4]

More recently, however, a small but increasing number of Christians who hold a high view of Scripture maintain that God possesses only Present Knowledge. That is, they contend that while God does know all that has occurred and is occurring now, God does not know (although can predict) what people will freely do (since until they make these choices there is nothing to be known).[5]

Third, Christians who hold a high view of Scripture differ significantly on the necessary and sufficient conditions for spending eternity in God's presence. All agree that Christ's redemptive action was necessary to reestablish (make possible again) the God-human relationship that had been severed by sin. But there are at least two widely held understandings of what humans must know and do to utilize Christ's redemptive act. Soteriological Exclusivists maintain that only those who have accepted Christ (and possibly "children") will spend eternity with God. Those who are intellectually capable but have not accepted (or rejected) Christ because they have never heard cannot enter into God's presence after death. Soteriological Inclusivists disagree. They agree that those who have accepted Christ will spend eternity with God. However, they add, it may well be that some who have not accepted Christ will also spend eternity with God as the result of meeting other sufficient conditions that a fair, just God has made available to them.[6]

---

2. Basinger, *Freewill Theism*, ch. 1.
3. Peterson et al., *Reason and Religious Belief*, 149–51, 168–9.
4. Basinger, *Freewill Theism*, ch. 2.
5. Pinnock et al., *Openness of God*, ch. 1.
6. Marbaniang, "Theology of Religions."

The main purpose of this essay is to explore this significant interpretive diversity. Or, to be more specific, I want to consider the question of why Christians who believe the Bible to be God's authoritative communication differ so significantly on what they believe is being taught concerning core doctrines.

## Inadequate Responses

I want first to consider briefly some responses that I consider inadequate. In general, we are not overly concerned with diverse perspectives when the disputants are clearly not equally knowledgeable. For example, I'm not troubled or challenged when the first-year philosophy student who has never read Kant's own words challenges an interpretation of Kant's perspective on some issue that has been offered by a respected Kantian scholar. Nor am I troubled or challenged when a Christian student who has never read the Koran disagrees with a respected Islamic scholar on the question of whether Islamic theology fosters violence.

In like manner, some have argued that the differences in interpretation on core doctrines among Christians with a high view of Scripture can largely be attributed to an inadequate understanding of how to engage in appropriate biblical interpretation on the part of those affirming one or more of the interpretive options. It must be acknowledged, it is granted, that "people without academic qualifications can have a sound interpretation of the Bible. But they're not as likely to be as accurate as those who have spent years and years of careful research and disciplined training in order to deal with the difficult matters of biblical interpretation."[7] Those without training often fail, for example, to apply good hermeneutics (the science of interpreting Scripture) by taking verses out of context or ignoring the wider context of the chapter or failing to understand the relevant historical/cultural context or failing to give preference to the interpretive option with the greatest amount of scriptural support. And once we recognize this fact and apply the appropriate hermeneutical principles, we will find that interpretive conflicts over core doctrines diminish greatly.

I don't deny at all that there is a wide range of academic training among the Christians in question or that such training is important. But the differing interpretive perspectives on core issues are, in each case with which I'm familiar, championed by a significant number of individuals with comparable hermeneutical training. So unless we want to go down the dubious, subjective road of ranking the institutions from which the individuals in question received their training, or assessing the extent to which they have mastered what they were taught, an appeal to hermeneutical training does not adequately address the interpretive diversity in question.

Another common response to such diversity focuses on the motives of the disputants. When considering disputes in general, it at times seems clear that some quite

---

7. Sproul, "Which Interpretation."

likely know the truth but simply do not want to acknowledge it. Many politicians at least at times fall into this category, as do most tobacco company executives when downplaying the dangers of tobacco use. In like manner, it has been argued, a significant portion of the interpretive diversity in question can be traced back to a lack of appropriate motives. It is argued, for instance, that many of the Christians involved in interpretational disputes don't base their scriptural interpretations on a search for the truth (which they actually know as such) but rather primarily on such things as "their own personal biases or pet doctrines" or an attempt to increase "personal advancement by promoting a 'new perspective' on Scripture"[8] or even the desire to justify what they know to be ungodly behavior.[9]

I don't deny that the scriptural interpretations offered by many Christians are influenced by factors other than a quest for truth. However, while it is quite likely the case that some Christians do have conscious agendas that shape their interpretive perspectives, I find no convincing objective evidence that most or even many are conscious manipulators of Scripture for personal gain or that those affirming one of differing interpretive options on core doctrinal issues—e.g., on the nature of God's power or knowledge—are more likely to fall into this category. So, I believe the important (but now further refined) question under consideration remains: Why do Christians who (1) believe the Bible to be God's authoritative communication and (2) cannot be shown to lack the requisite knowledgeable and sincerity, differ so significantly on what they believe to be the correct scriptural teaching on core doctrines?

I want next to discuss two potential responses that I believe, while ultimately inadequate, to be worthy of more detailed discussion.

We'll consider first the contention that interpretive diversity on core doctrines could be diminished significantly if more emphasis were placed on Christian tradition—on the teachings of the church or church fathers in the past. The contention here is not that considering other sources of relevant information—e.g., consulting current commentaries, talking with respected Christian leaders, etc.—is inappropriate or unhelpful. But, in the words of R. C. Sproul, we must not minimize the significance of "the recognized minds of Christian history. It's amazing to me the tremendous amount of agreement there is among Augustine, Aquinas, Anselm, Luther, Calvin, and Edwards—the recognized titans of church history. I always consult those because they're the best. If you want to know something, go to the pros."[10]

This doesn't mean, it is acknowledged, that Christians haven't historically held differing perspectives on many issues. But with respect to the core tenets of the faith—including the nature of God's power and knowledge and the necessary and sufficient conditions for salvation—there is an interpretive perspective (or at most a small set of interpretations) that has historically been affirmed by the majority of those with a

8. Houdmann, "Why So Many Christian Interpretations?"
9. Kercheville, "Why Different Interpretations?"
10. Sproul, "Which Interpretation?"

high view of Scripture, and these interpretive options should be retained unless we can produce very convincing reasons to believe otherwise. For example, some will argue that while Theological Determinism and Weak Free Will Theism have long traditions of support among those with a high view or Scripture, Strong Free Will Theism—which posits minimal direct divine intervention—does not. And many in this camp also claim that while Simple Foreknowledge and Middle Knowledge have long traditions of support, Present Knowledge does not.[11] While this alone doesn't entail that Weak Free Will Theism and Present Knowledge are false, they grant, the fact that few "titans of church history" have considered them to be viable interpretive options means that "new" interpretive options carry a heavy burden of proof. Specifically, it is incumbent on those offering these "new interpretations" to demonstrate convincingly that they should replace the historic perspectives (or at least be taken as serious contenders).

I don't deny that tradition should be taken seriously. However, I believe it wrong to assume that Church tradition gives us one standard interpretive understanding (or small set of understandings) of the core doctrines. Among those with a high view of Scripture, there have always been significantly different interpretive perspectives not only on such issues as God's power, God's knowledge, and the necessary and sufficient conditions for salvation, but even on who has the authority to discern scriptural truth.

And even if this were not so, to assume that a given historic (past) interpretation (or small set of interpretations) stands in a privileged position in relation to more current interpretations is misguided. The reasons why respected figures in the past held their interpretive perspectives should always be considered when assessing more current interpretations. But whatever strength these supporting arguments possess is not gained from the fact that those in the past, even those we respect, offered them or found them convincing. That is, the supporting arguments for historically held interpretations have no privileged apriori epistemic standing. While their origin may be in the past (even distant past), whatever strength they possess is atemporal. All reasons offered for given interpretive perspectives stand on equal footing when attempting to determine which option(s) are superior or can be justifiably affirmed today.

This brings us to the other important type of response to be considered before I share my own: that much of the diversity in question can be traced to insufficient openness to the guidance of the Holy Spirit. Many promoting this approach begin with 1 Cor 2:10–13, where we read that the Holy Spirit knows the mind of God (verse 11), which he reveals (verse 10), and teaches (verse 13), to those whom he indwells.[12] As they see it, when a person possesses the "intimate, indwelling reality of [Christ]," such a person is given a special type of relationship with God in which truth is more readily realized, perceived, and experienced"—i.e., a relationship in which God guides you in and toward "truth."[13]

11. Basinger, "Justifiably Deny Knowledge," 133–45.
12. Houdmann, "Why So Many Christian Interpretations?"
13. Cardoza, "Interpret Bible Differently."

Proponents of this perspective do not claim that those with whom they differ are necessarily lacking in academic knowledge or are insincere in the sense of having inappropriate motives. The contention, rather, is that God has, through the guidance of the Holy Spirit, made the truths of Scripture available (directly or through anointed spiritual leaders) to those who are in the type of relationship with God that allows this truth to be received.

While I don't deny that some individuals may through the Spirit have access to personal, subjective (what some call privileged) religious truth or at least that they might be justified in believing this to be so, I'm uneasy with appeals to privileged religious truth in general and privileged scriptural understanding in particular. First, those Christians maintaining they have this gift of scriptural discernment often offer us incompatible interpretive perspectives. Thus, because of the subjective source of these incompatible interpretations, we are left with no objective basis for determining which of the privileged scriptural discernments, if any, is actually God's truth.

Also, most of us know from our own experience that some Christians use purported privileged access to God's will through the Spirit as a means to avoid responsibility for their actions. For instance, I've known more than one Christian college student who has attempted to end a long-standing, but now undesired romantic relationship by saying (sometimes with tears) that, although she/he would like to keep dating, God has laid upon her/his heart that each could better serve God apart. Of course, purposeful misuse of alleged privileged divine information is not the norm. But because it does at times occur, and we are not normally in a position by the very nature of the subjective source of this information to determine objectively when such misuse is actually occurring, it is also difficult to know when it is not.

## My Response

My response to the interpretive disagreements among Christians with the same high view of Scripture is based on empirical assumptions about the nature of belief formation and epistemological assumptions about our ability to determine the truth of the matter.

As I see it, the formation and retention of all religious beliefs, including our beliefs about the teachings of Scripture, are significantly influenced by various factors beyond our control. Two of these factors are well-known and rather noncontroversial, although the extent to which they contribute to scriptural interpretation is open to debate.

First, it's widely accepted that subconscious cultural conditioning shapes our religious beliefs. I'm from a Mennonite culture. The Mennonite aversion to violent behavior is not primarily genetic, as is evidenced by the fact that the biological children of Mennonites not raised in a Mennonite culture are less pacifistic than those raised in a Mennonite culture, while the biological children of non-Mennonites raised in a Mennonite culture are just as pacifistic as those who were "born Mennonite." Nor does this pacifistic tendency appear to be solely or primarily the result of explicit indoctrination. It seems rather to be primarily the result of the subconscious absorption of this pacifistic view of the world within the Mennonite culture after birth.[14]

And the same is true, I maintain, for our beliefs about the teachings of Scripture. Our interpretive stance on many issues—e.g., what we believe Scripture to be teaching about the nature of God, race, sexual orientation, or the role of government in people's lives—has been subconsciously shaped in part by the worldviews (cultural paradigms) to which we have been exposed.

Second, no one denies that what we are explicitly taught early in life by authority figures—by parents, pastors, school teachers, and/or friends—influences religious belief formation and retention throughout our lives. For instance, although many of my students maintain that their religious beliefs are based primarily on their personal study of the Bible, class discussion reveals quickly that their understanding of what the Bible teaches on such basic issues as God's power or knowledge, the destiny of those who have never heard, or the proper Christian attitude toward wealth has been shaped profoundly (and sometimes almost solely) by the explicit teaching of a parent, pastor, or televangelist.

There is, though, a third factor in the formation and retention of religious belief in general and scriptural interpretation in particular that is gaining increasing consideration: the manner in which the brain forms and retains beliefs. This is still a relatively new field of study, but neurophysiologists are coming increasingly to agree on a number of findings. While not totally noncontroversial, I'm going to assume for our current purpose that the following claims about the belief-shaping functions of the brain are likely true:[15]

The normal functioning of our brain is not to proportion belief to the totality of the evidence but rather to make judgments in specific situations apart from all relevant data of which we are aware.[16] In fact, several studies have found no relationship or even a negative relationship between a person's confidence in her beliefs and the extent to which these beliefs have been subjected to comprehensive, objective scrutiny.[17] If true, this stands as a partial explanation for why it is so difficult for many to consider the full teaching of Scripture on an issue, focusing instead primarily on a small set of relevant texts ("proof texts") to support their favored interpretation.

Our brains subconsciously use currently held beliefs to filter the deluge of information we receive and guide our responses. Or, to state this important point more generally,

---

14. See Basinger, "Kantian Perspective," 52 for a fuller discussion. I have no objective support for this contention. However, my personal experience with Mennonite culture over the past 50 years leads me to believe firmly that pacifistic belief is primarily a function of early immersion in a pacifistic cultural context.

15. First discussed in Basinger, "Kantian Perspective," 53–54.

16. Goldman, "Cognitive Basis," 234–41.

17. Goldman, "Cognitive Basis," 238.

it appears that we are wired in such a way that our preconceptions or expectations significantly affect how we interpret and respond to new claims.[18] In fact, this effect is so dramatic that new information or counter-arguments seem to have little or no effect in many cases. If this is true, then it should not be surprising why it is so common for Christians, even sincere, educated Christians aware of diverse perspectives, to continue to affirm the same core interpretive perspectives over the course of their lives.

Our emotive attachment to beliefs strongly influences belief retention. Specifically, current studies seem to indicate that the more strongly we "feel" that our beliefs, including our beliefs about the teachings of Scripture, are true, the less predisposed we are to examine the evidential basis for these beliefs and thus, the less likely we are to modify these beliefs, even when we acknowledge counterevidence.[19] While the normal functioning of the brain strongly favors belief retention, conscious reflection on beliefs—e.g., conscious reflection on the reasons by which we and our interpretive competitors hold our respective positions—can result in belief modification, including beliefs about the teaching of Scripture.[20]

In summary, what I think we learn from current studies on religious belief formation, retention, and modification is that what we believe to be the teaching of Scripture on core doctrines is significantly, but not irrevocably, shaped by our subconscious cultural conditioning, the beliefs we acquired early in life from authority figures, and the way our brains normally process such data.

It's also important that I clarify my general epistemological position on our ability to determine which among a set of competing perspectives on a given issue is true or can be justifiably held.

Those often labelled evidentialists believe not only that our primary goal should be to attempt to uncover the truth of the matter, but that if we seriously and sincerely consider all the relevant evidence, we can resolve many, or at least a significant number, of religious disagreements. My position is less optimistic. In addition to my belief, noted earlier, that it is always appropriate to ensure that those offering differing interpretations of Scripture have comparable hermeneutical training, I also believe it is always appropriate to assess the self-consistency of interpretive perspectives. And these considerations can at times justifiably cause us to question certain interpretive options. For example, I'm wary of those who claim that God's ideal (as found in Scripture) has always been that men have authority over women in marriage without even considering Gen 3:15, where we find the first explicit scriptural reference to male authority as part of the curse placed upon women after the fall. And it's concerning to find those who claim as Theological Determinists that God controls all things (including how we think and act) also affirming as Freewill Theists that prayer changes things

18. Goldman, "Cognitive Basis," 236–7.
19. Goldman, "Cognitive Basis," 237–9, 241.
20. Taylor, "Where Belief Born."

in the sense that God sometimes fails to do what God would like to do because we have failed to ask for divine intervention.

However, I also believe, as noted earlier, that with respect to all important doctrines, we can find equally trained and knowledgeable Christians offering competing perspectives that are self-consistent. Moreover, I argued that neither an appeal to tradition nor an appeal to privileged access to truth through the Spirit will resolve many doctrinal disputes. Nor do I believe there to be any additional set of objective criteria to which we can turn for such adjudication. Accordingly, I am left to agree with those who maintain that there is no set of neutral, non-question-begging criteria in relation to which it can be established that any one of a number of comprehensive, self-consistent interpretive perspectives is the truth or even more reasonable (justified) than the others.

Or, to state in summary form the empirical and epistemological assumptions that inform my position on the pervasive, significant doctrinal disputes that exist among those Christians who affirm a high view of Scripture, I believe that:

Both the interpretive options of which we are aware and the options we affirm are very significantly shaped by our subconscious cultural conditioning, the beliefs we acquired early in life from authority figures, and the way our brain normally processes the relevant data.

While conscious recognition of these shaping factors can minimize their influence and thus lead to belief modification, we are not in an epistemic position to demonstrate objectively that our interpretive perspectives are superior to those self-consistent competing perspectives offered by those we cannot demonstrate to be less knowledgeable or sincere.[21] If we assume for the sake of argument I'm correct, where does this leave us? It might be argued that if competing interpretive perspectives are not, as I contend, subject to objective adjudication, there is actually little purpose, or at least a diminished purpose, for disputants to reflect seriously on the reasons why they and their competitors hold their respective interpretive positions. While I don't deny that my epistemic position prohibits any of us from demonstrating objectively that our scriptural interpretations are correct or more reasonable than those of all others, I reject the claim that there is, therefore, little reason for us, or our competitors, to reflect seriously on the reasons why we hold differing understandings of Scripture on core doctrines.

First, our understanding of what God is communicating to us in Scripture has practical consequences for our lives and the lives of others. For example, our beliefs on such issues as the status of men and women in marriage, the legal and moral status of various forms of appropriate sexual activity, and the appropriate use of personal and governmental force to defend the rights of the innocent will clearly impact both our lives and the lives of others. And our perspectives on God's power and knowledge

---

21. See Basinger, "Kantian Perspective," 55–57 for a fuller discussion.

often dictate how we as Christians explain and respond to sickness, sudden tragedies, and other challenges in our own lives.

Moreover, we all once held what we considered basic, fundamental truths about the world—beliefs that we just assumed were true and thus would never have considered questioning—that we now no longer hold or hold in a much more tentative manner. For instance, most of us find that we can identify beliefs related to race, gender, sexuality, and appropriate societal norms, etc. that we once considered obvious and non-negotiable but have since been abandoned or modified. And in almost all such cases, we find that belief modification was based in part on conscious reflection upon our beliefs (often including what we have assumed to be the relevant scriptural teaching) and the beliefs of others (including their relevant scriptural interpretations).

So, I agree with those who maintain that even if we can't resolve interpretive disputes objectively, reflecting seriously on why we and our epistemic competitors hold our respective stances can at least move us from interpretive positions bestowed on us by culture and authority figures to positions that are more fully our own, and that this is of value.

Nor does it follow from my epistemic position that we ought not attempt to convince others to adopt our interpretive perspectives. To acknowledge that our competitors are equally justified in holding their differing interpretations does not require that we also acknowledge we believe that their supporting reasons are as strong as our own. To acknowledge that our competitors justifiably hold their perspectives is simply to acknowledge that we cannot demonstrate in an objective, non-question-begging way that these perspectives are internally inconsistent or that our competitors have failed to consider all the relevant evidence to which they have access. And we can grant all this and still justifiably believe personally that our own interpretive perspectives should be considered superior and still justifiably attempt to convince others to agree.

Given that the interpretive perspectives of those with whom we differ have been significantly shaped by their culture, authority figures, and brain function, we should not expect any sudden significant change in their understanding of the teachings of Scripture, especially with respect to those scriptural interpretations that have strong emotive grounding. Any significant modification of a firmly held interpretation is more likely to be the result of a process over time, a process in which our competitors will come first to acknowledge our alternate perspective as possible but still clearly wrong, then as plausible but still probably wrong, then as a reasonable option not personally affirmed, and then finally as the new or modified interpretive perspective they now affirm as their own. But it is compatible with both the relevant scientific evidence and the reality of actual interpretive modification to maintain that the shaping influence of culture, authority figures, and natural brain function can be diminished to the point where those who differ with us will "convert" to our perspective, especially if we have been successful in our attempts to have our competitors engage in a comparative assessment of the supporting arguments for the interpretations in question.

In fact, it is not incompatible with my epistemic position to contend that encouraging Christians to consider the supporting reasons for both their own interpretive positions and those of their competitors can significantly help shape what Christians in general believe to be the teachings of Scripture on a given issue. Consider, for example, the pervasive change in Christian attitudes toward slavery over the past 150 years. In 1864, John Henry Hopkins spoke for many conservative Christians with a high view of Scripture when he wrote that:

> The Bible's defense of slavery is very plain. St. Paul was inspired, and knew the will of the Lord Jesus Christ, and was only intent on obeying it. And who are we, that in our modern wisdom presume to set aside the Word of God . . . and invent for ourselves a "higher law: than those of Holy Scriptures which are given to us as 'a light to our feet and a lamp to our paths', in the darkness of a sinful and a polluted world.[22]

Yet it seems perfectly clear today to the vast majority of Christians who affirm the same high view of Scripture as did Hopkins that we cannot find in the Word of God any defense for the type of slavery to which Hopkins is referring.

How can we best explain this change? It seems to me simplistic and inaccurate to claim that those Christians who believed Scripture supported some forms of slavery did so because they were lacking in hermeneutical training or were not sincerely attempting to live as God would have them live or were not open to the Spirit of God and, thus, that the change occurred primarily because their misguided views were finally supplanted by those of thoughtful, sincere Christians who were open to the Spirit's leading. I believe, rather, that many Christians considered some forms of slavery to be scriptural because the dominant worldview of the culture, the teachings of religious authority figures, and normal brain function led them to this belief, even as they were doing all in their power to believe and act in ways that would please God.

Accordingly, it seems more plausible to me to maintain that what brought about the change in question was in part the successful attempts over time by sincere, spirit-seeking Christians who did not see a biblical basis for slavery to convince those sincere, spirit-seeking Christians who did see a biblical basis for slavery to comparatively assess supporting arguments for each position and that, as a result, most who engaged in such assessment came ultimately to believe that slavery in any form was not sanctioned by God. And if I am correct, what this demonstrates is that encouraging Christians to engage in serious comparative assessment of the reasons for which divergent perspectives are held can, in some cases, lead Christians with a high view of Scripture to greater consensus.[23]

That's the "good news." But, given my position, it remains the case that we cannot objectively demonstrate that those scriptural interpretations we attempt to convince

---

22. Hopkins, "View of Slavery."
23. General point first discussed in Basinger, "Kantian Perspective," 57–59.

other Christians, either individually or corporately, to accept are in fact God's truth or superior to those self-consistent interpretations offered by our knowledgeable, sincere interpretive competitors. In fact, if we accept, as I do, that the teachings of Scripture affirmed by any of us today are no less shaped in part by the culture in which we live, the authority figures in our lives, and our brain function than the interpretive beliefs held by those in the past, we are left with the possibility that some of our most basic, fundamental religious beliefs—including some that seem to us today so obviously true—may well not appear at all obvious, or even true, to sincere Christians with a high view of Scripture who have, at a different place and time, been shaped differently by these factors. Which beliefs these might be I do not know; that there may well be some such beliefs I do not doubt.

It does not follow from all this, let me restate in closing, that we ought not continue to engage in serious assessment of our understandings of scriptural teaching. Since we cannot avoid holding and acting upon interpretations that have practical consequences for our lives and the lives of others, it is important for us to engage in the type of assessment that can clarify our beliefs, focus our belief options, and possibly lead to interpretive modification. However, I do believe we should engage in such assessment humbly, given that all of us who attempt seriously to discern the teachings of Scripture are shaped significantly by our socio-cultural time and place. I also believe, though, that the Spirit of God can work within any socio-cultural context to help those open to the Spirit's leading us better understand that which they are capable of understanding and better act in ways they are capable of acting. And while that may be too meager for many, it is sufficient for me.

## Bibliography

Basinger, David. "Can a Christian Justifiably Deny God's Exhaustive Knowledge of the Future?" *Christian Scholar's Review* 25 (1995) 133–45.

———. *The Case for Freewill Theism: A Philosophical Assessment.* Downers Grove, IL: InterVarsity, 1996.

———. "Religious Belief Formation: A Kantian Perspective Informed by Science." In *God in an Open Universe: Science, Metaphysics, and Open Theism.* Edited by Thomas Oord et al., 50–66. Eugene, OR: Pickwick Publications, 2011.

Cardoza, Freddy. "Why People Interpret the Bible Differently and Why It Matters." March 8, 2009. http://freddycardoza.wordpress.com/2009/03/.

DeLashmutt, Gary. "How Can Anyone Be Certain of the Bible's Meaning?" *Common Objections to Christianity.* Xenos Christian Fellowship. https://www.xenos.org/teachings/?teaching=854.

Goldman, Ronald L. "Is There a Cognitive Basis for Religious Belief?" *Journal of Psychology and Judaism* 24 (2000) 234–41.

Hopkins, John Henry. *A Scriptural, Ecclesiastical, and Historical View of Slavery, from the Days of the Patriarch Abraham, to the Nineteenth Century.* New York: Pooley, 1864.

Houdmann, S. Michael. "Why are there so many Christian interpretations?" Got Questions Ministries. http://www.gotquestions.org/interpretations-Christian.html.

Kercheville, Berry. "Why Are There So Many Different Interpretations of the Bible?" Brentwood Church of Christ. http://brentwoodchurch.com/different-interpretations-of-bible.php.

Marbaniang, Domenic. "Theology of Religions: Pluralism, Inclusivism, Exclusivism." Articlesbase, 2010. http://www.articlesbase.com/christianity-articles/theology-of-religions-pluralism-inclusivism exclusivism-2035225.html.

Peterson, Michael, et al. *Reason and Religious Belief: An Introduction to the Philosophy of Religion*. 5th ed. New York: Oxford University Press, 2013.

Pinnock, Clark, et al. *The Openness of God: A Biblical Challenge to the Traditional Understanding of God*. Downers Grove, IL: InterVarsity, 1994.

Sproul, R. C. "Which Interpretation Is Right?" Ligonier Ministries. http://www.ligonier.org/blog/which-interpretation-right/.

Taylor, Kathleen. Quoted in "Where Belief is Born." *The Guardian* (2007). http://www.guardian.co.uk/science/2005/jun/30/psychology.neuroscience.

# 22

## The Renewing of the Mind: Cognitive and Developmental Implications of Romans 12:2

— Jeffrey H. Altman

WHY DO SOME CHRISTIANS prosper spiritually and emotionally after conversion while others struggle? This is a perennial problem for the church, as can be seen from the exhortation sections of the New Testament epistles to the many modern self-help books on conquering this or that besetting sin. When faced with emotional, attitudinal, or behavioral problems, Christians are more often than not counseled to address their difficulties by ratcheting up faith, prayer, belief, trust, or whatever, with devotional formulas, or with a combination of spiritual practices and pastoral counsel. Fortunately, professional counseling and therapy have gained moderate acceptance lately, but there are still many struggling Christians who feel left on their own to deal with what, in truth, are normal human challenges. Such challenges as unwanted feelings, attitudes, thoughts, and behaviors certainly can benefit from prayer, scripture reading, and the grace of worship, but they are more complex than sin, per se.[1]

In the beginning of his exhortatory section of Romans (12:2),[2] St. Paul exhorts the church to be transformed by the renewal of the mind (*nous*). By mind he means more than mere cognitive abilities, but includes in his concept the moral aspects of thinking and reasoning, and even emotion—all that is antecedent to Christian behavior.[3] Traditional Christians universally agree that changes in perspective, attitude, thought life, and behavior accompany or should accompany Christian conversion, but until recently little was known about the mind, or the brain through which mind manifests itself.

To be sure, much has been written about discipleship, growth in grace, spiritual formation, and holiness of life. Yet few sources have addressed how spiritual practices inform and produce changes of mind, attitude, or habit. Even less has been written

---

1. Wesley, *Sermons*, 394–96.

2. "Do not conform any longer to the pattern of this world, but be transformed by the renewing of your mind" (Rom 12:2, NIV).

3. Kittel and Bromiley, *Theological Dictionary of the New Testament*, 958–59.

about the brain and its role in Christian growth and maturation. There has been little to say about how conversion changes the mind. It is as though conversion somehow rewrites years of personal history, experience, and belief in one grand flash of insight and will-power. In one sense conversion powerfully alters the person, profoundly so in some cases. Yet in other cases troubling remnants of the past endure for years and seem to resist even the most stalwart attempts at change.

We are fortunate to live at a time of great advance in the study of the human brain and its cognitive functions, as well as in the physical aspects of human behavior, including such things as personality, concept formation, belief systems, and so on. In this chapter I will address some of the research that opens our understanding to why people think and act as they do, and how these new findings inform Christian growth.

## Mind and Body

The first point of contact between New Testament anthropology and modern psychology is the affirmation of the mind/body connection. True to its Old Testament's foundation, the New Testament treats human beings not as entities with separable parts, physical and spiritual, but as beings with one nature where flesh and spirit interpenetrate each other in an inseparable union. The supposed philosophical dualism of mind and body never arises in Scripture. Human beings are one thing, with one purpose, and fully accountable for their lives, choices, behaviors, and attitudes. That is, the physical as well as the spiritual aspects of human beings are taken equally seriously—as are both the physical world in which we live and the moral constraints upon our nature and the natural order.

Similarly, much modern psychology identifies us with the natural cosmos; however, that identification reduces the spiritual to mere epiphenomenal functions of a material brain. Because of this reduction, physical determinism plays a greater role in some human attitude formation and behavior than in faith-based accounts. Nevertheless, secular research has identified a host of formative processes that have been shown to be precursors of the kinds of minds we develop. These include genetic factors, social factors, and experiential factors. Much of psychology in the last hundred years has dealt with understanding these factors and in either preventing or correcting maladaptations caused by negative influences on development. More recently, the goal has been to optimize positive development in children and adults.[4]

What we have learned through modern research is that physical phenomena powerfully affect mental development, so much so that specific mechanisms can be shown to causally change behavior, perception, belief, and emotion. For example, Steinmetz and others determined that specific areas in the rabbit brain encoded a learned blink response that was instantiated under given stimulus conditions—a puff

---

4. Seligman, *Happiness*.

of air to the eye, coupled with a light stimulus.[5] However, once the behavior was learned it could be eradicated by destruction of the cells where the memories were stored. More than eradicating the behavior, the deletion of these cells made it impossible for the animal ever to learn that response again.

At the human level, similar effects also occur, as in the case of Phineas Gage.[6] Gage was a railroad worker in the ninrteenth century who was a large, healthy man with a gentle demeanor, who was severely injured when a steel rod penetrated his frontal lobes. Although he survived the injury, his personality changed such that he became angry and defiant, garrulous, and tended to drink to excess. So damage to that part of his brain associated with judgment and internal control revealed a significant relationship between the physical brain and the more abstract construct of personality. Similar observations and countless studies have shown conclusively that every aspect of our environment influences who we are, what we think and believe, and what we do or do not perceive, and even how likely we are to respond to the spiritual claims made in holy Scripture.

The rest of this essay will review a few of the most prominent influences on human development as they shape formation of the mind. These are: genetic endowment, temperament, attachment, parenting, and information processing. I will end with a discussion of the implications for Christian growth and spiritual health.

## Genetic Endowments

Our physical nature is significantly shaped by the genetic program encoded in our chromosomes and genes. The human genome consists of twenty-three pairs of chromosomes, one set inherited from our fathers and one set inherited from our mothers. In calculating the number of possible combinations of our genes during conception, we reach the astounding number of 64 trillion possibilities[7]; that is, each of us has one chance in 64 trillion of being put together just the way we are. Even without reference to genetic flaws and known genetic disorders, it is evident that while each member of the human species is undeniably human, and that we are much more alike than different, still genetic differences of all kinds are possible and, in fact, render us more or less prone to certain kinds of physical as well as psychological outcomes. For example, we know from experience that we can classify human mood and temperament into categories such as happy, melancholy, aloof, distracted, persistent, and so on. While I will show later that some of these traits can be affected by environmental influences, it is also true that some of us are just "wired" to be more or less easy-going, persistent, or friendly.[8] Our genetic inheritance also determines

---

5. Steinmetz, "Behavioral Neuroscience," 878–87.
6. Beatty, *Human Brain*, 290–91.
7. Shaffer, *Development Psychology*, 76.
8. Seligman, *Happiness*.

our resistance to certain environmental elements, like high blood pressure, depression, or cancer. In such cases two people with different genetic endowments might be exposed to the same level of environmental toxins, with one person developing a cancer from the exposure, but the other person, who is more resistant, showing no ill effects to exposure of the same toxin.

In addition to the complexity of the known interactions of genes in traditional genetics, the new field of epigenetics has shown that the production of proteins governed by specific signals from the genes are regulated by RNA, which determines which genes are turned on and turned off.[9] Moreover, once these effects occur, they can be passed on as mutations to the next generation. For example, in families who habitually overeat, RNA can signal genes to code for storage of more fat cells to a much greater degree than would be the case in families whose diets are more moderate. Among those families who traditionally overeat, the encoding for fat storage is passed on to the next generation, and, if such behaviors continue, would continue to be passed on in that genetic line.[10]

All of these processes, both genetic and epigenetic, are further influenced by the tendency of some genetic traits to be highly *canalized*, that is, more likely to be expressed and to override environmental influences. For example, physical traits like height and weight, eye color, hair type and color, and so on, are highly constrained and unlikely to be significantly changed by environmental conditions as long as those conditions are within normal ranges. On the other hand, personality, religious affiliation, political attitudes, and such, are much less constrained by specific elements of the genome, but more influenced by our social surround. So developmental outcomes are influenced by the interaction of genes and environment, but the proportion of influence of one over the other varies.

Another factor in the expression of gene traits is known as *reaction range*, a phenomenon in which the expression of genes is directly associated with optimal or less than optimal environmental conditions. An example of reaction range can be shown in the expression of intelligence. A child may have a genetic endowment allowing high or very high cognitive function (IQ), however, in situations where health is compromised, nutrition is inadequate, or in the presence of significant physical or emotional trauma, the actual cognitive function could top out significantly lower than the potential. So it can be seen that genetic endowment and the interaction of environmental factors exert tremendous influence on the various aspects of human development, wellbeing, and even, as we will see later, concept formation.

---

9. Mariman, "Epigenetic Manifestations."
10. Mariman, "Epigenetic Manifestations."

## Gene and Environment Interaction

Temperament

Temperament describes a set of highly genetically determined personality-like traits that have been identified by researchers such as Chess and Thomas.[11] They have shown that, from birth, infants express traits relating to mood, sociability, and activity level that are grouped into one of three categories. The first of these, *easy temperament*, is made up of infants who show a cluster of traits including: rapid ability to adapt to different environments, responsiveness to both their caregivers and to strangers, and easy to soothe after being upset. The second temperament is that of the *difficult child*. Difficult children show traits exactly opposite those of easygoing children; that is, they have great difficulty adjusting to new circumstances; they are hard to habituate to routines; they are often fretful and difficult to soothe when they are upset, and indeed, they become upset quite easily. Some suggest that these children have more genetic sensitivity to stimuli, for example, intensity of light or sound, or physical discomfort. The third temperament is that of the so-called *slow to warm up* child. In their responses, these children fall somewhere between easy children and difficult children, where although they might demonstrate difficult responses, particularly, for example in the morning upon awakening or awakening after a nap, they simply need more time to adjust. However, they do adjust and become more content with their surroundings where permitted to take their own time.

These temperaments of easy, difficult, and slow to warm up tend to persist throughout childhood and, in some cases, even into adulthood. However, they have also been shown to be adaptable over time, if the social surround accommodates children's particular needs. In difficult children, for instance, where parents and siblings learn to cooperate with a difficult child, as the child matures, difficult traits often diminish and may disappear altogether. Therefore, it is not determined that one will go into adulthood burdened with negative patterns of interaction. The optimal environment for any given temperament, called *goodness of fit*,[12] is defined as an appropriately responsive environment vis-à-vis temperament displayed.

Temperament, then, although highly genetically determined in infancy and early childhood, does not necessarily persist into adulthood, but can. In adulthood, we define such traits as personality—as type B (laid-back type) personalities, or type A personalities, the more intense directive personality type.[13] Whatever the particular model of the personality used to describe adults, the scales always include some form of easy-going personality, some form of difficult personality, and something similar

---

11. Chess and Thomas, *Temperament*.
12. Strelau, "Temperament," 15–28.
13. Pervin, *Handbook of Personality*.

to the slow to warm up personality—such as the person who wishes to be left alone in the morning until after the first cup of coffee.

Temperament as a measure of predisposition to behavior is, then, a clear example of interaction between genetic makeup and quality of the social surround. It is interesting to note that even among Christians, we can identify those who, while exemplifying the Christian life in most ways, nevertheless, can be described as more or less easy to get along with. Similarly, there are those who are clearly Christians, yet tend to worry more than others, or to perceive more negatively than others, or to judge more rigidly than others. These moods and behaviors can, at least in part, be attributed to effects of temperament and personality type.

## Attachment and Parenting

Attachment theory describes another set of biologically driven human characteristics identified by researchers Bowly and Ainsworth as arising from genetically programmed needs for security.[14] In animal studies, Lorenz has shown that animals express a similar but more instinctive characteristic called *imprinting*.[15] For example, in young birds, imprinting occurs within the first thirty minutes after hatching; but young birds will imprint on anything that moves within their field of vision. The effect of the imprint is that the young bird will keep as near as possible to the imprinted object, ideally its mother. Imprinting assures that chicks will remain near their mothers and will respond to warning calls rapidly by darting under her wings.

The human mechanism of *attachment*, while functioning similarly to imprinting in animals, is less instinctive, taking much longer to form. However, the effect of an attachment seems also related to matters of security. In her *strange situation research paradigm*, Ainsworth used a familiar playroom setting to test the quality of infant attachments to their mothers.[16] In this paradigm mother and infant are introduced into a room set up comfortably as a playroom and sitting area for two adults, the mother and stranger. During the assessment, hidden observers note a child's reaction to his/her mother and to the stranger under a set of contrived events. In the first event sequence, after the child and mother enter the room observers note how the child reacts to the stranger; is she/he wary, comfortable, or indifferent? A child who is comfortable usually approaches the stranger with some gesture for interaction. Also noted are how the child interacts with its mother and how easily the child engages with attractive toys scattered around the room—where the child is free to explore and play. After about eight minutes the child's mother leaves the room without announcement; most children, even securely attached ones, exhibit distress at the mother's leaving. After a short interval the mother returns and sits in her chair, but without initiating

14. Bowlby, *Attachment*; Ainsworth, *Patterns*.
15. *Konrad Lorenz*, National Geographic Society.
16. Ainsworth, *Patterns*.

interaction with her child. At this point, observers note the child's reaction upon her return. Similar events occur several more times during the assessment. In all instances, what observers look for is the quality of interaction between the mother and child under these various circumstances.

Ainsworth found that *securely attached* infants show considerably more comfort having the stranger present, play more readily and inventively with the toys provided, engage both their mothers and the stranger by showing toys, chatting, and maintaining visual contact.[17] Although, as mentioned above, all infants show some distress when mothers leave the room, securely attached infants show great joy and welcoming behaviors when the mother returns to the room. In contrast, *insecurely attached* infants are much more constrained in their exploration of the room, uncomfortable with the stranger's presence, much less interactive with their mothers, and display more extreme negative reactions upon mothers leaving and returning to the room, including, in some cases, avoidance of mothers altogether.

One mediating factor in attachment formation is that we are capable of forming more than one attachment. In cases where children have at least one positive attachment, the effects of other negative attachments are significantly reduced. So it is possible that a person who is securely attached, either to another parent, to friends, or to siblings is also protected against negative developmental outcomes. So insecure attachments do not lead inevitably to poor developmental outcomes; however, a preponderance of insecure attachments is likely to cause maladjustment. Indeed, the impact of attachment has been shown to be much more persistent than the effects of initial temperament.[18]

Secure and insecure attachments persist through childhood into adulthood. Zayas identified adult attachment styles that correspond to infant attachment styles and accompanying behaviors.[19] For instance, securely attached adults have fewer problematic relationships, including romantic relationships, and they are much more comfortable expressing themselves, being open, and are more productive and creative. The persistence of attachment is a troubling phenomenon, because the quality of attachment styles seems to be passed on from one generation to another, such that insecurely attached mothers tend also to have insecurely attached infants. So while the basic mechanism is a biologically driven need for security, the formation of an attachment is significantly influenced by the nature of caregiver-infant interactions. In this regard we need to discuss briefly the nature of parenting and how parenting styles influence the quality of attachment.

---

17. Ainsworth, *Patterns*.
18. Main et al., "Security," 66–104.
19. Zayas and Aber, "Roots," 289–97.

## Parenting Styles

Baumrind has identified four styles of parenting that have profound influences on child developmental outcomes. These are classified as: authoritarian parenting, authoritative parenting, permissive parenting, and neglectful parenting.[20] We will look at each of these in turn.

### Authoritarian Parenting

Authoritarian parenting is defined as parenting with high levels of control, even coercive control, with low levels of parental warmth. The absence of warmth in the presence of coercive control results in a style that, on average, is experienced by children as harsh, unyielding, and uncaring. Authoritarian parents value being in charge and, therefore, attempt to hide their own doubts and weaknesses. They also treat resistance of any kind as a threat to their authority. This gives children the false notion that parents do not experience the world as they themselves do, and often come to believe that parents do not care or respect them. In the long-term, authoritarian parenting, especially in its extreme form, which can accompany physical and emotional abuse, is associated with continued social alienation and behavioral problems, such as acting out in school and engaging in self-destructive behaviors like drug and alcohol use and early sexual activity. Under this style of parenting it is likely for most children to rebel early and spend as much time away from parents as possible; it is also possible that children may become dispirited and beaten down or overly compliant and dependent on such parents. In either case, the outcomes are generally harmful to development as a whole, although some children have a resilience that carries them through such coercive and restrictive environments.

### Authoritative Parenting

In contrast, *authoritative parenting* is marked by parents who, while making reasonable demands for compliance to rules and order, also make expectations clear. These parents are also warm and loving, allowing children to question their authority in appropriate ways. They often engage children in decision-making and help guide them into making good judgments. Also, authoritative parents tend to teach desired behaviors, not by coercion, but by a process of *induction* where children at an early age are assisted in learning to internalize self-control. All this leads to greater maturity, social adjustment, and willingness to take responsibility as children mature into their teen years and on into adulthood. Authoritative parenting is therefore associated with more positive developmental outcomes.

---

20. Baumrind, "Parental Authority."

PART 3: EXPLORATION AND REFLECTIONS—THEOLOGICAL AND OTHERWISE

*Permissive Parenting*

*Permissive parenting* is defined as parenting with high levels of warmth but with little structure or supervision. Such parents allow high degrees of individual freedom for children to explore and manage life on their own. At one end of the spectrum of permissiveness would be parents who are aware of what their children are doing, but tend to stand back and let the children learn by experimentation, only intervening to protect young children from danger. At the other end, permissiveness can border on neglect, where parents are not always mindful of where children are or what may be happening in their children's lives. While permissive parenting can have positive outcomes such that children are creative and learn to problem solve on their own, one negative aspect is that children feel alone and wish to have more structure in their lives, more parental oversight. Another negative of this parenting style is that children may expect that taking matters into their own hands and doing things according to their own design is acceptable in all situations, for example, in school (where permissiveness is less tolerated). In such cases, these children can become disruptive by demanding freedoms they have come to expect and interpreting normal rules and regulations as coercive.

*Neglectful Parenting*

The most damaging of negative parenting styles is the *neglectful style* in which parents have low warmth and low supervision. These parents are truly neglectful in the sense that children do not feel psychologically or relationally supported by those they love, nor do they have adequate structure in their lives to help them navigate even simple life events. For example, they often have difficulty in developing and maintaining friendships, learning study habits, and problem solving. These children often feel abandoned and, like children of authoritarian parents, can become angry because they often do not know how to navigate routine aspects of life.

Negative outcomes for both authoritarian and neglectful are similar. Children may become angry, at first toward parents, but may generalize to other figures of authority. Also, anger can turn inward, where children feel something is wrong with them that can't be fixed. In such cases the anger can give rise to depression, anxiety, and various forms of acting-out to counterbalance insecurity. Where anger becomes global, it is often leveled at a world seemingly hostile and without meaning.

So parenting is an important environmental factor, interacting with some of the more genetically determined traits noted above, such as temperament and quality of attachment. It is not difficult, then, to see how parenting can either amend problems related to temperament or attachment or exacerbate such problems. Taken together, these early antecedents of development are powerful in shaping life adjustment.[21]

21. Bowlby, *Secure Base*; Robins, *Straight and Devious*, 116–32; Sperling, *Attachment*.

## Internal Working Models

Through life experiences we develop models of relationships called *internal working models*.[22] These are cognitive structures made up of our beliefs, attitudes, and expectations about who we are in the world, and about the roles of others with whom we interact. These models become incorporated in the *self-system*—another cognitive/emotional set of expectations that are antecedent to thoughts, feelings, and behavior. The *self-system* shapes how we respond to those within our social network, as well as how we judge ourselves. Internal working models that align with reality, in terms of how the world of people and things work, and which afford the individual a realistic image of themselves, are much more adaptive than models built on false assumptions, negative emotions and attitudes, and expectations. Moreover, in relation to the *self-system*, the quality of internal working models is associated with motivation, that is, the direction and intensity of engagement in life tasks.

## Engagement and Disaffection

Human beings are motivated creatures. That means, on one hand, that we are driven by our biology toward behavior that satisfies such needs as thirst, hunger, sex, and pain reduction.[23] On the other hand, we are also motivated toward satisfying more psychological needs such as needs for meaning, friendship, success, and individual freedom.[24]

Biological drives have to do with survival, safety, and physical comfort, while psychological needs have to do with higher-order needs for affiliation, success, and creativity. However, most researchers agree that biological needs typically must be satisfied before psychological needs arise. For example, individuals who are hungry or thirsty will address those issues before needs for affiliation, expertise, or creative impulses manifest themselves. As teachers in many poorer school districts can attest, hungry children are not interested much in reading, math, or art. Similarly, children under constant threat of violence are generally too distracted to do well in school.

In situations, however, where physical needs for survival and safety are cared for, the psychological needs come more to the fore. Such psychological motivating factors have been studied for more than one hundred years. In summarizing the research, Deci and Ryan noted that three basic psychological needs recur across the motivational literature, i.e., needs for *competence, autonomy*, and *relatedness* (CAR).[25] *Competence* is identified as the need to be effectively instrumental in one's environment; that is, able to act in and on the environment to bring about desired outcomes. The need for

---

22. Main et al., "Security," 66–104.
23. Freud, *Psychoanalysis*.
24. Maslow, *Motivation*.
25. Deci and Ryan, *Intrinsic Motivation*.

*autonomy* has to do with the necessity of our being able to freely choose what we do; that is, to experience the locus of causality within ourselves rather than external to us. *Relatedness* reflects our need to be in meaningful, nurturing relationships, to love and be loved; we are meant to be social, to live in communities.

These motivational factors are hypothesized to be universal among human beings and are also at the center of our experience of self. For example, when faced with failure—an assault on the need for competence—most of us experience some level of self-doubt, such that repeated failure undermines our confidence in our abilities in one area or another or instills the belief that we may not be competent at all. Similarly, living under coercive conditions in which our need for autonomy is thwarted causes us to feel trapped, helpless, and desperate to escape. Finally, failure to negotiate meaningful relationships results in feelings of isolation, loneliness, rejection, and abandonment.[26]

The degree to which these basic needs are satisfied can be measured precisely in terms of how motivated persons are to: (1) continue behaviors oriented toward gaining or maintaining competence, (2) pursue self-initiated agendas or cooperate with external expectations, and (3) seek and maintain reciprocal relationships.

Research in the fields of education, sports, and work have shown that where people live in supportive, nurturing environments, their experience of self includes feelings of competence, autonomy, and relatedness, and they are both happier and more productive.[27] In contrast, those who live in environments unsupportive or hostile to the fulfillment of these needs experience frustration, helplessness, confusion, detachment, and oppression—all of which reduce productive engagement in life tasks. For example, Deci has shown that seventy years under communism in Romania completely undermined the motivation to work, where no matter how engaged a person might have started out, years of stagnation in quality and productivity rendered the entire work force disillusioned and disengaged in meaningful labor.[28] Similarly, in educational settings where teachers provide appropriate guidance, directions, and practice opportunities when introducing new topics, students experience more success, and, therefore, more confidence to strive higher, whereas the opposite is true where adequate guidance and resources are lacking.

The same patterns of engagement and disaffection occur with respect to faith. Richard Ryan has shown that individuals who experience God as loving and supportive exhibit joy, hope, and meaning in relationships. In contrast, those who experience God as retributive and severe are more rigid, more legalistic, and less happy. Of note is the relationship between our view of God and the nature of religious communities in which faith is framed. As with other developmental processes, like attachment

---

26. Connell and Wellborn, "Competence."
27. Deci and Ryan, *Instrinic Motivation*, 245–332.
28. Deci, et.al., "Self-determination."

and parenting, authoritarian settings are detrimental to healthy faith formation, while authoritative settings lead to health in faith development.[29]

## Cognitive Development and Information Processing

Given the discussions above on genetic and environmental factors in human development, it remains to address how these processes fit together; this brings us to the domains of mind and brain. For us, consciousness is so immediate, so continuous, that we rarely stop to consider how it works. Most modern theorists reduce mind and consciousness to some epiphenomenal aspect of brain function, that is, a matter of brain physiology. For Christian theists, though, such an account is insufficient. Humans cannot be mere expressions of physical processes, but that does not mean we can just ignore our physical body, as though it has nothing to do with who and what we are in Christ.

Returning to our introductory question as to why some individuals thrive after conversion while others struggle, the intervening review of human development suggests that we must take our physical nature seriously as it relates to the image of God in us and to spiritual formation. Indeed, in the incarnation God has shown that our physical nature is entirely suitable for carrying his image. Hence, knowledge of physical maturation, especially maturation of the brain and its processes, is essential if we are to understand why Christians behave as they do.

To that end, it is necessary to acknowledge that consciousness itself depends on our physical makeup, and especially on the brain. Certainly, it must be possible for God to directly break into our awareness, but it would be impossible for us to make sense of it, or to convey its meaning, without thought, memory, words, syntax, and hundreds of other mental operations. All mental operations require precise networks of neurons to shuttle information; and information itself must be sorted, stored, and retrieved to be of use. We call these operations, collectively, information processing.

### Initial Information Processing

What we have learned through brain and cognitive research is that the foundations of human behavior are more complex than could have been imagined, even thirty years ago. Even familiar and apparently simple processes, such as remembering, rest on layers of neural activity that are both dependent on and shaped by dynamic, reciprocal interactions between internal biological/psychological factors and external/experiential factors, as we have noted above in regard to other processes. The brain is exquisitely tuned to its physical environment. Indeed, it is made to internalize the world in which it exists, to make sense of it. However, it takes time to build a brain.

---

29. Ryan, "Two Types of Religious Internalization."

For humans, eighteen to twenty-three years is required for most brains to mature. And maturation continues throughout the lifespan, so long as we remain physically and psychologically healthy. However, while some maturation processes are initiated by our genetic programming, many also require interaction with external stimuli. For example, while the sense of hearing develops *in utero*, as sounds penetrate to the developing infant from the outside world, vision develops only after a child is born, as light energy precipitates a cascade of developmental changes in the visual cortex of the brain—where we actually see. Indeed, without visual stimulation infants cannot develop visual acuity, depth vision, or pattern recognition.[30]

Hence, the first need for comprehending the world is for our five senses to be properly developed so that the brain can sense and perceive what is out there. Detection of stimuli through one of our senses is the first step in cognitive processing. Following detection, the brain must retain a stimulus and attend to it long enough to recognize it, forward it to short term memory (STM), recall information from long term memory to further classify the information in STM, and finally, either initiate an output response—like suppressing a sneeze—or encoding information for permanent storage in long term memory, e.g., a street address.[31]

Cognitive Schema

Everything we "know" is contained in neural networks called schemes (sometimes called mental representations) and schemes are essential for thinking—which includes judgment and evaluation, decision making, discrimination, planning, reflecting, creating, and almost everything else we do. Schemes are formed as we experience events, emotions, and physical surroundings, and encode concurrent inputs together by association. Individual schemes contain specific data—our knowledge of color, for instance—but many other schemes are connected by branching to related knowledge. For, example, thinking of the color red is likely to activate networks encoding red things, like flowers, fire trucks, or radishes. Thinking involves accessing stored knowledge from long-term memory (LTM) and processing it in short-term memory (our RAM memory) as it receives immediate perception. So deciding on the color for a new chair requires knowledge of color and knowing how to shop. Most acts of thinking are equally complex, and take years of learning, experience, and practice to master. And mastery depends on optimal conditions for detection of stimuli, interpretation of those stimuli, and encoding of important information.

Properly speaking, however, infants have no cognitions, or thoughts. Their world is an immediate experience of light, sound, smell, taste and touch sensations—what William James called a "booming, buzzing confusion."[32] Nothing is meaningful

30. Shafffer, *Development*, 198–206.
31. Reisberg, *Cognition*, 59–211.
32. James, *Psychology*.

cognitively because there is no stored knowledge, no memory, and no reference point—at least, not at first. The transition from sensation to perception (interpreted sensation) occurs very rapidly as the infant brain accommodates to physical stimuli and associate stimulus events with outcomes. For example, babes learn at about three weeks that crying brings comforting responses from their social surround—food, cuddling, diaper changes, and so on. In time, parental vocalizations and interactions create memories and expectations; these are the beginnings of making sense of the world and mapping external events into mental representations. The process begins with sensory data collected by infants' sensory organs—sound, smell, and so on. But sensory data must be strong enough to be detected; that is, light, sound, or pressure must reach a sensory threshold. Clearly, stimuli that are too weak to be detected are not further processed; they do not even register as being present. In addition to the strength of the signal, the sensory organs must be able to detect stimuli appropriately. Therefore, damaged or dysfunctional sensory receptors reduce available input, and, therefore, limit further cognitive processing.

As important as mere detection of stimuli is, there must also be a means of holding on to stimuli long enough for them to be perceived (interpreted). The sensory store is a cognitive function that holds on to stimulus data for about five to seven seconds, just long enough to pass it on to short-term memory. During that time we must become aware of a stimulus through the executive function of *attention*. Failure to attend to data results in its loss; it is written over with the next influx of stimuli and is not processed further. Attention, however, fixes inputs long enough to get them into short-term memory, or what is sometimes called the working memory. Information can exist in the short-term memory for up to 20 seconds. If our attention is interrupted while we hold information in STM, for example, trying to remember a telephone number while someone is talking to us, we can lose the information. Information lost from STM has no chance of getting into our more permanent long-term storage (LTM), but if conditions are right, STM transfers information to LTM. As far as we know, once information is encoded into LTM, it remains indefinitely. Encoded information that gets into long-term memory is then available for recall; however, whether or not it is ever recalled depends on how well it was encoded in the first place. Memories that are encoded with a great deal of precision and attention and are encoded into existing cognitive structures tend to be easier to recall than things that get into long-term memory by random assignment.

So it can be seen that the processes of gathering information, interpreting it, acting on it, and storing it for later retrieval are indeed complex operations with a number of pitfalls along the way. It is generally known, for example, that we only detect some of the stimuli in our immediate surroundings; of those, we attend to only a few, and of those, fewer still are processed into short-term memory. Then of what gets into short-term memory, we choose only some to store in long-term memory. But the story does not end there. In the process of recall, we again filter information so that we, in any given episode of recall, may not remember everything that was stored. For instance, one form of LTM, our autobiographical memory, is notoriously subject to reinterpretation. We tend to re-write accounts to make meaning of the past under the physical and psychological conditions of the present—the old joke about parents getting smarter as we get older captures this phenomenon in a humorous way.

It is also important to note that memories and other knowledge structures, as noted earlier, are in reality networks of neural connections. Once these cognitive structures form, they are incredibly stable, and it takes considerable effort to change them. So belief systems, interpretation of historical events, and opinions are resistant to change.

Therefore, all that we know, all that we remember, all that we believe, exist in knowledge structures that have been built up over time and quite varied experiences. It is not surprising, then, that how we think, what we think about the world, and what we think about ourselves, are all subject to certain levels of error. For example, the formation of a belief can include not only an event that we have personally witnessed but also the emotions we experienced during the event. So a fearful event like an accident can lead to a generalized and irrational fear of driving or riding in a car. Similarly, our notions and ideas about the world, people groups, relationships, and God can be faulty. Whatever the circumstances under which information becomes encoded, memories, feelings, and ideas are what they are because of the way the brain works. We have all dealt with people who, against all reason, maintain certain points of view, irrational beliefs, or indefensible attitudes, even though evidence refutes their position. Given, then, how concepts form, one can understand how stereotypes, biases, and racial hatred persist, and, in fact, are passed on through generations. Conversely, as exemplified in Moses's words in Deut 6:6–9, we observe the mechanisms by which good and positive perceptions are built and passed on from generation to generation.[33] That we are social beings also suggests that our development is both individual and communal. We turn, then, to the implications of the account given above.

## Implications

From this account of human development several implications follow: First, we may consider that sin is not the only cause of negative human behavior, neither at the level of the individual, nor that of the community.[34] As noted earlier, Wesley identified human weaknesses such as ignorance, errors of judgment, infirmities, mistakes, and

---

33. "And these words which I command you this day shall be upon your heart; and you shall teach them diligently to your children, and shall talk of them when you sit in your house, and when you walk by the way, and when you lie down, and when you rise. And you shall bind them as a sign upon your hand, and they shall be as frontlets between your eyes. And you shall write them on the doorposts of your house and on your gates." (Deut 6:6–9, ESV)

34. I include in the term *behavior* emotions, attitudes, and inclinations—as these are all precursors of action.

temptations that are not subject to moral perfection.[35] I argue here that a modern understanding of these fallibilities is that they are residual effects of genetic and environmental processes. As St. Paul says, we know in part, we reason childishly, and see incompletely (1 Cor 13:9–12). Indeed, his letters are peppered with such encouragement as: to work out our salvation with fear and trembling (Phil 2:12), to be free of anxiety (Phil 4:6), to be angry and not sin (Eph 4:26), to put away fear (Rom 8:15; see also 1 John 4:18), and to agree with each other in the Lord (Eph 4:2). These are matters addressed to Christians, who while learning to "put on the new man," are also learning to "put off the old man" (Eph 4:22–24).

Second, the complex antecedents to behavior imply that remediation of behavioral, attitudinal, social, and emotional frailties, is also complex. Always, we are beings of earth and of heaven. Our development is a process of interpenetrating spiritual and physical dynamics; therefore, we must differentiate between spiritual, physical, and mental pathways to wholeness. For most of church history, evidences of human imperfection have been addressed with spiritual solutions—as noted earlier. However, entrenched fear, depression, anger, insensitivity to others, obsessive/compulsive disorder, and autism, to name only a few categories, are not things that usually yield to devotional practices. Some emotional, psychological, and personality difficulties require the hard work of professional therapy and counseling.[36]

The third implication is that optimal development has both individual and collective aspects. I have said we are made for communities; we are made to love and be loved. Our greatest good derives from nurturing social environments that have shaped us, that have allowed us freedom to explore and experiment, and that have afforded us the tools to be instrumental in shaping the world around us. Therefore, just as we need the Body of Christ for our spiritual health, we need each other for our developmental health—from birth and throughout the lifespan. The church has not yet grasped this necessity in its full dimension, but it can become a place of healing. It can provide *goodness of fit* for those who are burdened with problematic temperaments; it can provide nurturance for those who have been pushed around and neglected; it can provide a safe place, where false beliefs and misperceptions can be gently corrected in the embrace of loving fellowship. So it is encouraging to see parish social services, support groups, and mental health initiatives cropping up in modern congregations. In addition to these, we need education to help the church understand needy people and how they can be helped, without being stereotyped or made to feel abnormal.

Finally, human infirmities are universal. Each of us has them, although some of us are fortunate enough to have ones considered "normal." Or, some of us are just good at hiding our oddities—often from ourselves, if not from our neighbors. In either case, we are called to two things: humility (Phil 2:3) and the refusal to judge (Matt 7:1–6).

---

35. Wesley, *Sermons*, 394–6.

36. In this regard, if one has to choose between a competent therapist and a Christian one, it is better to choose the competent professional.

# Bibliography

Ainsworth, M. D., et al. *Patterns of Attachment: A Psychological Study of the Strange Situation.* New York: Psychology Press, 1978.

Ames, Russell, and Carole Ames. *Research on Motivation in Education.* Orlando: Academic Press, 1984.

Baumrind, Diana. "Current Patterns of Parental Authority." *Developmental Psychology* 4 (1971) 1–103.

Beatty, Jackson. *The Human Brain: Essentials of Behavioral Neuroscience.* Thousand Oaks, CA: Sage, 2001.

Bowlby, John. *A Secure Base: Parent-Child Attachment and Healthy Human Development.* New York: Basic Books, 1988.

———. *Attachment and Loss.* Vol. 1. London: Hogarth, 1969.

Chess, Stella, and Alexander Thomas. *Temperament: Theory and Practice.* New York: Brunner/Mazel, 1996.

Connell, James P., and James G. Wellborn. "Competence, Autonomy, and Relatedness: A Motivational Analysis of Self-System Processes." In *Self Processes and Development*, 43–78. Hillsdale, NJ: Erlbaum, 1991.

Deci, Edward L., and Richard M. Ryan. *Intrinsic Motivation and Self-Determination in Human Behavior.* New York: Plenum, 1985.

Deci, Edward L., et al. "Self-determination in a Work Organization." *Journal of Applied Psychology* 74 (1989) 580–90.

Freud, Sigmund. *A General Introduction to Psychoanalysis.* New York: Liveright, 1920.

James, William. *Psychology.* New York: Holt, 1892.

Kittel, Gerhard, ed., and Geoffrey Bromiley, ed. and trans. *Theological Dictionary of the New Testament*, vol. 4. Grand Rapids: Eerdmans, 1967.

*Konrad Lorenz: Science of Animal Behavior.* Produced by National Geographic Society in association with Jack Kaufman Pictures, 1975.

Main, Mary, et al. "Security in Infancy, Childhood, and Adulthood: A Move to the Level of Representation." *Monographs of the Society for Research in Child Development* 50 (1985) 66–104.

Mariman, E. C. "Epigenetic Manifestations in Diet-Related Disorders." *Journal of Nutrigenetics and Nutrigenomics* 1 (2008) 232–9.

Maslow, Abraham H. *Motivation and Personality.* New York: Harper & Row, 1970.

Miller, Patricia H. *Theories of Developmental Psychology.* New York: Freeman, 1989.

Pervin, Lawrence A., and Oliver P. John. *Handbook of Personality: Theory and Research.* New York: Guilford, 1999.

Reisberg, Daniel. *Cognition: Exploring the Science of the Mind.* New York: Norton, 1997.

Rholes, W. Steven, and Jeffry A. Simpson. *Adult Attachment: Theory, Research, and Clinical Implications.* New York: Guilford, 2004.

Robins, Lee N., and Michael Rutter. *Straight and Devious Pathways from Childhood to Adulthood.* Cambridge: Cambridge University Press, 1990.

Ryan, Richard M., et al. "Two Types of Religious Internalization and Their Relations to Religious Orientations and Mental Health." *Journal of Personality and Social Psychology* 65 (1993) 586–96.

Seligman, Martin E.P. *Authentic Happiness: Using the New Positive Psychology to Realize Your Potential for Lasting Fulfillment.* New York: Free Press, 2002.

Shaffer, David R. *Developmental Psychology: Childhood and Adolescence*. Pacific Grove: Brooks/Cole, 1999.

Skinner, Ellen A. *Perceived Control, Motivation, and Coping*. Thousand Oaks, CA: Sage, 1995.

Sperling, Michael B., and William H. Berman. *Attachment in Adults: Clinical and Developmental Perspectives*. New York: Guilford, 1994.

Steinmetz, J. E. "Neural Basis of Classical Conditioning." In *Encyclopedia of Behavioral Neuroscience*, edited by George Koob et al. London: Elsevier, 2010.

Strelau, Jan, and A. Angleitner. "Temperament and the Concept of Goodness of Fit." In *Explorations in Temperament: International Perspectives on Theory and Measurement*, 15–28. London: Plenum, 1991.

Thomas, Alexander, and Stella Chess. *Temperament and Development*. New York: Brunner/Mazel, 1977.

Thomas, Alexander, et al. *Temperament and Behavior Disorders in Children*. New York: New York University Press, 1968.

Wesley, John. *Wesley's 52 Standard Sermons*. Salem, OH: Schmul, 1967.

Zayas, Vivian, and J. Aber. "For Review Only Roots of Adult Attachment: Maternal Caregiving at 18 Months Predicts Adult Peer and Partner Attachment." *Social Psychologist and Personality Science* 2 (2011) 289–97.

# 23

## Beauty Will Save the World: Literary Imagination and Ministry

— Thomas R. Worth

To my mind, a Dostoyevsky novel reads like a Russian soap opera and *The Idiot* especially so. It takes some perseverance (almost like being a pastor!) to keep up with all the chaotic relationships, romances, and the kaleidoscope of characters. Yet those who have read *The Idiot* feel like they've accomplished something important. Prince Myshkin, the main character in the novel, is a harmless, innocent nobleman, who is recovering from a debilitating mental ailment and is moving back into society. He has no agenda for the people who surround him and so is regarded by them as an idiot. Because Myshkin does not seek to use them, they grow to trust him more and more. He is a good listener, almost as if he had learned how to practice "Faith Sharing" from a contemporary spiritual director like Maryann Fackleman. An idea of Myshkin's, which helps him be who he is, and for which he is mocked more than once, is this: "beauty will save the world."[1]

That phrase has many interpretations, but this essay will understand beauty in the sense of art, especially literary art. For those of us in ministry, beauty can save us. Great literature can help nourish our souls, our sentiments, and our imaginations. It can provide us with legitimate sources of delight and enjoyment. It can help us step out of ourselves and behold human existence from the perspective of another. Great literature can give pointers in helping us love God, love our neighbor, and love ourselves. If we have been quickened and awakened by beauty in literature, we participate in a culture of universal metaphors and understandings—a vocabulary which helps us hear and communicate with many kinds of people. In fact, Eugene H. Peterson (one of our era's foremost teachers on pastoral and spiritual theology) said that if he were to start a seminary, he would have his students spend the first two years studying literature![2]

---

1. Dostoyevsky, *The Idiot*, 402, 543.
2. Cusick, "A Conversation with Eugene Peterson," 4.

Literature can help pry us loose from ourselves. If we are too full of our own story, it is difficult for us to hear another's. We listen impatiently and wait for the other to quit talking so we can tell our own story. But ministry involves precisely this: to somehow be liberated from being centered on "me" and "mine" so that we may hear and listen and be involved in the healing and redemption of another heart. There are many ways in which God will help us. At the deepest levels, the cross of Jesus is what frees us from self-centeredness. How the Lord brings the cross to bear in each of our lives is as individual and various as we are. Our churches, our families, our schools, our workplaces, our personal prayer, Bible study and reflection, can all be venues where we can be set free from self, if we submit to God's dealings in these situations. But this small essay seeks merely to promote the specific work of human growth and liberation which can take place in our private lives from reading great literature. I will grant that great literature is not the major instrument God uses with most of us. But for those in ministry who have a literary inclination, a good book can bring a Sabbath for the soul and somehow help us to become more human.

When Jesus was lifted up on the cross, he established an everlasting gravitational center which draws all to himself. All things now serve him because he has drawn them within the orbit of his great redemptive work (John 12:32; Ps 119:91). Great literature, which articulates the good, the true, and the beautiful, is among those matters and makings of human culture which can serve our Lord, whether their makers be Christian or not.

Literature is more than just a source for sermon illustrations. It is a way to nurture one's soul and sentiments. There is what I would call a literary Vincentian Canon—that which has nourished souls with a kind of humanistic catholicity. Just as Vincent of Lérins observed that true classical Christian doctrine was "that which has been believed everywhere, always and by all,"[3] so great literature is that which has an honest deep appeal to humanity transcending the borders of nations, times, and peoples. It can speak to readers in a multitude of times and situations, not the least of which could be: ministers of the gospel. These ministers are not only tasked with being able to appeal and speak to people at the deeper levels, they themselves must first have been spoken to. They themselves must bear the marks of what Frost called "an immortal wound."

> It is absurd to think that the only way to tell if a poem is lasting is to wait and see if it lasts. The right reader of a good poem can tell the moment it strikes him that he has taken an immortal wound—that he will never get over it.[4]

Literature can convey the good and the true in the guise of the beautiful. Like Jesus's parable of the Good Samaritan, beauty can get past our defenses and beguile

---

3. Moxon, *Commonitorium of Vincentius*, 10. (quod ubique, quod semper, quod ab omnibus creditum est)

4. Cox and Latham, *Selected Prose of Robert Frost*, 71.

us long enough to be changed and convicted, as it did with that lawyer who tried to justify himself by asking, "And who is my neighbor?" (Luke 10:25–37) It can speak truth to power as it did with Nathan's story to David of the rich man who took the poor man's sheep to feed his guests (2 Sam 12).

Literature can awaken a longing for what is truly good, that which was embodied perfectly in our Lord Jesus, but which also can be suggested or adumbrated in great works of fiction. It nourishes our sentiments. My wife and I have a friend in Bulgaria who is a brilliant English teacher and a wise believer in our Lord Jesus. She did her master's thesis on *The Lord of the Rings* by J. R. R. Tolkien. She told us how the story first captivated her when she was an adolescent. She was brought up under Communism and its version of reality. As she looked back on it, Tolkien's heroic romance awoke in her a desire for the goodness, truth, and beauty she read about in the fading kingdoms of Middle Earth. The tale served as a kind of proto-evangelium for her. When she came in contact with underground Christians as a teenager, her awakened desire met with the good news of Jesus Christ and she put her trust in him. Now, some twenty-five years later, she is a pillar in her church, and one of my most congenial interpreters when I go there to preach.

As I mentioned earlier, good books can help us as ministers take a Sabbath for our souls. They can help us to escape our situations, step outside of ourselves for a little while and recover strength, courage, and vision to continue. As Tolkien perspicaciously observed, those who don't want us to escape are the jailers![5]

During my recent convalescence from a broken leg and arm, as well as liver failure, I read *Gilead*, the Pulitzer Prize winning novel by Marilynne Robinson. It allowed me to step outside my misery for several hours at a time. I found myself on the prairie in a small town in Iowa called Gilead, reflecting on life with this old Congregational pastor and being awakened to the beauty of human existence and of life lived honestly in the fear of the Lord. The novel takes the form of an older pastor writing an extended letter to his young son. He knows he does not have long to live and he wants to pass on what is most meaningful to his son by leaving him this testimony, which he may read when he is old enough to comprehend it. Having been a pastor for many years myself, I could relate sympathetically to the record John Ames was leaving for his boy. But Robinson has the gift of making this character speak to many kinds of people. I doubt there are many pastors on the Pulitzer Prize committee, but evidently they discerned the novel's appeal was universal enough to speak to many kinds of readers.

I have never been on the prairie. I've seen it in movies and read about it in other books, but Robinson made me feel like I had grown up there and lived my whole life there. Her book was that evocative. I do know what the pastorate can be like, so that aspect was meaningful to me, but it was no new revelation. However, I wonder if those who've never been close to the family of a pastor, or perhaps have never even been to church, would nevertheless partake of Robinson's gift in this novel and understand

---

5. Tolkien, *Tree and Leaf*, 60.

what being a pastor involves, the same way I felt like I knew the prairie, even though I had never been there? Listen to C. S. Lewis on this matter:

> Literature enlarges our being by admitting us to experiences not our own. They may be beautiful, terrible, awe-inspiring, exhilarating, pathetic, comic, or merely piquant. Literature gives the entrée to them all. Those of us who have been true readers all our life seldom realize the enormous extension of our being that we owe to authors. We realize it best when we talk with an unliterary friend. He may be full of goodness and good sense but he inhabits a tiny world. In it, we should be suffocated. My own eyes are not enough for me . . . In reading great literature I become a thousand men and yet remain myself. Like the night sky in a Greek poem, I see with a thousand eyes, but it is still I who see. Here, as in worship, in love, in moral action, and in knowing, I transcend myself: and am never more myself than when I do.[6]

Maya Angelou gives an example of this power of a piece of great literature to lift a person out of herself. As a young girl she experienced a great trauma and then became mute to all but her younger brother. A perceptive neighbor used great books, such as *A Tale of Two Cities*, to lift her out of herself.

> I have tried often to search behind the sophistication of years for the enchantment I so easily found in those gifts. The essence escapes but the aura remains. To be allowed, no, invited, into the private lives of strangers, and to share their joys and fears, was a chance to exchange the Southern bitter wormwood for a cup of mead with Beowulf or a cup of hot tea and milk with Oliver Twist. When I said aloud, "It is a far, far better thing that I do, than I have ever done . . ." tears of love filled my eyes at my selflessness.[7]

Eugene H. Peterson has used literature to teach spiritual theology. In his course in spirituality he had his students write reviews of *Middlemarch* (George Eliot), *The Power and the Glory* (Graham Greene), and *The Book of the Dun Cow* (Walter Wangerin). He uses these works of literature to quicken his students' imaginations.

> The importance of poetry and novels is that Christian life involves the use of the imagination. After all, we are dealing with the invisible. And, imagination is our training in dealing with the invisible, making connections, looking for plot and character. I don't want to do away with or denigrate theology or exegesis, but our primary allies in this business are the artists. I want literature to be on par with those other things. They need to be brought in as full partners in this whole business. The arts reflect where we live: we live in narrative; we live in story. We don't live as exegetes.[8]

---

6. Lewis, *An Experiment in Criticism*, 140–41.
7. Angelou, *I Know Why the Caged Bird Sings*, 98.
8. Cusick, "A Conversation with Eugene Peterson," 4.

When Alexandr Solzhenitsyn was awarded the Nobel Prize for Literature in 1970, he was forced to reflect on the nature of literature in his acceptance speech. He would have much rather cut to the chase and have spoken directly about the social and political problems of Russia.[9] But instead he had to write about writing, whereby he left us with a rare and wonderful insight based on that phrase in Dostoyevsky's *The Idiot*, "beauty will save the world."[10]

In his Nobel lecture, Solzhenitsyn contrasts the flow of words pumped out by the Soviet media of his day which, while seeming smooth, plausible, and correct for a while to some, had no staying power, had no backbone of truth to give it substance. I am reminded of the insight of a friend of mine on the nature of the flood with which the dragon seeks to drown the woman in Revelation 12. Thirty years ago, before the pervasiveness of computers, Steve Wilber said, "That flood coming out of the dragon's mouth is *information*." And now, truly we are living in days when we are inundated with all kinds of information—we live in the information age. Solzhenitsyn asserted that great literature had the power to transcend that flow of words and images, which seek to drown us or at least, dilute the truth.

> Works steeped in truth and presenting it to us vividly alive will take hold of us, will attract us to themselves with great power—and no one, ever, even in a later age, will presume to negate them. And so perhaps that old trinity of Truth, Good, and Beauty is not just the formal outworn formula it used to seem to us during our heady, materialistic youth. If the crests of these three trees join together, as the explorers and investigators used to affirm, and if the too obvious and too straight branches of Truth and Good are crushed or amputated and cannot reach the light—yet perhaps the whimsical, unpredictable, unexpected branches of Beauty will make their way through and soar up TO THAT VERY PLACE and in this way perform the work of all three.
>
> *And in that case it was not a slip of the tongue for Dostoyevsky to say that "Beauty will save the world," but a prophecy. After all he was given the gift of seeing much; he was extraordinarily illumined.*
>
> And consequently perhaps art, literature, can in actual fact help the world of today.[11]

As Christians, we know that Jesus saves the world. "God so loved the world that he gave his only begotten Son" (John 3:16). What Jesus did at the cross was good; it was beautiful. Out of that place of cruelty, ugliness, and insane tragedy, Christ wrested our everlasting redemption and rose again the third day, sealing forever the happy end to the too often sad story of our world. And now the beauty of the Lord can be seen in the secret places of our private devotion and good works, the public places of our corporate

---

9. Scammell, *Solzhenitsyn*, 723.
10. Dostoyevsky, *The Idiot*, 543.
11. Solzhenitsyn, *The Nobel Lecture on Literature*, 6–7.

worship and service, and perhaps most of all, in the familiar places of our families and our friends. And I haven't even mentioned all that we could behold in creation, from the sunrise stealing upon us to the Pileated Woodpecker calling in the trees. But also in the temple of this whole creation, we can behold the beauty of the Lord, sometimes in the most unlikely places because the earth is the Lord's and the fullness thereof, not only by virtue of creation but also by virtue of redemption.

We ministers of the gospel need all the help we can get, not only to express the inexpressible beauty of the Lord, but also to be open to be nourished and awakened by the various ways which that glory, that beauty can come to us. Prayer, study, and reflection in the Scriptures, all the various ways we learn how to love people both within and without our families, churches, communities, and nations—all the various ways in which the Spirit leads us into loving our Lord—thank God for these ways within him who is the Way. I'm not as radical as Peterson; I'm not proposing two years of literature before we ever get started with theology in seminary. But let us not despise the blessing that a great work of fiction can be, at least for some of us. A good book could be the thing that keeps us from drowning.

Psalm 90 bears the superscription, "A prayer of Moses the man of God." Amid the relentless decay and demise of everything and everyone, he longs for that which is eternal, that which is beautiful. Don't we all? I will close this essay with a poem based on this psalm, which I wrote for Advent and Christmas. In the poem I quote from the English version of the French Carol, "Bring a Torch, Jeanette, Isabella." I found that the first stanza from this carol, already imbedded in our culture, served as a unit of vocabulary that helped me convey the point of the poem.

### From Wrath to Beauty

Lord, you have been our dwelling place
through every generation that has existed on this globe.
And what were you like before creation?
Before the mountains were heaved up into the sky
or this planet was formed,
you were who you were and are.
From everlasting to everlasting you have existed
in the beauty of your holiness and love,
in the glory of all that you were before the world was,
all that you will be, beyond the unfolding renewal of the world.

We, by contrast, have for so long been under this regime of finitude,
of the silent working of endings,
forever withering what was blooming,
bringing death to the living, loss to the loving. . .
And those who learned the ropes of this regime of wrath

taught us how to number our days
and live wisely while we yet lived.

But we ask you, O God, like Moses your friend has asked you—
to relent, to turn, to repent.
There must be something more than the prudent expenditure
of the time that we have.
The fact that we return to dust
is in itself a reminder of the original prediction.
Life passes so quickly and evanescently that, dreamlike,
we dissolve into the primary elements at the end.
The forward push of time
plows like a ship through the ocean of our existence.
And what is left in its wake,
but the closing waves of the sea of things as they were and always are?
Not only our lifetimes, but the centuries and the millennia
pass like the watches of the night itself.
We come and go . . .
And is this all there is?

Satisfy us, nourish us,
sustain us with that which is truly substantial—
even consubstantial with the Father and the Holy Ghost:
Your unfailing love, your covenant loyalty,
your merciful faithfulness, your faithful mercy—
that we may sing and have joy amid the relentless return to dust.

May the beauty of the Lord rest upon us . . .
the beauty which was with the Father and the Holy Spirit,
that glory, beauty, favor,
that incalculable grace which brings death to death,
subverts the regime of wrath, abrogates it
and supplants it with the nature and character of Jesus:
the glory of his centrally eccentric love for us—
his love for us dust-bound glimpses of human hope and yearning—
longing for something permanent,
something beyond the dust, something after it and before it—
*that* which is from everlasting to everlasting.

Let the beauty of the Lord, let his favor rest upon us—
yes!—that beauty that dwells at the Father's side,
the glory of the Only-Begotten
who came when shepherds were abiding in the fields,

> keeping watch over their flocks by night.
> And did this watch in the night seem like a thousand years
> or the day that had just gone by?
> And did we hear the heavenly hosts singing,
> Glory to God in the highest,
> and on earth (where wrath had reigned) peace
> to us on whom his favor (oh so unmerited!) now rested?
> Let the beauty of the Lord rest upon us!
>
> *Bring a torch, Jeanette, Isabella! Bring a torch, to the cradle run!*
> *It is Jesus, good folk of the village, Christ is born and Mary's calling,*
> *Ah! Ah! Beautiful is the Mother! Ah! Ah! Beautiful is her Son.*
>
> Arise, shine, for your Light has come;
> and the Glory, the Beauty of the Lord, has risen upon you![12]

## Bibliography

Angelou, Maya. *I Know Why the Caged Bird Sings*. New York: Random House, 1969.

Cox, Hyde, and Edward Connery Latham, eds. *Selected Prose of Robert Frost*. New York: Collier, 1968.

Cusick, Michael J. "A Conversation with Eugene Peterson." *Mars Hill Review* 3 (1995) 73–90. http://www.leaderu.com/marshill/mhr03/peter1.html

Dostoyevsky, Fyodor. *The Idiot*. Translated by Henry and Olga Carlisle. New York: Penguin, 1969.

Lewis, C. S. *An Experiment in Criticism*. Cambridge: Cambridge University Press, 1961.

Moxon, Reginald Stewart. *The Commonitorium of Vincentius of Lerins*. Cambridge: Cambridge University Press, 1915.

Robinson, Marilynne. *Gilead*. New York: Farrar, Straus & Giroux, 2004.

Solzhenitsyn, Aleksandr I. *The Nobel Lecture on Literature*. Trans. Thomas P. Whitney. New York: Harper & Row, 1972.

Scammell, Michael. *Solzhenitsyn: A Biography*. New York: Norton, 1984.

Tolkien, J. R. R. *Tree and Leaf*. Boston: Houghton Mifflin, 1965.

Worth, Thomas Ryder. *The Incarnation: Twenty-five Poems for Advent on the Word Made Flesh*. McAllen, TX: Evangalliance Publications, 2018.

---

12. Worth, *The Incarnation*, 55–57.

# 24

## Strong *Nabû*: The Form and Meaning of an Ancient Mesopotamian Prayer

— Joel H. Hunt[1]

Of the myriad Mesopotamian tablets, there are about one hundred brief Akkadian ritual prayers which bear the Sumerian rubric ŠU.ÍL.LA (Akkadian *šuilla*). This means "lifted hand" and indicates the posture of prayer. These texts are similar to biblical penitential psalms in their structure and outlook. This study is dedicated to one šuilla prayer addressed to Nabû, the patron god of scribes.

Generally speaking, *šuilla* prayers have a tripartite framework:

1. Address/Hymn—Praise with traditional titles and statements.
2. Request—Petitions regarding sickness, enemies, death, etc.
3. Thanks—Promise of future praise, service, or testimony.

Nabû 1 massages the request section of the basic tripartite outline to create a five-part prayer.[2] The hymnic introduction, lines 1–10, constitutes half of this *šuilla*, and is our major concern. These initial lines focus on Nabû's character, his word, and his ability to reconcile angry deities.

The petition section, lines 11–18, consists of three components: a description of the worshiper's righteous activity over time (lines 11–12), a complaint regarding the destruction of the sufferer's life (lines 13–16), and the petition proper (lines 17–18).

The closing praise (line 19) follows traditional models. The supplicant looks to the future and pledges continued praise of the deity. Nabû 1 reads:[3]

---

1. Since Paul Livermore was my first Hebrew teacher and instilled in me a love of the ancient Near East, I contribute this paper on a Babylonian psalm to Nabû, the god of the scribal arts. It seems appropriate for a volume honoring an educator of Paul's stature.

2. Mayer has edited this prayer in *Untersuchungen zur Formensprache der babylonischen "Gebetsbeschwörungen,"* 469–72. We will use his edition as the basis of our discussion.

3. The numbering of the text, Nabû 1, follows the work of Werner Mayer, *UFBG*. The square brackets [. . .] indicate breaks on the tablet. Where possible, we have supplied material from parallel passages.

1. [Strong Nabû], Legitimate Heir,
2. [Who holds] the stylus, Who opens understanding,
3. [. . .], Who collates years,
4. [Who saves] life, who repays,
5. [Foremost] of the gods, Honored Name.
6. The father, his creator, does not alter his command,
7. Tutu does not alter the command of Nabû his son.
8. Among the gods, his twins, his word is supreme.
9. He whose god was furious, you turn his neck,
10. He whose Fate is angry, you reconcile with him.
11. From my youth, with fidgets, I prayed here,
12. I am (now) old, to all gods my palms are open.
13. In my contrition my life is demolished,
14. Before humanity I am as in a tempest.
15. My days have gone away, My years have come to an end.
16. I did not see good, Benefit I did not have.
17. Legitimate [Heir], Strong Nabû,
18. [I besought you] with prayers, Show me the light!
19. Your greatness let me proclaim, Your fame let me praise!

## Hymnic Introduction

The prayer begins with ten lines of praise to Nabû. The following chart presents the transcribed Akkadian text, an English translation, and the structure of the hymn. We will treat the three stanzas in turn to understand how the poem communicates about Nabû.

| | | |
|---|---|---|
| 1. | [ÉN ᵈAG *gešr*]*u aplu kēnu* <br> [Firstborn Nabû], Legitimate Heir, | |
| 2. | [*ṣābit*] *qan ṭuppi pētû ḫasīssi* <br> [Who holds] the stylus, Who opens understanding, | Nabû's Character |
| 3. | [xxx].MEŠ *bārû šanāti* <br> [. . .], Who collates years, | |

4. [nāṣir] napišti mutēr gimilli
   [Who saves] life, who repays,                            Nabû's
5. [ašarēd] ilāni šumu kabtu                                Character
   [Foremost] of the gods, Honored Name.

6. zikiršu ul enni abu bānûšu
   The father, his creator, does not alter his command,

7. ᵈTU.TU ul enni zikir ᵈAG mārīšu                          Nabû's
   Tutu does not alter the command of Nabû his son.        Word

8. ina ilāni māšīšu amassu ṣīrat
   among the gods, his twins, his word is supreme.

9. ša ilšu isbusu tusaḫḫar kišāssu
   He whose god was furious, you turn his neck,
                                                           Nabû's
                                                           Reconciliation
10. ša zenât šīmtušu tusallam ittīšu
    He whose Fate is angry, you reconcile with him.

## Nabû's Character

This hymnic introduction, lines 1–10, breaks into three distinct stanzas on the basis of content and grammar. Noun Phrase (NP) statements dominate the first half of the hymn. This style contrasts with the sentences (S) of lines 6–10. In light of this grammatical alteration and their topical unity, we group lines 1–5 together as stanza one. These statements are more static than the verbal sentences encountered later in the hymn. The poet uses stylized terminology and common epithets of Nabû. Of course, this use of traditional titles is a boon for the modern interpreter attempting to reconstruct the initial word in the first five lines.

The shift away from NP statements to more complex sentences signals a break in the poem at line 6 and the focus in stanza two becomes more distant than in stanza one.

Additionally, the topic changes at line 6. Tutu, Nabû's father, becomes prominent. In this period the divine name (DN) Tutu was an alternative name for Marduk. Though Nabû remains in the spotlight and his word has authority, the poet communicates something regarding Nabû's rank among the gods vis-à-vis Tutu.

A final shift in both topic and grammar separates stanza two, lines 6–8, from stanza three, lines 9–10. Lines 9–10, which contain second person verbs that call directly to the deity, portray Nabû as both a willing and a capable advocate for human beings affected by the anger of their personal god or goddess. Significantly, these affirmations adjoin the complaint and request section.

| 1a. | NP | 1b. | NP |
|---|---|---|---|
| 2a. | NP | 2b. | NP |
| 3a. | [NP?] | 3b. | NP |
| 4a. | NP | 4b. | NP |
| 5a. | NP | 5b. | NP |
| 6. | S | Third Person Verb | |
| 7. | S | Third Person Verb | |
| 8. | S | Third Person Suffix | |
| 9. | S | Second Person Verb | |
| 10. | S | Second Person Verb | |

*Line 1 [$^d$AG geš r]u aplu kēnu; [Strong Nabû], Legitimate Heir*

INITIAL TERM

The first epithet of this hymn is broken. However, we suggest that line 1a spoke of Nabû in a fashion parallel to line 17, and introduced the deity by name.[4] In light of line 17, we have reconstructed [$^d$AG gešr]u. The chiastic recurrence of these terms in both the first line of the hymn and at the transition to the request proper forms an envelope and binds these materials together. Additionally, this restoration produces a three-fold repetition of the divine name AG to begin the *šuilla* (line 1), to connect the second stanza of the hymn to the first after a major grammatical shift (line 7), and to introduce the petition proper (line 17). Repetition is a common divider in Ancient Near Eastern texts and the Bible.[5]

SUCCESSION

After asserting Nabû's strength, the text shifts to recognize that Nabû's fortunes were intimately connected to those of his father Marduk. Line 1b expresses Nabû's relationship to Marduk. Pomponio proposed that Nabû was a god native to Syria in the III Millennium BC who was carried to Babylonia when the Amorites settled there. The Babylonian priests resolved the problem of the relationship between Marduk and

---

4. For a complete study of the history and character of the god Nabû, see Pomponio, *Nabû*.
5. Watson, *Classical Hebrew Poetry*, 26, 274–82.

Nabû by making the latter the scribe and minister of the former. When Marduk, assimilated to Asalluḫi, became firstborn offspring of Ea and was introduced into the pantheon of Eridu, Nabû followed him. Pomponio refers to the work of Thorkild Jacobsen who suggested that Marduk, "storm son," and the motif of a battle between the sea and the storm were originally at home along the Mediterranean coast and then brought to Babylon with the Amorites.[6] Despite Nabû's importance to the supplicant, he appears here in connection to his father.[7] But Nabû is not simply the first born of Marduk, he is the only legitimate heir of Marduk. Kēnu, when used with IBILA (aplu), expresses the idea of a legitimate heir within a man's household.

Nabû 1, 1b suggests royal succession, a concept not unknown in mythological contexts. For example, succession is an issue in Marduk's rise to power as described by *Enūma eliš*. In the later Babylonian period Nabû ascends the throne of the gods. As Oates writes:

> During the Ist millennium BC Nabu was popularized to such an extent (probably by the scribes themselves!) that at times he appears to rival Marduk and may indeed have been on the point of supplanting his father as supreme deity in the mythology.[8]

Pomponio attributes this rise in Nabû's fortunes to two factors and pushes the beginning of Nabû's rise into the II Millennium. First, the increasing prestige of Marduk in Babylonian religion must have produced a proportional re-evaluation of the entirety of his divine court, including the stature of Nabû, Marduk's scribe and minister. Second, the growing demand for scribes within the increasing administration in Babylonia, which began with the reign of Hammurabi (1792–1750), must have contributed to the increase of Nabû's importance.[9]

This *šuilla* hymn may reflect Nabû's accession over other deities in general and over Marduk in particular. Certainly, the *šuilla* originated within the circle of Nabû's devotees, so it is not surprising to find this high view of Nabû.

Babylon exerted cultural dominance even at the peak of Assyrian power. At both Nimrud and Khorsabad the largest temple was dedicated to Nabû. His worship was popularized by Semiramis and her son Adad-nirari III (810–783). The temple façade was decorated not in Assyrian styles but with individual insets of Babylonian fashion.[10] Pomponio briefly summarizes the evidence regarding the vicissitudes of Nabû's cult in Assyria, noting that the name of the god starts to appear in Assyrian onomastica of the 14–13th centuries. In the reign of Shamanesser I (1274–1245), the

---

6. Pomponio, *Nabû*, 237; Jacobsen, "The Battle Between Marduk and Tiamat," 105–8.

7. Regarding the slow movement of a deity from a subordinate within the palace to the supreme ruler, see Abusch's discussion of the changing roles of Marduk as presented by *BMS* 9 in "The Form and Meaning of a Babylonian Prayer to Marduk," 5.

8. Oates, *Babylon*, 172.

9. Pomponio, *Nabû*, 238.

10. Oates, *Babylon*, 126.

first sanctuary of Nabû in Assur is constructed. With Assurnasirpal II (883–859) and, especially, with Adad-nirari III (810–783), the number of the temples of the god in Assyria increases. In the royal inscriptions, beginning with those of Sargon II (721–705), Nabû begins to be cited among the protectors of the sovereign.[11]

Pomponio also notes that the massive presence of citations of the god in the inscriptions of Esarhaddon (680–669) and Assurbanipal (668–627?) and in the benediction formulae of contemporaneous letters, the erection of the temples in his honor in the cities of Kalah and Khorsabad and the important sanctuaries in Nineveh and Assur, his preeminence in the onomastica in Kalah, Balawat and Nineveh, and the religious politics of the final Assyrian sovereigns, Aššur-etel-ilāni (626?–623?) and Sin-šarra-iškun (622?–612), demonstrate that Nabû reached the apex of the Assyrian pantheon. This extraordinary increase of Nabû's cult in Assyria may have contributed to an increase in its prestige in Babylonia itself, especially in the comparisons with Marduk.[12] These worshipers present him as the powerful and legitimate heir of his father Marduk. Line 1b focuses on Nabû's legitimate claim to the throne. By line 5 the poem expands the image and presents Nabû's fitness for this role. He is most supreme among the gods.

*Line 2. [ṣābit] qan ṣuppi pētû ṣasīssi; [Who holds] the Stylus, Who Opens Understanding*

SCRIBE

Line 2 of the hymn turns to an area of Nabû's expertise. This one line presents two essential characteristics of Nabû. First, in texts covering over two and a half millennia, Nabû is the scribe god and patron of writing. Secondly, Nabû is a god of wisdom and knowledge, a characteristic he shared with the two principle divinities of the pantheon of Eridu and Babylon: Ea and Marduk.[13] The text specifies that Nabû is god of a significant, specialized knowledge, namely, the scribal arts. The poet begins to enlarge the portrait of Nabû in the middle portion of the first stanza through the use of traditional epithets. These titles are appropriate for the deity's role beyond his family relationships. Nabû bears his well-known emblem as ṣābit qan ṭuppi, "the one who holds the stylus."[14]

---

11. Pomponio, *Nabû*, 241–2.
12. Oates, *Babylon*, 126; Pomponio, *Nabû*, 241–2.
13. Pomponio, *Nabû*, 177–88.
14. Pomponio, in *Nabû* (181), notes Nabû's link with the materials necessary for the scribal art. Particularly, Nabû handles the stylus used to write on tablets.

## Wisdom Giver

Since Nabû's pedigree includes the wise gods Ea and Marduk, it is not surprising that he is *pētû ḫasīssi*.[15] In general, this phrase describes a person who is "open-minded," "open with respect to understanding," or "wise."[16]

The use of active participles throughout the first stanza argues in favor of a more active meaning of *pētû ḫasīssi*. These terms denote the bestowal of wisdom by the deity on another. The deity opens up another individual's ability to understand and to act. One sees this usage in an Esarhaddon text, which uses a finite verbal form: *ana uddus ilāni rabûti iptû ḫasīsī*, "they gave me understanding for the repairing of the (statues of the) great gods."[17]

*Line 3 [xxx].MEŠ[18] bārû šanāti; [. . .], Who Collates Years*

### Reconstruction of 3a

The second half of this line focuses on Nabû's ability to deal with time. We suggest that this middle line of stanza one, despite its fragmentary state, forms the heart of the *šuilla* hymn. If this reconstruction is accurate, this affirmation relates directly to the complaint section of the *šuilla*. Nabû looks over the passage of time, just as the discouraged supplicant will in line 15. Nabû observes the movement of days and years. Since this hymn introduces a protest and prayer, we assume that the poet believed that Nabû could bring meaning back to the life of a discouraged elderly person (line 12).

The term *bārû* in 3b suggests that the parallel term in 3a ought to relate to the idea of the priest or diviner, just as we have supplied "days" to parallel "years." Any of the words *āšipu, asû*, or the common Ea, Marduk, Nabû term *apkallu*, would provide a fitting parallel to *bārû šanāti*, "diviner of years," therefore, we suggest the synonymous concept "seer/sage of days." We recognize the tenuousness of this suggestion and await the discovery of another tablet of this *šuilla* to provide illumination.

### Collator

The affirmation of line 3, [xxx].MEŠ *bārû šanāti*, is significant for the *šuilla* as a whole. Seux's interpretation of the title as expressing Nabû's role as the guardian of the calendar is unconvincing, or at least incomplete. His idea does not adequately link the epithet to the *šuilla*.[19]

---

15. We are using the term "wisdom" to refer to the deity's acumen and skill.
16. For example, *CAD*, Ḫ (127) notes the phrase *pēt ḫasissi*, "wise" throughout Sargon II inscriptions.
17. *CAD*, Ḫ (127) refers to *BA* 3 289: 21.
18. Text B of line 3a preserves the only the plural marker MEŠ in the first half of the line.
19. Seux, *Hymnes*, 301, no. 3.

The title suggests more than the notion that Nabû notes the passage of time or helps to establish the regular rhythm of time's movement. Šamaš, the sun deity, is more suited to this view of calendrical observation. In a prayer dealing with the evaluation of one's life, however, it seems reasonable that the poet would go beyond asserting that Nabû marks the passage of time. A stronger affirmation is that Nabû notes the days and years of his devotees for their benefit. We suggest here that a fitting parallel to the motif in 3b would be some notion of the observation of days in 3a. Line 15 of the complaint section of the šuilla strengthens this idea since it describes the supplicant's own evaluation of days and years (*ittatlakū ūmīya iqtatâ šanātū'a*). It would make sense for the poet to address the deity with statements applicable to this evaluation by the disheartened soul. Nabû's identity as the divine scribe also supports our suggestion of his careful inspection of the times of his devotees.

Despite the well-known use of *bārû* as "diviner" from the Old Babylonian period onward, another use of the verb *barû* provides an analogy for its use here. *Barû* denotes the collating of a tablet to verify that everything that should have been written on a tablet has been written. This occurs, for instance, in Assurbanipal colophons. At the end of the tablet copied, the scribe wrote: *tikip santakki mala bašmu ina ṭuppāni asniq abrêma*, "I wrote down on tablets all the cuneiform signs (and) I collated carefully." This use of *barû* may clarify what is taking place in Nabû 1, 3. Nabû, the *ṣābit qan ṭuppi* of line 2, is like an expert scribe checking an inscribed clay tablet. He is the deity who checks the days of his followers to know how they are inscribed.[20]

*Line 4. [nāṣir] napišti mutēr gimilli; [Who saves] Life, Who Repays*

RECONSTRUCTION OF 4A

The fourth verse of this first stanza lauds Nabû's ability to reward people. Since the beginning of this line is broken, we must rely upon similar Nabû texts to supply appropriate epithets in the initial position. A participial form of a term such as *eṭēru*, *gamālu*, *naṣāru*, *šalāmu*, or *šūzubu* would affirm Nabû's ability to spare a person's life.[21] Nabû 3 reads *nāṣiru napišti andul dadmī ēṭir* (KAR) *nišī*, "(Nabu) protector of life, who shelters the human dwellings, who saves the people,"[22] and facilitates the suggested restoration of *nāṣir*. Regardless of the word restored, the concept seems clear: Nabû safeguards the lives of those who trust him.[23]

---

20. This understanding may be reflected in Mayer's "der die Jahre überprüft" in *UFBG* (471), but we are not sure that Mayer makes the connection between scribal collation and divine oversight.

21. For possible terms, see Mullo Weir, *A Lexicon of Accadian Prayers*, 235; see also Seux, *Hymnes*, 301, no. 4.

22. *BMS* 22: 6b–7 (= Nabû 3).

23. Mayer, *UFBG*, 469, 4 (1).

PART 3: EXPLORATION AND REFLECTIONS—THEOLOGICAL AND OTHERWISE

REPAYER

Line 4b can be understood in two mutually exclusive ways. Due to the possible *double entendre* of this phrase, we have translated *mutēr gimilli* by the neutral "one who repays." This epithet may connote either the wreaking of vengeance, or the returning of a kindness.

*Mutēr gimilli* may refer to one who avenges the wrong done to another.[24] CAD provides several examples from Enūma eliš of the idea "avenger" in reference to Nabû's father, Marduk.[25] These citations strengthen the supposition that one should understand Nabû 1, 4b as referring to Nabû's performance as a deity who works on the behalf of wronged people.

The rewarder, the *mutēr gimilli*, returns to another person what that person deserves. If the person has been kind, the deity responds with favor. If the person was unkind, perhaps seeking vengeance improperly, then the deity makes the person suffer punishment. According to Nabû 1, 4b, Nabû, the god who protects the life of his worshipers, provides the merited return. The supplicant will return to this question of getting what is deserved when evaluating life in lines 11–16.

*Line 5 [ašarēd] ilāni šumu kabtu; [Foremost] of the gods, Honored Name*

This climactic line of stanza one affirms Nabû's supremacy over all deities. He is the leader and one honored by the other gods. This concept of supremacy will be elucidated in the next stanza as the poet describes the nature of Nabû's lordship over divinities. Nabû has a powerful word that cannot be countermanded.

Line 5a is difficult. Out of several possible restorations, we follow Mayer's restoration of *ašarēd*, "foremost."[26] This suggestion makes sense since one may assume that the text affirms Nabû's supremacy over other divinities.

The second half of this verse, *šumu kabtu*, represents a slight modification of a common Nabû epithet, *šumu ṭābu* "good name."[27] The phrase *šumu kabtu* occurs in royal contexts as an affirmation of the monarch's power. Thus the substitution of *kabtu* for *ṭābu* makes sense since this verse details Nabû's chief rank among the deities. The Sumerian of *šumu kabtu* would be MU.DUGUD. This construction sounds similar to the abbreviated MU.DU$_{10}$.GA = *šumu ṭābu*. Perhaps in recitation, at some early phase of the text's history, a scribe heard MU.DUGUD instead of MU.DU$_{10}$.GA. The mistaken writer would thus create a new title for Nabû. However, instead of attributing

24. For example, *CAD*, G (73) notes the bilingual reference ad.a.ni šu.gar.ra gá: *mutīr gimillu abīšu*, "the avenger of his father" (*BA* 5 642: 5f.).
25. *CAD*, M/2, 299.
26. Mayer, *UFBG*, 469.
27. Seux noted, in *Hymnes* (152, n. 30), that *šumu ṭābu* is the Akkadian equivalent of an abbreviation of a Sumerian name of Nabû dmu–du10–ga–sa4–a (mu–du10–ga = *šumu ṭābu* "good name" and sa4–a = *nabû* "to name").

the unusual *šumu kabtu* to a scribal hearing error, one might suggest that a clever scribe maximized the homophonous relationship existing between MU.DU$_{10}$.GA and MU DUGUD to form an epithet affirming Nabû's royal stature.

*Summary*

The lines that frame this initial stanza, lines 1 and 5, place Nabû in the realm of other deities. The image develops from an initial view of Nabû as the strong son of Marduk (line 1) to a broader view of Nabû's prominence on the heavenly plane (line 5). Nabû has become superior to his erstwhile peers, and they honor his name.

Nabû's Word

The hymn shifts in lines 6–8 to an active perspective. The text changes from a static conception of Nabû's character and position to third person address regarding Nabû's actions.

A theme change in stanza two accompanies the grammatical alteration from stanza one. The poem initially affirms the person and nature of Nabû through a series of epithets. This view changes, in a manner similar to other *šuilla* prayers, to a description of the abilities of the deity. Here, instead of describing the deity's provision of food[28] or life,[29] the poet proclaims the prominence of the deity's word that none can countermand.[30] The text presents a twist to this theme, however, since Nabû is not totally supreme. Nabû's word reigns supreme among his former peers. But one god, Nabû's own father, potentially could reverse his pronouncements. Pomponio asserts that despite the rise in Nabû's popularity over time, Nabû never completely displaced Marduk, the deity to whom he was most intimately tied. There may be some clues to support the notion that Nabû's ascent developed in opposition to the god of Babylonia, for example, the gradual process of the transference of the Ezida of Borsippa from the cult of Marduk to that of Nabû. However, while Nabû may have risen to a rank alongside Marduk, he does not appear to have supplanted his father.[31] Nabû 1, 6–8 reflects this theology. Nabû has authority to command other deities, yet Marduk retains some measure of veto power.

Both father and son appear in more active capacities in stanza two than in stanza one. Stanza two moves from a static description of Nabû to a description of the deity in relation to others. The image of Marduk grows in stanza two as well. Stanza one alluded to Marduk as the unnamed father of the son and heir of line 1. Stanza two

---

28. See, Ea 1a, 35–36, Marduk 1, 5–9.
29. See, Ea 1a, 5.
30. See, Marduk 1, 2c: *ša lā uštamsaku ēpiš pīšu*, "the one whose order is not revoked."
31. Pomponio, *Nabû*, 161–5, 237–43.

sharpens the focus on Marduk. He is the father of Nabû and the one deity who might exercise power in support of or in opposition to his son's leadership.

## Nabû's Word and Nabû's Father

Line 6: *zikiršu ul enni abu bānûšu*; The father, his creator, does not alter his command.
Line 7: ᵈTU.TU *ul enni zikir* ᵈAG *mārīšu*; Tutu does not alter the command of Nabû his son.

The first two lines of stanza two express the continuing relationship of Nabû to his father Marduk. Lines 6–7, essentially identical in thought, vary in syntax and structure. The poet moves from a general statement in line 6 to a more specific affirmation in line 7.

## Zikru

Despite the grammatical and thematic changes noted above, the initial ambiguity of the word *zikru* in line 6 forms a link between stanzas one and two. Since *zikru* may refer to the name of a person or deity, it may be construed as a synonym for *šumu*. For example, in *Enūma eliš*, a text renowned for denominating dynamics, one reads, *likūnma annû zikiršu*, "May this name of his endure;"[32] and *ina zikri ḫanšā ilū rabûti ḫanšā šumīšu imbû*, "With the name, 'Fifty,' the great gods had given him his fifty names."[33]

The context of this *šuilla* prayer, however, clarifies that one should interpret *zikru* according to its general usage and not according to its more restricted sense. Clearly the poet intends the definition "word, command" in the second stanza. But the poet has juxtaposed the terms *zikru* and *šumu*. This juxtaposition connects stanza two to the preceding stanza and pushes the thought forward to the affirmation about Nabû's authority.

Biblical literature witnesses to the close affinity between *zakar/zikru* and *šem/šumu*. Generally, Akkadian contrasts with the other Semitic tongues with regard to the meaning of *zkr*. In Akkadian, the root *zkr* means "say, name," while *zkr* in the other languages indicates the more specific idea "remembering." Some biblical texts use *zakar* and *šem* in similar ways, especially when *zkr* connotes "memory." For instance, Proverbs 10:7 provides a perfect parallel between *zakar/zikru* and *šem/šumu*: "The memory (*zakar*) of the righteous is a blessing, but the name (*šem*) of the wicked will rot." This kind of biblical reference illuminates the close connection between the terms in lines 5–8 of this Nabû hymn. As both the Akkadian and biblical evidence shows, one could expect a meaning for *zikru* in line 6 that parallels *šumu* in line 5.[34]

---

32. *EE* VII, 54.

33. *EE* VII, 143; see also *ša* MUL.KAK.SI.SA: *ina šamê zikiršu*, *JRAS* Cent. Supp. pl. 2: 12.

34. For a discussion of this notion, with additional references, see Botterweck and Ringgren,

## Structure

Line 6 introduces the main idea and line 7 adds a "what's more" element.[35] Both lines contain the negated verb ul enni. The poet enhances the remaining terms in line 6 with a corresponding expression in line 7 in the following ways:

1. The poem replaces the general subject *abu*, "father" in line 6 with the more specific divine name ᵈTU.TU, in line 7. The divine name ᵈTU.TU forms a link between Nabû and Marduk.[36] ᵈTU.TU is one of Marduk's many names,[37] and praise to Marduk, as ᵈTU.TU, in *Enūma eliš* VII 9-34 shows that ᵈTU.TU expresses Marduk's creative capabilities.[38]

2. In both lines 6 and 7 the base of the object is the term *zikir*-, "command." The specifying *rectum* bound to the *regens* provides the variation. In line 6, the less specific *zikiršu*, "his command," anticipates the specific statement *zikir* ᵈAG, "Nabû's command," in line 7.

3. Finally, the poet shifts focus from the Begetter to the Begotten with the change from *bānûšu* in line 6 to *mārīšu* in line 7. These words clarify the relationship between ᵈTU.TU and Nabû. In line 6 *bānûšu* expands *abu*. In line 7 *mārīšu* further specifies the name ᵈAG.[39]

The major point of these two lines is that the firmness of Nabû's command rests on the will of Marduk.[40] Marduk declares the immutability of his son's pronouncements.

---

*Theological Dictionary of the Old Testament*, s.v. "Zakar" by H. Eising.

35. Kugel, *The Idea of Biblical Poetry*, 8.

36. *CH* III 10-15 reads, *na-ra-am* TU.TU *mu-ri-iš* uruBar-sí-páki *na-a'-du-um la mu-up-pa-ar-ku-ú-um a-na* É.ZI.DA, "beloved of Tutu, the one who brings joy to Borsippa, the devout one, who does not neglect Ezida." Pomponio, in *Nabû* (16, n. 8 and 17), believes that Tutu in Codex Hammurabi refers to Marduk. Furthermore, Pomponio deduces that Tutu, in OB and in the following periods, constituted a name of Marduk, which was occasionally employed in texts of the I Millennium to designate also Nabû, son of the god of Babylon.

37. See *EE* VII 9, 15, 19, 25, 33; *CT* 24: 27, 30a; *CT* 25: 34 II 18 13c; *KAV* 63 III 35.

38. In *Enūma Eliš* VII, 9-34, Marduk as dTU.TU accompanies other appellatives affirming Marduk's creativity. These four names are dZi.ukkin.na (VII 15-18), dZi.kù (VII 19-24), dAga.kù (VII 25-32), and dTu6.kù. These lines affirm Marduk's creativity in providing shrines for the deities, giving peace to the gods, achieving pre-eminence in the divine assembly, inspiring humanity, upholding purification, producing riches and abundance, turning scarcity into plenty, reviving the dying, showing mercy to the captured gods, creating humankind, and uprooting all the wicked with his pure incantation.

39. Additionally, the elements of lines 6 and 7 are arranged in reverse order. These elements are: a = *zikir* + *rectum*; b = the repeated *ul enni*; c = references to Marduk (*abu* and dTU.TU); and d = the appositional elements *bānûšu* and *mārīšu*.

40. Other texts affirm Marduk or other gods as possessing an unchangeable word. *CAD*, E (173) provides some examples: (Marduk) *ša amat qibītīšu mamman lā innû*, "whose word, once spoken, nobody can reverse . . ." (*AMT* 93, 3: 5). Note also (Šamaš) *ša annašu ilu mamman lā ennû*, "whose mercy no god has ever annulled" (*BMS* 60: 8); (Ninurta) *ša ina puḫur ilāni zikiršu ilu mamma* BAL-*ú*, "whose word none of the gods can reverse in the divine assembly," (*AKA* 257: 9); (Ninurta) *ša lā enû*

The term *mārīšu* is significant for the ideas of stanza two, though it may seem superfluous at first. This second stanza contains three important allegiance words bound to the suffix *–šu*. The words *bānûšu*, "his begetter," *mārīšu*, "his son," and *māšīšu*, "his twins," express significant relationships for Nabû, relationships in which Nabû is not the superior party. For the purposes of the hymn, these once significant affiliations recede into the background. Nabû no longer submits to his father's authority completely. Nabû has exceeded his former peers, they are no longer in the same league.[41]

## Nabû's Word and Nabû's Twins

This closing line of stanza two expands the horizon of the first two verses in an important respect. To do this, the poem affirms:

Line 8 *in a ilāni māšīšu amassu ṣīrat*; Among the gods, his twins, his word is supreme.

Whereas lines 6–7 deal with Nabû's word in relationship to his father Marduk, line 8 declares that his word carries weight among other divinities. Line 8 expresses the climax of stanza two and Marduk's establishment of his legitimate heir's command. Nabû's word is not overturned by his father or by anyone else. His utterance reigns supreme among the gods. The poem places these other gods in a subordinate position because of Nabû's powerful word. As in Assyrian practice, Marduk sets up his son as crown prince to ensure a successful transition of power.

## Māšīšu

*Māšīšu*, "his twins," joins the other relational words in lines 6–8, *abu*, *bānûšu*, and *mārīšu*, to bind these lines together.[42] "His twins" expresses a sibling or coequal relationship, and perhaps a past rivalry, between Nabû and unspecified deities.

The word *māšīšu*, "his twins," indicates the hymn's belief in Nabû's accession above divinities once his peers. As crown prince, a position suggested by the hymn's beginning (1b), Nabû surpasses all other deities as the proper heir to Marduk's throne. This hypothesis fits the general tenor of the hymn's exaltation of Nabû[43] and is in

---

*qibīt pīšu*, "who has never changed his word," (AKA 256 i 4); *ša lā enû milikšu*, (AKA 256 i 7); *ina qibītīšu ša lā eni balāssu liqbi*, "may (DN) decree life for him with his word that is not to be reversed," (Šurpu IV 90); *ina purussīšu ša lā enî*, (Streck, Asb. 180: 21); (Marduk) *kēnat amassu lā enât qibīssu šīt pīšu lā uštēpel ilu ayumma*, "his word is true, his command cannot be changed, no god shall change his word," (EE VII, 151).

41. The word *mārīšu* also forms a sound link to the term *māšīšu* of line 8 to help bind this stanza together.

42. This understanding of the term *māššīšu* is shared by a variety of interpreters, including Ebeling, AGH (11), "seinen Geschwistern," CAD, M/1 (402), "his twin brothers," Mayer, UFBG (471), "seinen göttlichen Brüdern," and Seux, Hymnes (301), "les dieux ses pairs."

43. Nabû 6, 10 provides additional support for this interpretation. In this complementary text

consonance with the general ideological thrust of *šuilla* hymns, since these texts exalt the deity addressed to the highest realms of the pantheon.[44]

Stanza two asserts that Nabû has ascended completely over other deities, with one significant exception. Nabû's command carries weight with other divinities, but Nabû remains in a somewhat subordinate role to his father Marduk.[45]

This poetic narrative of stanza two reflects Nabû's ascent, which is known to have occurred in Mesopotamian theology. Just as in the larger theological shift, stanza two recognizes that though Nabû may command former peers, he does not supplant his father. Marduk retains the right to countermand Nabû.[46]

Nabû's Reconciliation

After lauding the power of Nabû's word in stanza two, stanza three (lines 9–10) turns to the irresistible nature of Nabû's command. This stanza affirms the effectiveness of Nabû's divine will in human existence. Nabû can command the angry personal deities of a suffering supplicant to relent and Nabû's word is obeyed by offended deities for the benefit of Nabû's worshipers. Lines 9–10 affirm:

Line 9. *ša ilšu isbusu tusaḫḫar kišāssu*; He whose god was furious, you turn his neck,

Line 10. *ša zenât šīmtušu tusallam ittišu*; He whose Fate is angry, you reconcile with him.

Topical and grammatical alterations together distinguish stanza three, lines 9–10, from stanza two, lines 6–8. Stanza three directly addresses Nabû. This change

---

three main deities listen to Nabû's word (*zikru!*). For the text of Nabû 6, 10, see Mayer, "Sechs Šu-ila-Gebete," 462–463: *ša* ᵈAnu ᵈEllil *u* ᵈEa *šemû zikiršu*, "auf dessen Wort Anu, Ellil und Ea lauschen."

44. The resultant restructuring of the pantheon may or may not appear in other texts. In the case of Nabû 1, this suggestion is also consistent with broader theological movements. Nabû ascended over all deities and almost supplanted his father Marduk. See Pomponio, *Nabû*, 161–5 and 237–43.

45. One might contrast here *BMS* 9 and *EE*, texts in which Marduk successfully emerges from the household of his parents to assume total divine authority. For *BMS* 9, see Abusch, "Form and Meaning." One could still wonder whether the suffix–*šu* of *amassu* refers to Marduk instead of Nabû. We have chosen the later since this prayer is directed to Nabû, but the former is a possibility given Marduk's veto power.

46. Royal succession language resonates in the terminology of line 1, line 6, *abu bānûšu*, and the movement of stanza two. This fits with what we have said. Note these examples selected from *CAD*, B, 94: *abu bānûa ina puḫur aḫḫēya rēšīya kiniš ullīma*, "the father who engendered me formally raised my rank in the presence of all my brothers" (Borger, Esarh. 40 i 10 and *passim* in Esarh.); RN AD *ba-nu-u-a* (Streck, Asb. 6 i 54, and *passim* in Asb.); note RN AD AD DÙ–*ia* (ibid. 38 iv 71); Sargon AD AD AD DÙ–*ia* "my own great-grandfather (Thompson Esarh. pl. 17 v 39 (Asb.)); RN *šar Bābili a-ba ba-nu-u-a*, "Nabopolassar, king of Babylon, my own father." (*VAB* 4 136 vii 48 and *passim* in Nbk). Apparently this phrase is not commonly used for deities. Note Šamaš *u* Ištar . . . *ana* Sin *a-bi ba-ni-šu-nu*, (*VAB* 4 224 ii 41), *seebīt* Sin *a-bi ba-ni-šu-un*, (ibid. 31 (Nbn.)), also *ina maḫar* Aššur *abi ba-ni-ki*, (Streck, Asb. 190: 16).

to second person expressions, *tusaḫḫar* and *tusallam*, anticipates the call for action in subsequent sections of the *šuilla*. Lines 9–10 focus on Nabû's concern for the supplicant. The complaint, lines 11–16, alleges that the person has suffered a bad fate. Lines 17–18 do not request explicitly that Nabû should turn the protective deities toward the supplicant in favor, but this notion underlies the sufferer's plight.

Initial parallel relative phrases separate lines 9–10 from the preceding sentences. These relatives identify the problem: the sufferer experiences the wrath of angry personal divinities. After this statement of divine anger, second person D stem verbs declare Nabû's gracious activity. Though the personal god or goddess is angry, Nabû restores peace. The following arrangement shows the pattern of lines 9 and 10:

| Line 9  | Ša | ilšu  | isbusu  | tusaḫḫar | kišāssu |
| Line 10 | Ša | zenât | šīmtušu | tusallam | ittišu  |

## The Relative Phrases

As shown above, lines 9 and 10 begin with relative ša and a statement of divine anger describing an abstract problem that forms the background to the immediate issues of the supplicant. The lines reverse word order after ša. Line 9 has DINGIR + -*šu* followed by a G preterit subjunctive verb. Line 10 reverses this order: the offended goddess, designated by NAM, follows the G stative verb.[47]

Words expressing the anger of the personal deities are commonly used for this purpose. For instance, *š/sabāsu*, especially in the stative, describes gods or goddesses angry with their followers.

There are several examples of the use of these terms within the corpus of the šuilla prayers. For example, Ellil 1b includes both terms and a request for peace.

> *libbi iliya u ištariya zenûti šabsūti u kummulūti*
> *ša ittiya zenû šabsū u kamlū*
> *libbi ilūtika rabīti ittiya sullimamma*

> "The angry, furious and wrathful heart of my god and my goddess,
> which are angry, furious and wrathful with me,
> (and) the heart of your great divinity, reconcile to me!"

The term *šīmtu*, "fate," of Nabû 1, 10 replaces the word *ištaru*, "goddess," which parallels *ilu*, "god," in other texts. This replacement occurs occasionally in contexts where one would expect *ištaru*.[48]

---

47. Text B, 37 has the variant [. . .] dNAM.MEŠ–*šú*. We prefer the singular dNAM to parallel *ilšu* of line 9.

48. Oppenheim, *Ancient Mesopotamia*, 201–6; Zimmern, "Šimat, Sīma, Tyche, Manīt," 574–7.

Besides recognizing this alternation, we must determine the significance of the substitution of *šīmtu* for the more common *ištaru* in this *šuilla*. The terms *ištaru* and *šīmtu* are intertwined, with *šīmtu* displaying a more comprehensive connotation than the common English translation "fate" communicates.⁴⁹ The movement in making a *šīmtu* (*šīmta šâmu*) progresses from an authority to a subordinate, a movement that holds true in our text. Certainly, the goddess is greater than the suffering supplicant.

A further use of the term *šīmtu* is important for this *šuilla* text, especially with regard to the prayer's later evaluation of the quality of the supplicant's life. Šīmtu may indicate the "share" of the vicissitudes of life allotted to each person.⁵⁰ The use of *šīmtu* unites the two main dimensions of human existence—personality and death. The divinities predetermine the substance and span of an individual's life. In this regard, the *isqu*, "lot," and the *uṣurtu*, "blueprint," are ancillary and supporting notions to the *šīmtu*.⁵¹ Ultimately, the interchangeability of the terms *ištaru* and *šīmtu* may be attributed to the function of "the manifestation called ištaru and, sometimes, *šīmtu*, to be the mythological, personified representation and the carrier of the *šīmtu* of the individual that was to materialize in his 'history' from his birth to his death."⁵²

This is a plausible explanation for the substitution of *šīmtu* for *ištaru* in the Nabû 1 *šuilla*.⁵³ Especially in light of the complaint section (11–16), where the text relates that the petitioner's personal history has disturbed the petitioner and motivated the prayer. The sufferer assumes the hand of the *ištaru*/*šīmtu* behind the bad *šīmtu*

---

49. Note Oppenheim's extended excursus on the intertwining of these terms. In *Ancient Mesopotamia* (201–202), he writes, "Customarily, *šīmtu* is translated by the Assyriologist as 'destiny' or 'fate,' a translation that is inexact and misleading, since the two English words are endowed with connotations alien to the Akkadian term. Quite generally speaking, *šīmtu* denotes a disposition originating from an agency endowed with power to act and to dispose, such as the deity, the king, or any individual may do, acting under specific conditions and for specific purposes. Such a disposition confers in a mysterious way privileges, executive powers, rights, and—when originating from a deity—even qualities (attributes), upon other gods, persons, and objects, deriving its effectiveness solely from the power and the right of disposition inherent in the acting agency. Thus the gods endow the king with strength, superior intelligence, good health, and success; thus the king assigns income and offerings to the sanctuaries, pastures to cities, and executive power to the administrators of his realm; and thus the private citizen disposes of his property to his sons and heirs. All this is done by making a *šīmtu* (*šīmta šâmu*)."

50. Oppenheim, in *Ancient Mesopotamia* (202), writes, "In certain religious contexts, however, the establishing of the *šīmtu* refers typically to the specific act through which each man is allotted—evidently at birth, although this is nowhere stated explicitly—an individual and definite share of fortune and misfortune. This share determines the entire direction and temper of his life. Consequently, the length of his days and the nature and sequence of the events that are allotted to the individual are thought of as being determined by an act of an unnamed power that has established his šīmtu. It is in the nature of the *šīmtu*, the individual 'share,' that its realization is a necessity, not a possibility."

51. Oppenheim, *Ancient Mesopotamia*, 204.

52. Oppenheim, *Ancient Mesopotamia*, 205.

53. The reason for this substitution may vary in other texts where one expects *ištaru* paired with *ilu*. It may be shown to be a simple variant and not related to ideas of fate and life experience as we find in Nabû 1.

experienced. The seeker bids Nabû to check over the tablets of individual destiny and cause the angry "Fate" to recast life's lot.

Beyond connecting the goddess to the supplicant's life experience, this idea is meaningful in view of the theological tenet of Nabû as collator of the supplicant's life. The person begs Nabû, scribe of the deities, to change the *šīmtu* of the sufferer's life. The sufferer hopes that the setting of life's course can be altered so that it is not as negative as it currently appears. Since this bad fate resulted ostensibly from an angry god or goddess, perhaps Nabû, the *ṣābit qan ṭuppi*, can change this inscribing of fate.

### The Verbs

Though stanza three recognizes divine anger, the verbs of lines 9–10 express hope. Nabû asserts his power and turns the angry god toward the sufferer and pacifies the furious goddess.

In line 10 the petitioner asks Nabû to bring a state of peace (*tusallam*) between the sufferer and the one directly responsible for the unfortunate life experiences. The term *salāmu* is common in prayers seeking reconciliation with an angry deity. For example, note the imperative of *salāmu* in Ninurta 4, 19:

> *sullimamma ittiya ilu u ištau zenûti*
>
> "Reconcile with me angry god and goddess."

Nabû 1, 10, in the spirit and style of a hymn of praise, uses the indicative form instead of the imperative or precative that would fit the petition section. The hymn declares that Nabû does reconcile angry deities with their worshipers.

*Tusaḫḫar* (line 9) parallels *tusallam* (line 10). The hymn avers that Nabû is the superior deity who can change the mind of the personal god angry with a human being.[54]

### The Final Elements

Lines 9–10 both end with a word bound to the suffix -*šu*. The referent indicated by the suffix differs. For the purposes of a prayer for help, the -*šu* suffix of line 10 is more significant than its parallel member in 9. The -*šu* of line 9 refers to the angry god. In line 10 "him" refers to the supplicant, not to the deity. This shifts the focus slightly to the human member of the equation just prior to the complaint and request where the human being comes into focus.

---

54. The idiom *suḫḫuru kišādu* indicates turning toward someone in favor. Cee, Seux, *Hymnes*, 301, n. 8; *CAD*, S, 50; *CAD*, K, 446; *AHw*, 1007; *ZA* 61, 58: 188.

*Conclusion*

We have suggested the following progression for the hymn. Stanza one praised Nabû using traditional titles from Nabû's repertoire in a somewhat distant and stilted fashion. Stanza two focused on the unrivaled power of Nabû's word, focusing on Nabû's superiority to other deities by means of sentences referring to Nabû in the third person. Stanza three, which precedes the complaint and request for assistance, dealt with Nabû's ability to speak a word of reconciliation and addresses Nabû in the second person, as if the supplicant gained access into the presence of the deity. The command of this supreme deity pacifies a god and goddess angry with a sufferer.

As in other hymns, the power of the deity's word forms the core of this poem. However, this šuilla contains an unusual element. Nabû 1 does not exalt Nabû completely over all other divinities. The poem elevates Nabû as crown prince to the throne of his father. Within the boundaries of the hymn, Nabû does not emerge fully from his father's shadow. Marduk assures that his son's word is unrivaled.

Nabû's conditional supremacy enables him to command other deities to become beneficent toward humans feeling abandoned or persecuted by their personal god or goddess. Nabû's dominion gives the supplicant the confidence needed to offer the complaint and requests that follow with the expectation that life may become brighter.[55]

Petition Section

The supplicant approaches as an older person of longstanding faith in the gods. However, this one has found that life has not been kind. The worshiper asserts an ardent piety since youth (line 11), but this faith has seemingly failed in later years. The supplicant of Nabû 1 feels as though life is over and that its final evaluation is negative. The sufferer wonders what has gone awry and whether or not Nabû will bring good.

Though despondent, this supplicant does not give up hope of salvation. The offering of renewed praise to Nabû and an appeal for illumination in lines 17–18, attest to this spirit of hope. The supplicant asks Nabû to shatter the confusing darkness with light.

*Action of Supplicant*

Lines 11–12 describe the supplicant's past and present piety. This short section, placed between the hymn and the complaint, describes the activity of prayer. The description of acts of supplication compares with Marduk 28, 5, where the supplicant describes

---

55. For other examples of the final hymnic statement(s) describing the deity in terms appropriate to introduce the petitions, note Ea 1a, 13; Marduk 4, 2; Marduk 18, 3b; Marduk 28, 3; and Nabû 3, 7–8.

approaching the deity with a *šigû*, a praise, or with Marduk 18, 8–9, which describes bringing a libation.

Nabû 1, 11–12, however, contrasts other texts in an important respect. In those cases, the description of the petitioner's activity follows the complaint.[56] Here, in Nabû 1, 11–12, the supplicant presents a pattern of praying before complaining. This self-description of past and present devotion states:

> Line 11 *ina meṣḫarūtiya mašišūti usappâ*; From my youth, with fidgets, I prayed here,
>
> Line 12 *šēbāku ana kal ilāni petâ upnāya*; I am (now) old, to all gods my palms are open.

Line 11 focuses on the worshiper's past history of devotion. The person maintains that even as a youth, *ina meṣḫarūtiya*, there was a desire to pray. Youth is not viewed here as an excuse for sins of ignorance.[57] Rather, in Nabû 1, 11, the focus is the supplicant's activities of devotion while still young. *Suppû* expresses the call to the deity.[58]

Mašišūtu

The term *mašišūtu* of line 11 is challenging. There are three possible understandings of this word:

1. The writing *ma-ši-šu-ti/e* might be incorrect. It has been conjectured that the text should read *ina meṣḫarūtijama* EŠ$_4$.DAR-*ti/e usappâ*.[59] It is not clear how this reading arises from the text.[60] This interpretation seems to be based on positing some opposition between service to one god versus worship of the whole pantheon.[61]

2. In *AGH*, E. Ebeling translated *mašišūti* as "die Glänzenden," apparently relating *mašišūti* to the verb *mašāšu* "to wipe, polish."[62] Mayer follows this suggestion, interpreting *mašišūti* as an adverbial accusative of state from *\*mšš*, "abwischen," translated

---

56. Regarding complaints in these prayers, see Mayer, *UFBG*, 67–208.

57. Cee, Marduk 4, 18: *ša meṣḫiriš idû lā idû mišima*, "Forgive known and unknown of childhood and..."

58. Mayer, in *UFBG* (132), does not list this text as an example in his discussion of the term. We have interpreted the verb *usappâ* as the D preterite of *suppû*, which makes sense in the past focus of line 11. The final *–â* results from the combination of the expected /i/ theme vowel of the preterite and an appended ventive /a/. The supplicant has returned to the site of many prayers since the days of childhood. This reading is apparently accepted by *CAD*, M/2 (37), which has *usappâ*, and translates, "in my youth I prayed to Ištar," reading EŠ4-DAR-*ti* for our *mašišūtu*.

59. *CAD*, M/2, 37.

60. One could opt to leave this term untranslated, so Seux, *Hymnes*, 302, "Dans ma jeunesse j'ai prié..."

61. van der Toorn, *Sin and Sanction*, 209, n. 22.

62. Ebeling, *AGH*, 11.

as, "In meiner Jugend pflegte ich in gereinigten Zustand (?) zu beten."[63] Mayer and Ebeling focus on the polished or purified state of the supplicant. These interpretations look at the result of the polishing process.[64] It is not clear whether these translators intend this state as some kind of youthful innocence and purity that contrasts with youthful ignorance and perversity.

3. K. van der Toorn offers an intriguing alternative, one that looks to the process, not the product, of polishing. In his discussion of youth as an extenuating circumstance of an ignorant sinner's life, van der Toorn draws attention to the contrast between adolescence and maturity as a literary topic. He cites Nabû 1 and suggests that it "seems to stress the inability for prolonged concentration of youthful worshippers."[65]

Van der Toorn points to the work of K. Deller and K. Watanabe.[66] In contrast to Ebeling and Mayer, Deller and Watanabe understand *mšš to refer to the action of polishing and not the end result.[67] This fits with the description of praying as an activity of the worshiper. The action of the young devotee's hands that suggests a wiping or burnishing motion may indicate worry over the dire straits of the sufferer.

Van der Toorn sees this motion in another light, because of his focus on the peculiar problems associated with immature devotion. With regard to *mašišūti*, he writes, "It refers to the restlessness of the adolescent, as contrasted with the sustained devotion of the grown-up." To clarify these observations and suggestions, he translates this section "In my youth I prayed with ever fidgety hands, now that I am old my palms are (steadily) opened to all the gods."[68] This is a fitting interpretation of the word mašišūti in the context of Nabû 1.

In contrast to the fidgety hands of line 11, line 12 depicts the steady action associated with a *šuilla*, "raised-hand," prayer. The intent of *petâ upnāya*, "my palms are open," is more specific than the alternative *qātē našû*, "hands are raised." The petitioner approaches the divinity with unclenched palms, which may indicate both the emptiness of the supplicant's situation and the expectation of a gift from the divine helper.

Line 12 contrasts with and goes beyond the preceding line that described the suppliant's adolescent devotion. The present focus of the action in line 12 begins with the petitioner's self-description, "I am old." The supplicant draws attention not only to the passage of time, but also to a different kind of devotion. He asserts a continuity of

---

63. Mayer, *UFBG*, 472.

64. As we have suggested, these lines reflect the action of the supplicant. Mayer views lines 13–16 as a complaint unit, but we are unsure how he views the function of lines 11–12. Perhaps by focusing on the product of *mašāšu*, Mayer did not consider that lines 11–12 describe the petitioner's act of praying.

65. van der Toorn, *Sin and Sanction*, 96.

66. Deller and Watanabe, "*šukkulu(m)*, *šakkulu*," 216–8.

67. Deller and Watanabe, "*šukkulu(m)*, *šakkulu*," 217, point to Madānu 1, 24 to support this motion. That line reads: lim-ma-ši gíl-la-ti. They translate this half verse as something such as "wipe away my sin" instead of the more generic "forgive my sin."

68. Van der Toorn, *Sin and Sanction*, 209, n. 22.

## PART 3: EXPLORATION AND REFLECTIONS—THEOLOGICAL AND OTHERWISE

worship, but with development in the areas of steadiness of attention to the deity and expectation of grace.[69]

*Complaint*

Before offering the plea, the petitioner describes the melancholy lot in life that "Fate" has offered.[70]

Line 13. *ina lipin appiya takturu napištī*

Line 14. [*ina*] *pān amēlūti kīma meḫê anāku*

Line 15. *ittatlakū ūmīya iqtatâ šanātū'a*

Line 16. *ul āmur dumqa nēmelu lā arši*

The sufferer specifies no disease or detractor, but complains generally about his lot.[71] Lines 13–16 present three, chiastically-arranged thought pairs. Line 15 forms the heart of this complaint. Life is over for the sufferer. Evaluations of the quality of this finished life frame line 15. We will evaluate each pair of complaints in turn.

| General Category | Specific Statement |
|---|---|
| Quality of Life | [13] "In my contrition my life is demolished, |
| | [14] Before humanity I am as in a tempest. |
| Duration of Life | [15] My days have gone away, |
| | My years have come to an end. |
| Quality of Life | [16] I did not see good, |
| | Benefit I did not have." |

### Pair One: Quality of Life

Pair one, lines 13–14, offers a harsh assessment of the suppliant's quality of life. His life is disturbed, even blown up. Pair one focuses on the present poor state of affairs in contrast to pair three, line 16, which looks at past misery.

---

69. The stative *petâ* helps to make this point. Whereas line 11 asserted, by use of the verb *usappâ*, that the petitioner prayed in past years, line 12 declares that the person waits expectantly and humbly at that moment with open hands. The insertion of "now" at the beginning of line 12 is appropriate.

70. One exemplar, *STT* 55, 39, shows that the text logically breaks after the description of the supplicant's action by adding these introductory words: *anāku* NENNI.A.NENNI *ardu pāliḫka*. This line allowed a petitioner to personalize the *šuilla*. The self-introductory formula clearly signals the beginning of the complaint and request sections.

71. Mayer, in *UFBG* (78), lists lines 13–16 under the appropriate heading "Klage über einen schlechten Allgemeinzustand."

The person's primary complaint in lines 13–14 is that his piety has not worked as expected. Instead of a life of comfort, the petitioner has received nothing but turbulence in return for years of reverence.

1. *Takturu*

We followed Seux and Mayer in reading *takturu* in line 13. Seux suggests a comparison with the phrase *ik-te-ru na-pi[š-ti]* in BWL 245, 47, "they endangered my life."[72] Mayer translates "[Bei/trotz] meinen Huldigen bin ich dem Tode nahegekommen."[73]

The sufferer evaluates his life as a mess. Specifically, he views his life as utterly destroyed as though a tidal wave crashed over it. The experience of a tempestuous life prompts the call to the deity.[74]

2. *Kīma meḫê*

In Nabû 1, 14 the overpowering waters are *meḫû*, "tempest," not *abūbu*, "flood," but the concept of destruction is identical. The metaphoric use of kīma meḫê describes either the one whose power overflows or the devastation of the one overwhelmed. In the first case, the king subjugates his enemies with unbridled victory. For instance, Esarhaddon writes that *kīma ezzi ṭīb meḫê assuḫ šurussum*, "like a raging *meḫû*-storm I tore up their roots."[75]

In the second sense, *kīma meḫê* describes the destruction of a party "as in a *meḫû*-storm." Mayer argues that the idiom *kīma meḫê* stands for *kīma ina meḫê*, and this clearly is the sense intended by *kīma meḫê* in Nabû 1, 14. The supplicant complains about being a victim, not a victor.

In Nabû 1, 13–14, despair is all that remains after the results of past and present devotion are washed away in the tempest of life. The sufferer believes that *ina lipin appiya*, "in my acts of contrition," a tidal wave of misfortune, not a spring of comfort,

---

72. Seux, *Hymnes*, 302, n. 14. See, also *AHw*, 452b, *karû*, G, 3.

73. Mayer, *UFBG*, 471.

74. We are not completely satisfied with the reading *tak–tu–ru*, despite the good sense of the resulting translation. The apparent shift in theme vowel, from i class to u, disturbs us. One wonders whether the u theme vowel of the term in Nabû 1, 13 denotes a hollow verb and not a final weak verb. We have considered another option, one that does not change the meaning suggested by Seux's comparison. Perhaps TAG TU RU stands for *šumturu*, a Š verbal adjective from the root *natāru*, arising through dissimilation of the first /t/ in *šutturu*. *Šutturu* connotes "to break up, demolish," an image more disheartening than that expressed by takturu. In particular it describes irresistible and destructive royal power. For instance: *šadê maršūti ašrī pašqūti ina akkullāti ušattirma*, "... with pickaxes I cut through difficult mountains, narrow places" (OIP 2 114:37). A Nabonidus text presents a particularly suggestive occurrence: *ušaḫrib māḫāzīšun ušattir abūbiš*, "(The king of the Ummanmanda) laid waste their cult cities and tore them down like the Deluge" (*VAB* 4 274 ii 30). The Nabonidus text unites two ideas, destruction and flood, presented in the thought pair of Nabû 1, 13–14. For additional passages, see *CAD* N/2, 117 and/or *AHw*, 766. A problem remains: one would expect the reading *šunturat* since *napištī* is feminine.

75. Borger, *Esarh.* 58 v 16; see *CAD*, M/2, 6 for other examples.

was the reward. The sufferer is not alone in this perception, for [*ina*] *pān amēlūti*, "before humanity," the destructive waters overflow.

Pair Two: Duration of Life

Pair two, the heart of the complaint section, communicates the supplicant's evaluation of life's passage. The first verb, *ittatlakū*, expresses a movement of separation. The supplicant's days have walked away. The second verb, *iqtatâ*, goes beyond the first communicating completeness. The image expands from part a to b with the change from UD.MEŠ-*ia*, "my days," which might indicate a short time span, to the more comprehensive MU.MEŠ-*ia*, "my years." By this second verse half, the point is not that days have passed away, but that years are over.

The poet's use of two perfect verbs significantly communicates the utter despair of the petitioner. From the perspective of the sufferer, life is already over. Of course, the existence of the *šuilla* itself indicates that this person exercises faith that this harsh evaluation is not the final word and that Nabû will act. The man brings his complaint to the deity who watches over days and years (line 3) believing that Nabû can and will renew both his life and meaning.[76]

Pair Three: Quality of Life

The final pair, line 16, returns to the quality of the petitioner's, ostensibly ended, life. Second of the framing statements, line 16 escalates the complaint of prior statements: life is not only currently tempestuous, it has always been an unprofitable existence.

By assessing the whole life of the sufferer, the closing pair of the complaint is more bleak than the initial statement. The first pair acknowledges that life was in turmoil when the supplicant called to Nabû. The final pair portrays a sorry summation. The sufferer maintains that not only are things bleak now, but that they have never been good. These statements of current (lines 13–14) and enduring (line 16) problems encircle the despairing declaration that life has ended for the supplicant (line 15).

*Petition Proper*

A renewed call to Nabû signals the end of the complaint and introduces the petition proper. The petitioner has lauded Nabû, described past and present piety, and complained about his circumstances. Finally, he asks Nabû to intervene.

Line 17. [*aplu*] *kēnu* ᵈAG *gešru*; Legitimate [Heir], Strong Nabû,

---

76. As noted by Benjamin R. Foster, old age and death can be tropes for penitents who have lost divine favor and the highest form of divine favor is shown in salvation from death. See "Letters and Literature," 98.

Line 18. [*aṣbat*] *sīpēka kullimmanni nūru*; [I besought you] with prayers, Show me the light!"

Line 17 closes the hymn and complaint sections and introduces the petition. If our reconstruction of line 1 is correct, and the prayer begins with the divine name plus an appellative, then the final NP of line 17, divine name plus an appellative, is significant. This construction strengthens the connection of line 17 to the preceding hymn and its separation from the request proper in line 18. Regardless of the accuracy of our reconstruction, the material of lines 1–17 forms the basis of the petitioner's cry for help.

"I HAVE PRAYED."

Line 18a, [*aṣbat*] *sīpēka*, "I besought you with prayers," continues the notion of the activity of prayer described in lines 11–12. Line 18a recalls a significant motif in the text, the petitioner's past and present approach to the deity in supplication.

As Mayer has suggested, the idiom [*aṣbat*] *sīpēka* appears identical with the idiomatic use of *ṣabāti* + *suppê*, "to beseech with prayers."[77] For example, Nebuchadnezzar II prays: ᵈMarduk *bēlīya utnēn suppêšu aṣbatma amat libbī ištene'u aqbiš*, "I prayed to Marduk, my lord, I besought him with prayers, I expressed to him whatever my heart wanted."[78] In Nabû 1, 18a the author has varied the spelling of this word for entreaty.

"SHOW ME THE LIGHT!"

The supplicant seeks enlightenment from Nabû in line 18b, the main thrust of the request. The A tablet reads *kul-lim-ma-an-ni* ZALÁG, the B text presents the variant *lu-mur nu-ú-ru*.

The first style of the idiom, the D imperative of *kullumu* plus *nūru*, occurs in literary prayer contexts. For instance, a lengthy Marduk prayer connects illumination to the needs of a person in jail: *ša ina bit ṣi-bit-ti na-du-ú tu-kal-lam nu-úr [ana] ḫi-is-sat* ᵈMarduk *ib-lu-ṭu ka-mu-te ul iš-ku-nu na-piš-tú*, "[The one] who is thrown into prison you show light. [At] the mention of Marduk those in fetters survive and do not give up the ghost."[79] The ideas of emancipation of prisoners is linked to illumination in an extended prayer to Ištar. The combined image appears to be of an inmate leaving a dark cell and entering into the first burst of new light: *[k]a-sa-a ú-ram-mi [-t]um ú-kal-lam nu-ú-ra*, "she releases the prisoner, she shows light."[80] Šurpu, which lists

77. Mayer, *UFBG*, 472.
78. *VAB* 4 122 i 52. The translation is from *CAD* Ṣ, 32.
79. Lambert, "Three Literary Prayers," 66: 8–9.
80. Lambert, "Three Literary Prayers," 54: 212–213.

## PART 3: EXPLORATION AND REFLECTIONS—THEOLOGICAL AND OTHERWISE

varied aspects of Marduk's authority, offers additional examples: *šá É ṣi-bit šu-ṣu-u* ZALÁG *kul-lu-mu*, "To set free the prisoner, to show (him) daylight . . ."[81] Another long prayer to Marduk provides a larger context for the phrase *kullumu* plus *nūru*. Marduk gives light to a person in a prison more binding than jail:[82]

> [*a-mir-šú*] *ina sūqi (sila) lit-t[a-'-i]d ilu-ut-ka*
> *dmarduk-ma mītu (lú.úš) bul-[luṭ i-l]i-' li-iz-zak-ru*
> *ù ar-du šá [. . .] x tag-me-lu-šu*
> *a-na kul-lat nišī m[eš li-šá-]pi nar-bi-ka*
> [*l*]*id-lul šá mi-tu-us[-su . . .] ú-kal-li-mu-šú nūra (zalág)*

> "May he who sees him in the street mark your divinity,
> Let them say to one another, 'Marduk is able to raise the dead'.
> As for the slave whom [. . .] you spared,
> Let him make [known] your greatness to all peoples.
> Let him praise the one, who, while he was dead, [. . .] showed him light."

This idiom occurs in negative contexts to describe a duty one has neglected. The phrase describes the deeds of the ill, and apparently guilty, person who has not reflected the character of the deity in daily life. In Šurpu II 29–31 this suffering person is the one:

> *ṣab-ta la ú-maš-ši-ru ka-sa-a la ú-ram-mu-u*
> *šá É ṣi-bit-ti la ú-kal-li-mu nu-ú-ru*
> *a-na ṣa-ab-ti ṣa-bat-su-ma a-na ka-si-i ku-us-si-šú-ma iq-bu-u*

> "who did not free a captive, did not release a man in bonds,
> who did not let the prisoner see the light (of day),
> who said to the captive: 'leave him captive!',
> to the man in bonds: 'bind him tighter!'"

The second style of the idiom, using *lûmur* as found in the B text, occurs elsewhere in contexts similar to those noted for *kullumu*. For instance, in Šurpu V–VI, 82: *ma-mit lit-ta-ṣi-ma a-na-ku* ZALÁG *lu-mur*, "may the oath leave so that I may see the light!"

Regardless of the reading chosen, and we have selected the urgency of the imperative, the meaning of the idiom remains the same.[83] The supplicant prays, "Show me the light," or "Let me see the light" in the sense of "Make me free!"

The idiom of making one see light in the sense of freeing a person mixes the image of an earthly prison and the ultimate penitentiary, death. In the first use of the

---

81. Šurpu IV 31.

82. Lambert, "Three Literary Prayers," 60: 183–187.

83. Both of these terms were also bound with the divine name to form proper names. See, for instance, <sup>d</sup>Šamaš–*nūra*–*kul*-*li*-*man*-*ni* in BE 14 99a:3 and, without *nūru*, <sup>d</sup>Nabû–*kal*-*lim*-*an*-*ni* ADD App. No. 1 i 36 and <sup>d</sup>Nabû–ZALÁG–*ka*-*lu*-*mur* in VAS 3 25:12.

phrase, the penitent desires freedom from darkness to enjoy light. In the second use, the prisoner looks to find and enjoy life itself.

The petitioner in Nabû 1 has suffered a terrible fate and is imprisoned in a chamber leading to death. Life is at an end (line 15). He seeks the help of a powerful and compassionate deity, one who can bring him out of prison and into the light of day. Nabû, described in the hymn as the "collator of years" (line 3) and the "one who saves" (line 4), is just such a deity. The supplicant seeks relief from a despairing, unfair life sentence. The prayer is that crown prince Nabû will commute this sentence.

### Final Praise

Line 19 ends the prayer with a common form of concluding praise.[84] The petitioner vows:

> narbîka lušāpî dalīlīka ludlul
>
> "Your greatness let me proclaim,
> Your fame let me praise!"

In this simple praise the supplicant looks beyond past and present privations to a time of vitality when praise is possible. Line 19 demonstrates confidence that Nabû will answer the petitioner's prayer for life.

## Concluding Remarks

### General

This *šuilla* hymn, lines 1–10, which lauds Nabû with traditional epithets and statements, reasonably fits the overall context of the prayer. There is a general unity of composition, though we would not want this evaluation misinterpreted. The text makes good sense as a whole. However, this observation does not prove that only one author or editor was responsible for the text. The ten-line hymn is quite lengthy for a short prayer of only nineteen lines.

On the basis of grammatical and topical shifts, the hymn breaks into three stanzas that flow together to form a meaningful picture. Stanza one, lines 1–5, describes Nabû's character. Stanza two, lines 6–8, affirms the priority of Nabû's command within the pantheon. Finally, stanza three, lines 9–10, reports how Nabû's regal authority functions for the benefit of a needy worshiper.

As we have seen, there are some interesting modifications in the hymnic introduction and elsewhere in the prayer that intensify the poignancy of the petition. Though Nabû 1 follows Kunstmann's basic outline, the text demands a different level

---

84. Mayer, in *UFBG* (322–5), indicates that *narbîka lušāpî* occurs 19 times and that *dalīlīka ludlul* occurs 24 times in the *šuilla* texts he studied.

of subdivision. Nabû 1 goes beyond the basic tripartite outline by adding a description of the supplicant's pious activity (11–12) and a developed complaint (13–16) to supplement the hymn (1–10), the petition (17–18), and the praise (19).

Theme

A dominant theme provides a unifying framework regarding the question of the relation of the hymn to the rest of the šuilla. The significant motifs of Nabû 1 cluster around general and specific notions of age and death. In the hymn, notably the ideas of Nabû as the one who rescues the perishing (4a) and the one who collates years (3b) link to this theme. Nabû, as the deity who can change the mind of Fate on behalf of a sufferer (10), is the god able to give new life to the dying soul.

The section detailing the supplicant's pious action recalls the theme of death as well. Lines 11–12 depict the passage of life from adolescence to older adulthood. The pious petitioner has gradually aged and is at the threshold of death.

The complaint, lines 13–16, enlarges the view of death as it describes the despair of a person whose life is over. This is not simply an elderly person in prayer, this is an individual without hope that life has had meaning or that it will continue.

The request highlights the theme of death through its plea, "Show me the light!" As noted above, this call unites the concepts of a literal jail and the final prison, death. Nabû, the one who collates the years, frees the sufferer in death's grasp.

## Bibliography

Abusch, T. "The Form and Meaning of a Babylonian Prayer to Marduk." *Journal of the American Oriental Society* 103 (1983) 3–15.
Bergmann, E. *Codex Hammurabi: Textus Primigenius*. Scripta Pontificii Instituti Biblici 51. Rome: Pontificum Institutum Biblicum, 1953.
Botterweck, G. Johannes, and Helmer Ringgren, eds. *Theological Dictionary of the Old Testament*. Vol. 4. Translated by David E. Green. Grand Rapids: Eerdmans, 1980.
Dalglish, Edward R. *Psalm Fifty-One in the Light of Ancient Near Eastern Patternism*. Leiden: Brill, 1962.
Deller, Karlheinz, and Kazuko Watanabe. "šukkulu(m), šakkulu, abwischen, auswischen." *Zeitschrift für Assyriologie* 70 (1981) 198–226.
Ebeling, Erich. *Die Akkadische Gebetsserie "Handerhebung."* Deutsche Akademie der Wissenschaften zu Berlin, Institut für Orientforschung 20. Berlin: Akademie-Verlag, 1953.
Foster, Benjamin R. "Letters and Literature: A Ghost's Entreaty." In *The Tablet and the Scroll: Near Eastern Studies in Honor of William W. Hallo*, edited by Mark E. Cohen et al., 98–102. Bethesda, MD: CDL, 1993.
Gelb, I. J., et al., eds. *The Assyrian Dictionary of the Oriental Institute of the University of Chicago*. Chicago: University of Chicago, 1956–2010.

Gurney, O. R., and J. J. Finkelstein. *The Sultantepe Tablets, I.* Occasional Publications of the British Institute of Archaeology at Ankara, No. 3. London: British Institute of Archaeology at Ankara, 1957.

Gurney, O.R., and P. Hulin. *The Sultantepe Tablets, II.* Occasional Publications of the British Institute of Archaeology at Ankara, No. 7. London: The British Institute of Archaeology at Ankara, 1964.

Hunt, J. H. *Mesopotamian Šuilla Prayers to Ea, Marduk, and Nabû.* Lewiston, NY: Mellen, 2010

Jacobsen, Thorkild. "The Battle between Marduk and Tiamat." *Journal of the American Oriental Society* 88 (1968) 105–8.

King, L. W. *Babylonian Magic and Sorcery.* London: Luzac, 1896.

Kugel, James L. *The Idea of Biblical Poetry. Parallelism and its History.* New Haven: Yale University Press, 1981.

Kunstmann, Walter C. *Die babylonische Gebetsbeschwörung.* Leipziger Semitische Studien, N.F. 2. Leipzig: Hinrichs, 1932.

Lambert, W. G. *Babylonian Creation Myths.* Mesopotamian Civilizations 16. Winona Lake, IN: Eisenbrauns, 2013.

———. "Three Literary Prayers of the Babylonians." *Archiv für Orientforschung* 19 (1960) 47–66.

Mayer, W. "Sechs Åu-ila-Gebete." *Orientalia* N.S. 59 (1990) 449–90.

———. *Šu-ila-Gebete. Supplement zu L.W. King, Babylonian Magic and Sorcery.* Alter Orient und Altes Testament 34. Verlag Butzon & Bercker; Neukirchen-Vluyn: Neukirchener Verlag, 1978.

———. *Untersuchungen zur Formensprache der babylonischen "Gebetsbeschwörungen."* Studia Pohl: Series Maior 5. Rome: Biblical Institute Press, 1976.

Mullo Weir, C. J. *A Lexicon of Accadian Prayers in the Rituals of Expiation.* Oxford: Oxford University Press, 1934.

Musée du Louvre. *Huitiéme Campagne de Sargon.* Textes Cuneiformes du Louvre 3. Paris: Guethner, 1912.

Oates, J. *Babylon.* Rev. ed. London: Thames & Hudson, 1986.

Oppenheim, A. Leo. *Ancient Mesopotamia: Portrait of a Dead Civilization.* Rev. ed. Chicago: University of Chicago Press, 1977.

Pomponio, F. *Nabû. Il culto e la figura di un dio del Pantheon babilonese ed assiro.* Studi Semitici 51. Roma: Istituto di Studi del Vicino Oriente, 1978.

Reiner, Erica. *Šurpu: A Collection of Sumerian and Akkadian Incantations.* Archiv für Orientforschung 11. Graz: Weidner, 1958.

Seux, M.-J. *Hymnes et Prieres aux Dieux de Babylonie et d'Assyrie.* Litteratures Anciennes du Proche-Orient 8. Paris: Cerf, 1976.

Tallqvist, K. *Akkadische Götterepitheta.* Studia Orientalia 7. Helsingforsiae: Societas Orientalis Fennica, 1938. Repr., Hildesheim/New York: Olms, 1974.

van der Toorn, Karel. *Sin and Sanction in Israel and Mesopotamia: A Comparative Study.* Studia Semitica Neerlandica 22. Assen: Van Gorcum, 1985.

von Soden, W. *Akkadisches Handwörterbuch.* Wiesbaden: Harrassowitz, 1959–81.

Watson, W. G. E. *Classical Hebrew Poetry. A Guide to its Techniques.* Journal for the Study of the Old Testament Supplement Series 26. Sheffield: JSOT Press, 1986.

Zimmern, H. "Šimat, Sīma, Tyche, Manīt." *Islamica* 2 (1926–27) 574–77.

# 25

## Is Pastoral Visitation a Thing of the Past?

— Donald N. Bastian

During the first decade of the twentieth century a young immigrant couple settled in a shallow valley three miles south of the prairie town of Estevan, Saskatchewan. But the vast sweep of bald, rolling prairies was so different from the village the young woman had left behind in England, and the family and friends back home were at such a distance that she fell into a homesickness so deep she thought she would die.

Church was not a part of the couple's life but in a desperate effort to help his wife, the husband suggested they go to church. On the next Sunday morning they hitched up horse and buggy and drove to town. The pastor of the church they visited returned the visit to their homestead during the following week, but it seemed to them like a formality. They sensed in his call no real heart for them. They were immigrants. The same thing happened after attending another church the following Sunday.

On a third Sunday they went to a little white clapboard-sided church in town, a new building that had "Free Methodist" on its sign. After a day or two the pastor turned up at their homestead. He found them working in the garden. When the young English woman offered to make a cup of tea he accepted readily and followed them into their home, something the previous visitors had not had time for.

That pastor's visit made a connection that led eventually to the young woman's conversion, the couple's incorporation into a church family and a long-enduring Christian bond that passed to the next generation and beyond. The immigrant couple were my parents-to-be long before I was born.

In recent times, pastoral visitation has been somewhat set aside or diminished as a duty of the local church leader. Pastors are too busy, it is reasoned. Homes are not as open as they once were in less sophisticated times. Other modes of carrying out the pastoral task have been advanced. One well-placed leader confessed to another pastor that he never made hospital calls on parishioners. Some have wanted to be CEOs managing the church more as a business leader would.

Even so, pastoral visitation carried out faithfully can still be a significant element in the overall task of pastoring. So our thoughts begin with that down-to-earth title—pastor. It is one of many titles used in the Bible for church leaders (apostles, bishops, prophets, elders, etc.). Along with the other offices, pastors were persons God had gifted with a charisma to be used in service to the church. They were to build up the body of Christ bringing it to maturity (Eph 4:11–13). It was a sweeping and trusted assignment!

The title, pastor, may or may not be the most common leadership title used in the Bible. But it clearly stands for the minister of a local church and is in common use in churches to the very present. In the life of the church the pastoral assignment is both pivotal and fundamental.

Across church history, pastoral assignments have been repeatedly given. Pastors were to proclaim the word of God and teach the people over whom they had oversight the meaning and practice of the gospel in everyday life. They were to promote church order. They were to "do the work of an evangelist"—reaching beyond established borders with the gospel. Theirs was the task of shepherding a flock of the people of God.

One important aspect of pastoral care is pastoral visitation. That's what the pastor was doing when he drove his buggy three miles to my parent's homestead and went into their modest home to develop a Christ-motivated acquaintance with them. Visitation is a fundamental element in the pastoral task, done in the home, the hospital, the counseling room, and wherever human need can be carefully and thoughtfully isolated and addressed. The term, pastor, is honorable, and pastoral visitation fruitful.

The word, pastor, deserves further examination. It means shepherd, one who cares for God's people much as shepherds care for their sheep. Shepherds know their sheep by name and the sheep are attuned to the voices of their own shepherds. Shepherds attend to their flock's needs for food, water, and pasture; they protect them from predators, and heal their bruises. The relationship is close and bonding.

The shepherding motif is common in Scriptures. Moses was raised in an Egyptian ruler's palace, but was later called to the service of God after a long period of time during which he worked for his father-in-law as a shepherd in the lonely reaches of Midian. David, Israel's second king, was providentially moved in stages from the menial task of caring for his father's sheep to becoming king over Israel.

Later, when Ezekiel spoke forth God's words both of judgment and promise to the leaders of an exiled people he used the motif of the shepherd. He rebuked the leaders of Israel for living off the flock rather than caring for the sheep with diligence. In doing so he set forth the duties of Israel's spiritual shepherds—to strengthen the weak, heal the sick, bind up the injured, bring back the strays, and search for the lost (Ezek 34:1–4). In that metaphor he was really referring to people in various stages of need.

The Sovereign Lord's strong rebuke to the selfish and inattentive shepherds flows then into God's resolution: "I myself will search for my sheep and look after them" (Ezek 34:11).[1] Think of it, the Shepherd God—he who elsewhere is called the Creator of All, the Lord of Hosts, the Judge of all the earth, the Almighty—would nevertheless

---

1. All Bible translations are NIV.

walk among his people wherever they were and tend to their needs as shepherds tend to the needs of the sheep they love.

That promise of the Sovereign Lord to walk among his people was fulfilled in Jesus. He was God in human form. He made astounding claims, among them, "I am the good shepherd. The good shepherd lays down his life for the sheep." And, "I know my sheep and my sheep know me." There is a wholesome closeness between the shepherd and the sheep. Sheep do not see well but they are especially alert to the human voice, which they recognize. Jesus said, "My sheep know my voice."

For Jesus, laying claim to the title, shepherd, was no idle ploy. He lived out the title. Picture him laying a hand on Peter's wife when she lay fevered, rebuking the fever so she could arise and serve. That was a kindness shown during a social moment in a home. Picture him stopping along the way to take children on his lap to bless them. That's the sort of things pastors do to this very day.

If the assignment of today's pastors includes "to strengthen the weak... bring back the strays, and search for the lost" (Ezek 34:16), surely some pastoral ministries will involve exercising the shepherding function by going into homes to minister. To extend Ezekiel's list we might add, the pastor's purpose in visitation includes also to teach, to give comfort, to enrich an acquaintance, to present the gospel, to read Scriptures and to pray. Whatever is intended by the visit, it is to be spiritually motivated.

Whenever this aspect of pastoral ministry is emphasized the name of the great Seventeenth Century Puritan, Richard Baxter, enters the discussion. He ministered in Kidderminster, England from 1641 to 1661. Kidderminster was then a town of two thousand souls. Few if any in the town were converted when he began. When his labors ended it is reported there were few if any who were unconverted. God had visited Kidderminster in renewing power through the faithful ministrations of a shepherd.

Richard Baxter was a capable and broad-based theologian and preacher. He gave the pulpit its rightful place. He exercised the other duties both to local flock and the larger society. But he believed that "personal visitation was the backbone of his ministry." Some of his visitation was done in the manse itself when parishioners would be invited to come as a family. Before the visit was over, he would give personal spiritual attention to every member from the youngest to the oldest.

It could be argued that our times are different from the conditions of the seventeenth century. That would be true. Urbanization has created great sprawling cities so pastors are often a distance from their parishioners; urban life is fast paced and frenetic—and at the same time often anonymous; a household supported by two wage earners keeps adult members on the run; even the young often are occupied away from home in the evenings. And when the family is home they may be consumed with the viewing of favorite TV programs or isolated from one another by the various electronic devices they control individually. How can a pastor wedge family visitation into all this?

It can also be argued that as a congregation comes to trust their pastor's spirituality, biblical insight, and heartfelt passion they will become more open to an appointment for a visit made in advance. Indeed, there will be parishioners, adherents, and newcomers who will relish a visit. A well-executed visit need not consume more than an hour and sometimes less, unless there is some special reason to remain longer.

Occasionally, visits with the elderly may be made in the daytime. Hospital and nursing home visits are personal visits too. Pastors sometimes wisely equip their studies to be used for sessions with one or two. The state of modern life may actually enhance the possibilities of pastoral visitation to the lonely, the conflicted, the confused all caught in the maelstrom of modern life.

If a pastor were to set a goal to average even no more than two pastoral home visits a week that would amount to more than one hundred a year. Even if the number were reduced to seventy-five, the number on the face of it is significant. Good things happen in a pastoral visit, thus making the overcoming of obstacles worthwhile.

Whether a congregation is newly formed and meeting in a public school gymnasium or a megachurch drawing thousands to its several Sunday congregations, the saved and the searching must be personalized by more than a handshake at the door. Personalizing may be achieved somewhat by encouraging membership in a small group or assigning the task of friendship to a trusted person or couple already in the church or even by an invitation to a meal in a member's home. But the function of focused pastoral attention by a pastoral visit should never be lost sight of.

There's something about a pastor's seeing a couple or a family in the privacy and security of their own home that is unmatched, even though other meeting sites are sometimes necessary. When a pastor visits a family and prays with them in their home, on following Sundays they listen to that pastor with fresh attention and greater depth when he or she preaches.

Pastors do not do pastoral visitation to gain personal acclaim. But those who visit faithfully will report, after a lifetime of ministry, that the blessings keep returning unasked. Notes, phone calls, e-mails, casual visits—not every day, but often enough to confirm that heart-to-heart bonds created through visitation are rich and lasting.

I recently talked by telephone with a retired couple to whom I served as a pastor fifty-two years ago. We recalled the night I visited their home and at their dining room table presented the gospel to the husband. There and then he yielded his life to the Savior, which made them a couple united in Christ for the first time. He became a loyal churchman and a half-century later the faith still glows in their lives, and we are special to one another. Indeed, pastoral visitation is not a thing of the past. Spiritual conquests and great personal, long-lived blessings spring forth from it when it is carefully carried out.